England v Australia

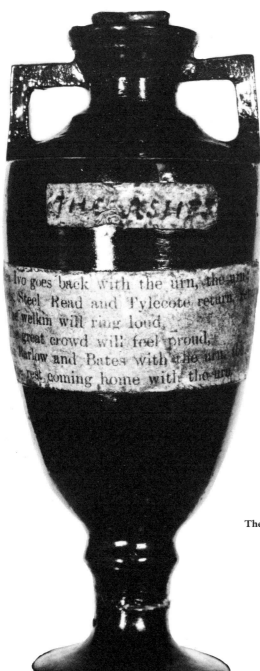

The urn containing the Ashes

RALPH BARKER
IRVING ROSENWATER

England v Australia

A compendium of Test Cricket
between the countries 1877-1968

B. T. Batsford Ltd | London

First published 1969
© *Ralph Barker & Irving Rosenwater, 1969*

Filmset by Filmtype Services, Scarborough, Yorkshire.
Printed in Great Britain by Fletcher & Son Ltd, Norwich, Norfolk.
and bound by Richard Clay (The Chaucer Press) Ltd, Bungay, Suffolk
for the Publishers B. T. Batsford Ltd, 4 Fitzhardinge Street,
London, W1

7134 0317 9

Preface

The story of 'Test' cricket begins with the tour of James Lillywhite's team of professionals to Australia in 1876-77 – although the phrase does not appear to have been applied to these games until some years later. Before this tour, England were unchallenged on level terms.

The first English team to tour Australia, in 1861-62, promoted by Messrs. Spiers and Pond, the caterers, and captained by H. H. Stephenson of Surrey, played 12 matches, all against odds, and won 6. Two years later, in 1863-64, at the invitation of the Melbourne Club, George Parr of Notts took out a strong and experienced side, which played 12 matches, all against odds, and returned unbeaten. There was no further tour until ten years later, in 1873-74, when W. G. Grace, at the age of 25, and again at the instance of the Melbourne Club, led a side which (again playing against odds) won 10 of its 15 matches and lost 3. This was followed by the tour of Lillywhite's team.

Since that first 'Test' Match of March 1877, the interchange of visits between the two countries has been continual, apart from breaks for the two world wars, and a total of 203 Test Matches has been played, the landmark of 200 being reached at Lord's in 1968 on the Australians' latest tour. Of these matches, Australia has won 80 and England 66, and 57 have been drawn.

We have not concerned ourselves overmuch with the reasons why some of the early matches were accorded Test Match status and some were not; but our researches have given us no grounds to quarrel with the established list of matches now sanctified by time.

In order to get each match account and its associated score-card into a single page – an essential for easy reference – it has been necessary to limit the text in each case to about 450 words. But we have found room to view each game against the background of the series of which it formed a part, and we have regarded the process of selection as an essential part of the story. Certain abbreviations – 'stumps' for 'close of play' and 'caught behind' for 'caught at the wicket' – have been employed, and except where confusion seemed likely to arise we have omitted to qualify statements of records achieved as being between England and Australia, taking it that this is implicit in the book's scope.

In the earlier matches the reader will generally find some clue to the style and method of the performer, but we have not thought it desirable to follow this practice so closely in later years, believing that many readers would be irritated to be told that Jim Laker bowled off-breaks or that Arthur Morris was a left-hander. Nevertheless where styles and methods seem to have special significance in a particular match, every effort has been made to find space to mention them.

We have taken the opportunity of carrying out a complete revision of the scores and statistics so far as original and contemporary sources have allowed; and we believe we have corrected many of the errors that have been perpetuated in the past. These vary from individual scores and methods of dismissal, details such as toss-winners, wicket-keepers, and the breakdown of extras, to bowling analyses and the fall of wickets, where by far the majority of the corrections have been made. From our revised figures we have compiled tables of statistics which we feel entitled to claim are more accurate, more detailed, and more informative than anything of the kind published before.

An indication of second-innings batting orders was, we felt, an obvious need; and we have therefore inserted a bracketed figure before the method of dismissal in all cases where the second-innings order was changed. Where a player batted in the same position, no annotation appears. We have also revised first-innings orders, where in some cases errors have stood uncorrected for more than 80 years.

Where it has been possible to determine which of the opening batsmen took first ball, that batsman has been shown first in the order. It has been the practice of some opening pairs to take first strike alternately, one in the first innings and the other in the second, but where the same pair opened in the second innings we have made no distinguishing mark, preferring to limit the annotations as far as possible. For the same reason, where a batsman who opened in the first innings has opened with a different partner in the second, the first-innings opener has been treated as batting in the same position whether or not he took first strike. Again, where only two batsmen went to the crease in a second innings, no distinguishing numbers have been allotted them.

Series averages have been included for all rubbers of three matches or more, the home country being shown first in each case.

For much detailed help and information we are indebted to Mr. Stephen Green, Curator of M.C.C.; Mr. A. R. Barnes, Secretary of the Australian Board of Control for International Cricket; Mr. B. J. Wakley, whose assistance on points of detail is gratefully acknowledged and whose book *Classic Centuries* we have frequently referred to; and Mr. David Frith, for allowing us access to various private memoranda on the two tours to Australia under A. E. Stoddart.

Copyright of the photographs is individually acknowledged below. We should like especially to thank Mr. Geoffrey A. Copinger for lending us many prints from his private collection.

June, 1969

Ralph Barker
Irving Rosenwater

ACKNOWLEDGMENT

The Authors and Publishers would like to thank the following for permission to reproduce the illustrations included in this book:

Central Press for figs. 88, 94, 97, 98, 101, 103, 106, 107, 110, 111, 112, 113, 115-26, 129-34; Geoffrey A. Copinger for figs. 29, 47, 58, 59, 70, 74 and 79; The Mansell Collection for figs. 8, 50, 55, 62 and 64; Marylebone Cricket Club for the frontispiece and figs. 2, 3, 4, 5, 12, 14, 15, 18, 21, 22, 26, 27, 30, 33, 36, 39, 56, 57, 63, 69, 72, 75, 76, 77, 78, 81, 87, 90, 93, 96, 99, 102, 108 and 114; Press Association for figs. 82, 83, 91, 92, 95 and 109; Public Library of Victoria for figs. 42 and 48; The Radio Times Hulton Picture Library for figs. 65 and 80; Sport and General for figs. 71 and 127.

Contents

Preface & Acknowledgment   Page v

Match Accounts & Score Cards   1–273

Series Averages   Page
1881–82; 1882–83 13
1884; 1884–85 25
1886; 1888 36
1891–92; 1893 53
1894–95; 1896 64
1897–98; 1899 75
1901–02; 1902 88

     Page
1903–04; 1905 101
1907–08; 1909 114
1911–12; 1912 127
1920–21; 1921 138
1924–25; 1926 151
1928–29; 1930 164
1932–33; 1934 177

     Page
1936–37; 1938 190
1946–47; 1948 202
1950–51; 1953 215
1954–55; 1956 228
1958–59; 1961 241
1962–63; 1964 254
1965–66; 1968 267

Appendices   Page
The results – series by series   274
The results   274
The grounds   275
The toss   275
Highest totals   275
Highest second innings totals   276
Highest totals in fourth innings   276
Lowest totals   276
Totals of less than 100 in each innings   277
Highest match aggregates   277
Lowest match aggregates   277
Biggest victories   277
Close finishes   277
Duration of matches   278
Most appearances   278
Most consecutive appearances   279
Most runs in a day by a side   279
Fewest runs in a day   279
Most runs by a side before lunch   279
Scoring rates per 100 balls   279
Youngest players   280
Oldest players   280
Oldest players on debut   280

The captains   280
Captains who sent opponents in   282
Declarations   282

The batsmen
Most runs   282
Most centuries   282
Centuries   283
Quickest time to 1,000 runs   284
Most runs in a series   285
Highest average in a series   285
Highest individual innings   285
Century in each innings   286
Three centuries in successive innings   286
Carrying bat through innings   286
Most runs in a day   287

     Page
Most boundaries in an innings   287
High percentage of runs in boundaries   287
Most boundaries in a day   288
Most boundaries before lunch   288
Hundreds before lunch   288
Youngest and oldest century-scorers   288
Centuries by batsmen low in order   289
Most sixes in an innings   289
Big hits   289
Fast innings   290
Fastest fifties   290
Fastest centuries   290
Fastest double-centuries   291
Longest innings   291
Longest period on field of play   291
Slow innings   291
Fewest runs before lunch   292
Slowest fifties   293
Slowest centuries   293
Slowest double-centuries   293
An hour before breaking duck   293
Record partnership for each wicket   293
Progressive partnership record   294
Highest partnerships   294
Fast partnerships   295
Fast partnerships for first wicket   296

The bowlers
Most wickets   296
Most wickets in a series   296
Lowest average in a series   297
Wicket frequency per match   297
Penetrative career bowling   297
Economical career bowling   298
Most wickets in an innings   298
Most wickets in a match   299
Most wickets in a day   299
Ten wickets in a match most times   299
Ten wickets on debut   300
Most runs conceded in an innings   300

     Page
Most runs conceded in a match   300
Five wickets in an innings most times   300
Bowling unchanged through completed innings   300
Hat-tricks   301
Three wickets in four balls   301

All-rounders   301

The wicketkeepers   301
Most dismissals in an innings   302
Most dismissals in a match   302
Most dismissals in a series   302
Wicketkeepers conceding no byes in high innings   302
Most runs by wicketkeepers   303

The fielders   303
Most catches in an innings   303
Most catches in a match   303
Most catches in a series   303
Most catches in career   303

Miscellanea
The over   303
The follow on   303
New ball   303
Intervals   304
Covering of wickets   304
Provisions regarding final Test   304
Record match receipts and attendances at major grounds   305
Record match receipts   305
Record receipts for series   305
Record match attendances   305
Record attendances for series   306
The Press   306

Career records   306

1876-77 First Test, Melbourne

March 15, 16, 17
Toss: Australia   *Result:* Australia won by 45 runs

Victories by Australian sides of 15 players or more, against Grace's touring XI in 1873-74 and Lillywhite's team of professionals in 1876-77, had created a desire in Australia to see how their leading cricketers would fare in an even-handed contest against an English XI. The best men of Sydney agreed to co-operate with the stars from Melbourne, and after negotiations it was decided to play a 4-day match in Melbourne on the return of Lillywhite's team from New Zealand. For various reasons three of Australia's best bowlers—Evans, Allan and Spofforth—were absent, which it was felt would destroy the home side's chances; but the Englishmen, who landed at Melbourne only the day before the game, were further handicapped by the absence of Pooley, their only wicket-keeper.

This first day of Test cricket began at 1.0 and finished at 5.0, with 50 minutes for lunch, and at the close Australia were 166 for 6, of which Charlie Bannerman, hitting with great freedom and vigour while first Horan and then Cooper defended doggedly, had made all but 40. The veteran round-arm bowlers Shaw and Southerton did best for England, Shaw's field including a short slip, cover, point, short leg, mid off, mid on, deep square leg, long on and a man straight

for the hit over the bowler's head. Armitage, a lob-bowler, whom Bannerman hit for 10 runs in his first over, tried to pitch the ball over the batsman's head on to the bails, to the crowd's amusement; a contemporary account records that these deliveries could only have been reached 'with a clothes' prop'. Armitage then resorted to 'grubbers', a style of bowling not seen in Melbourne for nearly 20 years, but he was soon taken off. Ulyett, who bowled fast and sometimes dangerously short, eventually split Bannerman's finger and caused his retirement. Out of Australia's total of 245 he made 165.

When England batted the Australian bowling and wicket-keeping touched a high standard, though the fielding did not compare with England's. Beginning confidently with some good batting by Jupp and Charlwood, England fell away in the middle and were led on first innings by 49. Australia were dismissed at the second attempt for 104, Shaw bowling throughout, but England, wanting 154 to win, were soon in trouble against Kendall, fast left-hand. Selby and Ulyett added 40 for the 5th wicket, but an Australian victory always looked probable. These were the days of 4-ball overs, and Shaw, the great 'length' bowler, sent down 89.3 overs, 50 of which were maidens, and took 8 for 89.

AUSTRALIA

C. Bannerman	retired hurt	165	b Ulyett	4
N. Thompson	b Hill	1	c Emmett b Shaw	7
T. P. Horan	c Hill b Shaw	12	c Selby b Ulyett	20
*D. W. Gregory	run out	1	(9)b Shaw	3
B. B. Cooper	b Southerton	15	b Shaw	3
W. E. Midwinter	c Ulyett b Southerton	5	c Southerton b Ulyett	17
E. J. Gregory	c Greenwood b Lillywhite	0	c Emmett b Ulyett	11
†J. McC. Blackham	b Southerton	17	lbw b Shaw	6
T. W. Garrett	not out	18	(4)c Emmett b Shaw	0
T. Kendall	c Southerton b Shaw	3	not out	17
J. Hodges	b Shaw	0	b Lillywhite	8
Extras	(b 4, lb 2, w 2)	8	(b 5, lb 3)	8
Total		**245**	Total	**104**

ENGLAND

H. Jupp	lbw b Garrett	63	(3)lbw b Midwinter	4
†J. Selby	c Cooper b Hodges	7	(5)c Horan b Hodges	38
H. R. J. Charlwood	c Blackham b Midwinter	36	(4)b Kendall	13
G. Ulyett	lbw b Thompson	10	(6)b Kendall	24
A. Greenwood	c E. Gregory b Midwinter	1	(2)c Midwinter b Kendall	5
T. Armitage	c Blackham b Midwinter	9	(8)c Blackham b Kendall	3
A. Shaw	b Midwinter	10	st Blackham b Kendall	2
T. Emmett	b Midwinter	8	(9)b Kendall	9
A. Hill	not out	35	(1)c Thompson b Kendall	0
*James Lillywhite	c and b Kendall	10	b Hodges	4
J. Southerton	c Cooper b Garrett	6	not out	1
Extras	(lb 1)	1	(b 4, lb 1)	5
Total		**196**	Total	**108**

FALL OF WICKETS

	AUSTRALIA	
Wkt.	1st	2nd
1st	2	7
2nd	40	27
3rd	41	31
4th	118	31
5th	142	35
6th	143	58
7th	197	71
8th	243	75
9th	245	75
10th	—	104

	ENGLAND	
Wkt.	1st	2nd
1st	23	0
2nd	79	7
3rd	98	20
4th	109	22
5th	121	62
6th	130	68
7th	145	92
8th	145	93
9th	168	100
10th	196	108

Umpires: Curtis A. Reid, B. Terry

ENGLAND	1st Innings				2nd Innings			
	O	M	R	W	O	M	R	W
Shaw	55.3	34	51	3	34	16	38	5
Hill	23	10	42	1	14	6	18	0
Ulyett	25	12	36	0	19	7	39	4
Southerton	37	11	61	3				
Armitage	3	0	15	0				
Lillywhite	14	5	19	1	1	0	1	1
Emmett	12	7	13	0				

AUSTRALIA	1st Innings				2nd Innings			
	O	M	R	W	O	M	R	W
Hodges	9	0	27	1	7	5	7	2
Garrett	18.1	10	22	2	2	0	9	0
Kendall	38	16	54	1	33.1	12	55	7
Midwinter	54	21	78	5	19	7	23	1
Thompson	17	10	14	1				
D. W. Gregory					5	1	9	0

1876–77 Second Test, Melbourne

March 31, April 2, 3, 4
Toss: Australia   *Result:* England won by four wickets

A return match was quickly arranged. Spofforth and Murdoch replaced E. J. Gregory and Horan in the Australian side and Kelly came in for Cooper. England, with only 11 fit players, were inevitably unchanged. The game attracted another large attendance, the members' enclosure being crowded with ladies and the grandstand well patronised; beneath it, a band played at intervals during the afternoon. At lunch on the first day, on a good wicket, Australia were 60 for 4, fast bowler Hill taking all the wickets. After lunch Jupp relieved Selby behind the wicket, but neither proved an efficient substitute for Pooley. Australia, however, never recovered from a moderate start and were all out for 122, Midwinter top-scoring with 31.

When England batted Spofforth bowled very fast, and interest centred on how Blackham would take him, Spofforth having missed the first Test through insisting that only Murdoch could keep wicket to him. In Spofforth's third over a very fast delivery lifted, and Blackham, standing up, stumped Shaw brilliantly. England were 7 for 2 at the close.

Next day the Australian attack was of a high quality, but the fielding was again markedly inferior to England's and several catches were missed. The bowling was eventually collared, the Australian captain

seeming to lack resource under pressure, and England built up a good lead, Greenwood, Ulyett, Emmett and Hill all making useful scores. But when Australia went in again 139 behind a fine opening stand between Thompson and Gregory reduced the arrears to 51, and by a mixture of stubborn defence and strong hitting all the way down the order the Australians eventually set England 121 to win.

At lunch-time on the fourth day England were 9 for 3, and half the side were out for 76. But the wicket was still good and the outfield fast, George Ulyett hit soundly and freely, and when he was sixth out at 112 the match was all but won. He had made top score in both innings.

In spite of this defeat the Australians regarded Lillywhite's team as the weakest ever to tour Australia. Ulyett was a brilliant hitter, and Jupp, Greenwood, Selby and Charlwood were respected as good average batsmen, but Kendall was thought far superior as a fast bowler to Ulyett, Emmett and Hill, while Southerton and Lillywhite were regarded as passé. 'We would counsel whoever may enter into future speculations for importing an England XI', advised one writer, 'to bear in mind the great improvement of colonial cricket, and not to imagine that anything will do for Australia.' Prophetic words indeed.

AUSTRALIA

Batsman	1st Innings		2nd Innings	
N. Thompson	lbw b Hill	18	b Lillywhite	41
C. Bannerman	b Hill	10	(3)c Jupp b Ulyett	30
†J. McC. Blackham	c Lillywhite b Hill	5	(10)lbw b Southerton	26
T. W. Garrett	b Hill	12	(7)c Jupp b Lillywhite	18
T. J. D. Kelly	b Ulyett	19	(4)b Southerton	35
W. E. Midwinter	c Emmett b Lillywhite	31	c Greenwood b Lillywhite	12
F. R. Spofforth	b Ulyett	0	(8)b Hill	17
W. L. Murdoch	run out	3	(5)c Shaw b Southerton	8
T. Kendall	b Lillywhite	7	b Southerton	12
*D. W. Gregory	not out	1	(2)c Ulyett b Lillywhite	43
J. Hodges	run out	2	not out	0
Extras	(b 8, lb 5, w 1)	14	(b 10, lb 7)	17
Total		**122**	**Total**	**259**

ENGLAND

Batsman	1st Innings		2nd Innings	
H. Jupp	b Kendall	0	b Kendall	1
A. Shaw	st Blackham b Spofforth	1	(8)not out	0
A. Greenwood	b Hodges	49	c Murdoch b Hodges	22
H. R. J. Charlwood	c Kelly b Kendall	14	b Kendall	0
†J. Selby	b Kendall	7	(2)b Spofforth	2
G. Ulyett	b Spofforth	52	(5)c Spofforth b Hodges	63
T. Emmett	c Kendall b Spofforth	48	(6)b Midwinter	8
A. Hill	run out	49	(7)not out	17
T. Armitage	c Thompson b Midwinter	21		
*James Lillywhite	not out	2		
J. Southerton	c Thompson b Kendall	0		
Extras	(b 5, lb 12, nb 1)	18	(b 8, lb 1)	9
Total		**261**	**Total (6 wkts)**	**122**

FALL OF WICKETS

AUSTRALIA

Wkt	1st	2nd
1st	29	88
2nd	29	112
3rd	50	135
4th	60	164
5th	96	169
6th	104	196
7th	108	203
8th	114	221
9th	119	259
10th	122	259

ENGLAND

Wkt	1st	2nd
1st	0	2
2nd	4	8
3rd	55	9
4th	72	54
5th	88	76
6th	162	112
7th	196	—
8th	255	—
9th	259	—
10th	261	—

Umpires: B. Terry,
S. Cosstick

ENGLAND	1st Innings					2nd Innings			
	O	M	R	W		O	M	R	W
Shaw	42	27	30	0	..	32	19	27	0
Lillywhite	29	17	36	2	..	41	15	70	4
Hill	27	12	27	4	..	21	9	43	1
Ulyett	14·1	6	15	2	..	19	9	33	0
Emmett					..	13	6	23	0
Southerton					..	28·3	13	46	4

AUSTRALIA	1st Innings					2nd Innings			
	O	M	R	W		O	M	R	W
Kendall	52·2	21	82	4	..	17	7	24	2
Spofforth	29	6	67	3	..	15	3	44	1
Midwinter	21	8	30	1	..	13·1	6	25	1
Hodges	12	2	37	1	..	6	2	13	2
Garrett	5	2	10	0	..	1	0	7	0
Thompson	11	6	17	0	..				

1. A. Shaw

2. C. Bannerman

3. England 1876–77
Back row: H. Jupp, T. Emmett, R. Humphrey, A. Hill, T. Armitage, G. Ulyett. *Middle row:* E. Pooley, J. Southerton, James Lillywhite (capt.), A. Shaw, A. Greenwood. *Front:* H. R. J. Charlwood, J. Selby.

1878-79 Only Test, Melbourne

January 2, 3, 4
Toss: England   *Result:* Australia won by ten wickets

Lord Harris's team was originally to have consisted entirely of amateurs, but a strong enough party could not be got together on these terms. Thus it was that the side toured under the banner of 'Gentlemen of England (with Ulyett and Emmett)'. Apart from the two professionals only Lucas had any status as a bowler, but the batting was strong, and the batsmen were expected to score heavily enough to make victory the inescapable conclusion of most games.

While the side were in Australia it was inevitable that they should be challenged by the Australian party recently returned from England; this was the tour on which they had beaten the MCC at Lord's by 9 wickets in a single day. There had been no full representative match on that tour. This game, billed as 'Gentlemen of England etc. v. *The* Australian XI', has come to be accepted as the third Test Match between the two countries.

In 1878 the Australians had shown that in Spofforth, Allan, Garrett and Boyle they had an attack far superior to anything England could field even at home. English batting was more stylish and technically correct, the running between the wickets showed more judgment, and the fielding was smarter; but the Australians had such an advantage

in bowling that they felt they must win. When the mighty Gentlemen of England (plus Ulyett and Emmett) had crashed to 26 for 7 on the first morning to Spofforth and Allan (left-arm medium), Australian confidence did not seem misplaced. Spofforth, indeed, did the hat trick.

A wonderful fight back by the captain, who defended soundly in partnership with the audacious, hard-hitting Absolom, brought England back into the game, and the score eventually reached 113. But although Ulyett and Emmett earned their money by sending down 121 of the 160 overs bowled, Emmett, fast left arm, taking 7 for 68, a patient innings by Alec Bannerman, already dubbed the 'little stonewaller', helped Australia, 95 for 3 at the end of the first day, to a lead of 143.

In the second innings Lord Harris again played the powerful bowling opposed to him in masterly style, but he had little support. A dampish wicket had materially assisted Spofforth on the first day, but there was no excuse this time. Moderating his pace and bowling with rare judgment and command, Spofforth came out with match figures of 13 for 110, and England only escaped an innings defeat with their last pair together. A return match had been arranged, but it was cancelled after a riot had spoiled a game against New South Wales at Sydney.

ENGLAND

G. Ulyett	b Spofforth	0	b Spofforth	14	
A. P. Lucas	b Allan	6	c Boyle b Allan	13	
A. J. Webbe	b Allan	4	lbw b Allan	0	
A. N. Hornby	b Spofforth	2	b Spofforth	4	
*Lord Harris	b Garrett	33	c Horan b Spofforth	36	
V. P. F. A. Royle	b Spofforth	3	c Spofforth b Boyle	18	
F. A. Mackinnon	b Spofforth	0	b Spofforth	5	
T. Emmett	c Horan b Spofforth	0	(9)not out	24	
C. A. Absolom	c A. Bannerman b Boyle	52	(8)c and b Spofforth	6	
†L. Hone	c Blackham b Spofforth	7	b Spofforth	6	
S. S. Schultz	not out	0	c and b Spofforth	20	
Extras	(b 4, lb 2)	6	(b 10, lb 4)	14	
Total		113	Total	160	

AUSTRALIA

C. Bannerman	b Emmett	15
W. L. Murdoch	c Webbe b Ulyett	4
T. P. Horan	c Hone b Emmett	10
A. C. Bannerman	b Schultz	73
F. R. Spofforth	c Royle b Emmett	39
T. W. Garrett	c Hone b Emmett	26
F. E. Allan	b Hornby	5
H. F. Boyle	c Royle b Emmett	28
†J. McC. Blackham	b Emmett	6
T. J. D. Kelly	c Webbe b Emmett	10
*D. W. Gregory	not out	12
Extras	(b 19, lb 2, w 7)	28
Total		256

	not out	15
	not out	4

Total (0 wkts) **19**

FALL OF WICKETS

ENGLAND

Wkt	1st	2nd
1st	0	26
2nd	7	28
3rd	10	28
4th	14	34
5th	26	78
6th	26	103
7th	26	103
8th	89	118
9th	113	128
10th	113	160

AUSTRALIA

Wkt	1st	2nd
1st	16	—
2nd	30	—
3rd	37	—
4th	101	—
5th	131	—
6th	158	—
7th	215	—
8th	224	—
9th	234	—
10th	256	—

Umpires: G. Coulthard, P. Coady

AUSTRALIA	1st Innings				2nd Innings			
	O	M	R	W	O	M	R	W
Spofforth	25	9	48	6	35	16	62	7
Allan	17	4	30	2	28	11	50	2
Garrett	5	0	18	1	10	6	18	0
Boyle	7	1	11	1	10	4	16	1

ENGLAND	1st Innings				2nd Innings			
	O	M	R	W	O	M	R	W
Emmett	59	31	68	7				
Ulyett	62	24	93	1	1	0	9	0
Lucas	18	6	31	0				
Schultz	6·3	3	16	1	1·3	0	10	0
Hornby	7	7	0	1				
Royle	4	1	6	0				
Lord Harris	3	0	14	0				

4. T. Emmett

5. F. R. Spofforth

6. **England 1878–79**
Back row: F. Penn, A. J. Webbe, C. A. Absolom, S. S. Schultz, L. Hone. *Middle row:* F. A. Mackinnon, A. N. Hornby, Lord Harris (capt.), H. C. Maul, G. Ulyett. *Front:* A. P. Lucas, V. P. F. A. Royle, T. Emmett.

1880 Only Test, Oval

September 6, 7, 8
Toss: England   *Result:* England won by five wickets

When the second Australian team visited England in 1880 they were largely cold-shouldered by the leading clubs due to the fracas at Sydney the previous year; but thanks to the initiative of the Surrey club, the first England v. Australia match on English soil took place at the Oval in September. The one regret was that Spofforth had injured a finger at Scarborough and was unable to play. The task of bowling England out twice on a perfect wicket thus lay principally with the two great medium-pacers Palmer and Boyle.

At 2.0 on the first day, after nearly 2½ hours' play, England were 167 for 1. Grace (W.G.) was still there with 82, and he reached his hundred soon after lunch. The 200 was passed with only one wicket down, Grace and Lucas putting on 120, and when Grace was out for 152 England were 281 for 4. They had reached 410 for 8 by the close.

A drizzling rain that evening was said not to have affected the wicket, but it may well have done so. Play started at 11.5, and Australia were batting at 11.40; at lunch they were 126 for 9 and doomed to follow on. 23 runs were added afterwards, but when Australia began their second innings, facing a deficit of 271, they made a deplorable start. Boyle, who had been sent in first, was run out, Bannerman and Groube failed,

and at 14 for 3 they were in an apparently hopeless position. Yet when the 19-year-old McDonnell joined Murdoch, who had gone in No. 3 this time, both men played with surprising freedom. McDonnell was lbw at 97, but Blackham played a useful innings, and Australia had reached 170 for 6 at stumps. Yet they were still 101 runs behind. Murdoch, who had batted 2½ hours, was not out 79.

Next morning Bonnor was out at 181 and Palmer at 187, but Alexander, the tour manager, helped Murdoch to add 52 for the ninth wicket, during which Murdoch completed his century, and when Alexander left Moule helped Murdoch to save the innings defeat. Australia, indeed, were not all out until the second over after lunch, when England were left with the apparent formality of making 57 to win.

Boyle and Palmer then took up the attack to such purpose that England were soon in complete disarray. G. F. Grace bagged a 'pair', Lucas was caught behind, Lyttelton was bowled, Barnes was caught at mid on and E. M. Grace was bowled second ball. 31 for 5. But a bearded, youthful if ample figure was striding from the pavilion; how Murdoch must have sighed in that moment for Spofforth! There were no more alarms and England won by 5 wickets.

ENGLAND

E. M. Grace	c Alexander b Bannerman	36	(6)b Boyle		0
W. G. Grace	b Palmer	152	(7)not out		9
A. P. Lucas	b Bannerman	55	c Blackham b Palmer		2
W. Barnes	b Alexander	28	(5)c Moule b Boyle		5
*Lord Harris	c Bonnor b Alexander	52			
F. Penn	b Bannerman	23	(4)not out		27
A. G. Steel	c Boyle b Moule	42			
†Hon. A. Lyttelton	not out	11	(1)b Palmer		13
G. F. Grace	c Bannerman b Moule	0	(2)b Palmer		0
A. Shaw	b Moule	0			
F. Morley	run out	2			
Extras	(b 8, lb 11)	19	(nb 1)		1
Total		**420**	**Total** (5 wkts)		**57**

AUSTRALIA

A. C. Bannerman	b Morley	32	c Lucas b Shaw		8
*W. L. Murdoch	c Barnes b Steel	0	(3)not out		153
T. U. Groube	b Steel	11	(4)c Shaw b Morley		0
P. S. McDonnell	c Barnes b Morley	27	(5)lbw b W. G. Grace		43
J. Slight	c G. F. Grace b Morley	11	(6)c Harris b W. G. Grace		0
†J. McC. Blackham	c and b Morley	0	(7)c E. M. Grace b Morley		19
G. J. Bonnor	c G. F. Grace b Shaw	2	(8)b Steel		16
H. F. Boyle	not out	36	(2)run out		3
G. E. Palmer	b Morley	6	c and b Steel		4
G. Alexander	c W. G. Grace b Steel	6	c Shaw b Morley		33
W. H. Moule	c Morley b W. G. Grace	6	b Barnes		34
Extras	(b 9, lb 3)	12	(b 7, lb 7)		14
Total		**149**	**Total**		**327**

AUSTRALIA	1st Innings					2nd Innings			
	O	M	R	W		O	M	R	W
Boyle	44	17	71	0	..	17	7	21	2
Palmer	70	27	116	1	..	16·3	5	35	3
Alexander	32	10	69	2	..				
Bannerman	50	12	111	3	..				
McDonnell	2	0	11	0	..				
Moule	12·3	4	23	3	..				

ENGLAND	1st Innings					2nd Innings			
	O	M	R	W		O	M	R	W
Morley	32	9	56	5	..	61	30	90	3
Steel	29	9	58	3	..	31	6	73	2
Shaw	13	5	21	1	..	33	18	42	1
W. G. Grace	1·1	0	2	1	..	28	10	66	2
Barnes					..	8·3	3	17	1
Lucas					..	12	7	23	0
Penn					..	3	1	2	0

FALL OF WICKETS

ENGLAND		
Wkt	1st	2nd
1st	91	2
2nd	211	10
3rd	269	22
4th	281	31
5th	322	31
6th	404	—
7th	410	—
8th	410	—
9th	413	—
10th	420	—

AUSTRALIA		
Wkt	1st	2nd
1st	28	8
2nd	39	13
3rd	59	14
4th	84	97
5th	84	101
6th	89	143
7th	97	181
8th	113	187
9th	126	239
10th	149	327

Umpires: R. Thoms, H. H. Stephenson

7. W. L. Murdoch

8. W. G. Grace

9 Australia 1880
Back row: G. E. Palmer, W. H. Moule, G. J. Bonnor, G. Alexander (manager), T. W. Groube. *Middle row:* F. R. Spofforth, H. F. Boyle, W. L. Murdoch (capt.), P. S. McDonnell, A. C. Bannerman. *Front:* A. H. Jarvis, J. Slight, J. McC. Blackham.

1881-82 First Test, Melbourne

December 31, January 2, 3 4
Toss: England   *Result:* Match Drawn

The England party this time was all-professional again, the first of three tours in the '80s under the management of Shaw, Shrewsbury and Lillywhite. Four matches judged representative were played, two against All-Australia to begin with and then two against a side picked from the party chosen to tour England that summer; but England did not win any of them. The first match, originally limited to three days to meet the tourists' sailing date for New Zealand, was extended into the fourth in an attempt to get a result, and there is evidence that the second and third Tests, although allotted a basic four days, might also have been extended if necessary.

England established a strong position at the outset in a fine second-wicket stand between Ulyett and Selby which added 137; while Ulyett played in his usual dashing style, Selby made most of his runs by delicate cuts and glances. A fine innings from Bates kept up the tempo, but later in the day the pace fell away, and by the close England were all out for 294. Evans, one of the earliest of the great Australian medium-pacers but playing in his first Test, bowled with machine-like accuracy, and W. H. Cooper, a leg-break bowler, was equally successful.

After Massie had been stumped off Midwinter—the same man who had played *against* England in Tests 1 and 2—Bannerman and Murdoch began a steady recovery, and Horan, going in just before lunch, put on 107 with Giffen and then batted through the rest of the day. Fine straight driving was a feature of his century, which he completed 15 minutes before stumps, when Australia were 277 for 6. The hours of play were 11.0 till 6.0, but there were one or two short interruptions for rain.

Next morning the last 4 wickets put on a further 43 runs, giving Australia a lead of 26, which Barlow and Ulyett wiped out in an opening stand of 37. Selby played another sound innings, laying back to cut Cooper and generally playing his shots while Barlow defended, and Bates again batted well, but Cooper's leg-breaks caused a collapse, and at 217 for 7 the innings was petering out with England in some danger. Scotton then gave convincing evidence of his quality as a stonewaller, Shaw was equally obdurate, and to make Australia's task more difficult 15 minutes were lost due to an injury to Blackham, Murdoch taking his place. 238 for 7 overnight, England eventually totalled 308.

Australia were left with only 2¼ hours in which to get 283, and with the wicket playing as well as ever the game was robbed of interest long before the Englishmen hurried off to their ship.

ENGLAND

R. G. Barlow	c Bannerman b Palmer	0	st Blackham b Palmer	33	
G. Ulyett	c McDonnell b Cooper	87	st Blackham b Cooper	23	
J. Selby	run out	55	c Boyle b Cooper	70	
W. Bates	c Giffen b Boyle	58	c Bannerman b Cooper	47	
A. Shrewsbury	c Blackham b Evans	11	b Cooper	16	
W. E. Midwinter	b Evans	36	c Massie b Cooper	4	
T. Emmett	b Evans	5	b Cooper	6	
W. H. Scotton	run out	21	not out	50	
*A. Shaw	c Boyle b Cooper	5	c Cooper b Boyle	40	
†R. Pilling	c Giffen b Cooper	5	b Palmer	3	
E. Peate	not out	4	run out	2	
Extras	(lb 6, nb 1)	7	(b 7, lb 2, nb 5)	14	
Total		294	Total	308	

AUSTRALIA

H. H. Massie	st Pilling b Midwinter	2			
A. C. Bannerman	b Ulyett	38	b Ulyett	8	
*W. L. Murdoch	b Ulyett	39	(4)not out	22	
P. S. McDonnell	b Midwinter	19	(5)not out	33	
T. P. Horan	run out	124	(3)c Emmett b Bates	26	
G. Giffen	b Emmett	30			
†J. McC. Blackham	b Emmett	2			
G. E. Palmer	c Pilling b Bates	34			
E. Evans	b Bates	3			
H. F. Boyle	not out	4			
W. H. Cooper	st Pilling b Peate	7	(1)b Bates	25	
Extras	(b 4, lb 11, w 3)	18	(b 9, lb 3, w 1)	13	
Total		320	Total (3 wkts)	127	

FALL OF WICKETS

ENGLAND

Wkt	1st	2nd
1st	5	37
2nd	142	96
3rd	151	179
4th	187	183
5th	227	188
6th	232	197
7th	277	217
8th	284	300
9th	289	305
10th	294	308

AUSTRALIA

Wkt	1st	2nd
1st	9	35
2nd	82	70
3rd	97	72
4th	113	—
5th	220	—
6th	226	—
7th	305	—
8th	309	—
9th	309	—
10th	320	—

Umpires: J. Swift, James Lillywhite, jnr.

AUSTRALIA

	1st Innings					2nd Innings			
	O	M	R	W		O	M	R	W
Palmer	36	9	73	1	..	77	19	77	2
Boyle	18	9	18	1	..	15	6	19	1
Bannerman	10	3	23	0	..				
Evans	71	35	81	3	..	75·2	45	63	0
Cooper	32·2	8	80	3	..	66	19	120	6
Giffen	3	0	12	0	..				
McDonnell					..	4	1	15	0

ENGLAND

	1st Innings					2nd Innings			
	O	M	R	W		O	M	R	W
Peate	59	24	64	1	..	11	5	22	0
Midwinter	39	21	50	2	..				
Bates	41	20	43	2	..	13	3	43	2
Emmett	35	12	61	2	..	16	11	19	0
Ulyett	20	5	41	0	..	15	3	30	1
Barlow	23	13	22	0	..				
Shaw	20	11	21	0	..				

10. G. Ulyett   11. G. E. Palmer

12. England 1881–82
Back row: G. Ulyett, R. Pilling, J. Lillywhite, J. Conway (manager), W. Midwinter, W. Bates. *Middle row:* A. Shrewsbury, A. Shaw (capt.), T. Emmett, E. Peate. *Front:* R. G. Barlow, W. H. Scotton, J. Selby.

1881-82 Second Test, Sydney

February 17, 18, 20, 21
Toss: England   *Result:* Australia won by five wickets

Australia were weakened by injuries, yet both bowling and batting proved adequate, and the fielding was described as the finest seen on the Sydney ground. Ulyett began for England in his usual aggressive style, but after he left at 39 wickets fell with depressing regularity. The only notable stand was the 25 added for the 7th wicket by the left-handers Scotton and Emmett, and England were all out on a good wicket for 133. Murdoch kept wicket, allowing Blackham to distinguish himself by some magnificent stops at mid off.

Australia went in at 4.45 and by 6.0 they were 86 for the loss of Massie, well on the way to a commanding lead. Massie, missed before he had scored, for once began steadily, but he hit freely when he was set. Next morning, assisted by two run outs, England got back into the game, and when the 7th wicket fell just after lunch Australia were only 7 runs ahead. Jones and Palmer, defending stubbornly, then added 27 for the 8th wicket in 37 overs, and another 29 were made for the last wicket, giving Australia a lead of 64. England were 8 for 0 when rain stopped play.

On the third morning the game was transformed as Ulyett and Barlow batted through to lunch, knocking off the deficit and putting England into the commanding position previously enjoyed by Australia. Ulyett should twice have been stumped by Murdoch (who was replaced by Blackham in the afternoon), and he was also missed at long off, but when he was out shortly after lunch England were 58 in front. Selby and Bates again failed, but Shrewsbury batted well, and England were re-establishing their hold on the game when Barlow, after a long and patient innings, was fourth out at 156. The batting then fell away before fine bowling from Garrett, quick-medium with a high action, and Palmer, and Australia were set 169 to win.

At stumps, when Australia were 35 for 2, the odds favoured England, and when Horan left next morning at 67 England still had the advantage. But McDonnell hit vigorously, and when he and Murdoch were out Garrett showed the right mixture of caution and aggression while Jones defended. Shaw tried 7 bowlers, but none of them reached the standard of Palmer, Garrett and Evans, while the Australian batting proved the more determined, no one failing on the vital fourth day. In England's first innings Palmer and Evans bowled unchanged for over 3 hours—a record that still stands.

ENGLAND

Batsman	Dismissal 1st	Runs	Dismissal 2nd	Runs
G. Ulyett	c Murdoch b Evans	25	lbw b Palmer	67
R. G. Barlow	b Palmer	31	c Boyle b Garrett	62
J. Selby	c and b Evans	6	c Blackham b Palmer	2
W. Bates	st Murdoch b Palmer	4	b Palmer	5
A. Shrewsbury	b Palmer	7	c McDonnell b Garrett	22
W. E. Midwinter	c Blackham b Palmer	4	b Palmer	8
W. H. Scotton	b Palmer	30	lbw b Garrett	12
T. Emmett	b Evans	10	c McDonnell b Garrett	9
*A. Shaw	c Massie b Palmer	11	b Evans	30
†R. Pilling	b Palmer	3	b Jones	9
E. Peate	not out	1	not out	1
Extras	(lb 1)	1	(b 3, lb 2)	5
Total		**133**		**232**

AUSTRALIA

Batsman	Dismissal 1st	Runs	Dismissal 2nd	Runs
H. H. Massie	c Shrewsbury b Bates	49	b Ulyett	22
J. McC. Blackham	c Shaw b Midwinter	40	c and b Bates	4
E. Evans	run out	11		
†*W. L. Murdoch	c Emmett b Bates	10	(3)c Barlow b Midwinter	49
T. P. Horan	run out	4	(4)b Ulyett	21
P. S. McDonnell	b Bates	14	(5)b Shaw	25
S. P. Jones	c Emmett b Ulyett	37	(6)not out	13
T. W. Garrett	c Shrewsbury b Peate	4	(7)not out	31
G. E. Palmer	b Bates	16		
H. F. Boyle	c Shrewsbury b Ulyett	0		
G. Coulthard	not out	6		
Extras	(b 1, lb 2, w 2, nb 1)	6	(b 3, lb 1)	4
Total		**197**	**Total (5 wkts)**	**169**

FALL OF WICKETS

ENGLAND

Wkt	1st	2nd
1st	39	122
2nd	47	124
3rd	64	130
4th	73	156
5th	77	165
6th	90	175
7th	115	183
8th	123	204
9th	132	230
10th	133	232

AUSTRALIA

Wkt	1st	2nd
1st	78	10
2nd	102	28
3rd	103	67
4th	111	113
5th	132	127
6th	133	—
7th	140	—
8th	167	—
9th	168	—
10th	197	—

Umpires: J. Swift,
James Lillywhite, jnr.

AUSTRALIA

	1st Innings				2nd Innings			
	O	M	R	W	O	M	R	W
Palmer	58	36	68	7	66	29	97	4
Evans	57	32	64	3	40·1	19	49	1
Garrett					36	12	62	4
Jones					11	4	19	1

ENGLAND

	1st Innings				2nd Innings			
	O	M	R	W	O	M	R	W
Peate	52	28	53	1	20	12	22	0
Midwinter	34	16	43	1	18	8	23	1
Emmett	6	2	24	0	6	3	17	0
Ulyett	22·2	16	11	2	15	4	48	2
Bates	72	43	52	4	24	11	37	1
Barlow	8	4	8	0	4	1	6	0
Shaw					21	15	12	1

1881-82 Third Test, Sydney

March 3, 4, 6, 7
Toss: England   *Result:* Australia won by six wickets

England were unfortunate, after winning the toss, to find themselves on a wicket below Test Match standard, while when the Australians' turn came they were permitted to select and prepare a fresh wicket. In the circumstances the England side performed well, Shrewsbury especially giving a wonderful display in both innings. Australia were still without Spofforth, but the side, chosen from the party to tour England that summer, was strengthened by the inclusion of Bannerman, Giffen and Boyle.

It was clear from the start that the ball would fly, and England struggled to 56 for 5. Shrewsbury then batted with consummate skill while Scotton defended, and 92 were put on for the 6th wicket. Emmett was soon out, Shaw was bowled by a shooter, and when Shrewsbury was 9th out at 164 he had made exactly half the total. Pilling and Peate added 24 for the last wicket, and then England hit back at once, Australia being 24 for 3 at the close. But Bannerman and McDonnell, the not out batsmen, were still together at lunch next day, and when play was abandoned during the afternoon after a heavy downpour Australia were 146 for 3, Bannerman and McDonnell

having already put on 130. The 21-year-old McDonnell, much the more aggressive, was 72 to Bannerman's 59.

On the third morning the wicket was dead and spongy and the England bowlers again failed to take a wicket. McDonnell hit Bates clean over the northern end of the pavilion, but he was missed for a second time by Shrewsbury at point just before completing his first century in first-class cricket. Australia were 215 for 3 at lunch, but immediately afterwards Bannerman was bowled by Midwinter, and Peate, who had found a spot on the drying wicket, then ran through the side. A margin of 72 was less than expected, but on this wicket it was a formidable lead.

Ulyett hit 23 quickly to follow up the roller, but Selby got one that squatted and when Shrewsbury went in England were 32 for 3. He was still there at the close, when England, after being 79 for 8, were 121 for 9, only 49 in front. On the fourth morning Australia were left with 63 to win, which considering the state of the wicket demanded steady play. Peate and Bates, bowling unchanged, took 4 good wickets between them before the winning hit was made in the 50th over.

ENGLAND

Batsman	1st Innings		2nd Innings	
G. Ulyett	b Palmer	0	b Garrett	23
R. G. Barlow	c Blackham b Garrett	4	c and b Garrett	8
J. Selby	c Massie b Palmer	13	b Palmer	1
W. Bates	c and b Palmer	1	c Bannerman b Garrett	2
A. Shrewsbury	c and b Boyle	82	c Boyle b Garrett	47
W. E. Midwinter	b Palmer	12	b Palmer	10
W. H. Scotton	c Jones b Garrett	18	b Palmer	1
T. Emmett	b Garrett	4	b Garrett	2
*A. Shaw	b Boyle	3	b Garrett	6
†R. Pilling	b Palmer	12	b Palmer	23
E. Peate	not out	11	not out	8
Extras	(b 22, lb 6)	28	(b 2, nb 1)	3
Total		188	Total	134

AUSTRALIA

Batsman	1st Innings		2nd Innings	
A. C. Bannerman	b Midwinter	70	c Pilling b Peate	14
H. H. Massie	b Bates	0	c Midwinter b Peate	9
*W. L. Murdoch	c Ulyett b Bates	6	c Midwinter b Bates	4
T. P. Horan	c and b Bates	1	not out	16
P. S. McDonnell	c Midwinter b Peate	147	c Emmett b Peate	4
G. Giffen	c Pilling b Peate	2		
†J. McC. Blackham	b Peate	4		
T. W. Garrett	b Peate	0		
G. E. Palmer	b Midwinter	6		
S. P. Jones	not out	7	(6) not out	10
H. F. Boyle	c Pilling b Peate	3		
Extras	(b 6, lb 8)	14	(b 2, lb 5, w 1, nb 1)	9
Total		260	Total (4 wkts)	66

FALL OF WICKETS

ENGLAND

Wkt	1st	2nd
1st	2	28
2nd	8	29
3rd	17	32
4th	35	42
5th	56	60
6th	148	70
7th	154	73
8th	159	79
9th	164	113
10th	188	134

AUSTRALIA

Wkt	1st	2nd
1st	0	14
2nd	10	21
3rd	16	39
4th	215	49
5th	228	—
6th	235	—
7th	244	—
8th	245	—
9th	252	—
10th	260	—

Umpires: J. Swift, James Lillywhite, jnr.

AUSTRALIA	1st Innings					2nd Innings			
	O	M	R	W		O	M	R	W
Palmer	45·2	23	46	5	..	40	19	44	4
Garrett	60	25	85	3	..	36·1	10	78	6
Boyle	27	18	18	2	..	4	1	9	0
Jones	8	5	11	0	..				

ENGLAND	1st Innings					2nd Innings			
	O	M	R	W		O	M	R	W
Peate	45	24	43	5	..	25	18	14	3
Bates	38	17	67	3	..	24·3	13	43	1
Ulyett	3	1	10	0	..				
Midwinter	62	25	75	2	..				
Shaw	8	4	14	0	..				
Emmett	16	6	37	0	..				

1881-82 Fourth Test, Melbourne

March 10, 11, 13, 14
Toss: England   *Result:* Match Drawn

Immediately after the third Test the two teams left Sydney by the evening train for Melbourne, where a second match was due to be played against the Australian touring party. The two tourists left out were Bonnor and Jones. In great heat, with an unpleasant hot wind, England were lucky to win the toss, and their innings of 309 was dominated by George Ulyett, who made 149, no one else reaching 30. Australia replied with 300, and at the end of the third day England were 234 for 2 in their second innings and seemed to have an outside chance of their only victory of the series. But at this point fate intervened. 'The weather', said one Melbourne report, 'which during the past week has been unpleasantly hot, underwent a very agreeable change yesterday ... about 11.0 a nice, steady, soaking rain began to fall.' It was all according to how you looked at it. Anyway, the fourth day, Tuesday 14 March, was washed out, and as the Australian team was leaving for England on the Thursday the game was not played out.

Ulyett, much more controlled than usual, was 30 not out at lunchtime on the first day, having survived a snick to the wicket-keeper which, fortunately for England, the umpire didn't hear. Driving and hitting to leg with more freedom in the afternoon, Ulyett was 95 not out at tea, and with all the bowlers mastered he made another 54 quickly afterwards, being 6th out at 239. England, 282 for 7 at the close, were all out next morning for 309.

Bannerman, although suffering from sunstroke, helped Murdoch to put on 110 for the Australian first wicket, and when Murdoch was out at 153 McDonnell and Massie attacked the tired bowlers, McDonnell hitting Midwinter into the crowd. 228 for 5 overnight, Australia failed to gain the expected advantage on the third morning and were all out after an hour's play for 300, 9 runs behind.

When they batted again all the England batsmen scored readily. Ulyett was caught on the boundary trying to put the hundred up for the first wicket, and Barlow, going for a third run, was brilliantly run out by Murdoch, throwing from the leg boundary to the bowler's end, but no other wicket fell. Blackham received some nasty knocks in this innings, but the wicket was still good, and a draw was in any case probable. The two draws in this series, both occasioned by sailing dates, were the last draws in Test Matches in Australia until 1946-47.

ENGLAND

G. Ulyett	c Blackham b Garrett	149	c Palmer b Boyle	64
R. G. Barlow	c Blackham b Garrett	16	run out	56
J. Selby	b Spofforth	7	not out	48
W. Bates	st Blackham b Garrett	23	not out	52
A. Shrewsbury	lbw b Palmer	1		
W. E. Midwinter	c Palmer b Boyle	21		
W. H. Scotton	st Blackham b Giffen	26		
T. Emmett	b Giffen	27		
*A. Shaw	c Murdoch b Garrett	3		
†R. Pilling	not out	6		
E. Peate	c and b Garrett	13		
Extras	(b 10, lb 7)	17	(b 12, lb 2)	14
Total		**309**	**Total** (2 wkts)	**234**

AUSTRALIA

*W. L. Murdoch	b Midwinter	85
A. C. Bannerman	c and b Midwinter	37
T. P. Horan	c and b Midwinter	20
P. S. McDonnell	c Barlow b Ulyett	52
H. H. Massie	c Emmett b Shaw	19
G. Giffen	c Scotton b Peate	14
†J. McC. Blackham	c Pilling b Midwinter	6
T. W. Garrett	c Ulyett b Bates	10
G. E. Palmer	c Ulyett b Bates	32
H. F. Boyle	c Shrewsbury b Bates	6
F. R. Spofforth	not out	3
Extras	(b 2, lb 7, w 6, nb 1)	16
Total		**300**

FALL OF WICKETS

ENGLAND		
Wkt	1st	2nd
1st	32	98
2nd	49	152
3rd	98	—
4th	109	—
5th	177	—
6th	239	—
7th	281	—
8th	284	—
9th	288	—
10th	309	—

AUSTRALIA		
Wkt	1st	2nd
1st	110	—
2nd	149	—
3rd	153	—
4th	189	—
5th	228	—
6th	237	—
7th	247	—
8th	280	—
9th	297	—
10th	300	—

Umpires: James Lillywhite, jnr.,
G. Coulthard

AUSTRALIA	1st Innings					2nd Innings			
	O	M	R	W		O	M	R	W
Garrett	54·2	23	80	5	..	27	6	62	0
Spofforth	51	14	92	1	..	15	3	36	0
Boyle	18	4	33	1	..	25	9	38	1
Palmer	23	5	70	1	..	20	5	47	0
Giffen	13	6	17	2	..	8·3	1	25	0
Bannerman					..	2	0	12	0

ENGLAND	1st Innings					2nd Innings			
	O	M	R	W		O	M	R	W
Bates	28·1	14	49	3	..				
Peate	20	6	38	1	..				
Emmett	19	14	22	0	..				
Ulyett	24	8	40	1	..				
Barlow	15	6	25	0	..				
Shaw	16	6	29	1	..				
Midwinter	41	9	81	4	..				

Averages: 1881-82

AUSTRALIA

BATTING	M.	Inns.	N.O.	Runs	H.S.	Av.
S. P. Jones	2	4	3	67	37	67·00
P. S. McDonnell	4	7	1	294	147	49·00
W. L. Murdoch	4	7	1	215	85	35·83
T. P. Horan	4	7	1	212	124	35·33
A. C. Bannerman	3	5	0	167	70	33·40
G. E. Palmer	4	4	0	88	34	22·00
H. H. Massie	4	6	0	101	49	16·83
G. Giffen	3	3	0	46	30	15·33
T. W. Garrett	3	4	1	45	31*	15·00
J. McC. Blackham	4	6	0	81	40	13·50
E. Evans	2	2	0	14	11	7·00
H. F. Boyle	4	4	1	13	6	4·33

PLAYED IN ONE TEST: W. H. Cooper 7, G. Coulthard 6*, F. R. Spofforth 3*.

BOWLING	Overs	Mds.	Runs	Wkts.	Av.
T. W. Garrett	213·3	76	367	18	20·38
G. E. Palmer	365·2	145	522	24	21·75
W. H. Cooper	98·2	27	200	9	22·22
H. F. Boyle	107	47	135	6	22·50
E. Evans	243·3	131	257	7	36·71

ALSO BOWLED: G. Giffen 24·3–7–54–2, S. P. Jones 19–9–30–1, F. R. Spofforth 66–17–128–1, A. C. Bannerman 12–3–35–0, P. S. McDonnell 4–1–15–0.

ENGLAND

BATTING	M.	Inns.	N.O.	Runs	H.S.	Av.
G. Ulyett	4	8	0	438	149	54·75
J. Selby	4	8	1	202	70	28·85
W. Bates	4	8	1	192	58	27·42
A. Shrewsbury	4	7	0	186	82	26·57
W. H. Scotton	4	7	1	158	50*	26·33
R. G. Barlow	4	8	0	210	62	26·25
E. Peate	4	7	5	40	13	20·00
A. Shaw	4	7	0	98	40	14·00
W. E. Midwinter	4	7	0	95	36	13·57
R. Pilling	4	7	1	61	23	10·16
T. Emmett	4	7	0	63	27	9·00

BOWLING	Overs	Mds.	Runs	Wkts.	Av.
W. Bates	241	121	334	16	20·87
G. Ulyett	99·2	37	180	8	22·50
E. Peate	232	117	256	11	23·27
W. E. Midwinter	194	79	272	10	27·20

ALSO BOWLED: A. Shaw 65–36–76–2, T. Emmett 98–48–180–2, R. G. Barlow 50–24–61–0.

Averages: 1882-83

AUSTRALIA

BATTING	M.	Inns.	N.O.	Runs	H.S.	Av.
A. C. Bannerman	4	8	1	255	94	36·42
J. McC. Blackham	4	7	1	204	58*	34·00
G. J. Bonnor	4	7	0	217	87	31·00
W. L. Murdoch	4	8	2	153	48	25·50
G. Giffen	4	7	0	162	41	23·14
P. S. McDonnell	3	5	0	59	43	11·80
H. H. Massie	3	6	0	69	43	11·50
F. R. Spofforth	4	6	2	31	14*	7·75
T. P. Horan	4	7	0	49	19	7·00
G. E. Palmer	4	6	2	20	7	5·00
T. W. Garrett	3	5	0	16	10	3·20

PLAYED IN ONE TEST: E. Evans 22* and 0, W. E. Midwinter 10 and 8*, H. F. Boyle 29.

BOWLING	Overs	Mds.	Runs	Wkts.	Av.
T. P. Horan	38	16	63	5	12·60
H. F. Boyle	63	25	87	5	17·40
G. E. Palmer	270·1	113	397	21	18·90
G. Giffen	81	23	164	8	20·50
F. R. Spofforth	244·1	93	408	18	22·66

ALSO BOWLED: A. C. Bannerman 11–2–17–1, W. E. Midwinter 70–37–71–4, T. W. Garrett 103–34–168–3, E. Evans 11–3–15–0, P. S. McDonnell 4–0–16–0.

ENGLAND

BATTING	M.	Inns.	N.O.	Runs	H.S.	Av.
A. G. Steel	4	7	1	274	135*	45·66
W. W. Read	4	7	0	228	75	32·57
W. Bates	4	7	1	172	55	28·66
C. T. Studd	4	7	0	160	48	22·85
E. F. S. Tylecote	4	7	0	142	66	20·28
R. G. Barlow	4	7	0	126	28	18·00
C. F. H. Leslie	4	7	0	106	54	15·14
W. Barnes	4	7	1	87	32	14·50
Hon. Ivo Bligh	4	7	1	62	19	10·33
G. B. Studd	4	7	0	31	9	4·42
F. Morley	3	5	2	4	2*	1·33

PLAYED IN ONE TEST: G. F. Vernon 11* and 3.

BOWLING	Overs	Mds.	Runs	Wkts.	Av.
W. Bates	192·3	87	286	19	15·05
A. G. Steel	130	49	195	11	17·72
F. Morley	150	85	150	8	18·75
R. G. Barlow	244	124	343	15	22·86
W. Barnes	108	40	170	6	28·33

ALSO BOWLED: C. F. H. Leslie 24–10–44–4, C. T. Studd 92–59–89–3, W. W. Read 8–2–27–0.

1882 Only Test, Oval

August 28, 29
Toss: Australia   *Result:* Australia won by 7 runs

English touring sides had lost matches in Australia, and Australian touring teams had had great victories in England, but against the full strength of English cricket in England it was taken for granted—except perhaps by the players themselves—that England must win. Confirmation of such a view came in the weeks before the game, when the Australians lost to the Players and to Cambridge University Past and Present. When it was known that George Palmer, one of their greatest bowlers, was unfit, victory for England seemed doubly sure.

Australia batted first on a wicket that had been drenched with rain in the previous two days and in 2¼ hours were dismissed for 63, their lowest score of the tour. 80 four-ball overs were bowled, and the two left-handers, Barlow and Peate, got 9 of the wickets. Difficult as the conditions were, the Australians offered no excuses for their wretched display. What they did do, however, was to hit back. Spofforth, bowling from the gasworks end, yorked Grace for 4 and had Barlow caught at 18, and although Ulyett, after a shaky start, hit cleanly for a time, England lost 6 wickets before passing the Australian score and were held to a lead of 38.

In the opinion of some people the ground next day was unfit for cricket, more heavy rain having fallen, but a start was made soon after midday. While the ground was wet and the ball soapy Massie took full advantage, and he and Bannerman knocked off the arrears. Massie, after being dropped in front of the pavilion by Lucas, reached 50 out of 61 in 45 minutes, a great piece of attacking cricket. The wicket, however, was beginning to take spin, and at 66 Massie lost his leg stump. Although Murdoch held one end a collapse followed and the Australians were all out at 3.20 for 122, leaving England only 85 to win.

The story of how the English batsmen, shivering in the chill of a bitter August afternoon, lost their nerve at a crisis after coming within 34 runs of victory with 8 wickets standing, has made this the most legendary of all cricket matches. In reality, however, they were bowled out on a responsive wicket by the tall, beak-nosed Spofforth and the bearded Boyle. Spofforth's match figures of 14 for 90 have never been bettered by an Australian.

Australian resolve to win this match was fortified by an incident in their second innings, when the 21-year-old Jones, after responding to a call for a single and completing the run, moved down the wicket to do some 'gardening' and was run out by Grace.

AUSTRALIA

A. C. Bannerman	c Grace b Peate	9	c Studd b Barnes	13	
H. H. Massie	b Ulyett	1	b Steel	55	
*W. L. Murdoch	b Peate	13	(4)run out	29	
G. J. Bonnor	b Barlow	1	(3)b Ulyett	2	
T. P. Horan	b Barlow	3	c Grace b Peate	2	
G. Giffen	b Peate	2	c Grace b Peate	0	
†J. McC. Blackham	c Grace b Barlow	17	c Lyttelton b Peate	7	
T. W. Garrett	c Read b Peate	10	(10)not out	2	
H. F. Boyle	b Barlow	2	(11)b Steel	0	
S. P. Jones	c Barnes b Barlow	0	(8)run out	6	
F. R. Spofforth	not out	4	(9)b Peate	0	
Extras	(b 1)	1	(b 6)	6	
Total		63	Total	122	

ENGLAND

R. G. Barlow	c Bannerman b Spofforth	11	(3)b Spofforth	0	
W. G. Grace	b Spofforth	4	c Bannerman b Boyle	32	
G. Ulyett	st Blackham b Spofforth	26	(4)c Blackham b Spofforth	11	
A. P. Lucas	c Blackham b Boyle	9	(5)b Spofforth	5	
†Hon. A. Lyttelton	c Blackham b Spofforth	2	(6)b Spofforth	12	
C. T. Studd	b Spofforth	0	(10)not out	0	
J. M. Read	not out	19	(8)b Spofforth	0	
W. Barnes	b Boyle	5	(9)c Murdoch b Boyle	2	
A. G. Steel	b Garrett	14	(7)c and b Spofforth	0	
*A. N. Hornby	b Spofforth	2	(1)b Spofforth	9	
E. Peate	c Boyle b Spofforth	0	b Boyle	2	
Extras	(b 6, lb 2, nb 1)	9	(b 3, nb 1)	4	
Total		101	Total	77	

FALL OF WICKETS

AUSTRALIA

Wkt	1st	2nd
1st	6	66
2nd	21	70
3rd	22	70
4th	26	79
5th	30	79
6th	30	99
7th	48	114
8th	53	117
9th	59	122
10th	63	122

ENGLAND

Wkt	1st	2nd
1st	13	15
2nd	18	15
3rd	57	51
4th	59	53
5th	60	66
6th	63	70
7th	70	70
8th	96	75
9th	101	75
10th	101	77

Umpires: R. Thoms, L. Greenwood

ENGLAND	1st Innings				2nd Innings			
	O	M	R	W	O	M	R	W
Peate	38	24	31	4	21	9	40	4
Ulyett	9	5	11	1	6	2	10	1
Barlow	31	22	19	5	13	5	27	0
Steel	2	1	1	0	7	0	15	2
Barnes					12	5	15	1
Studd					4	1	9	0

AUSTRALIA	1st Innings				2nd Innings			
	O	M	R	W	O	M	R	W
Spofforth	36·3	18	46	7	28	15	44	7
Garrett	16	7	22	1	7	2	10	0
Boyle	19	7	24	2	20	11	19	3

13. E. Peate

14. H. H. Massie

15. **Australia 1882**
Standing: G. E. Palmer, H. F. Boyle, W. L. Murdoch (capt.), P. S. McDonnell, F. R. Spofforth, T. P. Horan, S. P. Jones.
Seated: C. W. Beal (manager), G. Giffen, A. C. Bannerman, T. W. Garrett, H. H. Massie, G. J. Bonnor.

1882-83 First Test, Melbourne

December 30, January 1, 2
Toss: Australia   *Result:* Australia won by nine wickets

The body of English cricket having been cremated after the 1882 Oval Test and the Ashes taken to Australia (according to the famous obituary notice in the *Sporting Times*), an English team, strong though not fully representative, at once travelled in quest of them. It was a crusade, as others have since found, of many setbacks and frustrations. Morley, the only fast bowler in the party, suffered an injury on the voyage out which kept him out of seven matches, and the first Test was irrevocably lost when rain fell after the Australians had batted, though this misfortune was counter-balanced in the third Test. A fourth match was then played against a combined team after the three arranged against Murdoch's 1882 touring party, and in winning this Australia in effect squared the rubber, though the urn containing the 'Ashes' had been presented to the English captain after the third game.

Massie was soon out, but Bannerman and Murdoch batted patiently, and although Bligh tried 6 bowlers in the first session, including Read with underhand lobs, Australia were 46 for 1 at lunch. After lunch Bligh tried Leslie, fastish but erratic, and he met with surprising success. He yorked Murdoch, Barlow hung on to a fast-travelling

snick off him at deep slip to dismiss Horan, and Tylecote, standing up, stumped Bannerman, making Australia 96 for 4.

After one or two mishits against Steel's flighted slows, McDonnell and Giffen began to play more safely, and they put on 66 before McDonnell was bowled by the round-arm Bates. Bonnor came in and twice hit the ball into the crowd, but Giffen ran out to Steel's leg-breaks once too often and was stumped. The giant Bonnor went on swinging the bat, hitting Bates into the elm trees and being dropped by Read off a vast skier in front of the pavilion, and at stumps Australia were 258 for 7, Bonnor 60 not out.

20,000 people were present on the second day, and they saw some absorbing cricket. Heavy rain had fallen in the night, and after the last 3 Australian wickets had fallen for 33, the Englishmen struggled gamely against accurate bowling to stay in the match. Bates, missed twice, put on 51 with Read for the 6th wicket, and the graceful Tylecote, who opened when England followed on, played two fine knocks. He and Barlow began the England second innings by putting on 64, but the batting on the third day lacked assurance on a much improved wicket, and Murdoch's side were left with only 56 to win.

AUSTRALIA

A. C. Bannerman	st Tylecote b Leslie	30	not out	25	
H. H. Massie	c and b C. T. Studd	4	c and b Barnes	0	
*W. L. Murdoch	b Leslie	48	not out	33	
T. P. Horan	c Barlow b Leslie	0			
P. S. McDonnell	b Bates	43			
G. Giffen	st Tylecote b Steel	36			
G. J. Bonnor	c Barlow b Barnes	85			
†J. McC. Blackham	c Tylecote b C. T. Studd	25			
F. R. Spofforth	c Steel b Barnes	9			
T. W. Garrett	c C. T. Studd b Steel	0			
G. E. Palmer	not out	0			
Extras	(b 4, lb 2, w 2, nb 3)	11			
Total		**291**	**Total (1 wkt)**	**58**	

ENGLAND

R. G. Barlow	st Blackham b Palmer	10	b Spofforth	28	
*Hon. Ivo Bligh	b Palmer	0	(5)b Spofforth	3	
C. F. H. Leslie	c Garrett b Palmer	4	(7)b Giffen	4	
C. T. Studd	b Spofforth	0	(3)b Palmer	21	
A. G. Steel	b Palmer	27	(4)lbw b Giffen	29	
W. W. Read	b Palmer	19	b Giffen	29	
W. Bates	c Bannerman b Garrett	28	(8)c Massie b Palmer	11	
†E. F. S. Tylecote	b Palmer	33	(2)b Spofforth	38	
G. B. Studd	run out	7	c Palmer b Giffen	0	
W. Barnes	b Palmer	26	not out	2	
G. F. Vernon	not out	11	lbw b Palmer	3	
Extras	(b 8, lb 1, nb 3)	12	(lb 1)	1	
Total		**177**	**Total**	**169**	

FALL OF WICKETS

AUSTRALIA

Wkt	1st	2nd
1st	5	0
2nd	81	—
3rd	81	—
4th	96	—
5th	162	—
6th	190	—
7th	251	—
8th	289	—
9th	289	—
10th	291	—

ENGLAND

Wkt	1st	2nd
1st	2	64
2nd	7	75
3rd	8	105
4th	36	108
5th	45	132
6th	96	150
7th	96	164
8th	117	164
9th	156	164
10th	177	169

Umpires: J. Swift
E. H. Elliott

ENGLAND	1st Innings					2nd Innings			
	O	M	R	W		O	M	R	W
C. T. Studd	46	30	35	2	..	14	11	7	0
Barnes	30	11	51	2	..	13	8	6	1
Steel	33	16	68	2	..	9	4	17	0
Barlow	20	6	37	0	..	4	2	6	0
Bates	21	7	31	1	..	13.1	7	22	0
Read	8	2	27	0	..				
Leslie	11	1	31	3	..				

AUSTRALIA	1st Innings					2nd Innings			
	O	M	R	W		O	M	R	W
Spofforth	28	11	56	1	..	41	15	65	3
Palmer	52.2	25	65	7	..	36.1	11	61	3
Garrett	27	6	44	1	..	2	1	4	0
Giffen					..	20	7	38	4

16. G. J. Bonnor

17. A. G. Steel

18. England 1882-83
Back row: W. Barnes, F. Morley, C. T. Studd, G. F. Vernon, C. F. H. Leslie. *Middle row:* G. B. Studd, E. F. S. Tylecote, Hon. Ivo Bligh (capt.), A. G. Steel, W. W. Read. *Front:* R. G. Barlow, W. Bates.

1882-83 Second Test, Melbourne

January 19, 20, 22
Toss: England   *Result:* England won by an innings and 27 runs

Palmer, whose variations of pace and spin had dominated the previous game, beat Studd at 28 and Barlow at 35, but Leslie, a lively cricketer, scored rapidly at once, and with Steel supporting him cautiously England at lunch were 68 for 2. The game continued evenly in the afternoon. A brilliant pick up and return by Spofforth, whose bowling had made no impression, ran out Leslie at 106, and Steel went at 131. Spofforth tried a spell at top speed in vain, and Read and Barnes added 62 before Barnes, after several escapes, was bowled by the slow-medium Giffen. Tylecote and Bligh followed in quick succession, both bowled by the same bowler off the same spot, and England were 199 for 7. Then Bates, reckless at first but concentrating as his luck held (he was dropped in the outfield by Horan), stayed with Read until the close at 247 for 7, and the partnership had reached 88 next morning when Horan took a catch on the boundary from Bates very similar to the one he had missed the previous day. Australia were left with 15 minutes' batting before lunch, a potentially nerve-wracking period in which Massie answered criticism of his selection and delighted the crowd by making most of the 30 runs scored. When 40 went up after

lunch Massie had made 34 to Bannerman's 2, the crowd being vastly entertained at the way the fielders clustered round Bannerman and scattered in alarm for Massie. But when Massie was out at 56 the cricket became slow.

Bates, the fifth bowler to be tried, aimed for the spot at the northern end which he believed Giffen had hit, and he proceeded to use it with even greater effect. He clean bowled Bannerman, and after Barnes had leapt and hung on one-handed to a return catch from Horan he bowled McDonnell, took an easy caught and bowled from Giffen, and then, after a consultation, set a trap for Bonnor for the hat-trick ball, getting him caught at close mid on. While Murdoch defended (he batted 2½ hours) Bates went on to take three of the last four wickets, and although when Australia followed on he was withdrawn from the attack for three overs while Bonnor was hitting everything, he came back to take 7 wickets in the innings and 14 in the match. Besides doing the hat trick he thus became the first of only three cricketers to score 50 or more and take 10 wickets in the same match.

ENGLAND

R. G. Barlow	b Palmer		14
C. T. Studd	b Palmer		14
C. F. H. Leslie	run out		54
A. G. Steel	c McDonnell b Giffen		39
W. W. Read	c and b Palmer		75
W. Barnes	b Giffen		32
†E. F. S. Tylecote	b Giffen		0
*Hon. Ivo Bligh	b Giffen		0
W. Bates	c Horan b Palmer		55
G. B. Studd	b Palmer		1
F. Morley	not out		0
Extras	(b 3, lb 3, nb 4)		10
Total			**294**

AUSTRALIA

H. H. Massie	b Barlow	43	(7)c C. T. Studd b Barlow	10
A. C. Bannerman	b Bates	14	c Bligh b Bates	14
*W. L. Murdoch	not out	19	(1)b Bates	17
T. P. Horan	c and b Barnes	3	(5)c Morley b Bates	15
P. S. McDonnell	b Bates	3	(6)b Bates	13
G. Giffen	c and b Bates	0	(8)c Bligh b Bates	19
G. J. Bonnor	c Read b Bates	0	(4)c Morley b Barlow	34
†J. McC. Blackham	b Barnes	5	(3)b Barlow	6
T. W. Garrett	b Bates	10	c Barnes b Bates	6
G. E. Palmer	b Bates	7	c G. B. Studd b Bates	4
F. R. Spofforth	b Bates	0	not out	14
Extras	(b 6, lb 3, nb 1)	10	(b 1)	1
Total		**114**	**Total**	**153**

FALL OF WICKETS

ENGLAND

Wkt	1st	2nd
1st	28	—
2nd	35	—
3rd	106	—
4th	131	—
5th	193	—
6th	199	—
7th	199	—
8th	287	—
9th	293	—
10th	294	—

AUSTRALIA

Wkt	1st	2nd
1st	56	21
2nd	72	28
3rd	75	66
4th	78	72
5th	78	93
6th	78	104
7th	85	113
8th	104	132
9th	114	139
10th	114	153

Umpires: J. Swift,
E. H. Elliott

AUSTRALIA	1st Innings				2nd Innings			
	O	M	R	W	O	M	R	W
Spofforth	34	11	57	0	..			
Palmer	66·3	25	103	5	..			
Giffen	49	13	89	4	..			
Garrett	34	16	35	0	..			

ENGLAND	1st Innings				2nd Innings			
	O	M	R	W	O	M	R	W
C. T. Studd	4	1	22	0	..			
Morley	23	16	13	0	..	2	0	7	0
Barnes	23	7	32	2	..	3	1	4	0
Barlow	22	18	9	1	..	31	6	67	3
Bates	26·2	14	28	7	..	33	14	74	7

1882-83 Third Test, Sydney

January 26, 27, 29, 30
Toss: England *Result:* England won by 69 runs

C. T. Studd's classical forward play, and Spofforth's great pace with the wind behind him, were early features after England had won the toss. 40 went up without loss, but Murdoch, making frequent bowling changes, succeeded in gaining the advantage by lunch-time, when England were 67 for 3. After lunch Steel was yorked and Barnes got a good one, and when Tylecote joined Read at 75 for 5 with Spofforth and Garrett in full cry, game and rubber were clearly in the balance. Tylecote at once began to go for his strokes, and his partnership with Read, which added 116, proved to be the turning point. The play quietened down during a period of bad light in the afternoon, but the rain held off, and England reached the useful total of 247. Australia, batting as agreed on a fresh wicket to reduce the importance of the toss, were 8 for 0 at the close.

After heavy rain in the night, play began next morning under a leaden sky. The wicket, however, was dead, Bannerman and Giffen met the accurate English attack with great coolness, and at lunch Australia were 72 for 0. More rain squalls during the interval gave England a wet ball to bowl with, but it was noticeable that Bates was getting some turn, and he had Giffen stumped at 76. Soon after the 100 went up the game was interrupted by more heavy showers, and it was

not until 5.15 that play restarted. Then Bannerman and Murdoch, surviving a number of mistimed shots on the quickened turf, surprised everyone by holding on until the close.

At 133 for 1 Australia were well placed; but very heavy rain all day Sunday made the wicket treacherous on the third day, and they would never have reached their total of 218 but for a deplorable display by England in the field. England then batted on the same wicket they had used in their first innings, and some grand driving by Studd got them going, but when the wicket cut up their collapse was taken as a matter of course. On the fourth day the good weather returned and Australia, wanting 153 to win with all their wickets intact, looked to have a reasonable task, but disappointment and dismay followed as the quicker bowling cavorted in all directions on the treacherous turf. Barlow, left-hand medium, bowled a fuller length than Morley and took 7 for 40.

England having won the decider of the three matches arranged against Murdoch's team of 1882, a group of Australian ladies burned a bail, sealed the ashes in an urn and presented it to Bligh. This is the urn to be seen now in the memorial gallery at Lord's.

ENGLAND

Batsman	1st Innings		2nd Innings	
R. G. Barlow	c Murdoch b Spofforth	28	(3)c Palmer b Horan	24
C. T. Studd	c Blackham b Garrett	21	b Spofforth	25
C. F. H. Leslie	b Spofforth	0	(1)b Spofforth	8
A. G. Steel	b Garrett	17	lbw b Spofforth	6
W. W. Read	c Massie b Bannerman	66	b Horan	21
W. Barnes	b Spofforth	2	lbw b Spofforth	3
†E. F. S. Tylecote	run out	66	c Bonnor b Spofforth	0
W. Bates	c McDonnell b Spofforth	17	c Murdoch b Horan	4
G. B. Studd	b Palmer	3	(10)c Garrett b Spofforth	8
*Hon. Ivo Bligh	b Palmer	13	(9)not out	17
F. Morley	not out	2	b Spofforth	0
Extras	(b 8, lb 3, nb 1)	12	(b 5, lb 2)	7
Total		**247**		**123**

AUSTRALIA

Batsman	1st Innings		2nd Innings	
A. C. Bannerman	c Bates b Morley	94	c Bligh b Barlow	5
G. Giffen	st Tylecote b Bates	41	b Barlow	7
*W. L. Murdoch	lbw b Steel	19	c G. B. Studd b Morley	0
P. S. McDonnell	b Steel	0	(5)c Bligh b Morley	0
T. P. Horan	c Steel b Morley	19	(4)run out	8
H. H. Massie	c Bligh b Steel	1	c C. T. Studd b Barlow	11
G. J. Bonnor	c G. B. Studd b Morley	0	b Barlow	8
†J. McC. Blackham	b Barlow	27	b Barlow	26
T. W. Garrett	c Barlow b Morley	0	(11)b Barlow	0
G. E. Palmer	c G. B. Studd b Barnes	7	not out	2
F. R. Spofforth	not out	0	(9)c Steel b Barlow	7
Extras	(b 6, lb 2, nb 1, w 1)	10	(b 6, lb 2, w 1)	9
Total		**218**		**83**

FALL OF WICKETS

ENGLAND		
Wkt	1st	2nd
1st	41	13
2nd	44	45
3rd	67	55
4th	69	87
5th	75	92
6th	191	94
7th	223	97
8th	224	98
9th	244	115
10th	247	123

AUSTRALIA		
Wkt	1st	2nd
1st	76	11
2nd	140	12
3rd	140	18
4th	176	18
5th	177	30
6th	178	33
7th	196	56
8th	196	72
9th	218	80
10th	218	83

Umpires: J. Swift,
E. H. Elliott

AUSTRALIA

Bowler	1st Innings				2nd Innings			
	O	M	R	W	O	M	R	W
Giffen	12	3	37	0				
Palmer	38	21	38	2	9	3	19	0
Spofforth	51	19	73	4	41·1	23	44	7
Garrett	27	8	54	2	13	3	31	0
Bannerman	11	2	17	1				
McDonnell	4	0	16	0				
Horan					17	10	22	3

ENGLAND

Bowler	1st Innings				2nd Innings			
	O	M	R	W	O	M	R	W
Morley	34	16	47	4	35	19	34	2
Barlow	47·1	31	52	1	34·2	20	40	7
Bates	45	20	55	1				
Barnes	13	6	22	1				
C. T. Studd	14	11	5	0				
Steel	26	14	27	3				

February 17, 19, 20, 21
Toss: England   *Result:* Australia won by four wickets

Not satisfied with the experiment of batting on two separate tracks—or perhaps intoxicated by it—the captains decided on four separate wickets, one for each innings, for the match with the combined team. Bowling at medium pace into a gale-force wind throughout the first morning, Midwinter, who had changed his allegiance again, earned the comment that no one else would have been strong enough to do it, and his figures give a hint of what an asset he was in this game.

48 for 2 at lunch, England were going well and had reached 110 without further loss when Studd was run out after being sent back by Steel. Steel's leg hitting was thrilling to watch and he completely dominated the rest of the England innings, but he was missed twice. England were all out first thing next morning, and the Australians then took some time in selecting a wicket. When they were eventually ready the contrast in size and method between Bannerman and Bonnor struck the crowd as irresistibly comic, but the laughter was soon silenced by the cricket. At 39 for 3 Giffen, who had suffered a strain before the game and had been unable to bowl, came in with Murdoch to run for him, and at lunch he and Bonnor, thanks to dropped catches, were still together. Bonnor, too, was unwell, and his 87, valuable as

it was, was not one of his best innings. The workmanlike Blackham took over the run-getting when Bonnor was out.

One run ahead, England in their turn examined the square critically, and they had 40 up without loss before lunch on the third day. Spofforth then bowled at his fastest, Palmer was at his most deadly, and when Steel left England were 112 for 6. A fine attacking innings by Bates then gave them a chance, Australia beginning their second innings on the fourth morning needing 199 to win. But English sympathisers must have wondered what hope their team had when, after several stretches of turf had been carefully prepared, each one was tried out in turn by a fast bowler at either end and the results observed.

Bannerman, missed behind the wicket early on, discarded his normal role of stonewaller and played many thrilling strokes, but when he was out at 107 for 4 England were back in the game. Blackham and Giffen then put on 55, and after 6 wickets had fallen for 164 Blackham, in partnership now with Midwinter, knocked off the runs. The English team, who caused irritation by their continual conferences in midfield as the game went against them, earned praise afterwards for the way they fought the game out without losing heart.

ENGLAND

Batsman	1st Innings	Runs	2nd Innings	Runs
R. G. Barlow	c Murdoch b Midwinter	2	c Bonnor b Midwinter	20
C. T. Studd	run out	48	c Murdoch b Midwinter	31
C. F. H. Leslie	c Bonnor b Boyle	17	b Horan	19
A. G. Steel	not out	135	b Spofforth	21
W. W. Read	c Bonnor b Boyle	11	b Spofforth	7
†E. F. S. Tylecote	b Boyle	5	b Palmer	0
W. Barnes	b Spofforth	2	(9)c and b Boyle	20
W. Bates	c Bonnor b Midwinter	9	(7)not out	48
*Hon. Ivo Bligh	b Palmer	19	(8)c Murdoch b Horan	10
G. B. Studd	run out	3	c Murdoch b Boyle	9
F. Morley	b Palmer	0	c Blackham b Palmer	2
Extras	(b 4, lb 7, nb 1)	12	(b 8, lb 1, nb 1)	10
Total		**263**	**Total**	**197**

AUSTRALIA

Batsman	1st Innings	Runs	2nd Innings	Runs
A. C. Bannerman	c Barlow b Morley	10	c Bligh b C. T. Studd	63
G. J. Bonnor	c Barlow b Steel	87	(3)c G. B. Studd b Steel	3
*W. L. Murdoch	b Barlow	0	(2)c Barlow b Bates	17
T. P. Horan	c G. B. Studd b Morley	4	c and b Bates	0
G. Giffen	c G. B. Studd b Leslie	27	st Tylecote b Steel	32
W. E. Midwinter	b Barlow	10	(8)not out	8
†J. McC. Blackham	b Bates	57	(6)not out	58
G. E. Palmer	c Bligh b Steel	0		
E. Evans	not out	22	(7)c Leslie b Steel	0
F. R. Spofforth	c Bates b Steel	1		
H. F. Boyle	c G. B. Studd b Barlow	29		
Extras	(b 10, lb 3, w 2)	15	(b 10, lb 4, w 4)	18
Total		**262**	**Total (6 wkts)**	**199**

FALL OF WICKETS

ENGLAND

Wkt	1st	2nd
1st	13	54
2nd	37	55
3rd	110	77
4th	150	99
5th	156	100
6th	159	112
7th	199	137
8th	236	178
9th	263	192
10th	263	197

AUSTRALIA

Wkt	1st	2nd
1st	31	44
2nd	34	51
3rd	39	51
4th	113	107
5th	128	162
6th	160	164
7th	164	—
8th	220	—
9th	221	—
10th	262	—

Umpires: J. Swift, E. H. Elliott

AUSTRALIA

	1st Innings				2nd Innings			
	O	M	R	W	O	M	R	W
Palmer	24	9	52	2	43·3	19	59	2
Midwinter	47	24	50	2	23	13	21	2
Spofforth	21	8	56	1	28	6	57	2
Boyle	40	19	52	3	23	6	35	2
Horan	12	4	26	0	9	2	15	2
Evans	11	3	15	0				

ENGLAND

	1st Innings				2nd Innings			
	O	M	R	W	O	M	R	W
Barlow	48	21	88	3	37·1	20	44	0
Morley	44	23	45	2	12	9	4	0
Barnes	10	2	33	0	16	5	22	0
Bates	15	6	24	1	39	19	52	2
Leslie	5	2	11	1	8	7	2	0
Steel	19	6	34	3	43	9	49	3
C. T. Studd	6	2	12	0	8	4	8	1

1884 First Test, Old Trafford

July 10, 11, 12
Toss: England   *Result:* Match Drawn

The Oval game of 1882, and the halved series of matches in Australia in 1882-83, had stimulated so much interest that three matches were arranged for the Australian visit of 1884, in an effort to reach a clear decision. England, by winning the Lord's Test and escaping defeat in the other two, won the Ashes, but Australia, who brought much the same side as two years earlier, were still a great team and probably the better side.

After the first day at Old Trafford had been washed out, the ground on the second day was muddy and spongy, and England, struggling through the morning to 83 for 6 at lunch, would have been in a sorry position but for Shrewsbury, who as always on bad wickets batted in masterly style. The only batsmen to give him any support were Steel and Lucas. Spofforth and Boyle, who were always destructive in England under these conditions, took the wickets between them. Australia soon lost Bannerman, but McDonnell and Murdoch in their contrasting styles both batted well, Midwinter hit effectively, and by the end of the day Australia were 141 for 7. They added another 41 runs on the last morning, leaving England needing 87 to avoid an innings defeat.

The afternoon's cricket was utterly absorbing as the Australians strained after victory and England fought to keep them out. Lucas, who gave a difficult chance to Blackham early on, played superb defensive cricket, while Grace showed great judgment and skill. The wicket had dried a good deal, and the Australian bowlers were getting plenty of work on the ball. When Grace was out Ulyett soon followed, but Shrewsbury gave another fine display, putting on 26 with Lucas and 36 with Steel, so that with 90 minutes left England were 14 runs ahead with 7 wickets still to fall. The situation then changed completely: Shrewsbury, Steel and Barnes were all out in quick succession, and England with 6 wickets down were only 27 ahead. At this point Spofforth was brought back to finish off the tail.

There had been some surprise at the inclusion of T. C. O'Brien in the side, and in the first innings he had been bowled by Spofforth first ball. Normally a forcing bat, he now perpetrated such a succession of edges and flukes that England were soon safe from defeat. The Australians, however, had given a great display of bowling and fielding, and the abandoned first day almost certainly cost them the match.

ENGLAND

W. G. Grace	c Palmer b Boyle	8	b Palmer	31	
*A. N. Hornby	st Blackham b Boyle	0	(9)st Blackham b Palmer	4	
G. Ulyett	b Spofforth	5	c Bannerman b Boyle	1	
A. Shrewsbury	b Boyle	43	b Palmer	25	
A. G. Steel	c Midwinter b Spofforth	15	c Blackham b Bonnor	18	
A. P. Lucas	not out	15	(2)b Giffen	24	
W. Barnes	c and b Boyle	0	(6)b Palmer	8	
T. C. O'Brien	b Spofforth	0	c Bannerman b Spofforth	20	
R. G. Barlow	c Bonnor b Boyle	6	(7)not out	14	
†R. Pilling	c Scott b Boyle	0	b Spofforth	3	
E. Peate	b Spofforth	2	not out	8	
Extras	(lb 1)	1	(b 18, lb 5, nb 1)	24	
Total		**95**	**Total (9 wkts)**	**180**	

AUSTRALIA

P. S. McDonnell	c Pilling b Steel	36
A. C. Bannerman	lbw b Ulyett	6
*W. L. Murdoch	c Grace b Peate	28
G. Giffen	c and b Barnes	16
W. E. Midwinter	c Grace b Ulyett	37
G. J. Bonnor	hit wkt b Peate	6
†J. McC. Blackham	lbw b Steel	8
H. J. H. Scott	b Grace	12
G. E. Palmer	not out	14
F. R. Spofforth	c Shrewsbury b Peate	13
H. F. Boyle	b Ulyett	4
Extras	(lb 2)	2
Total		**182**

FALL OF WICKETS

ENGLAND

Wkt	1st	2nd
1st	6	41
2nd	13	44
3rd	13	70
4th	45	106
5th	83	108
6th	83	114
7th	84	139
8th	93	145
9th	93	154
10th	95	—

AUSTRALIA

Wkt	1st	2nd
1st	10	—
2nd	56	—
3rd	86	—
4th	90	—
5th	97	—
6th	118	—
7th	141	—
8th	157	—
9th	172	—
10th	182	—

Umpires: J. Rowbotham, C. K. Pullin

AUSTRALIA	1st Innings					2nd Innings			
	O	M	R	W		O	M	R	W
Spofforth	32	10	42	4	..	41	17	52	2
Boyle	25	9	42	6	..	20	8	27	1
Palmer	6	2	10	0	..	36	17	47	4
Giffen					..	29	15	25	1
Bonnor					..	4	1	5	1

ENGLAND	1st Innings					2nd Innings			
	O	M	R	W		O	M	R	W
Peate	49	25	62	3	..				
Ulyett	30	17	41	3	..				
Barlow	8	3	18	0	..				
Steel	13	5	32	2	..				
Barnes	19	10	25	1	..				
Grace	11	10	2	1	..				

1884 Second Test, Lord's

July 21, 22, 23
Toss: Australia   *Result:* England won by an innings and 5 runs

Thanks largely to a plucky and determined last-wicket stand by Scott and Boyle, Australia recovered so well from a bad start that by the end of the first day they were almost on terms. Four wickets fell for 46, all to Peate from the nursery end, but Giffen and Bonnor improved matters by adding 42, and at lunch Australia were 117 for 6. Scott, combining a strong defence with some clean cutting and leg hitting, continued to bat well, and after 9 wickets had fallen for 160 he and Boyle put on 69 for the last wicket. Scott was eventually caught at point by Murdoch, substituting for Grace, who was off the field with an injured finger. In spite of this injury he opened with Lucas when England began their reply at 4.50. The 50 was reached at 6.0 for the loss of Grace, and Lucas batted in his usual classic style for 28, but just when it seemed that Shrewsbury and Ulyett would play out time Shrewsbury was stumped off Giffen. At 90 for 3, England's advantage was scarcely perceptible.

When the 5th wicket fell at 135 next morning the match was in the balance, and the fieldsmen crowded round Barlow, but by stubborn defence he slowly wore down the bowling while Steel, who had begun

cautiously, opened up. Spofforth tried a spell at his fastest from the nursery end, packing the slips, with Blackham standing back, and he had Steel missed at short leg and Barlow missed at mid on; but by lunch-time the Lancashire pair had added 96 and England were two runs ahead. Barlow was out in the first over after lunch, but Steel found another good partner in Lyttelton and by fearless hitting reached his 100 in 2 hours 50 minutes. When the innings ended at 4.30 England had gained a lead of 150.

Australia made a useful start, but then Steel, who had bowled little in the first innings because of a back injury, came on and bowled McDonnell. Bannerman and Murdoch looked safe enough until Ulyett, bowling towards the pavilion end in failing light, dismissed them both and then held on one-handed to a fierce return from Bonnor. 73 for 4 at the close, Australia were saved from a complete rout next morning by another resolute innings by Scott. Ulyett, bowling at his fastest and breaking back from a worn patch caused by Spofforth's follow-through, took 7 for 36; Blackham, facing Ulyett without gloves, had to retire with a damaged finger.

AUSTRALIA

P. S. McDonnell	b Peate	0	b Steel	20	
A. C. Bannerman	b Peate	12	c and b Ulyett	27	
*W. L. Murdoch	lbw b Peate	10	c Shrewsbury b Ulyett	17	
G. Giffen	b Peate	63	c Peate b Ulyett	5	
W. E. Midwinter	b Peate	3	(7)b Ulyett	6	
G. J. Bonnor	c Grace b Christopherson	25	(5)c and b Ulyett	4	
†J. McC. Blackham	run out	0	(8)retired hurt	0	
H. J. H. Scott	c sub (W. L. Murdoch) b Steel	75	(6)not out	31	
G. E. Palmer	c Grace b Peate	7	b Ulyett	13	
F. R. Spofforth	c Barlow b Grace	0	c Shrewsbury b Barlow	11	
H. F. Boyle	not out	26	b Ulyett	10	
Extras	(b 5, lb 3)	8	(b 1)	1	
Total		**229**	**Total**	**145**	

ENGLAND

W. G. Grace	c Bonnor b Palmer	14
A. P. Lucas	c Bonnor b Palmer	28
A. Shrewsbury	st Blackham b Giffen	27
G. Ulyett	b Palmer	32
A. G. Steel	b Palmer	148
*Lord Harris	b Spofforth	4
R. G. Barlow	c Palmer b Bonnor	38
W. W. Read	b Palmer	12
†Hon. A. Lyttelton	b Palmer	31
E. Peate	not out	8
S. Christopherson	c Bonnor b Spofforth	17
Extras	(b 15, lb 5)	20
Total		**379**

FALL OF WICKETS

AUSTRALIA

Wkt	1st	2nd
1st	0	33
2nd	25	60
3rd	32	65
4th	46	73
5th	88	84
6th	93	90
7th	132	118
8th	155	133
9th	160	145
10th	229	—

ENGLAND

Wkt	1st	2nd
1st	37	—
2nd	56	—
3rd	90	—
4th	120	—
5th	135	—
6th	233	—
7th	272	—
8th	348	—
9th	351	—
10th	379	—

Umpires: F. H. Farrands, C. K. Pullin

ENGLAND	1st Innings					2nd Innings			
	O	M	R	W		O	M	R	W
Peate	40	14	85	6		16	4	34	0
Barlow	20	6	44	0		21	8	31	1
Ulyett	11	3	21	0		39·1	23	36	7
Christopherson	26	10	52	1		8	3	17	0
Grace	7	4	13	1					
Steel	1·2	0	6	1		10	2	26	1

AUSTRALIA	1st Innings					2nd Innings			
	O	M	R	W		O	M	R	W
Spofforth	55·1	19	112	2					
Palmer	75	26	111	6					
Giffen	22	4	68	1					
Boyle	11	3	16	0					
Bonnor	8	1	23	1					
Midwinter	13	2	29	0					

19. J. McC. Blackham

20. W. H. Scotton

21. Australia 1884
Back row: J. McC. Blackham, H. J. H. Scott, L. Greenwood, W. E. Midwinter, P. S. McDonnell, G. Alexander. *Middle row:* G. Giffen, H. F. Boyle, W. L. Murdoch (capt.), G. J. Bonnor, G. E. Palmer. *Front:* A. C. Bannerman, F. R. Spofforth.

1884 Third Test, Oval

August 11, 12, 13
Toss: Australia   *Result:* Match Drawn

The Australian batting in the 1884 season was not exceptional, yet on the first day of the final Test they achieved an extraordinary success, three batsmen scoring hundreds on the same day. For the third time their side was unchanged, Cooper, the 12th member of the party, having been injured, like Morley in the previous series, on the voyage over. For England, Scotton deputised for Lucas, who was not available, and Barnes replaced Christopherson.

On a hot day, with a fast wicket and outfield, Australia lost Bannerman soon after the start but nevertheless reached 130 for 1 by lunch. McDonnell, hitting as hard as ever but generally keeping the ball on the ground, was then 86, his only mistakes being two hard hits back to the bowler. At 3.10, when he was out, he had made two-thirds of the runs. Murdoch, uncertain at first after a long run of low scores in Tests, batted through the rest of the day with Scott; he was 145 not out at the close, and Scott was 101. Both men were missed once. Towards the end of the day Lyttelton took his pads off to bowl lobs, and Read, who had also bowled lobs earlier in the day, kept wicket.

One down in the series, Australia had everything to gain by going all out for a win; yet Murdoch batted another 2 hours 40 minutes next day for 66, and the scoring rate remained steady at under a run a minute. With the regular bowlers exhausted Lyttelton again bowled lobs from the gasworks end, taking the last 4 wickets for 8 runs; and when Shrewsbury was put on amidst loud laughter just before the end, all the England side had bowled.

After 9½ hours in the field, England reached 50 in 40 minutes and were 71 for 2 at the close. The only time the wicket was hit in the two days was when Spofforth was bowled by a lob.

By 3.0 on the last day England at 181 for 8 were by no means safe, the wicket showing signs of wear. Scotton, who had batted 3½ hours for 53, was then joined by a disgruntled no. 10 in Walter Read, and Read, taking it out on the bowlers, made a hundred in less than 2 hours and added 151 with Scotton in 2 hours 10 minutes to make the game safe. Although Scotton batted 5¾ hours in a great defensive innings, England still scored their runs faster than the Australians.

AUSTRALIA

A. C. Bannerman	c Read b Peate	4
P. S. Donnell	c Ulyett b Peate	103
*W. L. Murdoch	c Peate b Barnes	211
H. J. H. Scott	c Lyttelton b Barnes	102
G. Giffen	c Steel b Ulyett	32
G. J. Bonnor	c Read b Grace	8
W. E. Midwinter	c Grace b Lyttelton	30
†J. McC. Blackham	lbw b Lyttelton	31
G. E. Palmer	not out	8
F. R. Spofforth	b Lyttelton	4
H. F. Boyle	c Harris b Lyttelton	1
Extras	(b 7, lb 10)	17
Total		**551**

ENGLAND

W. G. Grace	run out	19			
W. H. Scotton	c Scott b Giffen	90			
W. Barnes	c Midwinter b Spofforth	19			
A. Shrewsbury	c Blackham b Midwinter	10	(3)c Scott b Giffen		37
A. G. Steel	lbw b Palmer	31			
G. Ulyett	c Bannerman b Palmer	10			
R. G. Barlow	c Murdoch b Palmer	0	(1)not out		21
*Lord Harris	lbw b Palmer	14	(4)not out		6
†Hon. A. Lyttelton	b Spofforth	8	(2)b Boyle		17
W. W. Read	b Boyle	117			
E. Peate	not out	4			
Extras	(b 8, lb 7, w 6, nb 3)	24	(b 3, lb 1)		4
Total		**346**	**Total** (2 wkts)		**85**

FALL OF WICKETS

AUSTRALIA

Wkt	1st	2nd
1st	15	—
2nd	158	—
3rd	365	—
4th	432	—
5th	454	—
6th	494	—
7th	532	—
8th	545	—
9th	549	—
10th	551	—

ENGLAND

Wkt	1st	2nd
1st	32	22
2nd	60	73
3rd	75	—
4th	120	—
5th	136	—
6th	136	—
7th	160	—
8th	181	—
9th	332	—
10th	346	—

Umpires: F. H. Farrands, C. K. Pullin

ENGLAND	1st Innings				2nd Innings			
	O	M	R	W	O	M	R	W
Peate	63	25	99	2	..			
Ulyett	56	24	96	1	..			
Steel	34	7	71	0	..			
Barnes	52	25	81	2	..			
Barlow	50	22	72	0	..			
Grace	24	14	23	1	..			
Read	7	0	36	0	..			
Scotton	5	1	20	0	..			
Harris	5	1	15	0	..			
Lyttelton	12	5	19	4	..			
Shrewsbury	3	2	2	0	..			

AUSTRALIA	1st Innings				2nd Innings			
	O	M	R	W	O	M	R	W
Bonnor	13	4	33	0	..			
Palmer	54	19	90	4	..	2	1	2	0
Spofforth	58	31	81	2	..	6	2	14	0
Boyle	13	7	24	1	..	8	1	32	1
Midwinter	31	16	41	1	..	3	0	15	0
Giffen	26	13	36	1	..	7	1	18	1
Scott	3	0	17	0	..			

Averages: 1884

ENGLAND

BATTING

	M.	Inns.	N.O.	Runs	H.S.	Av.
W. W. Read	2	2	0	129	117	64·50
A. G. Steel	3	4	0	212	148	53·00
A. P. Lucas	2	3	1	67	28	33·50
A. Shrewsbury	3	5	0	142	43	28·40
R. G. Barlow	3	5	2	79	38	26·33
E. Peate	3	4	3	22	8*	22·00
Hon. A. Lyttelton	2	3	0	56	31	18·66
W. G. Grace	3	4	0	72	31	18·00
G Ulyett	3	4	0	48	32	12·00
Lord Harris	2	3	1	24	14	12·00
W. Barnes	2	3	0	27	19	9·00

PLAYED IN ONE TEST: W. H. Scotton 90, S. Christopherson 17, T. C. O'Brien 0 and 20, A. N. Hornby 0 and 4, R. Pilling 0 and 3.

BOWLING

	Overs	Mds.	Runs	Wkts.	Av.
G. Ulyett	136·1	67	194	11	17·63
E. Peate	168	68	280	11	25·45

ALSO BOWLED: Hon. A. Lyttelton 12–5–19–4, W. G. Grace 42–28–38–3, A. G. Steel 58·2–14–135–4, W. Barnes 71–35–106–3, S. Christopherson 34–13–69–1, R. G. Barlow 99–39–165–1, W. W. Read 7–0–36–0, W. H. Scotton 5–1–20–0, Lord Harris 5–1–15–0, A. Shrewsbury 3–2–2–0.

AUSTRALIA

BATTING

	M.	Inns.	N.O.	Runs	H.S.	Av.
H. J. H. Scott	3	4	1	220	102	73·33
W. L. Murdoch	3	4	0	266	211	66·50
P. S. McDonnell	3	4	0	159	103	39·75
G. Giffen	3	4	0	116	63	29·00
G. E. Palmer	3	4	2	42	14*	21·00
W. E. Midwinter	3	4	0	76	37	19·00
H. F. Boyle	3	4	1	41	26*	13·66
J. McC. Blackham	3	4	1	39	31	13·00
A. C. Bannerman	3	4	0	49	27	12·25
G. J. Bonnor	3	4	0	43	25	10·75
F. R. Spofforth	3	4	0	28	13	7·00

BOWLING

	Overs	Mds.	Runs	Wkts.	Av.
H. F. Boyle	77	28	141	9	15·66
G. E. Palmer	173	65	260	14	18·57
F. R. Spofforth	192·1	79	301	10	30·10

ALSO BOWLED: G. J. Bonnor 25–6–61–2, G. Giffen 84–33–147–4, W. E. Midwinter 47–18–85–1, H. J. H. Scott 3–0–17–0.

Averages: 1884–85

AUSTRALIA

BATTING

	M.	Inns.	N.O.	Runs	H.S.	Av.
P. S. McDonnell	2	4	0	230	124	57·50
J. McC. Blackham	2	3	1	88	66	44·00
G. J. Bonnor	3	5	0	198	128	39·60
W. Bruce	2	4	1	98	45	32·66
T. W. Garrett	3	5	2	94	51*	31·33
J. W. Trumble	4	7	1	164	59	27·33
T. P. Horan	4	8	1	163	63	23·28
S. P. Jones	4	8	1	150	40	21·42
A. H. Jarvis	3	6	0	110	82	18·33
G. Giffen	3	5	0	77	47	15·40
A. C. Bannerman	4	7	0	97	51	13·85
F. R. Spofforth	3	5	0	55	50	11·00
H. J. H. Scott	2	4	0	29	19	7·25
G. E. Palmer	2	3	0	6	6	2·00

PLAYED IN ONE TEST: P. G. McShane 9 and 12*, J. Worrall 34 and 6, E. Evans 33 and 1, S. Morris 4 and 10*, H. H. Massie 2 and 21, H. Musgrove 4 and 9, G. Alexander 3 and 10, W. H. Cooper 0* and 6, F. H. Walters 7 and 5, W. L. Murdoch 5 and 7, A. P. Marr 0 and 5, R. J. Pope 0 and 3, H. F. Boyle 1 and 0*, W. R. Robertson 0 and 2.

BOWLING

	Overs	Mds.	Runs	Wkts.	Av.
T. P. Horan	55·1	29	80	6	13·33
S. P. Jones	43·2	16	80	5	16·00
F. R. Spofforth	194·1	84	306	19	16·10
G. E. Palmer	124·1	54	171	10	17·10
J. W. Trumble	89	41	112	5	22·40
G. Giffen	189·1	71	348	11	31·63
W. Bruce	106·1	35	191	6	31·83

ALSO BOWLED: S. Morris 34–14–73–2, H. F. Boyle 72–28–116–3, J. Worrall 56–28–97–1, W. H. Cooper 18–4–26–0, G. J. Bonnor 16–10–23–0, P. S. McDonnell 3–0–11–0, P. G. McShane 3–2–3–0, H. J. H. Scott 4–1–9–0, W. R. Robertson 11–3–24–0, G. Alexander 10–3–24–0, A. P. Marr 12–6–14–0, T. W. Garrett 32–17–65–0, E. Evans 8–2–17–0.

ENGLAND

BATTING

	M.	Inns.	N.O.	Runs	H.S.	Av.
W. Barnes	5	8	1	369	134	52·71
A. Shrewsbury	5	9	3	301	105*	50·16
W. Bates	5	7	0	222	64	31·71
J. Briggs	5	7	0	177	121	25·28
J. M. Read	5	7	0	143	56	20·42
W. H. Scotton	5	9	1	159	82	19·87
J. Hunter	5	7	2	93	39*	18·60
W. Flowers	5	8	0	144	56	18·00
G. Ulyett	5	7	0	87	68	12·42
W. Attewell	5	7	2	58	30	11·60
R. Peel	5	7	2	37	17*	7·40

BOWLING

	Overs	Mds.	Runs	Wkts.	Av.
W. Bates	93·1	41	148	10	14·80
W. Barnes	206·2	97	292	19	15·36
G. Ulyett	178·2	86	295	14	21·07
R. Peel	390·2	193	451	21	21·47
W. Flowers	179·3	81	249	11	22·63
W. Attewell	325·1	190	310	13	23·84

ALSO BOWLED: J. Briggs 8–3–13–0.

1884-85 First Test, Adelaide

December 12, 13, 15, 16
Toss: Australia   *Result:* England won by eight wickets

England, although taking a strong all-professional party, had left some of their finest players at home, so it seemed that the advantage would lie with Australia. But disputes over management and finance resulted in the Australians fielding scratch sides instead of a settled team, and this may well have cost them the series. It was hard fought enough as it was, with the issue open until the final match.

The Australian side for the first Test was selected from the touring party of 1884, but the players had been idle since returning from England and only McDonnell, Blackham and Giffen were in Adelaide in time for serious practice. Murdoch won the toss, and at lunch Australia were 56 for 2, 47 of them to McDonnell. Missed off a straight-forward catch to Bates at long-off when 79, McDonnell reached his second Test hundred in succession at 3.30, and the runs came very quickly during his stand of 95 with Blackham. Fourth out at 190, he batted for 3¼ hours. Australia were in a strong position at 220 for 4 when Bates came on and finished off the innings.

The second day, interrupted by a brief thunderstorm in the morning and rendered thoroughly unpleasant in the afternoon by dust-storms, was nevertheless highly successful for England. The wicket was unaffected, and although Shrewsbury failed, Ulyett hit hard, splitting Bannerman's hand, and whenever he skied the ball it fell safely. When he was out at 107 Scotton and Barnes settled into a partnership which lasted the rest of the day, although both were missed. England were 232 for 2 at the close. Next morning, on a wicket rendered none too easy by rain, Barnes reached his only Test hundred. A punishing off-side player, he batted 5 hours in all. Scotton batted three-quarters of an hour longer in another rock-like display.

Australia began their second innings at 3.10, 126 behind. McDonnell at once began playing with the same freedom as in the first innings, though he should have been stumped, and he was again missed by Bates, this time at mid off. Australia were on the point of clearing their arrears with only 2 wickets down when Giffen, troubled by lumbago, missed a call for an easy run and McDonnell was run out only 17 short of his second hundred of the match. Giffen fought hard to redeem this disaster, but Bannerman was absent, and the remaining batting failed a second time, leaving England only 66 to win.

AUSTRALIA

Batsman	1st Innings dismissal	1st	2nd Innings dismissal	2nd
A. C. Bannerman	lbw b Peel	2	absent hurt	—
P. S. McDonnell	b Attewell	124	run out	83
*W. L. Murdoch	c Hunter b Peel	5	b Peel	7
H. J. H. Scott	b Peel	19	(5)lbw b Peel	1
†J. McC. Blackham	c Attewell b Bates	66	(1)b Peel	11
G. Giffen	b Bates	4	(4)c Shrewsbury b Peel	47
G. J. Bonnor	c Read b Bates	4	c Peel b Barnes	19
G. E. Palmer	c Shrewsbury b Bates	6	b Barnes	0
H. F. Boyle	c Hunter b Bates	1	(10)not out	0
G. Alexander	run out	3	(9)st Hunter b Peel	10
W. H. Cooper	not out	0	(6)c Shrewsbury b Barnes	6
Extras	(b 7, w 2)	9	(b 7)	7
Total		243	Total	191

ENGLAND

Batsman	1st Innings dismissal	1st	2nd Innings dismissal	2nd
W. H. Scotton	st Blackham b Giffen	82	c Scott b Boyle	2
*A. Shrewsbury	b Boyle	0	(3)not out	26
G. Ulyett	c Alexander b Boyle	68		
W. Barnes	b Palmer	134	(4)not out	28
W. Bates	c Giffen b Palmer	18		
W. Flowers	lbw b Palmer	15		
J. M. Read	c and b Giffen	14		
J. Briggs	c Blackham b Palmer	1		
W. Attewell	not out	12		
R. Peel	b Palmer	4		
†J. Hunter	run out	1	(2)c Scott b Palmer	7
Extras	(b 18, lb 1, nb 1)	20	(b 4)	4
Total		369	Total (2 wkts)	67

FALL OF WICKETS

AUSTRALIA

Wkt	1st	2nd
1st	33	28
2nd	47	56
3rd	95	125
4th	190	139
5th	224	160
6th	227	171
7th	233	182
8th	239	191
9th	242	191
10th	243	—

ENGLAND

Wkt	1st	2nd
1st	11	8
2nd	107	14
3rd	282	
4th	306	—
5th	325	—
6th	344	—
7th	349	—
8th	349	—
9th	361	—
10th	369	—

Umpires: I. Fisher,
J. Travers

ENGLAND	1st Innings O	M	R	W	2nd Innings O	M	R	W
Peel	41	15	68	3	40·1	15	51	5
Attewell	50	23	48	1	18	10	26	0
Ulyett	10	3	23	0	2	1	3	0
Flowers	10	1	27	0	16	4	27	0
Barnes	14	2	37	0	31	10	51	3
Bates	24·1	10	31	5	9	3	26	0

AUSTRALIA	1st Innings O	M	R	W	2nd Innings O	M	R	W
Boyle	63	25	95	2	9	3	21	1
Giffen	56·2	26	80	2	6	0	19	0
Cooper	18	4	26	0				
Bonnor	16	10	23	0				
Palmer	73	37	81	5	16	5	23	1
McDonnell	3	0	11	0				
Scott	4	1	9	0				
Alexander	10	3	24	0				

22. England 1884-85

Top to bottom: (1) J. M. Read, (2) G. Ulyett, (3) W. H. Scotton, (4) R. Peel, (5) J. Hunter, (6) W. Attewell, (7) A. Shrewsbury, (8) A. Shaw (capt.), (9) W. Barnes, (10) James Lillywhite, (11) W. Flowers, (12) J. Briggs, (13) W. Bates.

23. P. S. McDonnell

24. W. Barnes

January 1, 2, 3, 5
Toss: England *Result:* England won by ten wickets

The demand of the 1884 Australian touring team for 50 per cent of the gate money at Melbourne resulted in a clean sweep for the second Test, and of the chosen XI all but Horan and Jones were new caps. Morris, Pope, Marr, Musgrove and Robertson were playing for Australia for the first and only time, and Trumble (J.W.), Jarvis, Worrall and Bruce were making their first appearance.

Shrewsbury, jumping in to the slows and lofting them into the open spaces, led the way for England with a fine 72, and Barnes played another sound innings; but, after Bates had made a quick 35, Flowers, Read and Ulyett failed and at 204 for 7 the innings seemed to be running out of steam. Briggs, however, jumping out like Shrewsbury to the slows but keeping the ball down, hit cleanly and hard, Attewell scored just as readily, and with useful support from Peel England were 303 for 9 at stumps, Briggs 65 not out. Even then the extent of England's recovery was not foreseen, as on the second morning the Australian bowling and fielding deteriorated and Briggs and Hunter put on 98 for the last wicket, England totalling 401.

Australia began their reply directly after lunch. Morris was out at once, and a great deal obviously depended on Horan. He lost Jones at 46 but found a determined if fortunate partner in Trumble, who was missed three times, and the score mounted slowly as both batsmen played with the application the situation demanded. By the time Horan was out Australia were 124 for 3, and with Jarvis starting in enterprising fashion the day ended at 151 for 3.

On the third day the England bowlers again tied the batsmen down, but the score had reached 190 before Trumble returned a catch to Barnes. With his quickish pace and jerky, round-arm delivery and slight turn to leg, Barnes seemed to cause the most trouble, and soon after lunch Australia were 203 for 7; but while Jarvis and Worrall were putting on 73 for the 8th wicket there seemed a good chance of saving the follow on. Then Briggs took a fine catch running back from mid on to dismiss Jarvis, Worrall was bowled soon afterwards, and Bruce was left high and dry. Horan sent Bruce in first when Australia followed on, and the left-hander played a fine innings, but the wicket was worn at one end, and the cadet Australian side did well to take the match into the fourth afternoon. Barnes, getting the ball to lift off a full length, was again the most successful bowler.

ENGLAND

*A. Shrewsbury	c Worrall b Morris	72	not out	0	
W. H. Scotton	b Bruce	13	not out	7	
W. Barnes	b Morris	58			
W. Bates	b Bruce	35			
W. Flowers	c Worrall b Bruce	5			
J. M. Read	b Jones	3			
J. Briggs	c Horan b Jones	121			
G. Ulyett	b Jones	0			
W. Attewell	c Jones b Worrall	30			
R. Peel	b Jones	5			
†J. Hunter	not out	39			
Extras	(b 7, lb 12, nb 1)	20			
Total		**401**	**Total** (0 wkts)	**7**	

AUSTRALIA

S. P. Jones	lbw b Peel	19	b Ulyett	9	
S. Morris	lbw b Attewell	4	(10) not out	10	
*T. P. Horan	c Shrewsbury b Peel	63	c Hunter b Barnes	16	
J. W. Trumble	c and b Barnes	59	c and b Barnes	11	
†A. H. Jarvis	c Briggs b Flowers	82	lbw b Peel	10	
R. J. Pope	c Flowers b Attewell	0	b Peel	3	
A. P. Marr	b Barnes	0	c and b Barnes	5	
H. Musgrove	c Read b Barnes	4	c Bates b Peel	9	
J. Worrall	b Flowers	34	c and b Barnes	6	
W. Bruce	not out	3	(2) c Hunter b Barnes	45	
W. R. Robertson	c Barnes b Peel	0	b Barnes	2	
Extras	(b 3, lb 4, w 2, nb 2)	11		0	
Total		**279**	**Total**	**126**	

FALL OF WICKETS

ENGLAND		
Wkt	*1st*	*2nd*
1st	28	—
2nd	144	—
3rd	161	—
4th	191	—
5th	194	—
6th	204	—
7th	204	—
8th	254	—
9th	303	—
10th	401	—

AUSTRALIA		
Wkt	*1st*	*2nd*
1st	4	29
2nd	46	66
3rd	124	80
4th	190	83
5th	193	86
6th	193	95
7th	203	99
8th	276	108
9th	278	116
10th	279	126

Umpires: E. H. Elliott,
James Lillywhite, jnr.

AUSTRALIA

	1st Innings				2nd Innings			
	O	M	R	W	O	M	R	W
Bruce	55	22	88	3	0·1	0	4	0
Worrall	56	28	97	1				
Marr	11	6	11	0	1	0	3	0
Trumble	23	9	41	0				
Robertson	11	3	24	0				
Morris	34	14	73	2				
Jones	25·2	9	47	4				
Horan	1	1	0	0				

ENGLAND

	1st Innings				2nd Innings			
	O	M	R	W	O	M	R	W
Flowers	29	12	46	2	11	6	11	0
Attewell	61	35	54	2	5	2	7	0
Barnes	50	27	50	3	38·3	26	31	6
Peel	102·1	56	78	3	44	26	45	3
Bates	17	11	17	0				
Ulyett	15	7	23	0	8	3	19	1
Briggs					8	3	13	0

1884–85 Third Test, Sydney

Test no. 19

February 20, 21, 23, 24
Toss: Australia   *Result:* Australia won by 6 runs

With a much more familiar side, but retaining Jones, Horan, Trumble and Jarvis, Australia won a great battle at Sydney. 40 for 0 at lunch, they were then held up by a hailstorm which covered the turf like snow. Afterwards Attewell and Flowers proved almost impossible to score from on the sodden wicket, and at stumps Australia were 97 for 8. But when Evans joined Garrett next morning with 9 wickets down, both batsmen played with confidence, and they put on 80 priceless runs before Ulyett got Evans caught at the wicket.

England had reached 31 comfortably enough on a fresh wicket when Shrewsbury was caught and bowled by Spofforth. Ulyett, swinging impatiently, was bowled, and Barnes was stumped off the wicket-keeper's pads. Then the fastish Horan, coming on to bowl when Garrett proved ineffective, found a spot made by Spofforth in his follow-through, and he got rid of Bates and Briggs cheaply and had Scotton caught at the wicket, a decision at which the batsman showed his displeasure. He had batted in his usual stubborn style, and with his dismissal England were 70 for 6. They eventually finished 48 behind.

Bonnor opened with Bannerman on the third morning and made 29 before he was bowled by a shooter, and Australia, 56 for 1 at lunch, lost Bannerman directly afterwards. After a long period of slow play

Horan hit Flowers into the pavilion, and when he was out there were useful contributions from Massie and Trumble; but the English fielding and catching at this point kept them in the match. Left with 214 to win, England had half an hour's batting, in which they lost Scotton and Ulyett (run out) for 29.

On the fourth morning, with 185 still needed, Barnes was soon out, and at 59 Spofforth produced a great ball to bowl Shrewsbury. Briggs went the same way, but Bates and Flowers added 31, Bates hitting Spofforth straight for 5 before being beautifully caught by Jarvis. At lunch England were 103 for 6—less than half way and only four wickets left. But after lunch Flowers and Read batted superbly, and for the first time in the match the Australian fielding, a decisive factor so far, wilted. At 137 Spofforth tried the southern end, but he came in for some rough treatment, and at 175 he was back at the northern end. 190 went up—only 24 to win. At last Spofforth got Read, trying to turn a straight one to leg, and then Attewell, over-anxious, ran himself out. Peel was caught behind at 199, but Flowers and Hunter were in sight of victory when Flowers cut Spofforth hard and was brilliantly caught at point by Evans.

AUSTRALIA

A. C. Bannerman	c Peel b Flowers	13	c Shrewsbury b Ulyett	16	
S. P. Jones	st Hunter b Flowers	28	(4)b Attewell	22	
T. P. Horan	c Hunter b Attewell	7	b Bates	36	
H. J. H. Scott	c Ulyett b Attewell	5	(5)c Barnes b Attewell	4	
G. J. Bonnor	c Barnes b Flowers	18	(2)b Ulyett	29	
J. W. Trumble	c Read b Attewell	13	c Ulyett b Bates	32	
*H. H. Massie	c Scotton b Flowers	2	b Bates	21	
†A. H. Jarvis	b Attewell	0	c and b Peel	2	
F. R. Spofforth	st Hunter b Flowers	3	(11)c Attewell b Bates	0	
T. W. Garrett	not out	51	not out	0	
E. Evans	c Hunter b Ulyett	33	(9)b Bates	1	
Extras	(b 3, lb 5)	8	(b 1, lb 1)	2	
Total		181	Total	165	

ENGLAND

W. H. Scotton	c Jarvis b Horan	22	b Spofforth	2	
*A. Shrewsbury	c and b Spofforth	18	b Spofforth	24	
G. Ulyett	b Spofforth	2	run out	4	
W. Barnes	st Jarvis b Spofforth	0	c Jarvis b Trumble	5	
W. Bates	c Evans b Horan	12	c Jarvis b Spofforth	31	
J. Briggs	c Scott b Horan	3	b Spofforth	1	
W. Flowers	c Jarvis b Spofforth	24	c Evans b Spofforth	56	
J. M. Read	c Evans b Horan	4	b Spofforth	56	
W. Attewell	b Horan	14	run out	0	
R. Peel	not out	8	c Jarvis b Trumble	3	
†J. Hunter	b Horan	13	not out	5	
Extras	(b 8, lb 3, nb 2)	13	(b 7, lb 9, w 1, nb 3)	20	
Total		133	Total	207	

FALL OF WICKETS

AUSTRALIA

Wkt	1st	2nd
1st	45	36
2nd	46	56
3rd	56	91
4th	73	95
5th	77	119
6th	83	151
7th	83	161
8th	94	165
9th	101	165
10th	181	165

ENGLAND

Wkt	1st	2nd
1st	31	14
2nd	33	18
3rd	33	29
4th	46	59
5th	56	61
6th	70	92
7th	82	194
8th	111	194
9th	111	199
10th	133	207

Umpires: E. Payne, J. Bryant

ENGLAND	1st Innings				2nd Innings			
	O	M	R	W	O	M	R	W
Attewell	71	47	53	4	58	36	54	2
Ulyett	12·2	8	17	1	39	25	42	2
Flowers	46	24	46	5	20	14	19	0
Bates	6	2	6	0	20	10	24	5
Peel	32	13	51	0	20	10	24	1

AUSTRALIA	1st Innings				2nd Innings			
	O	M	R	W	O	M	R	W
Spofforth	48	23	54	4	48·1	22	90	6
Garrett	6	2	17	0	16	8	31	0
Horan	37·1	22	40	6	9	4	23	0
Evans	4	1	9	0	4	1	8	0
Trumble					26	13	26	2
Jones					3	0	9	0

1884-85 Fourth Test, Sydney

March 14, 16, 17
Toss: England   *Result:* Australia won by eight wickets

A gem of an innings from Shrewsbury, who made 37 out of England's score of 52 for 1 at lunch, got the game away to a good start, and when he left at 76 Bates joined Barnes in a stand of 83 for the 4th wicket. While Barnes played steadily, making hardly a bad stroke, Bates, reckless at times, enjoyed his full share of luck. Spofforth, trying a very fast spell during the afternoon, was cut unmercifully by both batsmen as his length suffered, and most of the wickets fell to Giffen, Spofforth again cutting up the pitch. A brilliant caught and bowled by Jones, the seventh bowler to be tried, dismissed Bates, and for a time the innings faltered, but some fine attacking play by Maurice Read lifted the total to 269. Left with a few minutes' batting at the end of the day, Australia sent in the tail-enders on a fresh wicket and were 12 for 1 at the close.

On a cold, dull day with rain threatening, Australia had reached 56 for 3 by lunch. Garrett and Bannerman by steady play took the score to 98, but the improvement was not maintained, and when a fine catch by Barnes dismissed Horan Australia were 119 for 6. The ball was again inclined to lift at one end, and off-spinner Flowers, with the

wind behind him, tried for pace alone and trusted to the wicket to do the rest. At 134 for 7 the innings seemed about to disintegrate.

Bonnor began shakily, although his great height—he was 6ft. 6 in.—helped him to reach and smother the rising ball. After several risky hits he suddenly started to middle them, and with some neat cutting by Jones the outlook was transformed. Frequent bowling changes did not upset either batsman, and in 85 minutes after tea Bonnor made 113 runs in probably the finest display of hitting ever seen in a Test Match. Considering the risks he took, and the state of the wicket at one end, it is astonishing that the first chance he gave was to slip off Ulyett from the shot that gave him his hundred. He batted only 115 minutes in all. Jones' innings was hardly less valuable, and after heavy rain had fallen in the night Australia's lead of 40 runs assumed real significance. The English team decided to bat on the wicket used by the Australians, but it broke up badly and they were all out for 77. Australia then batted on the wicket used in the first innings by England and won comfortably by 8 wickets.

ENGLAND

G. Ulyett	b Giffen	10	c Garrett b Palmer	2
*A. Shrewsbury	b Giffen	40	c Bonnor b Spofforth	16
W. H. Scotton	c Blackham b Giffen	4	c Jones b Spofforth	0
W. Barnes	b Giffen	50	c Bannerman b Spofforth	20
W. Bates	c and b Jones	64	c Blackham b Palmer	1
J. M. Read	b Giffen	47	c Bannerman b Spofforth	6
W. Flowers	b Giffen	14	c Jones b Palmer	7
J. Briggs	c Palmer b Spofforth	3	run out	5
W. Attewell	b Giffen	1	not out	1
R. Peel	not out	17	c and b Spofforth	0
†J. Hunter	b Spofforth	13	b Palmer	4
Extras	(b 5, nb 1)	6	(b 14, nb 1)	15
Total		**269**	**Total**	**77**

AUSTRALIA

G. E. Palmer	b Ulyett	0		
T. W. Garrett	b Barnes	32		
J. W. Trumble	b Peel	5		
P. S. McDonnell	c Attewell b Ulyett	20		
A. C. Bannerman	c Shrewsbury b Flowers	51	(1)c Flowers b Peel	3
G. Giffen	c Attewell b Barnes	1	(2)b Barnes	8
T. P. Horan	c Barnes b Ulyett	9		
G. J. Bonnor	c Bates b Barnes	128	(3)not out	12
S. P. Jones	run out	40	(4)not out	15
†*J. McC. Blackham	not out	11		
F. R. Spofforth	c Read b Barnes	1		
Extras	(b 5, lb 1, w 2, nb 3)	11	(b 2)	2
Total		**309**	**Total** (2 wkts)	**40**

FALL OF WICKETS

ENGLAND

Wkt	1st	2nd
1st	19	5
2nd	52	16
3rd	76	19
4th	159	20
5th	186	27
6th	219	42
7th	222	63
8th	229	69
9th	252	69
10th	269	77

AUSTRALIA

Wkt	1st	2nd
1st	0	7
2nd	16	16
3rd	40	—
4th	98	—
5th	108	—
6th	119	—
7th	134	—
8th	288	—
9th	308	—
10th	309	—

Umpires: E. H. Elliott,
P. G. McShane

AUSTRALIA

	1st Innings					2nd Innings			
	O	M	R	W		O	M	R	W
Giffen	52	14	117	7	..				
Palmer	16	5	35	0	..	19·1	7	32	4
Spofforth	29	10	61	2	..	20	8	30	5
Garrett	2	1	5	0	..				
Trumble	12	5	16	0	..				
Horan	5	2	12	0	..				
Jones	10	5	17	1	..				

ENGLAND

	1st Innings					2nd Innings			
	O	M	R	W		O	M	R	W
Ulyett	54	25	91	3	..				
Peel	31	12	53	1	..	9	4	16	1
Attewell	18	13	22	0	..	3	1	4	0
Bates	17	5	44	0	..				
Barnes	35·3	17	61	4	..	9	3	15	1
Flowers	14	5	27	1	..	3·3	2	3	0

1884-85 Fifth Test, Melbourne

March 21, 23, 24, 25
Toss: Australia   *Result:* England won by an innings and 98 runs

For the final and deciding Test Australia were again weakened by disputes and disqualifications. England were unchanged, their only problem being that Briggs, who had injured his bowling hand early in the tour, was still unable to bowl. Australia's troubles, however, had hardly begun. Winning the toss, they batted on a wicket that had not dried out properly after heavy watering, and with Ulyett making the ball fly they lost 6 wickets for 45 runs in an hour's play before lunch, and the 9th wicket fell at 99. Spofforth then joined Trumble and at once ran out to meet the ball in apparently reckless style. The wicket meanwhile had dried out, and 64 runs were added before Spofforth, 'trying to play a puzzling ball several different ways', according to one account, was bowled. By close of play Scotton and Barnes, with the wicket now easy, had made 44 without being separated.

The morning session next day went in favour of Australia, but a stand of 44 between Barnes and Shrewsbury put England back on top. Barnes's 74 was a chanceless innings, more of his runs than usual coming on the leg side. Bates then joined Shrewsbury, and the ensuing stand brought victory within England's grasp. Bates was dropped so

many times that the crowd became derisive, but Shrewsbury's innings was without blemish apart from an easy chance to McShane behind the bowler at 23. Bates, who was very unwell, was forced to retire for a time when 54, but Flowers and Briggs batted usefully, and a last-wicket stand took England into a lead of 223 on the third morning and enabled Shrewsbury to reach his century after 5 hours 10 minutes at the crease. Many of his runs came from pulling off balls to the vacant leg side.

An interesting sidelight on the wicket is that the Australians did not have it rolled between innings in case it crumbled: this possibly explains the heavy watering beforehand. They started badly and were 26 for 3 at tea, and although Horan, Jones and Bruce all played defiant knocks the rubber was decided on the fourth morning. Despite the early ill feeling over finance, a friendly spirit shines through most of the matches, marred only by bad umpiring, from which both sides apparently suffered. In the final Test Hodges refused to come out after tea on the third day after the Englishmen had complained about his decisions, and his place was taken by Tom Garrett.

AUSTRALIA

A. C. Bannerman	c Peel b Ulyett	5	c sub (G. F. Vernon) b Ulyett		2
W. Bruce	c Briggs b Peel	15	(6)c Bates b Attewell		35
G. Giffen	b Ulyett	13	c Peel b Ulyett		12
*T. P. Horan	lbw b Ulyett	0	(5)b Attewell		20
S. P. Jones	lbw b Peel	0	(4)b Peel		17
F. H. Walters	b Ulyett	7	(8)c Attewell b Flowers		5
†A. H. Jarvis	c Hunter b Peel	15	(9)c Peel b Flowers		1
J. W. Trumble	not out	34	(7)lbw b Attewell		10
P. G. McShane	c Hunter b Barnes	9	(11)not out		12
T. W. Garrett	c Briggs b Barnes	6	(2)b Ulyett		5
F. R. Spofforth	b Attewell	50	(10)c sub (A. H. Jarvis) b Flowers		1
Extras	(b 5, lb 1, nb 3)	9	(b 5)		5
Total		**163**	**Total**		**125**

ENGLAND

W. H. Scotton	b Bruce	27
W. Barnes	c Horan b Bruce	74
J. M. Read	b Giffen	13
G. Ulyett	b Spofforth	1
*A. Shrewsbury	not out	105
W. Bates	c Walters b Bruce	61
W. Flowers	b Spofforth	16
J. Briggs	c Walters b Trumble	43
W. Attewell	c Bannerman b Trumble	0
R. Peel	b Trumble	0
†J. Hunter	b Giffen	18
Extras	(b 10, lb 14, nb 4)	28
Total		**386**

FALL OF WICKETS

AUSTRALIA

Wkt	1st	2nd
1st	21	4
2nd	21	17
3rd	21	26
4th	34	60
5th	34	60
6th	45	91
7th	67	100
8th	87	106
9th	99	108
10th	163	125

ENGLAND

Wkt	1st	2nd
1st	60	—
2nd	96	—
3rd	97	—
4th	141	—
5th	256	—
6th	324	—
7th	324	—
8th	335	—
9th	337	—
10th	386	—

Umpires: J. Hodges, J. Phillips

ENGLAND

	1st Innings				2nd Innings			
	O	M	R	W	O	M	R	W
Peel	41	26	28	3	30	16	37	1
Ulyett	23	7	52	4	15	7	25	3
Barnes	28	12	47	2				
Flowers	9	6	9	0	21	7	34	3
Attewell	5	1	18	1	36·1	22	24	3

AUSTRALIA

	1st Innings				2nd Innings			
	O	M	R	W	O	M	R	W
Giffen	74·3	31	132	2				
Bruce	51	13	99	3				
Spofforth	49	21	71	2				
Trumble	28	14	29	3				
Garrett	8	6	12	0				
McShane	3	2	3	0				
Jones	5	2	7	0				
Horan	3	0	5	0				

July 5, 6, 7
Toss: Australia   *Result:* England won by four wickets

The tourists, despatched under the aegis of the Melbourne Club, were not a happy party, quarrels developing from the start. The batting, lacking such great players as Murdoch, McDonnell, Bannerman and Horan, was disappointing, and even the bowling, with Spofforth handicapped by an injured finger and Evans and Palmer not the force they had been, lacked the bite of previous tours. They were up against an immensely strong and settled England side whose only deficiency lay in fast bowling, and the luck and the weather went against them, while at Lord's, where the conditions favoured them for a time, they were baulked by one of the greatest innings ever played. They were thus defeated in all three Tests. This was Spofforth's last series in England, and Lohmann's first.

Australia began well at Old Trafford by winning the toss, and at lunch they were 69 for 1. Jones and Jarvis then put on 63 in the best stand of the innings, and 134 for 3 should have been the basis of a substantial total, but of the remaining batsmen only J. W. Trumble reached double figures and the innings closed at 205. Jones, in his best innings for Australia, batted soundly for 2 hours 50 minutes for his 87. At the close England were 36 for 1.

On the second day the Australians made a determined and successful effort to get back into the game. Spofforth, bowling at his fastest, knocked Shrewsbury's leg stump out at 51, and although Walter Read played freely, England were 140 for 5 at lunch and 160 for 7 soon after. But Barlow stood firm, and he and Lohmann, who was missed early on, added 46 for the 8th wicket, helping England to a lead of 18. Jones and Scott knocked these off without loss, but after Jones left at 37 the Australian second innings slid to 55 for 4 at stumps. On the last morning Scott's admirable innings ended at 73 for 8, but the last two wickets added 50 runs and England were set 106 to win.

Beginning just after 3.0 England soon lost Grace and Shrewsbury, both to Giffen; their two best batsmen were gone. And at 24 Read was caught at mid off. But Barlow came in no. 5 and followed up his bowling (7 for 44 in Australia's second innings) with another determined innings, partnered first by Scotton and then by Steel, who was badly missed by Bonnor at slip. Barlow was out at 90 for 5, but England went on to win comfortably. Dropped catches, of which there were several, helped to turn the game.

AUSTRALIA

						FALL OF WICKETS

Player	1st innings dismissal	Runs	2nd innings dismissal	Runs
S. P. Jones	lbw b Grace	87	c Ulyett b Steel	12
*H. J. H. Scott	c Barlow b Ulyett	21	b Barlow	47
G. Giffen	b Steel	3	c Shrewsbury b Barlow	1
†A. H. Jarvis	c Scotton b Ulyett	45	c Lohmann b Barlow	2
G. J. Bonnor	c Lohmann b Barlow	4	c Barlow b Peate	2
J. W. Trumble	c Scotton b Steel	24	c Ulyett b Barlow	4
W. Bruce	run out	2	(8)c Grace b Barlow	0
T. W. Garrett	c Pilling b Lohmann	5	(9)c Grace b Ulyett	22
J. McC. Blackham	not out	7	(7)lbw b Barlow	2
G. E. Palmer	c Lohmann b Ulyett	4	c Pilling b Barlow	8
F. R. Spofforth	c Barlow b Ulyett	2	not out	20
Extras	(w 1)	1	(b 3)	3
Total		205	Total	123

FALL OF WICKETS

AUSTRALIA

Wkt	1st	2nd
1st	58	37
2nd	71	42
3rd	134	44
4th	141	53
5th	181	68
6th	187	70
7th	188	70
8th	192	73
9th	201	103
10th	205	123

ENGLAND

Player	1st innings dismissal	Runs	2nd innings dismissal	Runs
W. H. Scotton	c Trumble b Garrett	21	b Palmer	20
W. G. Grace	c Bonnor b Spofforth	8	c Palmer b Giffen	4
A. Shrewsbury	b Spofforth	31	c and b Giffen	4
W. W. Read	c Scott b Garrett	51	c Jones b Spofforth	9
*A. G. Steel	c Jarvis b Palmer	12	(6)not out	19
R. G. Barlow	not out	38	(5)c Palmer b Spofforth	30
G. Ulyett	b Spofforth	17	c Scott b Garrett	8
J. Briggs	c Garrett b Spofforth	1	not out	2
G. A. Lohmann	b Giffen	32		
E. Peate	st Jarvis b Palmer	6		
†R. Pilling	c Bruce b Palmer	2		
Extras	(b 2, lb 2)	4	(b 10, lb 1)	11
Total		223	Total (6 wkts)	107

ENGLAND

Wkt	1st	2nd
1st	9	7
2nd	51	15
3rd	80	24
4th	109	62
5th	131	90
6th	156	105
7th	160	—
8th	206	—
9th	219	—
10th	223	—

Umpires: J. West,
C. K. Pullin

ENGLAND	1st Innings					2nd Innings			
	O	M	R	W		O	M	R	W
Peate	19	7	30	0	..	46	35	45	1
Lohmann	23	9	41	1	..	5	3	14	0
Steel	27	5	47	2	..	8	3	9	1
Ulyett	36·1	20	46	4	..	6·3	3	7	1
Barlow	23	15	19	1	..	52	24	44	7
Grace	9	3	21	1	..	1	0	1	0

AUSTRALIA	1st Innings					2nd Innings			
	O	M	R	W		O	M	R	W
Spofforth	53	22	82	4	..	29·2	13	40	2
Giffen	32	15	44	1	..	24	9	31	2
Garrett	45	23	43	2	..	17	9	14	1
Palmer	17·2	4	41	3	..	7	3	11	1
Bruce	9	6	9	0	..				

25. J. Briggs

26. H. J. H. Scott

27. Australia 1886
Back row: G. Giffen, F. R. Spofforth, B. J. Wardill (manager). *Middle row:* F. H. Farrands (umpire), R. J. Pope, W. Bruce, J. McIlwraith, T. W. Garrett, E. Evans, J. W. Trumble, unknown official, R. A. Thoms (umpire). *Front:* G. J. Bonnor, J. McC. Blackham, H. J. H. Scott, S. P. Jones, G. E. Palmer. *On ground:* A. H. Jarvis.

1886 Second Test, Lord's

July 19, 20, 21
Toss: England *Result:* England won by an innings and 106 runs

Within 15 minutes of the start of the Lord's Test heavy rain held up play for 85 minutes, and when the game restarted the bowlers got plenty of work on the ball. There was no sun at first, however, the ball turned slowly, and at lunch England were 35 for 1. Afterwards the wicket threatened to become unplayable, the ball kicking and turning viciously, and Scotton, Read and Steel were all dismissed in this period, while Shrewsbury, who had earlier been missed at slip, might have been stumped on the leg side off Giffen.

When Barnes joined Shrewsbury at 4.40 the wicket was at its worst, yet the two Notts batsmen gave a masterly display, so that England at the close had somehow reached 202 for 4. In spite of Shrewsbury's two mistakes, players and spectators alike pronounced his innings the finest of its kind they had ever seen. He had batted at this point for just over 4 hours and had made 91. Barnes was 28. The wicket was easier next morning and Shrewsbury and Barnes added another 78 runs in 65 minutes before they were separated, Shrewsbury completing his century just before midday. None of the remaining batsmen was able

to adjust himself to the continual pace variations of the pitch, but Shrewsbury went serenely on. When he was last out just after 3.0 he had batted 6 hours 51 minutes and England, safe from defeat, had a day and a half in which to bowl Australia out twice.

Jones and Scott, as in the first Test, gave Australia a useful start, but from the moment Briggs and Steel came on as first and second change the batting faltered. Keeping a perfect length and turning only the occasional ball, Briggs had all the batsmen in difficulties, and from 45 for 1 Australia slumped to 67 for 6. Palmer and Blackham added 32, but at 5.55 the innings was over. Briggs got another wicket before the close, when Australia, 12 for 1, were still 220 behind.

Next morning the wicket looked good enough for a stern rearguard action, and a fine stand between Palmer and Trumble, the two surviving night-watchmen, encouraged hopes of a fighting draw. The turning point came when Briggs was brought back at the pavilion end, but the effort of George Palmer, who defended successfully for 2½ hours, suggests that Australia should have avoided defeat.

ENGLAND

W. G. Grace	c Jarvis b Palmer	18
W. H. Scotton	b Garrett	19
A. Shrewsbury	c Bonnor b Trumble	164
W. W. Read	c Spofforth b Giffen	22
*A. G. Steel	lbw b Spofforth	5
W. Barnes	c Palmer b Garrett	58
R. G. Barlow	c Palmer b Spofforth	12
G. Ulyett	b Spofforth	19
†E. F. S. Tylecote	b Spofforth	0
J. Briggs	c Jones b Trumble	0
G. A. Lohmann	not out	7
Extras	(b 24, lb 4, nb 1)	29
Total		**353**

AUSTRALIA

S. P. Jones	c Grace b Briggs	25	(4) b Briggs	17
*H. J. H. Scott	lbw b Briggs	30	(5) b Briggs	2
G. Giffen	b Steel	3	(6) b Barlow	1
†A. H. Jarvis	b Briggs	3	(7) not out	13
G. J. Bonnor	c Grace b Steel	0	(8) b Briggs	3
J. W. Trumble	c Tylecote b Briggs	0	(3) c Tylecote b Barnes	20
G. E. Palmer	c Shrewsbury b Barnes	20	(1) c Lohmann b Barlow	48
J. McC. Blackham	b Briggs	23	(9) b Briggs	5
T. W. Garrett	not out	7	(2) b Briggs	4
F. R. Spofforth	b Barnes	5	(11) c and b Briggs	0
E. Evans	c Ulyett b Barnes	0	(10) run out	0
Extras	(b 4, lb 1)	5	(b 13)	13
Total		**121**	**Total**	**126**

FALL OF WICKETS

ENGLAND

Wkt	1st	2nd
1st	27	—
2nd	77	—
3rd	112	—
4th	119	—
5th	280	—
6th	303	—
7th	333	—
8th	333	—
9th	340	—
10th	353	—

AUSTRALIA

Wkt	1st	2nd
1st	45	6
2nd	52	56
3rd	59	91
4th	60	95
5th	62	98
6th	67	105
7th	99	120
8th	109	126
9th	121	126
10th	121	126

Umpires: F. H. Farrands, C. K. Pullin

AUSTRALIA

	1st Innings				2nd Innings			
	O	M	R	W	O	M	R	W
Garrett	72	40	77	2				
Evans	36	20	37	0				
Palmer	38	15	45	1				
Spofforth	56	26	73	4				
Trumble	14	4	27	2				
Giffen	40	18	63	1				
Jones	3	1	2	0				

ENGLAND

	1st Innings				2nd Innings			
	O	M	R	W	O	M	R	W
Barnes	14·3	7	25	3	10	5	18	1
Lohmann	7	3	21	0	14	9	11	0
Briggs	34	22	29	5	38·1	17	45	6
Steel	21	8	34	2	16	9	14	0
Barlow	6	3	7	0	25	20	12	2
Ulyett					8	3	13	0

1886 Third Test, Oval

August 12, 13, 14
Toss: England   *Result:* England won by an innings and 217 runs

So completely did Grace dominate the early part of the England innings in the final Test that when he was out at 216 he had scored 170 of them. After lunch he hit with a freedom that he seldom achieved at this period in his career. But he owed much of his dominance to the fact that the batsman at the other end for most of the time was Scotton; and during the morning he had a very uncertain time, on a wicket that quickened up later. Missed four times before he reached his hundred, Grace batted for 4½ hours and hit 22 fours, one of them a huge on-drive off Spofforth which would count 6 today. Scotton batted 3¾ hours for 34. In the last hour Shrewsbury and Read added 63, bringing the score to 279 for 2. Blackham, replacing Jarvis behind the wicket, kept brilliantly all day.

As a last cruel blow to the Australians, rain that evening made it likely that the wicket would give the bowlers some help when their turn came to bat. Half an hour was lost next morning through an early shower, but England batted comfortably enough, and wickets were eventually lost in an attempt to get quick runs as the pitch began to dry. Read was caught in the long field when in sight of his hundred, and a typically busy innings by Briggs enlivened the finish. The bowling was good all through.

The Australians went in at 4.10 in bright sunshine and were all out just before 6.0 for 68, Lohmann and Briggs bowling unchanged. Both men turned the ball sharply, and although Lohmann's length was untidy at first he settled down. If some of the Australian batting appeared to lack resolution it cannot be wondered at. Following on, Scott sent McIlwraith and Evans in first and they survived the last 20 minutes.

With the wicket still difficult, and in bad light, it seemed impossible for the Australians to hold out through the third day, and wickets soon began to fall; when Palmer joined Giffen they were 30 for 4. Giffen, who had had a shocking series with the bat, then played firmly and safely while Palmer abandoned his normal steady game and hit out—an interesting comment on the comparison between the state of the wicket on the last day at Lord's and at the Oval. Giffen was out just before lunch after a fine innings, hitting a full toss straight back at Lohmann, and soon after 3.0 the game was over.

The Australians lost four other matches in addition to the Tests, and their experience at the Oval was an unfortunate ending to a disappointing tour.

ENGLAND

W. G. Grace	c Blackham b Spofforth	170
W. H. Scotton	b Garrett	34
A. Shrewsbury	c Jones b Trumble	44
W. W. Read	c Jones b Spofforth	94
W. Barnes	c Evans b Trumble	3
*A. G. Steel	st Blackham b Trumble	9
R. G. Barlow	c Trumble b Garrett	3
G. Ulyett	c McIlwraith b Garrett	0
J. Briggs	c Trumble b Spofforth	53
†E. F. S. Tylecote	not out	10
G. A. Lohmann	b Spofforth	7
Extras	(b 3, lb 2, nb 2)	7
Total		**434**

AUSTRALIA

S. P. Jones	c Grace b Lohmann	2	(3) c Read b Lohmann	2
G. E. Palmer	c Barlow b Briggs	15	(6) st Tylecote b Steel	35
G. Giffen	c Shrewsbury b Briggs	5	(4) c and b Lohmann	47
*H. J. H. Scott	c Tylecote b Lohmann	6	(5) c Grace b Lohmann	4
J. W. Trumble	c Read b Lohmann	13	(7) c Read b Briggs	18
J. McIlwraith	b Lohmann	2	(1) c Tylecote b Briggs	7
†J. McC. Blackham	c and b Briggs	0	(8) c Grace b Briggs	5
T. W. Garrett	c Grace b Lohmann	2	(10) c Shrewsbury b Lohmann	4
W. Bruce	c Ulyett b Lohmann	9	b Lohmann	11
E. Evans	not out	9	(2) run out	3
F. R. Spofforth	b Lohmann	1	not out	5
Extras	(b 4)	4	(b 7, lb 1)	8
Total		**68**	Total	**149**

FALL OF WICKETS

ENGLAND

Wkt	1st	2nd
1st	170	—
2nd	216	—
3rd	287	—
4th	293	—
5th	305	—
6th	314	—
7th	320	—
8th	410	—
9th	418	—
10th	434	—

AUSTRALIA

Wkt	1st	2nd
1st	2	11
2nd	11	14
3rd	22	26
4th	34	30
5th	35	84
6th	35	120
7th	44	129
8th	49	131
9th	67	137
10th	68	149

Umpires: F. H. Farrands, R. Carpenter

AUSTRALIA	1st Innings				2nd Innings			
	O	M	R	W	O	M	R	W
Giffen	62	32	96	0	..			
Garrett	99	55	88	3	..			
Palmer	47	21	80	0	..			
Bruce	6	2	9	0	..			
Spofforth	30·1	12	65	4	..			
Evans	13	10	6	0	..			
Trumble	47	14	83	3	..			

ENGLAND	1st Innings				2nd Innings			
	O	M	R	W	O	M	R	W
Lohmann	30·2	17	36	7	..	37	14	68	5
Briggs	30	17	28	3	..	32	19	30	3
Barlow					..	14	8	13	0
Barnes					..	7	4	10	0
Steel					..	7	1	20	1

Averages: 1886

ENGLAND

BATTING	M.	Inns.	N.O.	Runs	H.S.	Av.
A. Shrewsbury	3	4	0	243	164	60·75
W. G. Grace	3	4	0	200	170	50·00
W. W. Read	3	4	0	176	94	44·00
W. Barnes	2	2	0	61	58	30·50
R. G. Barlow	3	4	1	83	38*	27·66
W. H. Scotton	3	4	0	94	34	23·50
G. A. Lohmann	3	3	1	46	32	23·00
J. Briggs	3	4	1	56	53	18·66
A. G. Steel	3	4	1	45	19*	15·00
G. Ulyett	3	4	0	44	19	11·00
E. F. S. Tylecote	2	2	1	10	10*	10·00

PLAYED IN ONE TEST: E. Peate 6, R. Pilling 2.

BOWLING	Overs	Mds.	Runs	Wkts.	Av.
J. Briggs	134·1	75	132	17	7·76
R. G. Barlow	120	70	95	10	9·50
G. Ulyett	51	26	66	5	13·20
G. A. Lohmann	116·2	55	191	13	14·69
A. G. Steel	79	26	124	6	20·66

ALSO BOWLED: W. Barnes 31·3–16–53–4, W. G. Grace 10–3–22–1, E. Peate 65–42–75–1.

AUSTRALIA

BATTING	M.	Inns.	N.O.	Runs	H.S.	Av.
S. P. Jones	3	6	0	145	87	24·16
G. E. Palmer	3	6	0	130	48	21·66
A. H. Jarvis	2	4	1	63	45	21·00
H. J. H. Scott	3	6	0	110	47	18·33
J. W. Trumble	3	6	0	79	24	13·16
G. Giffen	3	6	0	60	47	10·00
T. W. Garrett	3	6	1	44	22	8·80
J. McC. Blackham	3	6	1	42	23	8·40
F. R. Spofforth	3	6	2	33	20*	8·25
W. Bruce	2	4	0	22	11	5·50
E. Evans	2	4	1	12	9*	4·00
G. J. Bonnor	2	4	0	9	4	2·25

PLAYED IN ONE TEST: J. McIlwraith 2 and 7.

BOWLING	Overs	Mds.	Runs	Wkts.	Av.
F. R. Spofforth	168·3	73	260	14	18·57
J. W. Trumble	61	18	110	5	22·00
T. W. Garrett	233	127	222	8	27·75
G. E. Palmer	109·2	43	177	5	35·40

ALSO BOWLED: G. Giffen 158–74–234–4, S. P. Jones 3–1–2–0, W. Bruce 15–8–18–0, E. Evans 49–30–43–0.

Averages: 1888

ENGLAND

BATTING	M.	Inns.	N.O.	Runs	H.S.	Av.
F. H. Sugg	2	2	0	55	31	27·50
W. Barnes	3	4	0	90	62	22·50
G. A. Lohmann	3	4	1	64	62*	21·33
R. Abel	3	4	0	81	70	20·25
W. G. Grace	3	4	0	73	38	18·25
J. Briggs	3	4	1	39	22*	13·00
R. Peel	3	4	0	48	25	12·00
W. W. Read	3	4	0	44	19	11·00
W. Gunn	2	3	0	25	15	8·33
G. Ulyett	2	2	0	0	0	0·00

PLAYED IN ONE TEST: J. Shuter 28, R. Pilling 17, A. G. Steel 3 and 10*, H. Wood 8, T. C. O'Brien 0 and 4, M. Sherwin 0* and 0.

BOWLING	Overs	Mds.	Runs	Wkts.	Av.
R. Peel	110·2	48	181	24	7·54
J. Briggs	84·1	42	94	12	7·83
W. Barnes	51	25	67	7	9·57
G. A. Lohmann	94·3	50	144	11	13·09

ALSO BOWLED: A. G. Steel 4·2–3–4–1.

AUSTRALIA

BATTING	M.	Inns.	N.O.	Runs	H.S.	Av.
J. J. Ferris	3	6	3	66	20*	22·00
P. S. McDonnell	3	6	0	70	32	11·66
C. T. B. Turner	3	6	0	59	26	9·83
J. D. Edwards	3	6	1	48	26	9·60
J. McC. Blackham	3	6	0	47	22	7·83
G. H. S. Trott	3	6	0	37	17	6·16
S. M. J. Woods	3	6	0	32	18	5·33
A. H. Jarvis	2	4	0	20	8	5·00
G. J. Bonnor	3	6	0	24	8	4·00
J. Worrall	3	6	2	14	8	3·50
A. C. Bannerman	3	6	0	19	13	3·16

PLAYED IN ONE TEST: J. J. Lyons 22 and 32.

BOWLING	Overs	Mds.	Runs	Wkts.	Av.
C. T. B. Turner	168	62	261	21	12·42
J. J. Ferris	119·2	59	167	11	15·18
S. M. J. Woods	54·1	18	121	5	24·20

ALSO BOWLED: J. Worrall 4–1–15–0, G. H. S. Trott 7–2–25–0.

1886-87 First Test, Sydney

January 28, 29, 31
Toss: Australia   *Result:* England won by 13 runs

Both games in this two-match series were played on rain-affected wickets at Sydney, both were low-scoring, and both were won by England. The all-professional touring party was again a strong one, while the Australians were again hampered by selection difficulties. The matches were poorly promoted and attendances suffered. Australian cricket, after its astonishing triumphs of only a few years earlier, was passing through a difficult period aggravated by contention and dispute, and this was reflected at the gate. Yet the first of these two Tests was a splendidly even game, and the matches introduced two great Australian bowlers to Test cricket in Turner and Ferris.

The start of the game was delayed by the completion of an inter-colonial match until 2.20, but even so it began a day earlier than the public expected. McDonnell won the toss and sent England in on a bowlers' wicket, but the utter demoralisation of the England side which followed was as much due to phenomenal catching as to the conditions. Bates began hitting at once and was caught on the boundary. Barnes was brilliantly caught third ball by Spofforth at point. McShane, coming into the side instead of the sick Palmer, brought off a difficult high catch at square leg to dismiss Shrewsbury. 13 for 3.

Barlow and Gunn were bowled at the same total, Spofforth made another astounding catch to dismiss Read, reaching out to a hard cut and holding it in his left hand, and Lohmann, caught off a big hit, was the only man to reach double figures. England's score of 45 remains their lowest.

Australia lost 2 wickets quickly, but they passed the England score without further loss. Jones, dropped on the boundary, mixed good strokes with bad, but Moses in his first Test batted steadily. At the close Australia were 76 for 4. But next morning, although conditions for batting were somewhat improved, their last 6 wickets fell after a dour struggle for 43, giving them a lead of 74.

Although the early English batsmen made a determined effort to retrieve the situation, the pitch was still helping the bowlers, and a sudden collapse left England 103 for 7 at the close—only 29 runs ahead. But on the third morning the last 3 wickets added 25, 25 and 31, 81 runs in all, leaving Australia 111 to win. The odds still looked on Australia, and when Moses and Midwinter were together they seemed likely to win; but Moses was out at 80, and the England attack, well handled by Shrewsbury, just got them home.

ENGLAND

W. Bates	c Midwinter b Ferris	8	b Ferris	24	
*A. Shrewsbury	c McShane b Ferris	2	b Ferris	29	
W. Barnes	c Spofforth b Turner	0	c Moses b Garrett	32	
R. G. Barlow	b Turner	2	c Jones b Ferris	4	
J. M. Read	c Spofforth b Ferris	5	b Ferris	0	
W. Gunn	b Turner	0	b Turner	4	
W. H. Scotton	c Jones b Turner	1	(9) c Spofforth b Garrett	6	
J. Briggs	c Midwinter b Turner	5	b Spofforth	33	
G. A. Lohmann	c Garrett b Ferris	17	(7) lbw b Ferris	3	
W. Flowers	b Turner	2	c McDonnell b Turner	14	
†M. Sherwin	not out	0	not out	21	
Extras	(b 2, lb 1)	3	(b 9, lb 5)	14	
Total		**45**	**Total**	**184**	

AUSTRALIA

†J. McC. Blackham	c Sherwin b Lohmann	4	b Barnes	5	
*P. S. McDonnell	b Barnes	14	lbw b Barnes	0	
H. Moses	b Barlow	31	c Shrewsbury b Barnes	24	
S. P. Jones	c Shrewsbury b Barnes	31	c Read b Barnes	18	
C. T. B. Turner	b Barlow	3	c and b Barnes	7	
A. C. Bannerman	not out	15	b Lohmann	4	
P. G. McShane	lbw b Briggs	5	b Briggs	0	
W. E. Midwinter	c Shrewsbury b Barlow	0	lbw b Barnes	10	
T. W. Garrett	b Lohmann	12	c Gunn b Lohmann	10	
F. R. Spofforth	b Lohmann	2	b Lohmann	5	
J. J. Ferris	c Barlow b Barnes	1	not out	0	
Extras	(b 1)	1	(b 12, lb 2)	14	
Total		**119**	**Total**	**97**	

FALL OF WICKETS

ENGLAND

Wkt	1st	2nd
1st	11	31
2nd	11	80
3rd	13	92
4th	13	92
5th	13	98
6th	17	99
7th	21	103
8th	29	128
9th	41	153
10th	45	184

AUSTRALIA

Wkt	1st	2nd
1st	8	4
2nd	18	5
3rd	64	29
4th	67	38
5th	86	58
6th	95	61
7th	96	80
8th	116	83
9th	118	95
10th	119	97

Umpires: C. Bannerman, H. Rawlinson

AUSTRALIA	1st Innings					2nd Innings			
	O	M	R	W		O	M	R	W
Turner	18	11	15	6	..	44.2	22	53	2
Ferris	17.3	7	27	4	..	61	30	76	5
Spofforth					..	12	3	17	1
Midwinter					..	4	1	10	0
Garrett					..	12	7	8	2
McShane					..	3	0	6	0

ENGLAND	1st Innings					2nd Innings			
	O	M	R	W		O	M	R	W
Barnes	22.1	16	19	2	..	46	29	28	6
Lohmann	21	12	30	3	..	24	11	20	3
Briggs	14	5	25	1	..	7	5	7	1
Barlow	35	23	25	3	..	13	6	20	0
Bates	21	9	19	1	..	17	11	8	0

1886-87 Second Test, Sydney

February 25, 26, 28, March 1
Toss: England   *Result:* England won by 71 runs

Rain had fallen in the night and Shrewsbury, who won the toss, would normally have put Australia in. But the experience of McDonnell in the previous Test, and his own experience in other recent matches, decided him to take first knock. England were without Barnes, the outstanding all-rounder of the previous match; in a hasty moment he had swung a punch at McDonnell, missed, and bruised his hand on a wall. Australia lacked Jones, for whom Cottam substituted, Trott was out with a strain, Spofforth was dropped, and several other players, including Bannerman and Giffen, were not available.

The start was delayed until 3.0, and more rain threatened. After a slow beginning England had lost 6 wickets for 50—5 of them to Turner—when Barlow joined Briggs. At 53 McDonnell made his first change, Garrett relieved Ferris, and soon afterwards Briggs was missed in the slips. He then hit the first 4 of the match, and he continued to bat with such audacity that McDonnell restored Ferris, who promptly sent his stumps flying. Flowers then joined Barlow in a long stand for the 8th wicket, 55 runs being added before stumps were drawn.

After further rain in the night England took their score to 151. It was a far better score than had seemed likely at one time, and under the conditions a good one. The Australian first innings closely paralleled England's until the fall of the 7th wicket, but when Moses, who had given another fine and determined display, was 8th out at 83 the innings folded up and Australia were left 67 runs behind. The medium-paced Lohmann took 8 for 35.

Opening again for England, Bates made a dashing 30, Barlow, no. 3 this time, batted 90 minutes for 10, and England struggled to 73 for 5. On the third morning, on an improved wicket, Briggs played another short but merry knock, and then Flowers and Barlow, heroes of the first innings, added 38 and ensured that Australia would face a formidable total. Barlow, who batted for more than 3 hours, once again held an England innings together, and Australia were set 222 to win.

McDonnell went in first and attacked the bowling, but he eschewed his favourite high hits into the outfield and kept the ball on the ground; his first false stroke cost him his wicket. Moses then took over the attacking role, hitting Lohmann over the grandstand fence, but when he was out the middle batting collapsed and England won on the fourth morning by 71 runs.

ENGLAND

*A. Shrewsbury	b Turner	9	b Turner	6		
W. Bates	c Ferris b Turner	8	b Turner	30		
J. M. Read	b Turner	11	(4)st Burton b Ferris	2		
W. Gunn	b Turner	9	(5)c Cottam b Ferris	10		
G. A. Lohmann	b Ferris	2	(6)b Ferris	6		
W. H. Scotton	b Turner	0	(7)b Ferris	2		
J. Briggs	b Ferris	17	(8)b Garrett	16		
R. G. Barlow	c Allen b Ferris	34	(3)not out	42		
W. Flowers	c Allen b Ferris	37	b Turner	18		
R. Wood	lbw b Ferris	6	hit wkt b Midwinter	0		
†M. Sherwin	not out	4	b Turner	5		
Extras	(b 9, lb 3, nb 2)	14	(b 12, lb 5)	17		
Total		151	Total	154		

AUSTRALIA

W. F. Giffen	b Lohmann	2	(6)b Briggs	0	
J. J. Lyons	b Lohmann	11	(4)c Gunn b Bates	0	
H. Moses	b Flowers	28	(2)st Sherwin b Bates	33	
R. Allen	b Lohmann	14	(3)c sub (C.T.B. Turner) b Bates	30	
*P. S. McDonnell	c Gunn b Lohmann	10	(1)c Gunn b Lohmann	35	
W. E. Midwinter	b Lohmann	1	(7)c Sherwin b Lohmann	4	
W. J. Cottam	hit wkt b Lohmann	1	(5)st Sherwin b Briggs	3	
C. T. B. Turner	c and b Flowers	9	c Briggs b Bates	9	
T. W. Garrett	b Lohmann	1	c Sherwin b Briggs	20	
J. J. Ferris	b Lohmann	1	run out	2	
†F. J. Burton	not out	0	not out	2	
Extras	(b 5, lb 1)	6	(b 9, lb 3)	12	
Total		84	Total	150	

FALL OF WICKETS

ENGLAND

Wkt	1st	2nd
1st	14	21
2nd	19	42
3rd	35	47
4th	38	59
5th	43	73
6th	50	77
7th	73	98
8th	130	136
9th	145	137
10th	151	154

AUSTRALIA

Wkt	1st	2nd
1st	12	51
2nd	15	86
3rd	40	86
4th	56	95
5th	59	95
6th	65	106
7th	82	121
8th	83	129
9th	83	135
10th	84	150

Umpires: C. Bannerman,
J. Swift and W. Gunn

AUSTRALIA	1st Innings				2nd Innings			
	O	M	R	W	O	M	R	W
Ferris	45	16	71	5	60	33	69	4
Turner	53	29	41	5	64·1	33	52	4
Garrett	6	2	12	0	10	6	7	1
Midwinter	3	1	2	0	6	3	9	1
Lyons	2	0	11	0				

ENGLAND	1st Innings				2nd Innings			
	O	M	R	W	O	M	R	W
Lohmann	25	12	35	8	40	16	52	2
Briggs	20	6	34	0	22	9	31	3
Flowers	8	3	9	2	13	5	17	0
Bates					26	13	26	4
Barlow					9	2	12	0

28. C. T. B. Turner

29. G. A. Lohmann

30. England 1886–87
Back row: W. Flowers, A. Shrewsbury (joint capt.), G. A. Lohmann, W. Gunn, W. Barnes, J. M. Read. *Front row:* W. Bates, A. Shaw (joint capt.), James Lillywhite (manager), M. Sherwin, W. H. Scotton, R. G. Barlow. *On ground:* J. Briggs.

1887-88 Only Test, Sydney

February 10, 11, 13, 14, 15
Toss: Australia   *Result:* England won by 126 runs

Nothing seemed less like a Test Match than this disappointing game, and perhaps it should never have been adjudged to be one. Two English parties toured Australia during the season, one organised by Lord Hawke at the invitation of the Melbourne Club, the other the third business venture under the management of Lillywhite, Shaw and Shrewsbury; and they got together to form a combined team for this match. Since each individual party had defeated representative Australian teams on its own, a case might be made for the admittance of further matches to Test status; indeed, the side beaten by Shaw's team only a few days before this game was almost identical with the Test Match XI. But what the Australians thought is worth quoting: 'The principal matches during the past fortnight by the English teams', said one writer, 'have been divested of all importance owing to the non-representative character of the colonial elevens opposing them.' The Australian teams were strong ones nevertheless; and the compromise of counting the last game as a Test Match may be the fairest.

The match was further downgraded by the state of the wicket, heavy rain having fallen before the game. No doubt McDonnell, after his experience of a year earlier, pondered long before sending England in to bat. Stoddart and Shrewsbury opened, both made use of the lofted drive, and they took the score to 27 before McShane brought off a fine running catch to dismiss Stoddart. The ball was turning so abruptly that some balls from Ferris were fielded by slip, and Blackham missed several stumping chances through failure to reach the ball. Walter Read had his middle stump knocked back by Turner, Maurice Read gave an easy return catch, and only Shrewsbury batted with any show of permanence, his 44, out of 86 for 6, being another masterly display. England were all out for 113, and at 5.0 Australia began their reply. The light was awful, the wicket was no better, and when stumps were drawn an hour later they were 35 for 8.

There was no play on the Saturday or the Monday through further heavy rain, by which time public interest had departed and all Test Match atmosphere had gone. Australia were all out for 42, and England, again performing well on a bad wicket, made 137 at the second attempt. Maurice Read, in a dashing if reckless display, made 39, and Australia were left wanting 209 to win. 47 for 5 at the close, they were all out on the third morning for 82. As usual after such a débâcle, the losing side were attacked for being lacking in spirit, but their task was hopeless.

ENGLAND

Batsman	1st innings			2nd innings	
A. E. Stoddart	c McShane b Turner	16		c Blackham b Turner	17
A. Shrewsbury	c Turner b Ferris	44		(6)b Ferris	1
G. Ulyett	c Burton b Turner	5		(2)b Ferris	5
*W. W. Read	b Turner	10		(3)b Turner	8
J. M. Read	c and b Turner	0		(4)c Bannerman b Turner	39
R. Peel	hit wkt b Ferris	3		(5)st Blackham b Turner	9
W. Newham	c Worrall b Ferris	9		(9)lbw b Turner	17
G. A. Lohmann	c Jones b Ferris	12		(7)c Blackham b Turner	0
J. Briggs	b Turner	0		(8)c Worrall b McShane	14
W. Attewell	not out	7		not out	10
†R. Pilling	run out	3		b Turner	5
Extras	(b 4)	4		(b 7, lb 5)	12
Total		113		Total	137

AUSTRALIA

Batsman	1st innings			2nd innings	
A. C. Bannerman	c Ulyett b Lohmann	2		c Attewell b Lohmann	2
S. P. Jones	c Shrewsbury b Peel	0		(4)c Shrewsbury b Lohmann	15
H. Moses	c W. W. Read b Lohmann	3		c Briggs b Lohmann	11
F. J. Burton	c Stoddart b Lohmann	1		(5)c Pilling b Peel	1
J. Worrall	st Pilling b Peel	6		(10)b Lohmann	1
P. G. McShane	c Shrewsbury b Peel	0		(8)b Peel	0
*P. S. McDonnell	b Lohmann	3		(2)b Peel	6
†J. McC. Blackham	c Shrewsbury b Peel	2		(9)not out	25
T. W. Garrett	c Pilling b Lohmann	10		(7)c Shrewsbury b Peel	1
C. T. B. Turner	not out	8		(6)lbw b Attewell	12
J. J. Ferris	c W. W. Read b Peel	0		c Shrewsbury b Peel	5
Extras	(b 6, w 1)	7		(b 2, lb 1)	3
Total		42		Total	82

FALL OF WICKETS

ENGLAND

Wkt	1st	2nd
1st	27	9
2nd	36	15
3rd	54	27
4th	54	54
5th	57	82
6th	88	82
7th	102	84
8th	103	111
9th	103	131
10th	113	137

AUSTRALIA

Wkt	1st	2nd
1st	2	8
2nd	2	8
3rd	10	20
4th	16	21
5th	18	44
6th	21	47
7th	23	53
8th	26	60
9th	37	61
10th	42	82

Umpires: C. Bannerman, J. Phillips

AUSTRALIA	1st Innings					2nd Innings			
	O	M	R	W		O	M	R	W
Turner	50	27	44	5	..	38	23	43	7
Ferris	47	25	60	4	..	16	4	43	2
Garrett	3	1	5	0	..				
McShane					..	21	7	39	1

ENGLAND	1st Innings					2nd Innings			
	O	M	R	W		O	M	R	W
Lohmann	19	13	17	5	..	32	18	35	4
Peel	18·3	9	18	5	..	33	14	40	5
Attewell					..	4·2	2	4	1

40

31. J. J. Ferris

32. A. Shrewsbury

33. England 1887–88
Back row: G. Brann, L. C. Docker, James Lillywhite (manager), J. M. Read, R. Pougher. *Middle row:* G. Ulyett, R. Pilling, C. A. Smith (capt.), A. Shrewsbury, G. A. Lohmann. *Front:* J. M. Preston, J. Briggs, W. Newham.

1888 First Test, Lord's

July 16, 17
Toss: Australia   *Result:* Australia won by 61 runs

Turner and Ferris, right-hand fast-medium and left-hand above medium respectively, showed themselves, in a summer favourable to bowlers, to be perhaps the most destructive pair ever to visit England, and the impression was that on rain-affected wickets, with orthodox batting skills at a discount, Australia were likely to win. This impression was confirmed in the first Test. But the general weakness of the Australian batting, and of the change bowling, was bound to catch up with them, and this it did in decisive manner in July and August, when five successive defeats were suffered leading up to the final Test. McDonnell made no attempt to develop proper support for Turner and Ferris, calling in the Cambridge blue Sammy Woods for the Test Matches, and the passing of the old quartet of Spofforth, Garrett, Palmer and Boyle (although Boyle was in the party he was hardly used at all) left a gap that not even Turner and Ferris could fill. For the batting failures it is less easy to account; but among batsmen who were unable to make the tour were Giffen and Moses, while the loss of Jones through illness was a serious blow.

On a mud wicket at Lord's Australia won the toss and started badly, losing Bannerman off a hard, low cut to Grace at point before a run had been scored. Trott soon skied Peel to cover, and McDonnell and Bonnor at once began hitting. Gunn misjudged a high Bonnor drive to long on, and a straight drive from McDonnell bounced out of Read's hands in the long field, but at 32 for 4 with both batsmen out the mistakes seemed unimportant. Blackham and Woods then added 33, Steel switching his bowlers until the stand was broken, and the 9th wicket fell at 82. Then Edwards and Ferris, in the longest and best stand of the innings, put on 34 for the last wicket.

Play had not begun until after 3.0, and England were left with 45 minutes' batting, in which they lost 3 wickets for 18 runs. Grace was soon out next morning, and the rest of the side failed abysmally under conditions bordering on the farcical, the wicket being even more difficult than on the first day. At 26 for 7 England actually looked like following on, the prescribed margin then being 80, but they avoided this humiliation. At 12.40 Australia batted again with a lead of 63, but they were soon 18 for 7, and only Ferris, slicing the ball clear of the field, had any success. Facing a total of 124 to win, England failed to appreciate that the only thing to do was to hit. Grace played the best innings of the match, but after he was out at 34 there was no stopping the Australians.

AUSTRALIA

A. C. Bannerman	c Grace b Lohmann	0	b Peel		0
*P. S. McDonnell	c O'Brien b Peel	22	b Lohmann		1
G. H. S. Trott	c Lohmann b Peel	0	b Lohmann		3
G. J. Bonnor	b Lohmann	6	c Lohmann b Peel		8
†J. McC. Blackham	b Briggs	22	run out		1
S. M. J. Woods	c Gunn b Briggs	18	c Grace b Peel		3
C. T. B. Turner	c Lohmann b Peel	3	c Grace b Briggs		12
J. D. Edwards	not out	21	c Sherwin b Lohmann		0
A. H. Jarvis	c Lohmann b Peel	3	(11)c Barnes b Peel		4
J. Worrall	c Abel b Briggs	2	b Lohmann		4
J. J. Ferris	c Sherwin b Steel	14	(9)not out		20
Extras	(b 5)	5	(b 3, lb 1)		4
Total		116	Total		60

ENGLAND

W. G. Grace	c Woods b Ferris	10	c Bannerman b Ferris		24
R. Abel	b Ferris	3	c Bonnor b Ferris		8
W. Barnes	c Jarvis b Turner	3	(9)st Blackham b Ferris		1
G. A. Lohmann	lbw b Turner	2	(10)st Blackham b Ferris		0
W. W. Read	st Blackham b Turner	4	(4)b Turner		3
T. C. O'Brien	b Turner	0	(5)b Turner		4
R. Peel	run out	8	(3)b Turner		4
*A. G. Steel	st Blackham b Turner	3	(6)not out		10
W. Gunn	c Blackham b Ferris	2	(7)b Ferris		8
J. Briggs	b Woods	17	(8)b Turner		0
†M. Sherwin	not out	0	c Ferris b Turner		0
Extras	(lb 1)	1			
Total		53			62

FALL OF WICKETS

AUSTRALIA

Wkt	1st	2nd
1st	0	1
2nd	3	1
3rd	28	13
4th	32	15
5th	65	18
6th	76	18
7th	76	18
8th	79	42
9th	82	49
10th	116	60

ENGLAND

Wkt	1st	2nd
1st	5	29
2nd	14	34
3rd	18	38
4th	22	39
5th	22	44
6th	22	55
7th	26	56
8th	35	57
9th	49	57
10th	53	62

Umpires: F. H. Farrands, C. K. Pullin

ENGLAND	1st Innings					2nd Innings			
	O	M	R	W		O	M	R	W
Lohmann	20	9	28	2	..	14	4	33	4
Peel	21	7	36	4	..	10·2	3	14	4
Briggs	21	8	26	3	..	4	1	9	1
Barnes	6	0	17	0	..				
Steel	3·2	2	4	1	..	1	1	0	0

AUSTRALIA	1st Innings					2nd Innings			
	O	M	R	W		O	M	R	W
Turner	25	9	27	5	..	24	8	36	5
Ferris	21	13	19	3	..	23	11	26	5
Woods	4	2	6	1	..				

34. J. J. Lyons

35. R. Peel

36. **Australia 1888**
Back row: C. W. Beal (manager), A. H. Jarvis, J. Worrall, S. P. Jones, F. H. Farrands (umpire), J. J. Lyons, J. McC. Blackham, J. Edwards, C. Lord (asst. manager). *Middle row:* H. F. Boyle, C. T. B. Turner, P. S. McDonnell (capt.), A. C. Bannerman, G. J. Bonnor. *Front:* J. J. Ferris, G. H. S. Trott.

August 13, 14

Toss: Australia   *Result:* England won by an innings and 137 runs

Formidable as they were on bad wickets, with Turner and Ferris to bowl sides out cheaply and batsmen ready to hit, the Australians proved no match for England on a hard, fast wicket. Yet their first-innings collapse in this match seems unaccountable—unless two amazing catches by Lohmann unsettled them. In the first over he picked up McDonnell low down and one-handed at slip before a run had been scored, and later in the morning, after Bannerman had defended for over 100 minutes, he jumped to his right from slip, arm outstretched, and held on to a hard cut as he fell. A fine defensive innings by Edwards found no support from the later batsmen, and after being 50 for 7 at lunch Australia were all out for 80.

Going in soon after 4.0, England also made an atrocious start. After 3 overs Grace reached far outside the off stump and was caught off Turner, and Ulyett did the same thing 4 runs later and was caught behind. Shuter and Read scored for a time with almost hysterical rapidity, but both were clean bowled by Turner, and England were 53 for 4. At this point Abel was joined by Barnes, and for the first time in the match the spectators saw batting of Test class. England were 185 for 5 at the close.

Next morning Abel soon ran himself out; he had batted 2 hours and given no chance. Sugg, missed twice, played a streaky innings, Briggs was out second ball, and England were 242 for 8. Partnered by Peel, Lohmann then thrilled the crowd with a wonderful display of clean hitting, and England gained a lead of 237, leaving Australia 17 minutes' batting before lunch, in which they made 18 off Lohmann and Briggs without loss. The wicket was still good and there seemed no reason why they should not make a fight of it, but after lunch, against Barnes and Peel, wickets tumbled. McDonnell made 32 of the first 34, and Bannerman held one end for 75 minutes, being 6th out at 62, but Australia were all out a second time in 2¼ hours. William Barnes, whose performances over the years made him one of England's best all-rounders, followed up his innings by taking 5 for 32 with his fast-medium bowling and 7 for 50 in the match. It was this match more than any other by which the touring party were judged. Surrey, champion county, championship leaders, and responsible for selection in this match, provided five of the England team.

AUSTRALIA

A. C. Bannerman	c Lohmann b Barnes	13	b Barnes	5		
*P. S. McDonnell	c Lohmann b Peel	0	b Peel	32		
G. H. S. Trott	b Briggs	13	st Wood b Peel	4		
G. J. Bonnor	b Briggs	0	c Wood b Barnes	5		
J. D. Edwards	b Lohmann	26	c Read b Barnes	0		
A. H. Jarvis	b Briggs	5	(9)b Peel	8		
S. M. J. Woods	run out	0	c Abel b Barnes	7		
C. T. B. Turner	b Briggs	0	b Peel	18		
†J. McC. Blackham	b Briggs	0	(10)c Lohmann b Barnes	4		
J. Worrall	c Grace b Barnes	8	(11)not out	0		
J. J. Ferris	not out	13	(6)run out	16		
Extras	(b 1, lb 1)	2	(lb 1)	1		
Total		**80**	**Total**	**100**		

ENGLAND

*W. G. Grace	c Edwards b Turner	1
J. Shuter	b Turner	28
G. Ulyett	c Blackham b Turner	0
W. W. Read	b Turner	18
R. Abel	run out	70
W. Barnes	c Worrall b Turner	62
F. H. Sugg	b Turner	31
R. Peel	b Woods	25
J. Briggs	b Woods	0
G. A. Lohmann	not out	62
†H. Wood	c Bannerman b Ferris	8
Extras	(b 6, lb 4, w 2)	12
Total		**317**

FALL OF WICKETS

AUSTRALIA

Wkt	1st	2nd
1st	0	34
2nd	22	38
3rd	22	43
4th	40	45
5th	49	62
6th	49	62
7th	50	72
8th	50	89
9th	63	98
10th	80	100

ENGLAND

Wkt	1st	2nd
1st	2	—
2nd	6	—
3rd	46	—
4th	53	—
5th	165	—
6th	191	—
7th	241	—
8th	242	—
9th	259	—
10th	317	—

Umpires: F. H. Farrands, R. Carpenter

ENGLAND	1st Innings				2nd Innings			
	O	M	R	W	O	M	R	W
Lohmann	29·3	21	21	1	6	4	11	0
Peel	8	4	14	1	28·2	13	49	4
Briggs	37	24	25	5	6	3	7	0
Barnes	16	9	18	2	29	16	32	5

AUSTRALIA	1st Innings				2nd Innings			
	O	M	R	W	O	M	R	W
Turner	60	24	112	6				
Ferris	35·2	15	73	1				
Trott	7	2	25	0				
Woods	32	10	80	2				
Worrall	4	1	15	0				

1888 Third Test, Old Trafford

August 30, 31

Toss: England   *Result:* England won by an innings and 21 runs

In spite of their disastrous sequence of defeats, Australia went into the last Test all-square with England; and when heavy rain fell for 48 hours before the start, the conditions seemed likely to favour them. For England, Pilling and Gunn replaced Wood and Shuter. Australia left out Jarvis, who had played twice in the series as a batsman, bringing in Lyons for the first time in England.

England batted on a soft wicket, but there was no sun, and an occasional shower deadened the pitch whenever it seemed likely to quicken. Abel was out without a run on the board, and Ulyett was bowled first ball, but Walter Read batted soundly while Grace played with exciting freedom; he hit Turner straight over the sight-screen, and took 10 runs in one over off Woods. Read was bowled at 58, and one run later an astonishing catch at long on removed Grace; Bonnor misjudged the catch completely but stuck out a hand at the last moment and pulled down the ball. The remaining batsmen, apart from Lohmann, who ran himself out, all contributed usefully, and a last-wicket stand between Briggs and Pilling, besides delighting the Lancashire crowd, added 36 runs. 172 under the conditions was a fair score.

The Australians went in at 5.40 and McDonnell attacked at once,

but he was soon caught off a skier. After a short break for rain Peel bowled Bannerman, and Australia finished the day 32 for 2. Next morning the weather was fine and the sun hot, and the effect on the wicket was soon apparent. Needing 61 to avoid the follow on with 8 wickets to fall, Australia lost 5 more wickets for 13 runs before Lyons joined Blackham in a stand that seemed certain to make England bat again. But 12 runs were still needed when Lyons was caught at slip, and they were not forthcoming.

Batting again on an impossible wicket Australia were soon 7 for 6; but Lyons, missed before he had scored, was then joined by Turner, and these two made a great but unavailing effort to save the innings defeat. Lyons, last out, was top scorer in both innings. In this shortest Test Match—it was over just before lunch on the second day—Australia were unlucky, but England were now as strong in bowling as in batting and were clearly the better side.

Both teams could claim that losing the toss had cost them one defeat, and it was fitting that the game at the Oval, where Australia won the toss on a good wicket, should prove the decider.

ENGLAND

*W. G. Grace	c Bonnor b Turner		38
R. Abel	b Turner		0
G. Ulyett	b Turner		0
W. W. Read	b Turner		19
W. Barnes	b Ferris		24
F. H. Sugg	b Woods		24
W. Gunn	lbw b Turner		15
R. Peel	lbw b Ferris		11
J. Briggs	not out		22
G. A. Lohmann	run out		0
†R. Pilling	c Bonnor b Woods		17
Extras	(b 2)		2
Total			**172**

AUSTRALIA

*P. S. McDonnell	c Grace b Peel	15	b Lohmann		0
A. C. Bannerman	b Peel	1	c Grace b Peel		0
G. H. S. Trott	st Pilling b Peel	17	run out		0
G. J. Bonnor	run out	5	c Grace b Peel		0
J. D. Edwards	b Peel	0	(9)c Grace b Peel		1
C. T. B. Turner	b Peel	0	(8)b Briggs		26
S. M. J. Woods	c Read b Briggs	4	b Lohmann		0
†J. McC. Blackham	c Read b Lohmann	15	(5)b Lohmann		5
J. J. Lyons	c Lohmann b Peel	22	(6)b Briggs		32
J. Worrall	b Peel	0	(11)not out		0
J. J. Ferris	not out	0	(10)c Abel b Peel		3
Extras	(b 2)	2	(b 2, lb 1)		3
Total		**81**	**Total**		**70**

FALL OF WICKETS

ENGLAND

Wkt	1st	2nd
1st	0	—
2nd	6	—
3rd	58	—
4th	59	—
5th	96	—
6th	115	—
7th	127	—
8th	135	—
9th	136	—
10th	172	—

AUSTRALIA

Wkt	1st	2nd
1st	16	0
2nd	32	0
3rd	35	1
4th	39	7
5th	39	7
6th	43	7
7th	45	55
8th	81	56
9th	81	70
10th	81	70

Umpires: F. H. Farrands, C. K. Pullin

AUSTRALIA	1st Innings				2nd Innings			
	O	M	R	W	O	M	R	W
Ferris	40	20	49	2	..			
Turner	59	21	86	5	..			
Woods	18·1	6	35	2	..			

ENGLAND	1st Innings				2nd Innings			
	O	M	R	W	O	M	R	W
Peel	26·2	17	31	7	..	16	4	37	4
Lohmann	17	9	31	1	..	8	3	20	3
Briggs	9	4	17	1	..	7·1	2	10	2

July 21, 22, 23
Toss: Australia   *Result:* England won by seven wickets

Losing more matches than they won, the Australians had a disappointing tour, while of the Test Matches one was washed out without a ball being bowled and England won the other two. Yet by their performances in these two matches Australia showed a characteristic ability for raising their game at the highest level. Once again Giffen and Moses were not available to tour, and although Murdoch returned after over five years' absence the batting was weak. The attack still relied almost entirely on Turner and Ferris, and several newcomers—among them S. E. Gregory and Hugh Trumble, later to set many records for Australia—failed completely. England, too, had their difficulties, five key players being absent from the second Test.

At Lord's in July the public proved better judges than the critics: ignoring forecasts of a one-sided game they turned up in strength. The early play, on a pitch deadened by rain, was startling in its brilliance, Lyons hitting 55 out of 66 in 45 minutes, including 50 of the first 55. But after Barnes had hit Lyons' leg stump with a yorker it took the Australians another 2 hours 10 minutes to double their score,

by which time they were all out. After lunch, which was taken at 109 for 4, the last 6 wickets fell for 23.

England began equally sensationally, Grace being out second ball, and after 40 minutes they were 20 for 4. Stimulated by their success the Australians bowled and fielded in exhilarating fashion, and the stand of 72 that followed between Ulyett and Maurice Read provided the best cricket of the series. England reached 108 for 5 overnight, but next morning, on an improving wicket, Lyons bowled his medium-pacers so successfully that England were held to a lead of 41.

Australia then began badly, but Lyons, coming in no. 4 this time, hit a quick 33, and the left-handed Barrett, who opened, batted patiently through to the close, when Australia were 168 for 9. Next morning Barrett carried his bat, the first time this had been done. Left with 136 to win and most of the day to get them in, England won comfortably, but the wicket and outfield were by this time at their best. Grace, whose slowness in the field had been noted, was missed when 44 but otherwise played with wonderful freedom. Not a single bye was conceded in the match.

AUSTRALIA

Batsman	1st Innings		2nd Innings	
J. J. Lyons	b Barnes	55	(4) c Attewell b Peel	33
C. T. B. Turner	b Attewell	24	lbw b Peel	2
*W. L. Murdoch	c and b Attewell	9	(5) b Lohmann	19
J. E. Barrett	c Grace b Ulyett	9	(1) not out	67
G. H. S. Trott	run out	12	(3) b Peel	0
S. E. Gregory	b Attewell	0	c Lohmann b Barnes	9
P. C. Charlton	st MacGregor b Peel	6	lbw b Grace	2
†J. McC. Blackham	b Peel	5	c Barnes b Grace	10
J. J. Ferris	b Attewell	8	lbw b Lohmann	8
K. E. Burn	st MacGregor b Peel	0	(11) c MacGregor b Attewell	19
H. Trumble	not out	1	(10) c Barnes b Lohmann	5
Extras	(lb 3)	3	(lb 2)	2
Total		132	Total	176

ENGLAND

Batsman	1st Innings		2nd Innings	
*W. G. Grace	c and b Turner	0	not out	75
A. Shrewsbury	st Blackham b Ferris	4	lbw b Ferris	13
W. Gunn	run out	14	c and b Ferris	34
W. W. Read	c and b Ferris	1	b Trumble	13
J. M. Read	b Lyons	34	not out	2
G. Ulyett	b Lyons	74		
R. Peel	c and b Trumble	16		
W. Barnes	b Lyons	9		
G. A. Lohmann	c and b Lyons	19		
†G. MacGregor	b Lyons	0		
W. Attewell	not out	0		
Extras	(lb 2)	2		
Total		173	Total (3 wkts)	137

FALL OF WICKETS

AUSTRALIA

Wkt	1st	2nd
1st	66	6
2nd	82	8
3rd	93	48
4th	109	84
5th	111	106
6th	113	109
7th	120	119
8th	131	136
9th	131	142
10th	132	176

ENGLAND

Wkt	1st	2nd
1st	0	27
2nd	14	101
3rd	20	135
4th	20	—
5th	92	—
6th	133	—
7th	147	—
8th	162	—
9th	166	—
10th	173	—

Umpires: A. Hill,
C. K. Pullin

ENGLAND	1st Innings				2nd Innings			
	O	M	R	W	O	M	R	W
Lohmann	21	10	43	0	29	19	28	3
Peel	24	11	28	3	43	23	59	3
Attewell	32	15	42	4	42·2	22	54	1
Barnes	6	2	16	1	6	3	10	1
Ulyett	3	3	0	1	6	2	11	0
Grace					14	10	12	2

AUSTRALIA	1st Innings				2nd Innings			
	O	M	R	W	O	M	R	W
Turner	35	17	53	1	22	12	31	0
Ferris	40	17	55	2	25	11	42	2
Trott	3	0	16	0				
Lyons	20·1	7	30	5	20	6	43	0
Trumble	12	7	17	1	8	1	21	1

37. J. M. Read

38. W. Bruce

39. Australia 1890
Back row: H. Trumble, J. McC. Blackham, K. E. Burn, J. E. Barrett, H. F. Boyle (manager). *Middle row:* F. H. Walters, G. H. S. Trott, W. L. Murdoch (capt.), J. J. Lyons, C. T. B. Turner. *Front:* S. E. Gregory, J. J. Ferris, R. J. Pope, S. P. Jones.

1890 Second Test, Oval

August 11, 12
Toss: Australia   *Result:* England won by two wickets

With Peel and Ulyett claimed by Yorkshire for a county match and Stoddart preferring to play for Middlesex, and with Briggs and Attewell unfit, three newcomers were brought in to the England side—Cranston, a left-handed batsman, Martin, a left-handed bowler of above medium pace with a high delivery, and Sharpe, of Surrey. Australia were unchanged.

Drenching rain which fell before the match destroyed the prospect of a hard wicket, and Australia were all out for 92, Trott alone batting with confidence. England did little better and were saved by Gunn, who batted 1¼ hours after an early 'life'. In the last few minutes Australia, 8 runs behind, lost 2 wickets for 5 runs, 22 wickets thus falling in the day.

The second day compared for excitement with the Ashes match of 1882. Lyons hit hard at first, but Martin and Lohmann turned the game so much England's way that Australia were only 46 in front with 3 wickets to fall. Then Trott, who had been defending skilfully, found a determined partner in Charlton, and 36 priceless runs were made before they were parted. England were left with 95 to win.

At 1.50 Grace cut his first ball straight into Trott's hands at point and out again—narrowly missing a 'king' pair; but soon after lunch both he and Shrewsbury were out. Gunn and Walter Read were both dropped, but they didn't last, and with 4 wickets down England still wanted 63. At this point Cranston joined Maurice Read; and while Cranston defended coolly, Read began to hit. 51 runs were added in 50 minutes, and the game looked won when there was another dramatic change, Read being caught at long on and Cranston taken at slip next ball off a prodigious break. Lohmann, over-anxious, soon skied Ferris to the wicket-keeper, and Barnes, after a beautiful cut for 4, was out next ball. Two runs to win, 2 wickets to fall. Sharpe played forward to a whole over from Ferris without making contact, the ball just beating the stumps, and after a single had been taken to level the scores there were 3 successive maidens before Sharpe hit a ball towards cover and began to run. Seconds later both batsmen were stranded in mid-pitch, but in his haste Barrett threw the ball in wildly, an overthrow resulted, and the game was lost and won. Martin, in his only Test, took 12 for 102.

AUSTRALIA

Batsman	1st innings		2nd innings	
J. J. Lyons	c W. W. Read b Martin	13	(4) b Martin	21
C. T. B. Turner	c Sharpe b Lohmann	12	(7) b Martin	0
*W. L. Murdoch	b Martin	2	(5) b Lohmann	6
J. E. Barrett	c Lohmann b Martin	0	(1) b Martin	4
G. H. S. Trott	c MacGregor b Martin	39	(6) c Cranston b Martin	25
K. E. Burn	c MacGregor b Lohmann	7	(2) b Martin	15
†J. McC. Blackham	b Martin	1	(8) b Lohmann	1
J. J. Ferris	c Lohmann b Sharpe	6	(3) lbw b Lohmann	1
P. C. Charlton	b Martin	10	b Sharpe	11
S. E. Gregory	b Lohmann	2	(11) not out	4
H. Trumble	not out	0	(10) b Martin	6
Extras		0	(b 7, lb 1)	8
Total		**92**	Total	**102**

ENGLAND

Batsman	1st innings		2nd innings	
*W. G. Grace	c Trumble b Ferris	0	c Trumble b Ferris	16
A. Shrewsbury	c Trott b Turner	4	lbw b Ferris	9
W. Gunn	b Ferris	32	st Blackham b Ferris	1
W. W. Read	b Turner	1	b Turner	6
J. Cranston	run out	16	(6) c Trumble b Turner	15
J. M. Read	c Murdoch b Charlton	19	(5) c Barrett b Turner	35
W. Barnes	c Murdoch b Charlton	5	(8) lbw b Ferris	5
G. A. Lohmann	c Gregory b Ferris	3	(7) c Blackham b Ferris	2
†G. MacGregor	c Turner b Ferris	1	not out	2
J. W. Sharpe	not out	5	not out	2
F. Martin	c Turner b Charlton	1		
Extras	(b 9, lb 3, nb 1)	13	(lb 1, nb 1)	2
Total		**100**	Total (8 wkts)	**95**

FALL OF WICKETS

AUSTRALIA

Wkt	1st	2nd
1st	16	4
2nd	27	5
3rd	27	36
4th	32	43
5th	39	49
6th	46	53
7th	70	54
8th	85	90
9th	92	92
10th	92	102

ENGLAND

Wkt	1st	2nd
1st	0	24
2nd	10	25
3rd	16	28
4th	55	32
5th	79	83
6th	90	83
7th	91	86
8th	93	93
9th	94	—
10th	100	—

Umpires: C. K. Pullin, J. Street

ENGLAND	1st Innings				2nd Innings			
	O	M	R	W	O	M	R	W
Martin	27	9	50	6	30.2	12	52	6
Lohmann	32.2	19	34	3	21	8	32	3
Sharpe	6	3	8	1	9	5	10	1

AUSTRALIA	1st Innings				2nd Innings			
	O	M	R	W	O	M	R	W
Turner	22	12	37	2	25	9	38	3
Ferris	25	14	25	4	23	8	49	5
Trumble	2	0	7	0				
Charlton	6	0	18	3	3	1	6	0

1891-92 First Test, Melbourne

January 1, 2, 4, 5, 6
Toss: Australia   *Result:* Australia won by 54 runs

Victory after a long sequence of reverses can seldom have been sweeter than Australia's triumphs in the first two games of this three-match series, which decided the rubber and won back the Ashes after nearly 10 years; and the tour as a whole brought a great revival of interest in cricket in Australia. England sent her strongest available side, led by W. G. Grace, and they had their chances in both games; but the maturing of Lyons and Bruce, the return to the international fold of George Giffen, and above all the recrudescence of Alec Bannerman (in the first two Tests he batted for 15 hours) brought just the required stiffening to the Australian side. Steadiness, as opposed to brilliance, became in this series a hallmark of Australian rather than English batting, the Englishmen missing the stability of Shrewsbury and Gunn, both of whom refused terms for the tour.

After the Australian players had appointed Blackham captain he won the toss, and Australia at lunch were 52 for 2. Scoring mostly by deflections, Bannerman and Bruce put on 87, but a collapse followed,

and with Moses wrenching his leg going for a short single Australia did well to reach 240 on the second morning. Sharpe, with a nice springy action and plenty of pace and stamina, was the best bowler.

The presence of Grace enlivened the series in more ways than one. Giffen said after his dismissal that he did not doubt the decision but he did question the taste of point (Grace) in appealing. And when Grace batted he was so discomfited by the placing of a close fieldsman that he asked Blackham whether he wanted a funeral in his team. Even so he and Abel gave England a great start. The fast-medium Bob McLeod then got Grace, Abel and Stoddart in a dozen balls, but Read and Bean put on 86, and England gained a lead of 24.

Profiting by some luck, Lyons then made 50 out of 65, and Bannerman and Bruce again batted well, but soon after lunch on the fourth day England began the wholly reasonable task of making 213 to win. Once again they got a great start, this time from Grace and Stoddart, but when they were separated Blackham boldly tried Trott's slow leg-breaks, and there was no recovery from the setback which followed.

AUSTRALIA

						FALL OF WICKETS
A. C. Bannerman	c Read b Sharpe	45	c Grace b Sharpe	41		AUSTRALIA
J. J. Lyons	c Grace b Peel	19	c Abel b Briggs	51		
G. Giffen	lbw b Peel	2	b Attewell	1		
W. Bruce	b Sharpe	57	c Lohmann b Sharpe	40		
H. Donnan	b Sharpe	9	(9)c and b Lohmann	2		
H. Moses	c Lohmann b Sharpe	23	run out	15		
G. H. S. Trott	c MacGregor b Sharpe	6	lbw b Attewell	23		
R. W. McLeod	b Sharpe	14	b Peel	31		
S. T. Callaway	b Attewell	21	(10)not out	13		
C. T. B. Turner	b Peel	29	(5)c Peel b Lohmann	19		
*J. McC. Blackham	not out	4	c MacGregor b Peel	0		
Extras	(b 5, lb 6)	11		0		
Total		**240**	Total	**236**		

Wkt	1st	2nd
1st	32	66
2nd	36	67
3rd	123	120
4th	136	152
5th	136	152
6th	148	182
7th	164	197
8th	191	210
9th	232	236
10th	240	236

ENGLAND

*W. G. Grace	b McLeod	50	c Bannerman b Turner	25	
R. Abel	b McLeod	32	(5)c Blackham b Turner	28	
A. E. Stoddart	c Giffen b McLeod	0	(2)b Callaway	35	
G. Bean	c Bruce b Giffen	50	(3)c McLeod b Trott	3	
J. M. Read	c and b Giffen	38	(4)b Trott	11	
R. Peel	b McLeod	19	b Turner	6	
G. A. Lohmann	lbw b Giffen	3	c Bannerman b Turner	0	
J. Briggs	c Bruce b Turner	41	c Trott b McLeod	4	
W. Attewell	c Bannerman b Turner	8	(10)c Donnan b Turner	24	
J. W. Sharpe	c Blackham b McLeod	2	(11)not out	5	
†G. MacGregor	not out	9	(9)c sub (S. E. Gregory) b Trott	16	
Extras	(b 7, lb 2, nb 3)	12	(b 1)	1	
Total		**264**	Total	**158**	

ENGLAND		
Wkt	1st	2nd
1st	84	60
2nd	85	60
3rd	85	71
4th	171	75
5th	179	93
6th	187	93
7th	232	98
8th	249	125
9th	256	139
10th	264	158

Umpires: J. Phillips,
T. Flynn

ENGLAND	1st Innings				2nd Innings			
	O	M	R	W	O	M	R	W
Sharpe	51	20	84	6	54	25	81	2
Peel	43	23	54	3	16·5	7	25	2
Attewell	21·1	11	28	1	61	32	51	2
Lohmann	28	14	40	0	39	15	53	2
Briggs	3	1	13	0	21	9	26	1
Stoddart	5	2	10	0				

AUSTRALIA	1st Innings				2nd Innings			
	O	M	R	W	O	M	R	W
Trott	10	2	25	0	19	2	52	3
Giffen	20	3	75	3	3	0	8	0
Turner	16	3	40	2	33·2	14	51	5
McLeod	28·4	12	55	5	23	8	39	1
Callaway	14	2	39	0	4	1	7	1
Bruce	3	0	18	0				

1891–92 Second Test, Sydney

January 29, 30, February 1, 2, 3
Toss: Australia   *Result:* Australia won by 72 runs

After Lyons had hit Briggs to the scoring board and lifted Lohmann to the top of the ladies' pavilion, Australia faltered on a lively wicket to 62 for 3 at lunch and were all out for 145, Blackham's decision to bat looking mistaken. Moses, although not fully recovered, batted well until his leg gave way again, but Grace had warned Blackham that he could expect no sympathy and a runner was not asked for. Nevertheless feeling against Grace amongst the crowd ran high. Then when England batted Moses limped about at slip in pitiful style; it was not until the second day that Grace allowed a substitute.

For the third time running the England opening stand reached 50, Abel especially batting crisply from the start on a plumb wicket. But the middle batting failed, and it was left to Briggs and Sharpe to see Abel to his hundred and England into a long lead. Abel, who batted 5 hours 25 minutes, was the first Englishman to carry his bat. 162 behind, the Australians had a few minutes' batting at the end of the second day, in which they lost Trott, and with Moses unable to bat the game looked lost.

On the third day the Australians gave a wonderful exhibition of determined batting. Although he scored quickly Lyons eschewed recklessness, collecting most of his runs by cuts and dabs to leg, while Bannerman took runs only when they were offered. The crowd, thin and despondent at first, increased dramatically as the stand developed. When he had made 49 Lyons twice snicked Sharpe to Abel at slip in one over, but neither chance was accepted and none other was offered; Lyons reached his hundred out of 129 and batted for just over 3 hours in all. At stumps Australia were 263 for 3, 101 in front, and Bannerman had batted 6 hours 23 minutes for 67.

On the fourth morning Australia added another 36 runs without loss before rain drenched the wicket. Bruce then chanced his arm successfully before Briggs finished the innings off with a hat trick. Rain came again before stumps, when England, wanting 230, were 11 for 3. The wicket rolled out well next day and Grace was criticised for not sending in the tail-enders overnight; as it was, despite a fine innings by Stoddart, England were never really in the hunt.

AUSTRALIA

A. C. Bannerman	c Abel b Lohmann	12	c Grace b Briggs	91
J. J. Lyons	c Grace b Lohmann	41	(3)c Grace b Lohmann	134
G. Giffen	c Abel b Lohmann	6	(4)lbw b Attewell	49
H. Moses	c Grace b Lohmann	29	absent hurt	—
C. T. B. Turner	c MacGregor b Lohmann	15	(7)not out	14
W. Bruce	c Bean b Attewell	15	(5)c Briggs b Sharpe	72
G. H. S. Trott	b Lohmann	2	(2)c Sharpe b Lohmann	1
R. W. McLeod	c Attewell b Lohmann	13	(6)c Read b Peel	18
W. F. Giffen	c and b Lohmann	1	(8)b Briggs	3
S. T. Callaway	run out	1	c Grace b Briggs	0
†*J. McC. Blackham	not out	3	(9)lbw b Briggs	0
Extras	(b 6, w 1)	7	(b 6, lb 2, w 1)	9
Total		**145**	Total	**391**

ENGLAND

R. Abel	not out	132	c W. Giffen b G. Giffen	1
*W. G. Grace	b Turner	26	c Blackham b Turner	5
G. Bean	b G. Giffen	19	c Lyons b Turner	4
A. E. Stoddart	c Blackham b McLeod	27	b Turner	69
J. M. Read	c Turner b G. Giffen	3	c and b G. Giffen	22
R. Peel	c G. Giffen b Turner	20	st Blackham b G. Giffen	6
G. A. Lohmann	b G. Giffen	10	c Bruce b G. Giffen	15
†G. MacGregor	lbw b McLeod	3	c and b G. Giffen	12
J. Briggs	lbw b Trott	28	c Trott b Turner	12
W. Attewell	b Trott	0	c and b G. Giffen	0
J. W. Sharpe	c Bannerman b G. Giffen	26	not out	4
Extras	(b 10, lb 2, w 1)	13	(b 5, lb 2)	7
Total		**307**	Total	**157**

FALL OF WICKETS

AUSTRALIA

Wkt	1st	2nd
1st	31	1
2nd	57	175
3rd	62	254
4th	90	347
5th	117	364
6th	123	376
7th	126	391
8th	132	391
9th	141	391
10th	145	—

ENGLAND

Wkt	1st	2nd
1st	50	2
2nd	79	6
3rd	123	11
4th	127	64
5th	152	83
6th	167	117
7th	178	133
8th	235	140
9th	235	140
10th	307	157

Umpires: J. Tooher,
T. Flynn

ENGLAND

	1st Innings					2nd Innings		
	O	M	R	W		O	M	R	W
Lohmann	43·2	18	58	8	..	51	14	84	2
Attewell	31	20	25	1	..	46	24	43	1
Briggs	10	2	24	0	..	32·4	8	69	4
Sharpe	10	1	31	0	..	35	7	91	1
Peel					..	35	13	49	1
Grace					..	15·3	2	34	0
Stoddart					..	4	1	12	0

AUSTRALIA

	1st Innings					2nd Innings		
	O	M	R	W		O	M	R	W
Turner	37	11	90	2	..	23·2	7	46	4
McLeod	18	6	55	2	..				
G. Giffen	28·2	5	88	4	..	28	10	72	6
Trott	14	3	42	2	..	5	0	11	0
Callaway	17	10	19	0	..	10	6	21	0

40. A. E. Stoddart

41. A. C. Bannerman

42. England 1891-92
Back row: H. Philipson, O. G. Radcliffe, W. Attewell, G. Bean, A. Shaw (manager). *Middle row:* A. E. Stoddart, G. A. Lohmann, W. G. Grace (capt.), R. Abel, J. M. Read. *Front:* G. MacGregor, J. Briggs, J. W. Sharpe.

1891-92 Third Test, Adelaide

March 24, 25, 26, 28
Toss: England   *Result:* England won by an innings and 230 runs

There was rough justice in England's good luck at Adelaide after their experience in Sydney. This was the first Test played at Adelaide, where the smooth, highly polished, grassless surface was a nightmare for bowlers until the rain fell.

Abel ran out to Trott at 47 and was stumped, but Grace and Stoddart then put on 74, Grace repeatedly walking out to the slower bowlers and hitting them in the air short of the deep field, while one big hit from Stoddart landed on the bicycle track. England were 209 for 2 at tea, after which Stoddart pulled Turner into the grandstand and Giffen into the crowd on the opposite side, and England were 313 for 4 at stumps. Stoddart gave only two possible chances before reaching his hundred: a catch and a stumping when he first came in off the same ball, Blackham thinking it would hit the wicket, and a high drive over long on at 50 which Lyons misjudged. A great many of his runs came on the leg side, the pull off the back foot and the forward glance, and he reached his hundred in 2¾ hours.

129 not out overnight, Stoddart was soon out next morning, but Peel and Briggs batted in entertaining fashion, although the fielding wilted during their partnership. Rain threatened and then began to fall, and the Australians were hampered by a wet ball, the umpires allowing play to continue for some time.

On the third morning the pitch was in a dreadful state, but when Australia batted Lyons attacked at once. One huge straight hit would have counted 5 on any ground but Adelaide, where the boundaries were exceptionally long behind the wickets but narrow on each side; and he then swung Lohmann into the crowd. But Bob McLeod, who ran out to almost every ball and played it on the full, was the only other batsman to reach 20. Doomed to defeat, Australia followed on, but Giffen joined with Lyons in a brief exhibition that showed there were no two harder or longer hitters in the world, and afterwards the slightly built Bruce hit almost as hard. Practically unplayable when the wicket was at its worst, Briggs took 12 for 136.

Six days was all the Englishmen's itinerary had permitted them for this final match of their tour, and had the weather held it would scarcely have been enough.

ENGLAND

*W. G. Grace	b McLeod	58
R. Abel	st Blackham b Trott	24
A. E. Stoddart	lbw b G. Giffen	134
J. M. Read	c Gregory b Turner	57
G. Bean	c McLeod b Lyons	16
R. Peel	c G. Giffen b Turner	83
G. A. Lohmann	lbw b G. Giffen	0
J. Briggs	b Turner	39
†H. Philipson	c Blackham b McLeod	1
G. MacGregor	run out	31
W. Attewell	not out	43
Extras	(b 5, lb 7, w 1)	13
Total		**499**

AUSTRALIA

A. C. Bannerman	c Bean b Lohmann	12	b Briggs	1	
J. J. Lyons	c Peel b Briggs	23	c Stoddart b Briggs	19	
G. Giffen	run out	5	c Bean b Attewell	27	
W. Bruce	lbw b Lohmann	5	lbw b Attewell	37	
C. T. B. Turner	c Lohmann b Briggs	10	c Grace b Briggs	5	
S. E. Gregory	c Abel b Briggs	3	c Peel b Briggs	7	
R. W. McLeod	b Briggs	20	c Grace b Lohmann	30	
G. H. S. Trott	b Briggs	0	st Philipson b Briggs	16	
W. F. Giffen	b Lohmann	3	c Peel b Briggs	2	
H. Donnan	c Bean b Briggs	7	not out	11	
†*J. McC. Blackham	not out	7	b Attewell	9	
Extras	(b 5)	5	(b 3, lb 2)	5	
Total		**100**	**Total**	**169**	

FALL OF WICKETS

ENGLAND

Wkt	1st	2nd
1st	47	—
2nd	121	—
3rd	218	—
4th	272	—
5th	327	—
6th	333	—
7th	412	—
8th	425	—
9th	425	—
10th	499	—

AUSTRALIA

Wkt	1st	2nd
1st	30	1
2nd	38	42
3rd	48	51
4th	48	85
5th	51	91
6th	66	99
7th	66	120
8th	73	124
9th	90	157
10th	100	169

Umpires: W. O. Whitridge,
G. Downes

AUSTRALIA

	1st Innings				2nd Innings			
	O	M	R	W	O	M	R	W
G. Giffen	51.1	17	154	2	..			
McLeod	41	11	78	2	..			
Trott	12	0	80	1	..			
Turner	46	17	111	3	..			
Donnan	9	2	22	0	..			
Lyons	5	0	22	1	..			
Bruce	4	3	19	0	..			

ENGLAND

	1st Innings				2nd Innings			
	O	M	R	W	O	M	R	W
Briggs	21.5	4	49	6	..	28	7	87	6
Lohmann	21	8	46	3	..	6	2	8	1
Attewell					..	34	10	69	3

Averages: 1891-92

AUSTRALIA

BATTING

	M.	Inns.	N.O.	Runs	H.S.	Av.
J. J. Lyons	3	6	0	287	134	47·83
W. Bruce	3	6	0	226	72	37·66
A. C. Bannerman	3	6	0	202	91	33·66
H. Moses	2	3	0	67	29	22·33
R. W. McLeod	3	6	0	126	31	21·00
C. T. B. Turner	3	6	1	92	29	18·40
G. Giffen	3	6	0	90	49	15·00
S. T. Callaway	2	4	1	35	21	11·66
H. Donnan	2	4	1	29	11*	9·66
G. H. S. Trott	3	6	0	48	23	8·00
J. McC. Blackham	3	6	3	23	9	7·66
W. F. Giffen	2	4	0	9	3	2·25

PLAYED IN ONE TEST: S. E. Gregory 3 and 7.

BOWLING

	Overs	Mds.	Runs	Wkts.	Av.
C. T. B. Turner	155·4	52	338	16	21·12
R. W. McLeod	110·4	37	227	10	22·70
G. Giffen	130·3	35	397	15	26·46
G. H. S. Trott	60	7	210	6	35·00

ALSO BOWLED: J. J. Lyons 5–0–22–1, S. T. Callaway 45–19–86–1, H. Donnan 9–2–22–0, W. Bruce 7–3–37–0.

ENGLAND

BATTING

	M.	Inns.	N.O.	Runs	H.S.	Av.
R. Abel	3	5	1	217	132*	54·25
A. E. Stoddart	3	5	0	265	134	53·00
W. G. Grace	3	5	0	164	58	32·80
R. Peel	3	5	0	134	83	26·80
J. M. Read	3	5	0	131	57	26·20
J. Briggs	3	5	0	124	41	24·80
W. Attewell	3	5	1	75	43*	18·75
J. W. Sharpe	2	4	2	37	26	18·50
G. Bean	3	5	0	92	50	18·40
G. MacGregor	3	5	1	71	31	17·75
G. A. Lohmann	3	5	0	28	15	5·60

PLAYED IN ONE TEST: H. Philipson 1.

BOWLING

	Overs	Mds.	Runs	Wkts.	Av.
J. Briggs	116·3	31	268	17	15·76
G. A. Lohmann	188·2	71	289	16	18·06
R. Peel	94·5	43	128	6	21·33
W. Attewell	193·1	97	216	8	27·00
J. W. Sharpe	150	53	287	9	31·88

ALSO BOWLED: W. G. Grace 15·3–2–34–0, A. E. Stoddart 9–3–22–0.

Averages: 1893

ENGLAND

BATTING

	M.	Inns.	N.O.	Runs	H.S.	Av.
A. Shrewsbury	3	5	1	284	106	71·00
F. S. Jackson	2	3	0	199	103	66·33
W. Gunn	3	5	1	208	102*	52·00
W. G. Grace	2	3	0	153	68	51·00
A. E. Stoddart	3	5	0	162	83	32·40
W. W. Read	2	3	1	64	52	32·00
A. Ward	2	3	0	68	55	22·66
G. MacGregor	3	3	1	22	12	11·00
W. H. Lockwood	2	3	0	32	22	10·66
J. Briggs	2	2	0	2	2	1·00
A. Mold	3	3	3	0	0*	

PLAYED IN ONE TEST: W. Flowers 35 and 4, R. Peel 12 and 0*, T. Richardson 16, E. Wainwright 1 and 26, W. Brockwell 11, J. M. Read 6 and 1.

BOWLING

	Overs	Mds.	Runs	Wkts.	Av.
T. Richardson	67·4	20	156	10	15·60
W. H. Lockwood	93	27	234	14	16·71
J. Briggs	120·1	40	293	16	18·31
A. Mold	98·1	32	234	7	33·42

ALSO BOWLED: W. Flowers 11–3–21–1, R. Peel 22–12–36–0, W. Brockwell 3–0–17–0, E. Wainwright 11–3–41–0, F. S. Jackson 16–4–43–0.

AUSTRALIA

BATTING

	M.	Inns.	N.O.	Runs	H.S.	Av.
W. Bruce	3	5	1	159	68	39·75
H. Graham	3	5	0	170	107	34·00
A. C. Bannerman	3	5	0	161	60	32·20
G. H. S. Trott	3	5	0	146	92	29·20
J. J. Lyons	3	5	0	117	33	23·40
J. McC. Blackham	3	5	3	44	23*	22·00
G. Giffen	3	5	0	91	53	18·20
S. E. Gregory	3	5	0	75	57	15·00
H. Trumble	3	5	1	58	35	14·50
C. T. B. Turner	3	5	0	34	27	6·80
R. W. McLeod	3	5	0	20	6	4·00

BOWLING

	Overs	Mds.	Runs	Wkts.	Av.
G. Giffen	171·4	59	342	16	21·37
C. T. B. Turner	175	72	315	11	28·63
W. Bruce	71	23	156	5	31·20
H. Trumble	105·2	30	234	6	39·00

ALSO BOWLED: R. W. McLeod 85–30–157–2, J. J. Lyons 7–1–26–0, G. H. S. Trott 17–3–76–0.

1893 First Test, Lord's

July 17, 18, 19
Toss: England   *Result:* Match Drawn

The Australian party of 1893, although potentially a great side, disappointed its followers, failed to win a Test Match, and lost the Ashes; and as they lost a good many other matches, one can only attribute their modest record to the superior all-round strength of English cricket at the time. Apart from Moses, who was again unable to tour, the side was fully representative, but on the hard, dry wickets prevalent that summer Turner was never quite the force he had been in the wet summers of 1888 and 1890, and Hugh Trumble, although a much improved bowler, was played comfortably enough. Giffen was the best bowler, though his batting suffered. England introduced a great Test batsman in F. S. Jackson and a great bowler in Lockwood, and when Lockwood was unfit they were able to substitute Richardson, whose record is second to none. How serious to England the absence of Shrewsbury and William Gunn had been in the previous series was amply shown.

England's performance on the first day in scoring 334 runs between 12.5 and 5.35 on a wicket damaged by rain was remarkable. When Jackson joined Shrewsbury at 31 for 2, 150 was the limit of expectation;

but 100 minutes later, when lunch was taken, 107 runs had been added, 74 of them to Jackson. After reaching 50 in 52 minutes Jackson was badly missed at mid on, and he was dropped again after lunch, as was Shrewsbury, but his driving and pulling were thrilling to see. With the wicket easier in the afternoon, Shrewsbury played with more freedom, and his hundred came in 4 hours.

33 for 2 overnight, Australia struggled next day against fine bowling by Lockwood to 75 for 5, and the subsequent fight back by their two youngest players, Graham and the diminutive Gregory, was as meritorious as the Shrewsbury-Jackson stand. Their running and aggression animated the game, and although both were missed they put on 142 in 100 minutes. With Bruce in the follow on was saved, and the deficit was eventually restricted to 65.

When England went in a second time Shrewsbury again batted finely, well supported by Gunn, but rain held up play after lunch on the last day at a time when Australia, 300 runs behind with 3¾ hours left, faced an uphill task to save the game. Grace, who had an injured finger, was missing his first home Test.

ENGLAND

A. Shrewsbury	c Blackham b Turner	106	b Giffen	81	
*A. E. Stoddart	b Turner	24	b Turner	13	
W. Gunn	c Lyons b Turner	2	c Graham b Giffen	77	
F. S. Jackson	c Blackham b Turner	91	c Bruce b Giffen	5	
J. M. Read	b Bruce	6	c McLeod b Bruce	1	
R. Peel	c Bruce b Trumble	12	(9)not out	0	
W. Flowers	b McLeod	35	(6)b Turner	4	
E. Wainwright	c Giffen b Turner	1	b Giffen	26	
W. H. Lockwood	b Bruce	22	(7)b Giffen	0	
†G. MacGregor	not out	5			
A. Mold	b Turner	0			
Extras	(b 19, lb 9, nb 2)	30	(b 16, lb 9, w 1, nb 1)	27	
Total		**334**	**Total** (8 wkts dec)	**234**	

AUSTRALIA

J. J. Lyons	b Lockwood	7
A. C. Bannerman	c Shrewsbury b Lockwood	17
G. Giffen	b Lockwood	0
G. H. S. Trott	c MacGregor b Lockwood	33
R. W. McLeod	b Lockwood	5
S. E. Gregory	c MacGregor b Lockwood	57
H. Graham	c MacGregor b Mold	107
W. Bruce	c Peel b Mold	23
C. T. B. Turner	b Flowers	0
H. Trumble	not out	2
†*J. McC. Blackham	lbw b Mold	2
Extras	(b 15, lb 1)	16
Total		**269**

FALL OF WICKETS

ENGLAND

Wkt	1st	2nd
1st	29	27
2nd	31	179
3rd	168	195
4th	189	198
5th	213	198
6th	293	198
7th	298	234
8th	313	234
9th	333	—
10th	334	—

AUSTRALIA

Wkt	1st	2nd
1st	7	—
2nd	7	—
3rd	50	—
4th	60	—
5th	75	—
6th	217	—
7th	264	—
8th	265	—
9th	265	—
10th	269	—

Umpires: J. Phillips,
W. Hearn

AUSTRALIA	1st Innings					2nd Innings			
	O	M	R	W		O	M	R	W
Turner	36	16	67	6	..	32	15	64	2
Bruce	22	4	58	2	..	20	10	34	1
Trumble	19	7	42	1	..	11	2	33	0
Trott	9	2	38	0	..	2	0	5	0
McLeod	21	6	51	1	..	25	11	28	0
Giffen	18	3	48	0	..	26·4	6	43	5

ENGLAND	1st Innings					2nd Innings			
	O	M	R	W		O	M	R	W
Peel	22	12	36	0	..				
Lockwood	45	11	101	6	..				
Mold	20·1	7	44	3	..				
Jackson	5	1	10	0	..				
Wainwright	11	3	41	0	..				
Flowers	11	3	21	1	..				

43. W. H. Lockwood

44. H. Graham

45. Australia 1893
Back row: R. Carpenter (umpire), V. Cohen (manager), A. H. Jarvis, W. F. Giffen, W. Bruce, A. C. Bannerman, R. A. Thoms (umpire).
Middle row: G. H. S. Trott, H. Trumble, G. Giffen, J. McC. Blackham (capt.), J. J. Lyons, R. W. McLeod, C. T. B. Turner.
Front: H. Graham, A. C. Y. Coningham, S. E. Gregory.

August 14, 15, 16
Toss: England *Result:* England won by an innings and 43 runs

Grace, Walter Read, Ward and Briggs replaced Maurice Read, Peel, Wainwright and Flowers in the England side. Flowers was unwell, and Ward would have played at Lord's had not Lancashire begged him off. The effect was to make the batting unusually strong but to weaken the bowling. Australia were unchanged. England batted on a wicket that gave the bowlers some help in the first hour, and Stoddart began shakily, but even so he reached 50 in 80 minutes. Grace, too, played one of his best innings, after which Shrewsbury and Ward put on 103. England were 311 for 5 with 45 minutes left when Jackson joined Read, and although the light was failing the tired bowlers were hit for 67 in this time, Jackson's share being 49. Dropped when 36 by Gregory at long on, Jackson was 98 next morning when he was joined by Mold with 9 wickets down, Giffen having run through the tail. Although Mold then ran between the wickets with extraordinary obtuseness, depriving Jackson of the strike, Jackson eventually reached his hundred with a tremendous drive to long on that landed on the covered stand next to the pavilion. Mold then immediately ran him out. He batted 2¼ hours and his on-side hitting was especially fine.

England's 483 was then their highest at home against Australia.

The Australian innings began well on a perfect wicket, but directly Briggs came on there was a sensational collapse. 32 for 3 at lunch, Australia were all out in 100 minutes for 91, the only redeeming features being the cool defence of Bruce and some spirited hitting by Blackham. Following on 392 behind, Australia did much better and were 158 for 2 at the close. Bannerman batted much more freely than usual, and he and the left-handed Bruce, who opened this time, had 50 up in 30 minutes. But Australia were still 234 behind, and next morning Giffen was yorked by Lockwood at 165. Then, after Gregory had failed, Trott and Graham put on a hundred in an hour, so that, approaching 300 with only 4 wickets down, Australia seemed to have a real chance of escaping. When they were separated, however, only a tremendous burst of firm-footed hitting by Lyons, who hit 3 fours in succession off Lockwood, the second pitching on the pavilion roof, delayed the end. Lockwood and Briggs, although often under pressure, bowled well throughout.

ENGLAND

*W. G. Grace	c Giffen b Trumble	68
A. E. Stoddart	b Turner	83
A. Shrewsbury	c Graham b Giffen	66
W. Gunn	b Giffen	16
A. Ward	c and b Giffen	55
W. W. Read	b Giffen	52
F. S. Jackson	run out	103
J. Briggs	b Giffen	0
W. H. Lockwood	c and b Giffen	10
†G. MacGregor	lbw b Giffen	5
A. Mold	not out	0
Extras	(b 19, lb 4, w 2)	25
Total		**483**

AUSTRALIA

A. C. Bannerman	c MacGregor b Lockwood	10	c Read b Lockwood		55
J. J. Lyons	b Briggs	19	(7)c Grace b Lockwood		31
G. H. S. Trott	b Lockwood	0	(4)c Read b Lockwood		92
S. E. Gregory	lbw b Briggs	9	(5)c Shrewsbury b Briggs		6
H. Graham	c MacGregor b Lockwood	0	(6)b Briggs		42
G. Giffen	c MacGregor b Lockwood	4	(3)b Lockwood		53
W. Bruce	not out	10	(2)c Jackson b Mold		22
H. Trumble	b Briggs	5	b Briggs		8
R. W. McLeod	c Lockwood b Briggs	2	c Jackson b Briggs		5
C. T. B. Turner	b Briggs	7	b Briggs		0
†*J. McC. Blackham	run out	17	not out		2
Extras	(b 5, lb 3)	8	(b 18, lb 15)		33
Total		**91**	**Total**		**349**

FALL OF WICKETS

ENGLAND

Wkt	1st	2nd
1st	151	—
2nd	151	—
3rd	200	—
4th	303	—
5th	311	—
6th	442	—
7th	442	—
8th	456	—
9th	478	—
10th	483	—

AUSTRALIA

Wkt	1st	2nd
1st	30	54
2nd	31	126
3rd	32	165
4th	32	189
5th	40	295
6th	48	311
7th	57	340
8th	59	342
9th	69	342
10th	91	349

Umpires: H. Draper, C. K. Pullin

AUSTRALIA

	1st Innings				2nd Innings			
	O	M	R	W	O	M	R	W
Turner	47	18	94	1	..			
Trumble	47	16	101	1	..			
McLeod	23	6	57	0	..			
Giffen	54	17	128	7	..			
Trott	6	1	33	0	..			
Bruce	3	0	19	0	..			
Lyons	7	1	26	0	..			

ENGLAND

	1st Innings				2nd Innings			
	O	M	R	W	O	M	R	W
Lockwood	19	9	37	4	29	7	96	4
Mold	4	0	12	0	23	8	73	1
Briggs	14.3	5	34	5	35	6	114	5
Jackson					11	3	33	0

1893 Third Test, Old Trafford

August 24, 25, 26
Toss: Australia   *Result:* Match Drawn

By winning at Old Trafford Australia could level the series and retain the Ashes; yet England were unable to field their best side. Lockwood was injured and was replaced by Richardson, which proved no handicap; but Jackson preferred to play for Yorkshire, and Peel, who was invited to play, was not released, although Yorkshire had already made sure of the championship. Australia won the toss, but this proved an uncertain advantage on a wicket on which every now and again a ball kicked following overnight rain.

After a hurricane start by Lyons, Bannerman and Giffen batted steadily. Briggs bowled intelligently, varying his pace and pitch, but McGregor had a bad time behind the wicket, missing two catches off Mold. Richardson replaced Mold and bowled Giffen, and the atmosphere changed as Australia slumped to 73 for 4. Bruce and Graham then improved matters by adding 56, and Bruce found another good partner in Hugh Trumble. Bruce was finally out at 194 to a wonderful left-handed catch at second slip by Read; his 68, made in 100 minutes, included many attractive leg-side strokes. England had 70 minutes' batting, finishing the day, at 54 for 2, on about even terms.

A keen and absorbing struggle filled the second day. Read was bowled by a ball that broke the width of the wicket, and in 2 hours 25 minutes before lunch England added only 91 for the loss of 4 wickets, Gunn then being 44 not out. After lunch, although wickets continued to fall, Gunn played in his most elegant style. Richardson, with some agricultural pulls, helped him add 42 for the ninth wicket, and Gunn reached a great hundred in 4 hours 10 minutes with hardly a bad stroke.

Australia raced to 56 in 35 minutes, wiping off the arrears, and they were 93 for 3 at the close, 54 in front, so a tremendous battle was in prospect on the last day. But an hour was lost through rain, and Australia were almost safe when Bruce, who had helped Bannerman put on 54, was caught off a kicker. Bannerman was then badly missed at slip by Read, but when he was 8th out shortly after lunch Australia were still only 143 in front. Blackham then played a characteristic innings, and England, with 135 minutes remaining and 198 needed, had no incentive to risk going for the runs.

AUSTRALIA

A. C. Bannerman	c MacGregor b Briggs	19	b Richardson	60	
J. J. Lyons	c MacGregor b Briggs	27	b Mold	33	
G. Giffen	b Richardson	17	c Brockwell b Richardson	17	
G. H. S. Trott	c Grace b Richardson	9	b Mold	12	
W. Bruce	c Read b Richardson	68	(6)c Shrewsbury b Richardson	36	
H. Graham	lbw b Mold	18	(7)st MacGregor b Briggs	3	
S. E. Gregory	b Briggs	0	(8)lbw b Richardson	3	
H. Trumble	b Richardson	35	(9)run out	8	
R. W. McLeod	b Briggs	2	(5)c Read b Richardson	6	
C. T. B. Turner	b Richardson	0	c Mold b Briggs	27	
*J. McC. Blackham	not out	0	not out	23	
Extras	(b 5, lb 4)	9	(b 4, lb 4)	8	
Total		**204**	Total	**236**	

ENGLAND

A. E. Stoddart	run out	0	c Gregory b Trumble	42	
*W. G. Grace	b Bruce	40	c Trott b McLeod	45	
A. Shrewsbury	c Bruce b Giffen	12	not out	19	
W. Gunn	not out	102	b Trumble	11	
A. Ward	c Blackham b Turner	13	b Trumble	0	
W. W. Read	b Giffen	12	not out	0	
W. Brockwell	c Gregory b Giffen	11			
J. Briggs	b Giffen	2			
†G. MacGregor	st Blackham b Turner	12			
T. Richardson	b Bruce	16			
A. Mold	b Trumble	0			
Extras	(b 17, lb 6)	23	(b 1)	1	
Total		**243**	Total (4 wkts)	**118**	

FALL OF WICKETS

AUSTRALIA

Wkt	1st	2nd
1st	32	56
2nd	59	79
3rd	69	92
4th	73	99
5th	129	153
6th	130	170
7th	194	173
8th	198	182
9th	201	200
10th	204	236

ENGLAND

Wkt	1st	2nd
1st	4	78
2nd	43	100
3rd	73	117
4th	93	117
5th	112	—
6th	136	—
7th	165	—
8th	196	—
9th	238	—
10th	243	—

Umpires: J. Phillips, C. Clements

ENGLAND

	1st Innings					2nd Innings			
	O	M	R	W		O	M	R	W
Mold	28	11	48	1	..	23	6	57	2
Richardson	23.4	5	49	5	..	44	15	107	5
Briggs	42	18	81	4	..	28.3	11	64	2
Brockwell	3	0	17	0	..				

AUSTRALIA

	1st Innings					2nd Innings			
	O	M	R	W		O	M	R	W
Giffen	67	30	113	4	..	6	3	10	0
Turner	53	22	72	2	..	7	1	18	0
Bruce	17	5	26	2	..	9	4	19	0
Trumble	3.2	1	9	1	..	25	4	49	3
McLeod					..	16	7	21	1

1894-95 First Test, Sydney

December 14, 15, 17, 18, 19, 20
Toss: Australia   *Result:* England won by 10 runs

The revival of interest in Test cricket in Australia begun three years earlier was more than maintained in this series, no sequence of matches having aroused such excitement. From the first day of the first Test the fortunes of two strong and evenly matched sides fluctuated, right through to the final Test when England went in wanting 297 in the fourth innings with the Ashes at stake. Ward and Brown, the last player to be chosen (when Abel declined the invitation) took the batting honours in company with Stoddart, who curbed his normal game to give the side stability, while Richardson proved himself the outstanding bowler of his time. George Giffen scored more runs and took more wickets than anyone on either side.

There was a sensational start when Richardson, on a perfect wicket, bowled Lyons off his pads, sent Trott's off stump twirling through the air, and then yorked Darling first ball—21 for 3. But Giffen and Iredale, helped by dropped catches behind the wicket off Richardson, held firm until lunch. Richardson tired in the heat of the afternoon, Lockwood ricked his back, and the England bowling suddenly looked thin. Iredale helped Giffen to add 171, and then Gregory, after an

uncertain start, played some magnificent shots off the back foot. At stumps Australia were 346 for 5. More dropped catches demoralised the bowlers on the second day, at the end of which England, facing a score of 586, were 130 for 3.

Rain over the weekend did not improve the wicket, but nearly all the England batsmen contributed usefully, aided by repeated mistakes in the field (Blackham had to retire with a split finger, which did not help), and the total reached 325. Following on 261 behind, England did even better, another fine defensive innings by Ward laying the foundations, and at the end of the fourth day they had cleared the arrears with 6 wickets still to fall. Sound cricket by the later batsmen left Australia on the fifth afternoon wanting 177 to win.

Richardson had a chill and bowled little, and at the close Australia, 113 for 2, wanted only 64. But the rain that had been threatening fell that night, and next morning, with the wicket a quagmire, England's two slow left-handers were unplayable. 15 runs were still wanted when the ninth wicket fell, and Blackham went to the wicket, but his thumb was too painful and he soon gave Peel a return catch.

AUSTRALIA

J. J. Lyons	b Richardson	1	b Richardson	25	
G. H. S. Trott	b Richardson	12	c Gay b Peel	8	
G. Giffen	c Ford b Brockwell	161	lbw b Briggs	41	
J. Darling	b Richardson	0	c Brockwell b Peel	53	
F. A. Iredale	c Stoddart b Ford	81	(6)c and b Briggs	5	
S. E. Gregory	c Peel b Stoddart	201	(5)c Gay b Peel	16	
J. C. Reedman	c Ford b Peel	17	st Gay b Peel	4	
C. E. McLeod	b Richardson	15	not out	2	
C. T. B. Turner	c Gay b Peel	1	c Briggs b Peel	2	
†*J. McC. Blackham	b Richardson	74	(11)c and b Peel	2	
E. Jones	not out	11	(10)c MacLaren b Briggs	1	
Extras	(b 8, lb 3, w 1)	12	(b 2, lb 1, nb 4)	7	
Total		586	Total	166	

ENGLAND

A. C. MacLaren	c Reedman b Turner	4	b Giffen	20	
A. Ward	c Iredale b Turner	75	b Giffen	117	
*A. E. Stoddart	c Jones b Giffen	12	c Giffen b Turner	36	
J. T. Brown	run out	22	c Jones b Giffen	53	
W. Brockwell	c Blackham b Jones	49	b Jones	37	
R. Peel	c Gregory b Giffen	4	b Giffen	17	
F. G. J. Ford	st Blackham b Giffen	30	c and b McLeod	48	
J. Briggs	b Giffen	57	b McLeod	42	
W. H. Lockwood	c Giffen b Trott	18	b Trott	29	
†L. H. Gay	c Gregory b Reedman	33	b Trott	4	
T. Richardson	not out	0	not out	12	
Extras	(b 17, lb 3, w 1)	21	(b 14, lb 8)	22	
Total		325	Total	437	

FALL OF WICKETS

AUSTRALIA		
Wkt	1st	2nd
1st	10	26
2nd	21	45
3rd	21	130
4th	192	135
5th	331	147
6th	379	158
7th	400	159
8th	409	161
9th	563	162
10th	586	166

ENGLAND		
Wkt	1st	2nd
1st	14	44
2nd	43	115
3rd	78	217
4th	149	245
5th	155	290
6th	211	296
7th	211	385
8th	252	398
9th	325	420
10th	325	437

Umpires J. Phillips, C. Bannerman

ENGLAND	1st Innings					2nd Innings			
	O	M	R	W		O	M	R	W
Richardson	55.3	13	181	5	..	11	3	27	1
Peel	53	14	140	2	..	30	9	67	6
Briggs	25	4	96	0	..	11	2	25	3
Brockwell	22	7	78	1	..				
Ford	11	2	47	1	..				
Stoddart	3	0	31	1	..				
Lockwood	3	2	1	0	..	16	3	40	0

AUSTRALIA	1st Innings					2nd Innings			
	O	M	R	W		O	M	R	W
Jones	18	6	44	1	..	19	0	57	1
Turner	44	16	89	2	..	35	14	78	1
Giffen	43	17	75	4	..	75	25	164	4
Trott	15	4	59	1	..	12.4	3	22	2
McLeod	14	2	25	0	..	30	6	67	2
Reedman	3.3	1	12	1	..	6	1	12	0
Lyons	2	2	0	0	..	2	0	12	0
Iredale					..	2	1	3	0

46. T. Richardson

47. G. Giffen

48. England 1894-95
Back row (standing): A. C. MacLaren, F. G. J. Ford, R. Peel, T. Richardson, A. Ward, L. H. Gay. *Middle row:* W. Brockwell,
A. E. Stoddart (capt.), J. Briggs, H. Philipson. *Front:* J. T. Brown, W. A. Humphreys.

1894-95 Second Test, Melbourne

December 29, 31, January 1, 2, 3
Toss: Australia *Result:* England won by 94 runs

With Blackham still unfit, Giffen took over as captain, and on winning the toss he put England in, heavy rain before the game having soaked the wicket. A watchful innings by Ward might have been the basis of a better score, but the attacking cricket that was called for was not forthcoming and England were all out in 2 hours for 75. The heavy roller was applied, and although the wicket was much improved Australia were soon 14 for 3. Darling then hit a quick 32 before Lockwood deceived him with his slower ball, and England's score was passed with only 4 wickets down. Richardson then removed Iredale, Giffen's slow but safe innings ended at 96, and the deficit was held to 48. The wicket was then rolled by mutual agreement for 15 minutes, and big scores were confidently forecast after the weekend.

An hour's batting on the Monday morning for the loss of MacLaren was enough for England to clear the arrears, and although Stoddart hit one drive over the pavilion gate the play was mostly steady on what was now a perfect wicket. After Ward was bowled at 101 the workmanlike Brown scored readily, and when he was out just on tea-time the score was 191, Stoddart 95 not out; his century came soon afterwards. Brockwell batted freely but did not last, and Peel came in

determined to stonewall. Stoddart confined himself to punishing the occasional loose ball, and both men set themselves to building a winning score. At stumps England were 239 ahead with 6 wickets left.

Stoddart's innings, which lasted 5 hours 20 minutes in all, seemed to have won the game for his side; and Peel batted on until after lunch next day, his 50 coming in 2 hours 48 minutes and containing 34 singles and no fours. A stand of 53 between Lockwood and Philipson for the 9th wicket looked like the last straw; but Australia had reached 98 for 1 by the end of the fourth day, and the wicket was still good.

Trott, who had opened with Bruce, carried on the good work next morning, and Australia had narrowed the gap to 246 before the second wicket fell, the fast-medium Brockwell inducing a false stroke from Giffen and then holding on to a terrific caught and bowled low down to dismiss Trott. Iredale then defended without support until Turner came in last with 160 still wanted. 60 of them were safely made that evening, but on the fifth morning Iredale was bowled by a long hop. England were two up, but it was clear that there was little to choose between the two sides.

ENGLAND

						FALL OF WICKETS		
						ENGLAND		
A. C. MacLaren	c Trott b Coningham	0	b Turner	15		Wkt	1st	2nd
A. Ward	c Darling b Trumble	30	b Turner	41		1st	0	24
*A. E. Stoddart	b Turner	10	b Giffen	173		2nd	19	101
J. T. Brown	c Trumble b Turner	0	c Jarvis b Bruce	37		3rd	23	191
W. Brockwell	c Iredale b Coningham	0	b Turner	21		4th	26	222
R. Peel	c Trumble b Turner	6	st Jarvis b Giffen	53		5th	44	320
F. G. J. Ford	c Giffen b Trumble	9	c Trott b Giffen	24		6th	58	362
W. H. Lockwood	not out	3	(9)not out	33		7th	60	385
J. Briggs	c Bruce b Turner	5	(8)lbw b Giffen	31		8th	70	402
†H. Philipson	c Darling b Turner	1	b Giffen	30		9th	71	455
T. Richardson	c Iredale b Trumble	0	c Gregory b Giffen	11		10th	75	475
Extras	(lb 9, nb 2)	11	(b 1, lb 2, nb 3)	6				
Total		**75**	**Total**	**475**				

AUSTRALIA

						AUSTRALIA		
						Wkt	1st	2nd
J. J. Lyons	b Richardson	2	(7)b Peel	14		1st	4	98
W. Bruce	c Ford b Peel	4	c Stoddart b Peel	54		2nd	12	191
*G. Giffen	c Philipson b Briggs	32	c Brown b Brockwell	43		3rd	14	206
S. E. Gregory	c Ward b Richardson	2	b Richardson	12		4th	53	214
J. Darling	b Lockwood	32	b Brockwell	5		5th	80	216
F. A. Iredale	b Richardson	10	b Peel	68		6th	96	241
G. H. S. Trott	run out	16	(1)c and b Brockwell	95		7th	108	254
A. Coningham	c Philipson b Richardson	10	(9)b Peel	3		8th	110	263
H. Trumble	b Richardson	1	(10)run out	2		9th	116	268
†A. H. Jarvis	c Brown b Briggs	11	(8)b Richardson	4		10th	123	333
C. T. B. Turner	not out	1	not out	26				
Extras	(w 2)	2	(b 5, lb 1, nb 1)	7		Umpires: J. Phillips,		
Total		**123**	**Total**	**333**			T. Flynn	

AUSTRALIA

	1st Innings					2nd Innings			
	O	M	R	W		O	M	R	W
Coningham	11	5	17	2	..	20	4	59	0
Turner	20	9	32	5	..	55	21	99	3
Trumble	9·1	4	15	3	..	26	6	72	0
Giffen					..	78·2	21	155	6
Lyons					..	2	1	3	0
Trott					..	17	0	60	0
Bruce					..	4	0	21	1

ENGLAND

	1st Innings					2nd Innings			
	O	M	R	W		O	M	R	W
Richardson	23	6	57	5	..	40	10	100	2
Peel	14	4	21	1	..	40·1	9	77	4
Lockwood	5	0	17	1	..	25	5	60	0
Briggs	13·5	2	26	2	..	12	0	49	0
Ford					..	6	2	7	0
Brockwell					..	14	3	33	3

1894-95 Third Test, Adelaide

January 11, 12, 14, 15
Toss: Australia   *Result:* Australia won by 382 runs

For this vital game, which they had to win to stay in the hunt, Australia had severe selection problems. Turner had a chill, Lyons and Graham were out of form, and Moses was still unfit. England, who had brought Philipson in for Gay in the previous Test, were unchanged. Australia won the toss for the third time running, and they had not been batting long when they began to be suspicious of the wicket. A new pitch, more central than the original one, had been selected only two days before the game, and it was probably underprepared, several balls tending to keep low. It improved somewhat as the match progressed; but it was never fast or difficult. The heat was intense, and even in the Australian first innings the Englishmen tired rapidly. But for two run outs, and magnificent bowling by Richardson, Australia would have made many more than 238; as it was they only reached that moderate figure after Albert Trott and Callaway, with the Englishmen exhausted, had added 81 for the last wicket. Earlier a promising innings by Harry Trott had been cut short when he sacrificed his wicket to save Giffen; Giffen went on to make 58 in 2¾ hours.

Physical weakness induced by heat and frequent showering has been blamed for the deplorable English batting that followed; to this can be added an exaggerated mistrust of the pitch, brilliant Australian fielding and catching, and some fine bowling by Giffen and the fast-medium Callaway. The only worthwhile stand was the 47 by Brown and Ford for the 7th wicket after England had plummeted to 64 for 6. With a lead of 114, Australia were saved from having to enforce the follow on by an amendment which had increased the margin to 120; otherwise England would have batted again when the wicket was at its best.

By the end of the second day Australia, 145 for 4 and 259 on, had reason to feel that the game was won. The innings began with another charming display by Bruce, was maintained by a century from Iredale, and ended with the Englishmen demoralised by the hitting of Albert Trott. Iredale, with an easy, upright stance and excelling in the off-drive, placed his shots well and showed a near-immaculate defence, although he was missed twice off Richardson; of the latter it was said after this match that 'the Australians now agree that he is the most perfect natural bowler they have ever seen'.

With the wicket showing signs of wear the fast-medium Albert Trott completed a remarkable debut, taking 8 for 43 in England's second innings. But England, anxious to get back to Sydney and Melbourne, showed little stomach for the fight.

AUSTRALIA

Batsman	1st Innings		2nd Innings	
W. Bruce	b Richardson	11	c Brockwell b Briggs	80
G. H. S. Trott	run out	48	b Peel	0
*G. Giffen	c Lockwood b Brockwell	58	c Ford b Peel	24
F. A. Iredale	b Richardson	7	c and b Peel	140
J. Darling	c Philipson b Briggs	10	c Philipson b Lockwood	3
S. E. Gregory	c Brown b Richardson	6	b Richardson	20
J. Harry	b Richardson	2	b Richardson	6
J. Worrall	run out	0	c Peel b Briggs	11
†A. H. Jarvis	c and b Lockwood	13	c Brown b Peel	29
A. E. Trott	not out	38	not out	72
S. T. Callaway	b Richardson	41	b Richardson	11
Extras	(b 2, w 1, nb 1)	4	(b 7, lb 7, nb 1)	15
Total		**238**		**411**

ENGLAND

Batsman	1st Innings		2nd Innings	
J. Briggs	b Callaway	12	(9)b A. Trott	0
A. C. MacLaren	b Callaway	25	c Iredale b A. Trott	35
W. Brockwell	c Harry b Callaway	12	(6)c and b A. Trott	24
A. Ward	c Bruce b Giffen	5	(1)b A. Trott	13
*A. E. Stoddart	b Giffen	1	(3)not out	34
J. T. Brown	not out	39	(5)b A. Trott	2
R. Peel	b Callaway	0	(7)c and b A. Trott	0
F. G. J. Ford	c Worrall b Giffen	21	b A. Trott	14
W. H. Lockwood	c Worrall b Giffen	0	(10)c Iredale b A. Trott	1
†H. Philipson	c Gregory b Giffen	7	(4)b Giffen	1
T. Richardson	c Worrall b Callaway	0	c A. Trott b Giffen	12
Extras	(b 2)	2	(b 5, lb 2)	7
Total		**124**		**143**

FALL OF WICKETS

AUSTRALIA

Wkt	1st	2nd
1st	31	0
2nd	69	44
3rd	84	142
4th	103	145
5th	120	197
6th	124	215
7th	137	238
8th	157	283
9th	157	347
10th	238	411

ENGLAND

Wkt	1st	2nd
1st	14	52
2nd	30	52
3rd	49	53
4th	50	64
5th	56	102
6th	64	102
7th	111	128
8th	111	128
9th	124	130
10th	124	143

Umpires: J. Phillips, G. Searcy

ENGLAND	1st Innings					2nd Innings			
	O	M	R	W		O	M	R	W
Richardson	21	4	75	5	..	31·2	8	89	3
Peel	16	1	43	0	..	34	6	96	4
Brockwell	20	13	30	1	..	10	1	50	0
Ford	8	2	19	0	..	6	0	33	0
Briggs	8	6	34	1	..	19	3	57	2
Lockwood	8	2	33	1	..	15	2	71	1

AUSTRALIA	1st Innings					2nd Innings			
	O	M	R	W		O	M	R	W
A. E. Trott	3	1	9	0	..	27	10	43	8
Giffen	28	11	76	5	..	22·1	12	74	2
Callaway	26·3	13	37	5	..	7	1	19	0

1894-95 Fourth Test, Sydney

February 1, 2, 4
Toss: England   *Result:* Australia won by an innings and 147 runs

With Moses and Graham in for Harry and Worrall, Australia were virtually at full strength. For England, Lockwood played although he had injured his hand. A spell of bad weather ruined the wicket, and a new pitch was prepared which was inevitably soft. It was the sort of toss that captains are glad to lose—and for the only time in the series Stoddart won it. He put Australia in.

Richardson began by lifting and breaking back from a length, Peel pushed the ball through, and the openers were soon out. Giffen, who had gone in no. 3, had meanwhile sent word to the pavilion to alter the order: Moses and Graham, whom he regarded as his two best wet-wicket batsmen, were to come in next. After pitching one outside the leg stump which broke across and missed the off, Peel bowled Giffen with a straight one, and when Moses, the first pawn in Giffen's tactical ploy, was bowled off his thigh by Richardson Australia were 26 for 4.

Seeing that Richardson was rising over the top of the wicket and that the keeper was standing back, Graham resolved to run out and hit at the pitch of the ball; as soon as he faced Richardson he put this plan into effect and lifted him high into the long field, the ball falling just short of the ring. After ducking as a bouncer passed over his head next ball, he rushed out and repeated the stroke, and again the ball bounced into the crowd. At the other end the astonished Gregory could only gape. But neither he nor Iredale lasted, and at 51 for 6, with Peel and Briggs in command, Stoddart's gamble had apparently paid off. Darling, however, came in no. 8 and hit Briggs into the tennis courts behind the pavilion—a vast blow of about 120 yards—and as the hitting continued the England fielding began to wilt. Several chances went to ground, and when Richardson bowled Darling at 119 for 7 the game had changed. Graham and Albert Trott then laid about them so vigorously that Richardson had to post two men at long on. 112 were added before Graham was out after batting 2¼ hours, and 45 more were put on for the last wicket. With only a few minutes left Giffen opened with the tempting slows of Harry Trott and MacLaren was stumped before the close.

It rained all day Saturday, and again on Sunday night. 'We shall be out twice in one day', was Stoddart's gloomy forecast. And he was right.

AUSTRALIA

G. H. S. Trott	c Brown b Peel	1
W. Bruce	c Brockwell b Peel	15
*G. Giffen	b Peel	8
H. Moses	b Richardson	1
H. Graham	st Philipson b Briggs	105
S. E. Gregory	st Philipson b Briggs	5
F. A. Iredale	c and b Briggs	0
J. Darling	b Richardson	31
A. E. Trott	not out	85
†A. H. Jarvis	c Philipson b Briggs	5
C. T. B. Turner	c Richardson b Lockwood	22
Extras	(b 3, lb 1, w 1, nb 1)	6
Total		**284**

ENGLAND

	1st		2nd	
A. C. MacLaren	st Jarvis b G. H. S. Trott	1	(4)c Bruce b Giffen	0
A. Ward	c and b Turner	7	c Darling b Giffen	6
J. Briggs	b G. H. S. Trott	11	(8)c Bruce b Giffen	6
*A. E. Stoddart	st Jarvis b G. H. S. Trott	7	(3)c Iredale b Turner	0
J. T. Brown	not out	20	(1)b Giffen	0
W. Brockwell	c Darling b Turner	1	(5)c Bruce b Turner	17
F. G. J. Ford	c G. H. S. Trott b Giffen	0	c Darling b Giffen	11
R. Peel	st Jarvis b Turner	0	(6)st Jarvis b Turner	0
†H. Philipson	c Graham b Giffen	4	c and b Turner	9
T. Richardson	c and b Giffen	2	not out	10
W. H. Lockwood	absent hurt	—	absent hurt	—
Extras	(b 7, lb 3, nb 2)	12	(b 5, lb 7, nb 1)	13
Total		**65**	**Total**	**72**

FALL OF WICKETS

AUSTRALIA

Wkt	1st	2nd
1st	2	—
2nd	20	—
3rd	26	—
4th	26	—
5th	51	—
6th	51	—
7th	119	—
8th	231	—
9th	239	—
10th	284	—

ENGLAND

Wkt	1st	2nd
1st	2	0
2nd	20	5
3rd	24	5
4th	31	12
5th	40	14
6th	43	29
7th	56	47
8th	63	52
9th	65	72
10th	—	—

Umpires: J. Phillips, C. Bannerman

ENGLAND	1st Innings				2nd Innings			
	O	M	R	W	O	M	R	W
Peel	24	5	74	3				
Richardson	22	5	78	2				
Briggs	22	4	65	4				
Brockwell	5	1	25	0				
Lockwood	8·2	3	22	1				
Ford	2	0	14	0				

AUSTRALIA	1st Innings				2nd Innings			
	O	M	R	W	O	M	R	W
G. H. S. Trott	14	5	21	3				
Turner	19	10	18	3	14·1	6	33	4
Giffen	5·5	1	14	3	15	7	26	5

1894-95 Fifth Test, Melbourne

Test no. 43

March 1, 2, 4, 5, 6
Toss: Australia   *Result:* England won by six wickets

Turner was left out of this deciding game, his place being taken by McKibbin, who turned the ball more on hard wickets. Turner was one of the three selectors and it is said he was outvoted by the other two, Blackham and Giffen; his omission caused much adverse comment. At lunch Australia were going well at 76 for 1, but after lunch Iredale was bowled by a bailer that ran on to the fence, and although Giffen made a chanceless 57 Australia were 152 for 4 at tea. Then Gregory and Darling took Australia to 282 for 4 at stumps. Both were quickly dismissed next day, but Lyons hit 55 in 70 minutes, and the fielding became ragged as the last pair added 47.

Once again Harry Trott took an early wicket, getting Brockwell stumped, but Stoddart and Ward put on 104. As with the Australians, it was the 5th wicket that provided the stuffing of the innings, and England, 200 for 4 overnight, were 295 for 4 at lunch on the third day. Twice Giffen fumbled return catches from MacLaren; but he had injured a finger batting, which may have accounted for it, also for the fact that he showed less than his habitual command over the ball. MacLaren's century came in just under 3 hours. Peel, after 4 noughts

in succession, helped him in a stand of 162. The later batting failed, however, and Australia, leading by 29, were 69 for 1 at the close.

It seemed now, with the fourth innings ahead of them, that only great bowling could preserve England's chance; and shortly after the hundred went up next morning with 2 wickets down, Peel suggested that he and Richardson change ends to get the best out of the cross wind that was blowing. From then on, despite a fighting knock by Darling, the Australian innings always looked likely to be kept within bounds. Even so, England were set 297 to win. 28 for 1 overnight, they lost Stoddart to the first ball of the fifth morning; but Brown, with rain threatening and possibly under orders to hit before it came, made 50 in the next half-hour; few 50s can compare with it for turning a game. The rain held off, Brown went on to make 140 in 2 hours 25 minutes while Ward defended, and England won comfortably in the end.

With the sides level at two games all beforehand, this match excited enormous interest, and there was nothing quite comparable until Allen's team reached a similar position 42 years later.

AUSTRALIA

G. H. S. Trott	b Briggs	42	b Peel	42	
W. Bruce	c MacLaren b Peel	22	c and b Peel	11	
*G. Giffen	b Peel	57	b Richardson	51	
F. A. Iredale	b Richardson	8	b Richardson	18	
S. E. Gregory	c Philipson b Richardson	70	b Richardson	30	
J. Darling	c Ford b Peel	74	b Peel	50	
J. J. Lyons	c Philipson b Lockwood	55	b Briggs	15	
H. Graham	b Richardson	6	lbw b Richardson	10	
A. E. Trott	c Lockwood b Peel	10	b Richardson	0	
†A. H. Jarvis	not out	34	not out	14	
T. R. McKibbin	c Peel b Briggs	23	c Philipson b Richardson	13	
Extras	(b 3, lb 10)	13	(b 5, lb 6, nb 2)	13	
Total		**414**	**Total**	**267**	

ENGLAND

A. Ward	b McKibbin	32	b G. H. S. Trott	93	
W. Brockwell	st Jarvis b G. H. S. Trott	5	c and b Giffen	5	
*A. E. Stoddart	st Jarvis b G. H. S. Trott	68	lbw b G. H. S. Trott	11	
J. T. Brown	b A. E. Trott	30	c Giffen b McKibbin	140	
A. C. MacLaren	hit wkt b G. H. S. Trott	120	not out	20	
R. Peel	c Gregory b Giffen	73	not out	15	
W. H. Lockwood	c G. H. S. Trott b Giffen	5			
F. G. J. Ford	c A. E. Trott b Giffen	11			
J. Briggs	c G. H. S. Trott b Giffen	0			
†H. Philipson	not out	10			
T. Richardson	lbw b G. H. S. Trott	11			
Extras	(b 8, lb 8, w 4)	20	(b 6, lb 5, w 2, nb 1)	14	
Total		**385**	**Total** (4 wkts)	**298**	

FALL OF WICKETS

AUSTRALIA

Wkt	1st	2nd
1st	40	32
2nd	101	75
3rd	126	125
4th	142	148
5th	284	179
6th	286	200
7th	304	219
8th	335	219
9th	367	248
10th	414	267

ENGLAND

Wkt	1st	2nd
1st	6	5
2nd	110	28
3rd	112	238
4th	166	278
5th	328	—
6th	342	—
7th	364	—
8th	364	—
9th	366	—
10th	385	

Umpires: J. Phillips, T. Flynn

ENGLAND	1st Innings					2nd Innings			
	O	M	R	W		O	M	R	W
Richardson	42	7	138	3		45·2	7	104	6
Peel	48	13	114	4		46	16	89	3
Lockwood	27	7	72	1		16	7	24	0
Briggs	23·4	5	46	2		16	3	37	1
Brockwell	6	1	22	0					
Ford	2	0	9	0					

AUSTRALIA	1st Innings					2nd Innings			
	O	M	R	W		O	M	R	W
Giffen	45	13	130	4		31	4	106	1
G. H. S. Trott	24	5	71	4		20	1	63	2
A. E. Trott	30	4	84	1		19	2	56	0
McKibbin	29	6	73	1		14	2	47	1
Bruce	5	1	7	0		3	1	10	0
Lyons						1	0	2	0

Averages: 1894-95

AUSTRALIA

BATTING

	M.	Inns.	N.O.	Runs	H.S.	Av.
A. E. Trott	3	5	3	205	85*	102·50
G. Giffen	5	9	0	475	161	52·77
H. Graham	2	3	0	121	105	40·33
S. E. Gregory	5	9	0	362	201	40·22
F. A. Iredale	5	9	0	337	140	37·44
G. H. S. Trott	5	9	0	264	95	29·33
J. Darling	5	9	0	258	74	28·66
W. Bruce	4	7	0	197	80	28·14
A. H. Jarvis	4	7	2	110	34*	22·00
J. J. Lyons	3	6	0	112	55	18·66
C. T. B. Turner	3	5	2	52	26*	17·33

PLAYED IN ONE TEST: J. C. Reedman 17 and 4, C. E. McLeod 15 and 2*, J. McC. Blackham 74 and 2, E. Jones 11* and 1, A. Coningham 10 and 3, J. Harry 2 and 6, J. Worrall 0 and 11, S. T. Callaway 41 and 11, T. R. McKibbin 23 and 13, H. Trumble 1 and 2, H. Moses 1.

BOWLING

	Overs	Mds.	Runs	Wkts.	Av.
S. T. Callaway	33·3	14	56	5	11·20
C. T. B. Turner	187·1	76	349	18	19·38
A. E. Trott	79	17	192	9	21·33
G. Giffen	343·2	111	820	34	24·11
G. H. S. Trott	102·4	18	296	12	24·66

ALSO BOWLED: J. C. Reedman 9·3–2–24–1, H. Trumble 35·1–10–87–3, A. Coningham 31–9–76–2, W. Bruce 12–2–38–1, C. E. McLeod 44–8–92–2, E. Jones 37–6–101–2, T. R. McKibbin 43–8–120–2, J. J. Lyons 7–3–17–0, F. A. Iredale 2–1–3–0.

ENGLAND

BATTING

	M.	Inns.	N.O.	Runs	H.S.	Av.
J. T. Brown	5	10	2	343	140	42·87
A. Ward	5	10	0	419	117	41·90
A. E. Stoddart	5	10	1	352	173	39·11
A. C. MacLaren	5	10	1	240	120	26·66
R. Peel	5	10	1	168	73	18·66
F. G. J. Ford	5	9	0	168	48	18·66
J. Briggs	5	9	0	164	57	18·22
W. H. Lockwood	5	7	2	89	33*	17·80
W. Brockwell	5	10	0	171	49	17·10
H. Philipson	4	7	1	62	30	10·33
T. Richardson	5	9	3	58	12*	9·66

PLAYED IN ONE TEST: L. H. Gay 33 and 4.

BOWLING

	Overs	Mds.	Runs	Wkts.	Av.
T. Richardson	291·1	63	849	32	26·53
R. Peel	305·1	77	721	27	26·70
J. Briggs	150·3	29	435	15	29·00
W. Brockwell	77	26	238	5	47·60
W. H. Lockwood	123·2	31	340	5	68·00

ALSO BOWLED: A. E. Stoddart 3–0–31–1, F. G. J. Ford 35–6–129–1.

Averages: 1896

ENGLAND

BATTING

	M.	Inns.	N.O.	Runs	H.S.	Av.
K. S. Ranjitsinhji	2	4	1	235	154*	78·33
A. E. Stoddart	2	4	1	103	41	34·33
R. Abel	3	6	0	184	94	30·66
A. A. Lilley	3	5	1	92	65*	23·00
F. S. Jackson	3	5	0	110	45	22·00
J. T. Brown	2	4	0	86	36	21·50
W. G. Grace	3	6	0	119	66	19·83
T. W. Hayward	2	4	1	38	13	12·66
A. C. MacLaren	2	4	0	41	20	10·25
J. T. Hearne	3	5	0	47	18	9·40
T. Richardson	3	5	2	20	10*	6·66

PLAYED IN ONE TEST: W. Gunn 25 and 13*, J. Briggs 0 and 16, E. G. Wynyard 10 and 3, G. A. Lohmann 1, R. Peel 0 and 0.

BOWLING

	Overs	Mds.	Runs	Wkts.	Av.
R. Peel	32	14	53	8	6·62
J. T. Hearne	127·1	56	211	15	14·06
T. Richardson	175·1	58	439	24	18·29

ALSO BOWLED: G. A. Lohmann 33–12–52–3, A. A. Lilley 5–1–23–1, J. Briggs 58–26–123–3, W. G. Grace 13–4–25–0, T. W. Hayward 13–3–61–0, F. S. Jackson 27–11–62–0, A. E. Stoddart 6–2–9–0.

AUSTRALIA

BATTING

	M.	Inns.	N.O.	Runs	H.S.	Av.
F. A. Iredale	2	4	0	152	108	38·00
G. H. S. Trott	3	6	0	206	143	34·33
S. E. Gregory	3	6	0	182	103	30·33
J. J. Kelly	3	6	3	72	27	24·00
T. R. McKibbin	2	3	1	44	28*	22·00
G. Giffen	3	6	0	119	80	19·83
J. Darling	3	6	0	112	47	18·66
H. Trumble	3	6	2	55	24	13·75
H. Donnan	3	6	0	46	15	7·66
C. Hill	3	6	0	30	14	5·00
E. Jones	3	5	0	18	4	3·60

PLAYED IN ONE TEST: C. J. Eady 10* and 2, H. Graham 0 and 10.

BOWLING

	Overs	Mds.	Runs	Wkts.	Av.
T. R. McKibbin	69·3	20	162	11	14·72
H. Trumble	170·1	58	339	18	18·83
G. Giffen	95	21	285	9	31·66
E. Jones	74	18	208	6	34·66

ALSO BOWLED: C. J. Eady 32–12–69–4, G. H. S. Trott 25–3–80–4.

1896 First Test, Lord's

June 22, 23, 24
Toss: Australia   *Result:* England won by six wickets

The team under Harry Trott had the best record of any Australian touring side since the great XIs of '82 and '84, and they were unfortunate not to regain the Ashes. The first two Tests, splendidly fought out, brought a win to each side, but the deciding game was spoiled by rain. England had the two outstanding players in Ranjitsinhji and Richardson, but Australia were the better all-round team.

The first morning at Lord's was surely the most sensational in Test cricket. 30,000 people crowded into the ground, spilling over on to the field of play, hampering the fielders, breaking out into rowdyism and throwing missiles when their view was obstructed. In the early tension Donnan ran himself out; then, after Giffen had been caught at the wicket off Lohmann, Richardson in his fourth over knocked out Trott's middle stump and soon afterwards bowled Gregory and Graham with successive balls. His pace and break were irresistible, and in 75 minutes the Australians on a fast, dry wicket, were bowled out for 53. Richardson, from the pavilion end, took 6 for 39, all clean bowled.

Grace, as so often in the past, set the England innings off on an infectious note of confidence, and Abel, badly missed in the slips off Jones when 9, stayed while 218 runs were added and was 5th out at 256; but the innings fell away after he left. Nevertheless when Australia went in again soon after midday on the second day they faced a deficit of 239.

Their troubles aggravated by an injury to Donnan, Australia began with Darling and Eady. Darling was bowled by Richardson without a run on the board, Eady was caught at the wicket 3 runs later, and Giffen and Trott were both troubled by Richardson's tremendous pace, scoring at first mostly by snicks. At 62 Richardson bowled Giffen; but there followed an extraordinary transformation as Trott and Gregory scored 90 runs in 65 minutes before lunch, and another 131 afterwards. Richardson and Hearne then reasserted themselves, and England were left with 109 to win. 16 of these were made overnight for the loss of Abel, but there was dismay next morning when it was found that rain had made an easy task difficult. A skilful little innings by Hayward when the wicket was at its worst helped England home, but with better support in the field Trumble and Jones might have pulled off a dramatic victory.

AUSTRALIA

H. Donnan	run out	1	(11)b Hearne	8	
J. Darling	b Richardson	22	b Richardson	0	
G. Giffen	c Lilley b Lohmann	0	b Richardson	32	
*G. H. S. Trott	b Richardson	0	c Hayward b Richardson	143	
S. E. Gregory	b Richardson	14	c Lohmann b Hearne	103	
H. Graham	b Richardson	0	b Richardson	10	
C. Hill	b Lohmann	1	b Hearne	5	
C. J. Eady	not out	10	(1)c Lilley b Richardson	2	
H. Trumble	b Richardson	0	(8)c Lilley b Hearne	4	
†J. J. Kelly	c Lilley b Lohmann	0	(9)not out	24	
E. Jones	b Richardson	4	(10)c Jackson b Hearne	4	
Extras	(b 1)	1	(b 7, lb 4, w 1)	12	
Total		**53**	**Total**	**347**	

ENGLAND

*W. G. Grace	c Trumble b Giffen	66	c Hill b Trumble	7	
A. E. Stoddart	b Eady	17	(5)not out	30	
R. Abel	b Eady	94	(2)c sub (F. A. Iredale) b Jones	4	
J. T. Brown	b Jones	9	c Kelly b Eady	36	
W. Gunn	c Kelly b Trumble	25	(6)not out	13	
F. S. Jackson	c Darling b Giffen	44			
T. Hayward	not out	12	(3)b Jones	13	
†A. A. Lilley	b Eady	0			
G. A. Lohmann	c sub (F. A. Iredale) b Giffen	1			
J. T. Hearne	c Giffen b Trott	11			
T. Richardson	c Hill b Trott	6			
Extras	(b 5, lb 2)	7	(b 3, lb 4, w 1)	8	
Total		**292**	**Total** (4 wkts)	**111**	

FALL OF WICKETS

AUSTRALIA

Wkt	1st	2nd
1st	3	0
2nd	3	3
3rd	4	62
4th	26	283
5th	26	289
6th	31	300
7th	41	304
8th	45	308
9th	46	318
10th	53	347

ENGLAND

Wkt	1st	2nd
1st	38	16
2nd	143	20
3rd	152	42
4th	197	82
5th	256	—
6th	266	—
7th	266	—
8th	267	—
9th	286	—
10th	292	—

Umpires: W. A. J. West, J. Phillips

ENGLAND

	1st Innings				2nd Innings			
	O	M	R	W	O	M	R	W
Richardson	11·3	3	39	6	47	15	134	5
Lohmann	11	6	13	3	22	6	39	0
Hayward					11	3	44	0
Hearne					36	14	76	5
Jackson					11	5	28	0
Grace					6	1	14	0

AUSTRALIA

	1st Innings				2nd Innings			
	O	M	R	W	O	M	R	W
Jones	26	6	64	1	23	10	42	2
Giffen	26	5	95	3	1	0	9	0
Eady	29	12	58	3	3	0	11	1
Trott	7·4	2	13	2	0·1	0	4	0
Trumble	19	3	55	1	20	10	37	1

1896 Second Test, Old Trafford

July 16, 17, 18
Toss: Australia   *Result:* Australia won by three wickets

The Lancashire committee brought MacLaren, Ranjitsinhji and Briggs into the England side for Hayward, Gunn and the injured Lohmann. This meant that England were again relying on only three front-line bowlers. The Australians substituted the spinner McKibbin for fast bowler Eady. The selection of Ranji caused raised eyebrows, but the Australians welcomed it; he rewarded their generosity by playing one of the greatest innings ever seen. Outplayed for the first two days, England got back into the match in dramatic fashion on the final afternoon.

Australia took full advantage of a shirt-front wicket and a limited attack to amass a score of 366 for 8 on the first day. Iredale and Giffen put on 131 for the 2nd wicket, Giffen hitting brilliantly later in his innings, while Iredale, although he never mastered Richardson, batted beautifully to reach his century in 3½ hours. When Iredale was 3rd out at 242, Trott and Gregory looked like repeating their Lord's effort, and in desperation Grace put Lilley on to bowl, Brown keeping wicket. He bowled rubbish, but broke the stand. Richardson, who had again been badly overworked, found the steam to get 3 late wickets, but next morning Kelly and McKibbin added 41 for the 9th wicket and

Australia totalled 412. On came Harry Trott to tease the England openers, both rose to the bait, and England were 23 for 2. Ranji and Abel saw the hundred up, but only an impassive innings by Lilley kept the margin to 181. Following on, England lost Grace, Stoddart, Abel and Jackson before stumps, when they were still 72 runs adrift.

The last day looked like being a formality; instead it produced a contest that can only be described as heroic. With 6 men out England were still 2 runs behind; but the 23-year-old Ranji, who had meanwhile reached 50 in 85 minutes, raced to his hundred in 2 hours 10 minutes, and with useful help from the later batsmen he finally made 154 not out. His skill in scoring on the leg side from straight balls was described as amazing. Australia went in again at 2.50 wanting 125 to win.

For the next 3 hours 10 minutes, as Australia fought desperately to hold on to her advantage, Richardson bowled without rest (there was no break for tea in those days) in perhaps the greatest sustained effort ever accomplished by a fast bowler, and one by one the great Australian batsmen were prized out. Yet in the end the task proved too much for one man—even for a Richardson—and Australia won by 3 wickets.

AUSTRALIA

F. A. Iredale	b Briggs	108	b Richardson	11	
J. Darling	c Lilley b Richardson	27	c Lilley b Richardson	16	
G. Giffen	c and b Richardson	80	c Ranjitsinhji b Richardson	6	
*G. H. S. Trott	c Brown b Lilley	53	c Lilley b Richardson	2	
S. E. Gregory	c Stoddart b Briggs	25	c Ranjitsinhji b Briggs	33	
H. Donnan	b Richardson	12	c Jackson b Richardson	15	
C. Hill	c Jackson b Richardson	9	c Lilley b Richardson	14	
H. Trumble	b Richardson	24	not out	17	
†J. J. Kelly	c Lilley b Richardson	27	not out	8	
T. R. McKibbin	not out	28			
E. Jones	b Richardson	4			
Extras	(b 6, lb 8, w 1)	15	(lb 3)	3	
Total		**412**	**Total** (7 wkts)	**125**	

ENGLAND

*W. G. Grace	st Kelly b Trott	2	c Trott b Jones	11	
A. E. Stoddart	st Kelly b Trott	15	b McKibbin	41	
K. S. Ranjitsinhji	c Trott b McKibbin	62	not out	154	
R. Abel	c Trumble b McKibbin	26	c McKibbin b Giffen	13	
F. S. Jackson	run out	18	c McKibbin b Giffen	1	
J. T. Brown	c Kelly b Trumble	22	c Iredale b Jones	19	
A. C. MacLaren	c Trumble b McKibbin	0	c Jones b Trumble	15	
†A. A. Lilley	not out	65	c Trott b Giffen	19	
J. Briggs	b Trumble	0	st Kelly b McKibbin	16	
J. T. Hearne	c Trumble b Giffen	18	c Kelly b McKibbin	9	
T. Richardson	run out	2	c Jones b Trumble	1	
Extras	(b 1)	1	(b 2, lb 3, w 1)	6	
Total		**231**	**Total**	**305**	

FALL OF WICKETS

AUSTRALIA

Wkt	1st	2nd
1st	41	20
2nd	172	26
3rd	242	28
4th	294	45
5th	294	79
6th	314	95
7th	325	100
8th	362	—
9th	403	—
10th	412	—

ENGLAND

Wkt	1st	2nd
1st	2	33
2nd	23	76
3rd	104	97
4th	111	109
5th	140	132
6th	140	179
7th	154	232
8th	166	268
9th	219	304
10th	231	305

Umpires: J. Phillips,
A. Chester

ENGLAND	1st Innings					2nd Innings			
	O	M	R	W		O	M	R	W
Richardson	68	23	168	7	..	42.3	16	76	6
Briggs	40	18	99	2	..	18	8	24	1
Jackson	16	6	34	0	..				
Hearne	28	11	53	0	..	24	13	22	0
Grace	7	3	11	0	..				
Stoddart	6	2	9	0	..				
Lilley	5	1	23	1	..				

AUSTRALIA	1st Innings					2nd Innings			
	O	M	R	W		O	M	R	W
Jones	5	2	11	0	..	17	0	78	2
Trott	10	0	46	2	..	7	1	17	0
Giffen	19	3	48	1	..	16	1	65	3
Trumble	37	14	80	2	..	29.1	12	78	2
McKibbin	19	8	45	3	..	21	4	61	3

49. K. S. Ranjitsinhji

50. H. Trumble

51. Australia 1896
Back row: F. Lemon (scorer), A. E. Johns, C. J. Eady, J. Darling, H. Donnan, T. R. McKibbin, H. Graham, H. Musgrove (manager). *Middle row:* H. Trumble, E. Jones, G. H. S. Trott (capt.), G. Giffen, F. A. Iredale. *Front:* J. J. Kelly, S. E. Gregory, C. Hill.

1896 Third Test, Oval

August 10, 11, 12
Toss: England *Result:* England won by 66 runs

After two of the most remarkable games ever played, with a win to each side, the final test was keenly anticipated, and it was a tragedy that it should have been utterly spoiled by the weather. The pre-match atmosphere, too, was marred by dispute. Five of the chosen England side—William Gunn, Richardson, Hayward, Abel and Lohmann—wrote to the Surrey committee demanding a match fee of £20, double the normal, but the committee refused even to negotiate. Richardson, Hayward and Abel retracted but Gunn did not, and he and Lohmann, who had been awaiting Gunn's decision, were left out. At the same time, unsavoury rumours about expenses granted to amateurs were denied by the Surrey club: Grace, they averred, got £10 a match, no more and no less. This admission, however, lent substance to the players' claim. Stoddart, who was also picked, was unfit to play.

A heavy shower on a ground already soft from previous downpours held up play until 4.55 on the first day, and in the 95 minutes remaining England did well to reach 69 for 1 on a slow wicket and in variable light. Next day, with the wicket drier, the ball came off much faster and turned more quickly. Jackson was well caught at mid on, Ranji was bowled by a break-back, and after MacLaren and Abel had promised better things Trumble, who had developed into a great

medium-pacer, crossed to the pavilion end and the last six wickets fell in 50 minutes for 31.

Aided by some luck and some loose bowling, both of which they to some extent compelled, Darling and Iredale then surprised everyone by hitting 75 in 45 minutes either side of lunch. But Iredale, going for a fifth run for a snick off Richardson, was magnificently thrown out by Ranji from a distance of well over 100 yards, and from this point the luck ran out. Bowling that had been made to look innocuous now pegged the batsmen down, and the last 9 wickets fell for 44, Hearne taking 6 for 41 despite missing two return catches. England were left with 85 minutes' batting, in which they struggled to 60 for 5, Abel playing another admirable fighting innings; the value of their lead of 86 would depend on the conditions next morning. As it happened, the wicket on the final day was at its most difficult and the batsmen on both sides were helpless, England winning by 66 runs.

While commiserating with the Australians in their failure to regain the Ashes with a side that possibly deserved to do so, many critics deplored the relaxed standards which allowed the actions of Jones and McKibbin to pass unchallenged throughout an English season.

ENGLAND

*W. G. Grace	c Trott b Giffen	24	b Trumble	9	
F. S. Jackson	c McKibbin b Trumble	45	b Trumble	2	
K. S. Ranjitsinhji	b Giffen	8	st Kelly b McKibbin	11	
R. Abel	c and b Trumble	26	c Giffen b Trumble	21	
A. C. MacLaren	b Trumble	20	b Jones	6	
T. Hayward	b Trumble	0	c Trott b Trumble	13	
E. G. Wynyard	c Darling b McKibbin	10	c Kelly b McKibbin	3	
R. Peel	b Trumble	0	b Trumble	0	
†A. A. Lilley	c Iredale b Trumble	2	c McKibbin b Trumble	6	
J. T. Hearne	b McKibbin	8	b McKibbin	1	
T. Richardson	not out	1	not out	10	
Extras	(lb 1)	1	(lb 2)	2	
Total		**145**	Total	**84**	

AUSTRALIA

J. Darling	c MacLaren b Hearne	47	b Hearne	0	
F. A. Iredale	run out	30	c Jackson b Hearne	3	
G. Giffen	b Hearne	0	(4)b Hearne	1	
*G. H. S. Trott	b Peel	5	(3)c sub (W. Brockwell) b Peel	3	
S. E. Gregory	b Hearne	1	c Richardson b Peel	6	
C. Hill	run out	1	b Peel	0	
H. Donnan	b Hearne	10	c Hayward b Peel	0	
†J. J. Kelly	not out	10	lbw b Peel	3	
H. Trumble	b Hearne	3	not out	7	
E. Jones	c MacLaren b Peel	3	b Peel	3	
T. R. McKibbin	b Hearne	0	c Abel b Hearne	16	
Extras	(b 8, lb 1)	9	(b 2)	2	
Total		**119**	Total	**44**	

FALL OF WICKETS

ENGLAND

Wkt	1st	2nd
1st	54	11
2nd	78	12
3rd	78	24
4th	114	50
5th	114	56
6th	131	67
7th	132	67
8th	135	67
9th	138	68
10th	145	84

AUSTRALIA

Wkt	1st	2nd
1st	75	0
2nd	77	3
3rd	82	7
4th	83	7
5th	84	11
6th	85	11
7th	112	14
8th	116	19
9th	119	25
10th	119	44

Umpires: J. Phillips,
W. Hearn

AUSTRALIA	1st Innings				2nd Innings			
	O	M	R	W	O	M	R	W
Giffen	32	12	64	2	1	0	4	0
Trumble	40	10	59	6	25	9	30	6
McKibbin	9·3	0	21	2	20	8	35	3
Jones					3	0	13	1

ENGLAND	1st Innings				2nd Innings			
	O	M	R	W	O	M	R	W
Peel	20	9	30	2	12	5	23	6
Hearne	26·1	10	41	6	13	8	19	4
Richardson	5	0	22	0	1	1	0	0
Hayward	2	0	17	0				

1897-98 First Test, Sydney

December 13, 14, 15, 16, 17
Toss: England   *Result:* England won by nine wickets

Even with a great bowling side the England batting in this series would hardly have been good enough; but as it was, all but Richardson and Hearne were innocuous. So desperate was the situation that Storer actually took his pads off to bowl leg-breaks in four of the five matches. MacLaren had a great series, and Ranjitsinhji might have had an even greater one had it not been for ill health; but Stoddart stood out of the first two Tests because of a family bereavement and never recovered his form, while Hayward, although batting consistently well, only twice reached the 70s. Seasoned professionals like Gunn, Abel, Ward and Brown were badly missed, the two young amateurs, Druce and Mason, being disappointing. Meanwhile for Australia the bowling was wonderfully varied and Darling and the 20-year-old Hill were magnificent with the bat.

A delay of three days before the match could start, due to heavy rain, allowed Ranji to recover to some extent from a throat infection; then, on a slow, easy wicket, England scored 337 for 5 on the first day, MacLaren reaching a chanceless hundred just before tea. Ranji, 39 not out overnight and virtually exhausted, was well enough next day to continue after treatment, and he farmed the expresses of Jones so successfully that he reached 175 before being last out.

Richardson, apparently overweight, laboured at first to get into top gear, but he took the first two wickets cheaply, Hearne, whose pace was above medium, took the next three, and at the end of the second day Australia were 86 for 5. Dropped catches next day helped Australia recover ground, and Charles McLeod, who had injured his hand in the field, batted stubbornly, but Australia followed on 314 behind. In one over from Richardson Iredale played at every ball without making contact, but generally in Australia's second innings Richardson was erratic.

Darling, 80 not out overnight, defended on the fourth day while Hill played brilliantly, but two run-outs spoiled Australia's chance, although they totalled 408. The first of these dismissals was especially unfortunate, McLeod, not hearing the umpire's call, walking out when bowled by a no ball, after which Storer impulsively ran him out. Apologies tendered afterwards were accepted. Left with 95 to win, England should have lost MacLaren to a catch behind the wicket when 5 (he was given not out), and Mason was dropped; it was just not Australia's match.

ENGLAND

J. R. Mason	b Jones	6	b McKibbin	32	
*A. C. MacLaren	c Kelly b McLeod	109	not out	50	
T. Hayward	c Trott b Trumble	72			
†W. Storer	c and b Trott	43			
N. F. Druce	c Gregory b McLeod	20			
G. H. Hirst	b Jones	62			
K. S. Ranjitsinhji	c Gregory b McKibbin	175	(3)not out	8	
E. Wainwright	b Jones	10			
J. T. Hearne	c and b McLeod	17			
J. Briggs	run out	1			
T. Richardson	not out	24			
Extras	(lb 11, w 1)	12	(b 5, nb 1)	6	
Total		**551**	**Total** (1 wkt)	**96**	

AUSTRALIA

J. Darling	c Druce b Richardson	7	c Druce b Briggs	101	
J. J. Lyons	b Richardson	3	(7)c Hayward b Hearne	25	
F. A. Iredale	c Druce b Hearne	25	(2)b Briggs	18	
C. Hill	b Hearne	19	b Hearne	96	
S. E. Gregory	c Mason b Hearne	46	run out	31	
*G. H. S. Trott	b Briggs	10	(8)b Richardson	27	
†J. J. Kelly	b Richardson	1	(9)not out	46	
H. Trumble	c Storer b Mason	70	(6)c Druce b Hearne	2	
C. E. McLeod	not out	50	(3)run out	26	
T. R. McKibbin	b Hearne	0	(11)b Hearne	6	
E. Jones	c Richardson b Hearne	0	(10)lbw b Richardson	3	
Extras	(b 1, lb 1, nb 4)	6	(b 12, lb 1, w 4, nb 10)	27	
Total		**237**	**Total**	**408**	

FALL OF WICKETS

	ENGLAND	
Wkt	1st	2nd
1st	26	80
2nd	162	—
3rd	224	—
4th	256	—
5th	258	—
6th	382	—
7th	422	—
8th	471	—
9th	477	—
10th	551	—

	AUSTRALIA	
Wkt	1st	2nd
1st	8	37
2nd	24	135
3rd	56	191
4th	57	269
5th	86	271
6th	87	318
7th	138	321
8th	228	382
9th	237	390
10th	237	408

Umpires: C. Bannerman, J. Phillips

AUSTRALIA	1st Innings				2nd Innings			
	O	M	R	W	O	M	R	W
McKibbin	34	5	113	1	5	1	22	1
Jones	50	8	130	3	9	1	28	0
McLeod	28	12	80	3				
Trumble	40	7	138	1	14	4	40	0
Trott	23	2	78	1				

ENGLAND	1st Innings				2nd Innings			
	O	M	R	W	O	M	R	W
Richardson	27	8	71	3	41	9	121	2
Hirst	28	7	57	0	13	3	49	0
Hearne	20·1	7	42	5	38	8	99	4
Briggs	20	7	42	1	22	3	86	2
Hayward	3	1	11	0	5	1	16	0
Mason	2	1	8	1	2	0	10	0

1897-98 Second Test, Melbourne

January 1, 3, 4, 5
Toss: Australia   *Result:* Australia won by an innings and 55 runs

England's dependence on MacLaren and Ranji had been clear at Sydney; and at Melbourne Ranji, by arrangement with the Australians, was allowed to absent himself for most of the first day in order to visit a doctor for the lancing of a throat abscess. For Australia, Noble replaced Lyons. Australia occupied the crease for almost the whole of the first two days, by the end of which the wicket had cracked into a mosaic, and although it did not play as badly as the Englishmen feared, the result by that time was certain.

After a burst of scoring from Darling, who hit 36 of the first 43, the early Australian batsmen settled down to compiling a big score. McLeod, who made only 19 in 80 minutes before lunch, scored more quickly afterwards, reaching his century in 3 hours 40 minutes, Hill and Gregory, who were both dropped, each reached 50 in just under 2 hours, and at stumps Australia were 283 for 3. The batsmen, although waging a war of attrition, found enough opportunities to keep the score moving, and the struggle had all the atmosphere and tension of a modern Test Match. Only one wicket fell next morning, and by lunch-time Australia, scoring at a run a minute, were 370 for 4. Iredale and Trott both played big innings, and long before the finish the regular

bowlers, whose form had been disappointing anyway, were exhausted. Yet MacLaren still did not think it worth while giving the ball to Wainwright, the Yorkshire off-spinner, who had done the double in England the previous season. Faced with half an hour's batting at the end of the day, England were 22 for 1 at the close.

A sensation was caused next morning when Jones, whose action had been called into question during the 1896 tour of England and again since the arrival of Stoddart's team, was no-balled for throwing by Phillips, the Australian umpire travelling with the tourists. Yet it was an isolated call, and the general opinion was that Jones' normal action was fair. MacLaren was not at his best, but Ranji batted with wonderful ease, and when England passed 200 with only 4 wickets down they looked like making a fight. But in the first over after tea Trumble bowled Ranji, Storer was seized by an attack of cramp and was dismissed immediately afterwards, and only a late stand between Druce and Briggs took England past 300. On the fourth morning, when they followed on, the English batsmen found the combination of Noble's away-swing and break-back too much for them on a crumbling wicket.

AUSTRALIA

J. Darling	c Hirst b Briggs	36
C. E. McLeod	b Storer	112
C. Hill	c Storer b Hayward	58
S. E. Gregory	b Briggs	71
F. A. Iredale	c Ranjitsinhji b Hirst	89
*G. H. S. Trott	c Wainwright b Briggs	79
M. A. Noble	b Richardson	17
H. Trumble	c Hirst b Mason	14
†J. J. Kelly	c Richardson b Hearne	19
E. Jones	run out	7
T. R. McKibbin	not out	2
Extras	(b 14, w 1, nb 1)	16
Total		**520**

ENGLAND

*A. C. MacLaren	c Trumble b McKibbin	35	c Trott b Trumble	38	
J. R. Mason	b McKibbin	3	b Trumble	3	
E. Wainwright	c Jones b Noble	21	(8)b Noble	11	
K. S. Ranjitsinhji	b Trumble	71	(3)b Noble	27	
T. Hayward	c Jones b Trott	23	(4)c Trumble b Noble	33	
†W. Storer	c Kelly b Trumble	51	(5)c Trumble b Noble	1	
G. H. Hirst	b Jones	0	(6)lbw b Trumble	3	
N. F. Druce	lbw b Trumble	44	(7)c McLeod b Noble	15	
J. T. Hearne	b Jones	1	(10)c Jones b Noble	0	
J. Briggs	not out	46	(9)c Trott b Trumble	12	
T. Richardson	b Trumble	3	not out	2	
Extras	(b 10, lb 3, nb 4)	17	(b 3, lb 1, w 1)	5	
Total		**315**	**Total**	**150**	

FALL OF WICKETS

AUSTRALIA

Wkt	1st	2nd
1st	43	—
2nd	167	—
3rd	244	—
4th	310	—
5th	434	—
6th	453	—
7th	478	—
8th	509	—
9th	515	—
10th	520	—

ENGLAND

Wkt	1st	2nd
1st	10	10
2nd	60	65
3rd	74	71
4th	133	75
5th	203	80
6th	208	115
7th	223	123
8th	224	141
9th	311	148
10th	315	150

Umpires: C. Bannerman, J. Phillips

ENGLAND	1st Innings				2nd Innings			
	O	M	R	W	O	M	R	W
Richardson	48	12	114	1	..			
Hirst	25	1	89	1	..			
Briggs	40	10	96	3	..			
Hearne	36	6	94	1	..			
Mason	11	1	33	1	..			
Hayward	9	4	23	1	..			
Storer	16	4	55	1	..			

AUSTRALIA	1st Innings				2nd Innings			
	O	M	R	W	O	M	R	W
McKibbin	28	7	66	2	4	0	13	0
Trumble	26·5	5	54	4	30·4	12	53	4
Jones	22	5	54	2				
Trott	17	3	49	1	7	0	17	0
Noble	12	3	31	1	17	1	49	6
McLeod	14	2	44	0	7	2	13	0

52. J. Darling

53. T. W. Hayward

54. **England 1897-98**
Back row: P. Sheridan (N.S.W.), G. H. Hirst, J. H. Board, J. R. Mason, T. Richardson, J. T. Hearne, N. F. Druce, H. Storer, B. J. Wardill (Vic.). *Front:* E. Wainwright, T. W. Hayward, A. E. Stoddart (capt.), K. S. Ranjitsinhji, A. C. MacLaren, J. Briggs.

1897-98 Third Test, Adelaide

Test no. 49

January 14, 15, 17, 18, 19
Toss: Australia   *Result:* Australia won by an innings and 13 runs

Stoddart returned to the England side at Adelaide to the exclusion of Wainwright, while for Australia Howell, a medium-pace off-cutter, replaced McKibbin. Darling again set the game in motion, making 54 of the 70 scored before lunch. The watchful McLeod, who was badly missed by Ranji at point off Hearne when 21, was out at 97, but with the arrival of Hill the game speeded up. Missed at 86 and again off a hot chance to Ranji at 98, Darling reached his hundred by pulling Briggs out of the ground, a feat rarely achieved at Adelaide; when Hill was out at 245, 148 runs had been added in 98 minutes. Darling went on hitting the tired bowlers until the close, when Australia were 309 for 2, but he was out in Richardson's first over next morning. He batted 4¾ hours.

England's troubles were by no means over. Gregory was missed by Stoddart at mid off. Richardson felt unwell and had to go off, though he came back after lunch and bowled splendidly. During the afternoon Hirst ricked his back and he too went off, to be followed after tea by Ranji, who injured a finger fielding. Hearne got Trott cheaply, and Richardson held one back for Noble, but when Iredale played on after batting 3 hours 20 minutes Australia were 493 for 7. They went on

concentrating on a mammoth score, taking their innings into the third day, troubled only by Richardson, who was unlucky with dropped catches and bowled far better than his figures suggest.

On a perfect wicket England began disastrously against top-class bowling and soon after lunch were 42 for 4. Hayward, batting soundly and without fuss, did his best to restore the position, helped first by Druce and then Hirst, who batted with a runner, and at the close England were 197 for 6. But a great catch by Jones, the outstanding fielder of the series, dismissed Stoddart next morning, and despite some lusty hitting by Richardson England followed on 295 behind. Mason, who was again sent in first, failed, but MacLaren, after surviving two difficult return catches, helped Ranji to add 142 for the 2nd wicket. Ranji, too, handicapped by his bruised finger, began with some streaky shots. With Jones suffering from a strain it looked at one point as though Australia would have to bat again, but a blustery wind that had caused a dust-storm suited Noble, while the middle batting fell to the variations of the fast-medium McLeod. MacLaren batted 5 hours for his 124, but England for the second match running were beaten by an innings.

AUSTRALIA

C. E. McLeod	b Briggs	31
J. Darling	c Storer b Richardson	178
C. Hill	c Storer b Richardson	81
S. E. Gregory	c Storer b Hirst	52
F. A. Iredale	b Richardson	84
*G. H. S. Trott	b Hearne	3
M. A. Noble	b Richardson	39
H. Trumble	not out	37
†J. J. Kelly	b Stoddart	22
E. Jones	run out	8
W. P. Howell	b Hearne	16
Extras	(b 16, lb 5, nb 1)	22
Total		**573**

ENGLAND

A. C. MacLaren	b Howell	14	c Kelly b Noble	124
J. R. Mason	b Jones	11	c Jones b Noble	0
K. S. Ranjitsinhji	c Noble b Trumble	6	c Trumble b McLeod	77
†W. Storer	b Howell	4	(5)c Hill b McLeod	6
T. Hayward	b Jones	70	(4)c and b McLeod	1
N. F. Druce	c Darling b Noble	24	b Noble	27
G. H. Hirst	c Trumble b Noble	85	lbw b McLeod	6
*A. E. Stoddart	c Jones b Howell	15	c Jones b McLeod	24
J. Briggs	c Kelly b Noble	14	not out	0
J. T. Hearne	b Howell	0	c and b Noble	4
T. Richardson	not out	25	c Jones b Noble	0
Extras	(b 2, lb 6, w 2)	10	(b 2, lb 6, w 3, nb 2)	13
Total		**278**	**Total**	**282**

FALL OF WICKETS

AUSTRALIA

Wkt	1st	2nd
1st	97	—
2nd	245	—
3rd	310	—
4th	374	—
5th	389	—
6th	474	—
7th	493	—
8th	537	—
9th	552	—
10th	573	—

ENGLAND

Wkt	1st	2nd
1st	24	10
2nd	30	152
3rd	34	154
4th	42	160
5th	106	212
6th	172	235
7th	206	262
8th	223	278
9th	224	282
10th	278	282

Umpires: J. Phillips,
C. Bannerman

ENGLAND	1st Innings				2nd Innings			
	O	M	R	W	O	M	R	W
Richardson	56	11	164	4	..			
Briggs	63	26	128	1	..			
Hearne	44·1	15	94	2	..			
Hirst	22	6	62	1	..			
Hayward	8	1	36	0	..			
Mason	11	2	41	0	..			
Storer	3	0	16	0	..			
Stoddart	4	1	10	1	..			

AUSTRALIA	1st Innings				2nd Innings			
	O	M	R	W	O	M	R	W
Howell	54	23	70	4	..	40	18	60	0
Jones	27	3	67	2	..	1	0	5	0
Trumble	17	3	39	1	..	16	5	37	0
Noble	24·5	5	78	3	..	33	7	84	5
Trott	4	0	14	0	..	6	0	18	0
McLeod					..	48	24	65	5

72

January 29, 31, February 1, 2
Toss: Australia   *Result:* Australia won by eight wickets

With the rubber at stake, and without Hirst, whose strain had not mended, the England opening bowlers made a tremendous effort at Melbourne in great heat after Australia had won the toss for the third time running. The wicket, which had been covered before the game, was two-paced, and with Hearne on the mark and Richardson bowling his fastest of the tour, Australia were soon 32 for 5. Hill then narrowly escaped being run out, the Englishmen afterwards agreeing that he just about deserved the benefit of the doubt; but Trott was out in the first over after lunch, and at 58 for 6 the Australian innings was in ruins. Hearne at that point had taken 4 for 20.

After lunch, however, the wicket played perfectly, Richardson and Hearne were forced by Hirst's absence to go on bowling long after they had tired, and Hill, partnered first by Trumble and then by Kelly, played the innings of his life. He gave one very difficult chance wide of Storer off Hearne at 65, and he played and missed at Hearne on one other occasion; otherwise he was never beaten all day. He reached his hundred in 2 hours 49 minutes, and at stumps he was 182 not out. Trumble, missed behind the wicket off Richardson when he had made

20, helped Hill to add 165, and then that other great stumbling-block, Kelly, stayed with him to the close, when Australia were 275 for 7. Another 48 runs were added next morning. Hill's 188 is the highest score in these matches by a batsman under 21.

In debilitating heat, and depressed perhaps by their change of fortune, England batted feebly, one batsman after another getting out when set. Fierce bush-fires around Melbourne filled the air with haze, and Australian commentators at a loss to explain England's failure blamed it on the strange smoke-laden atmosphere. So dense was the smoke when England followed on that from the Press Box the ball could not be seen when it was travelling at any pace.

England showed more determination at the second attempt, and there was a point when Ranji and Hayward were together when a good finish seemed in prospect; but the innings fell away. With Richardson unable to bowl due to a strain, and with Storer injured and unable to keep, Australia had no difficulty in knocking off the 115 they needed to win.

AUSTRALIA

C. E. McLeod	b Hearne	1	not out	64	
J. Darling	c Hearne b Richardson	12	c Druce b Hayward	29	
C. Hill	c Stoddart b Hearne	188	lbw b Hayward	0	
S. E. Gregory	b Richardson	0	not out	21	
F. A. Iredale	c Storer b Hearne	0			
M. A. Noble	c and b Hearne	4			
*G. H. S. Trott	c Storer b Hearne	7			
H. Trumble	c Mason b Storer	46			
†J. J. Kelly	c Storer b Briggs	32			
E. Jones	c Hayward b Hearne	20			
W. P. Howell	not out	9			
Extras	(b 3, w 1)	4	(nb 1)	1	
Total		**323**	**Total** (2 wkts)	**115**	

ENGLAND

A. C. MacLaren	b Howell	8	(3) c Iredale b Trumble	45	
E. Wainwright	c Howell b Trott	6	c McLeod b Jones	2	
K. S. Ranjitsinhji	c Iredale b Trumble	24	(4) b Noble	55	
T. Hayward	c Gregory b Noble	22	(5) c and b Trumble	25	
N. F. Druce	lbw b Jones	24	(7) c Howell b Trott	16	
†W. Storer	c and b Trumble	2	(9) c Darling b McLeod	26	
J. R. Mason	b Jones	30	(8) b Howell	26	
*A. E. Stoddart	c Darling b Jones	17	(6) b Jones	25	
J. Briggs	not out	21	(1) c Darling b Howell	23	
J. T. Hearne	c Trott b Jones	0	not out	4	
T. Richardson	b Trott	20	c Trumble b McLeod	2	
Extras		0	(b 1, lb 11, w 1, nb 1)	14	
Total		**174**	**Total**	**263**	

FALL OF WICKETS

AUSTRALIA

Wkt	1st	2nd
1st	1	50
2nd	25	50
3rd	25	—
4th	26	—
5th	32	—
6th	58	—
7th	223	—
8th	283	—
9th	303	—
10th	323	—

ENGLAND

Wkt	1st	2nd
1st	14	7
2nd	16	63
3rd	60	94
4th	60	147
5th	67	157
6th	103	192
7th	121	211
8th	148	259
9th	148	259
10th	174	263

Umpires: J. Phillips, C. Bannerman

ENGLAND	1st Innings					2nd Innings			
	O	M	R	W		O	M	R	W
Richardson	26	2	102	2	..				
Hearne	35·4	13	98	6	..	7	3	19	0
Hayward	10	4	24	0	..	10	4	24	2
Briggs	17	4	38	1	..	6	1	31	0
Stoddart	6	1	22	0	..				
Storer	4	0	24	1	..				
Wainwright	3	1	11	0	..	9	2	21	0
Mason					..	4	1	10	0
Ranjitsinhji					..	3·4	1	9	0

AUSTRALIA	1st Innings					2nd Innings			
	O	M	R	W		O	M	R	W
Howell	16	7	34	1	..	30	12	58	2
Trott	11·1	1	33	2	..	12	2	39	1
Noble	7	1	21	1	..	16	6	31	1
Trumble	15	4	30	2	..	23	6	40	2
Jones	12	2	56	4	..	25	7	70	2
McLeod					..	8·2	4	11	2

February 26, 28, March 1, 2
Toss: England   *Result:* Australia won by six wickets

Hirst returned for England, Wainwright held his place, and Stoddart stood down, while for Australia Iredale, who had been out of form, made way for Worrall. England won the right to take first knock for the first time since the opening match; and at first they seemed likely to take full advantage, MacLaren and Wainwright putting on 111. But when MacLaren was out Wainwright followed, and Ranji, jumping out to a high-flighted slow from Trott, was brilliantly caught at extra cover, so that England were 119 for 3. Hayward and Storer then put on 78, Druce followed with the best innings of the day, and England were 301 for 5 at stumps; but next morning Jones took 4 for 11 in 50 balls and the last 5 wickets fell for 34.

The Australian first innings was remarkable for a great piece of fast bowling by Richardson, in what proved to be his last Test match. Suffering less than usual from dropped catches, although his luck was often atrocious, and free from the rheumatism that had plagued him throughout the tour, he took 8 for 94 in 36·1 overs, on a good batting wicket which nevertheless had some life in it for the really quick bowler, as Jones had shown. After making 184 for 5 in the remainder of the second day Australia were all out on the third morning for 239, giving England a lead of 96.

Any fears that with the rubber decided the match might be lacking in atmosphere were dispelled in the bitter struggle that followed; indeed the atmosphere at times reached fever heat. MacLaren was out first ball chasing a wide one, Ranji was lbw to a ball he believed he had played first, and the first delivery Storer faced he loudly declared to be a throw. He and Hayward, however, put on 69, and although Jones and Trumble steadily bowled England out Australia were left wanting 275 to win.

Darling evidently believed that the match could only be won if Richardson were knocked off: his driving of the fast bowler was superb, although he was missed twice off scorching hits. Just before Darling reached his 50, however, Richardson, bowling round the wicket, appealed against him for lbw; Richardson said at lunch-time that he had never seen a clearer case. But he had run in front of Bannerman, who was bound to say not out. The incident resulted in ruffled tempers and an outbreak of crowd hooliganism, an unpleasant feature right through the tour. Nothing, however, could detract from Darling's great innings, which won the match for his side; his hundred came in 91 minutes and contained 20 fours. A redeeming feature was that the spirit between the teams was unaffected, the Australians suffering at times almost as much as the tourists from crowd rowdyism and abuse.

ENGLAND

						FALL OF WICKETS

Batsman	Dismissal 1st	R	Dismissal 2nd	R
*A. C. MacLaren	b Trott	65	c Darling b Jones	0
E. Wainwright	c Hill b Trumble	49	b Noble	6
K. S. Ranjitsinhji	c Gregory b Trott	2	lbw b Jones	12
T. Hayward	b Jones	47	c Worrall b Trumble	43
†W. Storer	b Jones	44	c Gregory b Trumble	31
N. F. Druce	lbw b Noble	64	c Howell b Trumble	18
G. H. Hirst	b Jones	44	c Trott b Jones	7
J. R. Mason	c Howell b Jones	7	b Trumble	11
J. Briggs	b Jones	0	b Howell	29
J. T. Hearne	not out	2	not out	3
T. Richardson	b Jones	1	b Howell	6
Extras	(b 2, lb 5, w 2, nb 1)	10	(lb 12)	12
Total		335	Total	178

FALL OF WICKETS

ENGLAND

Wkt	1st	2nd
1st	111	0
2nd	117	16
3rd	119	30
4th	197	99
5th	230	104
6th	308	121
7th	318	137
8th	324	148
9th	334	172
10th	335	178

AUSTRALIA

Batsman	Dismissal 1st	R	Dismissal 2nd	R
C. E. McLeod	b Richardson	64	b Hearne	4
J. Darling	c Mason b Briggs	14	c Wainwright b Richardson	160
C. Hill	b Richardson	8	b Richardson	2
J. Worrall	c Ranjitsinhji b Richardson	26	c Hirst b Hayward	62
S. E. Gregory	c Storer b Richardson	21	not out	22
M. A. Noble	c Storer b Richardson	31	not out	15
*G. H. S. Trott	c Ranjitsinhji b Hearne	18		
H. Trumble	b Richardson	12		
†J. J. Kelly	not out	27		
W. P. Howell	c MacLaren b Richardson	10		
E. Jones	c Storer b Richardson	1		
Extras	(b 5, w 1, nb 1)	7	(b 6, w 1, nb 4)	11
Total		239	Total (4 wkts)	276

AUSTRALIA

Wkt	1st	2nd
1st	36	23
2nd	45	40
3rd	99	233
4th	132	252
5th	137	—
6th	188	—
7th	188	—
8th	221	—
9th	232	—
10th	239	—

Umpires: J. Phillips, C. Bannerman

AUSTRALIA	1st Innings				2nd Innings			
	O	M	R	W	O	M	R	W
Noble	26	6	57	1	15	4	34	1
Howell	17	6	40	0	6·1	0	22	2
Trumble	26	4	67	1	24	7	37	4
Jones	26·2	3	82	6	26	3	61	3
Trott	23	6	56	2	7	1	12	0
McLeod	11	4	23	0				

ENGLAND	1st Innings				2nd Innings			
	O	M	R	W	O	M	R	W
Richardson	36·1	7	94	8	21·4	1	110	2
Briggs	17	4	39	1	5	1	25	0
Hearne	21	9	40	1	15	5	52	1
Storer	5	1	13	0				
Mason	13	7	20	0	11	1	27	0
Hayward	4	0	12	0	3	0	18	1
Hirst	4	1	14	0	7	0	33	0

Averages: 1897-98

AUSTRALIA

BATTING	M.	Inns.	N.O.	Runs	H.S.	Av.
J. Darling	5	8	0	537	178	67·12
C. E. McLeod	5	8	2	352	112	58·66
C. Hill	5	8	0	452	188	56·50
S. E. Gregory	5	8	2	264	71	44·00
F. A. Iredale	4	5	0	216	89	43·20
J. J. Kelly	5	6	2	147	46*	36·75
H. Trumble	5	6	1	181	70	36·20
M. A. Noble	4	5	1	106	39	26·50
G. H. S. Trott	5	6	0	144	79	24·00
W. P. Howell	3	3	1	35	16	17·50
E. Jones	5	6	0	39	20	6·50
T. R. McKibbin	2	3	1	8	6	4·00

PLAYED IN ONE TEST: J. Worrall 26 and 62, J. J. Lyons 3 and 25.

BOWLING	Overs	Mds.	Runs	Wkts.	Av.
M. A. Noble	150·5	33	385	19	20·26
C. E. McLeod	116·2	48	236	10	23·60
E. Jones	198·2	32	553	22	25·13
H. Trumble	232·3	57	535	19	28·15
W. P. Howell	163·1	66	284	9	31·55
G. H. S. Trott	110·1	15	316	7	45·14

ALSO BOWLED: T. R. McKibbin 71–13–214–4.

ENGLAND

BATTING	M.	Inns.	N.O.	Runs	H.S.	Av.
A. C. MacLaren	5	10	1	488	124	54·22
K. S. Ranjitsinhji	5	10	1	457	175	50·77
T. W. Hayward	5	9	0	336	72	37·33
G. H. Hirst	4	7	0	207	85	29·57
N. F. Druce	5	9	0	252	64	28·00
J. Briggs	5	9	3	146	46*	24·33
W. Storer	5	9	0	208	51	23·11
A. E. Stoddart	2	4	0	81	23	20·25
E. Wainwright	4	7	0	105	49	15·00
T. Richardson	5	9	3	83	25*	13·83
J. R. Mason	5	10	0	129	32	12·90
J. T. Hearne	5	9	3	31	17	5·16

BOWLING	Overs	Mds.	Runs	Wkts.	Av.
J. T. Hearne	217	66	538	20	26·90
T. Richardson	255·5	50	776	22	35·27
J. Briggs	190	56	485	9	53·88

ALSO BOWLED: A. E. Stoddart 10–2–32–1, T. W. Hayward 52–15–164–4, W. Storer 28–5–108–2, J. R. Mason 54–13–149–2, G. H. Hirst 99–18–304–2, W. Wainwright 12–3–32–0, K. S. Ranjitsinhji 3·4–1–9–0.

Averages: 1899

ENGLAND

BATTING	M.	Inns.	N.O.	Runs	H.S.	Av.
T. W. Hayward	5	7	1	413	137	68·83
K. S. Ranjitsinhji	5	8	2	278	93*	46·33
A. A. Lilley	4	5	1	181	58	45·25
F. S. Jackson	5	8	1	303	118	43·28
A. C. MacLaren	4	6	1	164	88*	32·80
C. B. Fry	5	8	0	187	60	23·37
W. M. Bradley	2	2	1	23	23*	23·00
H. Young	2	2	0	43	43	21·50
C. L. Townsend	2	3	0	51	38	17·00
W. G. Quaife	2	4	1	44	20	14·66
J. T. Tyldesley	2	4	0	50	22	12·50
W. Rhodes	3	4	1	18	8*	6·00
J. T. Hearne	3	3	1	8	4*	4·00

PLAYED IN ONE TEST: W. G. Grace 28 and 1, W. Gunn 14 and 3, W. Storer 4 and 3, G. H. Hirst 6, G. L. Jessop 51 and 4, W. Mead 7 and 0, J. T. Brown 27 and 14*, W. Brockwell 20, W. H. Lockwood 24, A. O. Jones 31, J. Briggs did not bat.

BOWLING	Overs	Mds.	Runs	Wkts.	Av.
W. H. Lockwood	55·3	24	104	7	14·85
H. Young	111·1	38	262	12	21·83
J. T. Hearne	199·3	87	321	13	24·69
W. Rhodes	146·2	37	341	13	26·23
W. M. Bradley	125	49	233	6	38·83
F. S. Jackson	119·3	42	284	5	56·80

ALSO BOWLED: J. Briggs 30–11–53–3, C. L. Townsend 28–5–75–3, K. S. Ranjitsinhji 15–5–30–1, T. W. Hayward 39–7–148–3, A. O. Jones 42–14–116–3, G. L. Jessop 43·1–10–124–3, G. H. Hirst 35–13–62–1, W. Mead 53–24–91–1, W. G. Grace 22–8–37–0, W. Brockwell 21–5–54–0, J. T. Brown 7–0–22–0, W. G. Quaife 3–1–6–0, C. B. Fry 2–1–3–0.

AUSTRALIA

BATTING	M.	Inns.	N.O.	Runs	H.S.	Av.
C. Hill	3	5	0	301	135	60·20
M. A. Noble	5	9	2	367	89	52·42
J. Worrall	4	8	1	318	76	45·42
H. Trumble	5	9	3	232	56	38·66
V. T. Trumper	5	9	1	280	135*	35·00
J. Darling	5	10	1	232	71	25·77
F. A. Iredale	3	5	1	102	36*	25·50
S. E. Gregory	5	8	0	188	117	23·50
J. J. Kelly	5	8	1	118	33	16·85
F. Laver	4	7	1	72	45	12·00
E. Jones	5	7	0	31	17	4·42
W. P. Howell	5	7	2	17	7	3·40

PLAYED IN ONE TEST: C. E. McLeod 31* and 77.

BOWLING	Overs	Mds.	Runs	Wkts.	Av.
H. Trumble	192·3	78	375	15	25·00
E. Jones	255·1	73	657	26	25·26
M. A. Noble	170·3	73	406	13	31·23
W. P. Howell	164	61	346	8	43·25

ALSO BOWLED: F. Laver 32–7–70–4, C. E. McLeod 48–15–131–1, J. Worrall 3–0–15–0.

June 1, 2, 3
Toss: Australia   *Result:* Match Drawn

What England had been up against in 1897-98 in Australia was amply demonstrated in 1899 when virtually the same side came to England. For the first time in England, five Test Matches were played, each of three days. The Australians, after outplaying England in the first, won the second easily; but the other three matches were drawn, Australia thus retaining the Ashes. This, in contemporary estimation, was the strongest Australian side since 1882; but Hill, the best batsman in the side, missed the last two Tests through a minor operation, and the side as a whole possibly suffered towards the end of its programme from the strain of a long tour in a dry summer. Thus England could claim at the finish to have had rather the better of the last three Tests and to be unlucky not to square the rubber.

The opening at Trent Bridge gave promise of an absorbing series, a slow but fluctuating day's play ending with Australia 238 for 8. Darling, Noble and Gregory all played useful innings, but Australia were only 167 for 5 when Kelly joined Hill. Missed at the wicket before scoring, Kelly helped Hill to add 62 against fine bowling from Hearne and Hirst, but 3 wickets then fell cheaply, and soon after noon next day Australia were all out for 252, Rhodes cleaning up the tail. Grace was in considerable difficulty against Jones when England batted, but he

and Fry put on 75, and with Fry batting particularly well England looked to be gaining command; then wickets began to fall, and when Hayward slipped and ran himself out England were 117 for 5. Ranji and Tyldesley put on 55, but both were subdued against good bowling, the pace of Jones generally proving too much. England were all out at 4.35 for 193, 59 behind, and although Darling was soon out, Noble and Hill had taken Australia to 93 for 1 by stumps.

On the last morning Australia tried to force the pace, but wickets fell with alarming frequency until Trumble and Kelly came together with 7 wickets down and put on 46. Hill, very strong on the leg side, batted 2 hours 40 minutes for his 80, but Gregory was unable to bat because of a damaged hand. Darling declared at lunch, leaving England just under 4 hours' batting in which to make 290. Grace was bowled in Howell's second over by a beautiful break-back, Jackson followed in the same over, and with Jones bowling at a tremendous pace and Trumble deceiving Fry, England were suddenly 19 for 4 and facing defeat. At 40 Hayward was badly missed by Darling himself at forward short leg; had the chance been taken England must surely have lost. As it was Ranji, in one of his greatest innings, played more and more freely and saw England through.

AUSTRALIA

*J. Darling	b Hearne	47		b Rhodes	14		
F. A. Iredale	c Hayward b Hearne	6	(4)	run out	20		
M. A. Noble	b Rhodes	41	(2)	lbw b Rhodes	45		
S. E. Gregory	b Hirst	48					
C. Hill	run out	52	(3)	c Grace b Jackson	80		
V. T. Trumper	b Hearne	0	(5)	b Jackson	11		
†J. J. Kelly	c Hirst b Hearne	26	(9)	not out	11		
F. Laver	b Rhodes	3	(7)	b Jackson	3		
W. P. Howell	c Hayward b Rhodes	0	(10)	not out	4		
H. Trumble	not out	16	(8)	c Ranjitsinhji b Rhodes	38		
E. Jones	c Fry b Rhodes	4	(6)	c Ranjitsinhji b Hearne	3		
Extras	(b 8, lb 1)	9		(lb 1)	1		
Total		**252**		**Total** (8 wkts dec)	**230**		

ENGLAND

*W. G. Grace	c Kelly b Noble	28	b Howell	1	
C. B. Fry	b Jones	50	c Jones b Trumble	9	
F. S. Jackson	c Darling b Noble	8	b Howell	0	
W. Gunn	b Jones	14	b Jones	3	
K. S. Ranjitsinhji	b Jones	42	not out	93	
T. Hayward	run out	0	b Trumble	28	
J. T. Tyldesley	c Laver b Howell	22	c Kelly b Trumble	10	
†W. Storer	b Jones	4	lbw b Jones	3	
G. H. Hirst	b Howell	6			
W. Rhodes	c Kelly b Jones	6			
J. T. Hearne	not out	4			
Extras	(lb 3, nb 6)	9	(b 5, w 1, nb 2)	8	
Total		**193**	**Total** (7 wkts)	**155**	

FALL OF WICKETS

AUSTRALIA

Wkt	1st	2nd
1st	14	18
2nd	85	111
3rd	109	151
4th	166	170
5th	167	173
6th	229	177
7th	229	180
8th	229	226
9th	248	—
10th	252	—

ENGLAND

Wkt	1st	2nd
1st	75	1
2nd	91	1
3rd	93	10
4th	116	19
5th	117	82
6th	172	140
7th	176	155
8th	178	—
9th	185	—
10th	193	—

Umpires: R. G. Barlow,
V. A. Titchmarsh

ENGLAND	1st Innings				2nd Innings			
	O	M	R	W	O	M	R	W
Rhodes	35.2	13	58	4	20	3	60	3
Hearne	59	28	71	4	29	10	70	1
Grace	20	8	31	0	2	0	6	0
Hirst	24	9	42	1	11	4	20	0
Jackson	11	3	27	0	26	8	57	3
Hayward	3	0	14	0	6	2	16	0

AUSTRALIA	1st Innings				2nd Innings			
	O	M	R	W	O	M	R	W
Jones	33	6	88	5	22	9	31	2
Howell	28.4	12	43	2	37	18	54	2
Trumble	13	7	17	0	29	16	39	3
Noble	16	4	36	2	11	5	23	0

50. E. Jones

55. (left) W. Rhodes

57. Australia 1899
Back row: V. T. Trumper, H. Trumble, A. E. Johns, W. P. Howell, B. J. Wardill (manager), M. A. Noble, F. Laver, C. E. McLeod.
Middle row: J. J. Kelly, C. Hill, J. Worrall, J. Darling (capt.), F. A. Iredale, E. Jones. *Front:* S. E. Gregory.

1899 Second Test, Lord's

June 15, 16, 17
Toss: England   *Result:* Australia won by ten wickets

The omission of Grace, who was dropped from a home Test Match for the first time, was foreshadowed at Nottingham; and Gunn, too, was left out of the England side. But the replacements were controversial. MacLaren came into the side as captain straight from the nets, with no first-class form, while several experienced Test batsmen were passed over to make room for all-rounders Townsend and Jessop. Even stranger was the dropping of Hearne and Hirst, leaving the bowling, on what promised to be a fast wicket, palely experimental. For Australia, Worrall replaced Iredale. Hill and Trumper, aged 22 and 21 respectively, were the batting stars for Australia, but the match-winner was the terrific pace of Jones, who broke through the early English batting in both innings.

After winning the toss, MacLaren was bowled in Jones' second over, Ranji gave a return catch trying to turn Jones to leg, Townsend was stumped off Howell, and after a period of steady play Fry, Hayward and Tyldesley were all out and England were 66 for 6, 4 of them to Jones. Jessop was jumpy at first, and at 69 Jackson, stranded in mid-pitch, should have been run out; but they settled down to play well, and at lunch England, after 2 hours 20 minutes, were 147 for 6. After lunch Jackson was missed in the slips off Jones, but the separation came

at 161 when Jessop was caught at long on. He and Jackson had put on 95 in just over an hour. Jackson, 8th out, batted with his usual sound judgment in a crisis for 2¼ hours, but the innings closed at 206.

By getting 3 men out for 59, England seemed at first to have restored the balance; but Hill and Noble then mastered the bowling, and at stumps Australia were 156 for 3. This stand, the turning point of the match, was continued next morning until it had put on 130, and after that Hill and Trumper put on 82. Hill, who was missed behind the wicket at 1 and 82—a stumping and a catch—reached his hundred in 3 hours, while Trumper played with astonishing grace and freedom for a young man in only his second Test. Australia led by 215.

Jones, from the nursery end as in the first innings, clean bowled Fry, had Hayward missed at the wicket, and then bowled Townsend after Howell had dismissed Ranji: 23 for 3. Hayward and Jackson then batted with every show of command, but Jackson, ultra-cautious, gave a return catch in the last over of the day, and although Hayward and MacLaren caused Darling some concern on the final day, the introduction of Laver with tempting half-volleys wide of the off stump broke the back of the innings and Australia won by 10 wickets.

ENGLAND

C. B. Fry	c Trumble b Jones	13	b Jones	4	
*A. C. MacLaren	b Jones	4	(6)not out	88	
K. S. Ranjitsinhji	c and b Jones	8	c Noble b Howell	0	
C. L. Townsend	st Kelly b Howell	5	b Jones	8	
F. S. Jackson	b Jones	73	c and b Trumble	37	
T. Hayward	b Noble	1	(2)c Trumble b Laver	77	
J. T. Tyldesley	c Darling b Jones	14	c Gregory b Laver	4	
G. L. Jessop	c Trumper b Trumble	51	c Trumble b Laver	4	
†A. A. Lilley	not out	19	b Jones	12	
W. Mead	b Jones	7	(11)lbw b Noble	0	
W. Rhodes	b Jones	2	(10)c and b Noble	2	
Extras	(b 2, lb 6, w 1)	9	(b 2, lb 2)	4	
Total		**206**	**Total**	**240**	

AUSTRALIA

J. Worrall	c Hayward b Rhodes	18	not out	11
*J. Darling	c Ranjitsinhji b Rhodes	9	not out	17
C. Hill	c Fry b Townsend	135		
S. E. Gregory	c Lilley b Jessop	15		
M. A. Noble	c Lilley b Rhodes	54		
V. T. Trumper	not out	135		
†J. J. Kelly	c Lilley b Mead	9		
H. Trumble	c Lilley b Jessop	24		
F. Laver	b Townsend	0		
E. Jones	c Mead b Townsend	17		
W. P. Howell	b Jessop	0		
Extras	(lb 4, nb 1)	5		
Total		**421**	**Total (0 wkts)**	**28**

FALL OF WICKETS

ENGLAND

Wkt	1st	2nd
1st	4	5
2nd	14	6
3rd	20	23
4th	44	94
5th	45	160
6th	66	166
7th	161	170
8th	184	212
9th	194	240
10th	206	240

AUSTRALIA

Wkt	1st	2nd
1st	27	—
2nd	28	—
3rd	59	—
4th	189	—
5th	271	—
6th	306	—
7th	386	—
8th	387	—
9th	421	—
10th	421	—

Umpires: T. Mycroft, W. A. J. West

AUSTRALIA

	1st Innings				2nd Innings			
	O	M	R	W	O	M	R	W
Jones	36.1	11	88	7	36	15	76	3
Howell	14	4	43	1	31	12	67	1
Noble	15	7	39	1	19.4	8	37	2
Trumble	15	9	27	1	15	6	20	1
Laver					16	4	36	3

ENGLAND

	1st Innings				2nd Innings			
	O	M	R	W	O	M	R	W
Jessop	37.1	10	105	3	6	0	19	0
Mead	53	24	91	1				
Rhodes	39	10	108	3	5	1	9	0
Jackson	18	6	31	0				
Townsend	15	1	50	3				
Ranjitsinhji	2	0	6	0				
Hayward	6	0	25	0				

1899 Third Test, Leeds

Test no. 54

June 29, 30, July 1
Toss: Australia   *Result:* Match Drawn

With Lockwood's fitness in doubt, and Kortright injured, England recalled Richardson at Leeds, but when heavy rain fell beforehand Briggs was preferred. Young, medium-pace left-hand, replaced his Essex colleague Mead, Hearne returned, and Brown and Quaife replaced Townsend and Jessop. Australia were unchanged.

Darling won the toss, and with the wicket likely to deteriorate he took first knock, sending Kelly in first with Worrall to see how the wicket would play. It was, in fact, slow at the beginning; yet Australia made a disastrous start, losing 3 for 24, all scored by Worrall. Joined by Hill, Worrall continued to force the pace, hitting with great power in front of the wicket, and he made his 76 out of 95 in just over 90 minutes. Young then bowled Trumper with a ball that went with his arm, and at lunch Australia were 131 for 6. Hill batted 1¾ hours for his 34, but Australia were all out at 3.45 for 172. Young, getting more pace from the pitch than Hearne, looked the best bowler, and Lilley was in good form behind the stumps.

England did not make quite such a bad start, but for a long time their innings closely paralleled Australia's, and it was not until Fry joined Quaife at 69 for 4 that the batsmen settled down. Quaife, oblivious of

the way the fieldsmen crowded round him, defended for 1¾ hours, and at stumps England were well enough placed at 119 for 4.

That evening a severe misfortune overtook England: Briggs, the only slow bowler in the side, had a violent fit during the show at the Empire Theatre Leeds and took no further part in the match. The Australian bowlers caused further shocks next morning, both Fry and Quaife being out without addition, but Hayward and Lilley averted disaster in a stand of 93, and England got a lead of 48.

The game continued full of incident when Australia batted again. Worrall and Darling made a quick 34, but after Worrall was caught at long off, Hearne did the hat trick, his victims being Hill, Gregory and Noble. Five runs later, when Darling mishit Young, Australia were 39 for 5, still 9 runs behind. But Kelly, joining Trumper, showed his nerve although continually beaten by Young, and when he was out Trumble played equally stubbornly. Trumper batted 100 minutes for his 32, and with the change bowling inadequate Trumble and Laver added 73. Needing 177 to win, England after some anxious moments were 19 for 0 at the close; but next day rain washed out this fascinating game.

AUSTRALIA

Batsman	1st Innings		2nd Innings	
J. Worrall	run out	76	c sub (J. T. Tyldesley) b Young	16
†J. J. Kelly	c Fry b Briggs	0	(7) c Lilley b Hayward	33
M. A. Noble	run out	0	(5) c Ranjitsinhji b Hearne	0
S. E. Gregory	c Lilley b Hearne	0	(4) c MacLaren b Hearne	0
C. Hill	c Lilley b Young	34	(3) b Hearne	0
*J. Darling	c Young b Briggs	9	(2) c Fry b Young	16
V. T. Trumper	b Young	12	(6) c Ranjitsinhji b Jackson	32
H. Trumble	not out	20	run out	56
F. Laver	st Lilley b Briggs	7	c Lilley b Hearne	45
E. Jones	b Young	5	c Brown b Hayward	2
W. P. Howell	c Ranjitsinhji b Young	7	not out	2
Extras	(b 2)	2	(b 17, lb 3, w 1, nb 1)	22
Total		**172**		**224**

ENGLAND

Batsman	1st Innings		2nd Innings	
J. T. Brown	c Trumble b Noble	27	not out	14
*A. C. MacLaren	c and b Trumble	9		
K. S. Ranjitsinhji	c Worrall b Noble	11		
W. G. Quaife	b Jones	20	not out	1
F. S. Jackson	b Trumble	9		
C. B. Fry	b Noble	38		
T. Hayward	not out	40		
†A. A. Lilley	c Hill b Trumble	55		
J. T. Hearne	b Trumble	3		
H. Young	c Kelly b Trumble	0		
J. Briggs	absent ill	—		
Extras	(b 3, lb 5)	8	(lb 4)	4
Total		**220**	Total (0 wkts)	**19**

FALL OF WICKETS

AUSTRALIA		
Wkt	1st	2nd
1st	8	34
2nd	17	34
3rd	24	34
4th	95	34
5th	114	39
6th	131	97
7th	132	140
8th	151	213
9th	164	215
10th	172	224

ENGLAND		
Wkt	1st	2nd
1st	27	—
2nd	38	—
3rd	53	—
4th	69	—
5th	119	—
6th	119	—
7th	212	—
8th	220	—
9th	220	—
10th	—	—

Umpires: W. Hearn, M. Sherwin

ENGLAND	1st Innings				2nd Innings			
	O	M	R	W	O	M	R	W
Hearne	23	5	69	1	31·3	12	50	4
Briggs	30	11	53	3				
Young	19·1	11	30	4	26	5	72	2
Jackson	5	1	18	0	11	6	13	1
Brown					7	0	22	0
Hayward					10	1	45	2

AUSTRALIA	1st Innings				2nd Innings			
	O	M	R	W	O	M	R	W
Trumble	39·3	16	60	5				
Noble	42	17	82	3	3	1	8	0
Howell	13	3	29	0				
Jones	21	9	34	1	4	2	7	0
Laver	3	1	7	0				

1899 Fourth Test, Old Trafford

July 17, 18, 19
Toss: England   *Result:* Match Drawn

This great match, full of fine cricket, ended in a draw; but it brought, in the following year, a change in the follow-on law (then compulsory after a difference of 120 runs), England, like many sides before them, wilting under the obligation of bowling and fielding through two successive innings in hot weather. For England, Hayward played one of the great Test innings, reminiscent of Shrewsbury, while for Australia Noble defied the English attack for 8½ hours in all, being the chief instrument in saving the game and ensuring the retention of the Ashes. England played Bradley, the Kent fast bowler, in place of Briggs, and Brockwell came in for the injured Brown. Iredale replaced Hill for Australia.

A heavy dew made the ball fly at first, and for the fourth time running England started badly, Hayward joining Jackson at 47 for 4. Jackson was caught off a bumper just before lunch, but his innings had been a vital one. Hayward then shared a short but spirited stand with Brockwell, but 6 men were out for 154. Then Hayward and Lilley, as at Leeds, turned the game England's way, adding 113. Hayward reached his hundred in just over 3½ hours, and the last 3 wickets put on 105. Facing a total of 372, Australia sent in the tail-enders and lost Laver before the close.

Another heavy dew, plus the pace of Bradley and more fine bowling from Young, reduced Australia to 57 for 7 next morning, but Mac-Laren left Bradley on too long, especially with a follow on in prospect; he bowled 18 overs before being rested. Meanwhile Noble, following a 'pair' at Leeds, was defending with consummate skill, and he and Trumble, who had been opening in some of the county matches, took the score to 130 for 7 at lunch. When Trumble was out Iredale gave further useful support, although often troubled by Bradley, and Australia totalled 196. Noble, who batted 3 hours 10 minutes for his 60 not out, went in first when Australia followed on just before 4.0, and he was still there at the close, when Australia, aided by dropped catches, were 142 for 2, 34 behind.

Soon after the 200 was reached on the last day, Hearne sent Trumper's middle stump flying and had Gregory caught, and Australia, only 37 in front with more than 5 hours remaining, were in grave danger. But Darling, missed at mid off when 3, stayed 2 hours 10 minutes, Noble batted until 2.45, Iredale stonewalled, and England's chance, real for much of the day, gradually faded. In the 65 minutes left to them by Darling, England raced somewhat recklessly to 94 for 3.

ENGLAND

W. G. Quaife	c Darling b Noble	8	c Iredale b Jones	15
C. B. Fry	b Jones	9	c Iredale b Trumble	4
K. S. Ranjitsinhji	c Worrall b Jones	21	not out	49
*A. C. MacLaren	b Noble	8	c Iredale b Trumble	6
F. S. Jackson	c Trumble b Jones	44	not out	14
T. Hayward	c Jones b Howell	130		
W. Brockwell	c Worrall b Noble	20		
†A. A. Lilley	lbw b Laver	58		
H. Young	b Howell	43		
J. T. Hearne	c Iredale b Trumble	1		
W. M. Bradley	not out	23		
Extras	(b 3, lb 3, w 1)	7	(b 4, nb 2)	6
Total		**372**	**Total** (3 wkts)	**94**

AUSTRALIA

†J. J. Kelly	b Young	9	(8)c Lilley b Ranjitsinhji	26
F. Laver	c Lilley b Bradley	0	(9)not out	14
W. P. Howell	b Bradley	0		
J. Worrall	b Bradley	14	(1)c Brockwell b Young	53
M. A. Noble	not out	60	(2)c and b Hearne	89
S. E. Gregory	lbw b Young	5	(5)c Ranjitsinhji b Hearne	1
V. T. Trumper	b Young	14	(4)b Hearne	63
*J. Darling	b Young	4	(6)c sub (W. Rhodes) b Young	39
H. Trumble	c MacLaren b Bradley	44	(3)c Ranjitsinhji b Bradley	7
F. A. Iredale	c Lilley b Bradley	31	(7)not out	36
E. Jones	b Jackson	0		
Extras	(b 14, w 1)	15	(b 14, lb 2, w 1, nb 1)	18
Total		**196**	**Total** (7 wkts dec)	**346**

FALL OF WICKETS

ENGLAND

Wkt	1st	2nd
1st	14	12
2nd	18	39
3rd	47	54
4th	47	—
5th	107	—
6th	154	—
7th	267	—
8th	324	—
9th	337	—
10th	372	—

AUSTRALIA

Wkt	1st	2nd
1st	1	93
2nd	6	117
3rd	14	205
4th	26	213
5th	35	255
6th	53	278
7th	57	319
8th	139	—
9th	195	—
10th	196	—

Umpires: A. Hide,
James Lillywhite, jnr.

AUSTRALIA	1st Innings				2nd Innings			
	O	M	R	W	O	M	R	W
Jones	42	9	136	3	8	0	33	1
Noble	28	19	85	3				
Trumble	29	10	72	1	13	3	33	2
Howell	19·1	7	45	2	6	2	22	0
Laver	13	2	27	1				

ENGLAND	1st Innings				2nd Innings			
	O	M	R	W	O	M	R	W
Young	29	10	79	4	37	12	81	2
Bradley	33	13	67	5	46	16	82	1
Brockwell	6	2	18	0	15	3	36	0
Hearne	10	6	7	0	47	26	54	3
Jackson	3·3	1	9	1	18	8	36	0
Ranjitsinhji	1	0	1	0	12	5	23	1
Quaife					3	1	6	0
Hayward					3	1	10	0

1899 Fifth Test, Oval

August 14, 15, 16
Toss: England   *Result:* Match Drawn

Frustrated at Leeds and again at Old Trafford, England approached the final Test determined to square the series, while Australia, with two defeats against the counties since the fourth Test, and still without Hill, began for the first time to look vulnerable. England omitted Brockwell and Quaife, and, less explicably, Young and Hearne, bringing in Lockwood, fit at last, Rhodes, Townsend and A. O. Jones. McLeod, out of form with the bat but in great form with the ball, replaced Laver for Australia.

Winning the toss, MacLaren by a happy inspiration sent Jackson and Hayward in first, and they put on 185 together, of which Jackson made 118. He had some luck, but his innings was distinguished by fine off-driving. Hayward took nearly 2½ hours to reach 50, but he doubled his score in the next 85 minutes, scoring mostly by perfect leg-side placings and on-drives. The orders then were to go for the runs, and at one point MacLaren and Fry added 110 in 65 minutes. England made 435 for 4 in the day and 576 in all, and when the Australians went in at 1.0 on the second day England had about 10½ hours in which to bowl them out twice.

The wicket remained perfect, but after lunch Jones, going round the wicket with his slows, dismissed Trumble and Trumper, and when Lockwood beat Noble with a break-back Australia were 85 for 3. Worrall, however, was playing a steady game, and after he left at 120, with about 2 hours left for play, Gregory and Darling continued the resistance. Twenty minutes were lost at one stage through bad light, and when play was resumed with the light not much improved Mac-Laren did not hesitate to use Bradley and Lockwood, but no further wicket fell until Darling was caught off Lockwood just before time, the score then being 220 for 5.

Play started on the last morning at 11.0, and despite fine bowling by Lockwood Australia held on for nearly 2 hours. Gregory played his best innings of the tour in making 117, while McLeod rediscovered all his powers of application. With rather less than 4½ hours remaining, Darling sent McLeod in first when Australia followed on, and while he again defended, Worrall this time played his natural game. They put on 116 for the 1st wicket in 90 minutes, making a draw virtually certain. Only Lockwood gave them any anxiety, and by the time he left the field in mid-afternoon, hampered by the strain that had bothered him all season, McLeod and Noble had made the game safe.

ENGLAND

F. S. Jackson	b Jones	118
T. Hayward	c Iredale b McLeod	137
K. S. Ranjitsinhji	c Howell b Jones	54
C. B. Fry	c Worrall b Jones	60
*A. C. MacLaren	c Trumper b Trumble	49
C. L. Townsend	b Jones	38
W. M. Bradley	run out	0
W. H. Lockwood	b Trumble	24
A. O. Jones	b Noble	31
†A. A. Lilley	c Iredale b Noble	37
W. Rhodes	not out	8
Extras	(b 9, lb 6, w 4, nb 1)	20
Total		**576**

AUSTRALIA

J. Worrall	c Hayward b Lockwood	55	c Lilley b Hayward	75
H. Trumble	c and b Jones	24	(7)not out	3
V. T. Trumper	c Lilley b Jones	6	(4)c and b Rhodes	7
M. A. Noble	b Lockwood	9	(3)not out	69
*J. Darling	c Fry b Lockwood	71	(6)run out	6
S. E. Gregory	c Jones b Lockwood	117	(5)b Rhodes	2
F. A. Iredale	b Lockwood	9		
†J. J. Kelly	lbw b Jones	4		
C. E. McLeod	not out	31	(2)b Rhodes	77
E. Jones	b Lockwood	0		
W. P. Howell	b Lockwood	4		
Extras	(b 5, lb 10, w 1, nb 6)	22	(b 7, w 4, nb 4)	15
Total		**352**	**Total** (5 wkts)	**254**

FALL OF WICKETS

ENGLAND

Wkt	1st	2nd
1st	185	—
2nd	316	—
3rd	318	—
4th	428	—
5th	436	—
6th	436	—
7th	479	—
8th	511	—
9th	551	—
10th	576	—

AUSTRALIA

Wkt	1st	2nd
1st	38	116
2nd	44	208
3rd	85	224
4th	120	228
5th	220	243
6th	242	—
7th	257	—
8th	340	—
9th	340	—
10th	352	—

Umpires: A. A. White,
W. Richards

AUSTRALIA	1st Innings				2nd Innings			
	O	M	R	W	O	M	R	W
Jones	53	12	164	4				
Noble	35·4	12	96	2				
Trumble	39	11	107	2				
McLeod	48	15	131	1				
Howell	15	3	43	0				
Worrall	3	0	15	0				

ENGLAND	1st Innings				2nd Innings			
	O	M	R	W	O	M	R	W
Bradley	29	12	52	0	17	8	32	0
Rhodes	25	2	79	0	22	8	27	3
Lockwood	40·3	17	71	7	15	7	33	0
Jones	30	12	73	3	12	2	43	0
Townsend	5	0	16	0	8	4	9	0
Jackson	14	7	39	0	13	2	54	0
Hayward					11	3	38	1
Fry					2	1	3	0

1901-02 First Test, Sydney

December 13, 14, 16
Toss: England   *Result:* England won by an innings and 124 runs

After the MCC had declined, MacLaren accepted an invitation from the Melbourne Club to take a touring side. This was the fifteenth and last English tour of Australia under private management. Although Hirst, Rhodes, Ranji, Jackson and Fry were not available, MacLaren got a strong party together. A surprise choice was Barnes, who was then playing in the Lancashire League: but Barnes had played several times for Lancashire under MacLaren.

The loss of Barnes through injury early in the Third Test upset the balance between the two sides. Even so, it was the failure of the batsmen, apart from MacLaren and Hayward, which cost England the series. The Australians soon showed that their batting in the first Test was an aberration, and Hill, who made 99, 98 and 97 in successive innings, was the rock on which English hopes foundered again and again.

England began the series in brilliant style with a century 1st-wicket partnership, and after the other specialist batsmen had failed Lilley and Braund added 124 for the 7th wicket. The last 3 wickets then put

on 68, and England achieved a massive 464. MacLaren's hundred came in 3 hours 7 minutes, and he gave only one chance, to slip off Jones at 46. England batted in all for 7 hours 37 minutes. A pleasing feature was the liveliness of the Australian out-cricket, especially the changing between overs, which was done with alacrity. 186 overs were bowled, at a rate of nearly 25 an hour. The English batsmen found the swerve bowling of Noble, McLeod and Laver disconcerting at times.

Australia had just over 1¾ hours' batting before the end of the second day and were 103 for 3 at the close, Barnes bowling throughout. When he was finally rested just before lunch next day he had bowled 32 overs and the Australian score was 152 for 8, and he came back directly after lunch and took the last two wickets, keeping a wonderful length all through.

Following on, Australia were out a second time in less than 3 hours. Blythe bowled effectively, but the man who puzzled them most in this innings was Braund with his leg-breaks. Some big hitting by Howell, who scored 16 in one over from Barnes and distorted his figures, enlivened the finish. The wicket stayed good to the end.

ENGLAND

*A. C. MacLaren	lbw b McLeod	116		
T. Hayward	c Hill b Trumble	69		
J. T. Tyldesley	c McLeod b Laver	1		
W. G. Quaife	b Howell	21		
G. L. Jessop	b McLeod	24		
A. O. Jones	c Kelly b Noble	9		
†A. A. Lilley	c Laver b McLeod	84		
L. C. Braund	c Jones b McLeod	58		
J. Gunn	c and b Jones	21		
S. F. Barnes	not out	26		
C. Blythe	c Trumble b Laver	20		
Extras	(b 6, lb 7, w 1, nb 1)	15		
Total		**464**		

AUSTRALIA

S. E. Gregory	c Braund b Blythe	48	(5)c MacLaren b Braund	43	
V. T. Trumper	c and b Barnes	2	c Lilley b Blythe	34	
C. Hill	b Barnes	46	b Braund	0	
M. A. Noble	st Lilley b Braund	2	c Lilley b Blythe	14	
W. P. Howell	c Braund b Blythe	9	(10)not out	31	
C. E. McLeod	b Barnes	0	b Blythe	0	
†J. J. Kelly	b Blythe	0	c Barnes b Blythe	12	
*J. Darling	c Quaife b Barnes	39	(1)c Jessop b Braund	3	
F. Laver	c Quaife b Braund	6	st Lilley b Braund	0	
H. Trumble	not out	5	(8)c Lilley b Barnes	26	
E. Jones	c Jessop b Barnes	5	c Jones b Braund	2	
Extras	(b 1, lb 3, nb 2)	6	(b 5, lb 2)	7	
Total		168	Total	172	

FALL OF WICKETS

ENGLAND

Wkt	1st	2nd
1st	154	—
2nd	163	—
3rd	193	—
4th	220	—
5th	236	—
6th	272	—
7th	396	—
8th	405	—
9th	425	—
10th	464	—

AUSTRALIA

Wkt	1st	2nd
1st	3	12
2nd	89	12
3rd	97	52
4th	112	59
5th	112	59
6th	112	89
7th	112	129
8th	142	136
9th	163	147
10th	168	172

Umpires: R. Callaway,
R. W. Crockett

AUSTRALIA

	1st Innings				2nd Innings			
	O	M	R	W	O	M	R	W
Jones	36	8	98	1				
Noble	33	17	91	1				
McLeod	44	17	84	4				
Howell	21	8	52	1				
Trumble	34	12	85	1				
Laver	17	6	39	2				
Trumper	1	1	0	0				

ENGLAND

	1st Innings				2nd Innings			
	O	M	R	W	O	M	R	W
Barnes	35·1	9	65	5	16	2	74	1
Braund	15	4	40	2	28·4	8	61	6
Gunn	5	0	27	0				
Blythe	16	8	26	3	13	5	30	4
Jessop	1	0	4	0				

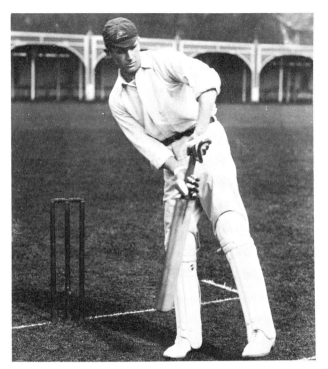

58. M. A. Noble

59. A. C. MacLaren

60. England 1901-02
Back row: J. Gunn, C. Blythe, S. F. Barnes, A. A. Lilley, T. W. Hayward, L. C. Braund. *Middle row:* H. G. Garnett, C. P. McGahey, A. C. MacLaren (capt.), C. Robson, A. O. Jones. *Front:* W. G. Quaife, J. T. Tyldesley.

1901–02 Second Test, Melbourne

January 1, 2, 3, 4
Toss: England *Result:* Australia won by 229 runs

With the wicket suffering from the effects of heavy rain, and with the sky overcast, MacLaren put Australia in. Trumper was out second ball, but the other batsmen attacked feverishly, and Australia did well to total 112. Barnes and Blythe bowled unchanged for nearly 2 hours and shared the wickets. The pitch was no better when England batted, and they were all out for 61 in 68 minutes, only Jessop, who hit 27 in 20 minutes, following the Australian example. Trumble and Noble also bowled unchanged, Noble taking 7 for 17. Darling then altered his order in an attempt to save some of his best batting for the second day, opening himself with Trumble. Australia were 48 for 5 at the close, only 99 ahead, but the weather had remained fine and the wicket was improving, Gregory was not out, and Hill, Trumper, Noble, Duff and Armstrong, in that order, were still to come.

The wicket rolled out well on the second morning and the game looked nicely poised. Barnes, Braund and Blythe did almost all the bowling between them, and they bowled well, but all the Australian batsmen who had been held back made useful scores. Gregory was sixth out at 98, but England lost a great chance of a break-through

when Hill was missed at cover off Blythe just before lunch. When Trumper was out to the first ball after the break England seemed likely to escape, but Hill, who batted stylishly for $3\frac{1}{2}$ hours, was not dismissed until another 105 runs had been added, and then Armstrong joined Duff in a last-wicket stand of 120. Both were playing in their first Test. Duff batted for 3 hours 26 minutes, and neither batsman gave a chance.

Barnes was not relieved in this innings until he had bowled 42 overs, taking 6 for 76, and the scoring then became so rapid that MacLaren had to bring him back. He bowled 64 overs in all and took 7 for 121, but he was over-bowled.

Wanting 405 to win, England lost wickets steadily in spite of cautious batting but had reached 147 for 5 at the end of the third day, at which point they wanted 258 to win—a very formidable task, though Tyldesley and Braund were together and batting well. Heavy rain next morning made the end a formality, the innings closing in 34 minutes. Trumble finished off the game with a hat trick, his victims being Jones, Gunn and Barnes.

AUSTRALIA

V. T. Trumper	c Tyldesley b Barnes	0	(8)	c Lilley b Barnes	16	
*J. Darling	c Lilley b Blythe	19		c Tyldesley b Barnes	23	
C. Hill	b Barnes	15	(7)	c Jones b Barnes	99	
H. Trumble	c Braund b Blythe	16	(1)	c Braund b Barnes	16	
M. A. Noble	c Lilley b Blythe	0	(9)	lbw b Blythe	16	
S. E. Gregory	st Lilley b Blythe	0		c Jones b Barnes	17	
R. A. Duff	c Braund b Barnes	32	(10)	b Braund	104	
†J. J. Kelly	c Quaife b Barnes	5	(4)	run out	3	
W. W. Armstrong	not out	4	(11)	not out	45	
W. P. Howell	b Barnes	1	(3)	c Hayward b Barnes	0	
E. Jones	c MacLaren b Barnes	14	(5)	c MacLaren b Barnes	5	
Extras	(b 6)	6		(b 7, lb 1, nb 1)	9	
Total		**112**		**Total**	**353**	

ENGLAND

*A. C. MacLaren	c Jones b Trumble	13		c Trumble b Noble	1	
T. Hayward	c Darling b Trumble	0		st Kelly b Trumble	12	
J. T. Tyldesley	c Gregory b Trumble	2		c Trumble b Noble	66	
W. G. Quaife	b Noble	0		b Noble	25	
G. L. Jessop	st Kelly b Noble	27		c Gregory b Noble	32	
J. Gunn	st Kelly b Noble	0	(9)	c Jones b Trumble	2	
†A. A. Lilley	c Trumper b Noble	6	(6)	c Darling b Noble	0	
A. O. Jones	c Kelly b Noble	0		c Darling b Trumble	6	
L. C. Braund	not out	2	(7)	c Darling b Noble	25	
S. F. Barnes	c and b Noble	1		c and b Trumble	0	
C. Blythe	c Trumper b Noble	4		not out	0	
Extras	(b 6)	6		(b 1, lb 1, nb 4)	6	
Total		**61**		**Total**	**175**	

FALL OF WICKETS

AUSTRALIA

Wkt	1st	2nd
1st	0	32
2nd	32	42
3rd	34	42
4th	34	42
5th	38	48
6th	81	98
7th	85	128
8th	90	167
9th	94	233
10th	112	353

ENGLAND

Wkt	1st	2nd
1st	5	2
2nd	16	29
3rd	16	80
4th	24	123
5th	36	123
6th	51	156
7th	51	173
8th	56	175
9th	57	175
10th	61	175

Umpires: R. Callaway, R. W. Crockett

ENGLAND	1st Innings				2nd Innings			
	O	M	R	W	O	M	R	W
Barnes	16·1	5	42	6	64	17	121	7
Blythe	16	2	64	4	31	7	85	1
Braund					53·2	17	114	1
Jessop					1	0	9	0
Gunn					6	1	13	0
Jones					1	0	2	0

AUSTRALIA	1st Innings				2nd Innings			
	O	M	R	W	O	M	R	W
Trumble	8	1	38	3	22·5	10	49	4
Noble	7·4	2	17	7	26	5	60	6
Jones					12	2	33	0
Howell					15	6	23	0
Armstrong					2	1	3	0
Trumper					2	1	1	0

1901-02 Third Test, Adelaide

January 17, 18, 20, 21, 22, 23
Toss: England   *Result:* Australia won by four wickets

Forecasts that the wicket wouldn't last proved mistaken, and Australia, set to get 315 to win in the fourth innings, achieved a brilliant victory. Both teams were hampered by injuries, Noble and Howell on the Australian side and Barnes and Blythe for England, but the major calamity was undoubtedly that of the loss of Barnes when Australia in their first innings were 57 for 1. After bowling only 7 overs, Barnes was forced to retire with a twisted knee.

As at Sydney, MacLaren and Hayward took part in a big 1st-wicket stand, but a collapse followed and half the side were out for 186, at which point Braund joined Quaife. They were still together at the close, and they had put on 108 when they were parted on the second morning after half an hour's play. At lunch England were 330 for 7, and Braund completed his hundred with the last man in; he had batted 3½ hours. Australia then made a spirited reply, and at lunch on the third day they were 248 for 4, Hill having made 98. But after lunch John Gunn, left-hand quick-medium, took 5 of the last 6 wickets and Australia, who had looked likely to gain a substantial lead, lagged by 67.

Before the close England had added 98 runs to their lead for the loss of MacLaren, and with rain falling that evening and the pitch worn at one end they seemed certain to win. Next day they had consolidated their position at 204 for 5 when a dust-storm ended play for the day. On the fifth day, on a wicket that was thought to be deteriorating, they lost their last 4 wickets for 43 runs, Barnes being unable to bat; but they still held the substantial margin of 314 runs.

Australia set about their fourth innings task just before lunch on a doubtful wicket, and although Barnes was off the field and Blythe was nursing a bruised bowling hand the target looked beyond them. Gunn bowled to the worn end and Hill, who batted no. 3, frequently jumped down the pitch to smother the ball, but with his score at 19 he should have been stumped off Braund. Three wickets were down for 98, but after tea a stand between Hill and Darling put Australia back in the game, and when play ended they were 201 for 4. Hill's second great innings of the match came to an end just before the close; he had batted 2 hours 52 minutes and narrowly missed a century for the third time running. The remaining Australian batsmen kept on doggedly on the sixth day until victory was achieved.

ENGLAND

*A. C. MacLaren	run out	67	b Trumble	44	
T. Hayward	run out	90	b Trumble	47	
J. T. Tyldesley	c and b Trumble	0	run out	25	
G. L. Jessop	c Trumper b Trumble	1	(5)b Trumble	16	
†A. A. Lilley	lbw b Trumble	10	(7)b McLeod	21	
W. G. Quaife	c Kelly b Howell	68	(4)lbw b Trumble	44	
L. C. Braund	not out	103	(6)b Howell	17	
A. O. Jones	run out	5	c and b Trumble	11	
J. Gunn	b Noble	24	lbw b Trumble	5	
S. F. Barnes	c Hill b Noble	5	absent hurt	—	
C. Blythe	c Hill b Noble	2	(10)not out	10	
Extras	(b 9, w 1, nb 3)	13	(b 7)	7	
Total		**388**	**Total**	**247**	

AUSTRALIA

*J. Darling	c MacLaren b Blythe	1	(5)c Hayward b Jessop	69	
V. T. Trumper	run out	65	b Gunn	25	
C. Hill	c Tyldesley b Braund	98	b Jessop	97	
R. A. Duff	lbw b Braund	43	(1)hit wkt b Gunn	4	
S. E. Gregory	c Blythe b Braund	55	(4)c Braund b Gunn	23	
W. W. Armstrong	c and b Gunn	9	(8)not out	9	
H. Trumble	b Gunn	13	(6)not out	62	
W. P. Howell	c Braund b Gunn	3			
M. A. Noble	b Gunn	14	(7)run out	13	
†J. J. Kelly	not out	5			
C. E. McLeod	b Gunn	7			
Extras	(b 2, lb 6)	8	(b 9, lb 3, nb 1)	13	
Total		**321**	**Total** (6 wkts)	**315**	

FALL OF WICKETS

ENGLAND

Wkt	1st	2nd
1st	149	80
2nd	160	113
3rd	164	126
4th	171	144
5th	186	165
6th	294	204
7th	302	218
8th	371	224
9th	384	247
10th	388	—

AUSTRALIA

Wkt	1st	2nd
1st	2	5
2nd	138	50
3rd	197	98
4th	229	194
5th	260	255
6th	288	287
7th	289	—
8th	302	—
9th	309	—
10th	321	—

Umpires: R. W. Crockett, P. Argall

AUSTRALIA	1st Innings					2nd Innings			
	O	M	R	W		O	M	R	W
Trumble	65	23	124	3	..	44	18	74	6
Noble	26	10	58	3	..	21	7	72	0
Howell	36	10	82	1	..	27	9	54	1
Armstrong	18	5	45	0	..	5	0	9	0
Trumper	6	3	17	0					
McLeod	19	5	49	0	..	14	3	31	1

ENGLAND	1st Innings					2nd Innings			
	O	M	R	W		O	M	R	W
Braund	46	9	143	3	..	14	5	79	0
Blythe	11	3	54	1	..	23	16	66	0
Barnes	7	0	21	0	..				
Gunn	42	14	76	5	..	22	14	88	3
Jessop	7	0	19	0	..	13	9	41	2
Hayward					..	4	0	28	0

1901–02 Fourth Test, Sydney

February 14, 15, 17, 18
Toss: England   *Result:* Australia won by seven wickets

Darling relinquished the captaincy for business reasons and Hugh Trumble took over. England needed to win this match to square the series, and Barnes had a try-out in the nets before the start but pronounced himself unfit. MacLaren again won the toss, and he and Hayward gave England another splendid start. They were 68 for 0 at lunch, and with Tyldesley also playing beautifully England were 174 for 1 at tea. Then Quaife, who had batted solidly in the series so far, failed, Jessop was out first ball, and England ended the day with 6 wickets down for 266. Saunders, slow left-hand, playing in his first Test, took four of the first 5 wickets.

Next morning England took their score to 317, and then Jessop, bowling at his fastest, caused a collapse, three batsmen being brilliantly caught at slip; when he came off at 53 for 4 he had bowled 9 overs for 25 runs and taken all 4 wickets, and England had more than re-established the position their early batting had won for them. But Noble, Duff and Armstrong, batting in solid style, began a recovery, and although Jessop was brought back he could not recapture his early pace. England still held the upper hand, but when play ceased early through rain Australia had fought their way back to 148 for 5, Noble having batted 2 hours 24 minutes before reaching 50. England soon dismissed the two not out batsmen on the third morning, and at lunch Australia were 201 for 7, but the tail-enders hit out so successfully (Howell making 35 in 14 minutes) that Australia got within 18 runs of England's total.

After this turn of fortune the psychological advantage lay with Australia, and this perhaps is the explanation for England's otherwise unaccountable collapse on a good wicket, though they were subjected to a splendid piece of attacking out-cricket, Noble and Saunders bowling unchanged backed up by keen fielding and brilliant wicket-keeping. None of the England batsmen was able to break out of the stranglehold imposed by the Australian captain and his team, and at stumps on the third day England were 77 for 7. There was no recovery next morning, and the demoralised England side dropped many catches and fielded raggedly as Australia knocked off the 118 runs they needed to win for the loss of 3 wickets. England thus lost the rubber, together with their chance of regaining the Ashes. Saunders had match figures of 9 for 162, but was left out of the final Test.

ENGLAND

*A. C. MacLaren	c Duff b Saunders	92	c Kelly b Noble	5
T. Hayward	b Saunders	41	b Noble	12
J. T. Tyldesley	c Kelly b Noble	79	c Trumble b Saunders	10
W. G. Quaife	c Kelly b Saunders	4	lbw b Noble	15
G. L. Jessop	c Noble b Saunders	0	b Saunders	15
L. C. Braund	lbw b Trumble	17	b Saunders	0
C. P. McGahey	b Trumble	18	c Kelly b Saunders	13
†A. A. Lilley	c Kelly b Noble	40	c Trumble b Noble	0
A. O. Jones	c Kelly b Trumble	15	c Kelly b Noble	6
J. Gunn	not out	0	not out	13
C. Blythe	b Noble	4	c Kelly b Saunders	8
Extras	(lb 5, nb 2)	7	(lb 2)	2
Total		**317**	**Total**	**99**

AUSTRALIA

*H. Trumble	c MacLaren b Jessop	6		
V. T. Trumper	c Braund b Jessop	7	lbw b Blythe	25
C. Hill	c Jones b Jessop	21	c Lilley b Gunn	30
S. E. Gregory	c Braund b Jessop	5	(5)not out	12
M. A. Noble	lbw b Braund	56		
R. A. Duff	c Lilley b Blythe	39	(1)not out	51
W. W. Armstrong	b Braund	55		
A. J. Hopkins	c Lilley b Braund	43		
†J. J. Kelly	not out	24		
W. P. Howell	c MacLaren b Gunn	35	(4)c sub (H. G. Garnett) b Gunn	0
J. V. Saunders	b Braund	0		
Extras	(b 7, nb 1)	8	(lb 1, nb 2)	3
Total		**299**	**Total** (3 wkts)	**121**

FALL OF WICKETS

ENGLAND

Wkt	1st	2nd
1st	73	5
2nd	179	24
3rd	188	36
4th	188	57
5th	225	57
6th	245	57
7th	267	60
8th	312	78
9th	312	88
10th	317	99

AUSTRALIA

Wkt	1st	2nd
1st	7	50
2nd	18	105
3rd	30	105
4th	48	—
5th	119	—
6th	160	—
7th	205	—
8th	252	—
9th	288	—
10th	299	—

Umpires: R. Callaway, C. Bannerman

AUSTRALIA	1st Innings					2nd Innings			
	O	M	R	W		O	M	R	W
Noble	33·2	12	78	3	..	24	7	54	5
Saunders	43	11	119	4	..	24·1	8	43	5
Howell	22	10	40	0	..				
Trumble	38	18	65	3	..				
Armstrong	2	1	8	0	..				

ENGLAND	1st Innings					2nd Innings			
	O	M	R	W		O	M	R	W
Braund	60	25	118	4	..	15	2	55	0
Gunn	16	5	48	1	..	8·3	1	17	2
Jessop	26	5	68	4	..	7	0	23	0
Blythe	37	17	57	1	..	6	0	23	1

February 28, March 1, 3, 4
Toss: Australia   *Result:* Australia won by 32 runs

Australia were again without Darling, and they brought in Eady and Travers in place of Howell and Saunders. England fielded the same side as in the fourth Test. Barnes again had a try-out before the game but was still unfit. Winning the toss for the first time in the series, Australia batted first on a wicket which after heavy rain played in a peculiar fashion; although slow it gave some assistance to the bowlers. 98 for 3 at lunch, Australia were all out inside 2½ hours for 144. Then Jessop, opening with MacLaren, hit 35 of the first 50 in 20 minutes, and although a collapse followed England were 133 for 5 at the close. The wicket changed its mind next morning under the effects of the roller and played faster and better as the day progressed. Braund and Lilley took their unbroken stand to 68, and England eventually totalled 189, giving them a useful lead of 45.

Australia, making up the deficit with one wicket down, were 128 for 2 at tea, a stylish and vigorous innings by Hill (who was missed twice by Lilley), with useful support from Gregory, taking them into the lead. The England bowlers, however, kept the score within bounds, and at stumps Australia had been held to a lead of 181 with 4 wickets to fall. On the third morning only 29 runs were added, so England were left with 211 to win.

Heavy showers that morning further affected the wicket, and there were more interruptions for rain during the day; but MacLaren and Hayward made a steady start, and when play was finally curtailed England, at 87 for 3, wanted 124 to win. The ball was now apt to kick off a length, however, and the outfield was dead, so England clearly faced a difficult task. On the last morning Jessop was caught at cover first ball, and wickets fell regularly until England, at 120 for 7, were still 90 behind. But Tyldesley was still there and batting well, as always when conditions favoured the bowlers, and he and Jones kept hope alive by adding 37 for the 8th wicket. When the last man joined Tyldesley 50 were still wanted; 17 of them were tensely made before Tyldesley was out.

Apart from 2 overs from Eady, Noble and Trumble bowled unchanged. They were helped by the wicket, and England were unlucky, but in the last resort it had again been the batting that failed. Australia thus won the rubber deservedly by four matches to one.

AUSTRALIA

Batsman	Dismissal 1st	Runs	Dismissal 2nd	Runs
V. T. Trumper	b Blythe	27	c McGahey b Braund	18
R. A. Duff	b Braund	10	c and b Braund	28
C. Hill	c Jones b Gunn	28	c Lilley b Hayward	87
S. E. Gregory	c Jones b Gunn	25	b Gunn	41
M. A. Noble	lbw b Hayward	7	c MacLaren b Gunn	16
*H. Trumble	c Quaife b Hayward	3	(7)b Blythe	22
W. W. Armstrong	not out	17	(6)lbw b Braund	20
A. J. Hopkins	c Lilley b Hayward	4	c MacLaren b Blythe	0
†J. J. Kelly	c Gunn b Hayward	0	not out	11
C. J. Eady	b Gunn	5	c Gunn b Braund	3
J. Travers	c Braund b Gunn	9	c and b Braund	1
Extras	(b 7, w 1, nb 1)	9	(b 3, lb 1, nb 4)	8
Total		**144**		**255**

ENGLAND

Batsman	Dismissal 1st	Runs	Dismissal 2nd	Runs
*A. C. MacLaren	c and b Trumble	25	run out	49
G. L. Jessop	c Hopkins b Trumble	35	(4)c Trumper b Trumble	16
W. G. Quaife	c Trumble b Noble	3	lbw b Noble	4
J. T. Tyldesley	c Kelly b Eady	13	(5)c Eady b Trumble	36
T. Hayward	c Trumper b Travers	19	(2)c Travers b Trumble	15
L. C. Braund	c Hopkins b Trumble	32	c Hill b Noble	2
†A. A. Lilley	c Eady b Trumble	41	c Duff b Noble	9
C. P. McGahey	b Trumble	0	c Hill b Noble	7
A. O. Jones	c Kelly b Eady	10	c and b Noble	28
J. Gunn	lbw b Eady	8	c Hill b Noble	4
C. Blythe	not out	0	not out	5
Extras	(b 1, lb 2)	3	(lb 2, nb 1)	3
Total		**189**		**178**

FALL OF WICKETS

AUSTRALIA

Wkt	1st	2nd
1st	16	30
2nd	54	52
3rd	81	131
4th	98	149
5th	104	208
6th	108	224
7th	112	249
8th	112	249
9th	124	255
10th	144	255

ENGLAND

Wkt	1st	2nd
1st	50	40
2nd	62	64
3rd	64	87
4th	91	87
5th	96	93
6th	164	104
7th	168	120
8th	173	157
9th	186	161
10th	189	178

Umpires: C. Bannerman, R. W. Crockett

ENGLAND	1st Innings O	M	R	W	2nd Innings O	M	R	W
Jessop	1	0	13	0				
Braund	10	2	33	1	26·1	4	95	5
Blythe	9	2	29	1	13	3	36	2
Hayward	16	9	22	4	22	4	63	1
Gunn	17	6	38	4	28	11	53	2

AUSTRALIA	1st Innings O	M	R	W	2nd Innings O	M	R	W
Noble	26	4	80	1	33	4	98	6
Trumble	25	4	62	5	30·3	7	64	3
Travers	8	2	14	1				
Eady	8·3	2	30	3	2	0	13	0

Averages: 1901-02

AUSTRALIA

BATTING	M.	Inns.	N.O.	Runs	H.S.	Av.
W. W. Armstrong	4	7	4	159	55*	53·00
C. Hill	5	10	0	521	99	52·10
R. A. Duff	4	8	1	311	104	44·42
S. E. Gregory	5	10	1	269	55	29·88
J. Darling	3	6	0	154	69	25·66
H. Trumble	5	9	2	169	62*	24·14
V. T. Trumper	5	10	0	219	65	21·90
A. J. Hopkins	2	3	0	47	43	15·66
M. A. Noble	5	9	0	138	56	15·33
W. P. Howell	4	7	1	79	35	13·16
J. J. Kelly	5	8	3	60	24*	12·00
E. Jones	2	4	0	26	14	6·50
C. E. McLeod	2	3	0	7	7	2·33

PLAYED IN ONE TEST: F. Laver 6 and 0, J. V. Saunders 0, C. J. Eady 5 and 3, J. Travers 9 and 1.

BOWLING	Overs	Mds.	Runs	Wkts.	Av.
J. V. Saunders	67·1	19	162	9	18·00
M. A. Noble	230	68	608	32	19·00
H. Trumble	267·2	93	561	28	20·03
C. E. McLeod	77	25	164	5	32·80

ALSO BOWLED: J. Travers 8–2–14–1, C. J. Eady 10·3–2–43–3, F. Laver 17–6–39–2, W. P. Howell 121–43–251–3, E. Jones 48–10–131–1, V. T. Trumper 9–5–18–0, W. W. Armstrong 27–7–65–0.

ENGLAND

BATTING	M.	Inns.	N.O.	Runs	H.S.	Av.
A. C. MacLaren	5	9	0	412	116	45·77
L. C. Braund	5	9	2	256	103*	36·57
T. W. Hayward	5	9	0	305	90	33·88
J. T. Tyldesley	5	9	0	232	79	25·77
A. A. Lilley	5	9	0	211	84	23·44
W. G. Quaife	5	9	0	184	68	20·44
G. L. Jessop	5	9	0	166	35	18·44
J. Gunn	5	9	2	77	24	11·00
S. F. Barnes	3	4	1	32	26*	10·66
C. Blythe	5	9	4	53	20	10·60
A. O. Jones	5	9	0	90	28	10·00
C. P. McGahey	2	4	0	38	18	9·50

BOWLING	Overs	Mds.	Runs	Wkts.	Av.
S. F. Barnes	138·2	33	323	19	17·00
J. Gunn	144·3	52	360	17	21·17
T. W. Hayward	42	13	113	5	22·60
C. Blythe	175	63	470	18	26·11
G. L. Jessop	56	14	177	6	29·50
L. C. Braund	268·1	76	738	21	35·14

ALSO BOWLED: A. O. Jones 1–0–2–0.

Averages: 1902

ENGLAND

BATTING	M.	Inns.	N.O.	Runs	H.S.	Av.
W. Rhodes	5	7	6	67	38*	67·00
Hon. F. S. Jackson	5	8	1	311	128	44·42
G. H. Hirst	4	5	1	157	58*	39·25
G. L. Jessop	4	5	0	190	104	38·00
J. T. Tyldesley	5	7	0	245	138	35·00
A. C. MacLaren	5	8	1	198	63	28·28
W. H. Lockwood	4	5	1	86	52*	21·50
R. Abel	2	4	0	73	38	18·25
L. C. Braund	5	7	0	115	65	16·42
L. C. H. Palairet	2	4	0	49	20	12·25
A. A. Lilley	5	7	0	46	16	6·57
K. S. Ranjitsinhji	3	4	0	19	13	4·75
C. B. Fry	3	4	0	5	4	1·25

PLAYED IN ONE TEST: F. W. Tate 5* and 4, T. W. Hayward 0 and 7, S. F. Barnes 7 and 5.

BOWLING	Overs	Mds.	Runs	Wkts.	Av.
W. H. Lockwood	81·1	18	206	17	12·11
S. F. Barnes	32	13	99	7	14·14
W. Rhodes	140·5	38	336	22	15·27
G. H. Hirst	79	18	208	9	23·11
L. C. Braund	76·5	13	210	7	30·00
Hon. F. S. Jackson	61·1	12	209	6	34·83

ALSO BOWLED: F. W. Tate 16–4–51–2, G. L. Jessop 10–2–26–0.

AUSTRALIA

BATTING	M.	Inns.	N.O.	Runs	H.S.	Av.
C. Hill	5	8	1	258	119	36·85
V. T. Trumper	5	8	0	247	104	30·87
H. Trumble	3	6	2	107	64*	26·75
A. J. Hopkins	5	7	1	117	40*	19·50
M. A. Noble	5	7	0	129	52	18·42
R. A. Duff	5	8	0	129	54	16·12
J. Darling	5	7	0	109	51	15·57
S. E. Gregory	5	8	1	100	29	14·28
W. W. Armstrong	5	7	0	97	26	13·85
J. J. Kelly	5	7	3	46	39	11·50
J. V. Saunders	4	6	1	6	3	1·20
E. Jones	2	1	0	0	0	0·00

PLAYED IN ONE TEST: W. P. Howell 0.

BOWLING	Overs	Mds.	Runs	Wkts.	Av.
H. Trumble	172·4	55	371	26	14·26
M. A. Noble	127	41	307	14	21·92
J. V. Saunders	131·1	23	473	18	26·27

ALSO BOWLED: A. J. Hopkins 17–5–49–2, E. Jones 39–13–107–3, V. T. Trumper 37–11–101–2, W. P. Howell 26–8–58–1, W. W. Armstrong 44–10–123–2.

1902 First Test, Edgbaston

Test no. 62

May 29, 30, 31
Toss: England *Result:* Drawn

Despite great performances by England in the last two Tests, Australia, who won on their merits at Sheffield and kept their heads at Old Trafford, retained the Ashes. They were lucky, though to escape the full consequences of losing the toss at Birmingham; and the luck stayed with them at Sheffield and Old Trafford, and even for a time at the Oval. The appointed England selectors, Lord Hawke, Gregor MacGregor and H. W. Bainbridge, who co-opted the captain and various others to help them, came in for much criticism, but their work, taking account of injuries and form, bears the closest inspection.

England began the first morning by losing 3 wickets for 35, but by lunch-time Jackson and Tyldesley had taken the score to 99 without further loss. Jackson was out at 112, and Lilley soon followed, so that England were 121 for 5, but Hirst then joined Tyldesley in a stand of 91 which set England on the road to a substantial score. Without Trumble (injured) the Australian bowling looked undistinguished and lacking in variety on an easy wicket, Jones having lost much of his pace,

and England were able to complete an impressive recovery. Tyldesley, badly missed when 43, played an otherwise splendid innings, his off-side play being especially fine, and at stumps England had reached 351 for 9.

Play did not start on the second day until 2.45 because of the state of the ground after heavy rain, and Lockwood and Rhodes then continued their unbroken last-wicket stand, the declaration not coming until 3.40. MacLaren, with less than a day and a half to get the Australians out twice, was presumably waiting for the pitch to start drying. In the event he judged his declaration beautifully, Australia being dismissed in 85 minutes for 36, their lowest score in Tests. Apart from one over from Braund to enable them to change ends, Hirst and Rhodes bowled throughout. Unable to get at Hirst, the Australians tried to hit Rhodes, with disastrous results, Trumper alone staying long.

Australia followed on, but bad light soon stopped play for the day, and only 75 minutes' cricket was possible on the third day, in which Australia comfortably saved the game.

ENGLAND

*A. C. MacLaren	run out	9
C. B. Fry	c Kelly b Jones	0
K. S. Ranjitsinhji	b Armstrong	13
Hon. F. S. Jackson	b Jones	53
J. T. Tyldesley	lbw b Howell	138
†A. A. Lilley	c Jones b Noble	2
G. H. Hirst	c Armstrong b Trumper	48
G. L. Jessop	c Hopkins b Trumper	6
L. C. Braund	b Jones	14
W. H. Lockwood	not out	52
W. Rhodes	not out	38
Extras	(lb 3)	3
Total	(9 wkts dec)	**376**

AUSTRALIA

V. T. Trumper	b Hirst	18	c Braund b Rhodes	14
R. A. Duff	c Jessop b Rhodes	2	c Fry b Braund	15
C. Hill	c Braund b Hirst	1	not out	10
S. E. Gregory	lbw b Hirst	0	not out	1
*J. Darling	c Jessop b Rhodes	3		
M. A. Noble	st Lilley b Rhodes	3		
W. W. Armstrong	c Lilley b Rhodes	0		
A. J. Hopkins	c Lilley b Rhodes	5		
†J. J. Kelly	not out	1		
E. Jones	c Jackson b Rhodes	0		
W. P. Howell	c Fry b Rhodes	0		
Extras	(b 3)	3	(lb 4, w 1, nb 1)	6
Total		**36**	**Total** (2 wkts)	**46**

FALL OF WICKETS

	ENGLAND	
Wkt	1st	2nd
1st	5	—
2nd	13	—
3rd	35	—
4th	112	—
5th	121	—
6th	212	—
7th	230	—
8th	264	—
9th	295	—
10th	—	—

	AUSTRALIA	
Wkt	1st	2nd
1st	9	16
2nd	10	41
3rd	14	—
4th	17	—
5th	25	—
6th	25	—
7th	31	—
8th	35	—
9th	35	—
10th	36	—

Umpires: J. Phillips, W. Hearn

AUSTRALIA	1st Innings				2nd Innings			
	O	M	R	W	O	M	R	W
Jones	28	9	76	3	..			
Noble	44	15	112	1	..			
Trumper	13	5	35	2	..			
Armstrong	25	6	64	1	..			
Howell	26	8	58	1	..			
Hopkins	6	2	28	0	..			

ENGLAND	1st Innings				2nd Innings			
	O	M	R	W	O	M	R	W
Hirst	11	4	15	3	..	9	6	10	0
Rhodes	11	3	17	7	..	10	5	9	1
Braund	1	0	1	0	..	5	0	14	1
Jackson					..	4	2	7	0

89

1902 Second Test, Lord's

June 12, 13, 14
Toss: England   *Result:* Match Drawn

England fielded the same side as at Birmingham, but Australia were still without Trumble, also Howell, while Darling and Noble had barely recovered from influenza, and Saunders had tonsilitis. As only 14 men had come on the tour there was a move to postpone the match, but it came to nothing.

In appalling weather that would have been more seasonable in January than June, spectators shivered in greatcoats waiting for play to start on the first day after heavy rain. Lunch was taken first, and when play eventually began at 2.45 England lost 2 wickets for no runs. The wicket was too slow for Jones, but Hopkins, a useful all-rounder who played 17 times against England without doing anything outstanding, and who in the previous match had taken 7 for 10 against the University at Cambridge, had Fry caught at short leg in his first over to what *Wisden* called 'a deplorable stroke' and bowled Ranji off his pads in his second. Rain then interrupted play with England 0 for 2. On the resumption Jackson, whose resistance at Birmingham on the first morning had laid the foundations of the England recovery, joined MacLaren, and after scoring a single he offered a sharp chance in the slips which if taken would have made the scoreboard read 1-3-1. From this point on Jackson's wonderful nerve and self-reliance were instrumental with MacLaren in reviving England's fortunes. Hopkins could not repeat his Cambridge success after all, and the other Australian bowlers were steadily mastered.

Rain intervened after England had been batting for 105 minutes, and the remaining two days were washed out altogether. This was the fifth consecutive drawn Test Match in England, but the general demand for more time to be allocated to these games had to be weighed against the serious interference with the county championship that would result. For Australia, deprived of two of their best bowlers, and with three other players below par, the rain, as in the first Test, was a fortunate circumstance.

ENGLAND

*A. C. MacLaren......	not out..................	47
C. B. Fry...........	c Hill b Hopkins..........	0
K. S. Ranjitsinhji.....	b Hopkins................	0
Hon. F. S. Jackson....	not out..................	55
Total...........	(2 wkts)..................	**102**

Did not bat: J. T. Tyldesley, †A. A. Lilley, G. H. Hirst, G. L. Jessop, L.C. Braund, W. H. Lockwood and W. Rhodes.

AUSTRALIA

V. T. Trumper, R. A. Duff, A. J. Hopkins, C. Hill, S. E. Gregory, *J. Darling, M. A. Noble, W. W. Armstrong, †J. J. Kelly, E. Jones and J. V. Saunders.

AUSTRALIA	*1st Innings*			
	O	M	R	W
Jones............	11	4	31	0
Hopkins.........	9	3	18	2
Saunders........	3	0	15	0
Trumper.........	8	1	33	0
Armstrong.......	5	0	5	0
Noble..........	2	2	0	0

FALL OF WICKETS
ENGLAND

Wkt	1st
1st	0
2nd	0

Umpires: V. A. Titchmarsh, C. E. Richardson

62. G. L. Jessop

61. (left) C. Hill

63. Australia 1902
Back row: J. J. Kelly, J. V. Saunders, H. Trumble, W. W. Armstrong, M. A. Noble, W. P. Howell, B. J. Wardill (manager).
Middle row: C. Hill, R. A. Duff, J. Darling (capt.), V. T. Trumper, E. Jones. *Front:* A. J. Hopkins, H. Carter, S. E. Gregory.

1902 Third Test, Sheffield

July 3, 4, 5
Toss: Australia   *Result:* Australia won by 143 runs

Australia for the first time were at full strength, while for England Barnes replaced Lockwood, who was out of form, and Abel, originally chosen to replace Fry, came in for the injured Ranji. This was the first and only Test Match between England and Australia played at Sheffield. The light for much of the game was appalling, the Sheffield smoke-stacks contributing their quota to the haze, but it did not prevent a fine piece of aggression by Trumper and Hill in the Australian second innings from deciding the issue.

Hirst and Braund opened the bowling for England, and Trumper was out in Braund's first over, which justified the captain's choice of bowlers; but when Barnes came on at 38 he took the wickets of the left-handers Hill and Darling in his first over, and when he got Duff caught behind 13 runs later he had taken 3 for 3 in 7 overs in his first spell in Test cricket in England. In addition, Gregory and Noble were both missed off his bowling, but at lunch England were well content to have Australia 98 for 5. The England attack looked formidable, but against this powerful array of bowlers Australia eventually reached 194.

England passed 100 with only 2 men out, but in a disastrous few minutes before bad light finally stopped play towards the end of the day they lost another 3 wickets and were 102 for 5 at the close. There was some rain in the night, and on a slowish wicket Noble and Saunders bowled well next day and England were all out in 45 minutes for 145, 49 behind.

The powerful England attack was now swept aside in a great innings by Trumper, who hit 62 out of 80 in 50 minutes, and after Barnes got Darling for a 'pair', Hill and Gregory put on 107 in 65 minutes, of which Hill's share was 77. Missed twice in the 70s, Hill reached his hundred in 1 hour 55 minutes. After he left, Hopkins and Armstrong again made useful scores and England faced a fourth innings target of 339.

Thanks to Jessop England had 50 up in half an hour and were 73 for 1 when bad light again stopped play, and next morning MacLaren and Jackson added 64 in less than an hour, but Noble's medium-pace break-backs on a wearing wicket eventually decided the issue.

AUSTRALIA

V. T. Trumper	b Braund	1	c Lilley b Jackson	62	
R. A. Duff	c Lilley b Barnes	25	c Hirst b Rhodes	1	
C. Hill	c Rhodes b Barnes	18	c MacLaren b Jackson	119	
*J. Darling	c Braund b Barnes	0	c Braund b Barnes	0	
S. E. Gregory	c Abel b Barnes	11	run out	29	
M. A. Noble	c Braund b Rhodes	47	b Jackson	8	
A. J. Hopkins	c Braund b Barnes	27	not out	40	
W. W. Armstrong	c and b Braund	25	b Rhodes	26	
†J. J. Kelly	b Barnes	0	c Hirst b Rhodes	0	
H. Trumble	c and b Jackson	32	b Rhodes	0	
J. V. Saunders	not out	0	b Rhodes	1	
Extras	(b 3, lb 5)	8	(lb 3)	3	
Total		**194**	**Total**	**289**	

ENGLAND

*A. C. MacLaren	b Noble	31	(4) c Trumper b Noble	63	
R. Abel	b Noble	38	c Hill b Noble	8	
J. T. Tyldesley	c Armstrong b Noble	22	b Trumble	14	
Hon. F. S. Jackson	c Gregory b Saunders	3	(6) b Noble	14	
C. B. Fry	st Kelly b Saunders	1	lbw b Trumble	4	
†A. A. Lilley	b Noble	8	(7) b Noble	9	
L. C. Braund	st Kelly b Saunders	0	(8) c Armstrong b Noble	9	
G. H. Hirst	c Trumble b Saunders	8	(9) b Noble	0	
G. L. Jessop	c Saunders b Noble	12	(1) lbw b Trumble	55	
W. Rhodes	not out	7	not out	7	
S. F. Barnes	c Darling b Saunders	7	b Trumble	5	
Extras	(b 4, lb 3, nb 1)	8	(b 4, lb 1, w 1, nb 1)	7	
Total		**145**	**Total**	**195**	

FALL OF WICKETS

AUSTRALIA

Wkt	1st	2nd
1st	3	20
2nd	39	80
3rd	39	80
4th	52	187
5th	73	214
6th	127	225
7th	137	277
8th	137	287
9th	194	287
10th	194	289

ENGLAND

Wkt	1st	2nd
1st	61	14
2nd	86	75
3rd	101	84
4th	101	98
5th	102	162
6th	106	165
7th	110	174
8th	130	174
9th	131	186
10th	145	195

Umpires: J. Phillips,
W. Richards

ENGLAND	1st Innings					2nd Innings			
	O	M	R	W		O	M	R	W
Hirst	15	1	59	0		10	1	40	0
Braund	13	4	34	2		12	0	58	0
Barnes	20	9	49	6		12	4	50	1
Jackson	5·1	1	11	1		17	2	60	3
Rhodes	13	3	33	1		17·1	3	63	5
Jessop						4	0	15	0

AUSTRALIA	1st Innings					2nd Innings			
	O	M	R	W		O	M	R	W
Trumble	18	10	21	0		21·5	3	49	4
Saunders	15·3	4	50	5		12	0	68	0
Trumper	4	1	8	0		6	0	19	0
Noble	19	6	51	5		21	4	52	6
Armstrong	5	2	7	0					

1902 Fourth Test, Old Trafford

July 24, 25, 26
Toss: Australia   *Result:* Australia won by 3 runs

That England came as near as they did to winning this match must be accounted one of the more remarkable feats of Test cricket. Winning the toss, Australia took full advantage of their good fortune. The ground was saturated, the wicket was slow and easy, and the run-ups were so greasy that Lockwood, back in the side for Barnes, was unable to bowl for over an hour. Both Trumper and Duff set a terrific pace, Trumper reached his hundred in just over 100 minutes out of 168, and the lunch score, after a delayed start, was 173 for 1. Then, before the afternoon sun had affected the surface, Hill and Darling put on 71, Darling twice hitting the ball out of the ground.

When England batted on a deteriorating wicket they were soon in trouble against Saunders and Trumble, but Jackson and Braund, coming together at 44 for 5, somehow survived until the close, when England were 70 for 5. The second day was one of England's greatest days. Jackson and Braund were not separated until they had added 141 in 2 hours, and Jackson, who was 77 when Braund was out, gained useful help from the tail-enders and was last out at 262, having batted 4¼ hours.

When Australia went in again at 4.15 with a lead of only 37 they were soon 10 for 3, and the crowd sensed an England victory. The score was still only 16 when Darling was missed on the square-leg boundary by Tate, who had come into the side at the last moment in preference to Hirst. Tate made some amends later by getting Gregory lbw, but by then the score had been advanced to 64. It was a crucial stand, in a fiercely partisan atmosphere, against a side poised for the kill; and when Gregory and Darling were out the side slid to 85 for 8 at stumps. Only one run was added next morning, leaving England 124 to win.

The wicket was still difficult, but MacLaren and Palairet knocked off 36 of the runs before lunch without being separated. After lunch Darling threw everything into the attack in a final gamble to snatch victory, and as rain threatened and twice drove the players off England advanced shakily towards their target, shedding batsmen at regular intervals on the way. The last pair were together with 8 wanted when rain again drove the players off. When they returned 45 minutes later, Tate hit Saunders for 4 and was then clean bowled.

Tate was not among those originally selected but it was announced the night before the game that he had been asked to attend. According to Fry, MacLaren chose Tate in preference to Hirst out of pique with Lord Hawke, who had refused to make Schofield Haigh available. But on the saturated wickets of 1902 Tate was having a great season.

AUSTRALIA

V. T. Trumper	c Lilley b Rhodes	104	c Braund b Lockwood	4	
R. A. Duff	c Lilley b Lockwood	54	b Lockwood	3	
C. Hill	c Rhodes b Lockwood	65	b Lockwood	0	
M. A. Noble	c and b Rhodes	2	(6)c Lilley b Lockwood	4	
S. E. Gregory	c Lilley b Rhodes	3	lbw b Tate	24	
*J. Darling	c MacLaren b Rhodes	51	(4)c Palairet b Rhodes	37	
A. J. Hopkins	c Palairet b Lockwood	0	c Tate b Lockwood	2	
W. W. Armstrong	b Lockwood	5	b Rhodes	3	
†J. J. Kelly	not out	4	not out	2	
H. Trumble	c Tate b Lockwood	0	lbw b Tate	4	
J. V. Saunders	b Lockwood	3	c Tyldesley b Rhodes	0	
Extras	(b 5, lb 2, w 1)	8	(b 1, lb 1, nb 1)	3	
Total		**299**	**Total**	**86**	

ENGLAND

L. C. H. Palairet	c Noble b Saunders	6	b Saunders	17	
R. Abel	c Armstrong b Saunders	6	(5)b Trumble	21	
J. T. Tyldesley	c Hopkins b Saunders	22	c Armstrong b Saunders	16	
*A. C. MacLaren	b Trumble	1	(2)c Duff b Trumble	35	
K. S. Ranjitsinhji	lbw b Trumble	2	(4)lbw b Trumble	4	
Hon. F. S. Jackson	c Duff b Trumble	128	c Gregory b Saunders	7	
L. C. Braund	b Noble	65	st Kelly b Trumble	3	
†A. A. Lilley	b Noble	7	c Hill b Trumble	4	
W. H. Lockwood	run out	7	b Trumble	0	
W. Rhodes	c and b Trumble	5	not out	4	
F. W. Tate	not out	5	b Saunders	4	
Extras	(b 6, lb 2)	8	(b 5)	5	
Total		**262**	**Total**	**120**	

FALL OF WICKETS

AUSTRALIA

Wkt	1st	2nd
1st	135	7
2nd	175	9
3rd	179	10
4th	183	64
5th	256	74
6th	256	76
7th	288	77
8th	292	79
9th	292	85
10th	299	86

ENGLAND

Wkt	1st	2nd
1st	12	44
2nd	13	68
3rd	14	72
4th	30	92
5th	44	97
6th	185	107
7th	203	109
8th	214	109
9th	235	116
10th	262	120

Umpires: J. Moss,
T. Mycroft

ENGLAND

	1st Innings				2nd Innings			
	O	M	R	W	O	M	R	W
Rhodes	25	3	104	4	14·4	5	26	3
Jackson	11	0	58	0				
Tate	11	1	44	0	5	3	7	2
Braund	9	0	37	0	11	3	22	0
Lockwood	20·1	5	48	6	17	5	28	5

AUSTRALIA

	1st Innings				2nd Innings			
	O	M	R	W	O	M	R	W
Trumble	43	16	75	4	25	9	53	6
Saunders	34	5	104	3	19·4	4	52	4
Noble	24	8	47	2	5	3	10	0
Trumper	6	4	6	0				
Armstrong	5	2	19	0				
Hopkins	2	0	3	0				

1902 Fifth Test, Oval

August 11, 12, 13
Toss: Australia *Result:* England won by one wicket

Jessop and Hirst were recalled for the final Test, to the exclusion of Ranji and Tate, and Hayward replaced Abel. Australia, having retained the Ashes and made certain of the rubber for the fourth series running, were again unchanged.

There had been a lot of rain, but a cold wind and no sun meant an easy wicket. Trumper as usual was away to a flying start and 45 runs came in the first half-hour, but the strong England attack pegged the Australians back and at lunch they were 107 for 4. When Hirst bowled Gregory after lunch he had taken all 5 wickets, but then Noble held the side together with a sound innings. At 175 for 7 England were still doing well, but Hopkins, Trumble and Kelly pulled the game round for their side, adding 81 for the 8th wicket and 68 for the 9th, and Australia totalled 324.

Rain in the night greatly enhanced the value of this score, and England had sunk to 94 for 6 at lunch. The wicket improved afterwards, and Hirst and Braund took their 7th wicket stand to 54, of which Hirst made 43, but when Lockwood joined Braund at 137 for 7, 38 were still needed to save the follow on. These runs were likely to be crucial, as the sun was coming out and it could not be long before the wicket responded. Soon afterwards Lockwood was missed by Hill

in the deep: if Tate's miss let Australia back into the fourth Test, Hill's gave England a chance in the fifth. The follow on was saved, and Australia had to bat when the wicket deteriorated; but with a lead of 141 they looked safe. Trumper quickly ran himself out, and none of the Australians batted with any confidence, even Hill being below his best. 114 for 8 at the close, Australia were soon all out on the third morning, leaving England 263 to win.

10 for 3 and 48 for 5, England seemed in a hopeless position; but at this point Jessop joined Jackson. Missed twice before lunch, Jessop launched a ferocious attack afterwards, and when Jackson was out Jessop found another unruffled partner in Hirst. He completed an astonishing hundred in 75 minutes, still the fastest century in these matches, but 76 were still wanted with only 3 wickets to go when he was out. Lockwood and Lilley between them helped Hirst to narrow the gap to 15, and then Hirst and Rhodes coolly knocked off the runs. Darling was criticised afterwards for over-bowling Trumble and Saunders; Trumble bowled unchanged throughout the match and took 12 for 173. Those who had kept their faith in Jessop despite his many failures were at last vindicated.

AUSTRALIA

V. T. Trumper	b Hirst	42	run out	2	
R. A. Duff	c Lilley b Hirst	23	b Lockwood	6	
C. Hill	b Hirst	11	c MacLaren b Hirst	34	
*J. Darling	c Lilley b Hirst	3	c MacLaren b Lockwood	15	
M. A. Noble	c and b Jackson	52	b Braund	13	
S. E. Gregory	b Hirst	23	b Braund	9	
W. W. Armstrong	b Jackson	17	b Lockwood	21	
A. J. Hopkins	c MacLaren b Lockwood	40	c Lilley b Lockwood	3	
H. Trumble	not out	64	(10)not out	7	
†J. J. Kelly	c Rhodes b Braund	39	(11)lbw b Lockwood	0	
J. V. Saunders	lbw b Braund	0	(9)c Tyldesley b Rhodes	2	
Extras	(b 5, lb 3, nb 2)	10	(b 7, lb 2)	9	
Total		**324**	**Total**	**121**	

ENGLAND

*A. C. MacLaren	c Armstrong b Trumble	10	b Saunders	2	
L. C. H. Palairet	b Trumble	20	b Saunders	6	
J. T. Tyldesley	b Trumble	33	b Saunders	0	
T. Hayward	b Trumble	0	c Kelly b Saunders	7	
Hon. F. S. Jackson	c Armstrong b Saunders	2	c and b Trumble	49	
L. C. Braund	c Hill b Trumble	22	c Kelly b Trumble	2	
G. L. Jessop	b Trumble	13	c Noble b Armstrong	104	
G. H. Hirst	c and b Trumble	43	not out	58	
W. H. Lockwood	c Noble b Saunders	25	lbw b Trumble	2	
†A. A. Lilley	c Trumper b Trumble	0	c Darling b Trumble	16	
W. Rhodes	not out	0	not out	6	
Extras	(b 13, lb 2)	15	(b 5, lb 6)	11	
Total		**183**	**Total** (9 wkts)	**263**	

FALL OF WICKETS
AUSTRALIA

Wkt	1st	2nd
1st	47	6
2nd	63	9
3rd	69	31
4th	82	71
5th	126	75
6th	174	91
7th	175	99
8th	256	114
9th	324	115
10th	324	121

ENGLAND

Wkt	1st	2nd
1st	31	5
2nd	36	5
3rd	62	10
4th	67	31
5th	67	48
6th	83	157
7th	137	187
8th	179	214
9th	183	248
10th	183	—

Umpires: C. E. Richardson, A. A. White

ENGLAND	1st Innings				2nd Innings			
	O	M	R	W	O	M	R	W
Lockwood	24	2	85	1	20	6	45	5
Rhodes	28	9	46	0	22	7	38	1
Hirst	29	5	77	5	5	1	7	1
Braund	16·5	5	29	2	9	1	15	2
Jackson	20	4	66	2	4	3	7	0
Jessop	6	2	11	0				

AUSTRALIA	1st Innings				2nd Innings			
	O	M	R	W	O	M	R	W
Trumble	31	13	65	8	33·5	4	108	4
Saunders	23	7	79	2	24	3	105	4
Noble	7	3	24	0	5	0	11	0
Armstrong					4	0	28	1

1903-04 First Test, Sydney

Test no. 67

December 11, 12, 14, 15, 16, 17
Toss: Australia   *Result:* England won by five wickets

England had lost four consecutive series, and no doubt this helped to stimulate the MCC into selecting and managing an Australian tour for the first time. Setting the two Melbourne games aside, where winning the toss meant winning the match, England came out with a strong advantage. With Fry, MacLaren and Jackson absent, Australia inevitably had the edge in batting; in Trumper they had the best batsman and in Noble the best all-rounder; but they had no fast bowler until Cotter appeared, and they could not match the variety of the England attack.

A fine opening spell by Arnold and Hirst on a fast wicket set Australia back to 12 for 3, but Noble and Armstrong added 106, and when Armstrong left Hopkins supported Noble in a fifth wicket stand of 82. Noble himself, after a cautious start, scored freely and gave no chance; he batted 4 hours 40 minutes in his only century for Australia. An overnight thunderstorm damaged the pitch, Australia went from 259 for 7 to 285 all out next morning, and England got away to a bad start. But Tyldesley, strong on the leg side and playing a succession of glorious off-drives, led a recovery, and at the close England were 243 for 4, Foster not out 73, Braund not out 67. Foster at this stage had batted nearly 3 hours; he had looked very uncertain at first, and had

been missed off Saunders at mid off when 51. But next morning, in the second phase of his innings, with the wicket playing faster, he batted more surely, reaching his hundred just ahead of Braund. England then lost several wickets cheaply, and soon after lunch they were 332 for 8. Partnered by Relf, Foster then embarked on the third phase of his innings. He made 94 between lunch and tea, and when Relf left at 447 he and Rhodes put on a record 130 for the last wicket in 66 minutes.

England led by 292, but a wonderful second innings fight-back by Australia, in which Trumper played perhaps his greatest innings, out-shining even Foster, nearly turned the game. Trumper reached his hundred in 94 minutes and went on to make 185, and England were set 194 to win. They faltered to 82 for 4, and Hirst was dropped before he had scored, but a patient knock by Hayward, with fine support from Hirst, saw them home.

When Hill was run out in the Australian second innings a section of the crowd demonstrated against umpire Crockett, and only a personal appeal from Noble dissuaded Warner from withdrawing his team.

AUSTRALIA

Batsman	Dismissal 1st	Score	Dismissal 2nd	Score
R. A. Duff	c Lilley b Arnold	3	(3)c Relf b Rhodes	84
V. T. Trumper	c Foster b Arnold	1	(5)not out	185
C. Hill	c Lilley b Hirst	5	(4)run out	51
*M. A. Noble	c Foster b Arnold	133	(6)st Lilley b Bosanquet	22
W. W. Armstrong	b Bosanquet	48	(7)c Bosanquet b Rhodes	27
A. J. Hopkins	b Hirst	39	(8)c Arnold b Rhodes	20
W. P. Howell	c Relf b Arnold	5	(10)c Lilley b Arnold	4
S. E. Gregory	b Bosanquet	23	(1)c Lilley b Rhodes	43
F. Laver	lbw b Rhodes	4	c Relf b Rhodes	6
†J. J. Kelly	c Braund b Rhodes	10	(2)b Arnold	13
J. V. Saunders	not out	11	run out	2
Extras	(nb 3)	3	(b 10, lb 15, w 2, nb 1)	28
Total		**285**	**Total**	**485**

ENGLAND

Batsman	Dismissal 1st	Score	Dismissal 2nd	Score
T. Hayward	b Howell	15	st Kelly b Saunders	91
*P. F. Warner	c Kelly b Laver	0	b Howell	8
J. T. Tyldesley	b Noble	53	c Noble b Saunders	9
E. G. Arnold	c Laver b Armstrong	27		
R. E. Foster	c Noble b Saunders	287		
L. C. Braund	b Howell	102	(4)st Kelly b Armstrong	19
G. H. Hirst	b Howell	0	(5)c Noble b Howell	0
B. J. T. Bosanquet	c Howell b Noble	2	(6)not out	60
†A. A. Lilley	c Hill b Noble	4	(7)not out	1
A. E. Relf	c Armstrong b Saunders	31		
W. Rhodes	not out	40		
Extras	(b 6, lb 7, w 1, nb 2)	16	(b 3, lb 1, w 2)	6
Total		**577**	**Total** (5 wkts)	**194**

FALL OF WICKETS

AUSTRALIA

Wkt	1st	2nd
1st	2	36
2nd	9	108
3rd	12	191
4th	118	254
5th	200	334
6th	207	393
7th	259	441
8th	263	468
9th	271	473
10th	285	485

ENGLAND

Wkt	1st	2nd
1st	0	21
2nd	49	39
3rd	73	81
4th	117	82
5th	309	181
6th	311	—
7th	318	—
8th	332	—
9th	447	—
10th	577	—

Umpires: R. W. Crockett, A. C. Jones

ENGLAND	1st Innings O	M	R	W		2nd Innings O	M	R	W
Hirst	24	8	47	2	..	29	1	79	0
Arnold	32	7	76	4	..	28	2	93	2
Braund	26	9	39	0	..	12	2	56	0
Bosanquet	13	0	52	2	..	23	1	100	1
Rhodes	17·2	3	41	2	..	40·2	10	94	5
Relf	6	1	27	0	..	13	5	35	0

AUSTRALIA	1st Innings O	M	R	W		2nd Innings O	M	R	W
Saunders	36·2	8	125	2	..	18·5	3	51	2
Laver	37	12	119	1	..	16	4	37	0
Howell	31	7	111	3	..	31	18	35	2
Noble	34	8	99	3	..	12	2	37	0
Armstrong	23	3	47	1	..	18	6	28	1
Hopkins	11	1	40	0	..				
Trumper	7	2	12	0	..				
Gregory	2	0	8	0	..				

1903-04 Second Test, Melbourne

January 1, 2, 4, 5
Toss: England *Result:* England won by 185 runs

Getting a full day's batting before the rain came, England won easily. Bosanquet and Arnold, injured, were replaced by Knight and Fielder, and for Australia, Trumble came in for Laver. England advanced slowly on the first day, scoring at little more than two runs an over, and at the close they were 221 for 2. Warner and Hayward put on 122 in 2 hours 35 minutes, and then Tyldesley and Foster added 99 without being separated. Next morning Foster was unable to resume his innings through illness, but on a rain-interrupted day England reached 306 for 6, Tyldesley being not out 97. On the third day, with the wicket sodden, England collapsed, and of the Australians only Trumper coped with the conditions. Driving magnificently, he was almost solely responsible for saving the follow on; even under these conditions he made his runs in only 112 minutes.

More heavy rain held play up until 3.20 on the third day. Tyldesley, hooking fiercely, and profiting from several escapes, played another fine innings under difficulties, making 62 out of 85 scored while he was in, and although of the rest only Relf reached double figures Australia were left with the impossible task of scoring 297 to win. Trumper and Hill attacked brilliantly for a time, but on this wicket against Rhodes it couldn't last, and in spite of a wonderful defensive display by Noble and an epidemic of dropped catches Australia were all out a second time for 111. Rhodes set up a record with match figures of 15 for 124.

Accurate as much of the Australian bowling was, and well as they performed when the conditions were favourable, the general sameness of the attack was noticeable from the first day. As it happened England did not miss Arnold or Bosanquet, but on hard wickets they were an essential part of the attack. Arnold bowled at a lively pace, making the ball lift and cutting it sometimes from leg to off, while Bosanquet, although expensive in the first Test, had often looked hard to play. With Hirst, Fielder, Braund, Rhodes and Relf also in the touring party, the problem was which bowlers to leave out.

After this match the captains agreed that for the remaining Tests the wicket should be rolled each evening if it had been raining, presumably to help it recover, and the outfield cut daily. In their second innings in the first Test at Melbourne, England had been considerably hampered by the length of the grass in the outfield.

ENGLAND

*P. F. Warner	c Duff b Trumble	68	c Trumper b Saunders	3	
T. Hayward	c Gregory b Hopkins	58	c Trumper b Trumble	0	
J. T. Tyldesley	c Trumble b Howell	97	c Trumble b Howell	62	
R. E. Foster	retired ill	49	absent ill	—	
L. C. Braund	c Howell b Trumble	20	(4)b Saunders	3	
A. E. Knight	b Howell	2	(7)lbw b Trumble	0	
G. H. Hirst	c Noble b Howell	7	(5)c Gregory b Howell	4	
W. Rhodes	lbw b Trumble	2	(6)lbw b Trumble	9	
†A. A. Lilley	c Howell b Trumble	4	(8)st Kelly b Trumble	0	
A. E. Relf	not out	3	(9)not out	10	
A. Fielder	b Howell	1	(10)c Hill b Trumble	4	
Extras	(lb 3, w 1)	4	(b 7, lb 1)	8	
Total		**315**	**Total**	**103**	

AUSTRALIA

V. T. Trumper	c Tyldesley b Rhodes	74	c Relf b Rhodes	35	
R. A. Duff	st Lilley b Rhodes	10	c Braund b Rhodes	8	
C. Hill	c Rhodes b Hirst	5	c Relf b Rhodes	20	
*M. A. Noble	c sub (H. Strudwick) b Rhodes	0	not out	31	
S. E. Gregory	c Hirst b Rhodes	1	c Rhodes b Hirst	0	
A. J. Hopkins	c sub (H. Strudwick) b Relf	18	c and b Rhodes	7	
H. Trumble	c sub (H. Strudwick) b Rhodes	2	c Braund b Rhodes	0	
W. W. Armstrong	c Braund b Rhodes	1	c Hayward b Rhodes	0	
†J. J. Kelly	run out	8	c Lilley b Rhodes	7	
W. P. Howell	c Fielder b Rhodes	0	c Hirst b Rhodes	3	
J. V. Saunders	not out	2	c Fielder b Hirst	0	
				0	
Extras	(lb 1)	1		0	
Total		**122**	**Total**	**111**	

FALL OF WICKETS

ENGLAND

Wkt	1st	2nd
1st	122	5
2nd	132	7
3rd	277	27
4th	279	40
5th	297	74
6th	306	74
7th	306	74
8th	314	90
9th	315	103
10th	—	—

AUSTRALIA

Wkt	1st	2nd
1st	14	14
2nd	23	59
3rd	23	73
4th	33	77
5th	67	86
6th	73	90
7th	97	90
8th	103	102
9th	116	105
10th	122	111

Umpires: R. W. Crockett, P. Argall

AUSTRALIA	1st Innings					2nd Innings			
	O	M	R	W		O	M	R	W
Trumble	50	10	107	4	..	10.5	2	34	5
Noble	6	3	4	0					
Saunders	16	3	60	0	..	8	0	33	2
Howell	34.5	14	43	4	..	8	3	25	2
Armstrong	25	6	43	0	..				
Hopkins	20	2	50	1	..	2	1	3	0
Trumper	1	0	4	0	..				

ENGLAND	1st Innings					2nd Innings			
	O	M	R	W		O	M	R	W
Rhodes	15.2	3	56	7	..	15	0	68	8
Hirst	8	1	33	1	..	14.4	4	38	2
Relf	2	0	12	1	..	1	0	5	0
Braund	5	0	20	0	..				

64. R. E. Foster

65. V. T. Trumper

66. England 1903–04
Back row: H. Strudwick, L. C. Braund, J. A. Murdoch (manager), A. E. Knight, E. G. Arnold, A. Fielder, W. Rhodes, R. E. Foster, A. E. Relf, J. T. Tyldesley. *Front:* T. W. Hayward, B. J. T. Bosanquet, P. F. Warner (capt.), G. H. Hirst, A. A. Lilley.

1903-04 Third Test, Adelaide

January 15, 16, 18, 19, 20
Toss: Australia   *Result:* Australia won by 216 runs

Bosanquet and Arnold returned for England, fast bowler Fielder was retained to the exclusion of all-rounder Relf, and Knight was left out. This left England with only four specialist batsmen, as in the first Test, and six front-line bowlers. Fielder, moreover, had not bowled a ball in the previous Test. Two down with three to play, Australia brought in Charles McLeod for Saunders, who had been expensive in England's first innings at Melbourne.

In spite of her array of bowlers England did not get a wicket until the last ball before lunch on the first morning, Duff then being dismissed for 79 out of 129, made in 90 minutes. For once he quite outpaced Trumper, his hooking being especially brilliant. Bosanquet, pitching a length, puzzled both batsmen with his googly, but Lilley too failed to read him correctly and one or two stumping chances went begging. When Hirst bowled the first maiden of the innings the score was 171, and the 200 came up in 2 hours. Trumper's hundred was his third in five Tests, and although the rate slowed later the close of play score was 355 for 6.

For once the later Australian batting failed, and then England, on a wicket that Warner afterwards described as the best he'd ever played on, suffered one of those unaccountable batting lapses that, although sometimes afflicting the strongest sides, seemed to reflect faulty selection here. Warner and Hayward put on 47 at the start, but at the end of the second day England were 199 for 8, only Hirst holding firm with 58. Despite a useful stand next morning between Arnold and Lilley England were all out for 245 (143 behind), and then the England bowlers took another mauling, Trumper getting a quick fifty and Noble and Gregory putting on 162 for the 4th wicket in just over two hours, of which Gregory's share was an exhilarating 112. 263 for 4 at the close, Australia advanced slowly next morning and were all out in mid-afternoon for 351, leaving England 495 to win.

Even on this wicket such a task looked beyond them, yet when Warner and Hayward put on 148 for the 1st wicket, England had to be given a chance. But when the opening stand was broken Arnold, the night-watchman, failed, and Warner was out on the fifth morning without adding to his score. Tyldesley did not last, Foster was suffering from a badly bruised thumb, and only Hirst of the remainder stayed long.

AUSTRALIA

Batsman	1st Innings		2nd Innings	
V. T. Trumper	b Hirst	113	lbw b Rhodes	59
R. A. Duff	b Hirst	79	c Braund b Hirst	14
C. Hill	c Lilley b Arnold	88	b Fielder	16
*M. A. Noble	st Lilley b Arnold	59	c Bosanquet b Braund	65
S. E. Gregory	c Tyldesley b Arnold	8	c Rhodes b Braund	112
A. J. Hopkins	b Bosanquet	0	(7)run out	7
W. W. Armstrong	lbw b Rhodes	10	(6)c Hirst b Bosanquet	39
H. Trumble	b Bosanquet	4	c and b Bosanquet	9
C. E. McLeod	run out	8	b Bosanquet	2
†J. J. Kelly	lbw b Bosanquet	1	st Lilley b Bosanquet	13
W. P. Howell	not out	3	not out	1
Extras	(b 7, lb 5, w 3)	15	(b 8, lb 2, w 3, nb 1)	14
Total		**388**	**Total**	**351**

ENGLAND

Batsman	1st Innings		2nd Innings	
*P. F. Warner	c McLeod b Trumble	48	c and b Trumble	79
T. Hayward	b Howell	20	lbw b Hopkins	67
J. T. Tyldesley	c Kelly b Hopkins	0	(4)c Noble b Hopkins	10
R. E. Foster	c Howell b Noble	21	(5)b McLeod	16
L. C. Braund	c Duff b Hopkins	13	(6)b Howell	25
G. H. Hirst	c Trumper b Trumble	58	(7)b Trumble	44
B. J. T. Bosanquet	c Duff b Hopkins	10	(9)c Trumper b Hopkins	10
W. Rhodes	c Armstrong b McLeod	9	(10)run out	8
E. G. Arnold	not out	23	(3)b Hopkins	1
†A. A. Lilley	run out	28	(8)c and b Howell	0
A. Fielder	b Trumble	6	not out	14
Extras	(b 4, lb 1, w 4)	9	(lb 2, w 2)	4
Total		**245**	**Total**	**278**

FALL OF WICKETS

AUSTRALIA

Wkt	1st	2nd
1st	129	48
2nd	272	81
3rd	296	101
4th	308	263
5th	310	289
6th	343	320
7th	360	324
8th	384	326
9th	384	350
10th	388	351

ENGLAND

Wkt	1st	2nd
1st	47	148
2nd	48	150
3rd	88	160
4th	99	160
5th	116	195
6th	146	231
7th	173	231
8th	199	256
9th	234	256
10th	245	278

Umpires: R. W. Crockett, P. Argall

ENGLAND

	1st Innings				2nd Innings			
	O	M	R	W	O	M	R	W
Fielder	7	0	33	0	25	11	51	1
Arnold	27	4	93	3	19	3	74	0
Rhodes	14	3	45	1	21	4	46	1
Bosanquet	30·1	4	95	3	15·5	0	73	4
Braund	13	1	49	0	21	6	57	2
Hirst	15	1	58	2	13	1	36	1

AUSTRALIA

	1st Innings				2nd Innings			
	O	M	R	W	O	M	R	W
McLeod	24	6	56	1	25	4	46	1
Trumble	28	9	49	3	33	8	73	2
Howell	13	4	28	1	20	5	52	2
Hopkins	24	5	68	3	28·1	9	81	4
Armstrong	10	3	25	0	7	2	15	0
Noble	3	0	10	1				
Trumper					4	0	7	0

1903–04 Fourth Test, Sydney

February 26, 27, 29, March 1, 2, 3
Toss: England   *Result:* England won by 157 runs

Needing to win to square the series, Australia introduced the 20-year-old Cotter in place of Howell, while Armstrong gave way to McAlister. England played Knight instead of Fielder. The wicket, which had some dampness in it, looked likely to improve as the match progressed, but in unsettled weather Warner chose to bat.

At this vital point in the series the England batting again faltered. Noble's fourth ball bowled Warner, and immediately after lunch, when Foster was out, England were 66 for 4. Cotter was fast but erratic, and the attack was left largely in the hands of Noble and Trumble. The wisdom of playing Knight was then proved as he and Braund batted throughout the afternoon session, and at tea England were on firmer ground at 142 for 4. 207 for 7 overnight, England added another 42 runs next morning, of which Knight, acting as anchor-man, scored only 6. He batted for 4 hours 20 minutes in all, and his innings gave England a chance.

The wicket, as expected, was faster and truer now, and the outfield quicker too. Duff was in his best form, but at 28 Braund bowled Trumper off his pads, and at 61 Arnold clean bowled Duff. All the England bowlers bowled well, there were several interruptions for rain, which served to quicken the wicket, and two fine catches left Australia 114 for 5 at the close. Some of the stoppages angered the crowd, and the hooting and bottle-throwing were worse than in the first Test on the same ground.

There was no play at all on the Monday, when the wicket was under water, and play did not restart until 4.0 on the Tuesday, when England finished the Australian innings off in 51 balls. The ball was cutting through, not turning, and the batting was weak. Hayward and Foster then gave England a good start, Hayward playing in his best watchful style, and when the wicket dried out on the sixth morning Warner and Rhodes added 55 for the last wicket, setting Australia 329 to win. The wicket was now in good order, and it was Bosanquet, coming on at 74 for 3, who finished off the match. Noble defended dourly, and he and Cotter put on 57 for the last wicket, but they could not prevent England regaining the Ashes.

Bosanquet's figures were rarely a true reflection of his value, but in this innings he took 6 for 51. His presence in the side was to many Australians the decisive factor in England's successful campaign.

ENGLAND

*P. F. Warner	b Noble	0	(9)not out	31	
T. Hayward	c McAlister b Trumble	18	lbw b Trumble	52	
J. T. Tyldesley	c Gregory b Noble	16	(4)b Cotter	5	
R. E. Foster	c McAlister b Noble	19	(1)c Noble b Hopkins	27	
A. E. Knight	not out	70	c McAlister b Cotter	9	
L. C. Braund	c Trumble b Noble	39	c McLeod b Hopkins	19	
G. H. Hirst	b Noble	25	c Kelly b McLeod	18	
B. J. T. Bosanquet	b Hopkins	12	c Hill b McLeod	7	
E. G. Arnold	lbw b Noble	0	(3)c Kelly b Noble	0	
†A. A. Lilley	c Hopkins b Trumble	24	b McLeod	6	
W. Rhodes	st Kelly b Noble	10	c McAlister b Cotter	29	
Extras	(b 6, lb 7, w 2, nb 1)	16	(b 1, lb 6)	7	
Total		**249**	Total	**210**	

AUSTRALIA

V. T. Trumper	b Braund	7	(4)lbw b Arnold	12	
R. A. Duff	b Arnold	47	b Arnold	19	
C. Hill	c Braund b Arnold	33	st Lilley b Bosanquet	26	
P. A. McAlister	c Arnold b Rhodes	2	(1)b Hirst	1	
A. J. Hopkins	b Braund	9	(7)st Lilley b Bosanquet	0	
C. E. McLeod	b Rhodes	18	(8)c Lilley b Bosanquet	6	
†J. J. Kelly	c Foster b Arnold	5	(10)c Foster b Bosanquet	10	
*M. A. Noble	not out	6	(5)not out	53	
S. E. Gregory	c Foster b Rhodes	2	(6)lbw b Bosanquet	0	
H. Trumble	c Lilley b Rhodes	0	(9)st Lilley b Bosanquet	0	
A. Cotter	c Tyldesley b Arnold	0	b Hirst	34	
Extras	(b 1, w 1)	2	(b 10)	10	
Total		**131**	Total	**171**	

FALL OF WICKETS

ENGLAND

Wkt	1st	2nd
1st	4	49
2nd	34	50
3rd	42	57
4th	66	73
5th	155	106
6th	185	120
7th	207	138
8th	208	141
9th	237	155
10th	249	210

AUSTRALIA

Wkt	1st	2nd
1st	28	7
2nd	61	35
3rd	72	59
4th	97	76
5th	101	76
6th	116	76
7th	124	86
8th	126	90
9th	130	114
10th	131	171

Umpires: R. W. Crockett, P. Argall

AUSTRALIA	*1st Innings*					*2nd Innings*			
	O	M	R	W		O	M	R	W
Cotter	14	1	44	0	..	17·3	3	41	3
Noble	41·1	10	100	7	..	19	8	40	1
Trumble	43	20	58	2	..	28	10	49	1
Hopkins	8	3	22	1	..	14	5	31	2
McLeod	8	5	9	0	..	20	5	42	3

ENGLAND	*1st Innings*					*2nd Innings*			
	O	M	R	W		O	M	R	W
Hirst	13	1	36	0	..	12·5	2	32	2
Braund	11	2	27	2	..	16	3	24	0
Rhodes	11	3	33	4	..	11	7	12	0
Arnold	15·3	5	28	4	..	12	3	42	2
Bosanquet	2	1	5	0	..	15	1	51	6

1903-04 Fifth Test, Melbourne

March 5, 7, 8
Toss: Australia   *Result:* Australia won by 218 runs

Straight from the fourth Test the two sides travelled to Melbourne for the fifth. England were unchanged, but for Australia Gehrs replaced Gregory. The game began with another dashing innings by Trumper, who batted 1 hour 50 minutes for his 88, and when he was out at 142 for 3 the hitting continued for a time, the 200 coming up in 165 minutes. McAlister and Hopkins played useful innings, but Australia missed the solidity of Armstrong and Gregory in the middle of the order, and after being 208 for 5 at tea they were all out for 247, the innings having lasted only 3 hours 50 minutes. Braund, pushing the ball through rather faster than usual, was punished at times but finished with 8 for 81.

With half an hour left for play Warner sent Rhodes in with Hayward, but Hayward was out without a run on the board and so was Arnold, the night-watchman, and England were 0 for 2. Warner and Rhodes then cautiously played out time. All day the wicket had been good, but during the night the weather broke up, and a resumption was not possible until 4.0 next day, when England were at a hopeless disadvantage. Cotter made the ball rear up dangerously from a length, and some batsmen drew away to avoid being hit on the head. Consider-

ing the conditions Foster and Tyldesley, who made the only real stand of the innings, batted with great skill, but England were all out in 102 minutes for 61.

In an effort to save his best batsmen for the morrow, when the wicket might have improved, Noble changed his batting order, and McAlister, McLeod and Cotter were dismissed for 13 runs before the close. More rain in the night deadened the wicket for a time, but Australia were soon 49 for 6. Duff and Noble then added 43, but after lunch the wicket became sticky again and Australia were all out for 133. England's task of making 320 to win was impossible on such a wicket, and they were also without Hayward, who had tonsilitis. They batted only 84 minutes, but there was time for Foster, who opened the innings, to leave his mark on the game with another superb display on a difficult wicket; he batted 46 minutes and was out to a wonderful one-handed overhead catch by Trumper at long on. Trumble, in his last Test, then did the hat trick, and the only other notable resistance came from Rhodes and Arnold, who made the best stand of the innings for the last wicket.

AUSTRALIA

R. A. Duff	b Braund	9	(7)c Warner b Rhodes	31	
V. T. Trumper	c and b Braund	88	(5)b Hirst	0	
C. Hill	c Braund b Rhodes	16	(6)c Warner b Hirst	16	
*M. A. Noble	c Foster b Arnold	29	(8)st Lilley b Rhodes	19	
P. A. McAlister	st Lilley b Braund	36	(1)c Foster b Arnold	9	
D. R. A. Gehrs	c and b Braund	3	(10)c and b Hirst	5	
A. J. Hopkins	c Knight b Braund	32	(9)not out	25	
C. E. McLeod	c Rhodes b Braund	8	(2)c Bosanquet b Braund	0	
H. Trumble	c Foster b Braund	6	(11)c Arnold b Hirst	0	
†J. J. Kelly	not out	6	(3)c and b Arnold	24	
A. Cotter	b Braund	6	(4)b Hirst	0	
Extras	(b 4, lb 4)	8	(b 1, lb 3)	4	
Total		**247**	**Total**	**133**	

ENGLAND

T. Hayward	b Noble	0	absent ill	—	
W. Rhodes	c Gehrs b Cotter	3	(8)not out	16	
E. G. Arnold	c Kelly b Noble	0	(10)c Duff b Trumble	19	
*P. F. Warner	c McAlister b Cotter	1	(5)c and b Trumble	11	
J. T. Tyldesley	c Gehrs b Noble	10	(3)c Hopkins b Cotter	15	
R. E. Foster	b Cotter	18	(2)c Trumper b Trumble	30	
G. H. Hirst	c Trumper b Cotter	0	(6)c McAlister b Trumble	1	
L. C. Braund	c Hopkins b Noble	5	(1)c McAlister b Cotter	0	
A. E. Knight	b Cotter	0	(4)c Kelly b Trumble	0	
B. J. T. Bosanquet	c Noble b Cotter	16	(7)c Gehrs b Trumble	4	
†A. A. Lilley	not out	6	(9)lbw b Trumble	0	
Extras	(b 1, nb 1)	2	(b 1, lb 4)	5	
Total		**61**	**Total**	**101**	

FALL OF WICKETS

AUSTRALIA

Wkt	1st	2nd
1st	13	9
2nd	67	9
3rd	142	13
4th	144	13
5th	159	43
6th	218	49
7th	221	92
8th	231	115
9th	235	133
10th	247	133

ENGLAND

Wkt	1st	2nd
1st	0	0
2nd	0	24
3rd	4	38
4th	5	47
5th	23	54
6th	26	61
7th	36	61
8th	36	61
9th	48	101
10th	61	—

Umpires: R. W. Crockett, P. Argall

ENGLAND	1st Innings					2nd Innings			
	O	M	R	W		O	M	R	W
Hirst	19	6	44	0	..	16.5	4	48	5
Braund	28.5	6	81	8	..	4	1	6	1
Rhodes	12	1	41	1	..	15	2	52	2
Arnold	18	4	46	1	..	8	3	23	2
Bosanquet	4	0	27	0	..				

AUSTRALIA	1st Innings					2nd Innings			
	O	M	R	W		O	M	R	W
Noble	15	8	19	4	..	6	2	19	0
Cotter	15.2	2	40	6	..	5	0	25	2
McLeod	1	1	0	0	..	5	0	24	0
Trumble					..	6.5	0	28	7

Averages: 1903-04

AUSTRALIA

BATTING	M.	Inns.	N.O.	Runs	H.S.	Av.
V. T. Trumper	5	10	1	574	185*	63·77
M. A. Noble	5	10	3	417	133	59·57
R. A. Duff	5	10	0	304	84	30·40
C. Hill	5	10	0	276	88	27·60
S. E. Gregory	4	8	0	189	112	23·62
W. W. Armstrong	3	6	0	125	48	20·83
A. J. Hopkins	5	10	1	157	39	17·44
P. A. McAlister	2	4	0	48	36	12·00
J. J. Kelly	5	10	1	97	24	10·77
A. Cotter	2	4	0	40	34	10·00
J. V. Saunders	2	4	2	15	11*	7·50
C. E. McLeod	3	6	0	42	18	7·00
W. P. Howell	3	6	2	16	5	4·00
H. Trumble	4	8	0	21	9	2·62

PLAYED IN ONE TEST: F. Laver 4 and 6, D. R. A. Gehrs 3 and 5.

BOWLING	Overs	Mds.	Runs	Wkts.	Av.
A. Cotter	51·5	6	150	11	13·63
H. Trumble	199·4	59	398	24	16·58
M. A. Noble	136·1	41	328	16	20·50
W. P. Howell	137·5	51	294	14	21·00
A. J. Hopkins	107·1	26	295	11	26·81
C. E. McLeod	83	21	177	5	35·40
J. V. Saunders	79·1	14	269	6	44·83

ALSO BOWLED: W. W. Armstrong 83–20–158–2, F. Laver 53–16–156–1, V. T. Trumper 12–2–23–0, S. E. Gregory 2–0–8–0.

ENGLAND

BATTING	M.	Inns.	N.O.	Runs	H.S.	Av.
R. E. Foster	5	9	1	486	287	60·75
A. E. Relf	2	3	2	44	31	44·00
T. W. Hayward	5	9	0	321	91	35·66
J. T. Tyldesley	5	10	0	277	70	27·70
P. F. Warner	5	10	1	249	79	27·66
G. H. Hirst	5	10	1	217	60*	24·11
L. C. Braund	5	10	0	226	102	22·60
W. Rhodes	5	9	2	126	40*	18·00
A. E. Knight	3	6	1	81	70*	16·20
E. G. Arnold	4	7	1	70	27	11·66
A. A. Lilley	5	9	1	72	28	9·00
B. J. T. Bosanquet	4	8	1	62	16	8·85
A. Fielder	2	4	1	25	14*	8·33

BOWLING	Overs	Mds.	Runs	Wkts.	Av.
W. Rhodes	172	36	488	31	15·74
B. J. T. Bosanquet	103	7	403	16	25·18
E. G. Arnold	159·3	31	475	18	26·38
L. C. Braund	136·5	30	359	13	37·61
G. H. Hirst	165·2	29	451	15	30·06

ALSO BOWLED: A. E. Relf 22–6–79–1, A. Fielder 32–11–84–1.

Averages: 1905

ENGLAND

BATTING	M.	Inns.	N.O.	Runs	H.S.	Av.
Hon. F. S. Jackson	5	9	2	492	144*	70·28
C. B. Fry	4	7	1	348	144	58·00
J. T. Tyldesley	5	9	1	424	112*	53·00
W. Rhodes	4	5	2	146	39*	48·66
R. H. Spooner	2	3	0	131	79	43·66
A. C. MacLaren	4	7	0	303	140	43·28
G. H. Hirst	3	4	1	105	40*	35·00
T. W. Hayward	5	9	0	305	82	33·88
E. G. Arnold	4	5	2	74	40	24·66
B. J. T. Bosanquet	3	6	2	85	27	21·25
A. A. Lilley	5	5	0	93	37	18·60
S. Haigh	2	2	0	25	14	12·50
W. Brearley	2	2	1	11	11*	11·00
A. O. Jones	2	4	0	40	30	10·00

PLAYED IN ONE TEST: J. Gunn 8, G. L. Jessop 0, D. Denton 0 and 12, A. R. Warren 7, C. Blythe 0.

BOWLING	Overs	Mds.	Runs	Wkts.	Av.
Hon. F. S. Jackson	67·5	8	201	13	15·46
A. R. Warren	39·2	9	113	6	18·83
W. Brearley	73·1	16	277	14	19·78
B. J. T. Bosanquet	58·4	3	201	9	22·33
E. G. Arnold	69	16	214	7	30·57
W. Rhodes	110·3	21	314	10	31·40
G. H. Hirst	62	13	212	6	35·33

ALSO BOWLED: C. Blythe 32–11–77–4, S. Haigh 37–12–95–4, G. L. Jessop 8–2–19–1, J. Gunn 6–2–27–1.

AUSTRALIA

BATTING	M.	Inns.	N.O.	Runs	H.S.	Av.
R. A. Duff	5	8	0	335	146	41·87
W. W. Armstrong	5	9	1	252	66	31·50
J. Darling	5	9	1	230	73	28·75
J. J. Kelly	5	7	4	73	42	24·33
S. E. Gregory	3	5	1	94	51	23·50
C. Hill	5	9	0	188	54	20·88
M. A. Noble	5	9	0	173	62	19·22
V. T. Trumper	5	8	1	125	31	17·85
A. Cotter	3	5	0	80	45	16·00
A. J. Hopkins	3	5	0	80	36	16·00
F. Laver	5	7	3	62	24	15·50
C. E. McLeod	5	8	1	47	13	6·71

PLAYED IN ONE TEST: D. R. A. Gehrs 0 and 11.

BOWLING	Overs	Mds.	Runs	Wkts.	Av.
F. Laver	189·3	55	510	16	31·87
A. Cotter	127	13	427	13	32·84
W. W. Armstrong	280·3	94	538	16	33·62
C. E. McLeod	202	54	525	10	52·50
M. A. Noble	148·2	37	409	6	68·16

ALSO BOWLED: R. A. Duff 30–8–85–4, A. J. Hopkins 38–10–115–4.

1905 First Test, Trent Bridge

May 29, 30, 31
Toss: England   *Result:* England won by 213 runs

After an initial failure at Trent Bridge the English batting was equal to all the demands made on it, the speed and certainty of the scoring putting the side in a winning position time and again. Darling, with a limited attack, was too often forced on the defensive, and the Australian batting lacked its accustomed steadiness. Trumper had a wretched series, and the decline of Noble as a bowler was another weakness. Jackson for England and Armstrong for Australia performed outstandingly well.

With Cotter bowling fast bumping long-hops which reached the wicket-keeper standing back stretching full length above his head, with the occasional yorker sandwiched in between, the England batsmen were quickly unsettled at Trent Bridge. Laver meanwhile varied his pace and length cleverly, and England were soon 49 for 4. Tyldesley alone played up to his reputation among the batsmen, but Lilley and Rhodes added a valuable 48 for the 9th wicket, and England reached 196. Australia also started disastrously, Duff being caught off Gunn and Trumper straining his back, but Hill and Noble batted through till after 6.0. Then Jackson, cutting back from the off, altered the game dramatically with 3 wickets in one over, and at stumps Australia were 158 for 4, with Trumper unlikely to bat again. Only

some big hitting by Cotter next morning saw them into a modest lead.

That there was nothing wrong with the pitch was shown when England batted again, MacLaren and Hayward putting on 145 for the 1st wicket. The Australians went on the defensive, Armstrong bowling down the leg side and McLeod swinging away to an off field, and at stumps England were 318 for 5. Tyldesley played another good innings, remarkable for its off-side play, and MacLaren's hooking of Cotter was thrilling to watch, his hundred coming in under 3 hours. Next morning Jackson and Rhodes added 108 in 75 minutes, and Australia were left with 4½ hours in which to get 401.

Duff and Darling began steadily and the game looked dead, but neither of them was playing Bosanquet with much confidence, and although his length was erratic Jackson kept him on. Eventually the Australians, paralysed by their own doubts when Bosanquet struck a length, and playing on in a light that was really unfit for cricket, faltered and were all out just before the rain came despite a defiant innings by Gregory.

Jessop, who could be really quick for a few overs, bowled short at the Australians in their first innings, and Cotter kept the ball up when England batted again.

ENGLAND

						FALL OF WICKETS

ENGLAND						
T. Hayward	b Cotter	5	c Darling b Armstrong	47		
A. O. Jones	b Laver	4	(4)b Duff	30		
J. T. Tyldesley	c Duff b Laver	56	c and b Duff	61		
A. C. MacLaren	c Kelly b Laver	2	(2)c Duff b Laver	140		
*Hon. F. S. Jackson	b Cotter	0	not out	82		
B. J. T. Bosanquet	b Laver	27	b Cotter	6		
J. Gunn	b Cotter	8				
G. L. Jessop	b Laver	0				
†A. A. Lilley	c and b Laver	37				
W. Rhodes	c Noble b Laver	29	(7)not out	39		
E. G. Arnold	not out	2				
Extras	(b 21, lb 5)	26	(b 11, lb 9, w 1)	21		
Total		**196**	**Total** (5 wkts dec)	**426**		

ENGLAND		
Wkt	*1st*	*2nd*
1st	6	145
2nd	24	222
3rd	40	276
4th	49	301
5th	98	313
6th	119	—
7th	119	—
8th	139	—
9th	187	—
10th	196	—

AUSTRALIA

R. A. Duff	c Hayward b Gunn	1	c and b Bosanquet	25	
V. T. Trumper	retired hurt	13	absent hurt	—	
C. Hill	b Jackson	54	(5)c and b Bosanquet	8	
M. A. Noble	c Lilley b Jackson	50	(3)st Lilley b Bosanquet	7	
W. W. Armstrong	st Lilley b Rhodes	27	(4)c Jackson b Bosanquet	6	
*J. Darling	c Bosanquet b Jackson	0	(2)b Bosanquet	40	
A. Cotter	c and b Jessop	45	b Rhodes	18	
S. E. Gregory	c Jones b Jackson	2	(6)c Arnold b Bosanquet	51	
C. E. McLeod	b Arnold	4	lbw b Bosanquet	13	
F. Laver	c Jones b Jackson	5	(8)st Lilley b Bosanquet	5	
†J. J. Kelly	not out	1	(10)not out	6	
Extras	(b 16, lb 2, w 1)	19	(b 4, lb 3, w 2)	9	
Total		**221**	**Total**	**188**	

AUSTRALIA		
Wkt	*1st*	*2nd*
1st	1	62
2nd	129	75
3rd	130	82
4th	130	93
5th	200	100
6th	204	139
7th	209	144
8th	216	175
9th	221	188
10th	—	—

Umpires: J. Carlin,
J. Phillips

AUSTRALIA	1st Innings					2nd Innings			
	O	M	R	W		O	M	R	W
Cotter	23	2	64	3	..	17	1	59	1
Laver	31·3	14	64	7	..	34	7	121	1
McLeod	8	2	19	0	..	28	9	84	0
Armstrong	6	3	4	0	..	52	24	67	1
Noble	3	0	19	0	..	7	1	31	0
Duff					..	15	2	43	2

ENGLAND	1st Innings					2nd Innings			
	O	M	R	W		O	M	R	W
Arnold	11	2	39	1	..	4	2	7	0
Gunn	6	2	27	1	..				
Jessop	7	2	18	1	..	1	0	1	0
Bosanquet	7	0	29	0	..	32·4	2	107	8
Rhodes	18	6	37	1	..	30	8	58	1
Jackson	14·5	2	52	5	..	5	3	6	0

68. R. A. Duff

67. (left) Hon. F. S. Jackson

69. Australia 1905
Back row: D. R. A. Gehrs, W. P. Howell, W. W. Armstrong, F. Laver (manager), A. J. Hopkins, P. M. Newland. *Middle row:* R. A. Duff, C. Hill, V. T. Trumper, J. Darling (capt.), M. A. Noble, C. E. McLeod, J. J. Kelly. *Front:* S. E. Gregory, A. Cotter.

1905 Second Test, Lord's

June 15, 16, 17
Toss: England   *Result:* Match Drawn

A prompt start at the advertised time was so rare in this period that it was liable to be praised as 'commendable punctuality', hence precise timings are sometimes difficult to arrive at. But a day's play in England generally meant 6-6½ hours on paper, and in Australia 4½-5 hours. For this match, rain over the previous few days made the wicket and outfield slow, and neither side chose a fast bowler.

Play on the first morning was castigated as slow, and Hayward spent 90 minutes over 16, but the pace of the wicket, and Darling's field placements and adjustments for each batsman, had a lot to do with restricting the scoring rate. Nevertheless England were 86 for 1 at lunch, thanks largely to MacLaren. In the afternoon Armstrong bowled down the leg side in his defensive style, only Tyldesley batting with any freedom after MacLaren was out, and from 208 for 4 an hour from the close England slumped to 258 for 8 at stumps. Fry batted 3½ hours for 73.

When more thundery rain came in the night and England reached 282 next morning, Australia looked in real danger. But Trumper and Duff, realising that the wicket would play easily at first, launched an immediate attack, and their hitting so demoralised the England bowlers that 57 were made in the first 33 minutes. A minor collapse followed, but determined batting by Armstrong and Darling averted the follow on, and the England lead was restricted to 101. England were batting again at 4.0, and although Hayward and Tyldesley made only modest contributions MacLaren attacked so successfully that he made 79 out of 136 before the close, hitting Armstrong so freely that the Australian changed his tactics, bowled at the wicket, and was at once much more difficult to play.

England were 252 ahead at the end of the second day with 5 wickets to fall, Fry having batted 1½ hours for 36 not out; but rain washed out what promised to be an exciting third day. Nevertheless this was one of the more interesting of drawn games. Australia had much the worst of the conditions, and for the enterprise of Trumper and Duff they deserved to avoid defeat. Rhodes and the fast-medium Haigh, who should have been ideally suited to the conditions, never recovered from the drubbing they received in the first few minutes. The wicket was no good to Bosanquet, and MacLaren kept him in cold storage.

ENGLAND

A. C. MacLaren	b Hopkins	56	b Armstrong	79
T. Hayward	lbw b Duff	16	c Laver b McLeod	8
J. T. Tyldesley	c Laver b Armstrong	43	b Noble	12
C. B. Fry	c Kelly b Hopkins	73	not out	36
*Hon. F. S. Jackson	c Armstrong b Laver	29	b Armstrong	0
A. O. Jones	b Laver	1	c Trumper b Armstrong	5
B. J. T. Bosanquet	c and b Armstrong	6	not out	4
W. Rhodes	b Hopkins	15		
†A. A. Lilley	lbw b McLeod	0		
S. Haigh	b Laver	14		
E. G. Arnold	not out	7		
Extras	(b 20, lb 2)	22	(b 2, lb 4, nb 1)	7
Total		**282**	**Total** (5 wkts)	**151**

AUSTRALIA

V. T. Trumper	b Jackson	31
R. A. Duff	c Lilley b Rhodes	27
C. Hill	c Bosanquet b Jackson	7
M. A. Noble	c Fry b Jackson	7
W. W. Armstrong	lbw b Jackson	33
*J. Darling	c Haigh b Arnold	41
S. E. Gregory	c Jones b Rhodes	5
A. J. Hopkins	b Haigh	16
C. E. McLeod	b Haigh	0
F. Laver	not out	4
†J. J. Kelly	lbw b Rhodes	2
Extras	(b 3, lb 5)	8
Total		**181**

FALL OF WICKETS
ENGLAND

Wkt	1st	2nd
1st	59	18
2nd	97	63
3rd	149	136
4th	208	136
5th	210	146
6th	227	—
7th	257	—
8th	258	—
9th	258	—
10th	282	—

AUSTRALIA

Wkt	1st	2nd
1st	57	—
2nd	73	—
3rd	73	—
4th	95	—
5th	131	—
6th	138	—
7th	171	—
8th	175	—
9th	175	—
10th	181	—

Umpires: J. Phillips,
W. Richards

AUSTRALIA	1st Innings				2nd Innings			
	O	M	R	W	O	M	R	W
McLeod	20	7	40	1	15	5	33	1
Laver	34	8	64	3	10	4	39	0
Noble	34	13	61	0	13	2	31	1
Duff	7	4	14	1				
Armstrong	30	11	41	2	10	2	30	3
Hopkins	15	4	40	3	2	0	11	0

ENGLAND	1st Innings				2nd Innings			
	O	M	R	W	O	M	R	W
Haigh	12	3	40	2				
Rhodes	16·1	1	70	3				
Jackson	15	0	50	4				
Arnold	7	3	13	1				

1905 Third Test, Leeds

July 3, 4, 5
Toss: England   *Result:* Match Drawn

On a wicket that was never plumb and which always gave the bowlers some help after recent rain, England, without MacLaren, totalled 301 after being 64 for 4. The credit for the recovery was largely Jackson's; he went in at 1.0 on the first morning when England were 57 for 3, and although beginning with great caution he reached his hundred in 3½ hours and then accelerated until he ran out of partners. Hirst, too, went in at a critical time and played steadily, helping Jackson in a 5th-wicket partnership of 69, and Bosanquet also gave valuable help. Next day Warren, in his first and only Test, bowled really fast and with plenty of life, and Australia were soon 36 for 3. Duff, Armstrong and Hopkins hit back, but the batting otherwise was brittle, and England gained a lead of 106. All that was left for Australia was to play for a draw, and their bowling was well suited to this. Armstrong reverted to aiming well outside the leg stump to a leg field, but in view of Warren's success Australia must have regretted leaving out Cotter.

275 runs on overnight, England forced the game on the last morning without recklessness, Tyldesley, who dealt with Armstrong by running away to square leg and thumping him on the off side, reaching a well-earned hundred in 2½ hours. Nevertheless Armstrong bowled 51 overs for 122 runs and took all the five wickets that fell.

401 behind when England declared, Australia were left with 20 minutes' batting before lunch, in which they lost Trumper to Warren. Duff left at 36 and Hill at 64, but Armstrong, joining Noble, came in and attacked just as he had in the first innings. 53 were added before Blythe, beginning a long spell at the pavilion end, had Armstrong lbw. Keeping an excellent length and turning the ball perceptibly, he then bowled both Darling and Hopkins, and Australia at 152 for 6 were in immediate danger. But Blythe (who was substituting for the injured Rhodes) then missed a return catch from Noble, Gregory, like Noble, defended with great patience and resource, and the other England bowlers failed altogether to produce their best form, so that Australia escaped. One up in the series, England may perhaps be forgiven for setting a target outside Australia's reach, but an earlier declaration might have brought victory. Even as it was, dropped catches helped Australia save the game.

ENGLAND

T. Hayward	b McLeod	26	c Hopkins b Armstrong	60
C. B. Fry	c Noble b McLeod	32	c Kelly b Armstrong	30
J. T. Tyldesley	b Laver	0	st Kelly b Armstrong	100
D. Denton	c Duff b McLeod	0	c Hill b Armstrong	12
*Hon. F. S. Jackson	not out	144	c Duff b Armstrong	17
G. H. Hirst	c Trumper b Laver	35	not out	40
B. J. T. Bosanquet	b Duff	20	not out	22
†A. A. Lilley	b Noble	11		
S. Haigh	c Noble b Armstrong	11		
A. R. Warren	run out	7		
C. Blythe	b Armstrong	0		
Extras	(b 10, lb 1, w 2, nb 2)	15	(b 1, lb 6, w 6, nb 1)	14
Total		**301**	**Total** (5 wkts dec)	**295**

AUSTRALIA

V. T. Trumper	b Warren	8	c Hirst b Warren	0
R. A. Duff	c Lilley b Blythe	48	b Hirst	17
C. Hill	c and b Hirst	7	c Warren b Haigh	33
M. A. Noble	c Hayward b Warren	2	st Lilley b Bosanquet	62
W. W. Armstrong	c Hayward b Warren	66	lbw b Blythe	32
*J. Darling	c Bosanquet b Warren	5	b Blythe	2
A. J. Hopkins	c Lilley b Jackson	36	b Blythe	17
S. E. Gregory	run out	4	not out	32
C. E. McLeod	b Haigh	8	not out	10
†J. J. Kelly	not out	1		
F. Laver	b Warren	3		
Extras	(b 4, lb 1, w 2)	7	(b 11, w 6, nb 2)	19
Total		**195**	**Total** (7 wkts)	**224**

FALL OF WICKETS

ENGLAND

Wkt	1st	2nd
1st	51	80
2nd	54	126
3rd	57	170
4th	64	202
5th	133	258
6th	201	—
7th	232	—
8th	282	—
9th	301	—
10th	301	

AUSTRALIA

Wkt	1st	2nd
1st	26	2
2nd	33	36
3rd	36	64
4th	96	117
5th	161	121
6th	161	152
7th	166	199
8th	191	—
9th	191	—
10th	195	

Umpires: J. Phillips,
V. A. Titchmarsh

AUSTRALIA	1st Innings				2nd Innings			
	O	M	R	W	O	M	R	W
Armstrong	26·3	6	44	2	51	14	122	5
Noble	23	6	59	1	20	3	68	0
Laver	29	10	61	2	10	4	29	0
McLeod	37	13	88	3	23	6	62	0
Hopkins	9	4	21	0				
Duff	4	1	13	1				

ENGLAND	1st Innings				2nd Innings			
	O	M	R	W	O	M	R	W
Hirst	11	1	37	1	10	2	26	1
Warren	19·2	5	57	5	20	4	56	1
Blythe	8	0	36	1	24	11	41	3
Jackson	4	0	10	1	8	2	10	0
Haigh	11	5	19	1	14	4	36	1
Bosanquet	4	0	29	0	15	1	36	1

1905 Fourth Test, Old Trafford

July 24, 25, 26
Toss: England   *Result:* England won by an innings and 80 runs

Perhaps to excite local interest, Brearley came in for Warren, and Rhodes and MacLaren returned for Blythe and Denton In the Australian side Cotter replaced Hopkins, and Gehrs came in for the injured Gregory. To regain the Ashes Australia needed to win this and the final Test.

On a wicket deadened by rain England made a steady start, Hayward especially showing good form. Spooner played a lovely innings in front of his own crowd, while Jackson once again proved his temperament in an innings which lasted 3 hours 43 minutes. The Australian bowling was collared and at times hardly looked of Test Match standard, but nearly all the bowlers suffered from the lack of a class slip. England were 352 for 6 at stumps, and next morning they added 94 in 100 minutes, suggesting that there was nothing much wrong with the wicket. Yet for Australia, half an hour's batting before lunch as the pitch began to dry proved disastrous. Brearley bowled very fast, making the ball lift and bringing it back at times from the off, Arnold varied his length and pace, and at the interval Australia were 27 for 3.

The Australian tactics from this point on seemed incomprehensible at the time, and they still seem unrealistic even in the light of the purpose with which *Wisden* subsequently credited them. By drawing this Test and winning at the Oval Australia could still halve the series, and one would have thought Darling would now have lowered his sights. But after lunch he drove the ball four times into the crowd and was missed a similar number of times, and under his direction all the other batsmen tried to score quickly. 197 in the circumstances was not a bad score, but Australia followed on 249 behind. Even then they continued to go for the runs, reaching 118 for one by the close.

On the last day the start was delayed until 12.10 by showers during the morning, and with more rain threatened Australia seemed to have a good chance of saving the game. Yet, on a wicket that was never so bad as to justify recklessness, one by one the Australian batsmen tried to hit before they were set, chasing after balls they could well have left alone and generally giving their wickets away. If, as *Wisden* avers, they were still trying to force a win, it seems in retrospect an extraordinarily forlorn hope. In the event the innings was finished off just before lunch; and to add to Australian chagrin, it rained for the rest of the day.

ENGLAND

A. C. MacLaren	c Hill b McLeod	14
T. Hayward	c Gehrs b McLeod	82
J. T. Tyldesley	b Laver	24
C. B. Fry	b Armstrong	17
*Hon. F. S. Jackson	c Cotter b McLeod	113
R. H. Spooner	c and b McLeod	52
G. H. Hirst	c Laver b McLeod	25
E. G. Arnold	run out	25
W. Rhodes	not out	27
†A. A. Lilley	lbw b Noble	28
W. Brearley	c Darling b Noble	0
Extras	(b 17, lb 20, w 1, nb 1)	39
Total		446

AUSTRALIA

M. A. Noble	b Brearley	7	(4)c Rhodes b Brearley	10
V. T. Trumper	c Rhodes b Brearley	11	lbw b Rhodes	30
C. Hill	c Fry b Arnold	0	c sub (A. O. Jones) b Arnold	27
W. W. Armstrong	b Rhodes	29	(5)b Brearley	9
R. A. Duff	c MacLaren b Brearley	11	(1)c Spooner b Brearley	60
*J. Darling	c Tyldesley b Jackson	73	c Rhodes b Brearley	0
D. R. A. Gehrs	b Arnold	0	(8)c and b Rhodes	11
C. E. McLeod	b Brearley	6	(9)c Arnold b Rhodes	6
A. Cotter	c Fry b Jackson	11	(10)run out	0
F. Laver	b Rhodes	24	(11)not out	6
†J. J. Kelly	not out	16	(7)c Rhodes b Arnold	5
Extras	(b 9)	9	(b 4, nb 1)	5
Total		197	Total	169

FALL OF WICKETS

ENGLAND

Wkt	1st	2nd
1st	24	—
2nd	77	—
3rd	136	—
4th	176	—
5th	301	—
6th	347	—
7th	382	—
8th	387	—
9th	446	—
10th	446	—

AUSTRALIA

Wkt	1st	2nd
1st	20	55
2nd	21	121
3rd	27	122
4th	41	133
5th	88	133
6th	93	146
7th	146	146
8th	146	158
9th	166	158
10th	197	169

Umpires: J. Carlin
J. E. West

AUSTRALIA	1st Innings				2nd Innings			
	O	M	R	W	O	M	R	W
Cotter	26	4	83	0	..			
McLeod	47	8	125	5	..			
Armstrong	48	14	93	1	..			
Laver	21	5	73	1	..			
Noble	15·5	3	33	2	..			

ENGLAND	1st Innings				2nd Innings			
	O	M	R	W	O	M	R	W
Hirst	2	0	12	0	..	7	2	19	0
Brearley	17	3	72	4	..	14	3	54	4
Arnold	14	2	53	2	..	15	5	35	2
Rhodes	5·5	1	25	2	..	11·3	3	36	3
Jackson	7	0	26	2	..	5	0	20	0

1905 Fifth Test, Oval

August 14, 15, 16
Toss: England *Result:* Match Drawn

When England, with the rubber decided, won the toss and batted for the fifth time running, the pattern of the series touched monotony. Yet the fluctuations on the last day were the most exciting of the series. On a heartbreaking wicket, and with the fielding often listless, Cotter in England's first innings kept up a good pace and bowled with much better length and control than previously, and his reward was 2 early wickets. But Hayward was watchful and correct, Fry played his best innings against the Australians, scoring many of his runs with powerful drives, and he and Jackson put on 151, so that by the end of the first day England, at 381 for 7, seemed safe from defeat in what was no more than a three-day game. Fry's innings gave especial pleasure after earlier failures; he batted only 3 hours 33 minutes, scored 92 between lunch and tea, and gave no chance.

When Australia batted Trumper and Hill were soon out, but Duff and Noble added 115 for the 3rd wicket, Noble's share being 25. Duff, who drove and hooked with tremendous power, should have been caught off a skier at slip when 78, but MacLaren and Hirst muffed the chance between them. During this innings Lilley split a finger and Darling allowed the substitute, A. O. Jones, to replace him

as wicket-keeper. Brearley again bowled finely, keeping the ball well up and maintaining his pace, but fearless hitting by Darling and sensible play by Kelly buttressed the Australian total after Duff was out for 146, and they finished only 67 behind.

On the last morning England suddenly found themselves 48 for 4, only 115 in front, and with Lilley unable to bat an Australian victory began to look possible; scenting this the team sprang to life. But appeals for a catch behind the wicket off Tyldesley and an lbw to Spooner were answered in England's favour, and the Australians showed their displeasure: unsatisfactory umpiring in this series had been remarked on by both sides. Tyldesley and Jackson gradually wore the bowlers down, after which Tyldesley and Spooner hit brilliantly, and England were able to declare 328 in front and leave Australia 2½ hours' batting. There was a point in the late afternoon when an England victory, too, looked possible, but Armstrong and Darling saw Australia safely through, and stumps were drawn half an hour before the advertised close. An earlier declaration might again have brought an England victory, but with Brearley indisposed, no wicket-keeper, and Jackson himself suffering from a strain, no chances were taken.

ENGLAND

A. C. MacLaren	c Laver b Cotter	6	(3)c Kelly b Armstrong	6
T. Hayward	hit wkt b Hopkins	59	lbw b Armstrong	2
J. T. Tyldesley	b Cotter	16	(4)not out	112
C. B. Fry	b Cotter	144	(5)c Armstrong b Noble	16
*Hon. F. S. Jackson	c Armstrong b Laver	76	(6)b Cotter	31
R. H. Spooner	b Cotter	0	(7)c sub (D. R. A. Gehrs) b Noble	79
G. H. Hirst	c Noble b Laver	5		
E. G. Arnold	c Trumper b Cotter	40	(1)b Cotter	0
W. Rhodes	b Cotter	36		
*A. A. Lilley	b Cotter	17		
W. Brearley	not out	11		
Extras	(b 11, lb 1, w 1, nb 7)	20	(b 4, lb 5, w 1, nb 5)	15
Total		**430**	**Total** (6 wkts dec)	**261**

AUSTRALIA

V. T. Trumper	b Brearley	4	c Spooner b Brearley	28
R. A. Duff	c and b Hirst	146		
C. Hill	c Rhodes b Brearley	18	b Arnold	34
M. A. Noble	c MacLaren b Jackson	25	b Hirst	3
W. W. Armstrong	c sub (A. O. Jones) b Hirst	18	not out	32
*J. Darling	b Hirst	57	not out	12
A. J. Hopkins	b Brearley	1	(2)run out	10
C. E. McLeod	b Brearley	0		
*J. J. Kelly	run out	42		
A. Cotter	c Fry b Brearley	6		
F. Laver	not out	15		
Extras	(b 17, lb 9, w 1, nb 4)	31	(b 4, lb 1)	5
Total		**363**	**Total** (4 wkts)	**124**

FALL OF WICKETS

ENGLAND

Wkt	1st	2nd
1st	12	0
2nd	32	8
3rd	132	13
4th	283	48
5th	291	103
6th	306	261
7th	322	—
8th	394	—
9th	418	—
10th	430	—

AUSTRALIA

Wkt	1st	2nd
1st	5	27
2nd	44	49
3rd	159	58
4th	214	92
5th	237	—
6th	247	—
7th	265	—
8th	293	—
9th	304	—
10th	363	—

Umpires: J. Phillips, W. A. J. West

AUSTRALIA	1st Innings					2nd Innings			
	O	M	R	W		O	M	R	W
Cotter	40	4	148	7	..	21	2	73	2
Noble	18	6	51	0	..	14·3	3	56	2
Armstrong	27	7	76	0	..	30	13	61	2
McLeod	13	2	47	0	..	11	2	27	0
Laver	17	3	41	2	..	3	0	18	0
Hopkins	11	2	32	1	..	1	0	11	0
Duff	4	1	15	0	..				

ENGLAND	1st Innings					2nd Innings			
	O	M	R	W		O	M	R	W
Hirst	23	6	86	3	..	9	2	32	1
Brearley	31·1	8	110	5	..	11	2	41	1
Arnold	9	0	50	0	..	9	2	17	1
Rhodes	21	2	59	0	..	8	0	29	0
Jackson	9	1	27	1	..				

1907-08 First Test, Sydney

December 13, 14, 16, 17, 18, 19
Toss: England   *Result:* Australia won by two wickets

The fortunes of the two sides fluctuated to a remarkable degree in this series, the outstanding feature being the extraordinary ability of the Australians to recover ground in their second innings. On the other hand, fears that the batting would prove short of class as a result of the absence through financial disagreements of several leading batsmen influenced the England selectors from the start. Jones, the captain, was unable to play at first through illness, and George Gunn, who happened to be in Australia although not a member of the touring party, was invited to play. To stiffen the batting further, Young, the reserve wicket-keeper, was chosen in place of Humphries. The first of these gambits proved successful; the second did not.

Gunn and Hutchings retrieved a bad start for England, adding 73 for the 3rd wicket, and then the foundation of a good score was laid in a partnership between Gunn and Braund which added 117 in 100 minutes. Gunn's powerful driving continually beat the field, and he hit 20 fours. But the later batsmen failed before the pace of Cotter and the guile of Armstrong, and England were all out for 273. Hill, Trumper and Noble then put Australia well on the way to a first-

innings lead, but a collapse followed and half the side were out for 184. Useful innings by Ransford, Macartney, Carter and Hazlitt, all playing in their first Test, eventually took Australia to a lead of 27. Gunn again batted finely in the second innings, he and Hardstaff putting on 113, and with rain threatening England were in a strong position at the end of the third day.

The rain duly came, but the wicket rolled out well, and Australia seemed to have a fair chance of getting the 274 they needed to win. When they had struggled against the hostile opening attack of Fielder and Barnes to 63 for 3, however, rain again intervened; yet after a blank fifth day the wicket still rolled out reasonably well. England worked their way steadily through the middle batting, and at 124 for 6 with 150 wanted Australia seemed to face certain defeat. But McAlister was missed behind the wicket, one of three vital catches missed in the match by Young, Carter played a fine innings, and Cotter and the 19-year-old Hazlitt knocked off the last 56 runs in 40 minutes to record an exciting win. Twice in this innings Crawford came on and took a vital wicket, but he was under-bowled.

ENGLAND

*F. L. Fane	c Trumper b Cotter	2	c Noble b Saunders	33	
†R. A. Young	c Carter b Cotter	13	(7)b Noble	3	
G. Gunn	c Hazlitt b Cotter	119	c Noble b Cotter	74	
K. L. Hutchings	c and b Armstrong	42	c Armstrong b Saunders	17	
L. C. Braund	b Cotter	30	(6)not out	32	
J. Hardstaff	b Armstrong	12	(5)b Noble	63	
W. Rhodes	run out	1	(2)c McAlister b Macartney	29	
J. N. Crawford	b Armstrong	31	c Hazlitt b Cotter	5	
S. F. Barnes	b Cotter	1	b Saunders	11	
C. Blythe	b Cotter	5	c Noble b Saunders	15	
A. Fielder	not out	1	lbw b Armstrong	6	
Extras	(b 7, lb 6, w 1, nb 2)	16	(b 2, w 3, nb 7)	12	
Total		**273**	**Total**	**300**	

AUSTRALIA

V. T. Trumper	b Fielder	43	b Barnes	3	
P. A. McAlister	c Hutchings b Barnes	3	(7)b Crawford	41	
C. Hill	c Gunn b Fielder	87	b Fielder	1	
*M. A. Noble	c Braund b Fielder	37	b Barnes	27	
W. W. Armstrong	c Braund b Fielder	7	b Crawford	44	
V. S. Ransford	c Braund b Rhodes	24	c and b Blythe	13	
C. G. Macartney	c Young b Fielder	35	(2)c Crawford b Fielder	9	
†H. Carter	b Braund	25	c Young b Fielder	61	
G. R. Hazlitt	not out	18	(10)not out	34	
A. Cotter	b Braund	2	(9)not out	33	
J. V. Saunders	c Braund b Fielder	9			
Extras	(b 4, lb 2, w 2, nb 2)	10	(b 6, nb 3)	9	
Total		**300**	**Total** (8 wkts)	**275**	

FALL OF WICKETS

ENGLAND

Wkt	1st	2nd
1st	11	56
2nd	18	82
3rd	91	105
4th	208	218
5th	221	223
6th	223	227
7th	246	241
8th	253	262
9th	271	293
10th	273	300

AUSTRALIA

Wkt	1st	2nd
1st	4	7
2nd	72	12
3rd	164	27
4th	171	75
5th	184	95
6th	222	124
7th	253	185
8th	279	219
9th	281	—
10th	300	—

Umpires: R. W. Crockett,
W. Hannah

AUSTRALIA	*1st Innings*					*2nd Innings*			
	O	M	R	W		O	M	R	W
Cotter	21·5	0	101	6	..	26	1	101	2
Saunders	11	0	42	0	..	23	6	68	4
Hazlitt	9	2	32	0	..	4	2	24	0
Armstrong	26	10	63	3	..	27	14	33	1
Macartney	3	0	5	0	..	14	2	39	1
Noble	6	1	14	0	..	15	5	23	2

ENGLAND	*1st Innings*					*2nd Innings*			
	O	M	R	W		O	M	R	W
Fielder	30·2	4	82	6	..	27·3	4	88	3
Barnes	22	3	74	1	..	30	7	63	2
Blythe	12	1	33	0	..	19	5	55	1
Braund	17	2	74	2	..	7	2	14	0
Crawford	5	1	14	0	..	8	2	33	2
Rhodes	5	2	13	1	..	7	3	13	0

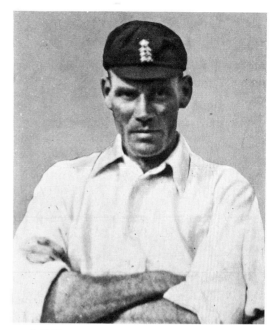

71. S. F. Barnes

70. (left) W. W. Armstrong

72. England 1907–08
Back row: R. A. Young, E. G. Hayes, A. Fielder, C. Blythe, J. Humphries, J. B. Hobbs. *Middle row:* J. N. Crawford, L. C. Braund, A. O. Jones (capt.), F. L. Fane, K. L. Hutchings, W. Rhodes. *Front:* S. F. Barnes, J. Hardstaff, Col. Philip Trevor (manager), G. Gunn.

1907-08 Second Test, Melbourne

January 1, 2, 3, 4, 6, 7
Toss: Australia *Result:* England won by one wicket

The impression of two evenly matched sides was strengthened at Melbourne, where England won with their last pair together. England included Hobbs and Humphries for Blythe, who was unwell, and Young. After an evenly contested first day Australia were all out next morning for 266, and England then progressed steadily, Hobbs batting for 3 hours 20 minutes in his first Test, but neither side gained much advantage until the last hour, in which Hutchings and Braund put on 91. Hutchings reached his hundred in 126 minutes, his second 50 coming in 51 minutes, and with Braund batting solidly England were 246 for 3 at the close.

The Australian score was passed on the third morning with only 3 wickets down, and the England position looked impregnable; but Cotter and Saunders came back strongly for Australia, and the lead was kept to 116. The match fluctuated again as Trumper and Noble knocked off the deficit without loss, and after 4 wickets had then fallen for the addition of only 36 runs, Armstrong and Macartney, by cricket that was alternately watchful and incisive, put on 106 at what looked to be the critical point of the match. Carter and Cotter again showed that Australia had no real tail, and the Australian second innings

finished only three short of 400. Crawford, given more work than anyone this time, was the most successful bowler.

At 1.0 on the fifth day England began the formidable task of making 282 to win. The wicket, although inevitably worn, was still playing well, and Hobbs and Fane began cautiously. But Hobbs and Gunn were both out at 54, and an unusually restrained Hutchings joined Fane. These two took the score to 121, when Fane was bowled by Armstrong, and at stumps England were 159 for 4, still wanting 123 to win.

Braund and Hutchings resumed on the last morning but neither stayed long. Hardstaff and Crawford were caught and Rhodes ran himself out, and England were 209 for 8—73 still wanted and the odds heavily on Australia. At this point Humphries joined Barnes, and by playing within their limitations, and by good running between the wickets, these two put on 34. Even so, 39 were still wanted when the last man, Fielder, came in. Barnes, a useful bat in Minor Counties and League cricket, farmed the bowling, Fielder struck a few solid blows, and in spite of all Noble's bowling changes and scientific field placings the runs were made.

AUSTRALIA

V. T. Trumper	c Humphries b Crawford	49	lbw b Crawford	63		
C. G. Macartney	b Crawford	37	(6)c Humphries b Barnes	54		
C. Hill	b Fielder	16	b Fielder	3		
*M. A. Noble	c Braund b Rhodes	61	(2)b Crawford	64		
W. W. Armstrong	c Hutchings b Crawford	31	b Barnes	77		
P. A. McAlister	run out	10	(4)run out	15		
V. S. Ransford	run out	27	c Hutchings b Barnes	18		
A. Cotter	b Crawford	17	(9)lbw b Crawford	27		
†H. Carter	not out	15	(8)c Fane b Barnes	53		
G. R. Hazlitt	b Crawford	1	b Barnes	3		
J. V. Saunders	b Fielder	0	not out	0		
Extras	(lb 1, w 1)	2	(b 12, lb 8)	20		
Total		266	Total	397		

ENGLAND

*F. L. Fane	b Armstrong	13	b Armstrong	50		
J. B. Hobbs	b Cotter	83	b Noble	28		
G. Gunn	lbw b Cotter	15	lbw b Noble	0		
K. L. Hutchings	b Cotter	126	c Cotter b Macartney	39		
L. C. Braund	b Cotter	49	b Armstrong	30		
J. Hardstaff	b Saunders	12	c Ransford b Cotter	19		
W. Rhodes	b Saunders	32	run out	15		
J. N. Crawford	c Ransford b Saunders	16	c Armstrong b Saunders	10		
S. F. Barnes	c Hill b Armstrong	14	not out	38		
†J. Humphries	b Cotter	6	lbw b Armstrong	16		
A. Fielder	not out	6	not out	18		
Extras	(b 3, lb 3, w 1, nb 3)	10	(b 9, lb 7, w 1, nb 2)	19		
Total		382	Total (9 wkts)	282		

FALL OF WICKETS

AUSTRALIA

Wkt	1st	2nd
1st	84	126
2nd	93	131
3rd	111	135
4th	168	162
5th	197	268
6th	214	303
7th	240	312
8th	261	361
9th	265	392
10th	266	397

ENGLAND

Wkt	1st	2nd
1st	27	54
2nd	61	54
3rd	160	121
4th	268	131
5th	287	162
6th	325	196
7th	353	198
8th	360	209
9th	369	243
10th	382	—

Umpires: R. W. Crockett, P. Argall

ENGLAND	1st Innings					2nd Innings			
	O	M	R	W		O	M	R	W
Fielder	27.5	4	77	2	..	27	6	74	1
Barnes	17	7	30	0	..	27.4	4	72	5
Rhodes	11	0	37	1	..	16	6	38	0
Braund	16	5	41	0	..	18	2	68	0
Crawford	29	1	79	5	..	33	6	125	3

AUSTRALIA	1st Innings					2nd Innings			
	O	M	R	W		O	M	R	W
Cotter	33	4	142	5	..	28	3	82	1
Saunders	34	7	100	3	..	30	9	58	1
Noble	9	3	26	0	..	22	7	41	0
Armstrong	34.2	15	36	2	..	30.4	10	53	3
Hazlitt	13	1	34	0	..	2	1	8	0
Macartney	12	2	34	0	..	9	3	21	1

1907-08 Third Test, Adelaide

January 10, 11, 13, 14, 15, 16
Toss: Australia   *Result:* Australia won by 245 runs

After outplaying their opponents for more than three days at Adelaide, England suddenly found the game slipping away from them, and soon, as Hartigan and Hill put on 243 for the 8th wicket—a record which still stands—the game was irretrievably lost. Hartigan was playing in his first Test, and another newcomer was O'Connor, a left-hand bat and medium-pace right-hand bowler, substituting for the injured Cotter.

When Australia batted first only Macartney of the early batsmen showed his best form, hitting a chanceless 75 in 2½ hours, and they owed much to a vigorous 8th wicket partnership between Hartigan and Carter which added 58. For England Hobbs and Fane again put on over 50 for the 1st wicket, Gunn played another responsible innings, not so forceful this time, and with Hardstaff batting freely England at the end of the second day were only 26 behind with 5 wickets in hand.

A bold innings by Crawford on the third morning gave England a lead of 78, which the Australians did not overtake in their second innings until they had lost 3 wickets, Barnes bowling Trumper for a duck. Noble then held the batting together, putting on 56 with Armstrong, and when Armstrong was out O'Connor was sent in as

night-watchman and survived. But Noble was out first thing next morning, at which point Australia were 135 for 5, only 57 runs on. The consistent Ransford then joined O'Connor in a partnership of left-handers which added 44 useful runs, but both were out in quick succession, and at 180 for 7, when Hill, coming in late because he was suffering from influenza (he had not fielded), joined Hartigan, it looked all over.

The heat, however, was intense, the temperature reaching 107 in the shade, and the bowlers were tiring; by close of play that evening both batsmen had made over a hundred and both were still not out. The combination of heat and mistakes in the field had demoralised the bowlers, the worst blunder being when Hill at 22 was missed at mid off by Barnes off Rhodes. Next morning Carter again showed his quality in a useful innings, and England were set 429 to win. Hill, after batting 5 hours 19 minutes, again did not field.

Hobbs had to retire with a strain, Fane was bowled for 0, and although Hardstaff and Braund put on 113 England never really shaped up to the task. Saunders and O'Connor shared the wickets, O'Connor, with Hartigan, completing a highly successful debut.

AUSTRALIA

V. T. Trumper	b Fielder	4	b Barnes		0
*M. A. Noble	c Hutchings b Barnes	15	c Gunn b Fielder		65
C. G. Macartney	lbw b Braund	75	b Barnes		9
P. A. McAlister	c Hutchings b Crawford	28	c Hutchings b Crawford		17
W. W. Armstrong	c Humphries b Fielder	17	c Hutchings b Braund		34
V. S. Ransford	b Barnes	44	(7) c Rhodes b Braund		25
C. Hill	c Humphries b Barnes	5	(9) c Gunn b Crawford		160
R. J. Hartigan	b Fielder	48	c sub (R. A. Young) b Barnes		116
†H. Carter	lbw b Hutchings	24	(10) not out		31
J. A. O'Connor	not out	10	(6) b Crawford		20
J. V. Saunders	b Fielder	1	run out		0
Extras	(b 3, lb 5, w 3, nb 3)	14	(b 20, lb 7, w 2)		29
Total		**285**	**Total**		**506**

ENGLAND

J. B. Hobbs	c Carter b Saunders	26	not out		23
*F. L. Fane	run out	48	b Saunders		0
G. Gunn	b O'Connor	65	c Trumper b O'Connor		11
K. L. Hutchings	c and b Macartney	23	b O'Connor		0
L. C. Braund	b Macartney	0	c Hartigan b O'Connor		47
J. Hardstaff	b O'Connor	61	c Macartney b Saunders		72
W. Rhodes	c Carter b O'Connor	38	c Armstrong b O'Connor		9
J. N. Crawford	b Armstrong	62	c and b Saunders		7
S. F. Barnes	c and b Armstrong	12	c McAlister b Saunders		8
†J. Humphries	run out	7	b O'Connor		1
A. Fielder	not out	0	c Ransford b Saunders		1
Extras	(b 12, lb 2, w 2, nb 5)	21	(b 3, nb 1)		4
Total		**363**	**Total**		**183**

FALL OF WICKETS

AUSTRALIA

Wkt	1st	2nd
1st	11	7
2nd	35	35
3rd	114	71
4th	140	127
5th	160	135
6th	191	179
7th	215	180
8th	273	423
9th	275	501
10th	285	506

ENGLAND

Wkt	1st	2nd
1st	58	8
2nd	98	9
3rd	138	15
4th	138	128
5th	194	138
6th	277	146
7th	282	162
8th	320	177
9th	363	182
10th	363	183

Umpires: R. W. Crockett, T. Laing

ENGLAND	1st Innings				2nd Innings			
	O	M	R	W	O	M	R	W
Barnes	27	8	60	3	42	9	83	3
Fielder	27.5	5	80	4	23	3	81	1
Rhodes	15	5	35	0	27	9	81	0
Crawford	14	0	65	1	45.5	4	113	3
Braund	9	1	26	1	23	3	85	2
Hutchings	2	1	5	1	7	0	34	0

AUSTRALIA	1st Innings				2nd Innings			
	O	M	R	W	O	M	R	W
Saunders	36	6	83	1	21.4	4	65	5
Macartney	18	3	49	2	4	1	17	0
O'Connor	40	8	110	3	21	6	40	5
Noble	18	4	38	0	7	1	14	0
Armstrong	18	4	55	2	10	1	43	0
Hartigan	2	0	7	0				

1907–08 Fourth Test, Melbourne

February 7, 8, 10, 11
Toss: Australia   *Result:* Australia won by 308 runs

By winning the fourth Test Australia regained the Ashes and demonstrated once again the astonishing resilience of the second half of their batting order; but England had all the worst of the conditions. A. O. Jones, recovered from his illness, replaced Fane, and Gregory came into the Australian side for Hartigan, who was not available. After a bad start Australia struggled through to a moderate total. Noble and McAlister, coming together at 35 for 2, put on 69, and Ransford and Armstrong added 91 for the 6th wicket, Ransford hitting to leg and cutting strongly. Otherwise the bowling, led by Barnes and Fielder, was on top. Rain delayed the resumption on the second day, and Hobbs, making up his mind to attack before the wicket got difficult, had 10 fours in his 57, but when he was 3rd out at 88 Saunders and Noble ran through the side, the last 7 wickets falling for 17.

With a lead of 109 Australia were soon in similar trouble, Trumper getting a 'pair'; Noble and McAlister also failed, and Australia were 28 for 3. Hill and Gregory, by daring running between the wickets, had taken the score to 49 for 3 by the close, but next morning, although the wicket appeared to have recovered, half the side were out for 77. Ransford then joined Armstrong and the score had been taken to 111

for 5 at lunch, Ransford playing his second attractive innings of the match at a critical point. When he was out at 162 Armstrong found further partners in Macartney, Carter and O'Connor, and with Crawford suffering from a strain England could not finish off the innings. The wicket had become slow and easy, and Barnes, although economic, was for once ineffective. Missed at slip off Braund when 44, Armstrong reached his hundred in 4 hours 8 minutes and immediately upon doing so drove Braund twice for 6. From 77 for 5 Australia thus reached 358 for 8 at stumps, and when England finally began their second innings they again needed a mammoth score—495 this time—to win.

The psychological effect of the kind of second innings recovery effected by the Australians was again shown, only Gunn displaying the degree of obduracy required, and England lost by 308 runs. This crushing defeat, unlucky though it was, underlined England's real weakness, the poor form of the spin bowlers after the three-pronged opening attack began to tire. In four Test Matches Rhodes and Braund had taken only 8 wickets between them, while Fielder, Barnes and Crawford had taken 63.

AUSTRALIA

Batsman	1st Innings dismissal	Runs	2nd Innings dismissal	Runs
*M. A. Noble	b Crawford	48	b Crawford	10
V. T. Trumper	c Crawford b Fielder	0	b Crawford	0
C. Hill	b Barnes	7	run out	25
P. A. McAlister	c Jones b Fielder	37	c Humphries b Fielder	4
S. E. Gregory	c Fielder b Crawford	10	lbw b Fielder	29
W. W. Armstrong	b Crawford	32	not out	133
V. S. Ransford	c Braund b Fielder	51	c Humphries b Rhodes	54
C. G. Macartney	c Hardstaff b Fielder	12	c Gunn b Crawford	29
†H. Carter	c and b Crawford	2	c Braund b Fielder	66
J. A. O'Connor	c Fielder b Crawford	2	c Humphries b Barnes	18
J. V. Saunders	not out	1	c Jones b Fielder	2
Extras	(b 1, lb 10, nb 1)	12	(b 7, lb 2, nb 6)	15
Total		**214**		**385**

ENGLAND

Batsman	1st Innings dismissal	Runs	2nd Innings dismissal	Runs
J. B. Hobbs	b Noble	57	c and b Saunders	0
G. Gunn	c and b Saunders	13	b Saunders	43
J. Hardstaff	c Carter b O'Connor	8	c Carter b Saunders	39
K. L. Hutchings	b Saunders	8	b Noble	3
L. C. Braund	run out	4	b Macartney	10
W. Rhodes	c McAlister b Saunders	0	c Carter b O'Connor	2
J. N. Crawford	b Saunders	1	c Carter b O'Connor	0
*A. O. Jones	b Noble	3	c Saunders b O'Connor	31
S. F. Barnes	c O'Connor b Noble	3	not out	22
†J. Humphries	not out	3	c Carter b Saunders	11
A. Fielder	st Carter b Saunders	1	b Armstrong	20
Extras	(b 1, lb 2, nb 1)	4	(lb 4, nb 1)	5
Total		**105**		**186**

FALL OF WICKETS

AUSTRALIA

Wkt	1st	2nd
1st	1	4
2nd	14	21
3rd	89	28
4th	103	65
5th	105	77
6th	196	162
7th	196	217
8th	198	329
9th	212	374
10th	214	385

ENGLAND

Wkt	1st	2nd
1st	58	0
2nd	69	61
3rd	88	64
4th	90	79
5th	90	85
6th	92	85
7th	96	128
8th	100	132
9th	103	146
10th	105	186

Umpires: R. W. Crockett, P. Argall

ENGLAND

	1st Innings				2nd Innings			
	O	M	R	W	O	M	R	W
Fielder	22	3	54	4	31	2	91	4
Barnes	23	11	37	1	35	13	69	1
Braund	12	3	42	0	7	0	48	0
Crawford	23.5	3	48	5	25	5	72	3
Rhodes	5	0	21	0	24	5	66	1
Hutchings					2	0	24	0

AUSTRALIA

	1st Innings				2nd Innings			
	O	M	R	W	O	M	R	W
O'Connor	6	1	40	1	21	3	58	3
Armstrong	1	0	4	0	3.1	0	18	1
Macartney	6	1	18	0	6	1	15	1
Saunders	15.2	8	28	5	26	2	76	4
Noble	6	0	11	3	12	6	14	1

1907–08 Fifth Test, Sydney

February 21, 22, 24, 25, 26, 27
Toss: England   *Result:* Australia won by 49 runs

For the final Test England were without Fielder and Humphries, who were both unfit, and Australia restored Hartigan for McAlister. Jones sent Australia in to bat on a rain-damaged wicket, but Noble countered by changing his batting order. Noble set the pace himself by trying to make runs quickly before the wicket became difficult, and Gregory batted doggedly, but Noble's tactics in holding back Hill and Trumper did not succeed. Australia were all out for 137, and although England lost Fane at once, Hobbs and Gunn batted through to the close on a much-improved wicket. England were then 116 for 1 and Jones' decision to put Australia in had been fully vindicated.

There were long stoppages for rain on the second and third days, rendering the wicket, if not treacherous, a difficult one to score runs on, but Gunn survived all these interruptions in a masterly innings, completing his hundred in 4 hours 23 minutes and batting nearly 5 hours in all, and England gained a lead of 144. What Barnes thought of the wicket towards the end of the third day was clear from the way he deliberately ran himself out to get the Australians to the wicket that evening, but they survived to make 18 without loss. In this period a unanimous appeal for a catch at the wicket off Barnes was answered in Noble's favour, the umpire apparently not being satisfied that the catch had been cleanly made. The crowd demonstrated against the Englishmen and for a few minutes feeling ran high.

Next day, although the wicket gradually improved under the influence of a drying wind, O'Connor and Noble were soon dismissed, and Trumper was dropped by Rhodes at short leg off a Barnes 'kicker' when he had scored a single. Gregory then batted with surprising freedom, and at lunch Australia were only 128 behind with 8 wickets to fall. On Gregory's departure at 166 the rate slowed down for a time, but Trumper was now playing in his best form, driving on both sides of the wicket and pulling fiercely. He made 166, and Australia built an unexpectedly long lead of 278. For the fourth match running they had scored far more runs at the second attempt.

The difficulty of England's task was greatly increased when rain fell again before they batted, and on the damaged wicket they lost 6 wickets for 87; but on the last morning the wicket rolled out well and a creditable fight was made. Once again England had gained a strong position only to surrender it when the Australians batted a second time.

AUSTRALIA

*M. A. Noble	b Barnes	35	lbw b Rhodes	34	
C. G. Macartney	c Crawford b Barnes	1	(5)c Jones b Crawford	12	
J. A. O'Connor	c Young b Crawford	9	(2)b Barnes	6	
S. E. Gregory	c and b Barnes	44	b Crawford	56	
C. Hill	c Hutchings b Barnes	12	(6)c Young b Crawford	44	
W. W. Armstrong	c and b Crawford	3	(7)c Gunn b Crawford	32	
V. T. Trumper	c Braund b Barnes	10	(3)c Gunn b Rhodes	166	
V. S. Ransford	c Gunn b Barnes	11	not out	21	
R. J. Hartigan	c and b Crawford	1	b Crawford	5	
†H. Carter	not out	1	c Hobbs b Rhodes	22	
J. V. Saunders	c Young b Barnes	0	c Young b Rhodes	0	
Extras	(b 9, lb 1)	10	(b 21, lb 3)	24	
Total		**137**	**Total**	**422**	

ENGLAND

J. B. Hobbs	b Saunders	72	c Gregory b Saunders	13	
F. L. Fane	b Noble	0	b Noble	46	
G. Gunn	not out	122	b Macartney	0	
K. L. Hutchings	run out	13	b Macartney	2	
J. Hardstaff	c O'Connor b Saunders	17	b Saunders	8	
J. N. Crawford	c Hill b Saunders	6	(10)not out	24	
L. C. Braund	st Carter b Macartney	31	(6)c Noble b Saunders	0	
W. Rhodes	c Noble b Armstrong	10	(7)b Noble	69	
†R. A. Young	st Carter b Macartney	0	(8)c O'Connor b Saunders	11	
*A. O. Jones	b Macartney	0	(9)b Armstrong	34	
S. F. Barnes	run out	1	b Saunders	11	
Extras	(b 6, lb 3)	9	(b 5, lb 6)	11	
Total		**281**	**Total**	**229**	

FALL OF WICKETS

AUSTRALIA

Wkt	1st	2nd
1st	10	25
2nd	46	52
3rd	46	166
4th	64	192
5th	73	300
6th	94	342
7th	124	373
8th	129	387
9th	137	422
10th	137	422

ENGLAND

Wkt	1st	2nd
1st	1	21
2nd	135	26
3rd	168	30
4th	189	51
5th	197	57
6th	245	87
7th	264	123
8th	271	176
9th	271	198
10th	281	229

Umpires: A. C. Jones, W. Hannah

ENGLAND	1st Innings				2nd Innings			
	O	M	R	W	O	M	R	W
Barnes	22·4	6	60	7	27	6	78	1
Rhodes	10	5	15	0	37·4	10	102	4
Crawford	18	4	52	3	36	10	141	5
Braund					20	3	64	0
Hobbs					7	3	13	0

AUSTRALIA	1st Innings				2nd Innings			
	O	M	R	W	O	M	R	W
Noble	28	9	62	1	24	6	56	2
Saunders	35	5	114	3	35·1	5	82	5
O'Connor	6	0	23	0	13	3	29	0
Macartney	15·1	3	44	3	15	4	24	2
Armstrong	12	2	29	1	18	7	27	1

Averages: 1907-08

AUSTRALIA

BATTING

	M.	Inns.	N.O.	Runs	H.S.	Av.
W. W. Armstrong	5	10	1	410	133*	45·55
H. Carter	5	10	3	300	66	42·85
R. J. Hartigan	2	4	0	170	116	42·50
M. A. Noble	5	10	0	396	65	39·60
C. Hill	5	10	0	360	160	36·00
S. E. Gregory	2	4	0	139	56	34·75
V. T. Trumper	5	10	0	338	166	33·80
V. S. Ransford	5	10	1	288	54	32·00
G. R. Hazlitt	2	4	2	56	34*	28·00
C. G. Macartney	5	10	0	273	75	27·30
A. Cotter	2	4	1	79	33*	26·33
P. A. McAlister	4	8	0	155	41	19·37
J. A. O'Connor	3	6	1	65	20	13·00
J. V. Saunders	5	5	2	13	9	1·85

BOWLING

	Overs	Mds.	Runs	Wkts.	Av.
J. V. Saunders	267·1	52	716	31	23·09
J. A. O'Connor	107	21	300	12	25·00
W. W. Armstrong	180·1	63	361	14	25·78
C. G. Macartney	102·1	20	266	10	26·60
M. A. Noble	147	32	299	11	27·18
A. Cotter	108·5	8	426	14	30·42

ALSO BOWLED: G. R. Hazlitt 28-6- 8-0, R. J. Hartigan 2-0-7-0.

ENGLAND

BATTING

	M.	Inns.	N.O.	Runs	H.S.	Av.
G. Gunn	5	10	1	462	122*	51·33
J. B. Hobbs	4	8	1	302	83	43·14
J. Hardstaff	5	10	0	311	72	31·10
K. L. Hutchings	5	10	0	273	126	27·30
L. C. Braund	5	10	1	233	49	25·88
F. L. Fane	4	8	0	192	50	24·00
W. Rhodes	5	10	0	205	69	20·50
J. N. Crawford	5	10	1	162	62	18·00
A. O. Jones	2	4	0	68	34	17·00
S. F. Barnes	5	10	2	121	38*	15·12
A. Fielder	4	8	4	53	20	13·25
J. Humphries	3	6	1	44	16	8·80
R. A. Young	2	4	0	27	13	6·75

PLAYED IN ONE TEST: C. Blythe 5 and 15.

BOWLING

	Overs	Mds.	Runs	Wkts.	Av.
J. N. Crawford	237·4	36	742	30	24·73
A. Fielder	216·3	31	627	25	25·08
S. F. Barnes	273·2	74	626	24	26·08
W. Rhodes	157·4	42	421	7	60·14
L. C. Braund	129	21	462	5	92·40

ALSO BOWLED: K. L. Hutchings 11-1-63-1, C. Blythe 31-6-88-1, J. B. Hobbs 7-3-13-0.

Averages: 1909

ENGLAND

BATTING

	M.	Inns.	N.O.	Runs	H.S.	Av.
J. Sharp	3	6	2	188	105	47·00
A. A. Lilley	5	7	4	106	47	35·33
C. B. Fry	3	6	2	140	62	35·00
K. L. Hutchings	2	2	0	68	59	34·00
W. Rhodes	4	7	2	168	66	33·60
A. O. Jones	2	3	0	62	28	30·66
J. B. Hobbs	3	6	1	132	62*	26·40
R. H. Spooner	2	4	0	99	58	24·75
J. T. Tyldesley	4	7	0	161	55	23·00
G. L. Jessop	2	1	0	22	22	22·00
A. C. MacLaren	5	7	0	85	24	12·14
G. H. Hirst	4	6	0	52	31	8·66
C. Blythe	2	2	0	2	1	1·00
S. F. Barnes	3	4	0	2	1	0·50

PLAYED IN ONE TEST: G. J. Thompson 6, T. W. Hayward 16 and 6, G. Gunn 1 and 0, J. H. King 60 and 4, A. E. Relf 17 and 3, S. Haigh 1* and 5, W. Brearley 6 and 4*, P. F. Warner 9 and 25, F. E. Woolley 8, E. G. Hayes 4 and 9, D. W. Carr 0.

BOWLING

	Overs	Mds.	Runs	Wkts.	Av.
C. Blythe	91·3	19	242	18	13·44
A. E. Relf	52·4	18	94	6	15·66
S. F. Barnes	155·3	54	340	17	20·00
G. H. Hirst	143·4	27	348	16	21·75
W. Rhodes	79	8	242	11	22·00
D. W. Carr	69	3	282	7	40·28

ALSO BOWLED: W. Brearley 38·2-7-78-3, J. H. King 27-5-99-1, E. G. Hayes 6-0-24-0, F. E. Woolley 10-1-37-0, S. Haigh 19-5-41-0, K. L. Hutchings 4-0-18-0, A. O. Jones 2-0-15-0, G. J. Thompson 4-0-19-0, J. Sharp 30·3-3-111-3.

AUSTRALIA

BATTING

	M.	Inns.	N.O.	Runs	H.S.	Av.
V. S. Ransford	5	9	3	353	143*	58·83
W. Bardsley	5	10	0	396	136	39·60
V. T. Trumper	5	9	1	211	73	26·37
S. E. Gregory	5	10	1	222	74	24·66
W. W. Armstrong	5	9	1	189	45	23·62
M. A. Noble	5	9	0	179	53	19·88
C. G. Macartney	5	9	1	148	51	18·50
P. A. McAlister	2	4	1	49	22	16·33
F. Laver	4	5	2	46	14	15·33
A. J. Hopkins	2	3	0	33	21	11·00
H. Carter	5	8	0	68	30	8·50
A. Cotter	5	8	0	66	19	8·25

PLAYED IN ONE TEST: J. A. O'Connor 8 and 13, W. J. Whitty 0* and 9*.

BOWLING

	Overs	Mds.	Runs	Wkts.	Av.
F. Laver	108·2	38	189	14	13·50
C. G. Macartney	127·2	33	258	16	16·12
W. W. Armstrong	140·2	51	293	14	20·92
A. Cotter	122·4	10	365	17	21·47

ALSO BOWLED: M. A. Noble 59·2-18-118-4, A. J. Hopkins 35-6-122-4, J. A. O'Connor 8·2-3-40-1, S. E. Gregory 3-0-25-0, W. J. Whitty 22-6-61-0.

1909 First Test, Edgbaston

May 27, 28, 29
Toss: Australia   *Result:* England won by ten wickets

Australia brought a side of about equal strength to the 1905 side and very similar to it, and they proved themselves a hard side to beat on good wickets in three days. The absence of Darling and Hill was compensated for in remarkable fashion by Bardsley and Ransford, while Macartney, if not quite a replacement for Duff, hardly weakened the side. England, potentially at full strength, could find room for only four of the 1907-08 touring party at Birmingham, but they might have done better if they had restricted their choice more than they did, 25 players being called upon in the series, only the captain and the wicket-keeper playing in all five Tests. The Australians for their part made few changes, fielded brilliantly under skilful leadership, and deserved their success.

Heavy rain before the start guaranteed a low-scoring game at Birmingham. Australia lost 2 wickets for 22 on an abbreviated first day and were all out on the second morning for 74, Hirst and Blythe bowling unchanged. England did little better at first, and although Jones and Tyldesley put on 48 they were soon 61 for 5. Jessop then hit 22 in 20 minutes to put England in front, but Armstrong, coming on with the score at 56 and with Jones and Tyldesley set, took 5 of the last 7 wickets for 27, and England's lead was kept to 47.

Only Gregory and Ransford offered much resistance to the swerve of Hirst and the wiles of Blythe when Australia batted again, although the wicket was not really treacherous; they came together at 16 for 2 and added 81 by sensible play. But the innings was remarkable for two wonderful catches, Jones taking Noble left-handed at short leg off a full blooded hit from a full toss, and Tyldesley catching Cotter off a ball that was going straight into the pavilion, leaning back and straining his side against the rails as he did so.

England were left with 105 to win, and a struggle was expected, but Hobbs and Fry, both out first ball in the first innings, knocked off the runs in 90 minutes without being separated, Hobbs playing with extraordinary brilliance on the damaged wicket. Australian ineptitude against the turning ball, following other batting failures in earlier matches, prompted many critics to write off their chances for the series, and the Australians themselves at this stage of their tour were greatly discouraged by their form and their lack of success.

AUSTRALIA

A. Cotter	c Hirst b Blythe	2	(9)c Tyldesley b Hirst	15	
W. Bardsley	c MacLaren b Hirst	2	(6)c Thompson b Blythe	6	
W. W. Armstrong	b Hirst	24	(7)c Jessop b Blythe	0	
V. T. Trumper	c Hirst b Blythe	10	(5)c Rhodes b Hirst	1	
*M. A. Noble	c Jessop b Blythe	15	(1)c Jones b Hirst	11	
S. E. Gregory	c Rhodes b Blythe	0	(3)c Thompson b Blythe	43	
V. S. Ransford	b Hirst	1	(4)b Blythe	43	
C. G. Macartney	c MacLaren b Blythe	10	(2)lbw b Blythe	1	
†H. Carter	lbw b Hirst	0	(8)c Hobbs b Hirst	1	
J. A. O'Connor	lbw b Blythe	8	c Lilley b Hirst	13	
W. J. Whitty	not out	0	not out	9	
Extras	(b 1, nb 1)	2	(b 7, lb 1)	8	
Total		**74**	Total	**151**	

ENGLAND

*A. C. MacLaren	b Macartney	5		
J. B. Hobbs	lbw b Macartney	0	not out	62
J. T. Tyldesley	b O'Connor	24		
C. B. Fry	b Macartney	0	not out	35
A. O. Jones	c Carter b Armstrong	28		
G. H. Hirst	lbw b Armstrong	15		
G. L. Jessop	b Armstrong	22		
W. Rhodes	not out	15		
†A. A. Lilley	c Ransford b Armstrong	0		
G. J. Thompson	run out	6		
C. Blythe	c Macartney b Armstrong	1		
Extras	(b 4, lb 1)	5	(b 5, lb 3)	8
Total		**121**	Total (0 wkts)	**105**

FALL OF WICKETS

AUSTRALIA

Wkt	1st	2nd
1st	5	4
2nd	7	16
3rd	30	97
4th	46	99
5th	47	103
6th	52	103
7th	58	106
8th	59	123
9th	71	125
10th	74	151

ENGLAND

Wkt	1st	2nd
1st	0	—
2nd	13	—
3rd	13	—
4th	61	—
5th	61	—
6th	90	—
7th	103	—
8th	107	—
9th	116	—
10th	121	—

Umpires: J. Carlin,
F. Parris

ENGLAND	1st Innings				2nd Innings			
	O	M	R	W	O	M	R	W
Hirst	23	8	28	4	23.5	4	58	5
Blythe	23	6	44	6	24	3	58	5
Thompson					4	0	19	0
Rhodes					1	0	8	0

AUSTRALIA	1st Innings				2nd Innings			
	O	M	R	W	O	M	R	W
Whitty	17	5	43	0	5	1	18	0
Macartney	17	6	21	3	11	2	35	0
Noble	1	0	2	0				
O'Connor	5	2	23	1	3.2	1	17	0
Armstrong	15.3	7	27	5	13	5	27	0

1909 Second Test, Lord's

June 14, 15, 16
Toss: Australia   *Result:* Australia won by nine wickets

For this Test Fry and Blythe were not available, and England brought in Gunn and Haigh, while King and Relf replaced Jessop and Thompson. England also left out Rhodes, and Hayward played although he hardly seemed to have recovered from a leg injury and was slow in the field and between the wickets. No fast bowler was included, although Brearley was invited at the last minute and declined. There seems little explanation for the many changes in the England side. Perhaps the selectors felt they could afford to experiment—the Australians had had a depressing start to their tour. McAlister and Laver replaced O'Connor and Whitty in the Australian side.

The wicket was expected to play tricks at first but to roll out later, and Noble put England in to bat, the first time this had been done in England. The type of wicket my be judged from the fact that Laver and Macartney opened the bowling. Hobbs and Hayward began steadily, but both were dismissed by Laver, and when Gunn was lbw to a ball which kept low, England were 44 for 3. A fighting 60 by the left-handed King, of Leicestershire, who was playing in his first Test at the age of 38 and whose selection had been much criticised, was the core of England's innings, but Tyldesley as always batted well when the pitch was difficult, helping King to add 79 for the 4th wicket,

Hirst played a useful innings, and Lilley hit out well towards the finish, so that England totalled 269.

The wicket and outfield were much quicker on the second day, and with no fast bowler the England attack looked commonplace. They were doing well enough at 119 for 4, but then Ransford and Trumper, who were both dropped, put on 79 for the 5th wicket, after which Ransford and Noble added 71. Missed three times, Ransford completed his hundred in $2\frac{3}{4}$ hours; his off-side play off the back foot was strong as always and he hit well to leg. Although a remarkably consistent player he rarely achieved the command necessary for big scores in Test cricket and this was his only Test century. Thanks largely to him Australia gained a lead of 81. The untiring Relf was England's best bowler, but he did not play again in the series.

By the time England had lost Hobbs at the end of the second day, Noble's tactics had been fully justified, and on the third day, with the wicket still fast, Armstrong turned his leg-breaks down the slope from the nursery end and England collapsed, leaving Australia only 41 to win.

This victory was the turning-point in the fortunes of Noble's team, and they did not lose a match in the next three months.

ENGLAND

Batsman	Dismissal 1st	Runs	Dismissal 2nd	Runs
T. Hayward	st Carter b Laver	16	run out	6
J. B. Hobbs	c Carter b Laver	19	c and b Armstrong	9
J. T. Tyldesley	lbw b Laver	46	st Carter b Armstrong	3
G. Gunn	lbw b Cotter	1	b Armstrong	0
J. H. King	c Macartney b Cotter	60	b Armstrong	4
*A. C. MacLaren	c Armstrong b Noble	7	(8)b Noble	24
G. H. Hirst	b Cotter	31	b Armstrong	1
A. O. Jones	b Cotter	8	(6)lbw b Laver	26
A. E. Relf	c Armstrong b Noble	17	(10)b Armstrong	3
†A. A. Lilley	c Bardsley b Noble	47	(9)not out	25
S. Haigh	not out	1	run out	5
Extras	(b 8, lb 3, w 3, nb 2)	16	(b 2, lb 3, nb 10)	15
Total		**269**	**Total**	**121**

AUSTRALIA

Batsman	Dismissal 1st	Runs	Dismissal 2nd	Runs
P. A. McAlister	lbw b King	22	not out	19
F. Laver	b Hirst	14		
W. Bardsley	b Relf	46	(2)c Lilley b Relf	0
W. W. Armstrong	c Lilley b Relf	12		
V. S. Ransford	not out	143		
V. T. Trumper	c MacLaren b Relf	28		
*M. A. Noble	c Lilley b Relf	32		
S. E. Gregory	c Lilley b Relf	14	(3)not out	18
A. Cotter	run out	0		
C. G. Macartney	b Hirst	5		
†H. Carter	b Hirst	7		
Extras	(b 16, lb 8, w 1, nb 2)	27	(b 4)	4
Total		**350**	**Total** (1 wkt)	**41**

FALL OF WICKETS

ENGLAND

Wkt	1st	2nd
1st	23	16
2nd	41	22
3rd	44	22
4th	123	23
5th	149	34
6th	175	41
7th	199	82
8th	205	90
9th	258	101
10th	269	121

AUSTRALIA

Wkt	1st	2nd
1st	18	4
2nd	84	—
3rd	90	—
4th	119	—
5th	198	—
6th	269	—
7th	317	—
8th	317	—
9th	342	—
10th	350	—

Umpires: J. Moss,
C. E. Dench

AUSTRALIA

	1st Innings				2nd Innings			
	O	M	R	W	O	M	R	W
Laver	32	9	75	3	14	5	24	1
Macartney	8	2	10	0				
Cotter	23	1	80	4	18	3	35	0
Noble	24·2	9	42	3	5	1	12	1
Armstrong	20	6	46	0	24·5	10	35	6

ENGLAND

	1st Innings				2nd Innings			
	O	M	R	W	O	M	R	W
Hirst	26·5	2	83	3	8	1	28	0
King	27	5	99	1				
Relf	45	14	85	5	7·4	4	9	1
Haigh	19	5	41	0				
Jones	2	0	15	0				

73. C. Blythe

74. C. G. Macartney

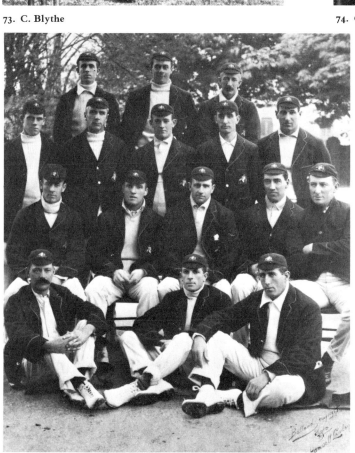

75. Australia 1909
Back row: V. S. Ransford, W. Bardsley, H. Carter.
Second row: W. J. Whitty, P. A. McAlister, A. Cotter,
R. J. Hartigan, J. A. O'Connor. *Third row:* V. T.
Trumper, A. J. Hopkins, M. A. Noble (capt.), F. Laver,
W. W. Armstrong. *Front:* S. E. Gregory, C. G.
Macartney, W. Carkeek.

1909 Third Test, Leeds

July 1, 2, 3
Toss: Australia *Result:* Australia won by 126 runs

As if five changes in the previous Test were not enough, England this time made six, Jessop, Brearley, Barnes, Rhodes, Sharp and Fry coming into the side. Australia were unchanged. The wicket was slow, but it gave just enough help to make batting difficult against top class bowling. McAlister was soon out, and after an hour's play Barnes and Hirst had bowled 20 overs for 29 runs. Then, when Australia had reached 47 for 1, England sustained a severe handicap, losing Jessop with a badly strained back. Gregory and Ransford put on 80 for the 2nd wicket, Gregory batting 2 hours 10 minutes for 46, and although Ransford never struck his best form he batted resolutely. But in 4 hours Australia were all out for 188, Rhodes, who came on for a second spell at 154, taking 4 of the last 5 wickets cheaply.

England began badly but Tyldesley and Sharp settled in and the score had reached 88 for 2 at stumps. Next day both men completed their 50s, but they were out soon afterwards, and Macartney then ran through the side, giving Australia a narrow but unexpected lead. Macartney turned the ball perceptibly from leg and got several wickets with the ball that went with the arm.

When Australia batted a second time Gregory was bowled at once by a prodigious swerver from Hirst, and McAlister again failed, but thanks to steady play by Ransford, Noble and Armstrong, Australia

recovered to be 103 for 3 at the close. Noble batted 80 minutes for 31 and Armstrong 2½ hours for 45. Splendid bowling, with Barnes outstanding, reduced the Australians to 127 for 7 on the third morning, 133 runs on with only three wickets in hand, but at this second crisis in the innings Macartney acted as anchor-man while 80 runs were put on for the last 3 wickets. Barnes, in his first Test Match in England for 7 years, bowled 60 overs in the match, 30 maidens, and took 7 for 100.

The absorbing struggle continued as England, wanting 214 to win, reached 56 for 2 overnight; but on the third morning they collapsed to Cotter and Macartney. Cotter's arm was now so low that he was almost round-arm, but he was still pacy, while Macartney's figures of 11 for 85, coupled with his steady batting in the second innings, made him the chief factor in the Australian victory, a victory which, as it transpired, decided the rubber.

When England reached 130 for 2 on the second morning they looked to have the match in hand, and their subsequent batting was severely censured. But the pitch always gave the bowlers a chance, and not even Hobbs, top scorer in the England second innings, ever looked comfortable.

AUSTRALIA

						FALL OF WICKETS

Batsman	1st Innings	1st	2nd Innings	2nd
P. A. McAlister	lbw b Hirst	3	c Sharp b Barnes	5
S. E. Gregory	b Barnes	46	b Hirst	0
V. S. Ransford	run out	45	lbw b Barnes	24
*M. A. Noble	b Hirst	3	(5)c Rhodes b Barnes	31
W. Bardsley	hit wkt b Rhodes	30	(7)c Lilley b Barnes	2
W. W. Armstrong	c Lilley b Brearley	21	(4)b Rhodes	45
V. T. Trumper	not out	27	(6)b Barnes	2
C. G. Macartney	c Fry b Rhodes	4	b Brearley	18
A. Cotter	b Rhodes	2	c MacLaren b Rhodes	19
†H. Carter	lbw b Rhodes	1	c Lilley b Barnes	30
F. Laver	c Lilley b Brearley	0	not out	13
Extras	(lb 4, w 1, nb 1)	6	(b 15, lb 2, nb 1)	18
Total		188		207

AUSTRALIA		
Wkt	1st	2nd
1st	6	0
2nd	86	14
3rd	100	52
4th	104	118
5th	140	122
6th	154	126
7th	167	127
8th	169	150
9th	171	183
10th	188	207

ENGLAND

Batsman	1st Innings	1st	2nd Innings	2nd
C. B. Fry	lbw b Cotter	1	b Cotter	7
J. B. Hobbs	b Macartney	12	b Cotter	30
J. T. Tyldesley	c Armstrong b Macartney	55	c and b Macartney	7
J. Sharp	st Carter b Macartney	61	b Cotter	11
*A. C. MacLaren	b Macartney	17	c Cotter b Macartney	1
W. Rhodes	c Carter b Laver	12	c Armstrong b Macartney	16
G. H. Hirst	b Macartney	4	(8)b Cotter	0
†A. A. Lilley	not out	4	(7)lbw b Cotter	2
S. F. Barnes	b Macartney	1	b Macartney	1
W. Brearley	b Macartney	6	not out	4
G. L. Jessop	absent hurt	—	absent hurt	—
Extras	(b 1, lb 4, nb 4)	9	(b 1, lb 1, w 1, nb 5)	8
Total		182		87

ENGLAND		
Wkt	1st	2nd
1st	8	17
2nd	31	26
3rd	137	60
4th	146	61
5th	157	61
6th	169	82
7th	171	82
8th	174	82
9th	182	87
10th	—	—

Umpires: W. A. J. West,
W. Richards

ENGLAND	1st Innings				2nd Innings			
	O	M	R	W	O	M	R	W
Hirst	26	6	65	2	17	3	39	1
Barnes	25	12	37	1	35	18	63	6
Brearley	14·1	1	42	2	24·1	6	36	1
Rhodes	8	2	38	4	19	3	44	2
Sharp					1	0	7	0

AUSTRALIA	1st Innings				2nd Innings			
	O	M	R	W	O	M	R	W
Cotter	17	1	45	1	16	2	38	5
Macartney	25·3	6	58	7	16·5	5	27	4
Armstrong	16	5	33	0	3	1	8	0
Laver	13	4	15	1	2	0	6	0
Noble	13	5	22	0				

1909 Fourth Test, Old Trafford

July 26, 27, 28
Toss: Australia   *Result:* Match Drawn

Heavy downpours the previous day and in the night damaged the pitch, and when the game started there was every prospect of a result within three days. England, who needed to win to maintain their challenge for the Ashes, made four changes, mostly forced on them by injuries or recoveries from injuries, while the Australians played Hopkins for McAlister. Varying his pace and pitch, Barnes bowled throughout the Australian first innings, 2 hours 50 minutes with a break for lunch, and Australia at one point were 66 for 6. But Armstrong, who came in at 48 for 4, played a stubborn defensive innings and held the side together, and under his guidance Australia reached 147, the last 3 wickets adding 60 runs.

The Australian attack on this tour was not highly regarded, but they always seemed to find a bowler to fit the conditions. This time it was Frank Laver. With a strong wind from square leg Laver swerved away just enough to be dangerous, varying his swerve with the off-break, and his ungainly run up to the wicket did not reduce his accuracy. In 18.2 overs he took 8 for 31. Thus in spite of a steady start the first-innings lead that England needed and seemed likely to get was denied them, and they lagged by 28.

The second day's play was curtailed through rain, Australia reaching 77 for 2, and on the third day the run-ups were slippery and Barnes couldn't at first get a foothold. Batting no. 3 this time, Macartney made a fine 51, and when at lunch-time Trumper and Ransford were still together and Australia were 214 runs ahead with only 5 wickets down, they were clearly safe from defeat. The wicket was playing easily, and although Trumper and Ransford began to score quickly, 89 runs coming in 70 minutes, Noble, one up in the series and not concerned to take any risks to force a win, batted on until a draw was virtually certain. He thus made sure of halving the series and of retaining the Ashes.

England were left with 2½ hours' batting, which they negotiated comfortably if laboriously, Spooner and Warner putting defeat out of the question in an opening stand of 78. Stumps were eventually drawn 15 minutes early. As a contest the match was spoiled by the loss of time on the second day.

During the Australian first-innings recovery Cotter, batting at the Stretford end to Blythe, hit a tremendous straight six out of the ground —a rare occurrence at Old Trafford.

AUSTRALIA

S. E. Gregory	b Blythe	21	b Hirst	5	
W. Bardsley	b Barnes	9	c MacLaren b Blythe	35	
V. S. Ransford	lbw b Barnes	4	(7)not out	54	
*M. A. Noble	b Blythe	17	b Blythe	13	
V. T. Trumper	c Hutchings b Barnes	2	(6)c Tyldesley b Rhodes	48	
W. W. Armstrong	not out	32	(5)lbw b Rhodes	30	
A. J. Hopkins	b Blythe	3	(8)c Barnes b Rhodes	9	
C. G. Macartney	b Barnes	5	(3)b Rhodes	51	
A. Cotter	c Tyldesley b Blythe	17	c MacLaren b Rhodes	4	
†H. Carter	lbw b Barnes	13	lbw b Barnes	12	
F. Laver	b Blythe	11			
Extras	(b 6, lb 7)	13	(b 9, lb 8, nb 1)	18	
Total		**147**	**Total** (9 wkts dec)	**279**	

ENGLAND

P. F. Warner	b Macartney	9	b Hopkins	25	
R. H. Spooner	c and b Cotter	25	b Laver	58	
J. T. Tyldesley	c Armstrong b Laver	15	b Hopkins	11	
J. Sharp	c Armstrong b Laver	3	not out	8	
W. Rhodes	c Carter b Laver	5	not out	0	
K. L. Hutchings	b Laver	9			
*A. C. MacLaren	lbw b Laver	16			
†A. A. Lilley	not out	26			
G. H. Hirst	c Hopkins b Laver	1			
S. F. Barnes	b Laver	0			
C. Blythe	b Laver	1			
Extras	(b 2, lb 3, nb 4)	9	(b 2, lb 4)	6	
Total		**119**	**Total** (3 wkts)	**108**	

FALL OF WICKETS

AUSTRALIA

Wkt	1st	2nd
1st	13	16
2nd	21	77
3rd	45	106
4th	48	126
5th	58	148
6th	66	237
7th	87	256
8th	110	262
9th	128	279
10th	147	—

ENGLAND

Wkt	1st	2nd
1st	24	78
2nd	39	90
3rd	44	102
4th	50	—
5th	63	—
6th	72	—
7th	99	—
8th	103	—
9th	103	—
10th	119	—

Umpires: W. A. J. West, W. Richards

ENGLAND	1st Innings					2nd Innings			
	O	M	R	W		O	M	R	W
Hirst	7	0	15	0	..	12	3	32	1
Barnes	27	9	56	5	..	22·3	5	66	1
Blythe	20·3	5	63	5	..	24	5	77	2
Sharp					..	1	0	3	0
Rhodes					..	25	0	83	5

AUSTRALIA	1st Innings					2nd Innings			
	O	M	R	W		O	M	R	W
Noble	8	2	11	0	..				
Macartney	18	6	31	1	..	7	2	16	0
Laver	18·2	7	31	8	..	21	12	25	1
Cotter	8	1	37	1	..	5	0	14	0
Armstrong					..	10	6	16	0
Hopkins					..	12	4	31	2

1909 Fifth Test, Oval

August 9, 10, 11
Toss: Australia   *Result:* Match Drawn

The England selectors left out Blythe and again failed to play a fast bowler although the wicket promised to be hard and true. But they were nothing if not unconventional, and they introduced a 37-year-old googly bowler named D. W. Carr, described as 'inclined to stoutness', a club player who was in his first season in county cricket. They also gave a trial to Woolley and Hayes. Noble won the toss for the fifth time, making up for Jackson's sequence of 1905, but the game began in sensational fashion with Carr, opening with his googlies from the Vauxhall end, hitting Gregory's off stump and getting Noble and Armstrong lbw, all in his first 7 overs. When Barnes bowled Ransford Australia were 58 for 4, and England looked well on the way to squaring the series. But with Bardsley resolute and Trumper aggressive a recovery was effected, and at lunch Australia were 132 for 4. Neither Bardsley nor Trumper had previously made a 50 in the series, but when they were parted they had added 118. As soon as Trumper was out MacLaren brought back Carr, but Macartney, who followed Trumper, played him confidently. Bardsley's hundred contained only one mistake—he was missed off Rhodes at slip by MacLaren at 77. Carr's

length did not survive the pressure exerted by Trumper and Bardsley and his figures reflected the rough treatment they gave him.

Making the ball fly at times, Cotter got 2 quick wickets when England batted towards the end of the day, but in the 2½-hour session next morning they took their score to 182 for 3, Fry and Rhodes adding 104. After a minor collapse following the break for lunch Sharp and Hutchings added 142 in 105 minutes, and England passed the Australian total with only 6 wickets down. But the tea interval, like the lunch interval, proved disastrous for England, and hopes of a substantial lead were dashed. The Australian fielding never wilted and Ransford in the deep saved many runs, while Cotter, inclined to be underrated because of his low arm, bowled very fast after each interval. Sharp, missed behind the wicket off Cotter when 93, batted 2¾ hours.

England needed quick wickets, but Australia were 76 for 0 at stumps and a draw was certain. As in the previous Test they made no attempt to force the game on the last day, and interest centred on whether Bardsley could get his second hundred of the match. It was the first time this had been done.

AUSTRALIA

						FALL OF WICKETS
S. E. Gregory	b Carr	1	run out	74		
W. Bardsley	b Sharp	136	lbw b Barnes	130		
*M. A. Noble	lbw b Carr	2	c MacLaren b Barnes	55		
W. W. Armstrong	lbw b Carr	15	c Woolley b Carr	10		
V. S. Ransford	b Barnes	3	not out	36		
V. T. Trumper	c Rhodes b Barnes	73	st Lilley b Carr	20		
C. G. Macartney	c Rhodes b Sharp	50	not out	4		
A. J. Hopkins	c Rhodes b Sharp	21				
A. Cotter	b Carr	7				
†H. Carter	lbw b Carr	4				
F. Laver	not out	8				
Extras	(b 1, lb 3, nb 1)	5	(b 4, lb 3, w 1, nb 2)	10		
Total		325	Total (5 wkts dec)	339		

AUSTRALIA		
Wkt	1st	2nd
1st	9	180
2nd	27	267
3rd	55	268
4th	58	294
5th	176	335
6th	259	—
7th	289	—
8th	300	—
9th	304	—
10th	325	—

ENGLAND

R. H. Spooner	b Cotter	13	c and b Macartney	3	
*A. C. MacLaren	lbw b Cotter	15			
W. Rhodes	c Carter b Cotter	66	(2)st Carter b Armstrong	54	
C. B. Fry	run out	62	not out	35	
J. Sharp	c Gregory b Hopkins	105	not out	0	
F. E. Woolley	b Cotter	8			
E. G. Hayes	lbw b Armstrong	4			
K. L. Hutchings	c Macartney b Cotter	59	(3)c sub (R. J. Hartigan) b Armstrong	9	
†A. A. Lilley	not out	2			
S. F. Barnes	c Carter b Hopkins	0			
D. W. Carr	b Cotter	0			
Extras	(b 8, lb 4, nb 6)	18	(lb 2, nb 1)	3	
Total		352	Total (3 wkts)	104	

ENGLAND		
Wkt	1st	2nd
1st	15	14
2nd	36	27
3rd	140	88
4th	187	—
5th	201	—
6th	206	—
7th	348	—
8th	348	—
9th	351	—
10th	352	—

Umpires: J. Moss, W. Richards

ENGLAND	1st Innings				2nd Innings			
	O	M	R	W	O	M	R	W
Carr	34	2	146	5	35	1	136	2
Barnes	19	3	57	2	27	7	61	2
Sharp	16·3	3	67	3	12	0	34	0
Woolley	4	1	6	0	6	0	31	0
Hayes	4	0	10	0	2	0	14	0
Rhodes	12	3	34	0	14	0	35	0
Hutchings					4	0	18	0

AUSTRALIA	1st Innings				2nd Innings			
	O	M	R	W	O	M	R	W
Cotter	27·4	1	95	6	8	1	21	0
Armstrong	31	7	93	1	7	4	8	2
Laver	8	1	13	0				
Macartney	16	2	49	0	8	2	11	1
Hopkins	15	2	51	2	8	0	40	0
Noble	8	1	29	0				
Gregory	1	0	4	0	2	0	21	0

1911-12 First Test, Sydney

December 15, 16, 18, 19, 20, 21
Toss: Australia *Result:* Australia won by 146 runs

The contrasting combination of Foster and Barnes proved irresistible in this series and largely accounted for the disappointing Australian batting after the first Test, though the luck ran strongly for England. Hobbs was the outstanding batsman, and Gunn was wonderfully consistent, but the decisive innings of the series was Hearne's 114 in the second Test, when he showed how to play Hordern's googlies.

England never really looked like breaking through in Australia's first innings, and at stumps Australia were 317 for 5, Trumper 95 not out. He and the hard-hitting Minnett put on 109 for the 6th wicket in 79 minutes, of which Minnett's share was 71. Trumper's controlled, chanceless innings lasted three hours 46 minutes, and Australia totalled 447.

Hobbs, who among other escapes was missed at silly mid on off Hordern when 39, helped England to a reasonable start, but he was out in the first over of the third morning, Gunn and Mead failed, and Foster joined Hearne at 142 for 5. The 20-year-old Hearne, in his first Test, was the only one to play Hordern safely, and he helped Foster to add 89 for the sixth wicket, of which Foster's share was a forceful 56.

At lunch England were 265 for 6, but when Woolley went at 293 the tail folded up. Hearne, last out, batted 2¾ hours for his 76.

129 ahead, Australia consolidated their advantage in a big 2nd-wicket stand between Kelleway and Hill. But the England attack, written off as lacking a class slow-bowler and 'presenting no difficulty' after the first innings, was never mastered in this innings; 119 for 1 overnight, Australia lost their last 9 wickets on the fourth day for 189, a glimpse of things to come. Wanting 438 to win, England set about their task in determined fashion, and at the end of the fourth day they were 65 for 1. Kinneir was soon out next morning, but Gunn and Mead batted through to lunch, and they had put on 72 for the 3rd wicket in 95 minutes when Mead, backing up too far, was run out. This was the end of any real chance of an England win, but a fine rearguard action led by Hearne, who stayed 2 hours 23 minutes this time, kept the game going into the sixth day. Hordern, who took 12 for 175 in his first Test, was already spoken of as the best bowler of his type in the world.

P. F. Warner, England's appointed captain for this series, was taken ill early in the tour, and Douglas took over as captain.

AUSTRALIA

W. Bardsley	c Strudwick b Douglas	30	b Foster	12	
C. Kelleway	c and b Woolley	20	b Douglas	70	
*C. Hill	run out	46	b Foster	65	
W. W. Armstrong	st Strudwick b Hearne	60	b Foster	28	
V. T. Trumper	c Hobbs b Woolley	113	c and b Douglas	14	
V. S. Ransford	c Hearne b Barnes	26	c Rhodes b Barnes	34	
R. B. Minnett	c Foster b Barnes	90	(8)b Douglas	17	
H. V. Hordern	not out	17	(7)b Foster	18	
A. Cotter	c and b Barnes	6	lbw b Douglas	2	
†H. Carter	b Foster	13	c Gunn b Foster	15	
W. J. Whitty	b Foster	0	not out	9	
Extras	(b 9, lb 15, nb 2)	26	(b 16, lb 7, nb 1)	24	
Total		**447**	**Total**	**308**	

ENGLAND

J. B. Hobbs	c Hill b Whitty	63	c Carter b Cotter	22	
S. P. Kinneir	b Kelleway	22	c Trumper b Hordern	30	
G. Gunn	b Cotter	4	c Whitty b Hordern	62	
W. Rhodes	c Hill b Hordern	41	(5)c Trumper b Hordern	0	
C. P. Mead	c and b Hordern	0	(4)run out	25	
J. W. Hearne	c Trumper b Kelleway	76	(7)b Hordern	43	
F. R. Foster	b Hordern	56	(6)c Ransford b Hordern	21	
F. E. Woolley	b Hordern	39	c Armstrong b Cotter	7	
*J. W. H. T. Douglas	c Trumper b Hordern	0	b Hordern	32	
S. F. Barnes	b Kelleway	9	b Hordern	14	
†H. Strudwick	not out	0	not out	12	
Extras	(b 3, lb 3, w 1, nb 1)	8	(b 14, lb 8, nb 1)	23	
Total		**318**	**Total**	**291**	

FALL OF WICKETS

AUSTRALIA

Wkt	1st	2nd
1st	44	29
2nd	77	150
3rd	121	169
4th	198	191
5th	278	218
6th	387	246
7th	420	268
8th	426	274
9th	447	283
10th	447	308

ENGLAND

Wkt	1st	2nd
1st	45	29
2nd	53	69
3rd	115	141
4th	129	141
5th	142	148
6th	231	167
7th	293	177
8th	293	263
9th	310	276
10th	318	291

Umpires: R. W. Crockett, W. Curran

ENGLAND	1st Innings				2nd Innings			
	O	M	R	W	O	M	R	W
Foster	29	6	105	2	31·3	5	92	5
Douglas	24	5	62	1	21	3	50	4
Barnes	35	5	107	3	30	8	72	1
Hearne	10	0	44	1	13	2	51	0
Woolley	21	2	77	2	6	1	15	0
Rhodes	8	0	26	0	3	1	4	0

AUSTRALIA	1st Innings				2nd Innings			
	O	M	R	W	O	M	R	W
Cotter	19	0	88	1	27	3	71	2
Whitty	28	13	60	1	20	8	41	0
Kelleway	16·5	3	46	3	19	6	27	0
Hordern	27	5	85	5	42·2	11	90	7
Armstrong	9	3	28	0	15	3	39	0
Minnett	2	1	3	0				

1911-12 Second Test, Melbourne

Test no. 88

December 30, January 1, 2, 3
Toss: Australia *Result:* England won by eight wickets

In a humid atmosphere and aided by a slight cross-wind Barnes proved almost unplayable. Swinging and breaking away from the right-hander to a field split 6-3, he occasionally brought the ball back sharply from the off. Opening the bowling this time with Foster, he bowled Bardsley with his first ball, and Kelleway, Hill and Armstrong also fell to him before lunch, when Australia, after a short interruption for rain, were 32 for 4. Barnes's figures were 9 overs, 6 maidens, 3 runs, 4 wickets. After lunch Foster bowled Trumper, Barnes dismissed Minnett, and Australia were 38 for 6. Foster, fast medium left-arm round, swinging into and across the batsman's body to a packed leg field, was the perfect foil.

During the afternoon Australia fought back steadily, led by Ransford, who made 43, but 7 wickets were down for 80 when Cotter joined Hordern. The weather had changed, the sun was hot, and the ball would no longer swing; the Australian tail, aided by a measure of luck, held on, and at tea the score was 129 for 8. Barnes, booed by the crowd during the afternoon for the elaborate care he took in adjusting his field, threw the ball down and refused to bowl until they were quiet. After this every run scored off him was cheered.

The last 2 wickets added another 55 runs after tea and Australia hit

back before the close by getting Hobbs cheaply. Douglas sent in Hearne to play out time, and next morning Rhodes and Hearne batted through to lunch, when England were 117 for 1, the feature of the play being Hearne's driving of Hordern. At tea England were 211 for 3, but then, mesmerised by Hordern, they were all out with a lead of 81. Hearne's chanceless 114 lasted $3\frac{3}{4}$ hours.

Australia again lost wickets to the new ball in their second innings but recovered later. At lunch on the third day they were 54 for 4, but in the afternoon Armstrong played a solid innings distinguished by hard driving, and Ransford helped him in a stand of 97 for the fifth wicket. The tail-enders all made useful contributions, Cotter hit Barnes straight for 6, and England were set 219 to win. They made a good start on the fourth morning and were 52 for 0 at lunch, after which Hobbs and Gunn settled the issue by putting on 112 for the 2nd wicket. Beaten and nearly bowled in Cotter's first over, Hobbs batted 3 hours 47 minutes and gave no chance. Hitch, who missed the first Test through injury, replaced Kinneir in the England side.

This was the first of Hobbs' 12 hundreds against Australia, in his 18th innings.

AUSTRALIA

C. Kelleway	lbw b Barnes	2	c Gunn b Foster	13		
W. Bardsley	b Barnes	0	run out	16		
*C. Hill	b Barnes	4	c Gunn b Barnes	0		
W. W. Armstrong	c Smith b Barnes	4	b Foster	90		
V. T. Trumper	b Foster	13	b Barnes	2		
V. S. Ransford	c Smith b Hitch	43	c Smith b Foster	32		
R. B. Minnett	c Hobbs b Barnes	2	(8)b Foster	34		
H. V. Hordern	not out	49	(7)c Mead b Foster	31		
A. Cotter	run out	14	c Hobbs b Foster	41		
†H. Carter	c Smith b Douglas	29	b Barnes	16		
W. J. Whitty	b Woolley	14	not out	0		
Extras	(b 5, lb 4, nb 1)	10	(b 14, lb 7, w 1, nb 2)	24		
Total		**184**	Total	**299**		

ENGLAND

W. Rhodes	c Trumper b Cotter	61	c Carter b Cotter	28
J. B. Hobbs	c Carter b Cotter	6	not out	126
J. W. Hearne	c Carter b Cotter	114	(4)not out	12
G. Gunn	lbw b Armstrong	10	(3)c Carter b Whitty	43
C. P. Mead	c Armstrong b Whitty	11		
F. R. Foster	c Hill b Cotter	9		
*J. W. H. T. Douglas	b Hordern	9		
F. E. Woolley	c Ransford b Hordern	23		
†E. J. Smith	b Hordern	5		
S. F. Barnes	lbw b Hordern	1		
J. W. Hitch	not out	0		
Extras	(b 2, lb 10, nb 4)	16	(b 5, lb 5)	10
Total		**265**	Total (2 wkts)	**219**

FALL OF WICKETS

AUSTRALIA

Wkt	1st	2nd
1st	0	28
2nd	5	34
3rd	8	34
4th	11	38
5th	33	135
6th	38	168
7th	80	232
8th	97	235
9th	140	298
10th	184	299

ENGLAND

Wkt	1st	2nd
1st	10	57
2nd	137	169
3rd	174	—
4th	213	—
5th	224	—
6th	227	—
7th	258	—
8th	260	—
9th	262	—
10th	265	—

Umpires: R. W. Crockett, D. Elder

ENGLAND	1st Innings					2nd Innings			
	O	M	R	W		O	M	R	W
Foster	16	2	52	1	..	38	9	91	6
Barnes	23	9	44	5	..	32·1	7	96	3
Hitch	7	0	37	1	..	5	0	21	0
Douglas	15	4	33	1	..	10	0	38	0
Hearne	1	0	8	0	..	1	0	5	0
Woolley	0·1	0	0	1	..	3	0	21	0
Rhodes					..	3	1	3	0

AUSTRALIA	1st Innings					2nd Innings			
	O	M	R	W		O	M	R	W
Cotter	22	2	73	4	..	14	5	45	1
Whitty	19	2	47	1	..	18	3	37	1
Hordern	23·1	1	66	4	..	17	0	66	0
Kelleway	15	7	27	0	..	7	0	15	0
Armstrong	15	6	20	1	..	8	1	22	0
Minnett	5	0	16	0	..	2	0	13	0
Ransford					..	1·1	0	11	0

76. H. V. Hordern

77. F. R. Foster

78. England 1911-12

Back row: S. P. Kinneir, E. J. Smith, F. E. Woolley, S. F. Barnes, J. Ironmonger, R. C. Campbell, J. Vine, H. Strudwick. *Middle row:* W. Rhodes, J. W. H. T. Douglas, P. F. Warner (capt.), F. R. Foster, T. Pawley (manager), J. B. Hobbs, G. Gunn. *Front:* J. W. Hearne, C. P. Mead (inset), J. W. Hitch.

1911-12 Third Test, Adelaide

January 12, 13, 15, 16, 17
Toss: Australia   *Result:* England won by seven wickets

The wicket had some early life in it and the Australian batsmen were again in trouble, Bardsley and Kelleway failing and Ransford, promoted to no. 4, retiring with a bruised thumb. In an attempt to protect his leading batsmen Hill batted Hordern no. 3, and the move succeeded in that Hordern, although lucky to survive, batted for 103 minutes. At lunch Australia were 45 for 2, Armstrong having replaced Ransford, and Armstrong continued in good form after lunch until he was beaten by Foster. Hordern was out soon afterwards, and then E. J. Smith, who usually stood back for Foster, saw his chance and stood up to the wicket to stump the left-handed Hill. When Foster knocked Minnett's middle stump out of the ground Australia, on a perfectly reasonable wicket and in excellent light, were 88 for 6.

The strength of the England pace attack was underlined when Hitch, brought on for the first time at 123 for 8, bowled Trumper with his first ball. Trumper had batted flawlessly for 65 minutes. The injured Ransford then joined Cotter, but he soon lost his partner and Australia were all out for 133.

In 63 minutes' play that evening Hobbs and Rhodes scored 49, and immediately after lunch next day, when the Australian score was overtaken, they were still together. Rhodes was out soon afterwards, but Hobbs reached a chanceless hundred in mid-afternoon with an off-drive to the boundary off Matthews, a leg-spinner who had been brought in for Whitty. Hobbs now began to jump in to Hordern and lift him into the deep, and as the Australians tired and catches were missed, England drove home their advantage. The Australians suffered another cruel blow when Trumper, in trying to field a fierce hit from Woolley, was struck on the leg and had to go off.

Beginning their second innings 368 behind, Australia were 96 for the loss of Kelleway at the end of the third day. Carter, who had gone in as night-watchman, helped Hill to put on 157, and all day the Australians rallied magnificently as England wilted in the heat. On the fifth day Ransford managed to help Matthews in a stand of 84, and had it not been for the injury to Trumper England might have been set a sizeable target. As it was, with 109 wanted, Rhodes and Gunn put victory beyond doubt in a 2nd-wicket stand of 97.

AUSTRALIA

						FALL OF WICKETS

Batsman	1st Innings dismissal	Runs	2nd Innings dismissal	Runs
W. Bardsley	c Smith b Barnes	5	b Foster	63
C. Kelleway	b Foster	1	b Douglas	37
H. V. Hordern	c Rhodes b Foster	25	(7)c and b Barnes	5
V. S. Ransford	not out	8	(8)b Hitch	38
W. W. Armstrong	b Foster	33	b Douglas	25
V. T. Trumper	b Hitch	26	(11)not out	1
*C. Hill	st Smith b Foster	0	(4)c Hitch b Barnes	98
R. B. Minnett	b Foster	0	(6)c Hobbs b Barnes	38
T. J. Matthews	c Mead b Barnes	5	b Barnes	53
A. Cotter	b Barnes	11	b Barnes	15
†H. Carter	c Gunn b Douglas	8	(3)c Smith b Woolley	72
Extras	(b 3, lb 6, nb 2)	11	(b 26, lb 3, nb 2)	31
Total		133	Total	476

AUSTRALIA

Wkt	1st	2nd
1st	6	86
2nd	6	122
3rd	65	279
4th	84	303
5th	88	342
6th	88	360
7th	97	363
8th	113	447
9th	123	475
10th	133	476

ENGLAND

Batsman	1st Innings dismissal	Runs	2nd Innings dismissal	Runs
J. B. Hobbs	c Hordern b Minnett	187	lbw b Hordern	3
W. Rhodes	lbw b Cotter	59	not out	57
G. Gunn	c Hill b Cotter	29	c Cotter b Kelleway	45
J. W. Hearne	c Hill b Kelleway	12	c Kelleway b Matthews	2
C. P. Mead	c and b Hordern	46	not out	2
F. R. Foster	b Armstrong	71		
*J. W. H. T. Douglas	b Minnett	35		
F. E. Woolley	c Cotter	20		
†E. J. Smith	c sub (J. Vine) b Cotter	22		
S. F. Barnes	not out	2		
J. W. Hitch	c sub (C. G. Macartney) b Hordern	0		
Extras	(b 7, lb 8, nb 3)	18	(b 1, lb 1, nb 1)	3
Total		501	Total (3 wkts)	112

ENGLAND

Wkt	1st	2nd
1st	147	5
2nd	206	102
3rd	260	105
4th	323	—
5th	350	—
6th	435	—
7th	455	—
8th	492	—
9th	501	—
10th	501	—

Umpires: R. W. Crockett, G. A. Watson

ENGLAND	1st Innings					2nd Innings			
	O	M	R	W		O	M	R	W
Foster	26	9	36	5	..	49	15	103	1
Barnes	23	4	71	3	..	46·4	7	105	5
Douglas	7	2	7	1	..	29	10	71	2
Hearne	2	0	6	0	..	10	0	61	0
Hitch	2	1	2	1	..	11	0	69	1
Woolley					..	7	1	30	1
Rhodes					..	1	0	6	0

AUSTRALIA	1st Innings					2nd Innings			
	O	M	R	W		O	M	R	W
Cotter	43	11	125	4	..	5	0	21	0
Hordern	47·1	5	143	2	..	11	3	32	1
Kelleway	23	3	46	1	..	7	3	8	1
Matthews	33	8	72	0	..	9·2	3	24	1
Minnett	17	3	54	2	..	4	1	12	0
Armstrong	14	0	43	1	..	6	1	12	0

1911-12 Fourth Test, Melbourne

February 9, 10, 12, 13
Toss: England   *Result:* England won by an innings and 225 runs

If Australia lost the fourth Test they lost the rubber; but they refused to panic, and fielded an unchanged side. Matthews, who had proved himself an economical bowler and a useful batsman at Adelaide, retained his place, and room could still not be found for Macartney, although Hill wanted him in the side. For England Vine replaced Hitch, who was suffering from a strain. Winning the toss, Douglas put Australia in.

In the event the wicket was never really difficult, but the Australians began defensively by putting Kelleway and Hordern in first. Both were out just before lunch, when Australia were 53 for 2. After lunch Trumper joined Bardsley, and the cricket brightened for a time, but wickets fell steadily to Foster and Barnes until at tea Australia were 146 for 6. After tea Minnett completed an attractive 50, but soon afterwards he was caught on the square-leg boundary. Facing a total of 191, Hobbs and Rhodes made 54 in 37 minutes before the close.

On the second day the wicket played perfectly, and although Hobbs and Rhodes were troubled at times by Hordern, the lunch and tea intervals found them still together. Both had reached their hundreds by tea, the afternoon session having brought 112 runs. After tea they went for the bowling and put on another 74 in 46 minutes before Hobbs was out. His hundred, scored in 143 minutes, had been flawless, but he gave a stumping chance off Matthews immediately after completing it, and was missed twice afterwards. The opening stand of 323 remains a record. Gunn, who had sat all day with his pads on, then joined Rhodes in a stand which was not broken until next morning, by which time 102 had been added. Rhodes' innings was not faultless but he batted solidly for nearly 7 hours while 425 runs were made.

At tea on the third day England were 522 for 6, but they were all out just before the close, and Australia made 8 without loss. Overnight showers then freshened the wicket, and Australia soon lost Kelleway and Bardsley, but Carter and Trumper defended dourly until lunch. Yet there was to be no repetition of the tremendous fight back in the previous Test, only Ransford batting with any freedom afterwards. Douglas' decision to put Australia in had been fully justified, he himself broke the back of Australia's second innings, and England regained the Ashes.

AUSTRALIA

Batsman		1st			2nd
C. Kelleway	c Hearne b Woolley	29		c Smith b Barnes	5
H. V. Hordern	b Barnes	19	(11)	c Foster b Douglas	5
W. Bardsley	b Foster	0		b Foster	3
V. T. Trumper	b Foster	17		b Barnes	28
*C. Hill	c Hearne b Barnes	22		b Douglas	11
W. W. Armstrong	b Barnes	7		b Douglas	11
R. B. Minnett	c Rhodes b Foster	56		b Douglas	7
V. S. Ransford	c Rhodes b Foster	4		not out	29
T. J. Matthews	c Gunn b Barnes	3	(10)	b Foster	10
A. Cotter	b Barnes	15	(9)	c Mead b Foster	8
†H. Carter	not out	6	(2)	c Hearne b Douglas	38
Extras	(b 1, lb 5, nb 7)	13		(b 9, lb 2, nb 7)	18
Total		**191**		**Total**	**173**

ENGLAND

J. B. Hobbs	c Carter b Hordern	178
W. Rhodes	c Carter b Minnett	179
G. Gunn	c Hill b Armstrong	75
J. W. Hearne	c Armstrong b Minnett	0
F. R. Foster	c Hordern b Armstrong	50
*J. W. H. T. Douglas	c Bardsley b Armstrong	0
F. E. Woolley	c Kelleway b Minnett	56
C. P. Mead	b Hordern	21
J. Vine	not out	4
†E. J. Smith	c Matthews b Kelleway	7
S. F. Barnes	c Hill b Hordern	0
Extras	(b 2, lb 4, w 4, nb 9)	19
Total		**589**

FALL OF WICKETS

AUSTRALIA

Wkt	1st	2nd
1st	53	12
2nd	53	20
3rd	69	76
4th	74	86
5th	83	101
6th	124	112
7th	152	117
8th	165	127
9th	170	156
10th	191	173

ENGLAND

Wkt	1st	2nd
1st	323	—
2nd	425	—
3rd	425	—
4th	486	—
5th	486	—
6th	513	—
7th	565	—
8th	579	—
9th	589	—
10th	589	—

Umpires: R. W. Crockett, W. Young

ENGLAND	1st Innings				2nd Innings			
	O	M	R	W	O	M	R	W
Foster	22	2	77	4	19	3	38	3
Barnes	29·1	4	74	5	20	6	47	2
Woolley	11	3	22	1	2	0	7	0
Rhodes	2	1	1	0				
Hearne	1	0	4	0	3	0	17	0
Douglas					17·5	6	46	5

AUSTRALIA	1st Innings				2nd Innings			
	O	M	R	W	O	M	R	W
Cotter	37	5	125	0				
Kelleway	26	2	80	1				
Armstrong	36	12	93	3				
Matthews	22	1	68	0				
Hordern	47·5	5	137	3				
Minnett	20	5	59	3				
Ransford	2	1	8	0				

February 23, 24, 26, 27, 28, 29, March 1
Toss: England   *Result:* England won by 70 runs

With the rubber lost Australia made changes. They recalled the 42-year-old S. E. Gregory, who had made 186 not out against MCC for New South Wales in the previous match, and they also brought in Macartney, Hazlitt, medium-pace off-cutters and swerve, and McLaren, fast. Bardsley, Cotter and Kelleway, who had played in the first four Tests, were left out, as was Matthews. Hitch, fit again, replaced Mead in the England side.

In the first Test, also at Sydney, Hordern had been the match-winner, and it was noticeable that all the batsmen played him cautiously. The early part of the innings was held together by Gunn, who batted 2 hours 23 minutes for 52, but half the side were out for 125. Woolley, however, was in form, and after a useful stand with Douglas he found another steady partner in Vine. At the close England were 204 for 6, Woolley having scored 62 of the 79 runs made since he came in.

Heavy rain fell in the night, but the wicket seemed unaffected. Woolley was missed at cover off Hazlitt, but at lunch he and Vine were still there, Woolley having completed his century in 2½ hours. He attacked all the bowlers, sometimes swinging Hordern high into the open spaces, and he and Vine put on 143 for the 7th wicket, of which Vine's share was 36.

Trumper and Gregory opened for Australia, and Foster, as he had done throughout the series, was soon rapping the batsmen on the hips and thighs. 'Bowl at the wicket', shouted the crowd. There was more catcalling when Barnes retired to the pavilion for repairs—a not infrequent occurrence on this tour. Meanwhile Trumper had been beautifully caught at third slip off Barnes and Hitch had got Hill caught behind. Four wickets were down for 82, and after Armstrong and Ransford had put on 51, Australia were 133 for 5 at the close. So far England were well on top.

There was a blank third day through rain, and the wicket and outfield were dead when play was eventually resumed. Australia were all out 148 behind, but after Hobbs and Rhodes had put up 50 in 36 minutes it was left to Gunn to hold the innings together. Wanting 363, Australia had got as far as 193 for 3 on the fifth day when rain and bad light intervened. The sixth day was blank through rain, and on the seventh, with 170 wanted, Barnes bumping shoulder high and Woolley kicking awkwardly, Australia did well to finish only 70 runs short. The luck had gone against them to the end.

ENGLAND

J. B. Hobbs	c Ransford b Hordern	32	c Hazlitt b Hordern	45
W. Rhodes	b Macartney	8	lbw b Armstrong	30
G. Gunn	st Carter b Hordern	52	b Hordern	61
J. W. Hearne	c Macartney b Armstrong	4	b Hordern	18
F. R. Foster	st Carter b Hazlitt	15	b McLaren	4
*J. W. H. T. Douglas	c Ransford b Hordern	18	b Armstrong	8
F. E. Woolley	not out	133	c Armstrong b Hazlitt	11
J. Vine	b Hordern	36	not out	6
†E. J. Smith	b Hordern	0	b Hordern	13
S. F. Barnes	c Hordern b Hazlitt	5	b Hordern	4
J. W. Hitch	c Hill b Hazlitt	4	c Ransford b Armstrong	4
Extras	(b 10, lb 4, w 1, nb 2)	17	(b 8, nb 2)	10
Total		**324**	Total	**214**

AUSTRALIA

V. T. Trumper	c Woolley b Barnes	5	c Woolley b Barnes	50
S. E. Gregory	c Gunn b Douglas	32	c Smith b Barnes	40
*C. Hill	c Smith b Hitch	20	b Foster	8
W. W. Armstrong	lbw b Barnes	33	b Barnes	33
R. B. Minnett	c Douglas b Hitch	0	c Woolley b Barnes	61
V. S. Ransford	c Hitch b Foster	29	b Woolley	9
†H. Carter	c sub (C. P. Mead) b Barnes	11	(8)c Woolley b Foster	23
C. G. Macartney	c and b Woolley	26	(7)c Woolley b Foster	27
H. V. Hordern	b Woolley	0	run out	4
G. R. Hazlitt	run out	1	c Rhodes b Foster	4
J. W. McLaren	not out	0	not out	0
Extras	(b 14, lb 2, w 2, nb 1)	19	(b 22, lb 8, w 1, nb 2)	33
Total		**176**	Total	**292**

FALL OF WICKETS

ENGLAND

Wkt	1st	2nd
1st	15	76
2nd	69	76
3rd	83	105
4th	114	110
5th	125	146
6th	162	178
7th	305	186
8th	305	201
9th	312	209
10th	324	214

AUSTRALIA

Wkt	1st	2nd
1st	17	88
2nd	59	101
3rd	81	117
4th	82	209
5th	133	220
6th	133	231
7th	171	278
8th	175	287
9th	176	287
10th	176	292

Umpires: R. W. Crockett, A. C. Jones

AUSTRALIA	1st Innings					2nd Innings			
	O	M	R	W		O	M	R	W
McLaren	16	2	47	0	..	8	1	23	1
Macartney	12	3	26	1	..	7	0	28	0
Hordern	37	8	95	5	..	25	5	66	5
Hazlitt	31	6	75	3	..	12	2	52	1
Armstrong	25	8	42	1	..	17·3	7	35	3
Minnett	8	1	22	0	..	1	1	0	0

ENGLAND	1st Innings					2nd Innings			
	O	M	R	W		O	M	R	W
Foster	16	0	55	1	..	30·1	7	43	4
Barnes	19	2	56	3	..	39	12	106	4
Hitch	9	1	31	2	..	6	1	23	0
Douglas	7	0	14	1	..	9	0	34	0
Woolley	2	1	1	2	..	16	5	36	1
Rhodes					..	2	0	17	0

Averages: 1911-12

AUSTRALIA

BATTING	M.	Inns.	N.O.	Runs	H.S.	Av.
W. W. Armstrong	5	10	0	324	90	32·40
V. S. Ransford	5	10	2	252	43	31·50
R. B. Minnett	5	10	0	305	90	30·50
V. T. Trumper	5	10	1	269	113	29·88
C. Hill	5	10	0	274	98	27·40
H. Carter	5	10	1	231	72	25·66
C. Kelleway	4	8	0	177	70	22·12
H. V. Hordern	5	10	2	173	49*	21·62
T. J. Matthews	2	4	0	71	53	17·75
W. Bardsley	4	8	0	129	63	16·12
A. Cotter	4	8	0	112	43	14·00
W. J. Whitty	2	4	2	23	14	11·50

PLAYED IN ONE TEST: S. E. Gregory 32 and 40, C. G. Macartney 26 and 27, G. R. Hazlitt 1 and 4, J. W. McLaren 0* and 0*.

BOWLING	Overs	Mds.	Runs	Wkts.	Av.
H. V. Hordern	277·3	43	780	32	24·37
R. B. Minnett	59	12	179	5	35·80
W. W. Armstrong	145·3	41	334	9	37·11
C. Kelleway	113·5	24	249	6	41·50
A. Cotter	167	26	548	12	45·66

ALSO BOWLED: G. R. Hazlitt 43–8–127–4, C. G. Macartney 19–3–54–1, W. J. Whitty 85–26–185–3, J. W. McLaren 24–3–70–1, T. J. Matthews 64·2–12–164–1, V. S. Ransford 3·1–1–19–0.

ENGLAND

BATTING	M.	Inns.	N.O.	Runs	H.S.	Av.
J. B. Hobbs	5	9	1	662	187	82·75
W. Rhodes	5	9	1	463	179	57·87
F. E. Woolley	5	7	1	289	133*	48·16
J. Vine	2	3	2	46	36	46·00
G. Gunn	5	9	0	381	75	42·33
J. W. Hearne	5	9	1	281	114	35·12
F. R. Foster	5	7	0	226	71	32·28
C. P. Mead	4	6	1	105	46	21·00
J. W. H. T. Douglas	5	7	0	102	35	14·57
E. J. Smith	4	5	0	47	22	9·40
S. F. Barnes	5	7	1	35	14	5·83
J. W. Hitch	3	4	1	8	4	2·66

PLAYED IN ONE TEST: S. P. Kinneir 22 and 30, H. Strudwick 0* and 12*.

BOWLING	Overs	Mds.	Runs	Wkts.	Av.
F. R. Foster	276·4	58	692	32	21·62
S. F. Barnes	297	64	778	34	22·88
J. W. H. T. Douglas	139·5	30	355	15	23·66
F. E. Woolley	68·1	13	209	8	26·12
J. W. Hitch	40	2	183	5	36·60

ALSO BOWLED: J. W. Hearne 41–2–196–1, W. Rhodes 19–3–57–0.

Averages: 1912

ENGLAND

BATTING	M.	Inns.	N.O.	Runs	H.S.	Av.
J. B. Hobbs	3	4	0	224	107	56·00
W. Rhodes	3	4	0	204	92	51·00
C. B. Fry	3	4	0	145	79	36·25
F. E. Woolley	3	4	0	99	62	24·75
F. R. Foster	3	4	1	55	20	18·33
J. W. Hearne	3	4	1	45	21*	15·00
E. J. Smith	3	4	1	22	14*	7·33
S. F. Barnes	3	3	1	8	7	4·00
R. H. Spooner	3	4	0	3	1	0·75
H. Dean	2	2	1	0	0*	0·00

PLAYED IN ONE TEST: P. F. Warner 4, S. Haigh 9, J. W. Hitch 4, J. W. H. T. Douglas 18 and 24.

BOWLING	Overs	Mds.	Runs	Wkts.	Av.
F. E. Woolley	23·2	7	55	10	5·50
H. Dean	54	19	97	6	16·16
W. Rhodes	21·2	6	60	3	20·00
S. F. Barnes	62	26	122	5	24·40
F. R. Foster	39	18	50	2	25·00

ALSO BOWLED: J. W. Hearne 12–1–31–0, S. Haigh 6–4–3–0.

AUSTRALIA

BATTING	M.	Inns.	N.O.	Runs	H.S.	Av.
C. G. Macartney	3	3	0	133	99	44·33
C. Kelleway	3	4	1	107	61	35·66
W. Bardsley	3	3	0	51	30	17·00
D. Smith	2	3	1	30	24*	15·00
C. B. Jennings	3	4	1	44	21	14·66
G. R. Hazlitt	3	3	1	26	19	13·00
W. Carkeek	3	2	1	5	5	5·00
S. E. Gregory	3	3	0	12	10	4·00
W. J. Whitty	3	2	0	3	3	1·50
T. J. Matthews	3	2	0	3	3	1·00

S. H. Emery played in two matches and E. R. Mayne in one match but did not bat.

PLAYED IN ONE TEST: R. B. Minnett 0 and 4.

BOWLING	Overs	Mds.	Runs	Wkts.	Av.
R. B. Minnett	10·1	3	34	4	8·50
G. R. Hazlitt	113·3	36	218	12	18·16
W. J. Whitty	110	42	252	12	21·00
S. H. Emery	19	2	68	2	34·00
C. G. Macartney	48	12	78	2	39·00
C. Kelleway	34	8	101	2	50·50
T. J. Matthews	49	16	113	2	56·50

1912 First Test, Lord's

June 24, 25, 26
Toss: England   *Result:* Match Drawn

Main interest in the Triangular Tournament of 1912 centred on the matches between England and Australia: England won all their three games against South Africa and Australia won two and drew one. After a squabble over the administration of the touring party, which had been brewing ever since the formation of the Australian Board of Control in 1905, Hill, Trumper, Armstrong, Cotter, Carter and Ransford, although originally invited, were left out. The side was thus seriously depleted, though no more so, perhaps, than several English touring sides of the period. The party was inevitably weak in reserves, but the Test Match side was still a strong one. Macartney, Minnett, Gregory, Hazlitt and McLaren had played in the final Test at Sydney in the February of that year, Bardsley and Kelleway had played in the first four Tests of that series and Matthews and Whitty in two. Hill and Trumper were 35 and new blood perhaps was needed, while Carkeek had been no. 2 to Carter in 1907-08. Yet when all that has been said, Australia were without five of their six most successful batsmen of the 1911-12 series and their only successful bowler. In addition they were hampered by a disastrously wet summer.

At Lord's rain restricted play on the first day to 3½ hours, in which England made 211 for 4. Hobbs and Rhodes put on 112 on a saturated pitch which gave the bowlers more help as the innings progressed, and as in Australia their running between the wickets, based on a perfect understanding, was exhilarating. Hobbs had the unusual experience of being outscored by Rhodes during most of their partnership, yet he reached his century in 2 hours 42 minutes, on a wicket that was treacherous as it dried.

Rain restricted play on the second day to little more than 20 minutes, and on the third morning the England batsmen, hurrying in and out when a wicket fell, took the score to 310 for 7, the declaration leaving the England bowlers 5 hours 40 minutes in which to bowl Australia out twice. For a time the fielders changed between overs at the double, believing perhaps that they had a chance of victory, but when Macartney came in, self-assertive and confident, he changed all this. The wicket had rolled out well, and Macartney, after reaching 50 in 90 minutes, pulled a short ball from Barnes for six. Meanwhile Kelleway, the most prolific batsman of the tournament after Hobbs, concentrated solely on survival. Foster, plying Macartney with in-swingers running down the leg side as he neared his hundred, got him to edge one at 99; he had batted only 2 hours 20 minutes. Disappointing as the match was as a contest, it had produced two innings of the highest class.

ENGLAND

J. B. Hobbs	b Emery	107
W. Rhodes	c Carkeek b Kelleway	59
R. H. Spooner	c Bardsley b Kelleway	1
*C. B. Fry	run out	42
P. F. Warner	b Emery	4
F. E. Woolley	c Kelleway b Hazlitt	20
F. R. Foster	c Macartney b Whitty	20
J. W. Hearne	not out	21
†E. J. Smith	not out	14
S. F. Barnes	} did not bat	
H. Dean		
Extras	(b 16, lb 4, nb 2)	22
Total	(7 wkts dec)	**310**

AUSTRALIA

C. B. Jennings	c Smith b Foster	21
C. Kelleway	b Rhodes	61
C. G. Macartney	c Smith b Foster	99
W. Bardsley	lbw b Rhodes	21
*S. E. Gregory	c Foster b Dean	10
D. Smith	not out	24
T. J. Matthews	b Dean	0
G. R. Hazlitt	b Rhodes	19
S. H. Emery	} did not bat	
W. J. Whitty		
†W. Carkeek		
Extras	(b 17, lb 5, w 1, nb 4)	27
Total	(7 wkts)	**282**

FALL OF WICKETS

ENGLAND		
Wkt	1st	2nd
1st	112	—
2nd	123	—
3rd	197	—
4th	211	—
5th	246	—
6th	255	—
7th	285	—
8th	—	—
9th	—	—
10th	—	—

AUSTRALIA		
Wkt	1st	2nd
1st	27	—
2nd	173	—
3rd	226	—
4th	233	—
5th	243	—
6th	243	—
7th	282	—
8th	—	—
9th	—	—
10th	—	—

Umpires: J. Moss,
A. E. Street

AUSTRALIA	1st Innings				2nd Innings			
	O	M	R	W	O	M	R	W
Whitty	12	2	69	1	..			
Hazlitt	25	6	68	1	..			
Matthews	13	4	26	0	..			
Kelleway	21	5	66	2	..			
Emery	12	1	46	2	..			
Macartney	7	1	13	0	..			

ENGLAND	1st Innings				2nd Innings			
	O	M	R	W	O	M	R	W
Foster	36	18	42	2	..			
Barnes	31	10	74	0	..			
Dean	29	10	49	2	..			
Hearne	12	1	31	0	..			
Rhodes	19·2	5	59	3	..			

79. S. E. Gregory

80. C. B. Fry

81. Australia 1912
Back row: R. B. Minnett, C. Kelleway, E. R. Mayne, D. Smith, S. H. Emery, G. S. Crouch (manager). *Middle:* J. W. McLaren, W. Carkeek, W. J. Whitty, S. E. Gregory (capt.), W. Bardsley, C. G. Macartney, G. R. Hazlitt. *Front:* H. Webster, C. B. Jennings, T. J. Matthews.

1912 Second Test, Old Trafford

July 29, 30, 31
Toss: England   *Result:* Match Drawn

Before he had scored Rhodes cut a rising ball from Whitty into and out of the hands of Hazlitt at point: from then on, on a wicket that was varying all the time as it dried and in a high wind that made the swerve of Whitty and Hazlitt disconcerting to all the other batsmen, Rhodes played a masterly innings. Five weeks earlier he had outshone Hobbs for a time at Lord's; now he played probably his greatest innings.

England, aware that in the first Test they had placed too much reliance on Foster and Barnes, played an extra bowler, bringing in Haigh and Hitch for Warner and Dean, while Australia, for whom Minnett was not available through injury, substituted Mayne for Smith.

Rain delayed the start, and it was after 2.0 before Fry tossed a coin in front of the pavilion and Gregory called wrongly. Fry, who as usual had been in the nets, was wearing pads. 42 runs came in the first hour for the loss of Hobbs and Spooner, both clean bowled by Whitty, and Fry spent an hour over 19 before being caught at long off. England should have been 84 for 4 soon afterwards, Hearne mishitting

a Matthews leg-break gently to Whitty at mid on, but the catch went down. Hearne then stayed to add 57 for the 4th wicket, of which his share was 9, and at the end of the day England were 185 for 6, Rhodes 92 not out. The tall left-hander Whitty, who had often looked unlucky in previous series, used the wind cleverly, brought the ball across sharply at times from leg, and bowled a dangerous yorker.

It was 5.0 on the second day, after many hours of rain, before the game could resume, and then there was only 75 minutes' cricket. Rhodes, who had batted 3¾ hours on the previous day, played on to his second ball. A self-taught batsman, not particularly graceful, Rhodes was a workman rather than an artist with the bat, and he was never thrilling to watch, but he showed true greatness in this innings. England did not last long after he left.

Australia had a few minutes' batting at the end of the day, and the third day was completely washed out. Supremacy in the Triangular Tournament thus depended on the final Test; but the break-up in the weather had so affected Australian performance that England were now firm favourites.

ENGLAND

J. B. Hobbs	b Whitty	19
W. Rhodes	b Whitty	92
R. H. Spooner	b Whitty	1
*C. B. Fry	c sub (J. W. McLaren) b Matthews	19
J. W. Hearne	b Hazlitt	9
F. E. Woolley	c Kelleway b Whitty	13
F. R. Foster	c and b Matthews	13
†E. J. Smith	c Emery b Hazlitt	4
S. Haigh	c Kelleway b Hazlitt	9
S. F. Barnes	not out	1
J. W. Hitch	b Hazlitt	4
Extras	(b 9, lb 9, nb 1)	19
Total		**203**

AUSTRALIA

C. B. Jennings	not out	9
C. Kelleway	not out	3
W. Bardsley		
*S. E. Gregory		
C. G. Macartney		
E. R. Mayne		
T. J. Matthews	did not bat	
S. H. Emery		
W. J. Whitty		
G. R. Hazlitt		
†W. Carkeek		
Extras	(b 2)	2
Total	(0 wkts)	**14**

FALL OF WICKETS

ENGLAND		
Wkt	1st	2nd
1st	37	—
2nd	39	—
3rd	83	—
4th	140	—
5th	155	—
6th	181	—
7th	185	—
8th	189	—
9th	199	—
10th	203	—

AUSTRALIA		
Wkt	1st	2nd
1st	—	—
2nd	—	—
3rd	—	—
4th	—	—
5th	—	—
6th	—	—
7th	—	—
8th	—	—
9th	—	—
10th	—	—

Umpires: G. Webb,
W. A. J. West

AUSTRALIA	1st Innings				2nd Innings			
	O	M	R	W	O	M	R	W
Hazlitt	40·5	12	77	4	..			
Whitty	27	15	43	4	..			
Kelleway	6	1	19	0	..			
Matthews	12	4	23	2	..			
Emery	7	1	22	0	..			

ENGLAND	1st Innings				2nd Innings			
	O	M	R	W	O	M	R	W
Foster	1	0	3	0	..			
Haigh	6	4	3	0	..			
Woolley	6	3	6	0	..			

1912 Third Test, Oval

August 19, 20, 21, 22
Toss: England   *Result:* England won by 244 runs

Early showers again prevented a punctual start. The wicket was wet and it was thought it might improve later, but with more rain threatened Fry took first knock. The adaptable Lancashire left-arm bowler Dean, who could suit his pace to the conditions, replaced Haigh, Hitch was left out, and Douglas came in at the last minute for Hayes, who was ill. Minnett (who on the wet wickets that were prevalent was having a disappointing tour) and Smith replaced Mayne and Emery for Australia. As the first two Tests had been drawn, this one was to be played to a finish.

In spite of interruptions England made 223 for 8 on the first day, which on a wicket never likely to be plumb looked a useful score. The pitch was soft and slow at the outset, but Hobbs batted only 1 hour 50 minutes for his 66, made out of 107 put on for the 1st wicket. Forcing the ball off his legs and steering it repeatedly for singles and twos, he refused to be kept quiet. Rhodes, in contrast, batted 3 hours for 49. Then Woolley, by hitting of exceptional power, had 11 fours in his 62.

A huge storm overnight meant another late start next morning. England were soon all out, and Australia struggled in bad light and against a close-set field to 51 for 2 at the day's end, further rain washing out the afternoon session. On the third morning Gregory had the heavy roller on, and the 3rd-wicket partnership prospered for a time, but after half an hour the pitch began to dry. Woolley came on at the pavilion end, Barnes crossed to the Vauxhall end, and Australia had no chance. Kelleway, who had batted two hours, was lbw to Woolley, a decision of which he clearly disapproved, indicating that the ball was too high, and Bardsley was bowled round his legs by a Barnes off-break. Only 21 runs were added after Kelleway's dismissal, and England went in again with a lead of 134.

After further rain had deadened the wicket, Hobbs led the way with a bright 32, and next morning Fry, after being bowled three times running in the nets beforehand, batted superbly. When in the 20s he apparently trod on his wicket—'But I had finished my shot,' he said, and he was given not out. The Australians, not unnaturally, were convinced that he was out. When the wicket began to dry, Hazlitt took the last 5 wickets for one run; and after a steady start following a further rolling Australia collapsed a second time. England's overwhelming victory obscured the fact that Australia had fully held her own when conditions were even.

ENGLAND

J. B. Hobbs	c Carkeek b Macartney	66	c Matthews b Whitty	32	
W. Rhodes	b Minnett	49	b Whitty	4	
R. H. Spooner	c Hazlitt b Macartney	1	c Jennings b Whitty	0	
*C. B. Fry	c Kelleway b Whitty	5	c Jennings b Hazlitt	79	
F. E. Woolley	lbw b Minnett	62	b Hazlitt	4	
J. W. Hearne	c Jennings b Whitty	1	c Matthews b Hazlitt	14	
J. W. H. T. Douglas	lbw b Whitty	18	lbw b Hazlitt	24	
F. R. Foster	b Minnett	19	not out	3	
†E. J. Smith	b Whitty	4	b Hazlitt	0	
S. F. Barnes	c Jennings b Minnett	7	c Whitty b Hazlitt	0	
H. Dean	not out	0	b Hazlitt	0	
Extras	(b 2, lb 10, nb 1)	13	(b 14, nb 1)	15	
Total		**245**	Total	**175**	

AUSTRALIA

*S. E. Gregory	c Rhodes b Barnes	1	(5) c Douglas b Dean	1	
C. Kelleway	lbw b Woolley	43	c Douglas b Dean	0	
C. G. Macartney	b Barnes	4	b Dean	30	
W. Bardsley	b Barnes	30	run out	0	
C. B. Jennings	c and b Woolley	0	(1) c Fry b Woolley	14	
R. B. Minnett	c Rhodes b Woolley	0	lbw b Woolley	4	
D. Smith	c Smith b Woolley	6	c Douglas b Dean	0	
T. J. Matthews	c Fry b Barnes	2	c and b Woolley	1	
W. J. Whitty	c Foster b Barnes	0	b Woolley	3	
G. R. Hazlitt	not out	2	c Dean b Woolley	5	
†W. Carkeek	c Barnes b Woolley	5	not out	0	
Extras	(b 12, lb 6)	18	(b 1, lb 5, w 1)	7	
Total		**111**	Total	**65**	

FALL OF WICKETS

ENGLAND

Wkt	1st	2nd
1st	107	7
2nd	109	7
3rd	131	51
4th	131	56
5th	144	91
6th	180	170
7th	216	171
8th	233	171
9th	239	175
10th	245	175

AUSTRALIA

Wkt	1st	2nd
1st	9	0
2nd	19	46
3rd	90	46
4th	90	47
5th	92	51
6th	96	51
7th	104	51
8th	104	54
9th	104	65
10th	111	65

Umpires: J. Moss,
A. E. Street

AUSTRALIA

	1st Innings				2nd Innings			
	O	M	R	W	O	M	R	W
Whitty	38	12	69	4	33	13	71	3
Matthews	14	5	43	0	10	3	21	0
Hazlitt	26	10	48	0	21·4	8	25	7
Macartney	19	6	22	2	22	5	43	0
Minnett	10·1	3	34	4				
Kelleway	7	2	16	0				

ENGLAND

	1st Innings				2nd Innings			
	O	M	R	W	O	M	R	W
Barnes	27	15	30	5	4	1	18	0
Dean	16	7	29	0	9	2	19	4
Foster	2	0	5	0				
Woolley	9·4	3	29	5	7·4	1	20	5
Rhodes					2	1	1	0

1920-21 First Test, Sydney

Test no. 95

December 17, 18, 20, 21, 22
Toss: Australia *Result:* Australia won by 377 runs

Preparatory to this first Test campaign for more than 8 years, England had displayed form which suggested a hard-fought series. Their batting looked strong and could not have been much improved, but the attack depended too much on Parkin's success as a 'mystery' bowler. Howell bowled well but suffered terribly from dropped catches, and England had no bowler to compare with J. M. Gregory for penetration and the ability to unsettle the best batsmen. The Australian batsmen, for their part, scored so heavily that Armstrong was able to give full rein to the genius of Mailey.

Apart from dropped catches, England had a good first day. Collins, who was not out 30 at lunch, when the score was 80 for 2, was dropped twice, but a brilliant return by Hendren ran out Kelleway after a typically stubborn innings and soon afterwards Hitch threw Collins' wicket down from square leg. When Armstrong was stumped on the leg side off Woolley in the last over before tea, half the side were out for 173. On the resumption Gregory was caught at the wicket, but a stand between Taylor and Pellew restored the balance, although Parkin was unlucky not to bowl them both. Next morning Ryder was the third batsman to be run out, and on a perfect wicket Australia were all out for 267. Russell was beaten by Kelleway's first ball, and at lunch England were 47 for 1.

Hearne was out soon after lunch, and Hobbs was bowled by Gregory, but Woolley and Hendren put on 74, and at tea England seemed fairly well placed at 158 for 4. But Mailey, who was put on as soon as Douglas went in, got all the later batsmen into a tangle, Gregory cleaned up the tail, and England were all out 77 runs behind. Collins and Bardsley had added 46 to this by the close.

Keeping up a rate of a run a minute throughout the third day, Australia reached 332 for 5. The England ground fielding remained good on the whole but more catches were missed. And England's ordeal was by no means over. On the fourth day Armstrong joined Kelleway, and driving with tremendous power he reached his hundred in 2 hours 4 minutes, while Kelleway batted 3½ hours for his 78. Hitch and Waddington were suffering from strains, and Australia ran up the record second-innings total of 581, setting England 659 to win. By tea on the fifth day England had made the creditable response of 228 for 5, but the end came soon after.

AUSTRALIA

Batsman	1st Innings		2nd Innings	
C. G. Macartney	b Waddington	19	(3)b Douglas	69
H. L. Collins	run out	70	c Waddington b Douglas	104
W. Bardsley	c Strudwick b Hearne	22	(1)b Hearne	57
C. Kelleway	run out	33	(6)c Russell b Woolley	78
*W. W. Armstrong	st Strudwick b Woolley	12	(7)b Parkin	158
J. M. Gregory	c Strudwick b Woolley	8	(9)run out	0
J. M. Taylor	lbw b Hearne	34	(4)c Woolley b Parkin	51
C. E. Pellew	c Hendren b Hearne	36	(5)lbw b Woolley	16
J. Ryder	run out	5	(8)run out	6
†W. A. Oldfield	c Hobbs b Parkin	7	c Strudwick b Parkin	16
A. A. Mailey	not out	10	not out	0
Extras	(b 4, lb 6, nb 1)	11	(b 17, lb 7, nb 2)	26
Total		**267**		**581**

ENGLAND

Batsman	1st Innings		2nd Innings	
J. B. Hobbs	b Gregory	49	lbw b Armstrong	59
A. C. Russell	b Kelleway	0	c Oldfield b Gregory	5
J. W. Hearne	c Gregory b Mailey	14	b Gregory	57
E. H. Hendren	c Gregory b Ryder	28	b Kelleway	56
F. E. Woolley	c Mailey b Ryder	52	st Oldfield b Mailey	16
*J. W. H. T. Douglas	st Oldfield b Mailey	21	c Armstrong b Mailey	7
W. Rhodes	c Gregory b Mailey	3	c Ryder b Mailey	45
J. W. Hitch	c Kelleway b Gregory	3	c Taylor b Gregory	19
A. Waddington	run out	7	b Kelleway	3
C. H. Parkin	not out	4	b Kelleway	4
†H. Strudwick	lbw b Gregory	2	not out	1
Extras	(b 3, lb 4)	7	(b 6, lb 3)	9
Total		**190**		**281**

FALL OF WICKETS
AUSTRALIA

Wkt	1st	2nd
1st	40	123
2nd	80	234
3rd	140	241
4th	162	282
5th	173	332
6th	176	519
7th	244	536
8th	249	540
9th	250	578
10th	267	581

ENGLAND

Wkt	1st	2nd
1st	0	5
2nd	50	105
3rd	70	149
4th	144	170
5th	145	178
6th	158	231
7th	165	264
8th	180	271
9th	188	279
10th	190	281

Umpires: A. C. Jones, R. W. Crockett

ENGLAND	1st Innings				2nd Innings			
	O	M	R	W	O	M	R	W
Hitch	10	0	37	0	8	0	40	0
Waddington	18	3	35	1	23	4	53	0
Parkin	26·5	5	58	1	35·3	5	102	3
Hearne	34	8	77	3	42	7	124	1
Woolley	23	7	35	2	36	11	90	2
Douglas	3	0	14	0	26	3	79	2
Rhodes					22	2	67	0

AUSTRALIA	1st Innings				2nd Innings			
	O	M	R	W	O	M	R	W
Kelleway	6	2	10	1	15·5	3	45	3
Gregory	23·1	3	56	3	33	6	70	3
Mailey	23	4	95	3	24	2	105	3
Ryder	6	1	20	2	17	6	24	0
Armstrong	1	0	2	0	10	0	21	1
Macartney					3	0	7	0

82. J. W. H. T. Douglas

83. (right) A. A. Mailey

84. England 1920-21
Back row: A. Dolphin, J. W. Hitch, C. H. Parkin, F.C. Toone (manager), F. E. Woolley, A. C. Russell, A. Waddington. *Middle row:* H. Strudwick, W. Rhodes, E. R. Wilson, J. W. H. T. Douglas (capt.), P. G. H. Fender, J. B. Hobbs. *Front row:* H. Howell, E. H. Hendren, J. W. Hearne, H. Makepeace.

1920–21 Second Test, Melbourne

December 31, January 1, 3, 4
Toss: Australia   *Result:* Australia won by an innings and 91 runs

Although before the rain came Australia, batting first, had compiled a winning score, England had some excuse for feeling, after this Test, that they might still make a fight of the series if their luck changed. In spite of dropped catches Australia were held to 282 for 6 on the first day, Ryder was out first thing next morning, and it was only when Gregory joined Pellew that Australia, in intense heat, slipped the reins. Pellew reached his hundred after lunch in 3 hours, and Gregory, who batted only 2 hours 17 minutes, made a century from no. 9. Their partnership for the 8th wicket added 173 in just over 2 hours.

Hearne was unable to field on the second day, or to bat in either innings, and England's final misfortune came when heavy rain flooded the ground over the weekend and was followed by hot sunshine on Monday morning, making the issue certain. Even then Hobbs and Hendren, who had fought back from a bad start with an unbroken stand of 61 on the Saturday evening, added another 81 runs in 57 minutes before the wicket became spiteful. Hobbs went on to complete a superb century on a wicket that became progressively more difficult

and on which none of the other England batsmen was able to survive. He batted for $3\frac{1}{2}$ hours and did not give a chance until he was past his hundred.

Had some of the catches been held in the Australian innings—Collins was dropped before he had scored and Pellew when he had made only 3—Australia might have been kept to a moderate total, and England might not then have had to follow on. As it was, England failed badly at the second attempt and were beaten by an innings.

The dropped catches were particularly depressing in a game in which the England ground fielding was magnificent. Howell was the chief sufferer, and when he was fresh he bowled really fast, some thought faster than Gregory. But nothing could gainsay the great length and strength of the Australian batting, or the lack of penetration of the England bowling. In the previous English season, indeed, many prewar players had said that runs had never been easier to get.

Australia, too, had their problems: Macartney was unwell and didn't play, and Mailey, although he played and would presumably have bowled if needed, was not called upon because of an arm injury.

AUSTRALIA

H. L. Collins	c Hearne b Howell	64
W. Bardsley	c Strudwick b Woolley	51
R. L. Park	b Howell	0
J. M. Taylor	c Woolley b Parkin	68
*W. W. Armstrong	lbw b Douglas	39
C. Kelleway	c Strudwick b Howell	9
C. E. Pellew	b Parkin	116
J. Ryder	c Woolley b Douglas	13
J. M. Gregory	c Russell b Woolley	100
†W. A. Oldfield	c and b Rhodes	24
A. A. Mailey	not out	8
Extras	(b 1, lb 3, w 1, nb 2)	7
Total		**499**

ENGLAND

J. B. Hobbs	c Ryder b Gregory	122	b Kelleway	20
W. Rhodes	b Gregory	7	c Collins b Armstrong	28
H. Makepeace	lbw b Armstrong	4	c Gregory b Armstrong	4
E. H. Hendren	c Taylor b Gregory	67	c and b Collins	1
A. C. Russell	c Collins b Gregory	0	c Armstrong b Collins	5
F. E. Woolley	b Gregory	5	b Ryder	50
*J. W. H. T. Douglas	lbw b Gregory	15	b Gregory	9
C. H. Parkin	c Mailey b Gregory	4	c Taylor b Armstrong	9
†H. Strudwick	not out	21	c Oldfield b Armstrong	24
H. Howell	st Oldfield b Armstrong	5	not out	0
J. W. Hearne	absent ill	—	absent ill	—
Extras	(nb 1)	1	(b 3, lb 3, nb 1)	7
Total		**251**	**Total**	**157**

FALL OF WICKETS

AUSTRALIA

Wkt	1st	2nd
1st	116	—
2nd	116	—
3rd	118	—
4th	194	—
5th	220	—
6th	251	—
7th	282	—
8th	455	—
9th	469	—
10th	499	—

ENGLAND

Wkt	1st	2nd
1st	20	36
2nd	32	53
3rd	174	54
4th	185	58
5th	201	70
6th	208	104
7th	213	141
8th	232	151
9th	251	157
10th	—	—

Umpires: R. W. Crockett, D. Elder

ENGLAND	1st Innings				2nd Innings			
	O	M	R	W	O	M	R	W
Howell	37	5	142	3				
Douglas	24	1	83	2				
Parkin	27	0	116	2				
Hearne	14	0	38	0				
Woolley	27	8	87	2				
Rhodes	8	1	26	1				

AUSTRALIA	1st Innings				2nd Innings			
	O	M	R	W	O	M	R	W
Gregory	20	1	69	7	12	0	32	1
Kelleway	19	1	54	0	12	1	25	1
Armstrong	24·3	8	50	2	15·2	5	26	4
Ryder	14	2	31	0	10	2	17	1
Park	1	0	9	0				
Collins	9	0	37	0	17	5	47	2
Pellew					1	0	3	0

1920-21 Third Test, Adelaide

January 14, 15, 17, 18, 19, 20
Toss: Australia   *Result:* Australia won by 119 runs

England needed to win this match to keep the rubber alive, and for three days they outplayed their opponents; but by the end of the fourth day Australia had played themselves back into a winning position, which they never surrendered. It was a classic encounter, in which the Australians displayed a batting depth of unparalleled power.

After being 96 for 4 and 176 for 5, Australia at the end of the first day anchored in the comparative shelter of 313 for 7, Collins having made 162. When 53 he mishit Howell to square leg and was dropped, and at 60 he was missed in the gully, again off Howell; but he made no other mistake. On the second morning, Australia were all out for 354, and then England began badly, Rhodes responding to a call from Hobbs and being run out, and Hobbs being brilliantly caught and bowled by Mailey. Makepeace and Hendren, however, scored readily, and when they were out Russell, who in the first two Tests had made only 10 in 4 innings, joined Woolley in a stand which took England to 233 for 4 at the close.

On the third morning Woolley was soon out, and Douglas as usual floundered at first against Mailey, but he held on, helping Russell to put on 124. Russell reached his hundred in 3 hours: he might have been

stumped off Mailey when 52; otherwise he played him well. All out soon after tea for 447, a lead of 93, England got Bardsley, Collins and Ryder for 71 runs before the close. Kelleway, missed in the slips off Howell before scoring, was not out 19.

Armstrong joined Kelleway next morning and the pair were not separated until twenty minutes after tea; they put on 194, of which Armstrong made 121. Taylor then batted stylishly for an hour, and before the close Pellew too began to plunder the tired bowling. Kelleway, who batted all day, reached his hundred in just over 5 hours. Only 2 wickets fell during the day.

Pellew completed a dashing century on the fifth day, while Gregory drove and hit vigorously, and Australia passed their record second-innings score of the first Test by one run. Wanting 490, England soon lost Rhodes, but Hobbs made 50 out of 66 before the close, completed his century before lunch next day, and batted only 2½ hours for 123, giving England a chance. While Hendren and Russell were together that chance remained, but after they were separated the result was inevitable.

AUSTRALIA

H. L. Collins	c Rhodes b Parkin	162	c Hendren b Parkin	24
W. Bardsley	st Strudwick b Douglas	14	b Howell	16
C. Kelleway	c Fender b Parkin	4	b Howell	147
J. M. Taylor	run out	5	(6)c Strudwick b Fender	38
W. W. Armstrong	c Strudwick b Douglas	11	b Howell	121
C. E. Pellew	run out	35	(7)c Strudwick b Parkin	104
J. M. Gregory	c Strudwick b Fender	10	(8)not out	78
J. Ryder	c Douglas b Parkin	44	(4)c Woolley b Howell	3
W. A. Oldfield	lbw b Parkin	50	b Rhodes	10
E. A. McDonald	b Parkin	2	b Rhodes	4
A. A. Mailey	not out	3	b Rhodes	13
Extras	(b 6, lb 8)	14	(b 5, lb 10, w 4, nb 5)	24
Total		**354**	**Total**	**582**

ENGLAND

J. B. Hobbs	c and b Mailey	18	b Gregory	123
W. Rhodes	run out	16	lbw b McDonald	4
H. Makepeace	c Gregory b Armstrong	60	c and b McDonald	30
E. H. Hendren	b Gregory	36	b Mailey	51
F. E. Woolley	c Kelleway b Gregory	79	b Gregory	0
A. C. Russell	not out	135	b Mailey	59
J. W. H. T. Douglas	lbw b Mailey	60	c Armstrong b Gregory	32
P. G. H. Fender	b McDonald	2	c Ryder b Mailey	42
C. H. Parkin	st Oldfield b Mailey	12	st Oldfield b Mailey	17
H. Strudwick	c Pellew b Mailey	9	c Armstrong b Mailey	1
H. Howell	c Gregory b Mailey	2	not out	4
Extras	(b 8, lb 5, nb 5)	18	(lb 3, nb 4)	7
Total		**447**	**Total**	**370**

FALL OF WICKETS

AUSTRALIA

Wkt	1st	2nd
1st	32	34
2nd	45	63
3rd	55	71
4th	96	265
5th	176	328
6th	209	454
7th	285	477
8th	347	511
9th	349	570
10th	354	582

ENGLAND

Wkt	1st	2nd
1st	25	20
2nd	49	125
3rd	111	183
4th	161	185
5th	250	243
6th	374	292
7th	391	308
8th	416	321
9th	437	341
10th	447	370

Umpires: R. W. Crockett, D. Elder

ENGLAND	1st Innings					2nd Innings			
	O	M	R	W		O	M	R	W
Howell	26	1	89	0	..	34	6	115	0
Douglas	24	6	69	2	..	19	2	61	0
Parkin	20	2	60	5	..	40	8	109	2
Woolley	21	6	47	0	..	38	4	91	0
Fender	12	0	52	1	..	22	0	105	1
Rhodes	5	1	23	0	..	25.5	8	61	3
Hobbs					..	7	2	16	0

AUSTRALIA	1st Innings					2nd Innings			
	O	M	R	W		O	M	R	W
McDonald	24	1	78	1	..	24	0	95	2
Gregory	36	6	108	2	..	20	2	50	3
Kelleway	11	4	25	0	..	8	2	16	0
Mailey	32.1	3	160	5	..	29.2	3	142	5
Armstrong	23	10	29	1	..	16	1	41	0
Ryder	6	0	29	0	..	9	2	19	0

1920-21 Fourth Test, Melbourne

February 11, 12, 14, 15, 16
Toss: England   *Result:* Australia won by eight wickets

Although Australia eventually coasted to victory by 8 wickets on the morning of the fifth day, this was another game of many fluctuations. Russell, who had done so well in the previous game, stood down with an injured thumb, Dolphin came in for Strudwick, and for Australia the 43-year-old Carter replaced Oldfield. Douglas won the toss for the first time in the series, and although the Australian fast bowlers got some early life from the wicket, England were 89 for 2 at lunch. Afterwards Hendren and Woolley were both out when set, but Douglas joined Makepeace in a stubborn stand of 106 for the 5th wicket. Makepeace, playing in his first series at the age of 38, reached his only hundred against Australia in 3 hours 50 minutes, a fine innings against top-class bowling. He was out in the last over of the day, in which Waddington, sent in as night-watchman ahead of Fender, also lost his wicket. 270 for 6 overnight, England were soon all out next morning, and by lunch-time Australia were 59 for no wicket.

After lunch Collins and Bardsley went steadily on to 117 before Fender and Woolley suddenly pulled out something extra with the ball, and with the whole side supporting them brilliantly, Australia found themselves 153 for 5, at which point Gregory (9 not out) was joined by Armstrong. With the Ashes won in the previous match, Armstrong was greeted, according to one account, by a 'demonstration of popularity absolutely unprecedented in the history of Australian cricket', and by the end of the day he had richly deserved it. He and Gregory put on 100 runs in the next 83 minutes and were still there at the close, when Australia were only 17 behind. Armstrong reached his third century of the series next morning. Although suffering from a severe attack of malaria he had once again tipped a game Australia's way.

Facing a deficit of 105, England lost Hobbs at 32, but Rhodes and Makepeace by cautious batting had cleared off the arrears by the close. Thus England began the fourth day in good heart. But soon it was their turn to slump, and at 152 for 4 they were only 47 runs on. Douglas, however, again batted well, and when Hendren got out a second time when well set, Fender batted freely and England passed 300 with only 5 wickets down. Then the vulnerable tail collapsed a second time, and Australia, with the wicket still good, needed only 211 to win.

ENGLAND

Batsman	Dismissal	R	Dismissal 2	R
J. B. Hobbs	c Carter b McDonald	27	lbw b Mailey	13
W. Rhodes	c Carter b Gregory	11	c Gregory b Mailey	73
H. Makepeace	c Collins b Mailey	117	lbw b Mailey	54
E. H. Hendren	c Carter b Mailey	30	b Kelleway	32
F. E. Woolley	lbw b Kelleway	29	st Carter b Mailey	0
*J. W. H. T. Douglas	c and b Mailey	50	st Carter b Mailey	60
A. Waddington	b Mailey	0	(8)st Carter b Mailey	6
P. G. H. Fender	c Gregory b Kelleway	3	(7)c Collins b Mailey	59
†A. Dolphin	b Kelleway	1	c Gregory b Mailey	0
C. H. Parkin	run out	10	c Bardsley b Mailey	4
H. Howell	not out	0	not out	0
Extras	(b 1, lb 5)	6	(b 5, lb 5, w 1, nb 3)	14
Total		**284**	**Total**	**315**

AUSTRALIA

Batsman	Dismissal	R	Dismissal 2	R
H. L. Collins	c Rhodes b Woolley	59	c Rhodes b Parkin	32
W. Bardsley	b Fender	56	run out	38
J. Ryder	lbw b Woolley	7	not out	52
J. M. Taylor	hit wkt b Fender	2		
J. M. Gregory	c Dolphin b Parkin	77		
C. E. Pellew	b Fender	12		
*W. W. Armstrong	not out	123	(4)not out	76
C. Kelleway	b Fender	27		
†H. Carter	b Fender	0		
A. A. Mailey	run out	13		
E. A. McDonald	b Woolley	0		
Extras	(b 1, lb 6, w 1, nb 5)	13	(b 5, lb 5, w 2, nb 1)	13
Total		**389**	**Total (2 wkts)**	**211**

FALL OF WICKETS

ENGLAND

Wkt	1st	2nd
1st	18	32
2nd	61	145
3rd	104	152
4th	164	152
5th	270	201
6th	270	305
7th	273	307
8th	274	307
9th	275	315
10th	284	315

AUSTRALIA

Wkt	1st	2nd
1st	117	71
2nd	123	81
3rd	128	—
4th	133	—
5th	153	—
6th	298	—
7th	335	—
8th	335	—
9th	376	—
10th	389	—

Umpires: R. W. Crockett, D. Elder

AUSTRALIA bowling

	1st Innings O	M	R	W		2nd Innings O	M	R	W
McDonald	19	2	46	1		23	2	77	0
Gregory	18	1	61	1		14	4	31	0
Mailey	29·2	1	115	4		47	8	121	9
Ryder	10	5	10	0		10	3	25	0
Armstrong	5	1	9	0					
Kelleway	18	2	37	3		23	8	47	1

ENGLAND bowling

	1st Innings O	M	R	W		2nd Innings O	M	R	W
Howell	17	2	86	0		10	1	36	0
Douglas	4	0	17	0		5	1	13	0
Waddington	5	0	31	0					
Parkin	22	5	64	1		12	2	46	1
Fender	32	3	122	5		13·2	2	39	0
Woolley	32·1	14	56	3		14	4	39	0
Rhodes						10	2	25	0

1920–21 Fifth Test, Sydney

February 25, 26, 28, March 1
Toss: England   *Result:* Australia won by nine wickets

Demoralised after four successive defeats, and facing a side bent on making it five, England were without Hearne, Hitch and Howell through injury and illness, Russell was still troubled by his hand injury, while Hobbs, although he played, was lame from a strained thigh-muscle which had prevented him from batting in the previous engagement. Nevertheless when Douglas won the toss Hobbs opened with Rhodes. For Australia, Macartney returned after missing three matches through illness.

In the best opening stand of the series for England Hobbs and Rhodes put on 54, but Makepeace and Hendren failed and England were 76 for 4. Woolley attacked the bowling and made 50 in 54 minutes, and Douglas as usual resisted stoutly, but England were all out for 204 and the fifth defeat looked certain. They hit back well by getting Collins and Bardsley cheaply, but by the close Australia were 70 for 2 and on the way to recovery. Next morning Taylor left at 89, but by lunch-time Macartney and Gregory had taken the score to 192 for 3. The bowling was treated almost contemptuously and the England score was passed in 2¼ hours' batting. Macartney's match-winning innings brought him his first century against England in his 16th Test

Match, and he and Gregory, scoring run for run, put on 198 in 135 minutes, by which time Australia looked certain to make 500. But Fender, in a remarkable second spell, took 5 for 56, and he and Wilson, by intelligent bowling, saved the game from developing into a rout.

When England batted again 188 behind, Woolley opened with Rhodes, but he and Makepeace were both out before the end of the second day, when England, at 24 for 2, faced an innings defeat. Hobbs played a useful innings next morning, but at lunch England were 91 for 5, and with Hendren out immediately afterwards the game looked over. Then Douglas put on 69 with Russell and 64 with Fender, and Australia were eventually set 93 to win, a task they accomplished for the loss of Collins on the morning of the fourth day.

The folly of allowing players—or gentlemen, for that matter—to comment on games in which they were playing was demonstrated when Wilson and Fender, who in their cables to English newspapers had taken exception to some ribaldry directed at Hobbs' lameness by a section of the crowd, were persistently barracked throughout the third day, by which time their comments had got back to Australia. Five defeats in a series was humiliation enough.

ENGLAND

J. B. Hobbs	lbw b Gregory	40	(5)c Taylor b Mailey	34	
W. Rhodes	c Carter b Kelleway	26	run out	25	
H. Makepeace	c Gregory b Mailey	3	c Gregory b Kelleway	7	
E. H. Hendren	c Carter b Gregory	5	(6)st Carter b Mailey	13	
F. E. Woolley	b McDonald	53	(1)c and b Kelleway	1	
A. C. Russell	c Gregory b Mailey	19	(8)c Gregory b Armstrong	35	
J. W. H. T. Douglas	not out	32	c and b Mailey	68	
P. G. H. Fender	c Gregory b Kelleway	2	(9)c Kelleway b McDonald	40	
E. R. Wilson	c Carter b Kelleway	5	(4)st Carter b Mailey	5	
C. H. Parkin	c Taylor b Kelleway	9	c Gregory b Mailey	36	
H. Strudwick	b Gregory	2	not out	5	
Extras	(b 3, lb 2, w 1, nb 2)	8	(b 3, lb 5, nb 3)	11	
Total		**204**	**Total**	**280**	

AUSTRALIA

H. L. Collins	c Fender b Parkin	5	c Strudwick b Wilson	37	
W. Bardsley	c Fender b Douglas	7	not out	50	
C. G. Macartney	c Hobbs b Fender	170	not out	2	
J. M. Taylor	c Hendren b Douglas	32			
J. M. Gregory	c Strudwick b Fender	93			
W. W. Armstrong	c Woolley b Fender	0			
J. Ryder	b Fender	2			
C. Kelleway	c Strudwick b Wilson	32			
H. Carter	c Woolley b Fender	17			
A. A. Mailey	b Wilson	5			
E. A. McDonald	not out	3			
Extras	(b 18, lb 6, nb 2)	26	(b 3, nb 1)	4	
Total		**392**	**Total** (1 wkt)	**93**	

FALL OF WICKETS

ENGLAND

Wkt	1st	2nd
1st	54	1
2nd	70	14
3rd	74	29
4th	76	75
5th	125	82
6th	161	91
7th	164	160
8th	172	224
9th	201	251
10th	204	280

AUSTRALIA

Wkt	1st	2nd
1st	16	91
2nd	22	—
3rd	89	—
4th	287	—
5th	287	—
6th	313	—
7th	356	—
8th	384	—
9th	384	—
10th	392	—

Umpires: R. W. Crockett, D. Elder

AUSTRALIA	1st Innings				2nd Innings			
	O	M	R	W	O	M	R	W
Gregory	16	4	42	3	16	3	37	0
McDonald	11	2	38	1	25	3	58	1
Kelleway	20	6	27	4	14	3	29	2
Mailey	23	1	89	2	36	5	119	5
Ryder					2	2	0	0
Armstrong					8	1	26	1

ENGLAND	1st Innings				2nd Innings			
	O	M	R	W	O	M	R	W
Douglas	16	0	84	2				
Parkin	19	1	83	1	9	1	32	0
Woolley	15	1	58	0	11	3	27	0
Wilson	15	4	28	2	6	1	8	1
Fender	20	2	90	5	1	0	2	0
Rhodes	7	0	23	0	7	1	20	0

Averages: 1920-21

AUSTRALIA

BATTING

	M.	Inns.	N.O.	Runs	H.S.	Av.
C. G. Macartney	2	4	1	260	170	86·66
W. W. Armstrong	5	7	1	464	158	77·33
J. M. Gregory	5	8	2	442	100	73·66
H. L. Collins	5	9	0	557	162	61·88
C. E. Pellew	4	6	0	319	116	53·16
C. Kelleway	5	7	0	330	147	47·14
W. Bardsley	5	9	1	311	57	38·87
J. M. Taylor	5	7	0	230	68	32·85
W. A. Oldfield	3	5	0	107	50	21·40
J. Ryder	5	8	1	132	52*	18·85
A. A. Mailey	5	7	4	52	13	17·33
H. Carter	2	2	0	17	17	8·50
E. A. McDonald	3	4	1	9	4	3·00

PLAYED IN ONE TEST: R. L. Park 0.

BOWLING

	Overs	Mds.	Runs	Wkts.	Av.
C. Kelleway	146·5	32	315	15	21·00
W. W. Armstrong	102·5	26	204	9	22·66
J. M. Gregory	208·1	30	556	23	24·17
A. A. Mailey	243·5	27	946	36	26·27
E. A. McDonald	126	10	392	6	65·33

ALSO BOWLED: J. Ryder 84–23–175–3, H. L. Collins 26–5–84–2, C. G. Macartney 3–0–7–0, R. L. Park 1–0–9–0, C. E. Pellew 1–0–3–0.

ENGLAND

BATTING

	M.	Inns.	N.O.	Runs	H.S.	Av.
J. B. Hobbs	5	10	0	505	123	50·50
J. W. H. T. Douglas	5	10	1	354	68	39·33
A. C. Russell	4	8	1	258	135	36·85
J. W. Hearne	2	2	0	71	57	35·50
H. Makepeace	4	8	0	279	117	34·87
E. H. Hendren	5	10	0	319	67	31·90
F. E. Woolley	5	10	0	285	79	28·50
P. G. H. Fender	3	6	0	148	59	24·66
W. Rhodes	5	10	0	238	73	23·80
H. Strudwick	4	8	3	65	24	13·00
C. H. Parkin	5	10	1	109	36	12·11
H. Howell	3	6	4	11	5*	5·50
A. Waddington	2	4	0	16	7	4·00

PLAYED IN ONE TEST: J. W. Hitch 3 and 19, A. Dolphin 1 and 0, E. R. Wilson 5 and 5.

BOWLING

	Overs	Mds.	Runs	Wkts.	Av.
P. G. H. Fender	100·2	7	410	12	34·16
C. H. Parkin	211·2	29	670	16	41·87
J. W. H. T. Douglas	121	13	420	8	52·50
F. E. Woolley	217·1	58	530	9	58·88
H. Howell	124	15	468	7	66·85

ALSO BOWLED: J. W. Hearne 90–15–239–4, W. Rhodes 84·5–15–245–4, A. Waddington 46–7–119–1, E. R. Wilson 21–5–36–3, J. W. Hitch 18–0–77–0, J. B. Hobbs 7–2–16–0.

Averages: 1921

ENGLAND

BATTING

	M.	Inns.	N.O.	Runs	H.S.	Av.
C. P. Mead	2	2	1	229	182*	229·00
A. C. Russell	2	3	1	216	102*	108·00
Hon. L. H. Tennyson	4	5	1	229	74*	57·25
G. Brown	3	5	0	250	84	50·00
F. E. Woolley	5	8	0	343	95	42·87
E. Tyldesley	3	4	1	124	78*	41·33
J. W. H. T. Douglas	5	7	1	176	75	29·33
P. G. H. Fender	2	3	1	50	44*	25·00
V. W. C. Jupp	2	4	0	65	28	16·25
D. J. Knight	2	4	0	54	38	13·50
C. H. Parkin	4	5	1	43	23	10·75
H. Strudwick	2	4	0	20	12	5·00
E. H. Hendren	2	4	0	17	10	4·25

PLAYED IN ONE TEST: A. E. Dipper 11 and 40, A. Ducat 3 and 2, F. J. Durston 6* and 2, A. J. Evans 4 and 14, N. E. Haig 3 and 0, C. Hallows 16*, H. T. W. Hardinge 25 and 5, J. W. Hearne 7 and 27, J. W. Hitch 18 and 51*, P. Holmes 30 and 8, H. Howell 0* and 4*, C. W. L. Parker 3*, T. L. Richmond 4 and 2, W. Rhodes 19 and 10, A. Sandham 21, J. C. White 1 and 6*, J. B. Hobbs did not bat.

BOWLING

	Overs	Mds.	Runs	Wkts.	Av.
C. H. Parkin	121·5	21	420	16	26·25
F. J. Durston	33·4	2	136	5	27·20
V. W. C. Jupp	39·1	4	142	5	28·40
J. W. H. T. Douglas	94	10	348	11	31·63
F. E. Woolley	109	38	248	7	35·42

ALSO BOWLED: P. G. H. Fender 34–9–112–2, N. E. Haig 23–4–88–2, J. W. Hearne 5–0–21–0, J. W. Hitch 19–3–65–2, H. Howell, 9–3–22–0, C. W. L. Parker 28–16–32–2, T. L. Richmond 19–3–86–2, W. Rhodes 13–3–33–2, J. C. White 36–7–107–3.

AUSTRALIA

BATTING

	M.	Inns.	N.O.	Runs	H.S.	Av.
W. Bardsley	5	8	2	281	88	46·83
E. A. McDonald	5	5	3	92	36	46·00
C. G. Macartney	5	8	1	300	115	42·85
T. J. E. Andrews	5	7	0	275	94	39·28
H. Carter	4	5	0	160	47	32·00
W. W. Armstrong	5	6	1	152	77	30·40
J. M. Taylor	5	6	0	173	75	28·83
C. E. Pellew	5	7	1	159	52	26·50
H. L. Collins	3	3	0	71	40	23·66
J. M. Gregory	5	6	0	126	52	21·00
H. S. T. L. Hendry	4	5	2	32	12*	10·66
A. A. Mailey	3	3	0	11	6	3·66

PLAYED IN ONE TEST: W. A. Oldfield 28*.

BOWLING

	Overs	Mds.	Runs	Wkts.	Av.
E. A. McDonald	205·5	32	668	27	24·74
W. W. Armstrong	127	50	212	8	26·50
J. M. Gregory	182·2	35	552	19	29·05
A. A. Mailey	124·4	18	398	12	33·16

ALSO BOWLED: H. S. T. L. Hendry 52–11–135–3, J. M. Taylor 8–1–26–1, T. J. E. Andrews 13–0–67–1, C. G. Macartney 13–4–30–0, C. E. Pellew 12–3–31–0, H. L. Collins 7–0–39–0.

May 28, 30
Toss: England   *Result:* Australia won by ten wickets

After their crushing defeat in Australia, England's cricketers needed time to lick their wounds. But there was no escape. Not only were they due to play another five Tests against the Australians that summer, but they actually had to travel back to England on the same boat. Australia fielded a settled side of proved ability, under a shrewd leader of unquestioned authority, while the England selectors jumped about like grasshoppers, and even changed the pilot in midstream. It was a shocking misfortune to lose Hobbs for virtually the entire series, but the permutation of a total of 30 players in one campaign must have undermined what confidence there was.

Some saw in the defeats that followed a condemnation of the English county system, where a handful of good bowlers were expending their energies in prodigal fashion for their counties right up to a few hours before a Test Match, and then travelling long distances, while the Australians cut short the playing time on the day before a Test Match in sensible if arbitrary fashion. Others pointed to the fact that, after the first Test, the only Yorkshire-born cricketer to find a place in either side was the Australian Carter.

At Trent Bridge the wicket was dampish and the weather unsettled and the Australians left out Mailey, fresh from his record of 36 wickets in a series. England played the leg-spinner Richmond. The course the series would take was firmly delineated in the first half-hour. Gregory and McDonald began the attack, and although in the course of the series McDonald was to prove himself much the more accurate bowler, Gregory was the great unsettler. In his third over he got Knight caught behind from an out-swinger; Tyldesley, beaten by pace, played on next ball; and in his fourth over Hendren was bowled by a break-back. At lunch, after 40 minutes had been lost through rain, England were 63 for 4. Holmes was still there with 26 not out; but he did not play again in the series. England collapsed after lunch and were all out for 112.

Bardsley played a fine if unspectacular innings for Australia, all but two of the remainder reached double figures, and Australia led by 120. Then when England batted again Gregory made the ball fly disconcertingly. Tyldesley was hit on the head by a bouncer which fell on his wicket, and Hendren faced a succession of bumpers, but Knight was batting well when Hendren called him for a run and sent him back too late. England finished only 28 in front, and Australia won by 10 wickets. The crowd showed their disapproval of Gregory, but the barracking was generally regarded as undeserved.

ENGLAND

D. J. Knight	c Carter b Gregory	8	run out		38
P. Holmes	b McDonald	30	c Taylor b McDonald		8
E. Tyldesley	b Gregory	0	b Gregory		7
E. H. Hendren	b Gregory	0	b McDonald		7
*J. W. H. T. Douglas	c Gregory b Armstrong	11	c Hendry b McDonald		13
F. E. Woolley	c Hendry b McDonald	20	c Carter b Hendry		34
V. W. C. Jupp	c Armstrong b McDonald	8	c Pellew b Gregory		15
W. Rhodes	c Carter b Gregory	19	c Carter b McDonald		10
*H. Strudwick	c Collins b Gregory	0	b Hendry		0
H. Howell	not out	0	not out		4
T. L. Richmond	c and b Gregory	4	b McDonald		2
Extras	(b 6, lb 6)	12	(b 4, lb 3, nb 2)		9
Total		**112**	Total		**147**

AUSTRALIA

W. Bardsley	lbw b Woolley	66
H. L. Collins	lbw b Richmond	17
C. G. Macartney	lbw b Douglas	20
J. M. Taylor	c Jupp b Douglas	4
*W. W. Armstrong	b Jupp	11
J. M. Gregory	lbw b Richmond	14
C. E. Pellew	c and b Rhodes	25
†H. Carter	b Woolley	33
T. J. E. Andrews	c and b Rhodes	6
H. S. T. L. Hendry	not out	12
E. A. McDonald	c Knight b Woolley	10
Extras	(b 8, lb 5, nb 1)	14
Total		**232**

not out		8
not out		22
Total (0 wkts)		**30**

FALL OF WICKETS
ENGLAND

Wkt	1st	2nd
1st	18	23
2nd	18	41
3rd	18	60
4th	43	63
5th	77	76
6th	78	110
7th	101	138
8th	107	138
9th	108	140
10th	112	147

AUSTRALIA

Wkt	1st	2nd
1st	49	—
2nd	86	—
3rd	98	—
4th	126	—
5th	138	—
6th	152	—
7th	183	—
8th	202	—
9th	212	—
10th	232	—

Umpires: J. Moss, H. R. Butt

AUSTRALIA	1st Innings				2nd Innings			
	O	M	R	W	O	M	R	W
Gregory	19	5	58	6	22	8	45	2
McDonald	15	5	42	3	22.4	10	32	5
Armstrong	3	3	0	1	27	10	33	0
Macartney					5	2	10	0
Hendry					9	1	18	2

ENGLAND	1st Innings				2nd Innings			
	O	M	R	W	O	M	R	W
Howell	9	3	22	0				
Douglas	13	2	34	2				
Richmond	16	3	69	2	3	0	17	0
Woolley	22	8	46	3				
Jupp	5	0	14	1	3.1	0	13	0
Rhodes	13	3	33	2				

1921 Second Test, Lord's

June 11, 13, 14
Toss: England   *Result:* Australia won by eight wickets

The England selectors made six changes, and might have made a seventh if Fry, who was invited to play at the age of 49, had not pleaded dissatisfaction with his form. Tennyson was not among those originally chosen but was brought in when Mead reported unfit, while Evans played on the strength of an innings of 69 not out for the MCC against the Australians: he had played in only 5 first-class matches since the war. Hobbs and Hearne were still unfit. Australia brought in Mailey for Collins, who had an injured thumb.

On a perfect wicket England made another disastrous start. Dipper was bowled, Knight caught at slip, and Hendren again got a good one. 25 for 3. Woolley and Douglas then batted through to lunch, when England were 77 for 3 and Armstrong's figures were 18 overs, 12 maidens, 1 for 9. In all they put on 83 in 2 hours.

The rest of the innings was dominated by Woolley. In trouble against Gregory at the start, Woolley played some beautiful strokes off him later, mostly off the back foot; but towards the end of his innings he hit out in desperation, none of the tail-enders seeming to concentrate on staying with him. He was missed twice in the slips off Gregory when 87, and was stumped chasing after Mailey soon afterwards.

When the Australians batted they treated the England bowlers with something very near contempt. The score was 116 for 2 after 65 minutes when the first maiden was bowled, and the fielding was fumbling and unathletic. By the end of the day Australia were 6 runs ahead with only 3 wickets down. Douglas and Durston hit back on the Monday morning, getting Bardsley and Armstrong for the addition of one run, but Gregory, who was missed twice, restored Australia's advantage, and the unpretentious Carter again made a nuisance of himself, helping in a last-wicket stand of 53.

155 behind, England soon lost Knight, but Woolley, who began by straight-driving McDonald to the rails, played a succession of glorious off drives and square cuts, and he and Dipper added 94. When he had made 93 Woolley hit a long hop straight at Hendry, who juggled with it but held on; he had missed Woolley earlier. Then Tennyson, uncomfortable at first, straight-drove the fast bowlers courageously, and at the close of the second day England were 243 for 8. Left next morning with 129 to win, Australia won by 8 wickets. Bardsley, with fine leg-side play and strong cutting, was again top-scorer.

ENGLAND

Batsman	1st Innings		2nd Innings	
D. J. Knight	c Gregory b Armstrong	7	c Carter b Gregory	1
A. E. Dipper	b McDonald	11	b McDonald	40
F. E. Woolley	st Carter b Mailey	95	c Hendry b Mailey	93
E. H. Hendren	b McDonald	0	c Gregory b Mailey	10
*J. W. H. T. Douglas	b McDonald	34	b Gregory	14
A. J. Evans	b McDonald	4	lbw b McDonald	14
Hon. L. H. Tennyson	st Carter b Mailey	5	not out	74
N. E. Haig	c Carter b Gregory	3	b McDonald	0
C. H. Parkin	b Mailey	0	c Pellew b McDonald	11
†H. Strudwick	c McDonald b Mailey	8	b Gregory	12
F. J. Durston	not out	6	b Gregory	2
Extras	(b 1, lb 11, w 1, nb 1)	14	(b 4, lb 3, nb 5)	12
Total		**187**	**Total**	**283**

AUSTRALIA

Batsman	1st Innings		2nd Innings	
W. Bardsley	c Woolley b Douglas	88	not out	63
T. J. E. Andrews	c Strudwick b Durston	9	lbw b Parkin	49
C. G. Macartney	c Strudwick b Durston	31	b Durston	8
C. E. Pellew	b Haig	43	not out	5
J. M. Taylor	lbw b Douglas	36		
*W. W. Armstrong	b Durston	0		
J. M. Gregory	c and b Parkin	52		
H. S. T. L. Hendry	b Haig	5		
†H. Carter	b Durston	46		
A. A. Mailey	c and b Parkin	5		
E. A. McDonald	not out	17		
Extras	(b 2, lb 5, nb 3)	10	(b 3, lb 2, nb 1)	6
Total		**342**	**Total (2 wkts)**	**131**

FALL OF WICKETS

ENGLAND
Wkt	1st	2nd
1st	20	3
2nd	24	97
3rd	25	124
4th	108	165
5th	120	165
6th	145	198
7th	156	202
8th	157	235
9th	170	263
10th	187	283

AUSTRALIA
Wkt	1st	2nd
1st	19	103
2nd	73	114
3rd	145	—
4th	191	—
5th	192	—
6th	230	—
7th	263	—
8th	277	—
9th	289	—
10th	342	—

Umpires: J. Moss,
W. Phillips

AUSTRALIA

	1st Innings				2nd Innings			
	O	M	R	W	O	M	R	W
Gregory	16	1	51	1	26·2	4	76	4
McDonald	20	2	58	4	23	3	89	4
Armstrong	18	12	9	1	12	6	19	0
Mailey	14·2	1	55	4	25	4	72	2
Hendry					4	0	15	0

ENGLAND

	1st Innings				2nd Innings			
	O	M	R	W	O	M	R	W
Durston	24·1	2	102	4	9·3	0	34	1
Douglas	9	1	53	2	6	0	23	0
Parkin	20	5	72	2	9	0	31	1
Haig	20	4	61	2	3	0	27	0
Woolley	11	2	44	0	3	0	10	0

85. J. M. Gregory

86. F. E. Woolley

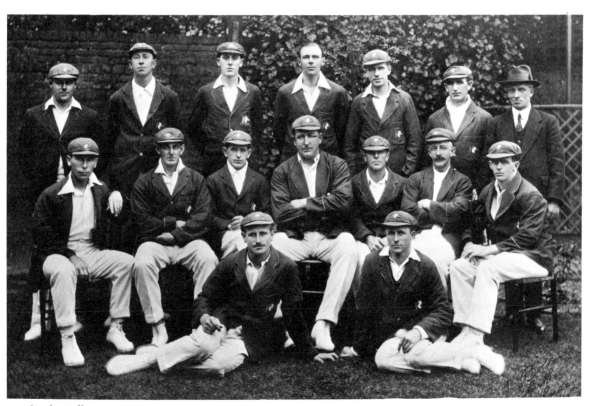

87. Australia 1921
Back row: W. Bardsley, J. Ryder, H. S. T. L. Hendry, J. M. Gregory, E. R. Mayne, T. J. E. Andrews, S. Smith (manager). *Middle row:* A. A. Mailey, E. A. McDonald, H. L. Collins, W. W. Armstrong (capt.), C. G. Macartney, H. Carter, J. M. Taylor. *Front:* C. E. Pellew, W. A. Oldfield.

1921 Third Test, Leeds

July 2, 4, 5
Toss: Australia   *Result:* Australia won by 219 runs

After his heartening display at Lord's, Tennyson was appointed captain and Douglas, after seven consecutive Test Match defeats, could not perhaps complain at being superseded. Yet his contribution had been a worthy one, and he retained his place in the side. And within an hour of the start he found himself captain again, Tennyson being obliged to leave the field after a Macartney drive had split his hand. Hobbs and Hearne, recovered from injury, were included, but Hobbs did not field after tea on the first day and later developed appendicitis. There were five other changes, so that of the side that played at Lord's only Tennyson, Douglas, Woolley and Parkin remained. Australia were unchanged.

After Douglas had taken the first 2 wickets, both as a result of magnificent slip catches by Woolley, Macartney and Pellew put on 101 so rapidly that the lunch score was 155 for 3. Parkin, who at various times tried to fill the role of fast bowler, had no success, and White was the only bowler to keep the batsmen quiet. Australia passed 250 with only 3 wickets down, but then Parkin came back to dismiss Gregory, Macartney and Hendry. Macartney, although not quite at his best, played many fine strokes in the only hundred made by an Australian in the series.

Armstrong, whose driving as usual was tremendous, now showed his best form, putting on 62 with Carter and 55 with McDonald, and when the innings closed at 5.30 the score was 407. Woolley was then bowled in the first over, Hearne lost his off stump at 13, and when bad light stopped play England looked hopelessly placed. On a dull, overcast Monday morning they struggled to 67 for 5, but then Brown, replacing Strudwick to strengthen the batting, held firm with Douglas in a stand of 97 that spanned the lunch interval, and Douglas then helped the handicapped Tennyson to add 88. Going in at 30 for 3, the deposed Douglas saw England to within 5 runs of saving the follow on before being 8th out at 253.

Parkin, amusing and terrifying the crowd with his antics, helped the heroic Tennyson make Australia bat again; but by close of play Australia were 143 for 2—291 ahead—and they continued on the last morning until 12.55, leaving England just under 4½ hours batting and arrears of 422. Brown, who opened this time, played another useful innings, but none of the other batsmen ever looked secure, and with Hobbs absent Australia won their eighth successive victory soon after tea.

AUSTRALIA

W. Bardsley	c Woolley b Douglas	6	b Jupp	25		
T. J. E. Andrews	c Woolley b Douglas	19	b Jupp	92		
C. G. Macartney	lbw b Parkin	115	c and b Woolley	30		
C. E. Pellew	c Hearne b Woolley	52	(5)c Ducat b White	16		
J. M. Taylor	c Douglas b Jupp	50	(6)c Tennyson b White	4		
J. M. Gregory	b Parkin	1	(8)c Jupp b White	3		
*W. W. Armstrong	c Brown b Douglas	77	not out	28		
H. S. T. L. Hendry	b Parkin	0	(9)not out	11		
†H. Carter	b Jupp	34	(4)lbw b Parkin	47		
E. A. McDonald	not out	21				
A. A. Mailey	c and b Parkin	6				
Extras	(b 16, lb 7, nb 3)	26	(b 10, lb 4, nb 3)	17		
Total		**407**	**Total** (7 wkts dec)	**273**		

ENGLAND

F. E. Woolley	b Gregory	0	(4)b Mailey	37		
H. T. W. Hardinge	lbw b Armstrong	25	c Gregory b McDonald	5		
J. W. Hearne	b McDonald	7	c Taylor b McDonald	27		
A. Ducat	c Gregory b McDonald	3	(6)st Carter b Mailey	2		
J. W. H. T. Douglas	b Armstrong	75	b Gregory	8		
V. W. C. Jupp	c Carter b Gregory	14	(7)c Carter b Armstrong	28		
†G. Brown	c Armstrong b Mailey	57	(1)lbw b Gregory	46		
J. C. White	b McDonald	1	(9)not out	6		
*Hon. L. H. Tennyson	c Gregory b McDonald	63	(8)b Armstrong	36		
C. H. Parkin	not out	5	b Mailey	4		
J. B. Hobbs	absent ill	—	absent ill	—		
Extras	(lb 3, nb 6)	9	(b 3)	3		
Total		**259**	**Total**	**202**		

FALL OF WICKETS
AUSTRALIA
Wkt	1st	2nd
1st	22	71
2nd	45	139
3rd	146	193
4th	255	223
5th	256	227
6th	271	227
7th	271	230
8th	333	—
9th	388	—
10th	407	

ENGLAND
Wkt	1st	2nd
1st	0	15
2nd	13	57
3rd	30	98
4th	47	124
5th	67	126
6th	164	128
7th	165	190
8th	253	197
9th	259	202
10th	—	—

Umpires: H. R. Butt,
A. Millward

ENGLAND	1st Innings				2nd Innings			
	O	M	R	W	O	M	R	W
Douglas	20	3	80	3	11	0	38	0
White	25	4	70	0	11	3	37	3
Parkin	20·1	0	106	4	20	0	91	1
Hearne	5	0	21	0				
Jupp	18	2	70	2	13	2	45	2
Woolley	5	0	34	1	18	4	45	1

AUSTRALIA	1st Innings				2nd Innings			
	O	M	R	W	O	M	R	W
Gregory	21	6	47	2	14	1	55	2
McDonald	26·1	0	105	4	15	2	67	2
Armstrong	19	4	44	2	3	0	6	2
Mailey	17	4	38	1	20·2	3	71	3
Hendry	10	4	16	0				

1921 Fourth Test, Old Trafford

July 23, 25, 26
Toss: England   *Result:* Match Drawn

Unfamiliarity with the laws of the game cost England their chance of a win at Manchester. After the first day had been lost through rain, Tennyson decided at 5.50 on the second day, with England 341 for 4, to declare the innings closed so as to get half an hour's bowling at the Australians that evening. But he had forgotten that he could not declare later than 100 minutes before close of play in what had become the first day of a two-day match. Signalling his team to remain on the field, Armstrong went off to point out Tennyson's blunder, but the argument was prolonged and eventually the whole team left the field. Suspecting that the Australians were quibbling, the crowd behaved so badly that even when the disagreement had been resolved and the England innings was about to continue, play could not restart until Tennyson and the umpires had explained the situation to them. Thus 25 minutes were lost. Armstrong, who had bowled the last over before the argument, was then allowed in the general confusion to bowl the next.

Because of the conditions Mailey had been left out, the dead wicket did not suit Gregory and McDonald, and at lunch England were 143 for 1. Russell, who had done well in Australia and who was having a great season, played for the first time in the series and made a hundred—although he was missed at slip by Armstrong off Gregory at 6 and again at 86. Basically an on-side player, Russell is said to have made 81 of his runs on the leg side. Woolley and Tyldesley both batted beautifully, but in the circumstances Mead was painfully slow, and had Tennyson appreciated the situation correctly he might have sent Tyldesley, Fender and himself in ahead of Mead after lunch and been in a position to declare at tea. As it was England were left with the task of bowling Australia out twice on the last day on a wicket that, although difficult for a time, never became really treacherous.

Bardsley, Macartney, Andrews and Taylor were all dismissed before the score had reached 50, and for the first time in the series England were on top. A further break-through might have put Australia in real danger; but Collins and Pellew stood firm, and long before tea, taken at 160 for 6, Australia were safe. The cricket was inevitably tedious, the innings lasting 318 minutes, of which Collins stayed 289 for his 40. Yet but for him (and he had missed the previous two Tests) Australia might have been pressed much more severely.

ENGLAND

A. C. Russell	b Gregory	101			
†G. Brown	c Gregory b Armstrong	31			
F. E. Woolley	c Pellew b Armstrong	41			
C. P. Mead	c Andrews b Hendry	47			
E. Tyldesley	not out	78			
P. G. H. Fender	not out	44			
C. Hallows			(1)not out	16	
C. H. Parkin			(2)c Collins b Andrews	23	
C. W. L. Parker			(3)not out	3	
*Hon. L. H. Tennyson	} did not bat				
J. W. H. T. Douglas					
Extras	(b 12, lb 5, nb 3)	20	(lb 2)	2	
Total	(4 wkts dec)	**362**	**Total** (1 wkt)	**44**	

AUSTRALIA

W. Bardsley	b Parkin	3
H. L. Collins	lbw b Parkin	40
C. G. Macartney	b Parker	13
T. J. E. Andrews	c Tennyson b Fender	6
J. M. Taylor	b Fender	4
C. E. Pellew	c Tyldesley b Parker	17
*W. W. Armstrong	b Douglas	17
J. M. Gregory	b Parkin	29
†H. Carter	b Parkin	0
H. S. T. L. Hendry	c Russell b Parkin	4
E. A. McDonald	not out	8
Extras	(b 22, lb 5, nb 7)	34
Total		**175**

FALL OF WICKETS
ENGLAND

Wkt	1st	2nd
1st	65	36
2nd	145	—
3rd	217	—
4th	260	—
5th	—	—
6th	—	—
7th	—	—
8th	—	—
9th	—	—
10th	—	—

AUSTRALIA

Wkt	1st	2nd
1st	9	—
2nd	33	—
3rd	44	—
4th	48	—
5th	78	—
6th	125	—
7th	161	—
8th	161	—
9th	166	—
10th	175	—

Umpires: J. Moss, A. E. Street

AUSTRALIA	1st Innings				2nd Innings			
	O	M	R	W	O	M	R	W
Gregory	23	5	79	1	..			
McDonald	31	1	112	0	..			
Macartney	8	2	20	0	..			
Hendry	25	5	74	1	4	1	12	0
Armstrong	33	13	57	2	..			
Andrews					5	0	23	1
Pellew					3	0	6	0
Taylor					1	0	1	0

ENGLAND	1st Innings				2nd Innings			
	O	M	R	W	O	M	R	W
Parkin	29·4	12	38	5	..			
Woolley	39	22	38	0	..			
Parker	28	16	32	2	..			
Fender	15	6	30	2	..			
Douglas	5	2	3	1	..			

1921 Fifth Test, Oval

August 13, 15, 16
Toss: England *Result:* Match Drawn

There had been six changes in the England side at Old Trafford, and there were two more at the Oval, Sandham and Hitch, both of Surrey, coming in for Hallows and Parker. Australia played Mailey for Hendry, and Oldfield replaced Carter. It was probably their strongest possible side. The England line-up, too, looked the strongest of the series, though Hitch was well past his best; and after the breaking of the sequence of defeats at Old Trafford a great tussle looked in prospect. Two factors, however, militated against it; one was the weather, the other the inevitable relaxation of effort of a great side when its mission is accomplished.

Rain delayed the start, and after a confident opening Russell was given out caught at the wicket. Tyldesley was missed by Collins in the gully, but Brown batted beautifully until he was out in the last over before lunch. England had reached 83 for 2 when heavy rain prevented any more play until 5.15, after which Woolley was brilliantly thrown out by Bardsley from deep third man, hesitating about a second run. Tyldesley, too, was out before the close, when England were 129 for 4. Armstrong followed the policy he had adopted throughout the series of using Gregory and McDonald in turn, apart from the opening assault, always keeping one of them fresh, and the rest of the work was done by Mailey.

An extraordinary transformation came over the game on the Monday morning. Sandham, who had batted coolly in bad light the previous evening, helped to put on 70, and when Tennyson came in at 191 he inspired Mead to a flurry of strokes. Mead, who had batted 70 minutes the previous evening for 19, made another 109 in the 2½ hours before lunch, when England were 303 for 5, and after lunch he went on to make 182.

Australia had just over 2 hours' batting, and a remarkable opening spell by Hitch would have had them in serious trouble but for dropped catches. Macartney and Andrews, however, played brilliantly, putting on 108 in quick time, and with only one day to go and the wicket easy a draw looked certain. This was duly achieved on the Tuesday, the proceedings becoming farcical when Armstrong, after a few overs of Gregory and McDonald, abandoned the game as a serious contest and allowed England to take runs as they pleased. Russell's century was some consolation for an unsatisfactory first-innings dismissal.

ENGLAND

A. C. Russell	c Oldfield b McDonald	13	not out	102
†G. Brown	b Mailey	32	c Mailey b Taylor	84
E. Tyldesley	c Macartney b Gregory	39		
F. E. Woolley	run out	23		
C. P. Mead	not out	182		
A. Sandham	b McDonald	21		
*Hon. L. H. Tennyson	b McDonald	51		
P. G. H. Fender	c Armstrong b McDonald	0	(3)c Armstrong b Mailey	6
J. W. Hitch	b McDonald	18	(4)not out	51
J. W. H. T. Douglas	not out	21		
C. H. Parkin	did not bat			
Extras	(lb 3)	3	(b 1)	1
Total	(8 wkts dec)	**403**	**Total** (2 wkts)	**244**

AUSTRALIA

H. L. Collins	hit wkt b Hitch	14
W. Bardsley	b Hitch	22
C. G. Macartney	b Douglas	61
T. J. E. Andrews	lbw b Parkin	94
J. M. Taylor	c Woolley b Douglas	75
C. E. Pellew	c Woolley b Parkin	1
*W. W. Armstrong	c Brown b Douglas	19
J. M. Gregory	st Brown b Parkin	27
†W. A. Oldfield	not out	28
E. A. McDonald	st Brown b Woolley	36
A. A. Mailey	b Woolley	0
Extras	(b 6, lb 3, w 2, nb 1)	12
Total		**389**

FALL OF WICKETS
ENGLAND
Wkt	1st	2nd
1st	27	158
2nd	54	173
3rd	84	—
4th	121	—
5th	191	—
6th	312	—
7th	312	—
8th	339	—
9th	—	—
10th	—	—

AUSTRALIA
Wkt	1st	2nd
1st	33	—
2nd	54	—
3rd	162	—
4th	233	—
5th	239	—
6th	288	—
7th	311	—
8th	338	—
9th	389	—
10th	389	—

Umpires: J. Moss,
W. Phillips

AUSTRALIA	1st Innings				2nd Innings			
	O	M	R	W	O	M	R	W
Gregory	38	5	128	1	3	0	13	0
McDonald	47	9	143	5	6	0	20	0
Mailey	30	4	85	1	18	2	77	1
Armstrong	12	2	44	0				
Pellew					9	3	25	0
Andrews					8	0	44	0
Taylor					7	1	25	1
Collins					7	0	39	0

ENGLAND	1st Innings				2nd Innings			
	O	M	R	W	O	M	R	W
Hitch	19	3	65	2				
Douglas	30	2	117	3				
Fender	19	3	82	0				
Parkin	23	4	82	3				
Woolley	11	2	31	2				

1924-25 First Test, Sydney

December 19, 20, 22, 23, 24, 26, 27
Toss: Australia   *Result:* Australia won by 193 runs

Beaten by four matches to one, England nevertheless did better than on the previous tour and improved as the series progressed, though they went down inexplicably in the final match to Grimmett, who took 11 for 82 in his first Test. On the single occasion on which they won the toss, in the fourth Test, they gained their first victory since the war, and had Tate been fit they would surely have won the third, which they lost by 11 runs. The final Test would then have been the decider. Tate, the outstanding bowler on either side, set up a record by taking 38 wickets in the series, but an accident to Gilligan in the previous summer deprived him of proper support; though Gilligan was a popular captain and inspiring fielder he did little as bowler or batsman. Hobbs and Sutcliffe batted superbly, Sutcliffe in his first series breaking many records, but the Australian batting was more even and this was decisive. Until the final Test Gregory and Mailey remained Australia's best bowlers, but they were rarely as penetrative as four years earlier. The 8-ball over was used for the first time.

Australia made 282 for 3 on the first day, Collins and Ponsford putting on 190 for the second wicket, both men making centuries, the latter in his first Test. Tate bowled as well as at any time in the series

but was frustrated by dropped catches and the obduracy of Collins, who had appreciated that Tate was the only bowler of menace and had set himself to wear Tate out. Despite a jarred toe which became progressively worse during the game Tate had a spell of 4 for 9 on the second day (Taylor, Hendry, Gregory and Kelleway), but a last wicket stand raised the Australian score to 450. England were 72 for 0 at stumps.

On the third morning Hobbs and Sutcliffe, in their first opening stand together, took the score to 157, but the remaining batsmen failed badly, the last 9 wickets falling for 141, of which Hendren made 74 not out. Australia thus led by 152. The fourth day, in which Australia converted their overnight 61 for 1 to 258 for 5, was curtailed by a violent wind, and on the fifth day England did well until a last-wicket stand by Taylor and Mailey added 127, Taylor after an uncertain start hitting 108.

Facing the enormous task of making 605 to win, Hobbs and Sutcliffe again began with a century partnership, and Sutcliffe and Woolley both made typical hundreds; but despite compiling a record fourth innings total England were never in touch with their target and lost by 193 runs. 189 of these had come in Australia's two last-wicket stands.

AUSTRALIA

Batsman	1st Innings	Runs	2nd Innings	Runs
*H. L. Collins	c Hendren b Tate	114	(4)c Chapman b Tate	60
W. Bardsley	c Woolley b Freeman	21	b Tate	22
W. H. Ponsford	b Gilligan	110	(5)c Woolley b Freeman	27
A. J. Richardson	b Hearne	22	(1)c and b Freeman	98
J. M. Taylor	c Strudwick b Tate	43	(8)b Tate	108
V. Y. Richardson	b Freeman	42	c Hendren b Tate	18
C. Kelleway	c Woolley b Tate	17	(3)b Gilligan	23
H. S. T. L. Hendry	c Strudwick b Tate	3	(7)c Strudwick b Tate	22
J. M. Gregory	c Strudwick b Tate	0	c Woolley b Freeman	2
†W. A. Oldfield	not out	39	c Strudwick b Gilligan	18
A. A. Mailey	b Tate	21	not out	46
Extras	(b 10, lb 8)	18	(b 2, lb 5, w 1)	8
Total		**450**	**Total**	**452**

ENGLAND

Batsman	1st Innings	Runs	2nd Innings	Runs
J. B. Hobbs	c Kelleway b Gregory	115	c Hendry b Mailey	57
H. Sutcliffe	c V. Richardson b Mailey	59	c Gregory b Mailey	115
J. W. Hearne	c sub (T. J. E. Andrews) b Mailey	7	b Gregory	0
F. E. Woolley	b Gregory	0	(6)c Mailey b Gregory	123
E. H. Hendren	not out	74	c Gregory b Hendry	9
A. Sandham	b Mailey	7	(7)c Oldfield b Mailey	2
A. P. F. Chapman	run out	13	(4)c Oldfield b Hendry	44
M. W. Tate	c sub (T. J. E. Andrews) b Mailey	7	c Ponsford b Kelleway	0
*A. E. R. Gilligan	b Gregory	1	b Kelleway	1
A. P. Freeman	b Gregory	0	not out	50
†H. Strudwick	lbw b Gregory	6	c Oldfield b Hendry	2
Extras	(b 1, lb 5, nb 3)	9	(b 4, lb 3, nb 1)	8
Total		**298**	**Total**	**411**

FALL OF WICKETS

AUSTRALIA

Wkt	1st	2nd
1st	46	40
2nd	236	115
3rd	275	168
4th	286	210
5th	364	241
6th	374	260
7th	387	281
8th	387	286
9th	388	325
10th	450	452

ENGLAND

Wkt	1st	2nd
1st	157	110
2nd	171	127
3rd	172	195
4th	202	212
5th	235	263
6th	254	269
7th	272	270
8th	274	276
9th	274	404
10th	298	411

Umpires: A. C. Jones,
A. P. Williams

ENGLAND	1st Innings O	M	R	W	2nd Innings O	M	R	W
Tate	55.1	11	130	6	33.7	8	98	5
Gilligan	23	0	92	1	27	6	114	2
Freeman	49	11	124	2	37	4	134	3
Hearne	12.1	3	28	1	25	2	88	0
Woolley	9	0	35	0				
Hobbs	2	0	13	0				
Chapman	2	0	10	0	3	1	10	0

AUSTRALIA	1st Innings O	M	R	W	2nd Innings O	M	R	W
Gregory	28.7	2	111	5	28	2	115	2
Kelleway	14	3	44	0	21	5	60	2
Mailey	31	2	129	4	32	0	179	3
Hendry	5	1	5	0	10.7	2	36	3
A. J. Richardson	1	1	0	0	5	0	13	0

1924-25 Second Test, Melbourne

January 1, 2, 3, 5, 6, 7, 8
Toss: Australia   *Result:* Australia won by 81 runs

Batting first on a wicket that had a surface like concrete, Australia made a record 600 runs. Yet at one point they had 3 wickets down for 47. Ponsford and Taylor then batted with wonderful confidence, and after lunch Ponsford began to cut freely, although with a deep-set field he did not hit a four until he was past his 50. At 63 he gave his only chance—to Tyldesley at forward short leg off Hearne. (Tyldesley and Douglas had replaced Freeman and Sandham.) Taylor was meanwhile driving well on either side of the wicket, but at 208 a bad call by Ponsford led to Taylor being thrown out from cover by Hobbs. Ponsford went on to reach a hundred in his second Test, having also got one in his first, and the day that had begun so well for England ended with Australia 300 for 4. Ponsford was out first thing next morning, but as the England bowlers faded in the heat the later batsmen doubled Australia's score.

England got a night's rest before their own innings, after which Hobbs and Sutcliffe batted through till stumps in a magnificent opening stand of 283, neither man giving a chance or indeed looking in any difficulty except occasionally against Mailey. The second ball of the fourth morning got Hobbs, however, and the last 9 wickets then fell for 196. Sutcliffe, 5th out at 404, batted 7 hours 11 minutes.

When Australia went in again with a lead of 121, Tate got 3 quick wickets, and although Collins and Taylor added 79, Australia at lunch on the fifth day were 139 for 5, Taylor then being 76. As well as driving cleanly he was very strong in front of the wicket off the back foot. He was eventually surprised by a ball from Tate that hastened off the pitch. Hearne, too, was bowling well, beginning to turn the ball a little both ways, and at 168 for 8 it was Australia's turn to fight back. So well did Gregory and Oldfield do so that 71 runs were added for the ninth wicket, and England were left with 372 to win. Beginning the sixth day at 54 for 1 they fought tenaciously on a wicket that was now taking spin, and at tea they were 200 for 3, but after beginning in exhilarating form Woolley lost confidence, and at stumps England were 259 for 6. Sutcliffe for the second time in the match had batted through the day, as well as completing his second hundred of the game and his third in succession; but on the seventh morning England's last 4 wickets fell in 45 minutes for 31.

Sutcliffe was the first Englishman to get two hundreds in a match in these games, although Bardsley had done it for Australia in 1909.

AUSTRALIA

						FALL OF WICKETS

AUSTRALIA

Batsman	1st dismissal	1st	2nd dismissal	2nd
*H. L. Collins	c Strudwick b Tate	9	b Hearne	30
W. Bardsley	c Strudwick b Gilligan	19	lbw b Tate	2
A. J. Richardson	run out	14	b Tate	9
W. H. Ponsford	b Tate	128	b Tate	4
J. M. Taylor	run out	72	b Tate	90
V. Y. Richardson	run out	138	c Strudwick b Hearne	8
C. Kelleway	c Strudwick b Gilligan	32	c and b Hearne	17
A. E. V. Hartkopf	c Chapman b Gilligan	80	lbw b Tate	0
J. M. Gregory	c Gilligan b Tate	44	not out	36
†W. A. Oldfield	not out	39	lbw b Hearne	39
A. A. Mailey	lbw b Douglas	1	b Tate	3
Extras	(b 18, lb 5, nb 1)	24	(b 11, lb 1)	12
Total		600	Total	250

FALL OF WICKETS — AUSTRALIA

Wkt	1st	2nd
1st	22	3
2nd	47	13
3rd	47	27
4th	208	106
5th	301	126
6th	424	166
7th	439	168
8th	499	168
9th	599	239
10th	600	250

ENGLAND

Batsman	1st dismissal	1st	2nd dismissal	2nd
J. B. Hobbs	b Mailey	154	lbw b Mailey	22
H. Sutcliffe	b Kelleway	176	c Gregory b Mailey	127
F. E. Woolley	b Gregory	0	(5)lbw b A. J. Richardson	50
J. W. Hearne	b Mailey	9	lbw b Gregory	23
E. H. Hendren	c Oldfield b Kelleway	32	(6)b Gregory	18
A. P. F. Chapman	c Oldfield b Gregory	28	(9)not out	4
J. W. H. T. Douglas	c Collins b A. J. Richardson	8	(8)b Mailey	14
R. Tyldesley	c Collins b Gregory	5	(7)c Ponsford b Mailey	0
M. W. Tate	b A. J. Richardson	34	(11)b Gregory	0
*A. E. R. Gilligan	not out	17	c and b Mailey	0
†H. Strudwick	b Hartkopf	4	(3)lbw b Gregory	22
Extras	(b 4, lb 4, nb 4)	12	(b 6, lb 2, nb 2)	10
Total		479	Total	290

FALL OF WICKETS — ENGLAND

Wkt	1st	2nd
1st	283	36
2nd	284	75
3rd	305	121
4th	373	211
5th	404	254
6th	412	255
7th	418	280
8th	453	289
9th	458	289
10th	479	290

Umpires: R. W. Crockett, C. Garing

ENGLAND	1st Innings					2nd Innings			
	O	M	R	W		O	M	R	W
Tate	45	10	142	3	..	33·3	8	99	6
Douglas	19·5	0	95	1	..	4	0	9	0
Tyldesley	35	3	130	0	..	2	0	6	0
Gilligan	26	1	114	3	..	11	2	40	0
Hearne	13	1	69	0	..	29	5	84	4
Woolley	11	3	26	0	..				

AUSTRALIA	1st Innings					2nd Innings			
	O	M	R	W		O	M	R	W
Gregory	34	4	124	3	..	27·3	6	87	4
Kelleway	30	10	62	2	..	18	4	42	0
Mailey	34	5	141	2	..	24	2	92	5
Hartkopf	26	1	120	1	..	4	1	14	0
A. J. Richardson	14	6	20	2	..	22	7	35	1
Collins					..	11	3	10	0

88. W. A. Oldfield

89. (right) M. W. Tate

90. England 1924–25
Back row: R. Tyldesley, H. Sutcliffe, A. Sandham, M. W. Tate, R. Kilner, J. W. Hearne. *Front row:* F. C. Toone (manager), A. P. F. Chapman, J. W. H. T. Douglas, A. E. R. Gilligan (capt.), F. E. Woolley, H. Strudwick.

1924-25 Third Test, Adelaide

January 16, 17, 19, 20, 21, 22, 23
Toss: Australia   *Result:* Australia won by 11 runs

The Adelaide wicket, which had been protected by tarpaulins before the game, sweated a little on the first morning and gave England the chance to nullify their continuing bad luck with the toss; otherwise their luck was out. Tate gave England a wonderful start by bowling Collins and getting Taylor lbw, but by that time he was in such pain from an injured foot that he had to go off. Australia recovered from 22 for 3 to 114 for 4, then slumped to 119 for 6. Gilligan, however, had to retire with a strain, Freeman injured his wrist fielding, and that left only Woolley and Kilner of the regular bowlers. England were so hopelessly handicapped that the last 4 Australian wickets put on 370.

With just over half an hour's batting at the end of the second day, Gilligan changed the order and England were 36 for 2 at the close. Next morning Chapman and Tate were soon out, and at 69 for 4 the main battle was joined. Hobbs and Sutcliffe, batting safely, had added 90 runs together when Sutcliffe was unexpectedly caught behind off Ryder. Woolley, who had bowled 43 8-ball overs in the Australian innings, did not stay long, but there was another determined partnership between Hobbs and Hendren which added 117 before Hobbs was

out after completing his ninth century. Hendren then took over the run-getting, but England finished up 124 behind.

At the end of the fourth day Australia in their second innings were 211 for 3, in an apparently impregnable position; but it rained next morning, and when the game was resumed 45 minutes late Kilner and Woolley took the last 7 wickets for 39 runs, leaving England needing 375 to win. A good start was essential, and Hobbs and Sutcliffe put on 63 while the wicket dried; then Hobbs pulled a long hop straight to square leg. Woolley and Hendren didn't last, but Whysall played a sound, hard-hitting innings, and when he and Chapman were together on the sixth morning England were going very strongly indeed. Both fell to brilliant catches, however, and with eight wickets down England still needed 63. Gilligan and Freeman had made 36 of them safely and England looked the likely winners when further rain set in; but 27 runs next morning, against a fresh attack, were a different matter, and Australia just got home by 11 runs, thus retaining the Ashes and winning the rubber.

AUSTRALIA

						FALL OF WICKETS
*H. L. Collins	b Tate	3	b Freeman	26		AUSTRALIA
A. J. Richardson	b Kilner	69	c Kilner b Woolley	14		Wkt	1st	2nd
J. M. Gregory	b Freeman	6	(9)c Hendren b Woolley	2		1st	10	36
J. M. Taylor	lbw b Tate	0	b Freeman	34		2nd	19	63
W. H. Ponsford	c Strudwick b Gilligan	31	c Hendren b Kilner	43		3rd	22	126
V. Y. Richardson	c Whysall b Kilner	4	(7)c Tate b Woolley	0		4th	114	215
J. Ryder	not out	201	(3)c and b Woolley	88		5th	118	216
T. J. E. Andrews	b Kilner	72	(6)c Whysall b Kilner	1		6th	119	217
C. Kelleway	c Strudwick b Woolley	16	(8)not out	22		7th	253	217
†W. A. Oldfield	lbw b Kilner	47	b Kilner	4		8th	308	220
A. A. Mailey	st Strudwick b Hendren	27	c Sutcliffe b Kilner	5		9th	416	242
Extras	(lb 9, nb 4)	13	(b 4, lb 4, nb 3)	11		10th	489	250
Total		**489**	Total	**250**		

ENGLAND

						ENGLAND
W. W. Whysall	b Gregory	9	(5)c and b Gregory	75		Wkt	1st	2nd
M. W. Tate	c Andrews b Mailey	27	(8)b Mailey	21		1st	15	63
†H. Strudwick	c Gregory b Kelleway	1	(11)not out	2		2nd	18	92
A. P. F. Chapman	b Gregory	26	(6)c Ryder b Kelleway	58		3rd	67	96
J. B. Hobbs	c Gregory b Mailey	119	(1)c Collins b A. J. Richardson	27		4th	69	155
H. Sutcliffe	c Oldfield b Ryder	33	(2)c Ponsford b Mailey	59		5th	159	244
F. E. Woolley	c Andrews b Mailey	16	(3)b Kelleway	21		6th	180	254
E. H. Hendren	c Taylor b Gregory	92	(4)lbw b Kelleway	4		7th	297	279
R. Kilner	lbw b A. J. Richardson	6	(7)c V. Y. Richardson b A. J. Richardson	24		8th	316	312
*A. E. R. Gilligan	c Collins b A. J. Richardson	9	(9)c V. Y. Richardson b Gregory	31		9th	326	357
A. P. Freeman	not out	6	(10)c Oldfield b Mailey	24		10th	365	363
Extras	(b 8, lb 10, nb 3)	21	(b 5, lb 5, w 1, nb 6)	17		Umpires: R. W. Crockett,
Total		**365**	Total	**363**		D. Elder

ENGLAND	1st Innings					2nd Innings			
	O	M	R	W		O	M	R	W
Tate	18	1	43	2	..	10	4	17	0
Gilligan	7·7	1	17	1	..				
Freeman	18	0	107	1	..	17	1	94	2
Woolley	43	5	135	1	..	19	1	77	4
Kilner	56	7	127	4	..	22·1	7	51	4
Hobbs	3	0	11	0	..				
Hendren	5·1	0	27	1	..				
Whysall	2	0	9	0	..				

AUSTRALIA	1st Innings					2nd Innings			
	O	M	R	W		O	M	R	W
Gregory	26·2	0	111	3	..	23	6	71	2
Kelleway	15	6	24	1	..	22	4	57	3
Mailey	44	5	133	3	..	30·2	4	126	3
A. J. Richardson	21	7	42	2	..	25	5	62	2
Ryder	6	2	15	1	..	2	0	11	0
Collins	5	1	19	0	..	9	4	19	0

1924-25 Fourth Test, Melbourne

February 13, 14, 16, 17, 18
Toss: England   *Result:* England won by an innings and 29 runs

England, although losing the toss on each occasion, had improved markedly with each Test, and it seemed that if they could get first knock they must have a good chance. At Melbourne Gilligan called correctly, and his batsmen responded so well that they occupied the crease for the whole of the first two days in making 548. Hobbs and Sutcliffe put on over a hundred for the fourth time in seven opening partnerships in the series, and Sutcliffe, although missed twice, batted through a day's play for the third time in the series and completed his fourth century—a record. At the close of the first day England were 282 for 2, and although they lost 3 wickets for 64 next morning they were steadied by a good innings from Hendren, after which Australia were forced on the defensive as Whysall and the left-handed Kilner put on 133.

There was a light shower before the resumption on the third morning, when Australia, after a confident opening, lost 2 wickets in an over to Tate, Collins being caught at short leg and Ryder being bowled off his pad second ball. Bardsley was going well when he attempted a short single to Hobbs at cover, whose underhand throw beat him to the bowler's wicket, and at 74 Richardson was bowled by Hearne. Australia went in to lunch in serious trouble at 95 for 4.

Another shower during lunch gave England a wet ball to bowl with, but at 109 Ponsford was caught behind off Hearne. Then Taylor and Andrews batted stylishly until, after further stoppages for rain, play was finally abandoned with Australia beginning to mount a recovery at 168 for 5, Taylor 42, Andrews 33. On the fourth morning the wicket, although drying slowly, helped the bowlers; Gregory, profiting from two dropped catches, helped Taylor to add 72 for the 8th wicket, but Australia followed on 279 behind. They lost Collins and Bardsley at once, and the wicket was still lively enough to compel Strudwick to stand back to Tate, but fine attacking play by Gregory, promoted to no. 3 by Collins, denied England further success before the wicket eased.

At tea Australia were 80 for 3, 199 behind, and the question was whether their great batting depth could mount a recovery that might turn the game. Another masterly display by Taylor received good support from Ryder and Kelleway, but Tate took 4 for 21 on the final morning and Australia lost by an innings—their first defeat for 13 years.

ENGLAND

J. B. Hobbs	st Oldfield b Ryder	66
H. Sutcliffe	lbw b Mailey	143
J. W. Hearne	c Bardsley b Richardson	44
F. E. Woolley	st Oldfield b Mailey	40
E. H. Hendren	b Ryder	65
A. P. F. Chapman	st Oldfield b Mailey	12
W. W. Whysall	st Oldfield b Kelleway	76
R. Kilner	lbw b Kelleway	74
*A. E. R. Gilligan	c Oldfield b Kelleway	0
M. W. Tate	c Taylor b Mailey	8
†H. Strudwick	not out	7
Extras	(b 6, lb 2, w 3, nb 2)	13
Total		**548**

AUSTRALIA

*H. L. Collins	c Kilner b Tate	22	c Whysall b Kilner	1
A. J. Richardson	b Hearne	19	(9)lbw b Hearne	3
J. Ryder	b Tate	0	(5)lbw b Woolley	38
W. Bardsley	run out	24	(2)b Tate	0
W. H. Ponsford	c Strudwick b Hearne	21	(8)b Tate	19
J. M. Taylor	c Hendren b Woolley	86	(4)c Woolley b Gilligan	68
T. J. E. Andrews	c Hearne b Kilner	35	(6)c Strudwick b Tate	3
C. Kelleway	lbw b Kilner	1	(7)c Strudwick b Tate	42
J. M. Gregory	c Woolley b Hearne	38	(3)c Sutcliffe b Kilner	45
†W. A. Oldfield	c Chapman b Kilner	3	b Tate	8
A. A. Mailey	not out	4	not out	8
Extras	(b 13, lb 2, nb 1)	16	(b 15)	15
Total		**269**	**Total**	**250**

FALL OF WICKETS

	ENGLAND	
Wkt	1st	2nd
1st	126	—
2nd	232	—
3rd	284	—
4th	307	—
5th	346	—
6th	394	—
7th	527	—
8th	527	—
9th	529	—
10th	548	—

	AUSTRALIA	
Wkt	1st	2nd
1st	38	5
2nd	38	5
3rd	64	64
4th	74	133
5th	109	190
6th	170	195
7th	172	225
8th	244	234
9th	257	238
10th	269	250

Umpires: R. W. Crockett, D. Elder

AUSTRALIA

	1st Innings				2nd Innings			
	O	M	R	W	O	M	R	W
Gregory	22	1	102	0	..			
Kelleway	29	5	70	3	..			
Mailey	43·6	2	186	4	..			
Ryder	25	5	83	2	..			
Richardson	26	8	76	1	..			
Collins	6	1	18	0	..			

ENGLAND

	1st Innings				2nd Innings			
	O	M	R	W	O	M	R	W
Tate	16	2	70	2	..	25·5	6	75	5
Gilligan	6	1	24	0	..	7	0	26	1
Hearne	19·3	1	77	3	..	20	0	76	1
Kilner	13	1	29	3	..	16	3	41	2
Woolley	9	1	53	1	..	6	0	17	1

February 27, 28, March 2, 3, 4
Toss: Australia   *Result:* Australia won by 307 runs

Australia introduced two new players in Kippax and Grimmett, resting Bardsley and Richardson. Kippax was a natural replacement, but the choice of leg-spinner Grimmett came as a surprise, though not perhaps to the England players, who had formed a high opinion of him. England dropped Chapman and brought in Sandham, who had scored a century in each innings against New South Wales in the previous match.

Australia were 77 for 3 at lunch. Collins was caught behind, Gregory swept and drove briefly and was then run out, and Ryder was bowled by Kilner. After lunch Andrews was caught at mid on, and when Taylor was picked up in the slips off Tate Australia were 103 for 5. This was the situation that faced Kippax on his debut, but he and Ponsford worked their way safely through to 189 at tea. Ponsford was then dropped twice, and at 208 Kippax was bowled. 31 runs later Ponsford was caught at forward short leg, and after an appeal against the light the day closed with Australia 239 for 7. Kilner, varying his pace and flight, had taken 4 for 82 in 29 overs. Next morning Tate got Kelleway lbw with his fourth ball, but the last 2 wickets added 56. Tate brought his total for the series to 33.

Hobbs glanced the fifth ball of Gregory's opening over a little too

fine and Oldfield leapt across to take a great catch; Sandham, playing Gregory into the covers and going for a single, was run out as Gregory sprang to take the throw and dived to break the bowler's wicket, dislocating a finger as he did so; and at 28 Sutcliffe was caught in the slips. Hendren failed, but Woolley and Hearne seemed to be mounting a recovery when Collins called up Grimmett, after which the England batting collapsed.

On the third morning Australia added purposefully to their unexpected lead of 128, Andrews employing all the strokes in a polished innings. But even so wickets fell steadily, and Australia were 156 for 6 when Kelleway joined Collins at the game's climax. These two dour players were still together at the close, and next day Kelleway found another stubborn partner in Oldfield, so that Australia eventually set England 454 to win. By taking the last 4 wickets Tate brought his aggregate for the series to a record 38.

Sutcliffe, who had had such a great series, was then bowled by Gregory for a duck, Hobbs was stumped off Grimmett, and the remaining batsmen again collapsed, Grimmett having match figures of 11 for 82.

AUSTRALIA

*H. Collins	c Strudwick b Gilligan	1	(7)lbw b Tate	28	
J. Ryder	b Kilner	29	b Gilligan	7	
J. M. Gregory	run out	29	(1)lbw b Hearne	22	
T. J. E. Andrews	c Whysall b Kilner	26	(3)c Woolley b Hearne	80	
J. M. Taylor	c Whysall b Tate	15	(4)st Strudwick b Tate	25	
W. H. Ponsford	c Woolley b Kilner	80	(5)run out	5	
A. F. Kippax	b Kilner	42	(6)c Whysall b Woolley	8	
C. Kelleway	lbw b Tate	9	c Whysall b Tate	73	
†W. A. Oldfield	c Strudwick b Tate	29	not out	65	
A. A. Mailey	b Tate	14	b Tate	0	
C. V. Grimmett	not out	12	b Tate	0	
Extras	(b 2, lb 5, nb 2)	9	(b 6, lb 4, w 1, nb 1)	12	
Total		**295**	**Total**	**325**	

ENGLAND

J. B. Hobbs	c Oldfield b Gregory	0	st Oldfield b Grimmett	13	
H. Sutcliffe	c Mailey b Kelleway	22	b Gregory	0	
A. Sandham	run out	4	lbw b Grimmett	15	
F. E. Woolley	b Grimmett	47	c Andrews b Kelleway	28	
E. H. Hendren	c Ponsford b Gregory	10	c Oldfield b Grimmett	10	
J. W. Hearne	lbw b Grimmett	16	lbw b Grimmett	24	
W. W. Whysall	lbw b Grimmett	8	st Oldfield b Grimmett	18	
R. Kilner	st Oldfield b Grimmett	24	c Ponsford b Collins	1	
M. W. Tate	b Ryder	25	c Mailey b Kelleway	33	
*A. E. R. Gilligan	st Oldfield b Grimmett	5	not out	0	
†H. Strudwick	not out	1	c Mailey b Grimmett	0	
Extras	(lb 4, nb 1)	5	(b 1, lb 3)	4	
Total		**167**	**Total**	**146**	

FALL OF WICKETS

AUSTRALIA

Wkt	1st	2nd
1st	3	7
2nd	55	43
3rd	64	110
4th	99	130
5th	103	152
6th	208	156
7th	239	209
8th	239	325
9th	264	325
10th	295	325

ENGLAND

Wkt	1st	2nd
1st	0	3
2nd	15	31
3rd	28	32
4th	58	60
5th	96	84
6th	109	99
7th	122	100
8th	157	146
9th	163	146
10th	167	146

Umpires: R. W. Crockett, D. Elder

ENGLAND	1st Innings					2nd Innings			
	O	M	R	W		O	M	R	W
Tate	39·5	6	92	4	..	39·3	6	115	5
Gilligan	13	1	46	1	..	15	2	46	1
Kilner	38	4	97	4	..	34	13	54	0
Hearne	7	0	33	0	..	22	0	84	2
Woolley	5	0	18	0	..	8	1	14	1

AUSTRALIA	1st Innings					2nd Innings			
	O	M	R	W		O	M	R	W
Gregory	9	1	42	2	..	10	0	53	1
Kelleway	15	1	38	1	..	7	1	16	2
Mailey	5	0	13	0	..				
Ryder	7	0	24	1	..				
Grimmett	11·7	2	45	5	..	19·4	3	37	6
Collins					..	8	2	36	1

Averages: 1924-25

AUSTRALIA

BATTING	M.	Inns.	N.O.	Runs	H.S.	Av.
J. Ryder	3	6	1	363	201*	72·60
J. M. Taylor	5	10	0	541	108	54·10
W. H. Ponsford	5	10	0	468	128	46·80
W. A. Oldfield	5	10	3	291	65*	41·57
T. J. E. Andrews	3	6	0	217	80	36·16
V. Y. Richardson	3	6	0	210	138	35·00
A. J. Richardson	4	8	0	248	98	31·00
H. L. Collins	5	10	0	294	114	29·40
C. Kelleway	5	10	1	252	73	28·00
J. M. Gregory	5	10	1	224	45	24·88
A. A. Mailey	5	10	3	129	46*	18·42
W. Bardsley	3	6	0	88	24	14·66

PLAYED IN ONE TEST: A. E. V. Hartkopf 80 and 0, A. F. Kippax 42 and 8, H. S. T. L. Hendry 3 and 22, C. V. Grimmett 12* and 0.

BOWLING	Overs	Mds.	Runs	Wkts.	Av.
C. V. Grimmett	31·3	5	82	11	7·45
C. Kelleway	171	39	413	14	29·50
A. J. Richardson	114	34	248	8	31·00
J. M. Gregory	208·4	22	816	22	37·09
A. A. Mailey	244	20	999	24	41·62

ALSO BOWLED: H. S. T. L. Hendry 15·7–3–41–3, J. Ryder 40–7–133–4, H. L. Collins 39–11–102–1, A. E. V. Hartkopf 30–2–134 1.

ENGLAND

BATTING	M.	Inns.	N.O.	Runs	H.S.	Av.
H. Sutcliffe	5	9	0	734	176	81·55
J. B. Hobbs	5	9	0	573	154	63·66
A. P. Freeman	2	4	2	80	50*	40·00
E. H. Hendren	5	9	1	314	92	39·25
W. W. Whysall	3	5	0	186	76	37·20
F. E. Woolley	5	9	0	325	123	36·11
A. P. F. Chapman	4	7	1	185	58	30·83
R. Kilner	3	5	0	129	74	25·80
J. W. Hearne	4	7	0	123	44	17·57
M. W. Tate	5	9	0	155	34	17·22
A. E. R. Gilligan	5	9	2	64	31	9·14
H. Strudwick	5	9	3	45	22	7·50
A. Sandham	2	4	0	28	13	7·00

PLAYED IN ONE TEST: J. W. H. T. Douglas 8 and 14, R. Tyldesley 5 and 0.

BOWLING	Overs	Mds.	Runs	Wkts.	Av.
M. W. Tate	316	62	881	38	23·18
R. Kilner	179·1	32	399	17	23·47
F. E. Woolley	110	11	375	8	46·87
J. W. Hearne	147·4	12	539	11	49·00
A. E. R. Gilligan	135·7	14	519	10	51·90
A. P. Freeman	121	16	459	8	57·37

ALSO BOWLED: E. H. Hendren 5·1–0–27–1, J. W. H. T. Douglas 23·5–0–104–1, R. Tyldesley 37–3–136–0, A. P. F. Chapman 5–1–20–0, J. B. Hobbs 5–0–24–0, W. W. Whysall 2–0–9–0.

Averages: 1926

ENGLAND

BATTING	M.	Inns.	N.O.	Runs	H.S.	Av.
J. B. Hobbs	5	7	1	486	119	81·00
H. Sutcliffe	5	7	1	472	161	78·66
E. H. Hendren	5	6	3	186	127*	62·00
A. P. F. Chapman	4	5	2	175	50*	58·33
R. Kilner	4	2	1	45	36	45·00
F. E. Woolley	5	6	0	237	87	39·50
M. W. Tate	5	3	1	61	33*	30·50
G. Geary	2	3	1	45	35*	22·50
G. T. S. Stevens	2	3	0	63	24	21·00
A. W. Carr	4	1	0	13	13	13·00
H. Strudwick	5	3	1	7	4*	3·50
H. Larwood	2	2	0	5	5	2·50

PLAYED IN ONE TEST: W. Rhodes 28 and 14, E. Tyldesley 81, G. G. Macaulay 76. C. F. Root played in three matches and J. W. Hearne in one match but did not bat.

BOWLING	Overs	Mds.	Runs	Wkts.	Av.
W. Rhodes	45	24	79	6	13·16
C. F. Root	107	47	194	8	24·25
H. Larwood	95	19	252	9	28·00
M. W. Tate	208·3	64	388	13	29·84
G. T. S. Stevens	64	7	184	5	36·80
R. Kilner	121·5	31	276	7	39·42

ALSO BOWLED: G. Geary 74·3–15–188–3, F. E. Woolley 15–1–63–1, G. G. Macaulay 32–8–123–1.

AUSTRALIA

BATTING	M.	Inns.	N.O.	Runs	H.S.	Av.
C. G. Macartney	5	6	1	473	151	94·60
W. Bardsley	5	5	1	231	193*	57·75
W. M. Woodfull	5	6	0	306	141	51·00
A. J. Richardson	5	5	0	155	100	31·00
W. A. Oldfield	5	6	2	112	33*	28·00
J. M. Gregory	5	6	0	149	73	24·83
J. Ryder	4	4	1	73	42	24·33
H. L. Collins	3	4	0	90	61	22·50
C. V. Grimmett	3	4	1	50	35	16·66
W. H. Ponsford	2	3	0	37	23	12·33
T. J. E. Andrews	5	6	0	49	15	8·16
J. M. Taylor	3	2	0	13	9	6·50
A. A. Mailey	5	5	1	9	6	2·25

BOWLING	Overs	Mds.	Runs	Wkts.	Av.
C. V. Grimmett	204	59	414	13	31·84
A. A. Mailey	172·4	25	592	14	42·28

ALSO BOWLED: C. G. Macartney 126·2–48–215–4, A. J. Richardson 150–57–273–4, J. M. Gregory 105–20–298–3, J. Ryder 49–8–142–1, H. L. Collins 2–0–11–0, T. J. E. Andrews 13–5–49–0.

1926 First Test, Trent Bridge

June 12, 14, 15
Toss: England   *Result:* Match Drawn

In 1921 the Australian fast attack, besides demoralising the England batting, had taken two-thirds of the wickets; but in 1926 Australia had to rely largely on spin. Mailey and Grimmett were great bowlers of contrasting styles, while Richardson and Macartney, medium-paced off-spin and left-arm slow respectively, were two of the most accurate bowlers in the world; but the kind of penetration needed to win matches in three days was lacking. The batting relied too much on Macartney and Woodfull in the Tests; Kippax and Victor Richardson should perhaps have toured, also Kelleway. Bardsley at 42 played one big innings but was otherwise disappointing, Collins, Ponsford and Hendry were all absent at various times through illness or injury, and Andrews and Taylor, great players in Australia, failed. At the crucial moment in the final Test Hobbs and Sutcliffe played perhaps their greatest innings, and for the same match England found two 'new' bowlers to win the game for them in Larwood and the 48-year-old Wilfred Rhodes. England had a period of grave danger at Leeds, where they followed on 200 runs behind after putting Australia in, but Hobbs and Sutcliffe put on 156 and made the game safe. The England open-ing pair never failed to put on at least 50 runs for any completed partnership.

England went into the first Test with no fast bowler, relying, as in Australia in 1924-25, on three front-line bowlers with Woolley and Hearne in support. Heavy rain before the game ruined the prepared wicket and an alternative pitch was chosen. Play eventually began about 12.15 under gloomy conditions, the light being none too good and the bowlers finding the run-ups greasy and the ball wet. Even so Gregory worked up a good pace, while at the other end Macartney kept down the runs, Collins' tactics of attacking at one end and defending at the other being clear from the start. Macartney bowled over the wicket and pitched mostly on or just outside the leg stump to three short legs, but when he bowled straight he looked more dangerous, twice beating the bat with balls that just missed the off stump. Gregory's attempt at reaching his old pace soon found out a knee weakness and after 45 minutes he came off; his last few overs caused him considerable pain. Then came the rain. The following day—Sunday—was warm and bright, but heavy rain on Monday and Tuesday washed out all hope of cricket and the gates were not opened again.

ENGLAND

J. B. Hobbs	not out	19
H. Sutcliffe	not out	13
F. E. Woolley		
J. W. Hearne		
E. H. Hendren		
A. P. F. Chapman		
R. Kilner	did not bat	
*A. W. Carr		
M. W. Tate		
C. F. Root		
†H. Strudwick		
Total	(0 wkts)	**32**

AUSTRALIA

*H. L. Collins, W. Bardsley, C. G. Macartney, J. M. Taylor, T. J. E. Andrews, W. M. Woodfull, J. Ryder, J. M. Gregory, A. J. Richardson, †W. A. Oldfield, A. A. Mailey.

AUSTRALIA	*1st Innings*			
	O	M	R	W
Gregory	8	1	18	0
Macartney	8·2	2	14	0
Richardson	1	1	0	0

Umpires: R. D. Burrows, F. Chester

91. **W. Bardsley**

92. **J. B. Hobbs**

93. **Australia 1926**

Back row: J. L. Ellis, H. S. T. L. Hendry, J. M. Gregory, J. Ryder, A. J. Richardson, S. C. Everett, S. Smith (manager). *Middle row*: A. A. Mailey, C. V. Grimmett, W. Bardsley, H. L. Collins (capt.), C. G. Macartney, T. J. E. Andrews, J. M. Taylor. *Front*: W. M. Woodfull, W. H. Ponsford, W. A. Oldfield.

1926 Second Test, Lord's

Test no. III

June 26, 28, 29
Toss: Australia   *Result:* Match Drawn

England played four front-line bowlers at Lord's, substituting Larwood for Hearne. Australia were unchanged. England got a great start when Collins played no stroke at a Root swerver and was bowled. Bardsley and Macartney put on 73, but Bardsley, often in trouble, was missed at the wicket off Tate. Yet it was Macartney who got out, caught at slip from one that lifted off a length. For Woodfull, Root placed five men in an arc from mid on to leg slip, and soon after lunch he had him caught at the wicket. Andrews looked vulnerable to Tate, but the bowler who dismissed him was Kilner, accepting a caught and bowled after dropping him the previous ball. Gregory hit across Larwood, Taylor was unlucky to get one that popped, and Australia were 208 for 6. Bardsley and Richardson then added 74 either side of the tea interval, and although Tate worried both batsmen Australia finished the day strongly at 338 for 8, Bardsley 173 not out. Bardsley was missed twice more by Strudwick after he got his hundred, but although he scored most of his runs off his legs and did not drive much he played a great knock. The England bowling was good all day. Australia added another 45 runs next morning, Bardsley carrying his bat.

When Hobbs and Sutcliffe began for England Gregory still looked fast, but he no longer compelled the hurried stroke, and he was soon replaced by Mailey. Both batsmen ran yards down the wicket to Mailey, or waited and cut or hooked, and it was not until Richardson came on, pitching on middle or middle and leg to four short legs, that the rate slowed. During the afternoon, indeed, when an acceleration seemed called for, the batsmen became curiously subdued; but when they were out after tea Woolley and Hendren enjoyed themselves in the last hour in the best batting of the day.

On the last morning England added 178 in 2½ hours and declared at lunch, 92 in front. Gregory was then caught off the first ball he received from Root, and Tate beat Collins time and again, but in circumstances that were not at first wholly without danger Macartney played the innings of the match. Impudent, experimental, unpredictable, he played the ball so late that it became impossible to place a field for him or to anticipate his stroke. Collins meanwhile batted two hours 25 minutes for 24. Wickets fell cheaply at the finish, but the game by then was dead.

Macartney's century was the first of 3 that he made after his 40th birthday, all in 1926. Armstrong also made 3, Hobbs 6, and Bardsley and Hendren one each. Bardsley, Hobbs and Macartney all performed the feat in this match.

AUSTRALIA

Batsman	Dismissal	Score	Dismissal (2nd)	Score
*H. L. Collins	b Root	1	c Sutcliffe b Larwood	24
W. Bardsley	not out	193		
C. G. Macartney	c Sutcliffe b Larwood	39	not out	133
W. M. Woodfull	c Strudwick b Root	13	(6)c Root b Woolley	0
T. J. E. Andrews	c and b Kilner	10	(4)b Root	9
J. M. Gregory	b Larwood	7	(2)c Sutcliffe b Root	0
J. M. Taylor	c Carr b Tate	9		
A. J. Richardson	b Kilner	35		
J. Ryder	c Strudwick b Tate	28	(7)not out	0
†W. A. Oldfield	c Sutcliffe b Kilner	19	(5)c Sutcliffe b Tate	11
A. A. Mailey	lbw b Kilner	1		
Extras	(b 12, lb 16)	28	(b 5, lb 12)	17
Total		**383**	**Total** (5 wkts)	**194**

ENGLAND

J. B. Hobbs	c Richardson b Macartney	119
H. Sutcliffe	b Richardson	82
F. E. Woolley	lbw b Ryder	87
E. H. Hendren	not out	127
A. P. F. Chapman	not out	50
*A. W. Carr		
R. Kilner		
M. W. Tate	did not bat	
C. F. Root		
H. Larwood		
†H. Strudwick		
Extras	(b 4, lb 4, w 1, nb 1)	10
Total	(3 wkts dec)	**475**

FALL OF WICKETS

AUSTRALIA

Wkt	1st	2nd
1st	11	2
2nd	84	125
3rd	127	163
4th	158	187
5th	187	194
6th	208	—
7th	282	—
8th	338	—
9th	379	—
10th	383	—

ENGLAND

Wkt	1st	2nd
1st	182	—
2nd	219	—
3rd	359	—
4th	—	—
5th	—	—
6th	—	—
7th	—	—
8th	—	—
9th	—	—
10th	—	—

Umpires: L. C. Braund,
A. E. Street

ENGLAND	1st Innings				2nd Innings			
	O	M	R	W	O	M	R	W
Tate	50	12	111	2	25	11	38	1
Root	36	11	70	2	19	9	40	2
Kilner	34·5	11	70	4	22	2	49	0
Larwood	32	2	99	2	15	3	37	1
Woolley	2	0	5	0	7	1	13	1

AUSTRALIA	1st Innings				2nd Innings			
	O	M	R	W	O	M	R	W
Gregory	30	3	125	0				
Macartney	33	8	90	1				
Mailey	30	6	96	0				
Richardson	48	18	73	1				
Ryder	25	3	70	1				
Collins	2	0	11	0				

1926 Third Test, Leeds

July 10, 12, 13
Toss: England   *Result*: Match Drawn

Carr had shown his readiness to get at the Australians by declaring on the last day at Lord's, and now, at Leeds, he put Australia in. Heavy rain the previous evening, and the anticipation of hot sun on a hastily prepared alternative wicket, prompted him to do so, but he did not act without consulting Ted Leyland, the groundsman, and Herbert Sutcliffe, whose home ground it was. The sun, however, was soon obscured, and Parker, the Gloucestershire slow left-arm bowler, was surprisingly left out. The Australians had even more serious problems: Collins had neuritis, Hendry scarlet fever, Ryder a doubtful ankle and Gregory a strained muscle, while Everett, Gregory's understudy, was unfit. Australia's state seemed parlous indeed when Bardsley flicked at Tate's first ball and was beautifully caught low down by Sutcliffe at slip.

Macartney came in and cut his first ball for 2. The next two balls came easily on to the bat, suggesting that the wicket was docile. But off the fifth ball Tate forced a hurried stroke and the ball flew to the left of Carr at third slip—a difficult catch. Carr got both hands to it, but it did not stick. Macartney then played an astonishing innings, reaching his hundred in 103 minutes and being 112 not out at lunch. Only Tate seemed able to bowl anything like a length to him, and

among the many adjectives applied to his innings the words 'insolent' and 'contemptuous' frequently recur. What impressed people most was Macartney's extraordinary ability to play virtually the same ball to widely different parts of the field, making scientific field-placing impossible. After lunch Macartney took his score to 151, made in 2 hours 52 minutes, and Carr's mistake was further rubbed in by Woodfull and Richardson, so that Australia had reached 366 for 3 when rain stopped play at 5.20.

Next morning good bowling by Tate and Geary prevented Australia from running away with the game, and when Hobbs and Sutcliffe went in directly after lunch with nothing to play for but a draw they put on 59 in 90 minutes. The Australian spinners then gained the upper hand, and England slumped to 182 for 8. But Geary and Macaulay played out time, and they added another 87 runs on the last morning in 100 minutes by restrained, sensible play, Macaulay especially playing the spinners with wonderful certainty. All Bardsley's permutations of bowlers failed, and it was ten past one before England followed on. Then Hobbs and Sutcliffe, on a wicket that showed some worn patches, put on 156 for the first wicket and England were safe.

AUSTRALIA

*W. Bardsley	c Sutcliffe b Tate	0			
W. M. Woodfull	b Tate	141			
C. G. Macartney	c Hendren b Macaulay	151			
T. J. E. Andrews	lbw b Kilner	4			
A. J. Richardson	run out	100			
J. M. Taylor	c Strudwick b Geary	4			
J. M. Gregory	c Geary b Kilner	26			
J. Ryder	b Tate	42			
*W. A. Oldfield	lbw b Tate	14			
C. V. Grimmett	c Sutcliffe b Geary	1			
A. A. Mailey	not out	1			
Extras	(b 2, lb 4, nb 4)	10			
Total		**494**			

ENGLAND

J. B. Hobbs	c Andrews b Mailey	49	b Grimmett	88	
H. Sutcliffe	c and b Grimmett	26	b Richardson	94	
F. E. Woolley	run out	27	c Macartney b Grimmett	20	
E. H. Hendren	c Andrews b Mailey	0	not out	4	
*A. W. Carr	lbw b Macaulay	13			
A. P. F. Chapman	b Macartney	15			
R. Kilner	c Ryder b Grimmett	36			
M. W. Tate	st Oldfield b Grimmett	5	(5)not out	42	
G. Geary	not out	35			
G. G. Macaulay	c and b Grimmett	76			
*H. Strudwick	c Gregory b Grimmett	1			
Extras	(b 4, lb 6, nb 1)	11	(b 5, lb 1)	6	
Total		**294**	**Total** (3 wkts)	**254**	

FALL OF WICKETS

AUSTRALIA

Wkt	1st	2nd
1st	0	—
2nd	235	—
3rd	249	—
4th	378	—
5th	385	—
6th	423	—
7th	452	—
8th	485	—
9th	492	—
10th	494	—

ENGLAND

Wkt	1st	2nd
1st	59	156
2nd	104	208
3rd	108	210
4th	110	—
5th	131	—
6th	140	—
7th	175	—
8th	182	—
9th	290	—
10th	294	—

Umpires: H. R. Butt,
W. Reeves

ENGLAND	1st Innings				2nd Innings			
	O	M	R	W	O	M	R	W
Tate	51	13	99	4	..			
Macaulay	32	8	123	1	..			
Kilner	37	6	106	2	..			
Geary	41	5	130	2	..			
Woolley	4	0	26	0	..			

AUSTRALIA	1st Innings				2nd Innings			
	O	M	R	W	O	M	R	W
Gregory	17	5	37	0	..	6	2	12	0
Macartney	41	13	51	2	..	4	1	13	0
Grimmett	49	11	88	5	..	29	10	59	2
Richardson	20	5	44	0	..	16	7	22	1
Mailey	21	4	63	2	..	18	2	80	0
Ryder					..	9	2	26	0
Andrews					..	4	0	36	0

1926 Fourth Test, Old Trafford

July 24, 26, 27
Toss: Australia   *Result:* Match Drawn

Leeds had been the fifth draw in succession in a Test Match in England, and the clamour for four-day Tests was becoming insistent, expecially from Australia. There was further frustration at Old Trafford, where, after a blank first morning, 10 balls were bowled and 6 runs scored before another downpour drove the players off for good. On the Sunday Carr went down with tonsilitis, and the leadership passed to Hobbs, England's first professional captain for 39 years. It had not been a happy series for Carr, his decisions at Lord's and Leeds drawing criticism, while in his only innings he had been lbw for 13. The writing, perhaps, was on the wall, especially as the selectors had shown themselves to be no respecters of persons: for this match they dropped Macaulay and Geary, heroes of the previous Test. The Australians due to Collins' illness were again led by Bardsley, while Ponsford replaced Taylor.

A heavy dew on Monday morning delayed the start, but the wicket was in good order. Hobbs changed his bowlers frequently, giving an early chance to Stevens with his leg-breaks, and at 29 Bardsley hit a long hop to short square leg, letting in Macartney. Without quite touching the brilliance of his display at Leeds, Macartney was in delightful form, while Woodfull showed that his short back-lift did not prevent him from getting power into his strokes with his wrists, playing the ball late. Despite steady bowling from Root, Kilner and Tate, 192 runs were put on before Macartney, reckless after reaching his hundred—his third in successive Test innings—was bowled by Root. This time Woodfull almost kept pace with him, being 93 when Macartney was out, and reaching his own century soon after. The rest of the Australian batting failed, mostly due to careless shots and one very good running catch in the long field by Chapman, substituting for Carr. Perhaps it seemed that there was not much to play for.

322 for 8 overnight, Australia batted on next morning, giving Tate a chance to improve his figures. When England went in Hobbs batted superbly, and although Sutcliffe was not at his best, 58 were made in the first hour. Tyldesley had some uncomfortable moments against Mailey, but he batted attractively as he settled down. Woolley hit two sixes, and Hendren, too, took some useful practice. A feature of the match was the umpiring, no bowler getting an lbw decision in spite of numerous appeals, while Andrews, after throwing the ball up on appeal, was adjudged not to have caught Tyldesley at silly point from a hard, low hit.

AUSTRALIA

W. M. Woodfull.....	c Hendren b Root.........	117
*W. Bardsley........	c Tyldesley b Stevens......	15
C. G. Macartney.....	b Root..................	109
T. J. E. Andrews.....	c sub (A. P. F. Chapman) b Stevens	8
W. H. Ponsford......	c and b Kilner.........	23
A. J. Richardson.....	c Woolley b Stevens.......	0
J. Ryder............	c Strudwick b Root.......	3
J. M. Gregory.......	c Kilner b Root..........	34
†W. A. Oldfield......	not out.................	12
C. V. Grimmett......	c Stevens b Tate...........	6
A. A. Mailey........	b Tate..................	1
Extras.............	(b 2, lb 1, w 1, nb 3).......	7
Total............	....	**335**

ENGLAND

J. B. Hobbs.........	c Ryder b Grimmett.......	74
H. Sutcliffe.........	c Oldfield b Mailey........	20
E. Tyldesley........	c Oldfield b Macartney.....	81
F. E. Woolley.......	c Ryder b Mailey.........	58
E. H. Hendren......	not out.................	32
G. T. S. Stevens.....	c Bardsley b Mailey........	24
R. Kilner...........	not out.............•....	9
*A. W. Carr.........		
M. W. Tate.........	did not bat	
C. F. Root.........		
†H. Strudwick.......		
Extras.............	(b 4, lb 3)..............	7
Total...........	(5 wkts).................	**305**

FALL OF WICKETS

AUSTRALIA

Wkt	1st	2nd
1st	29	—
2nd	221	—
3rd	252	—
4th	256	—
5th	257	—
6th	266	—
7th	300	—
8th	317	—
9th	329	—
10th	335	—

ENGLAND

Wkt	1st	2nd
1st	58	—
2nd	135	—
3rd	225	—
4th	243	—
5th	272	—
6th	—	—
7th	—	—
8th	—	—
9th	—	—
10th	—	—

Umpires: H. Young,
H. Chidgey

ENGLAND

	1st Innings				2nd Innings			
	O	M	R	W	O	M	R	W
Tate.............	36·2	7	88	2	..			
Root............	52	27	84	4	..			
Kilner..........	28	12	51	1	..			
Stevens.........	32	3	86	3	..			
Woolley.........	2	0	19	0	..			

AUSTRALIA

	1st Innings				2nd Innings			
	O	M	R	W	O	M	R	W
Gregory.........	11	4	17	0	..			
Grimmett........	38	9	85	1	..			
Mailey..........	27	4	87	3	..			
Ryder...........	15	3	46	0	..			
Richardson.......	17	3	43	0	..			
Macartney.......	8	5	7	1	..			
Andrews.........	9	5	13	0	..			

1926 Fifth Test, Oval

August 14, 16, 17, 18
Toss: England *Result:* England won by 289 runs

England recalled Rhodes, top of the bowling averages at 48, while Carr, whose health and form were doubtful, gave way to Chapman. Larwood replaced Root. For Australia, Collins returned to the exclusion of Ryder, Ponsford keeping his place.

The extraordinary perversity of cricket and cricketers was illustrated on the first day of this timeless Test, which paradoxically was fuller of incident than any in the series so far. Hobbs, according to one account, played 'divinely' until he missed a Mailey full toss. Hendren cut at a medium-paced long hop in the last over before lunch and played on. Chapman jumped out once too often and was stumped. Stevens hit Mailey into the pavilion, then pushed an identical ball to silly mid off. These and other misjudgments brought England to a modest 280 all out. Sutcliffe, most uncomfortable of the batsmen, was top scorer, while Mailey, the best bowler, was the most expensive. More was to come. Larwood was through Bardsley several times before getting him caught behind. Macartney, potentially in devastating mood, dragged a ball into his wicket. Ponsford ran himself out, Andrews was bowled by a perfect break-back. Collins, who had played only one innings of any account since the Lord's Test, joined Woodfull at 59 for 4, and they played out time.

Next morning Rhodes bowled Woodfull, and he came back later

to dismiss Richardson. But Collins defended while Gregory, beaten at first many times by Larwood, began to hit, and they put on 107. Oldfield and Grimmett afterwards added 67, and Australia led on first innings by 22. England faced an anxious last hour in which Hobbs and Sutcliffe moved serenely to 49 for 0.

After a tropical downpour in the night the sky was cloudy for the first hour and the wicket slow. Then the sun came out, after which most of the bowling was done by Richardson, off-breaks round the wicket from the Vauxhall end with a close leg field, and Macartney, left-arm over from the pavilion end. The ball kicked and turned viciously, but Hobbs and Sutcliffe not only survived but kept the score moving, Hobbs especially proving impossible to contain. Arguments as to whether the bowlers made the best use of the conditions still go on, but what remains beyond dispute is the masterly way in which the England pair dealt with the problems they faced. Hobbs made exactly 100 and Sutcliffe 161. When Australia batted on the fourth day after further rain, Larwood removed Woodfull, Macartney and Andrews, and the rest of the leading batsmen fell to Rhodes. 'From the moment he went on', said one account, 'the match was over.' England thus regained the Ashes after 14 years.

ENGLAND

Batsman	Dismissal 1st	R	Dismissal 2nd	R
J. B. Hobbs	b Mailey	37	b Gregory	100
H. Sutcliffe	b Mailey	76	b Mailey	161
F. E. Woolley	b Mailey	18	lbw b Richardson	27
E. H. Hendren	b Gregory	8	c Oldfield b Grimmett	15
*A. P. F. Chapman	st Oldfield b Mailey	49	b Richardson	19
G. T. S. Stevens	c Andrews b Mailey	17	c Mailey b Grimmett	22
W. Rhodes	c Oldfield b Mailey	28	lbw b Grimmett	14
G. Geary	run out	9	c Oldfield b Gregory	1
M. W. Tate	b Grimmett	23	not out	33
H. Larwood	c Andrews b Grimmett	0	b Mailey	5
†H. Strudwick	not out	4	c Andrews b Mailey	2
Extras	(b 6, lb 5)	11	(b 19, lb 18)	37
Total		280		436

AUSTRALIA

Batsman	Dismissal 1st	R	Dismissal 2nd	R
W. M. Woodfull	b Rhodes	35	c Geary b Larwood	0
W. Bardsley	c Strudwick b Larwood	2	(4)c Woolley b Rhodes	21
C. G. Macartney	b Stevens	25	c Geary b Larwood	16
W. H. Ponsford	run out	2	(2)c Larwood b Rhodes	12
T. J. E. Andrews	b Larwood	3	(6)c Tate b Larwood	15
*H. L. Collins	c Stevens b Larwood	61	(5)c Woolley b Rhodes	4
A. J. Richardson	c Geary b Rhodes	16	(8)b Rhodes	4
J. M. Gregory	c Stevens b Tate	73	(7)c Sutcliffe b Tate	9
†W. A. Oldfield	not out	33	b Stevens	23
C. V. Grimmett	b Tate	35	not out	8
A. A. Mailey	c Strudwick b Tate	0	b Geary	6
Extras	(b 5, lb 12)	17	(lb 7)	7
Total		302		125

FALL OF WICKETS

ENGLAND		
Wkt	1st	2nd
1st	53	172
2nd	91	220
3rd	108	277
4th	189	316
5th	213	373
6th	214	375
7th	231	382
8th	266	425
9th	266	430
10th	280	436

AUSTRALIA		
Wkt	1st	2nd
1st	9	1
2nd	44	31
3rd	51	31
4th	59	35
5th	90	63
6th	122	83
7th	229	83
8th	231	87
9th	298	114
10th	302	125

Umpires: F. Chester, H. Young

AUSTRALIA	1st Innings					2nd Innings			
	O	M	R	W		O	M	R	W
Gregory	15	4	31	1	..	18	1	58	2
Grimmett	33	12	74	2	..	55	17	108	3
Mailey	33.5	3	138	6	..	42.5	6	128	3
Macartney	6	3	16	0	..	26	16	24	0
Richardson	7	2	10	0	..	41	21	81	2

ENGLAND	1st Innings					2nd Innings			
	O	M	R	W		O	M	R	W
Tate	37.1	17	40	3	..	9	4	12	1
Larwood	34	11	82	3	..	14	3	34	3
Geary	27	8	43	0	..	6.3	2	15	1
Stevens	29	3	85	1	..	3	1	13	1
Rhodes	25	15	35	2	..	20	9	44	4

1928-29 First Test, Brisbane

Test no. 115

November 30, December 1, 3, 4, 5
Toss: England   *Result:* England won by 675 runs

Australia, at the end of a long period of dominance, and with nearly all their great players either retired or ageing, took far too long to reconstruct their side, while England, immensely strong in batting and far ahead of Australia in bowling, were inspired in the field by the wonderful catching of Chapman and the aggressive wicket-keeping of Duckworth. It was not until the final Test that Australia fielded anything like a young side, and then England, who left out their captain, missed chance after chance in the field and could not gather themselves together for a final effort, so that they suffered their only defeat of the tour. Hammond broke many records, while for Australia Bradman, also in his first series, gave warning of what was to come.

For the first Test Australia relied entirely on long-established players apart from Bradman, who had already made 295 runs against the tourists for twice out. Gregory, at 33 a veteran of 20 Tests, was their youngest bowler. Yet England were slow into their stride. Sutcliffe tried to hook a head-high bumper just before lunch and was caught at fine leg, Hobbs underestimated Bradman's speed and throw and was run out, Mead was beaten by Grimmett, and England were 108

for 3. Hammond and Jardine, both playing in their first Test, took England through a tense period to 160 for 3 at tea, and then Hendren, going for his shots from the start, made 50 in 77 minutes, and England were 272 for 5 at stumps. Hendren's 169, completed next day, lasted just over 5 hours in all, and with Larwood making 70 out of 124 in under 2 hours England reached 521.

In a disastrous last hour on the second day Australia lost 4 wickets for 44, Chapman starting the rout with a wonderful catch at fourth slip, and their chances of recovery were wrecked when Gregory, who had bowled with plenty of pace and life, was forced by a recurrence of his cartilage trouble to retire from all cricket, while Kelleway was taken ill with food poisoning. Tate got Bradman lbw with a slower ball, Ryder batted 83 minutes before mishitting a long hop, and in less than 2½ hours Australia were all out, Larwood taking 6 for 32.

England, in the context of a timeless Test, were obliged to bat again, but eventually Chapman declared—the first declaration in a Test in Australia—and after being 17 for 1 on the fourth evening Australia collapsed after heavy rain in the night, although Woodfull carried his bat. Hendren's great innings was the turning point of the match.

ENGLAND

J. B. Hobbs	run out	49	lbw b Grimmett	11	
H. Sutcliffe	c Ponsford b Gregory	38	c sub (F. C. Thompson) b Ironmonger	32	
C. P. Mead	lbw b Grimmett	8	lbw b Grimmett	73	
W. R. Hammond	c Woodfull b Gregory	44	c sub (F. C. Thompson) b Ironmonger	28	
D. R. Jardine	c Woodfull b Ironmonger	35	not out	65	
E. H. Hendren	c Ponsford b Ironmonger	169	c Ponsford b Grimmett	45	
*A. P. F. Chapman	c Kelleway b Gregory	50	c Oldfield b Grimmett	27	
M. W. Tate	c Ryder b Grimmett	26	c Bradman b Grimmett	20	
H. Larwood	lbw b Hendry	70	c Ponsford b Grimmett	37	
J. C. White	lbw b Grimmett	14			
†G. Duckworth	not out	5			
Extras	(lb 10, nb 3)	13	(lb 3, nb 1)	4	
Total		**521**	**Total** (8 wkts dec)	**342**	

AUSTRALIA

W. M. Woodfull	c Chapman b Larwood	0	not out	30	
W. H. Ponsford	b Larwood	2	c Duckworth b Larwood	6	
A. F. Kippax	c and b Tate	16	c and b Larwood	15	
H. S. T. L. Hendry	lbw b Larwood	30	c Larwood b White	6	
C. E. Kelleway	b Larwood	8	absent ill	—	
*J. Ryder	c Jardine b Larwood	33	(5) c Larwood b Tate	1	
D. G. Bradman	lbw b Tate	18	(6) c Chapman b White	1	
†W. A. Oldfield	lbw b Tate	2	(7) c Larwood b Tate	5	
C. V. Grimmett	not out	7	(8) c Chapman b White	1	
H. Ironmonger	b Larwood	4	(9) c Chapman b White	0	
J. M. Gregory	absent hurt	—	absent hurt	—	
Extras	(b 1, lb 1)	2	(nb 1)	1	
Total		**122**	**Total**	**66**	

FALL OF WICKETS

ENGLAND

Wkt	1st	2nd
1st	85	25
2nd	95	69
3rd	108	117
4th	161	165
5th	217	228
6th	291	263
7th	319	285
8th	443	342
9th	495	—
10th	521	—

AUSTRALIA

Wkt	1st	2nd
1st	0	6
2nd	7	33
3rd	24	46
4th	40	47
5th	71	49
6th	101	62
7th	105	66
8th	116	66
9th	122	—
10th	—	—

Umpires: D. Elder,
G. A. Hele

AUSTRALIA	1st Innings					2nd Innings			
	O	M	R	W		O	M	R	W
Gregory	41	2	142	3	..				
Kelleway	34	9	77	0	..				
Grimmett	40	2	167	3	..	44·1	8	131	6
Ironmonger	44·3	18	79	2	..	50	20	85	2
Ryder	6	2	23	0	..	14	3	43	0
Hendry	10	1	20	1	..	27	6	79	0

ENGLAND	1st Innings					2nd Innings			
	O	M	R	W		O	M	R	W
Larwood	14·4	4	32	6	..	7	0	30	2
Tate	21	6	50	3	..	11	3	26	2
Hammond	15	5	38	0	..	1	0	2	0
White					..	6·3	2	7	4

94. W. R. Hammond

95. C. V. Grimmett

96. **England 1928-29**
Back row: G. Duckworth, L. E. G. Ames, C. P. Mead, M. W. Tate, E. H. Hendren, G. Geary. *Middle row:* M. Leyland, S. J. Staples, W. R. Hammond, F. C. Toone (manager), H. Sutcliffe, H. Larwood, A. P. Freeman. *Front:* E. Tyldesley, J. C. White, A. P. F. Chapman (capt.), D. R. Jardine, J. B. Hobbs.

1928-29 Second Test, Sydney

December 14, 15, 17, 18, 19, 20
Toss: Australia   *Result:* England won by eight wickets

Apart from the changes that were forced on them the Australians did little to reconstruct their side. Nothling, not much above medium, came in for Gregory, Blackie, a 46-year-old off-spinner who had entered big cricket very late, came in for Kelleway, and Victor Richardson replaced Bradman. England, who had gone into the first Test with three bowlers plus Hammond, did not take this risk again, Geary, who came in for Mead, retaining his place for the series.

Woodfull and Richardson had 50 up in an hour, but then Larwood, who had come back for a second spell, hit Richardson's off stump as he played back, and at 65 Geary bowled Kippax. The ball actually cannoned off his pads from outside the leg stump and it was some time before it was established that he was out, Kippax believing at first that Duckworth had broken the wicket. Duckworth's habit of making frequent high-pitched appeals had already annoyed Australian crowds and with this incident the barracking of him intensified.

69 for 2 at lunch, Australia suffered yet another setback when Ponsford turned his back on a shortish ball—not a bumper—and was hit on the back of the left hand, fracturing a small bone. He took no further part in the series. Hendry then did much to justify his inclusion in a long stand with Woodfull that lasted until just before tea. But

both men were out in quick succession, and only a sturdy innings from Oldfield saw Australia to 251 for 8 at the close. Geary moved the ball about enough at medium pace to take 5 for 35.

Australia were quickly disposed of next morning, and after interruptions for bad light England were 126 for 2 at stumps. On the third day Jardine was run out at 148, but Hammond and Hendren, driving powerfully, put on 145 in just over two hours to take England into the lead with only three wickets down, Ryder being a long time in packing the covers. Hammond stayed until the fourth morning, batting 7 hours 41 minutes. All the England players reached double figures, and Australia began their second innings 383 behind.

Richardson, whose fielding had been exceptional, was out before a run had been scored, but Hendry, although never comfortable against Larwood, led a wonderful fight back with Woodfull. Powerful hitting by Ryder helped to ensure that England would have to bat again, but the task left to them was a formality. Tate was England's best bowler this time, but already at this stage in his career Larwood was causing batsmen to take risks to avoid facing him or to protect others. There was an impression, too, that at times he bowled at the batsman.

AUSTRALIA

						FALL OF WICKETS

						AUSTRALIA		
W. M. Woodfull	lbw b Geary	68	run out	111		*Wkt*	*1st*	*2nd*
V. Y. Richardson	b Larwood	27	c Hendren b Tate	0		1st	51	0
A. F. Kippax	b Geary	9	(4)lbw b Tate	10		2nd	65	215
W. H. Ponsford	retired hurt	5	absent hurt	—		3rd	152	234
H. S. T. L. Hendry	b Geary	37	(3)lbw b Tate	112		4th	153	246
*J. Ryder	lbw b Geary	25	(5)c Chapman b Larwood	79		5th	171	347
O. E. Nothling	b Larwood	8	(6)run out	44		6th	192	348
†W. A. Oldfield	not out	41	(7)lbw b Tate	0		7th	222	370
C. V. Grimmett	run out	9	(8)c Chapman b Geary	18		8th	251	397
D. D. J. Blackie	b Geary	8	(9)not out	11		9th	253	397
H. Ironmonger	c Duckworth b Larwood	1	(10)b Geary	0		10th	—	—
Extras	(b 4, lb 9, w 2)	15	(b 5, lb 6, w 1)	12				
Total		**253**	Total	**397**				

ENGLAND

						ENGLAND		
J. B. Hobbs	c Oldfield b Grimmett	40				*Wkt*	*1st*	*2nd*
H. Sutcliffe	c Hendry b Ironmonger	11				1st	37	8
W. R. Hammond	b Ironmonger	251				2nd	65	13
D. R. Jardine	run out	28				3rd	148	—
E. H. Hendren	c Richardson b Blackie	74				4th	293	—
*A. P. F. Chapman	c Ryder b Blackie	20				5th	341	—
H. Larwood	c Ryder b Grimmett	43				6th	432	—
G. Geary	lbw b Blackie	66	(1)b Hendry	8		7th	496	—
M. W. Tate	lbw b Blackie	25	(2)c sub (D. G. Bradman)			8th	523	—
			b Hendry	4		9th	592	—
†G. Duckworth	not out	39	(3)not out	2		10th	636	—
J. C. White	st Oldfield b Hendry	29	(4)not out	2				
Extras	(b 2, lb 3, w 4, nb 1)	10						
Total		**636**	Total (2 wkts)	**16**				

Umpires: D. Elder,
G. A. Hele

ENGLAND	1st Innings					2nd Innings			
	O	M	R	W		O	M	R	W
Larwood	26·2	4	77	3	..	35	5	105	1
Tate	21	9	29	0	..	46	14	99	4
White	38	10	79	0	..	30	5	83	0
Geary	18	5	35	5	..	31·4	11	55	2
Hammond	5	0	18	0	..	9	0	43	0

AUSTRALIA	1st Innings					2nd Innings			
	O	M	R	W		O	M	R	W
Nothling	42	15	60	0	..	4	0	12	0
Grimmett	64	14	191	2	..				
Ironmonger	68	21	142	2	..				
Blackie	59	10	148	4	..				
Hendry	23·1	4	52	1	..	3	2	4	2
Ryder	11	3	22	0	..				
Kippax	5	3	11	0	..				

1928-29 Third Test, Melbourne

December 29, 31, January 1, 2, 3, 4, 5
Toss: Australia   *Result:* England won by three wickets

Bradman returned for Ponsford, while Nothling and Ironmonger were replaced by a'Beckett, fast-medium, and Oxenham, medium. Australia began badly, losing 3 for 57: if another wicket fell cheaply the rubber was surely lost. But Kippax, a tall, graceful stylist, and Ryder, rugged but forceful, put on 161 at a run a minute, and when Kippax was out Bradman joined Ryder in another good stand, so that Australia were 276 for 4 at stumps. Ryder seemed to have made his position as captain secure: he had been appointed for the first two Tests only, and had not been confirmed as captain for this match until just before the game.

Australia were 287 for 6 next morning, but a'Beckett then helped Bradman to put on 86. Tate bowled at his best in this period, but Bradman's defence was great. Bradman had batted 3¼ hours when Hammond hit his leg stump, and a'Beckett took 2 hours 22 minutes over his 41. England were 47 for 1 at stumps, only 168 runs being scored in the day.

On the third day England reached 161 before losing Sutcliffe: hesitant all through, he batted 3½ hours for his 58. With rain threatening, Chapman and Hendren went in ahead of Jardine, but neither took root, and Jardine was with Hammond at the close, when England were

312 for 4, Hammond 169 not out. On the fourth day the bowlers pegged away at Hammond's leg stump, but he reached his second successive double century after 6 hours 29 minutes. He was out soon afterwards, and England's lead was held to 20.

118 for 2 overnight, Australia had a good fifth day, Woodfull completing a chanceless century and Bradman, after spending 2 hours over his first 40, accelerating afterwards. Larwood had a pulled muscle and bowled little. By the close Australia were 347 for 8 and England, tired out in the heat, were already facing a fourth innings target of over 300. Their chance seemed gone when rain fell in the night.

The game resumed nearly an hour late, with a hot sun to make the wicket sticky. The ball kicked up and hit the batsmen's shoulders and arms and even the head and neck. Hobbs gave an early chance to Hendry at slip, but he and Sutcliffe, playing back to nearly every ball, somehow survived until tea, when England were 78 for 0. Hobbs had signalled for Jardine to come in no. 3, and when Hobbs was out Sutcliffe and Jardine skilfully saw the day through. Only 14 were wanted when Sutcliffe's great innings ended on the seventh day, and although 3 more wickets were lost the result was then hardly in doubt.

AUSTRALIA

W. M. Woodfull	c Jardine b Tate	7	c Duckworth b Tate	107	
V. Y. Richardson	c Duckworth b Larwood	3	b Larwood	5	
H. S. T. L. Hendry	c Jardine b Larwood	23	st Duckworth b White	12	
A. F. Kippax	c Jardine b Larwood	100	b Tate	41	
*J. Ryder	c Hendren b Tate	112	b Geary	5	
D. G. Bradman	b Hammond	79	c Duckworth b Geary	112	
†W. A. Oldfield	b Geary	3	b White	7	
E. L. a'Beckett	c Duckworth b White	41	b White	6	
R. K. Oxenham	b Geary	15	b White	39	
C. V. Grimmett	c Duckworth b Geary	5	not out	4	
D. D. J. Blackie	not out	2	b White	0	
Extras	(b 4, lb 3)	7	(b 6, lb 7)	13	
Total		**397**	**Total**	**351**	

ENGLAND

J. B. Hobbs	c Oldfield b a'Beckett	20	lbw b Blackie	49	
H. Sutcliffe	b Blackie	58	lbw b Grimmett	135	
W. R. Hammond	c a'Beckett b Blackie	200	(4)run out	32	
*A. P. F. Chapman	b Blackie	24	(6)c Woodfull b Ryder	5	
E. H. Hendren	c a'Beckett b Hendry	19	b Oxenham	45	
D. R. Jardine	c and b Blackie	62	(3)b Grimmett	33	
H. Larwood	c and b Blackie	0			
G. Geary	lbw b Grimmett	1	not out	4	
M. W. Tate	c Kippax b Grimmett	21	(7)run out	0	
†G. Duckworth	b Blackie	3	(9)not out	0	
J. C. White	not out	8			
Extras	(b 1)	1	(b 15, lb 14)	29	
Total		**417**	**Total** (7 wkts)	**332**	

FALL OF WICKETS

AUSTRALIA

Wkt	1st	2nd
1st	5	7
2nd	15	60
3rd	57	138
4th	218	143
5th	282	201
6th	287	226
7th	373	252
8th	383	345
9th	394	351
10th	397	351

ENGLAND

Wkt	1st	2nd
1st	28	105
2nd	161	199
3rd	201	257
4th	238	318
5th	364	326
6th	364	328
7th	381	328
8th	385	—
9th	391	—
10th	417	—

Umpires: D. Elder, G. A. Hele

ENGLAND	1st Innings				2nd Innings			
	O	M	R	W	O	M	R	W
Larwood	37	3	127	3	16	3	37	1
Tate	46	17	87	2	47	15	70	2
Geary	31·5	4	83	3	30	4	94	2
Hammond	8	4	19	1	16	6	30	0
White	57	30	64	1	56·5	20	107	5
Jardine	1	0	10	0				

AUSTRALIA	1st Innings				2nd Innings			
	O	M	R	W	O	M	R	W
a'Beckett	37	7	92	1	22	5	39	0
Hendry	20	8	35	1	23	5	33	0
Grimmett	55	14	114	2	42	12	96	2
Oxenham	35	11	67	0	28	10	44	1
Blackie	44	13	94	6	39	11	75	1
Ryder	4	0	14	0	5·5	1	16	1

1928-29 Fourth Test, Adelaide

February 1, 2, 4, 5, 6, 7, 8
Toss: England *Result:* England won by 12 runs

Hobbs and Sutcliffe again put on over a hundred, Hobbs' footwork and timing being a joy. But both were out at 143, Jardine was immediately lbw, and when Hendren missed a break-back England were 179 for 4. Chapman helped Hammond to add 67 at a critical period, and then Duckworth went in to play out time. England on a perfect wicket had been held to 246 for 5, Grimmett bowling beautifully. Hammond, not out 47, had batted for 2 hours 10 minutes; but next morning, farming the bowling, he made 72 of the last 88.

When Australia batted on the second afternoon they made another atrocious start, losing three wickets for 19; but Ryder again helped in a splendid recovery, while the 19-year-old Jackson, fluent and wristy, square and late cut prettily and employed a succession of lovely forcing shots on the leg side. At stumps Australia were 131 for 3, and although they lost Ryder next morning, Jackson, in his first Test, reached his hundred off the first ball after lunch after batting 4 hours 10 minutes. At the end of the third day Australia were 365 for 9, by which time Larwood was down to medium pace, Geary was off with a strain, and the bulk of the work fell to White, whose accuracy and endurance, as in the previous Test, were phenomenal.

On the fourth morning, against a deficit of 35, England lost Hobbs and Sutcliffe for 21; but Hammond and Jardine took part in a record stand which put England back in the game. Hammond was slow, Jardine stodgy, but the atmosphere for many hours was one of intense conflict and both men batted admirably; they put on 262 before they were separated on the fifth afternoon. Jardine batted for 5¾ hours and Hammond for 7 hours 20 minutes. All the other batsmen failed until Tate made 47 in a burst of hitting at the end.

Wanting 349, Australia at stumps on the fifth day were 24 for 0, but they were pegged down next morning, and when Hendry mistimed a pull directly after lunch they were 74 for 3. Ryder used his feet to get at White, but at 26 he survived a simple return catch. He went on to add 137 with Kippax, and again the ascendancy passed to Australia. Then two good catches were taken, one a glorious diving catch at slip by Hammond, and at stumps Australia were 260 for 6—89 still wanted. On the last morning more fine catching and an accurate pick-up and throw by Hobbs which ran out Bradman robbed Australia of a great victory.

ENGLAND

J. B. Hobbs	c Ryder b Hendry	74	c Oldfield b Hendry	1	
H. Sutcliffe	st Oldfield b Grimmett	64	c Oldfield b a'Beckett	17	
W. R. Hammond	not out	119	c and b Ryder	177	
D. R. Jardine	lbw b Grimmett	1	c Woodfull b Oxenham	98	
E. H. Hendren	b Blackie	13	c Bradman b Blackie	11	
*A. P. F. Chapman	c a'Beckett b Ryder	39	c Woodfull b Blackie	0	
†G. Duckworth	c Ryder b Grimmett	5	(11)lbw b Oxenham	1	
H. Larwood	b Hendry	3	(7)lbw b Oxenham	5	
G. Geary	run out	3	(8)c and b Grimmett	6	
M. W. Tate	b Grimmett	2	(9)lbw b Oxenham	47	
J. C. White	c Ryder b Grimmett	0	(10)not out	4	
Extras	(b 3, lb 7, w 1)	11	(b 6, lb 10)	16	
Total		**334**	**Total**	**383**	

AUSTRALIA

W. M. Woodfull	c Duckworth b Tate	1	c Geary b White	30	
A. A. Jackson	lbw b White	164	c Duckworth b Geary	36	
H. S. T. L. Hendry	c Duckworth b Larwood	2	c Tate b White	5	
A. F. Kippax	b White	3	c Hendren b White	51	
*J. Ryder	lbw b White	63	c and b White	87	
D. G. Bradman	c Larwood b Tate	40	run out	58	
E. L. a'Beckett	b White	36	c Hammond b White	21	
R. K. Oxenham	c Chapman b White	15	c Chapman b White	12	
†W. A. Oldfield	b Tate	32	not out	15	
C. V. Grimmett	b Tate	4	c Tate b White	9	
D. D. J. Blackie	not out	3	c Larwood b White	0	
Extras	(lb 5, w 1)	6	(b 9, lb 3)	12	
Total		**369**	**Total**	**336**	

FALL OF WICKETS

ENGLAND

Wkt	1st	2nd
1st	143	1
2nd	143	21
3rd	149	283
4th	179	296
5th	246	297
6th	263	302
7th	270	327
8th	308	337
9th	312	381
10th	334	383

AUSTRALIA

Wkt	1st	2nd
1st	1	65
2nd	6	71
3rd	19	74
4th	145	211
5th	227	224
6th	287	258
7th	323	308
8th	336	320
9th	365	336
10th	369	336

Umpires: D. Elder,
G. A. Hele

AUSTRALIA

	1st Innings					2nd Innings			
	O	M	R	W		O	M	R	W
a'Beckett	31	8	44	0	..	27	9	41	1
Hendry	31	14	49	2	..	28	11	56	1
Grimmett	52.1	12	102	5	..	52	15	117	1
Oxenham	34	14	51	0	..	47.4	21	67	4
Blackie	29	6	57	1	..	39	11	70	2
Ryder	5	1	20	1	..	5	1	13	1
Kippax					..	2	0	3	0

ENGLAND

	1st Innings					2nd Innings			
	O	M	R	W		O	M	R	W
Larwood	37	6	92	1	..	20	4	60	0
Tate	42	10	77	4	..	37	9	75	0
White	60	16	130	5	..	64.5	21	126	8
Geary	12	3	32	0	..	16	2	42	1
Hammond	9	1	32	0	..	14	3	21	0

1928-29 Fifth Test, Melbourne

March 8, 9, 11, 12, 13, 14, 15, 16
Toss: England   *Result:* Australia won by five wickets

Australia brought in Fairfax, Wall and Hornibrook for Hendry, a'Beckett and Blackie, fielding their youngest side of the series. For England, Sutcliffe and Hammond had been ordered to rest, Chapman had had influenza, White had a strained shoulder and Ames a broken finger. Of these only Hammond and White played.

Wall and Hornibrook, fast-medium and left-hand slow-medium, opened the bowling, but Hobbs, in his twelfth and last century against Australia, dominated the first day, making 142 out of the first 235. Next day Australia were without Grimmett (bruised knee) and England took a firm grip on the game, Hendren playing a great attacking innings. Leyland, missed in the gully when 13, drove powerfully and reached his hundred during a useful last-wicket stand with White, in his first Test against Australia.

The Australian innings followed much the same pattern; a sound start, a century from an opener, a big stand in the middle, and a nuisance stand at the end. Woodfull batted 5½ hours, while Bradman, missed by Geary at mid on when 46, otherwise drove and cut unerringly, and he and the solid Fairfax put on 183. England, on the defensive, dispensed with slip fielders almost entirely. Only 14 wickets fell in the first four days.

Rain delayed the start on the fifth day, and then Geary, helped by a cross-wind, pinned all the batsmen down. Then came the frustrating last-wicket stand, after which Jardine was out first ball. Larwood, the night-watchman, was out next morning, as was Hammond, and in a fatal period after lunch England lost 3 more wickets for 20 runs. Grimmett, back in the attack, got two, and Wall, getting some lift after overnight rain, got the other and always looked dangerous. Tate made 50 in 52 minutes while Leyland stood firm, but Australia's final target of 286 did not look quite out of reach.

Sent in to survive a few minutes at the end of the sixth day, Oldfield and Hornibrook lasted right through until the last ball before lunch. The fielding was good but the catching was far below the standard of previous matches, Chapman being sorely missed. Oldfield stayed for 2½ hours—an innings of immense value—but he was dropped by Hammond when 8. Hammond, however, was the best of the bowlers. At 129 Woodfull was bowled—for the first time in first-class cricket for 27 months—and the grim struggle continued until bad light stopped play at 173 for 4. On the eighth day Kippax was run out, but although England kept up the tension and were well led by White they missed further chances and Ryder and Bradman took Australia to victory. The match won few adherents for time-limitless cricket.

ENGLAND

J. B. Hobbs	b Ryder	142	c Fairfax b Grimmett	65
D. R. Jardine	c Oldfield b Wall	19	c Oldfield b Wall	0
W. R. Hammond	c Fairfax b Wall	38	(4)c Ryder b Fairfax	16
E. Tyldesley	c Hornibrook b Ryder	31	(5)c Oldfield b Wall	21
†G. Duckworth	c Fairfax b Hornibrook	12	(11)lbw b Oxenham	9
E. H. Hendren	c Hornibrook b Fairfax	95	b Grimmett	1
M. Leyland	c Fairfax b Oxenham	137	not out	53
H. Larwood	b Wall	4	(3)b Wall	11
G. Geary	b Hornibrook	4	(9)b Wall	3
M. W. Tate	c sub (E. L. a'Beckett) b Hornibrook	15	(8)c Fairfax b Hornibrook	54
*J. C. White	not out	9	(10)c Oxenham b Wall	4
Extras	(b 4, lb 6, w 1, nb 2)	13	(b 19, lb 1)	20
Total		**519**	**Total**	**257**

AUSTRALIA

W. M. Woodfull	c Geary b Larwood	102	(3)b Hammond	35
A. A. Jackson	run out	30	(4)b Geary	46
A. F. Kippax	c Duckworth b White	38	(5)run out	28
*J. Ryder	c Tate b Hammond	30	(6)not out	57
D. G. Bradman	c Tate b Geary	123	(7)not out	37
A. G. Fairfax	lbw b Geary	65		
R. K. Oxenham	c Duckworth b Geary	7		
†W. A. Oldfield	c and b Geary	6	(1)b Hammond	48
C. V. Grimmett	not out	38		
T. W. Wall	c Duckworth b Geary	9		
P. M. Hornibrook	lbw b White	26	(2)b Hammond	18
Extras	(b 6, lb 9, w 2)	17	(b 12, lb 6)	18
Total		**491**	**Total** (5 wkts)	**287**

FALL OF WICKETS

ENGLAND		
Wkt	1st	2nd
1st	64	1
2nd	146	19
3rd	235	75
4th	240	119
5th	261	123
6th	401	131
7th	409	212
8th	428	217
9th	470	231
10th	519	257

AUSTRALIA		
Wkt	1st	2nd
1st	54	51
2nd	143	80
3rd	203	129
4th	203	158
5th	386	204
6th	399	—
7th	409	—
8th	420	—
9th	432	—
10th	491	—

Umpires: G. A. Hele,
A. C. Jones

AUSTRALIA	1st Innings					2nd Innings			
	O	M	R	W		O	M	R	W
Wall	49	8	123	3	..	26	5	66	5
Hornibrook	48	8	142	3	..	19	5	51	1
Oxenham	45·1	15	86	1	..	10·3	1	34	1
Grimmett	25	11	40	0	..	24	7	66	2
Fairfax	27	4	84	1	..	7	0	20	1
Ryder	18	5	29	2	..				
Kippax	3	1	2	0	..				

ENGLAND	1st Innings					2nd Innings			
	O	M	R	W		O	M	R	W
Larwood	34	7	83	1	..	32·1	5	85	0
Tate	62	26	108	0	..	38	13	72	0
Geary	81	36	105	5	..	20	5	31	1
White	75·3	22	136	2	..	18	8	28	0
Hammond	16	3	31	1	..	26	8	53	3
Leyland	3	0	11	0	..				

Averages: 1928-29

AUSTRALIA

BATTING	M.	Inns.	N.O.	Runs	H.S.	Av.
A. A. Jackson	2	4	0	276	164	69·00
D. G. Bradman	4	8	1	468	123	66·85
J. Ryder	5	10	1	492	112	54·66
W. M. Woodfull	5	10	1	491	111	54·55
A. F. Kippax	5	10	0	311	100	31·10
H. S. T. L. Hendry	4	8	0	227	112	28·37
E. L. a'Beckett	2	4	0	104	41	26·00
W. A. Oldfield	5	10	2	159	48	19·87
R. K. Oxenham	3	5	0	88	39	17·60
C. V. Grimmett	5	9	3	95	38*	15·83
V. Y. Richardson	2	4	0	35	27	8·75
D. D. J. Blackie	3	6	3	24	11*	8·00
W. H. Ponsford	2	3	1	13	6	6·50
H. Ironmonger	2	4	0	5	4	1·25

PLAYED IN ONE TEST: C. Kelleway 8, O. E. Nothling 8 and 44, A. G. Fairfax 65, T. W. Wall 9, P. M. Hornibrook 26 and 18. J. M. Gregory did not bat.

BOWLING	Overs	Mds.	Runs	Wkts.	Av.
T. W. Wall	75	13	189	8	23·62
D. D. J. Blackie	210	51	444	14	31·71
J. Ryder	68·5	16	180	5	36·00
H. S. T. L. Hendry	165·1	51	328	8	41·00
C. V. Grimmett	398·2	95	1024	23	44·52
R. K. Oxenham	200·2	72	349	7	49·85
H. Ironmonger	162·3	59	306	6	51·00

ALSO BOWLED: J. M. Gregory 41–2–142–3, P. M. Hornibrook 67–13–193–4, A. G. Fairfax 34–4–104–2, E. L. a'Beckett 117–29–216–2, A. F. Kippax 10–4–16–0, O. E. Nothling 46–15–72–0, C. Kelleway 34–9–77–0.

ENGLAND

BATTING	M.	Inns.	N.O.	Runs	H.S.	Av.
W. R. Hammond	5	9	1	905	251	113·12
E. H. Hendren	5	9	0	472	169	52·44
H. Sutcliffe	4	7	0	355	135	50·57
J. B. Hobbs	5	9	0	451	142	50·11
D. R. Jardine	5	9	1	341	98	42·62
A. P. F. Chapman	4	7	0	165	50	23·57
H. Larwood	5	8	0	173	70	21·62
M. W. Tate	5	10	0	214	54	21·40
J. C. White	5	8	4	70	29	17·50
G. Duckworth	5	9	4	76	39*	15·20
G. Geary	4	8	1	95	66	13·57

PLAYED IN ONE TEST: M. Leyland 137 and 53*, C. P. Mead 8 and 73, E. Tyldesley 31 and 21.

BOWLING	Overs	Mds.	Runs	Wkts.	Av.
G. Geary	240·3	70	477	19	25·10
J. C. White	406·4	134	760	25	30·40
H. Larwood	259·1	41	728	18	40·44
M. W. Tate	371	122	693	17	40·76
W. R. Hammond	119	30	287	5	57·4

ALSO BOWLED: D. R. Jardine 1–0–10–0, M. Leyland 3–0–11–0.

Averages: 1930

ENGLAND

BATTING	M.	Inns.	N.O.	Runs	H.S.	Av.
H. Sutcliffe	4	7	2	436	161	87·20
K. S. Duleepsinhji	4	7	0	416	173	59·42
A. P. F. Chapman	4	6	0	259	121	43·16
R. W. V. Robins	2	4	2	70	50*	35·00
W. R. Hammond	5	9	0	306	113	34·00
E. H. Hendren	2	4	0	134	72	33·50
J. B. Hobbs	5	9	0	301	78	33·44
M. Leyland	3	5	1	103	44	25·75
M. W. Tate	5	8	0	148	54	18·50
F. E. Woolley	2	4	0	74	41	18·50
H. Larwood	3	5	1	63	19	15·75
G. Duckworth	5	8	2	87	33	14·50
I. A. R. Peebles	2	3	2	9	6	9·00
R. Tyldesley	2	3	0	12	6	4·00

PLAYED IN ONE TEST: J. C. White 23* and 10, G. O. Allen 3 and 57, R. E. S. Wyatt 64 and 7, W. W. Whysall 13 and 10, M. S. Nichols 7*, G. Geary 0. T. W. Goddard did not bat.

BOWLING	Overs	Mds.	Runs	Wkts.	Av.
R. Tyldesley	89	23	234	7	33·42
R. W. V. Robins	85·2	7	338	10	33·80
M. W. Tate	280·1	82	574	15	38·26
I. A. R. Peebles	126	17	354	9	39·33
W. R. Hammond	148·2	35	302	5	60·40

ALSO BOWLED: J. C. White 53–7–166–3, H. Larwood 101–18–292–4, G. Geary 35–10–95–1, M. S. Nichols 21–5–33–2, T. W. Goddard 32·1–14–49–2, R. E. S. Wyatt 14–1–58–1, F. E. Woolley 9–1–38–0, M. Leyland 35–9–95–0, G. O. Allen 34–7–115–0.

AUSTRALIA

BATTING	M.	Inns.	N.O.	Runs	H.S.	Av.
D. G. Bradman	5	7	0	974	334	139·14
W. M. Woodfull	5	7	1	345	155	57·50
W. H. Ponsford	4	6	0	330	110	55·00
A. F. Kippax	5	7	1	329	83	54·83
A. G. Fairfax	4	5	2	150	53*	50·00
A. A. Jackson	2	2	0	74	73	37·00
S. J. McCabe	5	7	1	210	54	35·00
V. Y. Richardson	4	5	0	98	37	19·60
W. A. Oldfield	5	6	1	96	43*	19·20
C. V. Grimmett	5	5	0	80	50	16·00
P. M. Hornibrook	5	5	1	16	7	4·00
T. W. Wall	5	5	2	12	8*	4·00

PLAYED IN ONE TEST: E. L. a'Beckett 29.

BOWLING	Overs	Mds.	Runs	Wkts.	Av.
S. J. McCabe	87	21	221	8	27·62
A. G. Fairfax	134·2	34	335	12	27·91
C. V. Grimmett	349·4	78	925	29	31·89
P. M. Hornibrook	196·1	50	471	13	36·23
T. W. Wall	229·4	44	593	13	45·61

ALSO BOWLED: E. L. a'Beckett 39–12–66–1, D. G. Bradman 1–0–1–0.

1930 First Test, Trent Bridge

June 13, 14, 16, 17
Toss: England *Result:* England won by 93 runs

The lessons of 1926 and of 1928–29 had been well learnt by the Australians, and they sent a touring party of whom nine were in their twenties and no less than six were 23 or under. The biggest surprise was the supplanting of Ryder by Woodfull. England on the other hand were an ageing and disintegrating side. Hobbs was 47, Hendren 41, White 39, Geary 36, Tate 35, while Chapman had played little first-class cricket since the previous series and Jardine even less. Yet England, like the Australians in 1928, felt obliged to begin with an experienced side. Victory came somewhat luckily in the first Test, and defeat should have been avoided at Lord's, but from that point on Australia were clearly the more effective side. The avalanche of runs from Bradman finally proved suffocating, while Grimmett gained an ascendancy over England's batsmen that was at least as important psychologically. For England, the fading of Hobbs and the temporary eclipse of Hammond left them with no answer to Bradman and Grimmett.

Lack of confidence against Grimmett was the theme of the opening day at Trent Bridge. Hobbs and Sutcliffe put on 53, but 4 wickets fell cheaply before Chapman, whose inclusion had been strongly criticised, knocked Grimmett off in a partnership of 82 with Hobbs. Undisturbed by interruptions for rain and bad light, Hobbs batted 3 hours 35 minutes and was 7th out at 218, after which Robins batted well, but England were 241 for 8 at stumps.

Heavy rain fell in the night, and it was mid-afternoon before the Australians began their reply to England's 270. Tate bowled Ponsford at 4, then crossed over to Larwood's end and had Woodfull magnificently caught in the gully by Chapman, and a fine innings by Kippax on the drying wicket did not save Australia from a deficit of 126. The pitch had now recovered, and Hobbs made an exemplary 74. Sutcliffe had to retire with an injured hand, but Hendren held the innings together, and Australia were left wanting 429 to win.

60 for 1 at the end of the third day, Australia were 198 for 3 at lunch on the final day with Bradman and McCabe going well, so that another 231 runs in four hours did not seem impossible, especially as Larwood was off with gastritis and Robins' length was erratic. But McCabe was brilliantly caught by substitute Copley falling forward at mid on, and Bradman, after 4 hours 20 minutes of careful batting, was bowled by a googly that he did not attempt to play. The suspicion that the England team was riddled with holes was somewhat allayed by the victory.

ENGLAND

J. B. Hobbs	c Richardson b McCabe	78	st Oldfield b Grimmett	74	
H. Sutcliffe	c Hornibrook b Fairfax	29	retired hurt	58	
W. R. Hammond	lbw b Grimmett	8	lbw b Grimmett	4	
F. E. Woolley	st Oldfield b Grimmett	0	b Wall	5	
E. H. Hendren	b Grimmett	5	c Richardson b Wall	72	
*A. P. F. Chapman	c Ponsford b Hornibrook	52	b Wall	29	
H. Larwood	b Grimmett	18	(9)b Grimmett	7	
R. W. V. Robins	not out	50	b McCabe	4	
M. W. Tate	b Grimmett	13	(7)c Kippax b Grimmett	24	
R. Tyldesley	c Fairfax b Wall	1	b Grimmett	5	
†G. Duckworth	lbw b Fairfax	4	not out	14	
Extras	(b 4, lb 7, nb 1)	12	(b 5, lb 1)	6	
Total		270		302	

AUSTRALIA

*W. M. Woodfull	c Chapman b Tate	2	c Chapman b Larwood	4	
W. H. Ponsford	b Tate	3	b Tate	39	
A. G. Fairfax	c Hobbs b Robins	14	(7)c Robins b Tate	14	
D. G. Bradman	b Tate	8	(3)b Robins	131	
A. F. Kippax	not out	64	(4)c Hammond b Robins	23	
S. J. McCabe	c Hammond b Robins	4	(5)c sub (S. H. Copley) b Tate	49	
V. Y. Richardson	b Tyldesley	37	(6)lbw b Tyldesley	29	
†W. A. Oldfield	c Duckworth b Robins	4	c Hammond b Tyldesley	11	
C. V. Grimmett	st Duckworth b Robins	0	c Hammond b Tyldesley	0	
P. M. Hornibrook	lbw b Larwood	0	c Duckworth b Robins	5	
T. W. Wall	b Tyldesley	0	not out	8	
Extras	(b 4, lb 4)	8	(b 17, lb 5)	22	
Total		144		335	

FALL OF WICKETS
ENGLAND

Wkt	1st	2nd
1st	53	125
2nd	63	137
3rd	63	147
4th	71	211
5th	153	250
6th	188	260
7th	218	283
8th	241	283
9th	242	302
10th	270	—

AUSTRALIA

Wkt	1st	2nd
1st	4	12
2nd	6	93
3rd	16	152
4th	57	229
5th	61	267
6th	105	296
7th	134	316
8th	140	322
9th	141	324
10th	144	335

Umpires: J. Hardstaff, snr., W. R. Parry

AUSTRALIA

	1st Innings O	M	R	W		2nd Innings O	M	R	W
Wall	17	4	47	1		26	4	67	3
Fairfax	21·4	5	51	2		15	4	58	0
Grimmett	32	6	107	5		30	4	94	5
Hornibrook	12	3	30	1		11	4	35	0
McCabe	7	3	23	1		14	3	42	1

ENGLAND

	1st Innings O	M	R	W		2nd Innings O	M	R	W
Larwood	15	8	12	1		5	1	9	1
Tate	19	8	20	3		50	20	69	3
Tyldesley	21	8	53	2		35	10	77	3
Robins	17	4	51	4		17·2	1	81	3
Hammond						29	5	74	0
Woolley						3	1	3	0

1930 Second Test, Lord's

June 27, 28, 30, July 1
Toss: England   *Result:* Australia won by seven wickets

The chief danger to England was clearly Grimmett, and a glorious hour of Woolley on the first morning at Lord's hardly compensated for the continuing absence of Leyland. Larwood was omitted as he was adjudged not fully fit: his place was taken by Allen. Duleepsinhji came into the side for the injured Sutcliffe, and White replaced Tyldesley. Australia were unchanged.

England lost Hobbs early, Hammond was never timing the ball well, and three wickets were down for 105. Duleepsinhji and Hendren put on 104 in 90 minutes, but Chapman and Allen failed and 6 wickets were down for 239. Then some bold hitting by Tate, who took part in a stand of 98 with Duleepsinhji, made the score look more substantial. Duleepsinhji was beaten several times at the start by Grimmett, and later by Fairfax and Wall with the second new ball, but he batted gracefully for 4¾ hours, finally being caught at long off trying to force the pace at the end of the day.

England's last wicket added a useful 38 runs, but by mid-afternoon on the second day Australia were 150 for 0 and the England total looked shrunken and inadequate. The bowling seemed ordinary, and the critics sighed for Larwood. England had made their runs so quickly that Australia had plenty of time; but when Bradman came in at 162 the rate galloped ahead, Bradman showing a unique ability to get the good

length ball to the fence. Woodfull was out at 393 after batting 5½ hours; he and Bradman put on 231 in 154 minutes, but he should have been stumped off Robins when 52. At the close Australia were 404 for 2, Bradman having batted 2 hours 40 minutes for 155 not out, an innings of almost absolute perfection.

On the Monday Bradman and Kippax added 192, in the course of which Bradman passed Murdoch's record 211, made in 1884. The Australians then went for quick runs, declaring at tea 304 in front. England began their second innings at 4.50, but Grimmett dismissed both Hobbs and Woolley, and with a day to go England were 93 for 2.

On the last morning Grimmett got Hammond and Hendren, and at 147 for 5 England looked a beaten side. Then Chapman, who had put up an awkward skier before making a run, took part in a fighting stand with Allen in which Allen, driving strongly, actually reached his fifty before Chapman. At lunch England were 262 for 5, with a chance of saving the game. But Allen was out soon afterwards, and although Chapman rightly continued to hit, the other batsmen failed to supply the contrast needed and Australia had plenty of time to get 72 to win. England came back strongly by getting Ponsford, Bradman and Kippax for 22, but Woodfull and McCabe were unmoved.

ENGLAND

J. B. Hobbs	c Oldfield b Fairfax	1	b Grimmett	19	
F. E. Woolley	c Wall b Fairfax	41	hit wkt b Grimmett	28	
W. R. Hammond	b Grimmett	38	c Fairfax b Grimmett	32	
K. S. Duleepsinhji	c Bradman b Grimmett	173	c Oldfield b Hornibrook	48	
E. H. Hendren	c McCabe b Fairfax	48	c Richardson b Grimmett	9	
*A. P. F. Chapman	c Oldfield b Wall	11	c Oldfield b Fairfax	121	
G. O. Allen	b Fairfax	3	lbw b Grimmett	57	
M. W. Tate	c McCabe b Wall	54	c Ponsford b Grimmett	10	
R. W. V. Robins	c Oldfield b Hornibrook	5	not out	11	
J. C. White	not out	23	run out	10	
†G. Duckworth	c Oldfield b Wall	18	lbw b Fairfax	0	
Extras	(b 2, lb 7, nb 1)	10	(b 16, lb 13, w 1)	30	
Total		**425**	**Total**	**375**	

AUSTRALIA

*W. M. Woodfull	st Duckworth b Robins	155	not out	26	
W. H. Ponsford	c Hammond b White	81	b Robins	14	
D. G. Bradman	c Chapman b White	254	c Chapman b Tate	1	
A. F. Kippax	b White	83	c Duckworth b Robins	3	
S. J. McCabe	c Woolley b Hammond	44	not out	25	
V. Y. Richardson	c Hobbs b Tate	30			
†W. A. Oldfield	not out	43			
A. G. Fairfax	not out	20			
C. V. Grimmett	⎱				
P. M. Hornibrook	⎰ did not bat				
T. W. Wall					
Extras	(b 6, lb 8, w 5)	19	(b 1, lb 2)	3	
Total	(6 wkts dec)	**729**	**Total** (3 wkts)	**72**	

FALL OF WICKETS

ENGLAND

Wkt	1st	2nd
1st	13	45
2nd	53	58
3rd	105	129
4th	209	141
5th	236	147
6th	239	272
7th	337	329
8th	363	354
9th	387	372
10th	425	375

AUSTRALIA

Wkt	1st	2nd
1st	162	16
2nd	393	17
3rd	585	22
4th	588	—
5th	643	—
6th	672	—
7th	—	—
8th	—	—
9th	—	—
10th	—	—

Umpires: F. Chester, T. W. Oates

AUSTRALIA

	1st Innings					2nd Innings			
	O	M	R	W		O	M	R	W
Wall	29·4	2	118	3	..	25	2	80	0
Fairfax	31	6	101	4	..	12·4	2	37	2
Grimmett	33	4	105	2	..	53	13	167	6
Hornibrook	26	6	62	1	..	22	6	49	1
McCabe	9	1	29	0	..	3	1	11	0
Bradman					..	1	0	1	0

ENGLAND

	1st Innings					2nd Innings			
	O	M	R	W		O	M	R	W
Allen	34	7	115	0	..				
Tate	64	16	148	1	..	13	6	21	1
White	51	7	158	3	..	2	0	8	0
Robins	42	1	172	1	..	9	1	34	2
Hammond	35	8	82	1	..	4·2	1	6	0
Woolley	6	0	35	0	..				

97. H. Sutcliffe

98. (right) D. G. Bradman

99. Australia 1930
Back row: A. A. Jackson, S. J. McCabe, P. M. Hornibrook, A. Hurwood, T. W. Wall, E. L. a'Beckett, W. H. Ponsford, C. V. Grimmett, A. F. Kippax, C. W. Walker. *Front:* A. G. Fairfax, V. Y. Richardson, W. M. Woodfull (capt.), D. G. Bradman, W. A. Oldfield

1930 Third Test, Leeds

Test no. 122

July 11, 12, 14, 15
Toss: Australia   *Result:* Match Drawn

At Lord's the England bowling had been tamed before Bradman came in. But at Leeds Tate got Jackson in his first over and Bradman had to face the new ball. Nevertheless he reached 50 in 49 minutes and a hundred before lunch in 99 minutes, while Woodfull was making 29. The slightest departure from a perfect length was punished unmercifully, the placing of the ball to avoid the fielders was unerring, and as at Lord's even the good-length ball was somehow got to the boundary. Bradman reached 200 in 3 hours 34 minutes, out of 266 made from the time he came in, and partnered by Kippax he passed R. E. Foster's 287 and reached his treble century in 5 hours 36 minutes, being 309 not out at the close. Australia were then 458 for 3, a rate of nearly 75 an hour.

Bradman made most of his runs in front of the wicket in this innings, yet there was always an array of fielders, generally including two slips, behind. The field was set for the bowler rather than the batsman, which for a player like Bradman was bound to be costly. Yet Chapman was facing an insoluble problem. Next day Australia's last 7 wickets, including Bradman's, fell for 108, and England at lunch were 17 for 0. But the wicket had already begun to go, and England at tea were 136 for 3. Leyland batted defiantly, hitting two sixes off Grimmett, and

Hammond at the close was 61 not out, having batted 2 hours 50 minutes, but England were then 212 for 5, 354 behind with two days left. 'Only a cloudburst can save us', said one English writer. And on the third morning a cloudburst duly came.

The long delay before the game was resumed annoyed the Australians, who rightly thought that play should have been restarted earlier. And when England followed on Hobbs and Sutcliffe were jeered by the crowd when they went off after a perfectly reasonable light appeal. Another light appeal ended the game 40 minutes early, and England escaped. Hammond's 113 lasted 5 hours 25 minutes, Woodfull successfully blocking his off shots, but there was nothing but a draw to play for when he went in. He was missed behind the wicket off Wall when 52.

England had Sutcliffe back, but Larwood and Tyldesley, who returned for Allen and Robins, were disappointing, Larwood being not fully fit, while Robins was missed in the field. Leyland and Geary replaced Woolley and White. For Australia, Jackson and a'Beckett came in for Ponsford and Fairfax, who were both unwell.

Of his 309 runs on the first day Bradman scored 105 before lunch, 115 in the afternoon, and 89 between tea and close of play.

AUSTRALIA

*W. M. Woodfull	b Hammond	50
A. A. Jackson	c Larwood b Tate	1
D. G. Bradman	c Duckworth b Tate	334
A. F. Kippax	c Chapman b Tate	77
S. J. McCabe	b Larwood	30
V. Y. Richardson	c Larwood b Tate	1
E. L. a'Beckett	c Chapman b Geary	29
†W. A. Oldfield	c Hobbs b Tate	2
C. V. Grimmett	c Duckworth b Tyldesley	24
T. W. Wall	b Tyldesley	3
P. M. Hornibrook	not out	1
Extras	(b 5, lb 8, w 1)	14
Total		566

ENGLAND

		1st		2nd	
J. B. Hobbs	c a'Beckett b Grimmett	29	run out	13
H. Sutcliffe	c Hornibrook b Grimmett	32	not out	28
W. R. Hammond	c Oldfield b McCabe	113	c Oldfield b Grimmett	35
K. S. Duleepsinhji	b Hornibrook	35	c Grimmett b Hornibrook	10
M. Leyland	c Kippax b Wall	44	not out	1
G. Geary	run out	0		
†G. Duckworth	c Oldfield b a'Beckett	33		
*A. P. F. Chapman	b Grimmett	45		
M. W. Tate	c Jackson b Grimmett	22		
H. Larwood	not out	10		
R. Tyldesley	c Hornibrook b Grimmett	6		
Extras	(b 9, lb 10, nb 3)	22	(lb 8)	8
Total		391	Total (3 wkts)	95

FALL OF WICKETS

AUSTRALIA

Wkt	1st	2nd
1st	2	—
2nd	194	—
3rd	423	—
4th	486	—
5th	491	—
6th	508	—
7th	519	—
8th	544	—
9th	565	—
10th	566	—

ENGLAND

Wkt	1st	2nd
1st	53	24
2nd	64	74
3rd	123	94
4th	206	—
5th	206	—
6th	289	—
7th	319	—
8th	370	—
9th	375	—
10th	391	—

Umpires: W. Bestwick, T. W. Oates

ENGLAND		1st Innings				2nd Innings		
	O	M	R	W	O	M	R	W
Larwood	33	3	139	1				
Tate	39	9	124	5				
Geary	35	10	95	1				
Tyldesley	33	5	104	2				
Hammond	17	3	46	1				
Leyland	11	0	44	0				

AUSTRALIA		1st Innings				2nd Innings		
	O	M	R	W	O	M	R	W
Wall	40	12	70	1	10	3	20	0
a'Beckett	28	8	47	1	11	4	19	0
Grimmett	56.2	16	135	5	17	3	33	1
Hornibrook	41	7	94	1	11.5	5	14	1
McCabe	10	4	23	1	2	1	1	0

1930 Fourth Test, Old Trafford

July 25, 26, 28, 29
Toss: Australia   *Result:* Match Drawn

England dropped Larwood, Geary and Tyldesley and brought in Nichols, Goddard and Peebles, and their bowling looked their best since the opening match. Australia, their invalids recovered, fielded the same side as at Trent Bridge and Lord's. On a pitch deadened by rain Australia laboured to 75 for o at lunch, Woodfull 37, Ponsford 30, and the first 100 runs took 2½ hours. Then Woodfull, who had been in considerable trouble facing Peebles, was caught behind off Tate. Bradman, apparently off colour, was nearly bowled first ball by Peebles, and he was then missed twice before being caught at slip. Kippax, too, was uncomfortable facing Peebles, but he settled down to make some delightful drives. Ponsford was bowled by a perfect off-break from Hammond after batting extremely well for 3 hours 50 minutes, McCabe was lbw to a googly, and seven wickets were down for 243. Fairfax and Grimmett, however, could not be separated, and next morning they took their unbroken stand to 87, Australia totalling 345. Modest as this total was compared with the two previous Tests, it might have been considerably less had there been a specialist slow left-hander in the England side.

England had just over half-an-hour's batting before lunch, in which Hobbs and Sutcliffe made 29. Sutcliffe especially was in brilliant form, for once outpacing Hobbs, and when the 100 went up Sutcliffe was 63 to Hobbs' 29. Hobbs was caught slashing at a widish ball at 108, and then Sutcliffe hooked once too often at Wall and was splendidly caught on the boundary at long leg, Bradman taking the ball above his head before falling among the spectators. Hammond, after a curiously inept innings, played on at 119, and the Australian total began to look formidable. Duleepsinhji and Leyland put on 73, but 2 wickets then fell quickly and England were 199 for 5. Tate then stayed with Leyland until the close at 221 for 5, Leyland having batted solidly for 2 hours.

On the third day there was only 45 minutes' cricket, and when bad light stopped play England were 251 for 8. The last day was washed out altogether. Once again England had given a disappointing display with the bat, but it was difficult to see how the first five in the order could be improved upon. Of the bowlers, Tate had bowled consistently well and borne the brunt of the attack, Larwood would presumably return if fit, and Peebles, although he was having trouble with his leg-break and was bowling mostly googlies, seemed certain to play. The need for some stiffening of the batting for the deciding Test, and perhaps for a class slow left-hander, remained.

AUSTRALIA

*W. M. Woodfull	c Duckworth b Tate	54
W. H. Ponsford	b Hammond	83
D. G. Bradman	c Duleepsinhji b Peebles	14
A. F. Kippax	c Chapman b Nichols	51
S. J. McCabe	lbw b Peebles	4
V. Y. Richardson	b Hammond	1
A. G. Fairfax	lbw b Goddard	49
†W. A. Oldfield	b Nichols	2
C. V. Grimmett	c Sutcliffe b Peebles	50
P. M. Hornibrook	c Duleepsinhji b Goddard	3
T. W. Wall	not out	1
Extras	(b 23, lb 3, nb 7)	33
Total		**345**

ENGLAND

J. B. Hobbs	c Oldfield b Wall	31
H. Sutcliffe	c Bradman b Wall	74
W. R. Hammond	b Wall	3
K. S. Duleepsinhji	c Hornibrook b McCabe	54
M. Leyland	b McCabe	35
*A. P. F. Chapman	c Grimmett b Hornibrook	1
M. W. Tate	c Ponsford b McCabe	15
M. S. Nichols	not out	7
I. A. R. Peebles	c Richardson b McCabe	6
†G. Duckworth	not out	0
T. W. Goddard	did not bat	
Extras	(b 13, lb 12)	25
Total	(8 wkts)	**251**

FALL OF WICKETS

AUSTRALIA

Wkt	1st	2nd
1st	106	—
2nd	138	—
3rd	184	—
4th	189	—
5th	190	—
6th	239	—
7th	243	—
8th	330	—
9th	338	—
10th	345	—

ENGLAND

Wkt	1st	2nd
1st	108	—
2nd	115	—
3rd	119	—
4th	192	—
5th	199	—
6th	222	—
7th	237	—
8th	247	—
9th	—	—
10th	—	—

Umpires: F. Chester, J. Hardstaff, snr.

ENGLAND	1st Innings				2nd Innings			
	O	M	R	W	O	M	R	W
Nichols	21	5	33	2	..			
Tate	30	11	39	1	..			
Goddard	32·1	14	49	2	..			
Peebles	55	9	150	3	..			
Leyland	8	2	17	0	..			
Hammond	21	6	24	2	..			

AUSTRALIA	1st Innings				2nd Innings			
	O	M	R	W	O	M	R	W
Wall	33	9	70	3	..			
Fairfax	13	5	15	0	..			
Grimmett	19	2	59	0	..			
Hornibrook	26	9	41	1	..			
McCabe	17	3	41	4	..			

August 16, 18, 19, 20, 21, 22
Toss: England   *Result:* Australia won by an innings and 39 runs

England solved their problems—or sought to solve them—by dropping Chapman and a bowler and bringing in two batsmen. The men they chose were Wyatt and Whysall. Whysall at 42 had not played for England for six years, but it was thought that his solid style would be valuable in a match to be played to a finish. For the same reason Wyatt was preferred to Chapman, as batsman and leader. In view of his brilliant fielding and catching Chapman seemed to have done his share, however, and his omission was seen as a blow to the morale of the side. A place could not be found for Hendren, while the possibility of substituting Ames for Duckworth was rejected. Australia made only one change, playing Jackson for Richardson.

Hobbs and Sutcliffe began carefully, and they had 68 on the board when Hobbs, who had looked eminently safe, mistimed a leg hit just before lunch. Whysall was lbw to Wall at 97, Duleepsinhji made a dashing if somewhat anachronistic 50, Hammond failed, Leyland was bowled by a Grimmett leg-break, and Wyatt, in his first match against Australia, went in just before tea at 197 for 5 with only the tail to come, surely one of the most daunting situations that ever faced an England captain. But he stayed with Sutcliffe until close of play, when England were 316 for 5, Sutcliffe 138, Wyatt 39; and next morning he and Sutcliffe made their partnership worth 170 in all. Sutcliffe batted 6 hours 43 minutes, and England totalled 405.

Australia then demonstrated their batting superiority beyond all doubt. At lunch they were 36 for 0 and at tea 159 for 0, Ponsford reaching his century in 135 minutes. But both he and Woodfull were missed by Duckworth off Tate in the early part of their innings. 216 for 2 overnight, Australia progressed towards a huge score on a third day truncated by rain, Bradman, who gave a hard chance to Duckworth off Hammond at 82, reaching what had always seemed an inevitable century. On the fourth day, when the wicket was lively after the rain, Bradman mastered the conditions in a stand of 243 with Jackson, although for a time after being hit in the chest he drew away from Larwood. In contrast to his innings at Lord's and Leeds he scored the majority of his runs behind the wicket, adapting his game to the match conditions.

Australia finally totalled 695, and then England lost Hobbs before the end of the day. The fifth day was entirely blank through rain, and it was ironical that Hornibrook, a type of bowler consistently omitted by England except at Lord's, should finally bowl them out. Bradman's figures for this series have never been approached, while Grimmett's record of 29 wickets, the best for an Australian in England, has been equalled (G. D. McKenzie, 1964) but not beaten.

ENGLAND

						FALL OF WICKETS

J. B. Hobbs	c Kippax b Wall	47	b Fairfax	9	
H. Sutcliffe	c Oldfield b Fairfax	161	c Fairfax b Hornibrook	54	
W. W. Whysall	lbw b Wall	13	c Hornibrook b Grimmett	10	
K. S. Duleepsinhji	c Fairfax b Grimmett	50	c Kippax b Hornibrook	46	
W. R. Hammond	b McCabe	13	c Fairfax b Hornibrook	60	
M. Leyland	b Grimmett	3	b Hornibrook	20	
*R. E. S. Wyatt	c Oldfield b Fairfax	64	b Hornibrook	7	
M. W. Tate	st Oldfield b Grimmett	10	run out	0	
H. Larwood	lbw b Grimmett	19	c McCabe b Hornibrook	9	
†G. Duckworth	b Fairfax	3	b Hornibrook	15	
I. A. R. Peebles	not out	3	not out	0	
Extras	(lb 17, nb 2)	19	(b 16, lb 3, nb 2)	21	
Total		**405**	**Total**	**251**	

ENGLAND

Wkt	1st	2nd
1st	68	17
2nd	97	37
3rd	162	118
4th	190	135
5th	197	189
6th	367	207
7th	379	208
8th	379	220
9th	391	248
10th	405	251

AUSTRALIA

*W. M. Woodfull	c Duckworth b Peebles	54
W. H. Ponsford	b Peebles	110
D. G. Bradman	c Duckworth b Larwood	232
A. F. Kippax	c Wyatt b Peebles	28
A. A. Jackson	c Sutcliffe b Wyatt	73
S. J. McCabe	c Duckworth b Hammond	54
A. G. Fairfax	not out	53
†W. A. Oldfield	c Larwood b Peebles	34
C. V. Grimmett	lbw b Peebles	6
T. W. Wall	lbw b Peebles	0
P. M. Hornibrook	c Duckworth b Tate	7
Extras	(b 22, lb 18, nb 4)	44
Total		**695**

AUSTRALIA

Wkt	1st	2nd
1st	159	—
2nd	190	—
3rd	263	—
4th	506	—
5th	570	—
6th	594	—
7th	670	—
8th	684	—
9th	684	—
10th	695	—

Umpires: J. Hardstaff, snr.,
W. R. Parry

AUSTRALIA	1st Innings					2nd Innings			
	O	M	R	W		O	M	R	W
Wall	37	6	96	2		12	2	25	0
Fairfax	31	9	52	3		10	3	21	1
Grimmett	66·2	18	135	4		43	12	90	1
McCabe	22	4	49	1		3	1	2	0
Hornibrook	15	1	54	0		31·2	9	92	7

ENGLAND	1st Innings					2nd Innings			
	O	M	R	W		O	M	R	W
Larwood	48	6	132	1					
Tate	65·1	12	153	1					
Peebles	71	8	204	6					
Wyatt	14	1	58	1					
Hammond	42	12	70	1					
Leyland	16	7	34	0					

1932-33 First Test, Sydney

December 2, 3, 5, 6, 7
Toss: Australia   *Result:* England won by ten wickets

Fast bowling to a close leg field, short of a length on the line of the body, was conceived of plumb wickets and frustration with off theory and born of the heavy scoring of the period, and especially that of Bradman in 1930. Nurtured and developed by a shrewd, scientific mind, and executed by a bowler of exceptional pace and accuracy, it was let loose on the surprised Australians in the early matches of the tour, and they never recovered from the complex it gave them. Jardine believed there was nothing novel or dangerous about it, and it is true that no one was badly hurt when Larwood was bowling it; but it certainly looked dangerous from the ring, and the batsmen themselves were in no doubt. The Australians resented it because it presented an insoluble problem, one that they felt was outside the spirit of cricket. The only antidote was retaliation, and this they had neither the ability nor the will to exercise. Great innings were played against it, but the batsmen concerned lived dangerously. So bitter did the controversy become that it seemed when indignant cables were exchanged between the governing bodies after the third Test that the tour would be abandoned, but it was allowed to run its course. Hated but admired for his austere courage, Jardine never wavered, and England won the series by four matches to one.

The sensational atmosphere in which the first Test was fermenting was intensified by doubts of Bradman's eligibility and fitness—he had signed a newspaper contract in defiance of a Board of Control ruling, and in six innings against the tourists he had totalled only 103 runs. The newspaper contract was abandoned, but on the day before the game Bradman was pronounced unfit. Larwood and Voce opened the bowling to Woodfull and Ponsford, and in Voce's sixth over Woodfull went to hook and was caught behind. Ponsford and Fingleton held out until lunch, but both were dismissed by Larwood soon afterwards, Kippax followed, and Australia were 87 for 4. There followed a magnificent partnership between McCabe and Richardson which added 129. Chancing his arm, hooking and pulling fiercely but never desperately, McCabe went on to make 187 not out, and Australia totalled 360.

By close of play on the second day England were 260 for 1, both Sutcliffe and Hammond being at their best, and later the Nawab of Pataudi completed a painstaking century. England looked like getting a huge lead, but the Australian bowlers fought hard all through, England's last 5 wickets fell for 54, and the lead was kept to 164. Apart from Fingleton and McCabe, however, the Australians crumpled before Larwood in their second innings and England won by 10 wickets.

AUSTRALIA

W. M. Woodfull	c Ames b Voce	7	b Larwood	0	
W. H. Ponsford	b Larwood	32	b Voce	2	
J. H. Fingleton	c Allen b Larwood	26	c Voce b Larwood	40	
A. F. Kippax	lbw b Larwood	8	(6)b Larwood	19	
S. J. McCabe	not out	187	(4)lbw b Hammond	32	
V. Y. Richardson	c Hammond b Voce	49	(5)c Voce b Hammond	0	
W. A. Oldfield	c Ames b Larwood	4	c Leyland b Larwood	1	
C. V. Grimmett	c Ames b Voce	19	c Allen b Larwood	5	
L. E. Nagel	b Larwood	0	not out	21	
W. J. O'Reilly	b Voce	4	(11)b Voce	7	
T. W. Wall	c Allen b Hammond	4	(10)c Ames b Allen	20	
Extras	(b 12, lb 4, nb 4)	20	(b 12, lb 2, w 1, nb 2)	17	
Total		**360**	Total	**164**	

ENGLAND

H. Sutcliffe	lbw b Wall	194	not out	1	
R. E. S. Wyatt	lbw b Grimmett	38	not out	0	
W. R. Hammond	c Grimmett b Nagel	112			
Nawab of Pataudi	b Nagel	102			
M. Leyland	c Oldfield b Wall	0			
D. R. Jardine	c Oldfield b McCabe	27			
H. Verity	lbw b Wall	2			
G. O. Allen	c and b O'Reilly	19			
L. E. G. Ames	c McCabe b O'Reilly	0			
H. Larwood	lbw b O'Reilly	0			
W. Voce	not out	0			
Extras	(b 7, lb 17, nb 6)	30			
Total		**524**	Total (0 wkts)	**1**	

FALL OF WICKETS

AUSTRALIA		
Wkt	1st	2nd
1st	22	2
2nd	65	10
3rd	82	61
4th	87	61
5th	216	100
6th	231	104
7th	299	105
8th	300	113
9th	305	151
10th	360	164

ENGLAND		
Wkt	1st	2nd
1st	112	—
2nd	300	—
3rd	423	—
4th	423	—
5th	470	—
6th	479	—
7th	519	—
8th	522	—
9th	522	—
10th	524	—

Umpires: G. A. Hele,
G. Borwick

ENGLAND	1st Innings				2nd Innings			
	O	M	R	W	O	M	R	W
Larwood	31	5	96	5	18	4	28	5
Voce	29	4	110	4	17.3	5	54	2
Allen	15	1	65	0	9	5	13	1
Hammond	14.2	0	34	1	15	6	37	2
Verity	13	4	35	0	4	1	15	0

AUSTRALIA	1st Innings				2nd Innings			
	O	M	R	W	O	M	R	W
Wall	38	4	104	3				
Nagel	43.4	9	110	2				
O'Reilly	67	32	117	3				
Grimmett	64	22	118	1				
McCabe	15	2	42	1	0.1	0	1	0
Kippax	2	1	3	0				

1932–33 Second Test, Melbourne

December 30, 31, January 2, 3
Toss: Australia   *Result:* Australia won by 111 runs

Australian faith in Bradman, which at this time amounted almost to religious fervour, was triumphantly restored in this match, despite the keen disappointment of his being bowled first ball in the first innings. Recovered from his indisposition, he was back in the side to the exclusion of Kippax, while Ironmonger and O'Brien, left-handed bowler and left-handed bat, replaced Nagel and Ponsford. England, taking a wrong view about the wicket, played an all-fast attack, Bowes coming in for Verity. It was Bowes who got Bradman for a duck, playing on when going for a hook, but otherwise the move was a failure.

The wicket was lacking in firmness, and Australia's first innings score of 228 was the highest of the match. Larwood began with off theory but soon switched to leg theory, Voce bowled leg theory from the start, and head-high bumpers kept both batsmen ducking. But the wicket was too slow for this to worry the batsmen unduly. Woodfull was bowled by Allen at 29, and most of the 42 runs that accrued before lunch came from Fingleton's strokes through the leg trap. In great heat Jardine used his bowlers in short spells, and at tea Australia had crawled to 120 for 3, Fingleton being 67 not out. He had played a few poor strokes, and had run out O'Brien, but although taking a good many

knocks he had handled the leg theory well, letting the ball pass by whenever he could. It was a hard fight all day against the shock attack, and after a useful innings from Richardson Australia at stumps were 194 for 7.

England were batting early next day and were 24 for 0 at lunch. Sutcliffe was dropped by McCabe at slip and enjoyed various other escapes in a lucky fifty, but of the others only Leyland and Allen reached twenty, and England were all out on the third morning 59 behind.

Allowing for the state of the wicket and the quality of the bowling, Bradman played no greater innings than the one which followed. Retreating when he could against Larwood's leg theory, he sought to bang the ball back into the open spaces beyond the bowler, Larwood opening with no fielder on the off side in front of point, and although due to the slow wicket it could not be said that he mastered leg theory, his defence and general tactics were superb. Woodfull and Richardson helped in useful stands, and England were set 251 to win. Sutcliffe and Leyland made 43 of them together on the third evening, but O'Reilly's googlies and Ironmonger's spinners running away to the off gave England no chance on the last day.

AUSTRALIA

J. H. Fingleton	b Allen	83	c Ames b Allen	1	
*W. M. Woodfull	b Allen	10	c Allen b Larwood	26	
L. P. J. O'Brien	run out	10	b Larwood	11	
D. G. Bradman	b Bowes	0	not out	103	
S. J. McCabe	c Jardine b Voce	32	b Allen	0	
V. Y. Richardson	c Hammond b Voce	34	lbw b Hammond	32	
†W. A. Oldfield	not out	27	b Voce	6	
C. V. Grimmett	c Sutcliffe b Voce	2	b Voce	0	
T. W. Wall	run out	1	lbw b Hammond	3	
W. J. O'Reilly	b Larwood	15	c Ames b Hammond	0	
H. Ironmonger	b Larwood	4	run out	0	
Extras	(b 5, lb 1, w 2, nb 2)	10	(b 3, lb 1, w 4, nb 1)	9	
Total		**228**	**Total**	**191**	

ENGLAND

H. Sutcliffe	c Richardson b Wall	52	b O'Reilly	33	
R. E. S. Wyatt	lbw b O'Reilly	13	(7)lbw b O'Reilly	25	
W. R. Hammond	b Wall	8	(4)c O'Brien b O'Reilly	23	
Nawab of Pataudi	b O'Reilly	15	(3)c Fingleton b Ironmonger	5	
M. Leyland	b O'Reilly	22	(2)b Wall	19	
*D. R. Jardine	c Oldfield b Wall	1	(5)c McCabe b Ironmonger	0	
†L. E. G. Ames	b Wall	4	(6)c Fingleton b O'Reilly	2	
G. O. Allen	c Richardson b O'Reilly	30	st Oldfield b Ironmonger	23	
H. Larwood	b O'Reilly	9	c Wall b Ironmonger	4	
W. Voce	c McCabe b Grimmett	6	c O'Brien b O'Reilly	0	
W. E. Bowes	not out	4	not out	0	
Extras	(b 1, lb 2, nb 2)	5	(lb 4, nb 1)	5	
Total		**169**	**Total**	**139**	

FALL OF WICKETS

AUSTRALIA

Wkt	1st	2nd
1st	29	1
2nd	67	27
3rd	67	78
4th	131	81
5th	156	135
6th	188	150
7th	194	156
8th	200	184
9th	222	186
10th	228	191

ENGLAND

Wkt	1st	2nd
1st	30	53
2nd	43	53
3rd	83	70
4th	98	70
5th	104	77
6th	110	85
7th	122	135
8th	138	137
9th	161	138
10th	169	139

Umpires: G. A. Hele, G. Borwick

ENGLAND	1st Innings				2nd Innings			
	O	M	R	W	O	M	R	W
Larwood	20·3	2	52	2	15	2	50	2
Voce	20	3	54	3	15	2	47	2
Allen	17	3	41	2	12	1	44	2
Hammond	10	3	21	0	10·5	2	21	3
Bowes	19	2	50	1	4	0	20	0

AUSTRALIA	1st Innings				2nd Innings			
	O	M	R	W	O	M	R	W
Wall	21	4	52	4	8	2	23	1
O'Reilly	34·3	17	63	5	24	5	66	5
Grimmett	16	4	21	1	4	0	19	0
Ironmonger	14	4	28	0	19·1	8	26	4

100. S. J. McCabe

101. H. Larwood

102. England 1932-33
Back row: G. Duckworth, T. B. Mitchell, Nawab of Pataudi, M. Leyland, H. Larwood, E. Paynter, W. F. Ferguson (scorer).
Middle row: P. F. Warner (manager), L. E. G. Ames, H. Verity, W. Voce, W. E. Bowes, F. R. Brown, M. W. Tate, R. C. N. Palairet (manager). *Front:* H. Sutcliffe, R. E. S. Wyatt, D. R. Jardine (capt.), G. O. Allen, W. R. Hammond.

January 13, 14, 16, 17, 18, 19
Toss: England   *Result:* England won by 338 runs

Before the Adelaide game ended the volcano that had been activating since before the series began finally erupted and the sensational events on the field were dwarfed by political moves which threatened the abandonment of the tour. Yet the game itself was dramatic enough. At lunch on the first day England were 37 for 4, but a wonderful stand between Leyland and Wyatt added 156. Leyland off-drove vigorously, Wyatt pulled and hooked savagely, and with Paynter following Leyland's lead and Verity presenting a straight bat England totalled 341. Then when Australia batted on the second afternoon Woodfull was struck over the heart by a shortish but straight ball from Larwood, and although he batted on he was in a collapsed state when he was out. Visiting him in the Australian dressing-room to enquire how he felt, Warner, joint manager of the touring side, was told that of the two sides engaged in the match only one was playing cricket; Woodfull's outburst was leaked to the Press, and the Australian Board of Control were put on the spot. Either they dropped Woodfull or they supported him and sent the cable to London that they were already rumoured to be drafting. A subsequent head injury to Oldfield which was no fault of the bowler inflamed the situation still further, pressure on the Board of Control became irresistible, and a cable was sent which denounced bodyline as unsportsmanlike. The MCC, like the Board of Control,

could only express confidence in their appointed captain, and they reluctantly offered to abandon the tour. But a face-saving formula was found. Whatever the dangers and implications of bodyline it was not illegal and legislation against it could hardly be introduced in the middle of a series.

Australia had begun almost as badly as England, and when Woodfull was out they were 51 for 4. But Ponsford and Richardson pulled the game round, and Oldfield batted with great determination for two hours before touching a short ball into his head when trying to pull. Australia finished 119 behind, and England, after losing Sutcliffe early, set out slowly and laboriously to consolidate. Australia were eventually set 532 to win.

Although he must have been under intense mental as well as physical strain Woodfull batted for just under 4 hours and carried his bat; but Bradman was audacious to the point of recklessness, and apart from Richardson no one else reached double figures. Richardson kept wicket in the England second innings, but England were even more seriously handicapped through injuries to Voce and Paynter. Changes in the sides were Paynter for Pataudi, Verity for Bowes and Ponsford for O'Brien.

ENGLAND

H. Sutcliffe	c Wall b O'Reilly	9	c sub (L. P. J. O'Brien) b Wall	7
*D. R. Jardine	b Wall	3	lbw b Ironmonger	56
W. R. Hammond	c Oldfield b Wall	2	(5)b Bradman	85
†L. E. G. Ames	b Ironmonger	3	(7)b O'Reilly	69
M. Leyland	b O'Reilly	83	(6)c Wall b Ironmonger	42
R. E. S. Wyatt	c Richardson b Grimmett	78	(3)c Wall b O'Reilly	49
E. Paynter	c Fingleton b Wall	77	(10)not out	1
G. O. Allen	lbw b Grimmett	15	(4)lbw b Grimmett	15
H. Verity	c Richardson b Wall	45	(8)lbw b O'Reilly	40
W. Voce	b Wall	8	(11)b O'Reilly	8
H. Larwood	not out	3	(9)c Bradman b Ironmonger	8
Extras	(b 1, lb 7, nb 7)	15	(b 17, lb 11, nb 4)	32
Total		**341**	**Total**	**412**

AUSTRALIA

J. H. Fingleton	c Ames b Allen	0	b Larwood	0
*W. M. Woodfull	b Allen	22	not out	73
D. G. Bradman	c Allen b Larwood	8	(4)c and b Verity	66
S. J. McCabe	c Jardine b Larwood	8	(5)c Leyland b Allen	7
W. H. Ponsford	b Voce	85	(3)c Jardine b Larwood	3
V. Y. Richardson	b Allen	28	c Allen b Larwood	21
†W. A. Oldfield	retired hurt	41	absent hurt	—
C. V. Grimmett	c Voce b Allen	10	(7)b Allen	6
T. W. Wall	b Hammond	6	(8)b Allen	0
W. J. O'Reilly	b Larwood	0	(9)b Larwood	5
H. Ironmonger	not out	0	(10)b Allen	0
Extras	(b 2, lb 11, nb 1)	14	(b 4, lb 2, w 1, nb 5)	12
Total		**222**	**Total**	**193**

FALL OF WICKETS

ENGLAND		
Wkt	1st	2nd
1st	4	7
2nd	16	91
3rd	16	123
4th	30	154
5th	186	245
6th	196	296
7th	228	394
8th	324	395
9th	336	403
10th	341	412

AUSTRALIA		
Wkt	1st	2nd
1st	1	3
2nd	18	12
3rd	34	100
4th	51	116
5th	131	171
6th	194	183
7th	212	183
8th	222	192
9th	222	193
10th	—	—

Umpires: G. A. Hele,
G. Borwick

AUSTRALIA	1st Innings					2nd Innings			
	O	M	R	W		O	M	R	W
Wall	34·1	10	72	5	..	29	6	75	1
O'Reilly	50	19	82	2	..	50·3	21	79	4
Ironmonger	20	6	50	1	..	57	21	87	3
Grimmett	28	6	94	2	..	35	9	74	1
McCabe	14	3	28	0	..	16	0	42	0
Bradman					..	4	0	23	1

ENGLAND	1st Innings					2nd Innings			
	O	M	R	W		O	M	R	W
Larwood	25	6	55	3	..	19	3	71	4
Allen	23	4	71	4	..	17·2	5	50	4
Hammond	17·4	4	30	1	..	9	3	27	0
Voce	14	5	21	1	..	4	1	7	0
Verity	16	7	31	0	..	20	12	26	1

1932-33 Fourth Test, Brisbane

February 10, 11, 13, 14, 15, 16
Toss: Australia   *Result:* England won by six wickets

On a lifeless pitch England toiled in the heat throughout the first day, at the end of which the mild barracking with which bodyline had been greeted in the morning had entirely subsided as Australia advanced to 251 for 3. Richardson, who had always stood up well to leg theory, helped Woodfull to put on 133 for the 1st wicket; both men dealt with Larwood by ducking or letting the leg-side balls pass harmlessly by. At the end of the day Bradman and Ponsford were together and going well, but they had not had to face Larwood when he was fresh: that came next morning. Bradman, who had shown repeatedly that he was not prepared to risk being hit, backed away and was bowled leg stump trying to cut, while Ponsford was bowled round his legs. Australia's last 7 wickets added only 89 runs, and in rather more than 2½ hours before stumps Sutcliffe and Jardine made 99.

At lunch on the third day England were going steadily at 151 for 1, but from then on batsman after batsman established himself with exaggerated care only to lose his wicket when apparently set. At 216 for 6, facing the prospect of the fourth innings, England were 124 behind; and with the new ball recently taken they were in a very tight corner. But at this stage Paynter, who had been in hospital with

tonsilitis and had not been expected to bat, went to the wicket, and he was still there at stumps, when England were 271 for 8. He and Verity carried on throughout the fourth morning, putting on 92 in all, and England gained an unexpected lead of 16.

Australia opened their second innings strongly, but at 46 Richardson was brilliantly caught at mid off. Bradman, stepping away to crack Larwood on the off side, was caught at deep point, Larwood took a spectacular diving catch at leg slip to dismiss Ponsford, Woodfull followed a leg-break and was caught at slip, and at stumps Australia were 100 for 4 and facing defeat. Darling was going strongly next morning when he was run out through a misunderstanding with Love, and England were left wanting 160 to win. They lost Sutcliffe almost at once, but Jardine, as well as batting two hours 12 minutes for 24, had the inspiration of sending Leyland in no. 3, and this proved a match-winning move. Paynter, whose first-innings knock had made victory possible, had the satisfaction of winning the match and the Ashes with a six. The Australians had dropped Fingleton and Grimmett for Darling and Bromley, and Love replaced the injured Oldfield. Voce's absence with influenza gave Mitchell his chance for England.

AUSTRALIA

V. Y. Richardson	st Ames b Hammond	83	c Jardine b Verity	32	
*W. M. Woodfull	b Mitchell	67	c Hammond b Mitchell	19	
D. G. Bradman	b Larwood	76	c Mitchell b Larwood	24	
S. J. McCabe	c Jardine b Allen	20	(5)b Verity	22	
W. H. Ponsford	b Larwood	19	(4)c Larwood b Allen	0	
L. S. Darling	c Ames b Allen	17	run out	39	
E. H. Bromley	c Verity b Larwood	26	c Hammond b Allen	7	
†H. S. B. Love	lbw b Mitchell	5	lbw b Larwood	3	
T. W. Wall	not out	6	c Jardine b Allen	2	
W. J. O'Reilly	c Hammond b Larwood	6	b Larwood	4	
H. Ironmonger	st Ames b Hammond	8	not out	0	
Extras	(b 5, lb 1, nb 1)	7	(b 13, lb 9, nb 1)	23	
Total		**340**	**Total**	**175**	

ENGLAND

*D. R. Jardine	c Love b O'Reilly	46	lbw b Ironmonger	24	
H. Sutcliffe	lbw b O'Reilly	86	c Darling b Wall	2	
W. R. Hammond	b McCabe	20	(4)c Bromley b Ironmonger	14	
R. E. S. Wyatt	c Love b Ironmonger	12			
M. Leyland	c Bradman b O'Reilly	12	(3)c McCabe b O'Reilly	86	
†L. E. G. Ames	c Darling b Ironmonger	17	(5)not out	14	
G. O. Allen	c Love b Wall	13			
E. Paynter	c Richardson b Ironmonger	83	(6)not out	14	
H. Larwood	b McCabe	23			
H. Verity	not out	23			
T. B. Mitchell	lbw b O'Reilly	0			
Extras	(b 6, lb 12, nb 3)	21	(b 2, lb 4, nb 2)	8	
Total		**356**	**Total** (4 wkts)	**162**	

FALL OF WICKETS

AUSTRALIA

Wkt	1st	2nd
1st	133	46
2nd	200	79
3rd	233	81
4th	264	91
5th	267	136
6th	292	163
7th	315	169
8th	317	169
9th	329	171
10th	340	175

ENGLAND

Wkt	1st	2nd
1st	114	5
2nd	157	78
3rd	165	118
4th	188	138
5th	198	—
6th	216	—
7th	225	—
8th	264	—
9th	356	—
10th	356	—

Umpires: G. A. Hele,
G. Borwick

ENGLAND	1st Innings					2nd Innings			
	O	M	R	W		O	M	R	W
Larwood	31	7	101	4		17.3	3	49	3
Allen	24	4	83	2		17	3	44	3
Hammond	23	5	61	2		10	4	18	0
Mitchell	16	5	49	2		5	0	11	1
Verity	27	12	39	0		19	6	30	2

AUSTRALIA	1st Innings					2nd Innings			
	O	M	R	W		O	M	R	W
Wall	33	6	66	1		7	1	17	1
O'Reilly	67.4	27	120	4		30	11	65	1
Ironmonger	43	19	69	3		35	13	47	2
McCabe	23	7	40	2		7.4	2	25	0
Bromley	10	4	19	0					
Bradman	7	1	17	0					
Darling	2	0	4	0					

1932-33 Fifth Test, Sydney

Test no. 129

February 23, 24, 25, 27, 28
Toss: Australia   *Result:* England won by eight wickets

Woodfull won the toss for the fourth time out of five, but in Larwood's opening over Richardson was caught at fourth slip. Runs then came steadily until Larwood's second spell, when Woodfull was bowled off his hip and Bradman round his legs trying to glance. O'Brien and McCabe got the innings going again, and they added 99 before O'Brien, who had come into the side for Ponsford, mistimed a pull. McCabe continued to play with great coolness, putting on 81 with Darling, and Darling and Oldfield, the latter recovered from his injury, put on another 52 before stumps, when Australia were 296 for 5. Australia were lucky with dropped catches, and they put on another 115 next morning, England looking a tired and jaded side.

When England batted Australia, too, dropped catches, and Hammond, going for his shots from the start, survived two very sharp chances and put on 122 with Sutcliffe, who also showed his best form. 159 for 2 at stumps, England used Larwood as night-watchman and on the third morning he played an innings far above his normal standard, full of fine straight driving, missing his century by only 2 runs and getting a wonderful reception from the Sydney crowd. But Hammond had got out to a careless shot just after reaching his own century, and with Leyland and Ames run out and Paynter failing,

England were indebted to a scratchy 51 from Wyatt and a forceful 48 from Allen for their lead of 19.

When Australia went in again on the fourth morning Richardson was caught off his glove in the first over trying to hook. Bradman began with an astonishing tennis-racket slam at a Larwood bumper, and he went on batting with a quick-footed abandon that met its inevitable end when he moved out to Verity and was yorked. Larwood had to go off with a foot injury, but apart from another courageous innings from Woodfull the batting failed lamentably against Verity, England needing only 164 to win.

That evening Jardine drew attention to footmarks made by Alexander, the replacement for the injured Wall, as had been done in England's first innings; and all the animosity of previous months boiled to the surface again as the crowd booed Jardine and cheered when a ball from Alexander struck him on the body. Ironmonger was well equipped to use the worn patches as Verity had done, but with so few runs to spare he was not inclined to pitch the ball up, and although he bowled 22 overs next day for 29 runs and the wickets of Jardine and Leyland, Hammond and Wyatt finished off the game and the series with a flourish.

AUSTRALIA

V. Y. Richardson	c Jardine b Larwood	0	c Allen b Larwood	0	
*W. M. Woodfull	b Larwood	14	b Allen	67	
D. G. Bradman	b Larwood	48	b Verity	71	
L. P. J. O'Brien	c Larwood b Voce	61	c Verity b Voce	5	
S. J. McCabe	c Hammond b Verity	73	c Jardine b Voce	4	
L. S. Darling	b Verity	85	c Wyatt b Verity	7	
†W. A. Oldfield	run out	52	c Wyatt b Verity	5	
P. K. Lee	c Jardine b Verity	42	b Allen	15	
W. J. O'Reilly	b Allen	19	b Verity	1	
H. H. Alexander	not out	17	lbw b Verity	0	
H. Ironmonger	b Larwood	1	not out	0	
Extras	(b 13, lb 9, w 1)	23	(b 4, nb 3)	7	
Total		**435**	Total	**182**	

ENGLAND

*D. R. Jardine	c Oldfield b O'Reilly	18	c Richardson b Ironmonger	24	
H. Sutcliffe	c Richardson b O'Reilly	56			
W. R. Hammond	lbw b Lee	101	(4)not out	75	
H. Larwood	c Ironmonger b Lee	98			
M. Leyland	run out	42	(3)b Ironmonger	0	
R. E. S. Wyatt	c Ironmonger b O'Reilly	51	(2)not out	61	
†L. E. G. Ames	run out	4			
E. Paynter	b Lee	9			
G. O. Allen	c Bradman b Lee	48			
H. Verity	c Oldfield b Alexander	4			
W. Voce	not out	7			
Extras	(b 7, lb 7, nb 2)	16	(b 6, lb 1, nb 1)	8	
Total		**454**	Total (2 wkts)	**168**	

FALL OF WICKETS

AUSTRALIA

Wkt	1st	2nd
1st	0	0
2nd	59	115
3rd	64	135
4th	163	139
5th	244	148
6th	328	161
7th	385	177
8th	414	178
9th	430	178
10th	435	182

ENGLAND

Wkt	1st	2nd
1st	31	43
2nd	153	43
3rd	245	—
4th	310	—
5th	330	—
6th	349	—
7th	374	—
8th	418	—
9th	434	—
10th	454	—

Umpires: G. A. Hele, G. Borwick

ENGLAND	1st Innings					2nd Innings			
	O	M	R	W		O	M	R	W
Larwood	32·2	10	98	4	..	11	0	44	1
Voce	24	4	80	1	..	10	0	34	2
Allen	25	1	128	1	..	11·4	2	54	2
Hammond	8	0	32	0	..	3	0	10	0
Verity	17	3	62	3	..	19	9	33	5
Wyatt	2	0	12	0					

AUSTRALIA	1st Innings					2nd Innings			
	O	M	R	W		O	M	R	W
Alexander	35	1	129	1	..	11	2	25	0
McCabe	12	1	27	0	..	5	2	10	0
O'Reilly	45	7	100	3	..	15	5	32	0
Ironmonger	31	13	64	0	..	26	12	34	2
Lee	40·2	11	111	4	..	12·2	3	52	0
Darling	7	5	3	0	..	2	0	7	0
Bradman	1	0	4	0	..				

176

Averages: 1932–33

AUSTRALIA

BATTING	M.	Inns.	N.O.	Runs	H.S.	Av.
D. G. Bradman	4	8	1	396	103*	56·57
S. J. McCabe	5	10	1	385	187*	42·77
L. S. Darling	2	4	0	148	85	37·00
W. M. Woodfull	5	10	1	305	73*	33·88
V. Y. Richardson	5	10	0	279	83	27·90
W. A. Oldfield	4	7	2	136	52	27·20
J. H. Fingleton	3	6	0	150	83	25·00
W. H. Ponsford	3	6	0	141	85	23·50
L. P. J. O'Brien	2	4	0	87	61	21·75
C. V. Grimmett	3	6	0	42	19	7·00
W. J. O'Reilly	5	10	0	61	19	6·10
T. W. Wall	4	8	1	42	20	6·00
H. Ironmonger	4	8	3	13	8	2·60

PLAYED IN ONE TEST: A. F. Kippax 8 and 19, L. E. Nagel 0 and 21*, E. H. Bromley 26 and 7, H. S. B. Love 5 and 3, P. K. Lee 42 and 15, H. H. Alexander 17* and 0.

BOWLING	Overs	Mds.	Runs	Wkts.	Av.
T. W. Wall	170·1	33	409	16	25·56
W. J. O'Reilly	383·4	144	724	27	26·81
H. Ironmonger	245·1	96	405	15	27·00
C. V. Grimmett	147	41	326	5	65·20

ALSO BOWLED: P. K. Lee 52·4–14–163–4, S. J. McCabe 92·5–17–215–3, H. H. Alexander 46–3–154–1, L. E. Nagel 43·4–9–110–2, D. G. Bradman 12–1–44–1, L. S. Darling 11–5–14–0, E. H. Bromley 10–4–19–0, A. F. Kippax 2–1–3–0.

ENGLAND

BATTING	M.	Inns.	N.O.	Runs	H.S.	Av.
E. Paynter	3	5	2	184	83	61·33
H. Sutcliffe	5	9	1	440	194	55·00
W. R. Hammond	5	9	1	440	112	55·00
R. E. S. Wyatt	5	9	2	327	78	46·71
Nawab of Pataudi	2	3	0	122	102	40·66
M. Leyland	5	9	0	306	86	34·00
H. Verity	4	5	1	114	45	28·50
H. Larwood	5	7	1	145	98	24·16
G. O. Allen	5	7	0	163	48	23·28
D. R. Jardine	5	9	0	199	56	22·11
L. E. G. Ames	5	8	1	113	69	16·14
W. Voce	4	6	2	29	8	7·25

PLAYED IN ONE TEST: W. E. Bowes 4* and 0*, T. B. Mitchell 0.

BOWLING	Overs	Mds.	Runs	Wkts.	Av.
H. Larwood	220·2	42	644	33	19·51
H. Verity	135	54	271	11	24·63
W. Voce	133·3	24	407	15	27·13
G. O. Allen	170·6	29	593	21	28·23
W. R. Hammond	120·5	27	291	9	32·33

ALSO BOWLED: W. E. Bowes 23–2–70–1, T. B. Mitchell 21–5–60–3, R. E. S. Wyatt 2–0–12–0.

Averages: 1934

ENGLAND

BATTING	M.	Inns.	N.O.	Runs	H.S.	Av.
M. Leyland	5	8	1	478	153	68·28
H. Sutcliffe	4	7	1	304	69*	50·66
C. F. Walters	5	9	1	401	82	50·12
E. H. Hendren	4	6	0	298	132	49·66
L. E. G. Ames	5	7	1	261	120	43·50
G. O. Allen	2	3	0	106	61	35·33
H. Verity	5	7	3	103	60*	25·75
R. E. S. Wyatt	4	6	0	135	44	22·50
G. Geary	2	3	0	62	53	20·66
W. R. Hammond	5	8	0	162	43	20·25
T. B. Mitchell	2	3	1	14	9	7·00
W. E. Bowes	3	3	1	12	10*	6·00
J. L. Hopwood	2	3	1	12	8	6·00
K. Farnes	2	3	0	2	1	0·66
E. W. Clark	2	3	3	6	2*	–

PLAYED IN ONE TEST: Nawab of Pataudi 12 and 10, W. W. Keeton 25 and 12, F. E. Woolley 4 and 0.

BOWLING	Overs	Mds.	Runs	Wkts.	Av.
K. Farnes	81·2	18	228	10	22·80
H. Verity	271·2	93	576	24	24·00
W. E. Bowes	144·3	27	483	19	25·42
E. W. Clark	101·2	15	324	8	40·50
W. R. Hammond	120·3	23	364	5	72·80
G. O. Allen	87	10	369	5	73·80

ALSO BOWLED: G. Geary 88–17–203–4, T. B. Mitchell 57–7–225–1, J. L. Hopwood 77–32–155–0, M. Leyland 13–1–55–0, R. E. S. Wyatt 4–0–28–0, E. H. Hendren 1–0–4–0.

AUSTRALIA

BATTING	M.	Inns.	N.O.	Runs	H.S.	Av.
W. H. Ponsford	4	7	1	569	266	94·83
D. G. Bradman	5	8	0	758	304	94·75
S. J. McCabe	5	9	1	483	137	60·37
W. A. Brown	5	9	0	300	105	33·33
A. G. Chipperfield	5	8	1	200	99	28·57
W. M. Woodfull	5	8	0	228	73	28·50
W. J. O'Reilly	5	8	4	100	30*	25·00
W. A. Oldfield	5	8	2	108	42*	18·00
L. S. Darling	4	6	0	77	37	12·83
C. V. Grimmett	5	8	1	87	39	12·42
T. W. Wall	4	5	1	20	18	5·00

PLAYED IN ONE TEST: E. H. Bromley 4 and 1, A. F. Kippax 28 and 8, H. I. Ebeling 2 and 41.

BOWLING	Overs	Mds.	Runs	Wkts.	Av.
W. J. O'Reilly	333·4	128	698	28	24·92
C. V. Grimmett	396·3	148	668	25	26·72
A. G. Chipperfield	79	19	222	5	44·40
T. W. Wall	172	25	472	6	78·66

ALSO BOWLED: H. I. Ebeling 31–9–89–3, S. J. McCabe 92–22–219–4, L. S. Darling 16–2–51–0.

1934 First Test, Trent Bridge

June 8, 9, 11, 12
Toss: Australia   *Result:* Australia won by 238 runs

Residual resentments from the bodyline series still smouldered when the Australians toured England in 1934, though an uneasy truce was maintained. No legislation banning bodyline bowling had been introduced, but the England selectors had their problems on this score largely solved for them by the retirement of Jardine and by Larwood's highly publicised refusal to take the field against the visitors. Voce, whose methods had upset some of the counties, was apparently not considered. Deprived of the two Notts bowlers, the England attack was never penetrative enough on good wickets to prepare the way for victory. The Australians, too, were a disappointing side: Woodfull, Wall and Kippax fell away, and of the newcomers Brown and Chipperfield were only marginally successful and Darling was a failure. Yet they proved themselves a team, which England, partly due to injuries to key players, never did. The sides went into the final game all square, but the outcome was determined by two record partnerships—388 and 451— between Bradman and Ponsford and the wonderful bowling throughout the summer of O'Reilly and Grimmett.

Walters, playing in his first Test, took over from Wyatt, the appointed captain, who had broken a thumb. At 77 Farnes, in his second spell, had Ponsford caught behind, and Woodfull soon

followed. Brown, Bradman and Darling were all dismissed cheaply, and at 153 for 5 Chipperfield, playing in his first Test, joined McCabe. Play finished early through bad light, but when he was out next morning McCabe had made 65 out of an invaluable partnership of 81. With Grimmett and Oldfield giving Chipperfield unobtrusive support, Australia then established a strong position. 99 not out at lunch, Chipperfield was out to the first ball after the break.

Hammond had played little in the previous month through a back injury, and apart from Sutcliffe the early England batsmen did little. On the third morning England were 165 for 6—60 wanted to save the follow on—but Hendren, who had already taken two hundreds off the tourists, righted the ship with Geary in a stand of 101.

106 behind on first innings, England got Woodfull, Ponsford and Bradman cheaply, but Brown played very straight while McCabe again attacked brilliantly, and when Woodfull declared on the fourth morning England faced $4\frac{3}{4}$ hours' batting on a wearing wicket, the target, 380, being out of reach.

Sutcliffe and Walters survived until half-an-hour after lunch, and although England were 115 for 5 at tea, Leyland and Ames held on for 70 minutes and looked like forcing a draw. But with O'Reilly bowling to the dusty end and Grimmett giving the batsmen no peace, Australia won in a thrilling finish with ten minutes to spare.

AUSTRALIA

*W. M. Woodfull	c Verity b Farnes	26	b Farnes	2	
W. H. Ponsford	c Ames b Farnes	53	b Hammond	5	
W. A. Brown	lbw b Geary	22	c Ames b Verity	73	
D. G. Bradman	c Hammond b Geary	29	c Ames b Farnes	25	
S. J. McCabe	c Leyland b Farnes	65	c Hammond b Farnes	88	
L. S. Darling	b Verity	4	c Hammond b Farnes	14	
A. G. Chipperfield	c Ames b Farnes	99	c Hammond b Farnes	4	
†W. A. Oldfield	c Hammond b Mitchell	20	not out	10	
C. V. Grimmett	b Geary	39	(10)not out	3	
W. J. O'Reilly	b Farnes	7	(9)c Verity b Geary	18	
T. W. Wall	not out	0			
Extras	(b 4, lb 5, nb 1)	10	(b 22, lb 9)	31	
Total		**374**	**Total** (8 wkts dec)	**273**	

ENGLAND

*C. F. Walters	lbw b Grimmett	17	b O'Reilly	46	
H. Sutcliffe	c Chipperfield b Grimmett	62	c Chipperfield b O'Reilly	24	
W. R. Hammond	c McCabe b O'Reilly	25	st Oldfield b Grimmett	16	
Nawab of Pataudi	c McCabe b Wall	12	c Ponsford b Grimmett	10	
M. Leyland	c and b Grimmett	6	(6)c Oldfield b O'Reilly	18	
E. H. Hendren	b O'Reilly	79	(5)c Chipperfield b O'Reilly	3	
†L. E. G. Ames	c Wall b O'Reilly	7	b O'Reilly	12	
G. Geary	st Oldfield b Grimmett	53	c Chipperfield b Grimmett	0	
H. Verity	b O'Reilly	0	not out	0	
K. Farnes	b Grimmett	1	c Oldfield b O'Reilly	0	
T. B. Mitchell	not out	1	lbw b O'Reilly	4	
Extras	(b 5)	5	(b 4, lb 3, nb 1)	8	
Total		**268**	**Total**	**141**	

FALL OF WICKETS

AUSTRALIA

Wkt	1st	2nd
1st	77	2
2nd	88	32
3rd	125	69
4th	146	181
5th	153	219
6th	234	231
7th	281	244
8th	355	267
9th	374	—
10th	374	

ENGLAND

Wkt	1st	2nd
1st	45	51
2nd	102	83
3rd	106	91
4th	114	103
5th	145	110
6th	165	134
7th	266	135
8th	266	137
9th	266	137
10th	268	141

Umpires: F. Chester,
A. Dolphin

ENGLAND	1st Innings				2nd Innings			
	O	M	R	W	O	M	R	W
Farnes	40·2	10	102	5	25	3	77	5
Geary	43	8	101	3	23	5	46	1
Hammond	13	4	29	0	12	5	25	1
Verity	34	9	65	1	17	8	48	1
Mitchell	21	4	62	1	13	2	46	0
Leyland	1	0	5	0				

AUSTRALIA	1st Innings				2nd Innings			
	O	M	R	W	O	M	R	W
Wall	33	7	82	1	13	2	27	0
McCabe	7	2	7	0	2	0	7	0
Grimmett	58·3	24	81	5	47	28	39	3
O'Reilly	37	16	75	4	41·4	24	54	7
Chipperfield	3	0	18	0	4	1	6	0

103. W. M. Woodfull and W. H. Ponsford

104. H. Verity

105. Australia 1934
Back row: W. F. Ferguson (scorer), W. A. Brown, E. H. Bromley, T. W. Wall, H. Bushby (manager), W. J. O'Reilly, L. O'B. Fleetwood-Smith, L. S. Darling, C. V. Grimmett, W. C. Bull (treasurer). *Middle row:* H. I. Ebeling, A. G. Chipperfield, D. G. Bradman, W. M. Woodfull (capt.), A. F. Kippax, S. J. McCabe, W. A. Oldfield. *Front:* B. A. Barnett, W. H. Ponsford.

1934 Second Test, Lord's

June 22, 23, 25
Toss: England   *Result:* England won by an innings and 38 runs

Although Verity took full advantage of conditions that for the most part were not really treacherous, England could not have hoped to square the series at Lord's without help from the weather. Before the rain Australia seemed likely to head England's first innings score; afterwards they were always struggling. Wyatt captained England although his thumb still needed protection, and Farnes, who had had some tendon trouble, reported fit. Pataudi dropped out, and Bowes came in for Mitchell. Australia were without Ponsford, who had influenza, Bromley substituting.

Sutcliffe and Hammond were both dismissed by the occasional leg-breaks of Chipperfield, and at lunch England were 83 for 2. Walters, missed twice but otherwise playing freely and in classical style, was caught in O'Reilly's leg trap at 130, and half the side were out for 182. Leyland was playing the spinners well, however, and with Ames driving powerfully the atmosphere changed. At stumps England were 293 for 5, Leyland 95, Ames 44, and next day both men ran to their centuries, although Ames had one huge slice of luck when he was missed at the wicket at 96. Wyatt was severely criticised for allowing the innings to run its course into the afternoon.

Wickets in England in 1934 were generally dry but slow, and Lord's was no exception; thus the England attack, relying principally on pace,

had a formidable task. By close of play Australia were 192 for 2, and although Woodfull and Bradman were out, Brown and McCabe had made the bowling look ordinary, Brown's very correct hundred coming in 2 hours 43 minutes. Farnes was limping, Hammond's back was troubling him, Geary had a knee-strain, and England were already a team of crocks. But heavy rain over the weekend produced a wicket that, although not much more than a slow turner, was foreign to the Australians, giving England the chance to undermine their morale. There were no bowlers apart from Verity to do it, and only 99 were needed to save the follow on, but with Bowes to close up one end Verity embarked on the task of bowling Australia out twice at the other.

If Australia could save the follow on the chances were that they would escape; but in spite of a fine defensive innings by Chipperfield and good support from Oldfield they failed to do so by 7 runs, thoroughly justifying Wyatt's earlier decision to bat on. The final disaster came when Bradman, lashing out wildly at Verity in the Australian second innings, skied the ball and was caught. There was notable defiance from Woodfull and Chipperfield, but with the wicket briefly spiteful later in the afternoon Australia lost by an innings. Verity took 14 wickets in the day.

ENGLAND

C. F. Walters	c Bromley b O'Reilly	82	
H. Sutcliffe	lbw b Chipperfield	20	
W. R. Hammond	c and b Chipperfield	2	
E. H. Hendren	c McCabe b Wall	13	
*R. E. S. Wyatt	c Oldfield b Chipperfield	33	
M. Leyland	b Wall	109	
†L. E. G. Ames	c Oldfield b McCabe	120	
G. Geary	c Chipperfield b Wall	9	
H. Verity	st Oldfield b Grimmett	29	
K. Farnes	b Wall	1	
W. E. Bowes	not out	10	
Extras	(lb 12)	12	
Total		**440**	

AUSTRALIA

*W. M. Woodful	b Bowes	22	c Hammond b Verity	43	
W. A. Brown	c Ames b Bowes	105	c Walters b Bowes	2	
D. G. Bradman	c and b Verity	36	(4) c Ames b Verity	13	
S. J. McCabe	c Hammond b Verity	34	(3) c Hendren b Verity	19	
L. S. Darling	c Sutcliffe b Verity	0	b Hammond	10	
A. G. Chipperfield	not out	37	c Geary b Verity	14	
E. H. Bromley	c Geary b Verity	4	c and b Verity	1	
†W. A. Oldfield	c Sutcliffe b Verity	23	lbw b Verity	0	
C. V. Grimmett	b Bowes	9	c Hammond b Verity	0	
W. J. O'Reilly	b Verity	4	not out	8	
T. W. Wall	lbw b Verity	0	c Hendren b Verity	1	
Extras	(b 1, lb 9)	10	(b 6, nb 1)	7	
Total		**284**	**Total**	**118**	

FALL OF WICKETS

ENGLAND		
Wkt	1st	2nd
1st	70	—
2nd	78	—
3rd	99	—
4th	130	—
5th	182	—
6th	311	—
7th	359	—
8th	409	—
9th	410	—
10th	440	—

AUSTRALIA		
Wkt	1st	2nd
1st	68	10
2nd	141	43
3rd	203	57
4th	204	94
5th	205	94
6th	218	95
7th	258	95
8th	273	95
9th	284	112
10th	284	118

Umpires: F. Chester, J. Hardstaff, snr.

AUSTRALIA	1st Innings				2nd Innings			
	O	M	R	W	O	M	R	W
Wall	49	7	108	4	..			
McCabe	18	3	38	1	..			
Grimmett	53·3	13	102	1	..			
O'Reilly	38	15	70	1	..			
Chipperfield	34	10	91	3	..			
Darling	6	2	19	0	..			

ENGLAND	1st Innings				2nd Innings			
	O	M	R	W	O	M	R	W
Farnes	12	3	43	0	..	4	2	6	0
Bowes	31	5	98	3	..	14	4	24	1
Geary	22	4	56	0	..			
Verity	36	15	61	7	..	22·3	8	43	8
Hammond	4	1	6	0	..	13	0	38	0
Leyland	4	1	10	0	..			

1934 Third Test, Old Trafford

July 6, 7, 9, 10
Toss: England   *Result:* Match Drawn

Forced to rebuild their attack by injuries to Farnes and Geary, the England selectors made a job of it and dropped Bowes as well. Ignoring current form they went for two fast bowlers who had done little or nothing that year and whose fitness was in doubt—Allen and the left-handed Clark—and as no leg-spinner took their fancy they chose Hopwood, slow-medium left arm, which did not make for a balanced attack. Australia were back to full strength on paper, but several players suffered from a debilitating throat infection in the course of the game, Bradman and Chipperfield being the worst affected.

In heat and humidity more typical of Adelaide than Old Trafford, England were 68 for 0 after an hour. A stoppage for drinks was then prolonged by a complaint about the ball, a replacement was selected, and on the resumption Sutcliffe played a maiden over from Grimmett. O'Reilly then had Walters caught at short leg off his first ball after the break, Wyatt was bowled by the second, Hammond glanced the third for four and was bowled by the fourth. 68 for 0 had become 72 for 3. Yet in spite of this dramatic over England continued to score at a run a minute and were 128 for 3 at lunch.

Sutcliffe was out at 149, but the 45-year-old Hendren continued his mastery of the Australian spinners, Leyland played equally well in a stand of 191, both scored centuries, Ames helped Leyland to add 142, and by lunch on the second day England were 533 for 8. Batting on in the hope of tiring his opponents, wearing the wicket, and making sure of a follow on, Wyatt delayed his declaration until 4.0.

Another sensational over, though of a different kind, began the Australian innings, Allen sending down four no-balls and three wides in an over of 13 balls. Australia were 136 for 1 at stumps, and on the third morning Brown defended while McCabe square cut, pulled and hooked fiercely, reaching his hundred in $2\frac{1}{2}$ hours; but Australia still needed 236 to save the follow on when these two were out. Woodfull, missed at slip first ball, should have been stumped at 31, Darling should have been run out, several other chances were missed or didn't go to hand, and Bradman and Chipperfield went to the wicket and held the bowlers up still further. Even so, at stumps Australia still needed 55 to save the follow on with only 2 wickets to fall. The England bowlers finally exhausted themselves taking these two wickets on the final morning, and the follow on was saved. But on this over-prepared wicket a draw had always seemed likely.

ENGLAND

C. F. Walters	c Darling b O'Reilly	52	not out	50		
H. Sutcliffe	c Chipperfield b O'Reilly	63	not out	69		
*R. E. S. Wyatt	b O'Reilly	0				
W. R. Hammond	b O'Reilly	4				
E. H. Hendren	c and b O'Reilly	132				
M. Leyland	c sub (B. A. Barnett) b O'Reilly	153				
†L. E. G. Ames	c Ponsford b Grimmett	72				
J. L. Hopwood	b O'Reilly	2				
G. O. Allen	b McCabe	61				
H. Verity	not out	60				
E. W. Clark	not out	2				
Extras	(b 6, lb 18, w 2)	26	(b 2, lb 1, w 1)	4		
Total	(9 wkts dec)	**627**	**Total** (0 wkts dec)	**123**		

AUSTRALIA

W. A. Brown	c Walters b Clark	72	c Hammond b Allen	0	
W. H. Ponsford	c Hendren b Hammond	12	not out	30	
S. J. McCabe	c Verity b Hammond	137	not out	33	
*W. M. Woodfull	run out	73			
L. S. Darling	b Verity	37			
D. G. Bradman	c Ames b Hammond	30			
†W. A. Oldfield	c Wyatt b Verity	13			
A. G. Chipperfield	c Walters b Verity	26			
C. V. Grimmett	b Verity	0			
W. J. O'Reilly	not out	30			
T. W. Wall	run out	18			
Extras	(b 20, lb 13, w 4, nb 6)	43	(b 1, lb 2)	3	
Total		**491**	**Total** (1 wkt)	**66**	

FALL OF WICKETS

ENGLAND

Wkt	1st	2nd
1st	68	—
2nd	68	—
3rd	72	—
4th	149	—
5th	340	—
6th	482	—
7th	492	—
8th	510	—
9th	605	—
10th	—	

AUSTRALIA

Wkt	1st	2nd
1st	34	1
2nd	230	—
3rd	242	—
4th	320	—
5th	378	—
6th	409	—
7th	411	—
8th	419	—
9th	454	—
10th	491	—

Umpires: J. Hardstaff, snr.,
F. Walden

AUSTRALIA	1st Innings					2nd Innings			
	O	M	R	W		O	M	R	W
Wall	36	3	131	0	..	9	0	31	0
McCabe	32	3	98	1	..	13	4	35	0
Grimmett	57	20	122	1	..	17	5	28	0
O'Reilly	59	9	189	7	..	13	4	25	0
Chipperfield	7	0	29	0	..				
Darling	10	0	32	0	..				

ENGLAND	1st Innings					2nd Innings			
	O	M	R	W		O	M	R	W
Clark	40	9	100	1	..	4	1	16	0
Allen	31	3	113	0	..	6	0	23	1
Hammond	28·3	6	111	3	..	2	1	2	0
Verity	53	24	78	4	..	5	4	2	0
Hopwood	38	20	46	0	..	9	5	16	0
Hendren					..	1	0	4	0

1934 Fourth Test, Leeds

July 20, 21, 23, 24
Toss: England   *Result:* Match Drawn

England gave a display of batting so feeble that it was hard to reconcile it with their form at Lord's and Old Trafford. In the absence of Sutcliffe, injured, a place might have been found for Paynter, but Keeton, who had no experience of Grimmett and O'Reilly, was chosen, and he opened with Walters. Keeton was caught behind off O'Reilly at 43, Walters gave an easy return catch at 85, and Hendren came in to face the last 10 minutes before lunch. He and Hammond withstood the main spin attack and then, at 135, succumbed to Wall and Chipperfield. Struggling on painfully through the afternoon, England were all out soon after 5.30 for 200.

Australia seemed to be weathering the last 45 minutes when Bowes, crossing to the grandstand end, bowled Brown at 37 and then had Oldfield, the night-watchman, caught behind. Coming in himself with only two minutes left Woodfull played on, and the day closed with Australia 39 for 3. In 10 balls since changing ends Bowes had taken 3 for 0.

There were two balls of Bowes' unfinished over left when Bradman took guard next morning; both were short of a length, and both were despatched to the boundary. For the rest of the day Bradman, betraying no hint of the recklessness that had characterised much of his play in

this series, played superb but orthodox cricket, not accelerating until the final session, in which he made 102. His partnership with Ponsford of 388 broke all records, and Ponsford himself played almost equally well. It was not until 5.51, after the stand had lasted 5 hours 41 minutes, that Ponsford was out, and then he trod on his wicket. Bradman at the close was 271 not out, and Ponsford's was the only wicket to fall during the day. There were a few edged strokes but only two possible chances, one to cover from Ponsford and one to square leg from Bradman, both just before lunch, both very hot chances, both off Bowes.

On the third morning Australia's last 6 wickets fell for 90, Bradman being bowled for 304. Keeton was beaten by Grimmett in the last over before lunch, Hammond was tragically run out, and when Walters was out England were 87 for 3. Going in at 3.10 Hendren batted through till stumps, but he lost Wyatt at 5.30, bowled round his legs sweeping at Grimmett. Leyland held on for the last hour, but England faced the last day in a seemingly hopeless position, 196 behind with six wickets to fall. Heavy rain that night and next day, however, upset all calculations of defeat and resistance, and the match was eventually abandoned.

ENGLAND

C. F. Walters	c and b Chipperfield	44	b O'Reilly	45	
W. W. Keeton	c Oldfield b O'Reilly	25	b Grimmett	12	
W R. Hammond	b Wall	37	run out	20	
E. H. Hendren	b Chipperfield	29	lbw b O'Reilly	42	
*R. E. S. Wyatt	st Oldfield b Grimmett	19	b Grimmett	44	
M. Leyland	lbw b O'Reilly	16	not out	49	
†L. E. G. Ames	c Oldfield b Grimmett	9	c Brown b Grimmett	8	
J. L. Hopwood	lbw b O'Reilly	8	not out	2	
H. Verity	not out	2			
T. B. Mitchell	st Oldfield b Grimmett	9			
W. E. Bowes	c Ponsford b Grimmett	0			
Extras	(lb 2)	2	(b 1, lb 6)	7	
Total		200	Total (6 wkts)	229	

AUSTRALIA

W. A. Brown	b Bowes	15
W. H. Ponsford	hit wkt b Verity	181
†W. A. Oldfield	c Ames b Bowes	0
*W. M. Woodfull	b Bowes	0
D. G. Bradman	b Bowes	304
S. J. McCabe	b Bowes	27
L. S. Darling	b Bowes	12
A. G. Chipperfield	c Wyatt b Verity	1
C. V. Grimmett	run out	15
W. J. O'Reilly	not out	11
T. W. Wall	lbw b Verity	1
Extras	(b 8, lb 9)	17
Total		584

FALL OF WICKETS

ENGLAND

Wkt	1st	2nd
1st	43	28
2nd	85	70
3rd	135	87
4th	135	152
5th	168	190
6th	170	213
7th	189	—
8th	189	—
9th	200	—
10th	200	—

AUSTRALIA

Wkt	1st	2nd
1st	37	—
2nd	39	—
3rd	39	—
4th	427	—
5th	517	—
6th	550	—
7th	551	—
8th	557	—
9th	574	—
10th	584	—

Umpires: A. Dolphin,
J. Hardstaff, snr.

AUSTRALIA	1st Innings					2nd Innings			
	O	M	R	W		O	M	R	W
Wall	18	1	57	1	..	14	5	36	0
McCabe	4	2	3	0	..	5	4	5	0
Grimmett	30·4	11	57	4	..	56·5	24	72	3
O'Reilly	35	16	46	3	..	51	25	88	2
Chipperfield	18	6	35	2	..	9	2	21	0

ENGLAND	1st Innings					2nd Innings			
	O	M	R	W		O	M	R	W
Bowes	50	13	142	6	..				
Hammond	29	5	82	0	..				
Mitchell	23	1	117	0	..				
Verity	46·5	15	113	3	..				
Hopwood	30	7	93	0	..				
Leyland	5	0	20	0	..				

1934 Fifth Test, Oval

August 18, 20, 21, 22
Toss: Australia   *Result:* Australia won by 562 runs

The England selectors, rightly judging that the only Australian weakness was against fast bowling, dropped two of the three spinners who had played at Leeds and picked Allen and Clark as well as Bowes. The only other change was forced on them through an injury to Hendren. This was a serious loss, but it did give the selectors a chance to improve the fielding. Instead they chose the 47-year-old Woolley: Woolley was having a great season, but to expect him to come back to Test cricket was asking too much, and he presented Wyatt with an insoluble problem in the field. Australia substituted Ebeling for Wall, who was injured, and Kippax for Darling.

The fate of the Ashes was virtually decided on the first day, in which Australia, thanks to another record stand between Bradman and Ponsford, made 475 for 2. The attack inevitably lacked variety; but the decisive factors were the magnificent batting of Bradman and the disastrous England catching and fielding. Wyatt was forced to spend many overs on the boundary himself; his own fielding and catching, in which he had previously set a fine example, let him down and he missed Ponsford twice. Ponsford continued his habit of turning his back on the shortish ball, and he was missed so often that the greatness of his innings must rest on its size; but Bradman's innings, apart from

one or two balls that got past the bat, was faultless, one of the finest he ever played. After Clark had bowled Brown at 21, he and Ponsford added 451, of which Bradman's share was 244; he was out 7 minutes before the close, having batted 5 hours 16 minutes. Ponsford at stumps was 205 not out, and he stayed until just before lunch on the Monday. Australia eventually totalled 701.

Walters and Sutcliffe had made 90 without being separated by the close, and a creditable reply looked likely; but in a disastrous 75 minutes next morning 5 wickets fell for 52. Ames then joined Leyland in a stand that promised to be face-saving until Ames was forced to retire with back trouble, and with Bowes also under medical care for a fistula Leyland was 8th and last out for an aggressive and chanceless 110.

Two substitutes, Gregory and McMurray, showed the best fielding of the series as Bradman and McCabe took Australia to 182 for 2 that evening, but on the fourth morning Bowes, bowling at not much above medium pace and keeping the ball well up, took 5 for 55, sharing the wickets with Clark. Woolley kept wicket. Grimmett bowled superbly when England batted again, and Australia won by 562.

AUSTRALIA

W. A. Brown	b Clark	10	c Allen b Clark	1
W. H. Ponsford	hit wkt b Allen	266	c Hammond b Clark	22
D. G. Bradman	c Ames b Bowes	244	b Bowes	77
S. J. McCabe	b Allen	10	c Walters b Clark	70
*W. M. Woodfull	b Bowes	49	b Bowes	13
A. F. Kippax	lbw b Bowes	28	c Walters b Clark	8
A. G. Chipperfield	b Bowes	3	c Woolley b Clark	16
†W. A. Oldfield	not out	42	c Hammond b Bowes	0
C. V. Grimmett	c Ames b Allen	7	c Hammond b Bowes	14
H. I. Ebeling	b Allen	2	c Allen b Bowes	41
W. J. O'Reilly	b Clark	7	not out	15
Extras	(b 4, lb 14, w 2, nb 13)	33	(b 37, lb 8, w 1, nb 4)	50
Total		**701**	**Total**	**327**

ENGLAND

C. F. Walters	c Kippax b O'Reilly	64	b McCabe	1
H. Sutcliffe	c Oldfield b Grimmett	38	c McCabe b Grimmett	28
F. E. Woolley	c McCabe b O'Reilly	4	c Ponsford b McCabe	0
W. R. Hammond	c Oldfield b Ebeling	15	c and b O'Reilly	43
*R. E. S. Wyatt	b Grimmett	17	(6)c Ponsford b Grimmett	22
M. Leyland	b Grimmett	110	(5)c Brown b Grimmett	17
†L. E. G. Ames	retired hurt	33	absent ill	—
G. O. Allen	b Ebeling	19	(7)st Oldfield b Grimmett	26
H. Verity	b Ebeling	11	(8)c McCabe b Grimmett	1
E. W. Clark	not out	2	not out	2
W. E. Bowes	absent ill	—	(9)c Bradman b O'Reilly	2
Extras	(b 4, lb 3, nb 1)	8	(lb 1, nb 2)	3
Total		**321**	**Total**	**145**

FALL OF WICKETS

AUSTRALIA

Wkt	1st	2nd
1st	21	13
2nd	472	42
3rd	488	192
4th	574	213
5th	626	224
6th	631	236
7th	638	236
8th	676	256
9th	682	272
10th	701	327

ENGLAND

Wkt	1st	2nd
1st	104	1
2nd	108	3
3rd	111	67
4th	136	89
5th	142	109
6th	263	122
7th	311	138
8th	321	141
9th	—	145
10th	—	—

Umpires: F. Chester, F. Walden

ENGLAND

	1st Innings				2nd Innings			
	O	M	R	W	O	M	R	W
Bowes	38	2	164	4	11·3	3	55	5
Allen	34	5	170	4	16	2	63	0
Clark	37·2	4	110	2	20	1	98	5
Hammond	12	0	53	0	7	1	18	0
Verity	43	7	123	0	14	3	43	0
Wyatt	4	0	28	0				
Leyland	3	0	20	0				

AUSTRALIA

	1st Innings				2nd Innings			
	O	M	R	W	O	M	R	W
Ebeling	21	4	74	3	10	5	15	0
McCabe	6	1	21	0	5	3	5	2
Grimmett	49·3	13	103	3	26·3	10	64	5
O'Reilly	37	10	93	2	22	9	58	2
Chipperfield	4	0	22	0				

1936-37 First Test, Brisbane

Test no. 135

December 4, 5, 7, 8, 9
Toss: England   *Result:* England won by 322 runs

Legislation designed to outlaw bodyline bowling had been passed in November 1934, and although Larwood, top of the 1936 averages, did not wish to be considered, Voce placed himself unreservedly at the disposal of the selectors and was England's best bowler. The choice of Allen as captain narrowed the field for fast bowlers, Bowes and Gover being left behind, but Farnes did well when given the chance. The weakness, however, lay fundamentally in spin bowling; England had none of top class, and the batsmen chosen to replace Walters, Sutcliffe and Hendren had scant experience of it. Thus a mistake was made in not taking Paynter. England suffered severely from injuries, the most serious being to Wyatt and Robins, the latter being unable to spin the ball much after breaking a finger. After a bad start to the tour, England surprised everyone by winning the first two Tests; but the return to form of Bradman, the pairing of Fleetwood-Smith with O'Reilly, and a change in the luck, enabled Australia to come from behind and clinch the series, the first time this had been done. So close was the struggle that all attendance records were broken.

The Australian side at Brisbane was as experimental as England's, but they made a great start, getting 3 wickets down for 20, including Hammond first ball. The situation was not unfamiliar to Leyland, and he and Barnett were still there at lunch. Dour and often troubled by O'Reilly, Leyland took 2 hours 19 minutes to reach 50, but Barnett drove strongly and played O'Reilly well. The close of play score of 263 for 6 represented a recovery, thanks chiefly to Leyland, but it was still nothing like enough. Australia, as short of pace as England were of spin, had been without McCormick with lumbago since his opening spell.

England did well to add another 95 runs next day; but although Badcock played on at 13, they were on the defensive by tea-time. After tea Bradman was caught at backward point, but Fingleton and McCabe batted comfortably through to stumps at 151 for 2.

On the third morning Voce, producing a disconcerting lift allied to subtle pace variations, got McCabe, Robinson and Chipperfield, and although Fingleton completed a watchful hundred the innings was finished off by the new ball. 124 ahead, England struggled against fine spin bowling from Ward to 144 for 6, but Allen and Hardstaff put on 61 at a critical time and Australia were set 381 to win. Voce bowled Fingleton that evening, and the overnight rain that caused a collapse next morning could not detract from the ascendancy England had established over the first four days.

ENGLAND

Batsman	1st Innings		2nd Innings	
T. S. Worthington	c Oldfield b McCormick	0	st Oldfield b McCabe	8
C. J. Barnett	c Oldfield b O'Reilly	69	c Badcock b Ward	26
A. E. Fagg	c Oldfield b McCormick	4	st Oldfield b Ward	27
W. R. Hammond	c Robinson b McCormick	0	hit wkt b Ward	25
M. Leyland	b Ward	126	c Bradman b Ward	33
†L. E. G. Ames	c Chipperfield b Ward	24	b Sievers	9
J. Hardstaff	c McCabe b O'Reilly	43	(8)st Oldfield b Ward	20
R. W. V. Robins	c sub (W. A. Brown) b O'Reilly	38	(9)c Chipperfield b Ward	0
*G. O. Allen	c McCabe b O'Reilly	35	(7)c Fingleton b Sievers	68
H. Verity	c Sievers b O'Reilly	7	lbw b Sievers	19
W. Voce	not out	4	not out	2
Extras	(b 1, lb 3, nb 4)	8	(b 14, lb 4, nb 1)	19
Total		358		256

AUSTRALIA

Batsman	1st Innings		2nd Innings	
J. H. Fingleton	b Verity	100	b Voce	0
C. L. Badcock	b Allen	8	c Fagg b Allen	0
*D. G. Bradman	c Worthington b Voce	38	(5)c Fagg b Allen	0
S. J. McCabe	c Barnett b Voce	51	(6)c Leyland b Allen	7
R. H. Robinson	c Hammond b Voce	2	(7)c Hammond b Voce	3
A. G. Chipperfield	c Ames b Voce	7	(8)not out	26
M. W. S. Sievers	b Allen	8	(3)c Voce b Allen	5
†W. A. Oldfield	c Ames b Voce	6	(4)b Voce	10
W. J. O'Reilly	c Leyland b Voce	3	b Allen	0
F. A. Ward	c Hardstaff b Allen	0	b Voce	1
E. L. McCormick	not out	1	absent ill	—
Extras	(b 4, lb 1, nb 5)	10	(nb 6)	6
Total		234		58

FALL OF WICKETS

ENGLAND

Wkt	1st	2nd
1st	0	17
2nd	20	50
3rd	20	82
4th	119	105
5th	162	122
6th	252	144
7th	311	205
8th	311	205
9th	343	247
10th	358	256

AUSTRALIA

Wkt	1st	2nd
1st	13	0
2nd	89	3
3rd	166	7
4th	176	7
5th	202	16
6th	220	20
7th	229	35
8th	231	41
9th	231	58
10th	234	—

Umpires: G. Borwick, J. D. Scott

AUSTRALIA	1st Innings				2nd Innings			
	O	M	R	W	O	M	R	W
McCormick	8	1	26	3				
Sievers	16	5	42	0	19.6	9	29	3
O'Reilly	40.6	13	102	5	35	15	59	0
Ward	36	3	138	2	46	16	102	6
Chipperfield	11	3	32	0	10	2	33	0
McCabe	2	0	10	0	6	1	14	1

ENGLAND	1st Innings				2nd Innings			
	O	M	R	W	O	M	R	W
Allen	16	2	71	3	6	0	36	5
Voce	20.6	5	41	6	6.3	0	16	4
Hammond	4	0	12	0				
Verity	28	11	52	1				
Robins	17	0	48	0				

106. **W. Voce**

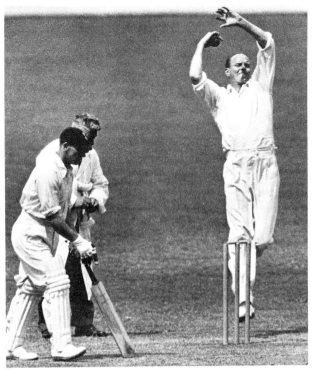

107. **W. J. O'Reilly**

108. **England 1936-37**
Back row: W. F. Ferguson (scorer), L. B. Fishlock, T. S. Worthington, A. E. Fagg, J. Hardstaff, Capt. R. Howard (manager).
Middle row: T. H. Wade, H. Verity, C. J. Barnett, K. Farnes, W. H. Copson, J. M. Sims, W. Voce. *Front:* L. E. G. Ames, W. R. Hammond, R. W. V. Robins, G. O. Allen (capt.), R. E. S. Wyatt, M. Leyland, G. Duckworth.

1936-37 Second Test, Sydney

December 18, 19, 21, 22
Toss: England   *Result:* England won by an innings and 22 runs

Brown, who had missed the first Test through injury, was still not fit, and Badcock was taken ill on the first morning. There was not much luck about the strong position built up by England on the first two days, Hammond's innings being chanceless until he was past 200; but rain then enabled Allen to declare and get the Australians in on a damp wicket. Australia brought in O'Brien for Robinson, while England played Sims for Worthington.

Another hostile opening spell by McCormick unsettled Fagg, Hammond was not far from playing on soon after he came in, and Barnett was missed by Chipperfield at slip from a Ward leg-break, but from then on the innings prospered. Barnett was always ready to drive O'Reilly, and at lunch England were 100 for 1. Barnett was bowled by Ward at 118, but Leyland, although playing a most untypical innings, stayed with Hammond for over 2½ hours and helped him put on 129. He was eventually out under the new lbw rule. O'Reilly and Ward bowled leg theory for long periods, but Hammond and Leyland got the blame for the inevitable slow play. Hammond, in fact, displayed a greater variety of strokes than usual, sweeping, square cutting, even hooking, and playing a stream of on-side shots

off his toes, in addition to the drive. After 5 hours England were 279 for 3.

Ames was out in the last over before lunch next day, having helped to put on 104, and after a short break for rain England had reached 426 for 6 just after tea when rain finally stopped play. There was an early morning thunderstorm on the third day, and on a wicket of uncertain pace Australia collapsed for 80, O'Reilly taking advantage of one or two speculative overs of spin to make 37.

Although the probability was that the wicket would roll out absolutely plumb, Allen preferred to chance the weather ahead and keep his second innings in hand, and he enforced the follow on; thus by close of play that evening Australia were 145 for 1, still 201 behind but with Bradman and Fingleton entrenched. For half-an-hour on the fourth morning Bradman and Fingleton played themselves in: then Sims, with his fourth ball, bowled Fingleton with a perfectly pitched googly. Bradman missed a pull at a shortish ball from Verity at 186, and although McCabe fought with great artistry the innings victory was achieved. Allen was a dynamic leader and England's best bowlers were Hammond and Voce.

ENGLAND

A. E. Fagg	c Sievers b McCormick	11		
C. J. Barnett	b Ward	57		
W. R. Hammond	not out	231		
M. Leyland	lbw b McCabe	42		
†L. E. G. Ames	c sub (R.H.Robinson) b Ward	29		
*G. O. Allen	lbw b O'Reilly	9		
J. Hardstaff	b McCormick	26		
H. Verity	not out	0		
J. M. Sims	⎫			
R. W. V. Robins	⎬ did not bat			
W. Voce	⎭			
Extras	(b 8, lb 8, w 1, nb 4)	21		
Total	(6 wkts dec)	**426**		

AUSTRALIA

J. H. Fingleton	c Verity b Voce	12	b Sims	73	
L. P. J. O'Brien	c Sims b Voce	0	c Allen b Hammond	17	
*D. G. Bradman	c Allen b Voce	0	b Verity	82	
S. J. McCabe	c Sims b Voce	0	lbw b Voce	93	
A. G. Chipperfield	c Sims b Allen	13	b Voce	21	
M. W. S. Sievers	c Voce b Verity	4	(7)run out	24	
†W. A. Oldfield	b Verity	1	(8)c Ames b Voce	1	
W. J. O'Reilly	not out	37	(9)b Hammond	3	
E. L. McCormick	b Allen	10	(10)lbw b Hammond	0	
F. A. Ward	b Allen	0	(11)not out	1	
C. L. Badcock	absent ill	—	(6)lbw b Allen	2	
Extras	(b 1, lb 1, nb 1)	3	(lb 3, nb 4)	7	
Total		**80**	**Total**	**324**	

FALL OF WICKETS

ENGLAND

Wkt	1st	2nd
1st	27	—
2nd	118	—
3rd	247	—
4th	351	—
5th	368	—
6th	424	—
7th	—	—
8th	—	—
9th	—	—
10th	—	—

AUSTRALIA

Wkt	1st	2nd
1st	1	38
2nd	1	162
3rd	1	186
4th	16	220
5th	28	226
6th	30	318
7th	31	319
8th	80	323
9th	80	323
10th	—	324

Umpires: G. Borwick,
J. D. Scott

AUSTRALIA	1st Innings				2nd Innings			
	O	M	R	W	O	M	R	W
McCormick	20	1	79	2				
Sievers	16·2	4	30	0				
Ward	42	8	132	2				
O'Reilly	41	17	86	1				
Chipperfield	13	2	47	0				
McCabe	9	1	31	1				

ENGLAND	1st Innings				2nd Innings			
	O	M	R	W	O	M	R	W
Voce	8	1	10	4	19	4	66	3
Allen	5·7	1	19	3	19	4	61	1
Verity	3	0	17	2	19	7	55	1
Hammond	4	0	6	0	15·7	3	29	3
Sims	2	0	20	0	17	0	80	1
Robins	1	0	5	0	7	0	26	0

1936-37 Third Test, Melbourne

January 1, 2, 4, 5, 6, 7
Toss: Australia   *Result:* Australia won by 365 runs

The first half-hour against the England fast attack brought only 7 runs, and then Brown was caught behind hooking at a bouncer. When Verity came on at 33 he got Bradman at short leg with his first ball, and after lunch Rigg was caught at short leg off Allen—all on a lifeless wicket. (Brown and Rigg had come in for O'Brien and Badcock, while Darling was replacing Chipperfield.) Fingleton was caught in the covers off a long hop after batting 2 hours for 38, and Australia were 129 for 5 at tea, the rubber apparently lost. Ames then stumped Sievers, but McCabe and Oldfield counter-attacked until a shower drove the players off. Further rain ended play for the day at 181 for 6.

Later in the day England had been handicapped by a wet ball; and in the night the luck turned right against them, heavy rain ruining the wicket. Play restarted at 2.15, and at 200 for 9 Bradman declared. Hammond and Leyland were the only batsmen who were not bewildered by the conditions, and they put on 42 in the only stand of the innings; but both went to brilliant catches by Darling at short leg. At 76 for 9 Allen declared, Sievers, substituting for the injured McCormick, having taken 5 for 21 at medium pace; but Bradman sent the tail-enders in first, and the 35 minutes that remained was reduced by bad light.

3 for 1 overnight, Australia lost Fleetwood-Smith to the third ball next morning, but Ward and Rigg defended stubbornly while the wicket improved, and when Ward was out after an hour Brown did the same. After lunch Brown pulled a long hop to square leg, and a 5th wicket fell at 97 when Rigg was lbw to Sims; but at this point, with the wicket fully recovered, Bradman joined Fingleton. Wary at the start, Bradman began to hit fiercely as more rain fell and the ball became greasy; but as the weather cleared he and Fingleton settled in, and by the close they had doubled the score. Next day they took their stand to 346, the highest ever recorded in Australia; only one wicket fell during the day.

Bradman had batted under the handicap of a severe chill, and when England went in on the fifth afternoon to make 689 to win, McCabe took over as captain. Hammond promised well before getting out to a careless stroke, and the brightest batting came from Leyland and Robins, who put on 111 in 65 minutes; but defeat always looked certain. Fleetwood-Smith, who would have played in the first two Tests but for injury, greatly strengthened the Australian attack.

AUSTRALIA

J. H. Fingleton	c Sims b Robins	38	(6)c Ames b Sims		136
W. A. Brown	c Ames b Voce	1	(5)c Barnett b Voce		20
*D. G. Bradman	c Robins b Verity	13	(7)c Allen b Verity		270
K. E. Rigg	c Verity b Allen	16	lbw b Sims		47
S. J. McCabe	c Worthington b Voce	63	(8)lbw b Allen		22
L. S. Darling	c Allen b Verity	20	(9)b Allen		0
M. W. S. Sievers	st Ames b Robins	1	(10)not out		25
*W. A. Oldfield	not out	27	(11)lbw b Verity		7
W. J. O'Reilly	c Sims b Hammond	4	(1)c and b Voce		0
F. Ward	st Ames b Hammond	7	(3)c Hardstaff b Verity		18
L. O'B. Fleetwood-Smith	did not bat		(2)c Verity b Voce		0
Extras	(b 2, lb 6, nb 2)	10	(b 6, lb 2, w 1, nb 10)		19
Total	(9 wkts dec)	**200**	**Total**		**564**

ENGLAND

T. S. Worthington	c Bradman b McCabe	0	c Sievers b Ward		16
C. J. Barnett	c Darling b Sievers	11	lbw b O'Reilly		23
W. R. Hammond	c Darling b Sievers	32	b Sievers		51
M. Leyland	c Darling b O'Reilly	17	not out		111
J. M. Sims	c Brown b Sievers	3	(10)lbw b Fleetwood-Smith		0
*L. E. G. Ames	b Sievers	3	(5)b Fleetwood-Smith		19
R. W. V. Robins	c O'Reilly b Sievers	0	(8)b O'Reilly		61
J. Hardstaff	b O'Reilly	3	(6)c Ward b Fleetwood-Smith		17
*G. O. Allen	not out	0	(7)c Sievers b Fleetwood-Smith		11
H. Verity	c Brown b O'Reilly	0	(9)c McCabe b O'Reilly		11
W. Voce	not out	0	c Bradman b F-Smith		0
Extras	(b 5, lb 1, nb 1)	7	(lb 3)		3
Total	(9 wkts dec)	**76**	**Total**		**323**

FALL OF WICKETS

AUSTRALIA

Wkt	1st	2nd
1st	7	0
2nd	33	3
3rd	69	38
4th	79	74
5th	122	97
6th	130	443
7th	183	511
8th	190	511
9th	200	549
10th	—	564

ENGLAND

Wkt	1st	2nd
1st	0	29
2nd	14	65
3rd	56	155
4th	68	155
5th	71	179
6th	71	195
7th	76	306
8th	76	322
9th	76	323
10th	—	323

Umpires: G. Borwick, J. D. Scott

ENGLAND

		1st Innings				2nd Innings		
	O	M	R	W	O	M	R	W
Voce	18	3	49	2	29	2	120	3
Allen	12	2	35	1	23	2	84	2
Sims	9	1	35	0	23	1	109	2
Verity	14	4	24	2	37·7	9	79	3
Robins	7	0	31	2	11	2	46	0
Hammond	5·3	0	16	2	22	3	89	0
Worthington					4	0	18	0

AUSTRALIA

		1st Innings				2nd Innings		
	O	M	R	W	O	M	R	W
McCabe	2	1	7	1	8	0	32	0
Sievers	11·2	5	21	5	12	2	39	1
O'Reilly	12	5	28	3	21	6	65	3
Fleetwood-Smith	3	1	13	0	25·6	2	124	5
Ward					12	1	60	1

1936-37 Fourth Test, Adelaide

January 29, 30, February 1, 2, 3, 4
Toss: Australia *Result:* Australia won by 148 runs

For the vital fourth Test Australia played Chipperfield and the 20-year-old Gregory for Darling and Ward, and with McCormick back for Sievers the side looked their best of the series. For England Wyatt, fit for the first time, replaced Worthington, while a third fast bowler, Farnes, displaced Sims, there being some doubt about Voce's fitness. The luck of the toss evened out, Australia batting first, but at 26 Fingleton ran himself out. 72 for 1 at lunch, Australia lost Brown and Rigg to Farnes directly afterwards, while Bradman batted unimpressively for 68 minutes before being bowled trying to hook Allen. McCabe played brilliantly while Gregory defended, and his first bad stroke cost him his wicket when at 206 he tried to pull Robins against the break and was brilliantly caught at square leg. Hammond got Gregory with the new ball, and Oldfield was smartly run out by Leyland, but Chipperfield batted soundly and at stumps Australia were 267 for 7.

England went in next morning facing the modest total of 288. Their highest opening stand had been 29, and this time Verity helped Barnett to put on 53; but Hammond spooned up a catch off O'Reilly, and England were 108 for 2. By careful play Barnett and Leyland took the score to 174 by the close, Barnett 92, Leyland 35, and once again

England seemed in sight of the Ashes. But on the third morning Leyland and Wyatt were both out in the first half-hour, and although Barnett and Ames took the score to 253 for 4 at lunch, and England went into the lead with only 5 wickets down, no one but Ames looked happy against the spin attack after Barnett left and England's lead was kept to 42. Hammond then had Fingleton lbw, but Bradman came in no. 3 and the arrears were cleared off before the close without further loss.

Inadequate batting had cost England their chance of establishing a commanding position; and on the fourth day, as Bradman played one of his most disciplined and purposeful innings, the initiative passed to Australia. Stands of 109 with McCabe and 135 with Gregory saw them into a big lead by the fifth morning despite spirited bowling and fielding, and although wickets fell quickly after Bradman was out just on lunch-time England needed 392 to win. Hardstaff showed a marked improvement against the spinners, and at stumps England were 148 for 3, with everything depending on the not out batsmen, Hammond and Leyland; but Fleetwood-Smith bowled Hammond in his first over next morning and later got Leyland and Ames, and although he was sometimes punished he was, with Bradman, the match-winner.

AUSTRALIA

J. H. Fingleton	run out	10	lbw b Hammond	12	
W. A. Brown	c Allen b Farnes	42	c Ames b Voce	32	
K. E. Rigg	c Ames b Farnes	20	(5)c Hammond b Farnes	7	
*D. G. Bradman	b Allen	26	(3)c and b Hammond	212	
S. J. McCabe	c Allen b Robins	88	(4)c Wyatt b Robins	55	
R. G. Gregory	lbw b Hammond	23	run out	50	
A. G. Chipperfield	not out	57	c Ames b Hammond	31	
†W. A. Oldfield	run out	5	c Ames b Hammond	1	
W. J. O'Reilly	c Leyland b Allen	7	c Hammond b Farnes	1	
E. L. McCormick	c Ames b Hammond	4	b Hammond	1	
L. O'B. Fleetwood-Smith	b Farnes	1	not out	4	
Extras	(lb 2, nb 3)	5	(b 10, lb 15, w 1, nb 1)	27	
Total		**288**	**Total**	**433**	

ENGLAND

H. Verity	c Bradman b O'Reilly	19	b Fleetwood-Smith	17	
C. J. Barnett	lbw b Fleetwood-Smith	129	c Chipperfield b F-Smith	21	
W. R. Hammond	c McCormick b O'Reilly	20	(4)b Fleetwood-Smith	39	
M. Leyland	c Chipperfield b F-Smith	45	(5)c Chipperfield b F-Smith	32	
R. E. S. Wyatt	c Fingleton b O'Reilly	3	(6)c Oldfield b McCabe	50	
†L. E. G. Ames	b McCormick	52	(7)lbw b Fleetwood-Smith	0	
J. Hardstaff	c and b McCormick	20	(3)b O'Reilly	43	
*G. O. Allen	lbw b Fleetwood-Smith	11	c Gregory b McCormick	9	
R. W. V. Robins	c Oldfield b O'Reilly	10	b McCormick	4	
W. Voce	c Rigg b Fleetwood-Smith	8	b Fleetwood-Smith	1	
K. Farnes	not out	0	not out	7	
Extras	(b 6, lb 2, w 1, nb 4)	13	(b 12, lb 2, nb 6)	20	
Total		**330**	**Total**	**243**	

FALL OF WICKETS

AUSTRALIA

Wkt	1st	2nd
1st	26	21
2nd	72	88
3rd	73	197
4th	136	237
5th	206	372
6th	226	422
7th	249	426
8th	271	427
9th	283	429
10th	288	433

ENGLAND

Wkt	1st	2nd
1st	53	45
2nd	108	50
3rd	190	120
4th	195	149
5th	259	190
6th	299	190
7th	304	225
8th	318	231
9th	322	235
10th	330	243

Umpires: G. Borwick, J. D. Scott

ENGLAND

	1st Innings				2nd Innings			
	O	M	R	W	O	M	R	W
Voce	12	0	49	0	20	2	86	1
Allen	16	0	60	2	14	1	61	0
Farnes	20·6	1	71	3	24	2	89	2
Hammond	6	0	30	2	15·2	1	57	5
Verity	16	4	47	0	37	17	54	0
Robins	7	1	26	1	6	0	38	1
Barnett					5	1	15	0
Leyland					2	0	6	0

AUSTRALIA

	1st Innings				2nd Innings			
	O	M	R	W	O	M	R	W
McCormick	21	2	81	2	13	1	43	2
McCabe	9	2	18	0	5	0	15	1
Fleetwood-Smith	41·4	10	129	4	30	1	110	6
O'Reilly	30	12	51	4	26	8	55	1
Chipperfield	9	1	24	0				
Gregory	3	0	14	0				

1936-37 Fifth Test, Melbourne

Test no. 139

February 26, 27, March 1, 2, 3
Toss: Australia   *Result:* Australia won by an innings and 200 runs

For the first time since 1894-95 the sides went into the final Test with two wins each. Chipperfield was injured and was replaced by Badcock, and the Australians strengthened their attack by playing fast bowler Nash instead of Brown. England, taking the opposite view, made a last attempt to stiffen the batting by playing Worthington for Robins. The latter had had an undistinguished series with bat and ball but had fielded with outstanding brilliance. The three-pronged fast attack was retained. The game was watched by the sole survivor of the first Test of all 60 years earlier—the 78-year-old Tom Garrett.

So far the side winning the toss had won the match; and when Australia batted first on a perfect wicket and in great heat the luck seemed to be running finally towards them. But England struck two early blows. Farnes had Rigg caught at the wicket at 42; and immediately after lunch Fingleton was caught at slip. McCabe was then missed at short square leg by Allen, and the next 100 runs came in 71 minutes as McCabe played brilliantly if at times chancily and Bradman batted as though making a hundred in a deciding Test was the most natural, inevitable thing in the world. Although the bowlers stuck to their task and the ground fielding rarely wilted, severe punishment was meted out as 249 runs were added in 163 minutes. Bradman reached his hundred in 2 hours 5 minutes, his third in successive Tests and his twelfth in all, and Australia at the close were 342 for 3, Bradman 165 not out.

When Bradman was bowled by Farnes early next morning the history of the series strongly suggested that England would soon be back in the game. But the two youngest players in the side, the solidly-built Badcock and the frail Gregory, put Australia's supremacy beyond all reasonable doubt in a stand of 161. Going in on the third morning facing a total of 604, England lost their first four wickets for 140, and the stand that developed between Hardstaff (73 not out) and Wyatt towards the end of the day seemed a forlorn hope. Even more did it seem so next morning after heavy rain in the night. A tired and beaten side, England batted apathetically and were all out for a second time on the fifth morning.

For Australia, the batting of Bradman and the bowling of Fleetwood-Smith were decisive, while O'Reilly, although often bowling defensively, was never mastered. England lost their impetus too soon, and Allen wore himself out. But Ames emerged as a class wicket-keeper, and Hardstaff gained a great reputation as an outfielder.

AUSTRALIA

J. H. Fingleton	c Voce b Farnes	17
K. E. Rigg	c Ames b Farnes	28
*D. G. Bradman	b Farnes	169
S. J. McCabe	c Farnes b Verity	112
C. L. Badcock	c Worthington b Voce	118
R. G. Gregory	c Verity b Farnes	80
†W. A. Oldfield	c Ames b Voce	21
L. J. Nash	c Ames b Farnes	17
W. J. O'Reilly	b Voce	1
E. L. McCormick	not out	17
L. O'B. Fleetwood-Smith	b Farnes	13
Extras	(b 1, lb 5, w 1, nb 4)	11
Total		**604**

ENGLAND

C. J. Barnett	c Oldfield b Nash	18	lbw b O'Reilly	41
T. S. Worthington	hit wkt b Fleetwood-Smith	44	c Bradman b McCormick	6
J. Hardstaff	c McCormick b O'Reilly	83	b Nash	1
W. R. Hammond	c Nash b O'Reilly	14	c Bradman b O'Reilly	56
M. Leyland	b O'Reilly	7	c McCormick b F-Smith	28
R. E. S. Wyatt	c Bradman b O'Reilly	38	run out	9
†L. E. G. Ames	b Nash	19	c McCabe b McCormick	11
*G. O. Allen	c Oldfield b Nash	0	c Nash b O'Reilly	7
H. Verity	c Rigg b Nash	0	not out	2
W. Voce	st Oldfield b O'Reilly	3	c Badcock b F-Smith	1
K. Farnes	not out	0	c Nash b Fleetwood-Smith	0
Extras	(lb 12, nb 1)	13	(lb 3)	3
Total		**239**	**Total**	**165**

FALL OF WICKETS

AUSTRALIA
Wkt	1st	2nd
1st	42	—
2nd	54	—
3rd	303	—
4th	346	—
5th	507	—
6th	544	—
7th	563	—
8th	571	—
9th	576	—
10th	604	—

ENGLAND
Wkt	1st	2nd
1st	33	9
2nd	96	10
3rd	130	70
4th	140	121
5th	202	142
6th	236	142
7th	236	153
8th	236	162
9th	239	165
10th	239	165

Umpires: G. Borwick, J. D. Scott

ENGLAND

	1st Innings O	M	R	W	2nd Innings O	M	R	W
Allen	17	0	99	0				
Farnes	28·5	5	96	6				
Voce	29	3	123	3				
Hammond	16	1	62	0				
Verity	41	5	127	1				
Worthington	6	0	60	0				
Leyland	3	0	26	0				

AUSTRALIA

	1st Innings O	M	R	W	2nd Innings O	M	R	W
McCormick	13	1	54	0	9	0	33	2
Nash	17·5	1	70	4	7	1	34	1
O'Reilly	23	7	51	5	19	6	58	3
Fleetwood-Smith	18	3	51	1	13·2	3	36	3
McCabe					1	0	1	0

Averages: 1936-37

AUSTRALIA

BATTING	M.	Inns.	N.O.	Runs	H.S.	Av.
D. G. Bradman	5	9	0	810	270	90·00
S. J. McCabe	5	9	0	491	112	54·55
R. G. Gregory	2	3	0	153	80	51·00
J. H. Fingleton	5	9	0	398	136	44·22
A. G. Chipperfield	3	6	2	155	57*	38·75
C. L. Badcock	3	4	0	128	118	32·00
W. A. Brown	2	4	0	95	42	23·75
K. E. Rigg	3	5	0	118	47	23·60
M. W. S. Sievers	3	6	1	67	25*	13·40
W. A. Oldfield	5	9	1	79	27*	9·87
E. L. McCormick	4	6	2	33	17*	8·25
W. J. O'Reilly	5	9	1	56	37*	7·00
L. O'B. Fleetwood-Smith	3	4	1	18	13	6·00
F. A. Ward	3	6	1	27	18	5·40

PLAYED IN ONE TEST: L. J. Nash 17, L. S. Darling 20 and 0, L. P. J. O'Brien 0 and 17, R. H. Robinson 2 and 3.

BOWLING	Overs	Mds.	Runs	Wkts.	Av.
M. W. S. Sievers	75·2	25	161	9	17·88
L. J. Nash	24·5	2	104	5	20·80
W. J. O'Reilly	247·6	89	555	25	22·20
L. O'B. Fleetwood-Smith	131·4	20	463	19	24·36
E. L. McCormick	84	6	316	11	28·72
F. A. Ward	136	28	432	11	39·27

ALSO BOWLED: S. J. McCabe 42–5–128–4, R. G. Gregory 3–0–14–0, A. G. Chipperfield 43–8–136–0.

ENGLAND

BATTING	M.	Inns.	N.O.	Runs	H.S.	Av.
W. R. Hammond	5	9	1	468	231*	58·50
M. Leyland	5	9	1	441	126	55·12
C. J. Barnett	5	9	0	395	129	43·88
J. Hardstaff	5	9	0	256	83	28·44
R. E. S. Wyatt	2	4	0	100	50	25·00
R. W. V. Robins	4	6	0	113	61	18·83
G. O. Allen	5	9	1	150	68	18·75
L. E. G. Ames	5	9	0	166	52	18·44
A. E. Fagg	2	3	0	42	27	14·00
T. S. Worthington	3	6	0	74	44	12·33
H. Verity	5	9	2	75	19	10·71
K. Farnes	2	4	3	7	7*	7·00
W. Voce	5	8	3	19	8	3·80
J. M. Sims	2	2	0	3	3	1·50

BOWLING	Overs	Mds.	Runs	Wkts.	Av.
W. Voce	162·1	20	560	26	21·53
K. Farnes	73·3	8	256	11	23·27
W. R. Hammond	88·4	8	301	12	25·08
G. O. Allen	128·7	12	526	17	30·94
H. Verity	195·7	57	455	10	45·50

ALSO BOWLED: R. W. V. Robins 56–3–220–4, J. M. Sims 51–2–244–3, T. S. Worthington 10–0–78–0, M. Leyland 5–0–32–0, C. J. Barnett 5–1–15–0.

Averages: 1938

ENGLAND

BATTING	M.	Inns.	N.O.	Runs	H.S.	Av.
L. Hutton	3	4	0	473	364	118·25
E. Paynter	4	6	2	407	216*	101·75
J. Hardstaff	2	3	1	184	169*	92·00
W. R. Hammond	4	6	0	403	240	67·16
L. E. G. Ames	2	3	0	135	83	45·00
C. J. Barnett	3	5	0	215	126	43·00
D. C. S. Compton	4	6	1	214	102	42·80
H. Verity	4	6	2	52	25*	13·00
D. V. P. Wright	3	5	2	39	22	13·00
W. J. Edrich	4	6	0	67	28	11·16
K. Farnes	4	3	1	14	7	7·00
W. E. Bowes	2	2	0	3	3	1·50

PLAYED IN ONE TEST: M. Leyland 187, A. Wood 53, A. W. Wellard 4 and 38, R. A. Sinfield 6, W. F. F. Price 0 and 6.

BOWLING	Overs	Mds.	Runs	Wkts.	Av.
W. E. Bowes	75·4	12	188	10	18·80
H. Verity	154·1	53	354	14	25·28
K. Farnes	179·4	32	581	17	34·17
D. V. P. Wright	120	20	426	12	35·50

ALSO BOWLED: M. Leyland 8·1–0–30–1, W. J. Edrich 35·2–6–139–4, A. W. Wellard 32–3–126–3, R. A. Sinfield 63–16–123–2, C. J. Barnett 1–0–10–0, W. R. Hammond 33–12–67–0.

AUSTRALIA

BATTING	M.	Inns.	N.O.	Runs	H.S.	Av.
D. G. Bradman	4	6	2	434	144*	108·50
W. A. Brown	4	8	1	512	206*	73·14
S. J. McCabe	4	8	0	362	232	45·25
B. A. Barnett	4	8	1	195	57	27·85
A. L. Hassett	4	8	0	199	56	24·87
J. H. Fingleton	4	6	0	123	40	20·50
L. O'B. Fleetwood-Smith	4	5	3	30	16*	15·00
W. J. O'Reilly	4	5	1	60	42	15·00
C. L. Badcock	4	8	1	32	9	4·57
M. G. Waite	2	3	0	11	8	3·66
E. L. McCormick	3	3	0	2	2	0·66

PLAYED IN ONE TEST: S. G. Barnes 41 and 33, F. A. Ward 2 and 7*, A. G. Chipperfield 1.

BOWLING	Overs	Mds.	Runs	Wkts.	Av.
W. J. O'Reilly	263	78	610	22	27·72
E. L. McCormick	114	20	345	10	34·50
L. O'B. Fleetwood-Smith	217·5	34	727	14	51·92

ALSO BOWLED: S. G. Barnes 38–3–84–1, S. J. McCabe 103–19–293–2, M. G. Waite 92–23–190–1, D. G. Bradman 2·2–1–6–0, A. G. Chipperfield 8·4–0–51–0, A. L. Hassett 13–2–52–0, F. A. Ward 30–2–142–0.

1938 First Test, Trent Bridge

June 10, 11, 13, 14
Toss: England   *Result:* Match Drawn

In halving the rubber and retaining the Ashes Australia owed almost everything to Bradman, Brown and O'Reilly, and to a wonderful innings by McCabe at Trent Bridge. Hassett, Fingleton and Badcock did little, while injuries restricted the appearances of Barnes and Chipperfield. McCormick was only fleetingly effective and Fleetwood-Smith was expensive; but although O'Reilly, like everyone else, suffered from overprepared wickets, he won the match for Australia when the chance came at Leeds. England's misfortune in losing Hutton and Ames through injury for this match, however, was a major factor, as was the failure of the selectors to reconstruct the side. As in 1934, the wicket and weather at the Oval gave the side batting first an overwhelming advantage.

In the first over Barnett cut McCormick into the gully, where Brown missed a difficult catch, and in the third over Hutton played on without disturbing a bail. Barnett then unleashed a stream of strokes, making 51 out of 70 inside an hour, and although dropped by Bradman from a hard hit to mid off he made 98 before lunch out of 169, reaching his century from the first ball after the break. The 22-year-old Hutton batted for 3 hours 20 minutes, and after Edrich and

Hammond had gone cheaply Paynter and Compton took the score to 422 for 4 by the close. Paynter, 36, gave an object lesson in the playing of slow spin, Compton, 20, made a brilliant hundred in 2¼ hours, and when they were parted they had put on 206. England declared at 3.15 on the second afternoon, and Australia began badly when Fingleton pulled a ball on to his wicket in Wright's first over. Bradman and Brown were both out before stumps, when Australia were 138 for 3.

Next morning Ward, the night-watchman, was bowled by Farnes, Hassett was caught driving at a leg-break, and Badcock was bowled by Wright—194 for 6. The left-handed Barnett then helped McCabe in a stand of 69, Hammond relying on spin until after lunch, when Barnett was immediately out to the new ball. McCabe then outwitted all Hammond's manoeuvres to deprive him of the strike and by brilliant stroke-play made 127 out of 148 in 80 minutes after the 7th wicket fell.

Hammond had saved Verity for the follow on; but the lack of a second fast bowler was again felt, and Australia, 247 runs behind, held on for more than eight hours with grim concentration, surviving skilfully on the last day when the ball began to turn. Brown batted 5 hours 20 minutes and radman 6 hours 5 minutes, his hundred containing 56 singles and only two fours.

ENGLAND

C. J. Barnett	b McCormick	126
L. Hutton	lbw b Fleetwood-Smith	100
W. J. Edrich	b O'Reilly	5
*W. R. Hammond	b O'Reilly	26
E. Paynter	not out	216
D. C. S. Compton	c Badcock b F-Smith	102
†L. E. G. Ames	b Fleetwood-Smith	46
H. Verity	b Fleetwood-Smith	3
R. A. Sinfield	lbw b O'Reilly	6
D. V. P. Wright	not out	1
K. Farnes	did not bat	
Extras	(b 1, lb 22, nb 4)	27
Total	(8 wkts dec)	**658**

AUSTRALIA

	1st innings		2nd innings	
J. H. Fingleton	b Wright	9	c Hammond b Edrich	40
W. A. Brown	c Ames b Farnes	48	c Paynter b Verity	133
*D. G. Bradman	c Ames b Sinfield	51	not out	144
S. J. McCabe	c Compton b Verity	232	c Hammond b Verity	39
F. A. Ward	b Farnes	2	(8)not out	7
A. L. Hassett	c Hammond b Wright	1	(5)c Compton b Verity	2
C. L. Badcock	b Wright	9	(6)b Wright	5
†B. A. Barnett	c Wright b Farnes	22	(7)lbw b Sinfield	31
W. J. O'Reilly	c Paynter b Farnes	9		
E. L. McCormick	b Wright	2		
L. O'B. Fleetwood-Smith	not out	5		
Extras	(b 10, lb 10, w 1)	21	(b 5, lb 16, nb 5)	26
Total		**411**	**Total** (6 wkts dec)	**427**

FALL OF WICKETS

ENGLAND

Wkt	1st	2nd
1st	219	—
2nd	240	—
3rd	244	—
4th	281	—
5th	487	—
6th	577	—
7th	597	—
8th	626	—
9th	—	—
10th	—	—

AUSTRALIA

Wkt	1st	2nd
1st	34	89
2nd	111	259
3rd	134	331
4th	144	337
5th	151	369
6th	194	417
7th	263	—
8th	319	—
9th	334	—
10th	411	—

Umpires: F. Chester, E. Robinson

AUSTRALIA

	1st Innings				2nd Innings			
	O	M	R	W	O	M	R	W
McCormick	32	4	108	1	..			
O'Reilly	56	11	164	3	..			
McCabe	21	5	64	0	..			
Fleetwood-Smith	49	9	153	4	..			
Ward	30	2	142	0	..			

ENGLAND

	1st Innings				2nd Innings			
	O	M	R	W	O	M	R	W
Farnes	37	11	106	4	24	2	78	0
Hammond	19	6	44	0	12	6	15	0
Sinfield	28	8	51	1	35	8	72	1
Wright	39	6	153	4	37	8	85	1
Verity	7·3	0	36	1	62	27	102	3
Edrich					13	2	39	1
Barnett					1	0	10	0

1938 Second Test, Lord's

June 24, 25, 27, 28
Toss: England   *Result:* Match Drawn

On a green wicket, against some hostile fast bowling by McCormick, England lost 3 wickets in half an hour for 31. Nevertheless they were 134 for 3 at lunch, Hammond, safe and dominant from the start, running to his 50 in 68 minutes and Paynter showing something of Sutcliffe's ability to stick when not quite in touch. Hammond's hundred came in 2 hours 25 minutes. Paynter actually outscored him after lunch, but was lbw to O'Reilly when 99. Apart from a vicious drive into the covers at 87 to which O'Reilly got a hand, Hammond gave no chance, his innings being packed with glorious strokes, and at stumps England were 409 for 5, Hammond 210, Ames 50.

Facing a total of 494, Fingleton and Brown made a sound start, but Bradman chopped on a ball from Verity that came in with the arm, and when McCabe was brilliantly caught off a meaty cut Australia were 152 for 3. Hassett helped Brown to add 124, and the shine had long since departed from the second new ball when Wellard got Hassett lbw. Two balls later he bowled Badcock, and at stumps Australia were 299 for 5, Brown 140 not out.

On the third morning Verity at once dismissed Barnett; and Chipperfield, who had injured a finger fielding, was lbw at 308 for 7. 37 were still required to save the follow on, but the England attack again failed at a critical time, O'Reilly hitting two sixes and helping Brown to put on 85 in 46 minutes. Farnes was baulked of a hat trick when Compton dropped Fleetwood-Smith at slip, and after 3 hours had been lost through rain Australia finished only 72 behind. Missed off Wellard at 184, Brown carried his bat in a match-saving innings.

Apprehensions that England might find themselves in difficulties on the damp wicket suddenly acquired force as McCormick made the ball lift nastily and England lost 2 wickets for 39 before stumps. On the last morning Edrich was caught hooking and Verity had his off stump knocked back, and when Hammond, incommoded by a strain, was 5th out at 76 England were only 148 in front. Paynter and Compton added 52 while the wicket dried out, but Paynter ran himself out, Ames, who had broken a finger, was caught at slip off the second ball after lunch, and only free scoring by Compton and Wellard removed all danger. Australia were left to survive the last 170 minutes, and Bradman, never seeming to consider the possibility of defeat, batted almost light-heartedly and reached his century just before the close.

B

ENGLAND

Batsman	1st Innings			2nd Innings	
C. J. Barnett	c Brown b McCormick	18		c McCabe b McCormick	12
L. Hutton	c Brown b McCormick	4		c McCormick b O'Reilly	5
W. J. Edrich	b McCormick	0		(4)c McCabe b McCormick	10
*W. R. Hammond	b McCormick	240		(6)c sub (M. G. Waite) b McCabe	2
E. Paynter	lbw b O'Reilly	99		run out	43
D. C. S. Compton	lbw b O'Reilly	6		(7)not out	76
†L. E. G. Ames	c McCormick b F-Smith	83		(8)c McCabe b O'Reilly	6
H. Verity	b O'Reilly	5		(3)b McCormick	11
A. W. Wellard	c McCormick b O'Reilly	4		b McCabe	38
D. V. P. Wright	b Fleetwood-Smith	6		not out	10
K. Farnes	not out	5			
Extras	(b 1, lb 12, w 1, nb 10)	24		(b 12, lb 12, w 1, nb 4)	29
Total		**494**		**Total (8 wkts dec)**	**242**

AUSTRALIA

Batsman	1st Innings			2nd Innings	
J. H. Fingleton	c Hammond b Wright	31		c Hammond b Wellard	4
W. A. Brown	not out	206		b Verity	10
*D. G. Bradman	b Verity	18		not out	102
S. J. McCabe	c Verity b Farnes	38		c Hutton b Verity	21
A. L. Hassett	lbw b Wellard	56		b Wright	42
C. L. Badcock	b Wellard	0		c Wright b Edrich	0
†B. A. Barnett	c Compton b Verity	8		c Paynter b Edrich	14
A. G. Chipperfield	lbw b Verity	1			
W. J. O'Reilly	b Farnes	42			
E. L. McCormick	c Barnett b Farnes	0			
L. O'B. Fleetwood-Smith	c Barnett b Verity	7			
Extras	(b 1, lb 8, nb 6)	15		(b 5, lb 3, w 2, nb 1)	11
Total		**422**		**Total (6 wkts)**	**204**

FALL OF WICKETS

ENGLAND

Wkt	1st	2nd
1st	12	25
2nd	20	28
3rd	31	43
4th	253	64
5th	271	76
6th	457	128
7th	472	142
8th	476	216
9th	483	—
10th	494	—

AUSTRALIA

Wkt	1st	2nd
1st	69	8
2nd	101	71
3rd	152	111
4th	276	175
5th	276	180
6th	307	204
7th	308	—
8th	393	—
9th	393	—
10th	422	—

Umpires: E. J. Smith, F. Walden

AUSTRALIA	1st Innings				2nd Innings			
	O	M	R	W	O	M	R	W
McCormick	27	1	101	4	24	5	72	3
McCabe	31	4	86	0	12	1	58	2
Fleetwood-Smith	33·5	2	139	2	7	1	30	0
O'Reilly	37	6	93	4	29	10	53	2
Chipperfield	8·4	0	51	0				

ENGLAND	1st Innings				2nd Innings			
	O	M	R	W	O	M	R	W
Farnes	43	6	135	3	13	3	51	0
Wellard	23	2	96	2	9	1	30	1
Wright	16	2	68	1	8	0	56	1
Verity	35·4	9	103	4	13	5	29	2
Edrich	4	2	5	0	5·2	0	27	2

109. **M. Leyland**

110. **L. O'B. Fleetwood-Smith**

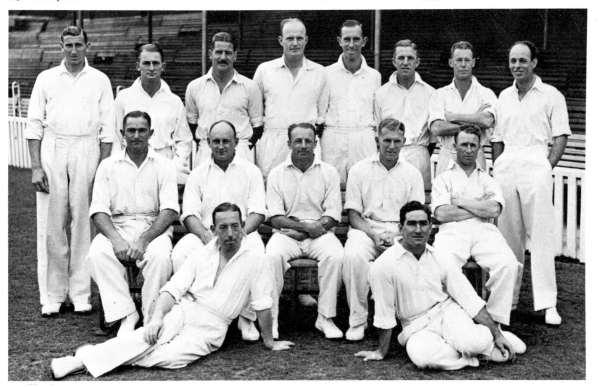

111. **Australia 1938**
Back row: E. L. McCormick, M. G. Waite, L. O'B. Fleetwood-Smith, W. J. O'Reilly, E. S. White, F. A. Ward, W. A. Brown, J. H. W. Fingleton. *Middle row:* S. G. Barnes, S. J. McCabe, D. G. Bradman (capt.), B. A. Barnett, C. W. Walker. *Front:* A. L. Hassett, C. L. Badcock.

July 22, 23, 25
Toss: England *Result:* Australia won by five wickets

After one of the most thrilling Tests ever played, Australia won by 5 wickets at Leeds; and as the Manchester Test had been entirely washed out, England could do no more than square the series if they won at the Oval, so Australia retained the Ashes. It was a bitter disappointment for England after their showing in the first two games, and the background to their defeat is as fascinating as the match itself.

Most significant was the absence through injury of Hutton, Ames and Leyland. In anticipation of a feather-bed wicket, the pace bowlers chosen at Manchester had been Nichols and Smailes; but at Leeds, preparation of the wicket had been hampered by rain, and with the prospect of a pitch with some life in it the selectors chose Farnes and Bowes. This strengthened the attack but weakened the batting. Gibb, chosen to keep wicket, did not recover in time from injury, and at this point the whole selection ought to have been reviewed and the side reconstructed; but the selectors kept to their policy of playing the strongest possible attack, simply replacing Gibb with Price. Perhaps England's heavy scoring in the first two Tests had blinded the selectors to the menace of O'Reilly. Anyway, when England won the toss at Leeds their line-up was six batsmen plus Price, Verity, Wright, Farnes and Bowes.

Bradman seems to have appreciated from the start that Australia's chance had come. The ball turned, the first hour produced only 29 runs, and England at lunch were 62 for 2—against 169 for 0 at Trent Bridge. Barnett batted 2 hours 25 minutes for 30, and only Hammond played with any freedom until Verity and Wright hit out at the end. With wicket-keeper Barnett sent in as night-watchman, Australia at stumps were 32 for 1, 191 behind.

The powerful England attack was held up next day by a workmanlike knock from B. A. Barnett, but the decisive innings came from Bradman. With rain threatening, and in light that for much of the day was appalling, Bradman cut, drove, deflected and swept his way to a remarkable century while his team strove desperately to provide him with partners. Australia led by 19, and before stumps Barnett and Edrich had put England ahead in a stand of 49; but next day O'Reilly destroyed the shallow England batting, the tail gave no trouble, and Australia were left with only 105 to win.

Once again the Australians batted through sepulchral light, determined to take their chance before the rain came; and although England had four wickets down for 61, including Bradman's, and the game was wide open again, an aggressive vignette of an innings from Hassett (who was missed at slip second ball) carried the day.

ENGLAND

W. J. Edrich	b O'Reilly	12	st Barnett b F-Smith	28	
C. J. Barnett	c Barnett b McCormick	30	c Barnett b McCormick	29	
J. Hardstaff	run out	4	b O'Reilly	11	
*W. R. Hammond	b O'Reilly	76	c Brown b O'Reilly	0	
E. Paynter	st Barnett b F-Smith	28	not out	21	
D. C. S. Compton	b O'Reilly	14	c Barnett b O'Reilly	15	
†W. F. F. Price	c McCabe b O'Reilly	0	lbw b Fleetwood-Smith	6	
H. Verity	not out	25	b Fleetwood-Smith	0	
D. V. P. Wright	c Fingleton b F-Smith	22	c Waite b Fleetwood-Smith	0	
K. Farnes	c Fingleton b F-Smith	2	b O'Reilly	7	
W. E. Bowes	b O'Reilly	3	lbw b O'Reilly	0	
Extras	(lb 4, nb 3)	7	(lb 4, w 1, nb 1)	6	
Total		**223**	**Total**	**123**	

AUSTRALIA

J. H. Fingleton	b Verity	30	lbw b Verity	9
W. A. Brown	b Wright	22	lbw b Farnes	9
†B. A. Barnett	c Price b Farnes	57	(7)not out	15
*D. G. Bradman	b Bowes	103	(3)c Verity b Wright	16
S. J. McCabe	b Farnes	1	(4)c Barnett b Wright	15
C. L. Badcock	b Bowes	4	not out	5
A. L. Hassett	c Hammond b Wright	13	(5)c Edrich b Wright	33
M. G. Waite	c Price b Farnes	3		
W. J. O'Reilly	c Hammond b Farnes	2		
E. L. McCormick	b Bowes	0		
L. O'B. Fleetwood-Smith	not out	2		
Extras	(b 2, lb 3)	5	(b 4, nb 1)	5
Total		**242**	**Total** (5 wkts)	**107**

FALL OF WICKETS

ENGLAND

Wkt	1st	2nd
1st	29	60
2nd	34	73
3rd	88	73
4th	142	73
5th	171	96
6th	171	116
7th	172	116
8th	213	116
9th	215	123
10th	223	123

AUSTRALIA

Wkt	1st	2nd
1st	28	17
2nd	87	32
3rd	128	50
4th	136	61
5th	145	91
6th	195	—
7th	232	—
8th	240	—
9th	240	—
10th	242	—

Umpires: F. Chester, E. J. Smith

AUSTRALIA	1st Innings					2nd Innings			
	O	M	R	W		O	M	R	W
McCormick	20	6	46	1	..	11	4	18	1
Waite	18	7	31	0	..	2	0	9	0
O'Reilly	34.1	17	66	5	..	21.5	8	56	5
Fleetwood-Smith	25	7	73	3	..	16	4	34	4
McCabe	1	1	0	0	..				

ENGLAND	1st Innings					2nd Innings			
	O	M	R	W		O	M	R	W
Farnes	26	3	77	4	..	11.3	4	17	1
Bowes	35.4	6	79	3	..	11	0	35	0
Wright	15	4	38	2	..	5	0	26	3
Verity	19	6	30	1	..	5	2	24	1
Edrich	3	0	13	0	..				

1938 Fourth Test, Oval

August 20, 22, 23, 24
Toss: England   *Result:* England won by an innings and 579 runs

After their experience at Leeds England had every excuse for packing their side with batting, but with Farnes, Bowes and Verity as their only front-line bowlers they were lucky to win the toss—for the fourth time. Wright was injured, Barnett dropped, and Wood replaced Price. Altogether with the recall of Leyland the side contained five Yorkshiremen. Australia's problems for this timeless Test were similar, and they answered them in the same way. McCormick was not fully fit, and instead of bringing in another bowler they preferred to play Barnes, relying on O'Reilly and Fleetwood-Smith, anticipating perhaps that the toss must go their way. Thus when Hutton and Edrich opened for England on a wicket made to last they faced nothing more hostile than Waite and McCabe.

O'Reilly threatened briefly to cut the match down to size when he dismissed Edrich at 29; but he was then confronted by an old antagonist in the 38-year-old Maurice Leyland. While Hutton, playing entirely from the crease, scored steadily with drives, cuts and deflections to leg, Leyland frequently moved in to the pitch of the ball to get his powerful forearms working, and between them they took the score to 347 for 1 at stumps, Hutton 160, Leyland 156. 35 minutes were lost through rain on Monday morning, after which the two Yorkshiremen continued

until their stand was worth 382; then the Australian fielding, which had been brilliant all through, brought about the downfall of Leyland. At lunch England were 434 for 2. Hutton and Hammond put on 135; but in a period of rain and bad light following Hammond's dismissal England lost Paynter and Compton for the addition of only 9 runs. 555 for 5, with only Hardstaff of the batsmen to come, was by no means a winning position: Australia's scores in the previous two Oval Tests—1930 and 1934—had been 695 and 701.

At stumps on the second day England were 634 for 5—Hutton 300, Hardstaff 40. Hutton had already batted longer than any man had batted before; and next morning the whole Australian team strove to defend their captain's record of 334. In this period no one bowled better than Fleetwood-Smith; but after 12 hours 19 minutes at the crease Hutton took his score to 335.

The pitch was still perfect, Hardstaff completed his hundred, and as injuries deprived Australia of first Fingleton and then Bradman, Hammond eventually declared. Brown, last out in the Australian first innings, just missed carrying his bat for the second time in the series, but otherwise the demoralisation of the Australians was complete.

ENGLAND

L. Hutton	c Hassett b O'Reilly	364
W. J. Edrich	lbw b O'Reilly	12
M. Leyland	run out	187
*W. R. Hammond	lbw b Fleetwood-Smith	59
E. Paynter	lbw b O'Reilly	0
D. C. S. Compton	b Waite	1
J. Hardstaff	not out	169
†A. Wood	c and b Barnes	53
H. Verity	not out	8
K. Farnes	} did not bat	
W. E. Bowes		
Extras	(b 22, lb 19, w 1, nb 8)	50
Total	(7 wkts dec)	**903**

AUSTRALIA

W. A. Brown	c Hammond b Leyland	69	c Edrich b Farnes	15
C. L. Badcock	c Hardstaff b Bowes	0	b Bowes	9
S. J. McCabe	c Edrich b Farnes	14	c Wood b Farnes	2
A. L. Hassett	c Compton b Edrich	42	lbw b Bowes	10
S. G. Barnes	b Bowes	41	lbw b Verity	33
†B. A. Barnett	c Wood b Bowes	2	b Farnes	46
M. G. Waite	b Bowes	8	c Edrich b Verity	0
W. J. O'Reilly	c Wood b Bowes	0	not out	7
L. O'B. Fleetwood-Smith	not out	16	c Leyland b Farnes	0
*D. G. Bradman	absent hurt	—	absent hurt	—
J. H. Fingleton	absent hurt	—	absent hurt	—
Extras	(b 4, lb 2, nb 3)	9	(b 1)	1
Total		**201**	**Total**	**123**

FALL OF WICKETS

ENGLAND

Wkt	1st	2nd
1st	29	—
2nd	411	—
3rd	546	—
4th	547	—
5th	555	—
6th	770	—
7th	876	—
8th	—	—
9th	—	—
10th	—	—

AUSTRALIA

Wkt	1st	2nd
1st	0	15
2nd	19	18
3rd	70	35
4th	145	41
5th	147	115
6th	160	115
7th	160	117
8th	201	123
9th	—	—
10th	—	—

Umpires: F. Chester, F. Walden

AUSTRALIA	1st Innings				2nd Innings			
	O	M	R	W	O	M	R	W
Waite	72	16	150	1				
McCabe	38	8	85	0				
O'Reilly	85	26	178	3				
Fleetwood-Smith	87	11	298	1				
Barnes	38	3	84	1				
Hassett	13	2	52	0				
Bradman	2·2	1	6	0				

ENGLAND	1st Innings				2nd Innings			
	O	M	R	W	O	M	R	W
Farnes	13	2	54	1	12·1	1	63	4
Bowes	19	3	49	5	10	3	25	2
Edrich	10	2	55	1				
Verity	5	1	15	0	7	3	15	2
Leyland	3·1	0	11	1	5	0	19	0
Hammond	2	0	8	0				

1946-47 First Test, Brisbane

November 29, 30, December 2, 3, 4
Toss: Australia *Result:* Australia won by an innings and 332 runs

Whereas Australia, as in 1920-21, jumped back into Test cricket with one of their strongest sides ever, English cricket was slow to recover from the war. The batting looked secure enough, but Hutton and Compton did little in the first three Tests, and the failure of Hammond was the tragedy of the series. Although Bedser and Wright strove manfully, the bowling was weak, the only support coming from Yardley and Edrich, who were among the successes of the tour. Australia showed considerable batting strength, with the left-handed Morris the outstanding newcomer apart from the all-rounder Miller; but the principal difference in the sides lay in the bowling. Lindwall and Miller were the most formidable opening pair since Gregory and McDonald, and the spin bowling was so strong and varied that the problem became who to leave out; no less than five bowlers took 10 or more wickets in the series. England had cruel luck with the umpiring, especially when Bradman, beginning uncertainly in the innings that was clearly to determine his future as a Test player, sliced a Voce half-volley to second slip, where Ikin made what seemed a perfectly good catch: Bradman was given not out, and he went on to make 187 in that innings and 234 in his 1.ext. The series introduced two great wicket-keepers in Tallon and Evans.

At 12.15 on the first day, after Morris had been caught at slip off Bedser, Bradman at the age of 38, after a long period of ill health, made his first appearance in Test cricket since his unhappy exit eight years earlier. Several snicks and pushes all but went to hand as he tried to establish himself, Barnes was out at 46, and just before lunch came the incident of the Ikin catch. After lunch Bradman began to look more assured, and with Hassett a model of correct technique the score was taken to 292 for 2 at stumps, Bradman 162, Hassett 81. By this time Bradman's confidence was fully restored.

Next day Hassett continued his long defensive innings, reaching 100 in 5 hours 44 minutes. Miller hit his first 50 in 80 minutes, and on a docile wicket the England bowling limitations were fully exposed as McCool and Johnson added 131. When England batted the fast bowling at once forced the hurried stroke, but the innings was soon interrupted by showers and bad light.

A violent thunderstorm in the night gave England a spiteful wicket to bat on, and although Edrich and Hammond showed wonderful skill as England struggled to 117 for 5, a second thunderstorm made saving the match impossible, invalidating the result as any measure of relative strength.

AUSTRALIA

S. G. Barnes	c Bedser b Wright	31
A. R. Morris	c Hammond b Bedser	2
*D. G. Bradman	b Edrich	187
A. L. Hassett	c Yardley b Bedser	128
K. R. Miller	lbw b Wright	79
C. L. McCool	lbw b Wright	95
I. W. Johnson	lbw b Wright	47
†D. Tallon	lbw b Edrich	14
R. R. Lindwall	c Voce b Wright	31
G. E. Tribe	c Gibb b Edrich	1
E. R. H. Toshack	not out	1
Extras	(b 5, lb 11, w 2, nb 11)	29
Total		**645**

ENGLAND

Batsman	1st Innings	Runs	2nd Innings	Runs
L. Hutton	b Miller	7	c Barnes b Miller	0
C. Washbrook	c Barnes b Miller	6	c Barnes b Miller	13
W. J. Edrich	c McCool b Miller	16	lbw b Toshack	7
D. C. S. Compton	lbw b Miller	17	c Barnes b Toshack	15
*W. R. Hammond	lbw b Toshack	32	b Toshack	23
J. T. Ikin	c Tallon b Miller	0	b Tribe	32
N. W. D. Yardley	c Tallon b Toshack	29	c Hassett b Toshack	0
†P. A. Gibb	b Miller	13	lbw b Toshack	11
W. Voce	not out	1	c Hassett b Tribe	18
A. V. Bedser	lbw b Miller	0	c and b Toshack	18
D. V. P. Wright	c Tallon b Toshack	4	not out	10
Extras	(b 8, lb 3, w 2, nb 3)	16	(b 15, lb 7, w 1, nb 2)	25
Total		**141**		**172**

FALL OF WICKETS

AUSTRALIA

Wkt	1st	2nd
1st	9	—
2nd	46	—
3rd	322	—
4th	428	—
5th	465	—
6th	596	—
7th	599	—
8th	629	—
9th	643	—
10th	645	—

ENGLAND

Wkt	1st	2nd
1st	10	0
2nd	25	13
3rd	49	33
4th	56	62
5th	56	65
6th	121	65
7th	134	112
8th	136	114
9th	136	143
10th	141	172

Umpires: G. Borwick, J. D. Scott

ENGLAND	1st Innings O	M	R	W	2nd Innings O	M	R	W
Voce	28	9	92	0	..			
Bedser	41	5	159	2	..			
Wright	43·6	4	167	5	..			
Edrich	25	2	107	3	..			
Yardley	13	1	47	0	..			
Ikin	2	0	24	0	..			
Compton	6	0	20	0	..			

AUSTRALIA	1st Innings O	M	R	W	2nd Innings O	M	R	W
Lindwall	12	4	23	0	..			
Miller	22	4	60	7	..	11	3	17	2
Toshack	16·5	11	17	3	..	20·7	2	82	6
Tribe	9	2	19	0	..	12	2	48	2
McCool	1	0	5	0	..			
Barnes	1	0	1	0	..			

112. T. G. Evans

113. A. R. Morris

114. **England 1946-47**
Back row: James Langridge, D. C. S. Compton, T. G. Evans, L. Hutton. *Middle row:* D. V. P. Wright, C. Washbrook, J. T. Ikin, A. V. Bedser, R. Pollard, T. P. B. Smith, R. Howard (manager). *Front row:* W. Voce, P. A. Gibb, N. W. D. Yardley, W. R. Hammond (capt.), W. J. Edrich, L. B. Fishlock, J. Hardstaff.

1946-47 Second Test, Sydney

December 13, 14, 16, 17, 18, 19
Toss: England   *Result:* Australia won by an innings and 33 runs

Apart from Edrich the England batsmen were wretchedly firm-footed against the leg-spin of McCool and the flighted off-breaks of Johnson, and although Ikin played coolly and firmly England were all out on a perfect wicket for 255. Australia missed Lindwall (chickenpox), but the innings was broken by McCool, who got Compton and Hammond cheaply after two wickets had fallen for 88. Bradman was off the field with a strain on the second morning, when the England innings closed, but rain and bad light delayed the Australian reply and at stumps they were 27 for 1.

After a dry weekend the wicket rolled out perfectly on the third morning, and when Johnson, the night-watchman, was disposed of England were confronted by the masterly defence of Barnes and Hassett. Wright beat them both without getting them out, but after lunch Hassett was caught at long leg. Miller played well until he was caught at slip off Smith, who had come into the side for Voce, and Bradman entered at 159 for 4. Before close of play at 252 for 4 Barnes had reached 109 in 6 hours and Bradman had passed his 50. Barnes had batted the entire day for 88.

The partnership continued for most of the fourth day until Bradman, who had been assimilating rather than seeking runs, began to hit out and was lbw, having just overhauled Barnes. He had batted 6½ hours and although beaten at times by Wright had given no chance. Barnes was out a moment later, having shown impregnable defence for 10 hours 42 minutes. The partnership yielded 405, a record in Australia.

After inspecting the pitch on the fifth morning Bradman batted on, declaring to leave England 24 minutes' batting before lunch, facing a deficit of 404. In a thrilling display against a close-set field Hutton then made 37 out of 49 but lost his grip on his bat to the last ball before lunch and hit his wicket.

England's fortunes were reviving after lunch until Washbrook was caught close in, and at tea England were 153 for 2; although Compton was never comfortable it seemed that defeat might still be avoided. But Compton flashed at the new ball 20 minutes from time, and England began the last day at 247 for 3, Edrich 86, Hammond 15. At 12.45 they were batting confidently on a wicket eased by a shower; but then Hammond was caught behind the bowler and resistance crumbled. Edrich's patient innings lasted 5 hours 14 minutes and contained 63 singles. Evans, replacing Gibb, did not concede a single bye.

ENGLAND

L. Hutton	c Tallon b Johnson	39	hit wkt b Miller	37	
C. Washbrook	b Freer	1	c McCool b Johnson	41	
W. J. Edrich	lbw b McCool	71	b McCool	119	
D. C. S. Compton	c Tallon b McCool	5	c Bradman b Freer	54	
*W. R. Hammond	c Tallon b McCool	1	c Toshack b McCool	37	
J. T. Ikin	c Hassett b Johnson	60	b Freer	17	
N. W. D. Yardley	c Tallon b Johnson	25	b McCool	35	
T. P. B. Smith	lbw b Johnson	4	c Hassett b Johnson	2	
†T. G. Evans	b Johnson	5	st Tallon b McCool	9	
A. V. Bedser	b Johnson	14	not out	3	
D. V. P. Wright	not out	15	c Tallon b McCool	0	
Extras	(b 4, lb 11)	15	(b 8, lb 6, w 1, nb 2)	17	
Total		**255**	**Total**	**371**	

AUSTRALIA

S. G. Barnes	c Ikin b Bedser	234
A. R. Morris	b Edrich	5
I. W. Johnson	c Washbrook b Edrich	7
A. L. Hassett	c Compton b Edrich	34
K. R. Miller	c Evans b Smith	40
*D. G. Bradman	lbw b Yardley	234
C. L. McCool	c Hammond b Smith	12
†D. Tallon	c and b Wright	30
F. W. Freer	not out	28
G. E. Tribe	not out	25
E. R. H. Toshack	did not bat	
Extras	(lb 7, w 1, nb 2)	10
Total	(8 wkts dec)	**659**

FALL OF WICKETS

ENGLAND

Wkt	1st	2nd
1st	10	49
2nd	88	118
3rd	97	220
4th	99	280
5th	148	309
6th	187	327
7th	197	346
8th	205	366
9th	234	369
10th	255	371

AUSTRALIA

Wkt	1st	2nd
1st	24	—
2nd	37	—
3rd	96	—
4th	159	—
5th	564	—
6th	564	—
7th	595	—
8th	617	—
9th	—	—
10th	—	—

Umpires: G. Borwick,
J. D. Scott

AUSTRALIA	1st Innings				2nd Innings			
	O	M	R	W	O	M	R	W
Miller	9	2	24	0	11	3	37	1
Freer	7	1	25	1	13	2	49	2
Toshack	7	2	6	0	6	1	16	0
Tribe	20	3	70	0	12	0	40	0
Johnson	30·1	12	42	6	29	7	92	2
McCool	23	2	73	3	32·4	4	109	5
Barnes					3	0	11	0

ENGLAND	1st Innings				2nd Innings			
	O	M	R	W	O	M	R	W
Bedser	46	7	153	1				
Edrich	26	3	79	3				
Wright	46	8	169	1				
Smith	37	1	172	2				
Ikin	3	0	15	0				
Compton	6	0	38	0				
Yardley	9	0	23	1				

1946-47 Third Test, Melbourne

January 1, 2, 3, 4, 6, 7
Toss: Australia   *Result:* Match Drawn

Despite early misfortunes when Edrich was hit on the shin by a hook from Barnes and had to go off and Voce retired with a strain, the remaining England bowlers reacted magnificently. Bedser got Morris lbw at 32 and after lunch dismissed Barnes. Hassett, passive for nearly an hour, was caught at slip, and soon after tea Bradman played on to Yardley. With his next ball Yardley had Johnson lbw, and when Miller was caught at the wicket Australia were 192 for 6. McCool and Tallon, however, had taken the score to 255 for 6 by stumps.

Edrich had recovered sufficiently to bowl the opening over next morning and with his first ball he had Tallon caught behind; and at 272 Bedser bowled Lindwall. But McCool was scoring freely, mostly with clean strokes off the back foot, and thanks largely to his opportune hundred Australia totalled 365.

Hutton soon fell to a perfect Lindwall out-swinger, and Washbrook was troubled by the left-arm medium Toshack, but Edrich played his shots from the start and the tension lifted. At stumps England were 147 for 1. The two batsmen were settling in next morning when Edrich was lbw after by all accounts getting a touch; Compton played no stroke to Toshack but was lbw, Hammond was deceived by Dooland, and when Washbrook was caught England's innings

paralleled Australia's. Fortunately a similar recovery was forthcoming, Yardley and Ikin showing great resolution in a stand of 113, and England finished only 14 behind. Barnes and Morris had added 33 to this by stumps.

Barnes was out on the fourth morning, Bradman reached 49 and then miscued a Yardley long hop, and Hassett was bowled by a googly; but Morris reached a patient hundred in 4 hours 25 minutes. 293 for 4 overnight, Australia lost both their not out batsmen to Bedser on the fifth morning, and the presence of another penetrative bowler might have turned the game. But Voce was still unfit, and England went to pieces as Tallon and Lindwall hit 154 for the 8th wicket in 88 minutes, mostly by wonderful driving, Tallon batting for 104 minutes and Lindwall for 113. 551 was a hopeless target, but Hutton and Washbrook had made 91 together by the close.

On the last day the wicket was easier than ever and the ball seldom turned, but although Washbrook square cut and pulled his way to 112 the other batting faltered, and when Bedser joined Yardley at 249 for 6 there were still 90 minutes left. Yardley remained imperturbable, however, but Bedser played very straight, and with the help of a short break for rain England escaped. But the result decided the Ashes.

AUSTRALIA

S. G. Barnes	lbw b Bedser	45	c Evans b Yardley	32
A. R. Morris	lbw b Bedser	21	b Bedser	155
*D. G. Bradman	b Yardley	79	c and b Yardley	49
A. L. Hassett	c Hammond b Wright	12	b Wright	9
K. R. Miller	c Evans b Wright	33	c Hammond b Yardley	34
I. W. Johnson	lbw b Yardley	0	(7)run out	0
C. L. McCool	not out	104	(6)c Evans b Bedser	43
†D. Tallon	c Evans b Edrich	35	c and b Wright	92
R. R. Lindwall	b Bedser	9	c Washbrook b Bedser	100
B. Dooland	c Hammond b Edrich	19	c Compton b Wright	1
E. R. H. Toshack	c Hutton b Edrich	6	not out	2
Extras	(nb 2)	2	(b 14, lb 2, nb 3)	19
Total		**365**	**Total**	**536**

ENGLAND

L. Hutton	c McCool b Lindwall	2	c Bradman b Toshack	40
C. Washbrook	c Tallon b Dooland	62	b Dooland	112
W. J. Edrich	lbw b Lindwall	89	lbw b McCool	13
D. C. S. Compton	lbw b Toshack	11	run out	14
*W. R. Hammond	c and b Dooland	9	b Lindwall	26
J. T. Ikin	c Miller b Dooland	48	c Hassett b Miller	5
N. W. D. Yardley	b McCool	61	not out	53
†T. G. Evans	b McCool	17	(9)not out	0
W. Voce	lbw b Dooland	0		
A. V. Bedser	not out	27	(8)lbw b Miller	25
D. V. P. Wright	b Johnson	10		
Extras	(b 1, lb 12, nb 2)	15	(b 15, lb 6, w 1)	22
Total		**351**	**Total** (7 wkts)	**310**

FALL OF WICKETS

AUSTRALIA

Wkt	1st	2nd
1st	32	68
2nd	108	159
3rd	143	177
4th	188	242
5th	188	333
6th	192	335
7th	255	341
8th	272	495
9th	355	511
10th	365	536

ENGLAND

Wkt	1st	2nd
1st	8	138
2nd	155	163
3rd	167	186
4th	176	197
5th	179	221
6th	292	249
7th	298	294
8th	298	—
9th	324	—
10th	351	—

Umpires: G. Borwick,
J. D. Scott

ENGLAND

	1st Innings				2nd Innings			
	O	M	R	W	O	M	R	W
Voce	10	2	40	0	6	1	29	0
Bedser	31	4	99	3	34.3	4	176	3
Wright	26	2	124	2	32	3	131	3
Yardley	20	4	50	2	20	0	67	3
Edrich	10.3	2	50	3	18	1	86	0
Hutton					3	0	28	0

AUSTRALIA

	1st Innings				2nd Innings			
	O	M	R	W	O	M	R	W
Lindwall	20	1	64	2	16	2	59	1
Miller	10	0	34	0	11	0	41	2
Toshack	26	5	88	1	16	5	39	1
McCool	19	3	53	2	24	9	41	1
Dooland	27	5	69	4	21	1	84	1
Johnson	6.5	1	28	1	12	4	24	0

1946-47 Fourth Test, Adelaide

January 31, February 1, 3, 4, 5, 6
Toss: England   *Result:* Match Drawn

The opening attack of Lindwall and Miller was on the whole contained in this series, and never more successfully than at Adelaide, where Hutton and Washbrook put on a hundred in both innings. The pitch was of comfortable pace, Hutton took avoiding action when Miller tried a succession of bumpers, and the England openers put on 137. Dooland then found the edge of Washbrook's bat with a leg-spinner, after which he caught and bowled Edrich, Hutton was lbw to a McCool top-spinner, and when Hammond played across Toshack England were 202 for 4. Bradman kept the spinners going, but Compton and Hardstaff, restricting their back-lift, played out time. Hardstaff was replacing Voce.

When Hardstaff played on to a Miller bouncer after lunch next day England had recovered to 320 for 5. Compton, slow to his 50, then accelerated to his hundred. When he was out Lindwall took the last 3 wickets in 4 balls, all clean bowled.

Harvey, substituting for the injured Barnes, played on, Bradman was completely beaten by Bedser, and Australia at stumps were 24 for 2. But on the third day Morris and Hassett stayed together until 4.40. Great heat and humidity slowed the tempo, but England bowled 70 overs in the day. Although Hassett batted austerely Australia added 269, Morris making a chanceless 122 and Miller and Johnson putting

on 71 together before the close. Next morning by brilliant hitting Miller made 67 in 71 minutes, and although Yardley applied the brake with an accurate leg stump attack Miller saw Australia to a lead of 27.

A sharp thunderstorm held up play for 23 minutes, but the wicket was unaffected and in 21 overs Hutton and Washbrook made 96, hooking the frequent bouncers projected by Lindwall and Miller and scoring so freely that the first 87 came in 57 minutes. But Washbrook went to a doubtful catch on the fifth morning, Hutton was bowled by Johnson, and Toshack sent England to the brink of defeat by taking 4 for 26 in the afternoon. Compton and Yardley then compelled Bradman to take the new ball, which accounted for Yardley and Bedser. At this point England were 228 in front, with only Compton's skill and the character and wit of Evans standing between Australia and victory.

England were 274 for 8 at stumps with a day to go, still facing defeat; but Evans, who was 95 minutes before scoring, stayed with Compton until lunch, and immediately after lunch Hammond declared, leaving Australia 3¼ hours to get 314. The challenge, if challenge it was, was not accepted, but there was time for Morris to emulate Compton by completing his second century of the match.

ENGLAND

L. Hutton	lbw b McCool	94	b Johnson	76
C. Washbrook	c Tallon b Dooland	65	c Tallon b Lindwall	39
W. J. Edrich	c and b Dooland	17	c Bradman b Toshack	46
*W. R. Hammond	b Toshack	18	c Lindwall b Toshack	22
D. C. S. Compton	c and b Lindwall	147	not out	103
J. Hardstaff	b Miller	67	b Toshack	9
J. T. Ikin	c Toshack b Dooland	21	lbw b Toshack	1
N. W. D. Yardley	not out	18	c Tallon b Lindwall	18
A. V. Bedser	b Lindwall	2	c Tallon b Miller	3
†T. G. Evans	b Lindwall	0	not out	10
D. V. P. Wright	b Lindwall	0		
Extras	(b 4, lb 5, w 2)	11	(b 5, lb 3, w 2, nb 3)	13
Total		**460**	**Total** (8 wkts dec)	**340**

AUSTRALIA

M. Harvey	b Bedser	12	b Yardley	31
A. R. Morris	c Evans b Bedser	122	not out	124
*D. G. Bradman	b Bedser	0	not out	56
A. L. Hassett	c Hammond b Wright	78		
K. R. Miller	not out	141		
I. W. Johnson	lbw b Wright	52		
C. L. McCool	c Bedser b Yardley	2		
†D. Tallon	b Wright	3		
R. R. Lindwall	c Evans b Yardley	20		
B. Dooland	c Bedser b Yardley	29		
E. R. H. Toshack	run out	0		
Extras	(b 16, lb 6, w 2, nb 4)	28	(lb 2, nb 2)	4
Total		**487**	**Total** (1 wkt)	**215**

FALL OF WICKETS

ENGLAND

Wkt	1st	2nd
1st	137	100
2nd	173	137
3rd	196	178
4th	202	188
5th	320	207
6th	381	215
7th	455	250
8th	460	255
9th	460	—
10th	460	—

AUSTRALIA

Wkt	1st	2nd
1st	18	116
2nd	18	—
3rd	207	—
4th	222	—
5th	372	—
6th	389	—
7th	396	—
8th	423	—
9th	486	—
10th	487	—

Umpires: G. Borwick, J. D. Scott

AUSTRALIA	1st Innings				2nd Innings			
	O	M	R	W	O	M	R	W
Lindwall	23	5	52	4	17.1	4	60	2
Miller	16	0	45	1	11	0	34	1
Toshack	30	13	59	1	36	6	76	4
McCool	29	1	91	1	19	3	41	0
Johnson	22	3	69	0	25	8	51	1
Dooland	33	1	133	3	17	2	65	0

ENGLAND	1st Innings				2nd Innings			
	O	M	R	W	O	M	R	W
Bedser	30	6	97	3	15	1	68	0
Edrich	20	3	88	0	7	2	25	0
Wright	32.4	1	152	3	9	0	49	0
Yardley	31	7	101	3	13	0	69	1
Ikin	2	0	9	0				
Compton	3	0	12	0				

1946-47 Fifth Test, Sydney

February 28, March 1, 3, 4, 5
Toss: England   *Result:* Australia won by five wickets

On a wicket that gave the bowlers some help after heavy rain before the game, Hutton was again the target for a barrage of bouncers. But it was Washbrook who left early, bowled by a good-length ball. Hutton and Edrich then put on 150, Hutton being the dominant partner before lunch and Edrich driving strongly afterwards, but Fishlock, deputising for Hammond (fibrositis), was bowled at 188. Other changes due to injury were Smith for Hardstaff and Hamence for Johnson, while Tribe was preferred to Dooland.

When the new ball was taken at 207 England faced another barrage of bumpers, this time in failing light. Compton, protecting his face, trod on his wicket, and after two unsuccessful light appeals Yardley and Ikin also lost their wickets before stumps, when England were 237 for 6. Hutton had batted 5 hours but had been missed three times. Rain washed out the second day, and with Sunday intervening the wicket on the third day was much as it had been at the start. But Hutton was ill with tonsilitis, and England did well to total 280.

Australia went in at 1.15, and while Barnes, returning in place of Harvey, was ostentatiously watchful, Morris leaned into his strokes. But it was Barnes who led the scoring after lunch, making 71 out of 126. Bedser eventually dismissed both openers, Bradman swept across

a flighted leg-spinner from Wright, and Miller was also out before the close, when Australia were 189 for 4. After their moderate score the Englishmen bowled and fielded with zest. On the fourth morning the ball turned sharply and Wright bowled to three slips. A great diving catch by Ikin got rid of Hassett, and Australia finished up 27 behind. Wright's figures on the fourth day were 5 for 41, while Bedser held the other end for 100 minutes for 14 runs.

All England now had to do to win, it seemed, was play steadily and set Australia about 250. But Fishlock was beaten for pace first ball, and with Hutton still unable to bat England were virtually 0 for 2. McCool troubled everyone except Compton, and although Evans and Smith gave useful support Australia went in just before lunch on the 5th day wanting only 214 to win.

Wright went on after three overs, but the wicket was easier and Barnes and Morris attacked. After Morris was run out England had a great chance when Bradman edged Wright to Edrich at slip, but the chance went down. Barnes left at 51 for 2, but Bradman and Hassett gained Australia the advantage in a stand of 98. The result was still open at 180 for 5, but Miller, under orders to hit before the wicket deteriorated, knocked off the runs.

ENGLAND

L. Hutton	retired ill	122	absent ill	—	
C. Washbrook	b Lindwall	0	b McCool	24	
W. J. Edrich	c Tallon b Lindwall	60	st Tallon b McCool	24	
L. B. Fishlock	b McCool	14	(1)lbw b Lindwall	0	
D. C. S. Compton	hit wkt b Lindwall	17	(4)c Miller b Toshack	76	
*N. W. D. Yardley	c Miller b Lindwall	2	b McCool	11	
J. T. Ikin	b Lindwall	0	(5)st Tallon b McCool	0	
†T. G. Evans	b Lindwall	29	(7)b Miller	20	
T. P. B. Smith	b Lindwall	2	(8)c Tallon b Lindwall	24	
A. V. Bedser	not out	10	(9)st Tallon b McCool	4	
D. V. P. Wright	c Tallon b Miller	7	(10)not out	1	
Extras	(b 7, lb 8, w 1, nb 1)	17	(b 1, lb 1)	2	
Total		**280**	**Total**	**186**	

AUSTRALIA

S. G. Barnes	c Evans b Bedser	71	c Evans b Bedser	30	
A. R. Morris	lbw b Bedser	57	run out	17	
*D. G. Bradman	b Wright	12	c Compton b Bedser	63	
A. L. Hassett	c Ikin b Wright	24	c Ikin b Wright	47	
K. R. Miller	c Ikin b Wright	23	not out	34	
R. A. Hamence	not out	30	c Edrich b Wright	1	
C. L. McCool	c Yardley b Wright	3	not out	13	
†D. Tallon	c Compton b Wright	0			
R. R. Lindwall	c Smith b Wright	0			
G. E. Tribe	c Fishlock b Wright	9			
E. R. H. Toshack	run out	5			
Extras	(b 7, lb 6, nb 6)	19	(b 4, lb 1, nb 4)	9	
Total		**253**	**Total** (5 wkts)	**214**	

FALL OF WICKETS
ENGLAND

Wkt	1st	2nd
1st	1	0
2nd	151	42
3rd	188	65
4th	215	65
5th	225	85
6th	225	120
7th	244	157
8th	269	184
9th	280	186
10th	—	—

AUSTRALIA

Wkt	1st	2nd
1st	126	45
2nd	146	51
3rd	146	149
4th	187	173
5th	218	180
6th	230	—
7th	230	—
8th	233	—
9th	245	—
10th	253	—

Umpires: G. Borwick, J. D. Scott

AUSTRALIA

	1st Innings					2nd Innings			
	O	M	R	W		O	M	R	W
Lindwall	22	3	63	7	..	12	1	46	2
Miller	15·3	2	31	1	..	6	1	11	1
Tribe	28	2	95	0	..	14	0	58	0
Toshack	16	4	40	0	..	4	1	14	1
McCool	13	0	34	1	..	21·4	5	44	5
Barnes					..	3	0	11	0

ENGLAND

	1st Innings					2nd Innings			
	O	M	R	W		O	M	R	W
Bedser	27	7	49	2	..	22	4	75	2
Edrich	7	0	34	0	..	2	0	14	0
Smith	8	0	38	0	..	2	0	8	0
Wright	29	4	105	7	..	22	1	93	2
Yardley	5	2	8	0	..	3	1	7	0
Compton					..	1·2	0	8	0

Averages: 1946-47

AUSTRALIA

BATTING	M.	Inns.	N.O.	Runs	H.S.	Av.
D. G. Bradman	5	8	1	680	234	97·14
K. R. Miller	5	7	2	384	141*	76·80
S. G. Barnes	4	6	0	443	234	73·83
A. R. Morris	5	8	1	503	155	71·85
C. L. McCool	5	7	2	272	104*	54·40
A. L. Hassett	5	7	0	332	128	47·42
R. R. Lindwall	4	5	0	160	100	32·00
D. Tallon	5	6	0	174	92	29·00
I. W. Johnson	4	5	0	106	52	21·20
G. E. Tribe	3	3	1	35	25*	17·50
B. Dooland	2	3	0	49	29	16·33
E. R. H. Toshack	5	5	2	14	6	4·66

PLAYED IN ONE TEST: F. W. Freer 28*, M. Harvey 12 and 31, R. A. Hamence 30* and 1.

BOWLING	Overs	Mds.	Runs	Wkts.	Av.
R. R. Lindwall	122·1	20	367	18	20·38
K. R. Miller	122·3	15	334	16	20·87
E. R. H. Toshack	178·4	50	437	17	25·70
C. L. McCool	182	27	491	18	27·27
I. W. Johnson	124·6	35	306	10	30·60
B. Dooland	98	9	351	8	43·87

ALSO BOWLED: F. W. Freer 20–3–74–3, G. E. Tribe 95–9–330–2, S. G. Barnes 7–0–23–0.

ENGLAND

BATTING	M.	Inns.	N.O.	Runs	H.S.	Av.
L. Hutton	5	9	1	417	122*	52·12
D. C. S. Compton	5	10	1	459	147	51·00
W. J. Edrich	5	10	0	462	119	46·20
C. Washbrook	5	10	0	363	112	36·30
N. W. D. Yardley	5	10	2	252	61	31·50
W. R. Hammond	4	8	0	168	37	21·00
J. T. Ikin	5	10	0	184	60	18·40
A. V. Bedser	5	10	3	106	27*	15·14
T. G. Evans	4	8	2	90	29	15·00
W. Voce	2	3	1	19	18	9·50
D. V. P. Wright	5	8	3	47	15*	9·40
T. P. B. Smith	2	4	0	32	24	8·00

PLAYED IN ONE TEST: P. A. Gibb 13 and 11, J. Hardstaff 67 and 9, L. B. Fishlock 14 and 0.

BOWLING	Overs	Mds.	Runs	Wkts.	Av.
N. W. D. Yardley	114	15	372	10	37·20
D. V. P. Wright	240·2	23	990	23	43·04
W. J. Edrich	115·3	13	483	9	53·66
A. V. Bedser	246·3	38	876	16	54·75

ALSO BOWLED: T. P. B. Smith 47–1–218–2, L. Hutton 3–0–28–0, J. T. Ikin 7–0–48–0, D. C. S. Compton 16·2–0–78–0, W. Voce 44–12–161–0.

Averages: 1948

ENGLAND

BATTING	M.	Inns.	N.O.	Runs	H.S.	Av.
D. C. S. Compton	5	10	1	562	184	62·44
C. Washbrook	4	8	1	356	143	50·85
L. Hutton	4	8	0	342	81	42·75
W. J. Edrich	5	10	0	319	111	31·90
T. G. Evans	5	9	2	188	50	26·85
J. C. Laker	3	6	1	114	63	22·80
A. V. Bedser	5	9	1	176	79	22·00
J. F. Crapp	3	6	1	88	37	17·60
N. W. D. Yardley	5	9	0	150	44	16·66
H. E. Dollery	2	3	0	38	37	12·66
J. A. Young	3	5	2	17	9	5·66
R. Pollard	2	2	1	3	3	3·00

PLAYED IN ONE TEST: J. Hardstaff 0 and 43, D. V. P. Wright 13* and 4, A. Coxon 19 and 0, C. J. Barnett 8 and 6, J. G. Dewes 1 and 10, K. Cranston 10 and 0, G. M. Emmett 10 and 0, A. J. Watkins 0 and 2, W. E. Hollies 0 and 0*.

BOWLING	Overs	Mds.	Runs	Wkts.	Av.
N. W. D. Yardley	84	22	204	9	22·66
W. E. Hollies	56	14	131	5	26·20
A. V. Bedser	274·3	75	688	18	38·22
R. Pollard	102	29	218	5	43·60
J. C. Laker	155·2	42	472	9	52·44
J. A. Young	156	64	292	5	58·40

ALSO BOWLED: A. Coxon 63–13–172–3, W. J. Edrich 53–5–238–3, D. V. P. Wright 40·3–12–123–2, K. Cranston 21·1–1–79–1, D. C. S. Compton 37–6–156–1, A. J. Watkins 4–1–19–0, L. Hutton 4–1–30–0, C. J. Barnett 17–5–36–0.

AUSTRALIA

BATTING	M.	Inns.	N.O.	Runs	H.S.	Av.
A. R. Morris	5	9	1	696	196	87·00
S. G. Barnes	4	6	2	329	141	82·25
D. G. Bradman	5	9	2	508	173*	72·57
R. N. Harvey	2	3	1	133	112	66·50
E. R. H. Toshack	4	4	3	51	20*	51·00
S. J. E. Loxton	3	3	0	144	92	48·00
A. L. Hassett	5	8	1	310	137	44·28
R. R. Lindwall	5	6	0	191	77	31·83
K. R. Miller	5	7	0	184	74	28·26
D. Tallon	4	4	0	112	53	28·00
W. A. Brown	2	3	0	73	32	24·33
W. A. Johnston	5	5	2	62	29	20·66
I. W. Johnson	4	6	1	51	21	10·20

PLAYED IN ONE TEST: R. A. Saggers 5, D. T. Ring 9.

BOWLING	Overs	Mds.	Runs	Wkts.	Av.
R. R. Lindwall	222·5	57	530	27	19·62
K. R. Miller	138·1	43	301	13	23·15
W. A. Johnston	309·2	92	630	27	23·33
E. R. H. Toshack	173·1	70	364	11	33·09
I. W. Johnson	183	60	427	7	61·00

ALSO BOWLED: S. J. E. Loxton 63–10–148–3, D. T. Ring 28–13–44–1, S. G. Barnes 5–2–11–0, A. R. Morris 8–1–24–0.

1948 First Test, Trent Bridge

June 10, 11, 12, 14, 15
Toss: England   *Result:* Australia won by eight wickets

Never has a touring side had such a triumphant progress as that of the Australians in 1948. Of their 31 first-class matches they won 23, including 4 of the Tests, and they were never beaten. Bradman was superb as batsman and leader, Morris was a left-hander in the great Australian tradition, Hassett and Barnes were Test batsmen of the highest class, and if Miller's figures were disappointing he was nevertheless a match-winner. Australia's principal advantage, indeed, lay in fast bowling, where Lindwall, Miller and even Johnston produced a pace to which English batsmen were unaccustomed; but they were greatly assisted by the experimental rule which allowed a new ball every 55 overs. The same rule restricted the opportunities of the spinners, Bradman's policy being to contain the batsmen until the new ball became due. England's four leading batsmen, with Compton outstanding, did well enough, but the bowling lacked distinction. England won the toss four times out of five, but in most respects the luck ran for Australia.

The England batsmen struggled for survival on the first day after interruptions for rain during the morning had put some dampness in the wicket. Edrich batted gamely while the ball was flying, and it was Johnston, with variations of pace and swing, who destroyed the middle

batting, reducing England to 74 for 8. Lindwall, however, had had to retire with a strain, and after tea Laker, with stubborn support from Bedser, hooked and drove so strongly that the score was more than doubled, 89 runs coming in 73 minutes. England totalled 165, and at stumps Australia were 17 for 0.

England gave nothing away next morning. Morris left at 73 and Barnes at 121, and Miller was caught at slip at the same total, all three wickets falling to Laker. Yardley then elected to take the new ball, and by stumps Australia were 293 for 4, 276 runs having been added in the day in 130 overs.

Bradman's careful innings ended next morning, but Hassett, even more watchful, also made a hundred, and with the last 3 wickets adding 144 England faced a deficit of 344. Hutton then batted in such exhilarating fashion that England recovered well from a bad start, and some fast bumpers from Miller, although antagonising the crowd, did not upset him. But Miller levelled his off stump next morning, and then Compton, in bad light which caused frequent interruptions, played the innings of the match. Lindwall was still absent, and Hardstaff, Yardley and Evans gave Compton good support. On the last day a draw was still possible until Compton lost his balance to a short-pitched ball and fell on his wicket.

ENGLAND

L. Hutton	b Miller	3	b Miller	74
C. Washbrook	c Brown b Lindwall	6	c Tallon b Miller	1
W. J. Edrich	b Johnston	18	c Tallon b Johnson	13
D. C. S. Compton	b Miller	19	hit wkt b Miller	184
J. Hardstaff	c Miller b Johnston	0	c Hassett b Toshack	43
C. J. Barnett	b Johnston	8	c Miller b Johnston	6
*N. W. D. Yardley	lbw b Toshack	3	c and b Johnston	22
†T. G. Evans	c Morris b Johnston	12	c Tallon b Johnston	50
J. C. Laker	c Tallon b Miller	63	b Miller	4
A. V. Bedser	c Brown b Johnston	22	not out	3
J. A. Young	not out	1	b Johnston	9
Extras	(b 5, lb 5)	10	(b 12, lb 17, nb 3)	32
Total		165	Total	441

AUSTRALIA

S. G. Barnes	c Evans b Laker	62	not out	64
A. R. Morris	b Laker	31	b Bedser	9
*D. G. Bradman	c Hutton b Bedser	138	c Hutton b Bedser	0
K. R. Miller	c Edrich b Laker	0		
W. A. Brown	lbw b Yardley	17		
A. L. Hassett	b Bedser	137		
I. W. Johnson	b Laker	21		
†D. Tallon	c and b Young	10		
R. R. Lindwall	c Evans b Yardley	42		
W. A. Johnston	not out	17		
E. R. H. Toshack	lbw b Bedser	19	(4)not out	21
Extras	(b 9, lb 4, w 1, nb 1)	15	(lb 2, w 1, nb 1)	4
Total		509	Total (2 wkts)	98

FALL OF WICKETS

ENGLAND		
Wkt	*1st*	*2nd*
1st	9	5
2nd	15	39
3rd	46	150
4th	46	243
5th	48	264
6th	60	321
7th	74	405
8th	74	413
9th	163	423
10th	165	441

AUSTRALIA		
Wkt	*1st*	*2nd*
1st	73	38
2nd	121	48
3rd	121	—
4th	185	—
5th	305	—
6th	338	—
7th	365	—
8th	472	—
9th	476	—
10th	509	—

Umpires: F. Chester, E. Cooke

AUSTRALIA	1st Innings					2nd Innings			
	O	M	R	W		O	M	R	W
Lindwall	13	5	30	1					
Miller	19	8	38	3		44	10	125	4
Johnston	25	11	36	5		59	12	147	4
Toshack	14	8	28	1		33	14	60	1
Johnson	5	1	19	0		42	15	66	1
Morris	3	1	4	0					
Barnes						5	2	11	0

ENGLAND	1st Innings					2nd Innings			
	O	M	R	W		O	M	R	W
Edrich	18	1	72	0		4	0	20	0
Bedser	44·2	12	113	3		14·3	4	46	2
Barnett	17	5	36	0					
Young	60	28	79	1		10	3	28	0
Laker	55	14	138	4					
Compton	5	0	24	0					
Yardley	17	6	32	2					

1948 Second Test, Lord's

June 24, 25, 26, 28, 29
Toss: Australia   *Result:* Australia won by 409 runs

Wright, who came into the England side for Young, had missed the first Test through injury, but Hardstaff, unfit, gave way to Dollery. By substituting Coxon for Barnett, England played an extra bowler. Australia were unchanged.

In conditions favourable to swing bowlers Australia began badly, losing Barnes at 3, and immediately after lunch Bradman, who had never looked comfortable, was caught at short fine leg. But Morris, after a careful start when the ball was swinging, began to time his off hits and deflections to leg beautifully, and with Hassett showing his usual composure despite accurate bowling and some dropped catches, the score was taken to 166. Then Morris, just after reaching a chanceless hundred, was caught in the gully, after which Miller was lbw. A partial recovery was checked when Yardley came on to dismiss Hassett and Brown in quick succession, and Johnson too was out before stumps, when Australia were 258 for 7, made off 111 overs. Hassett spent nearly 3 hours over his 47.

When Bedser removed Lindwall at 275 next morning the end seemed in sight. But Yardley persisted with his faster bowlers against the firm-footed tail-enders, and it was not until he introduced Wright that the last wicket fell, by which time Australia had reached 350. England had 45 minutes' batting before lunch, and although Miller was unable to

bowl the opening speed attack lost little in hostility. Washbrook was caught at the wicket, and after Johnson had squeezed an off-break between Hutton's bat and pad, Lindwall sent Edrich's middle stump flying and shattered Dollery's wicket two balls later. Yardley thus joined Compton at 46 for 4, and the stand that followed aroused hopes of a real recovery; but all too soon a new ball became due, and with it Johnston had Compton caught at slip and Lindwall bowled Yardley. 207 for 9 at stumps, England again found themselves facing defeat at the end of the second day.

The third day was all Australia as they built up an overwhelming lead. Barnes and Morris put on 122, and Bradman after another uncertain start produced a flow of strokes. Barnes celebrated his hundred by hitting 20 off five balls from Laker, but Bradman missed his, falling to Bedser for the fifth time in succession. Some glorious driving by Miller and Lindwall next morning enabled Bradman to declare at 3.15 on the fourth afternoon, and although showers caused interruptions they also enlivened the wicket, so that Hutton and Washbrook took many knocks from short-pitched balls. Compton and Dollery had steered England to 106 for 3 by stumps, but when they were parted first thing next morning the match was soon over.

AUSTRALIA

S. G. Barnes	c Hutton b Coxon	0	c Washbrook b Yardley	141	
A. R. Morris	c Hutton b Coxon	105	b Wright	62	
*D. G. Bradman	c Hutton b Bedser	38	c Edrich b Bedser	89	
A. L. Hassett	b Yardley	47	b Yardley	0	
K. R. Miller	lbw b Bedser	4	c Bedser b Laker	74	
W. A. Brown	lbw b Yardley	24	c Evans b Coxon	32	
I. W. Johnson	c Evans b Edrich	4	(8)not out	9	
†D. Tallon	c Yardley b Bedser	53			
R. R. Lindwall	b Bedser	15	(7)st Evans b Laker	25	
W. A. Johnston	st Evans b Wright	29			
E. R. H. Toshack	not out	20			
Extras	(b 3, lb 7, nb 1)	11	(b 22, lb 5, nb 1)	28	
Total		350	Total (7 wkts dec)	460	

ENGLAND

L. Hutton	b Johnson	20	c Johnson b Lindwall	13	
C. Washbrook	c Tallon b Lindwall	8	c Tallon b Toshack	37	
W. J. Edrich	b Lindwall	5	c Johnson b Toshack	2	
D. C. S. Compton	c Miller b Johnston	53	c Miller b Johnston	29	
H. E. Dollery	b Lindwall	0	b Lindwall	37	
*N. W. D. Yardley	b Lindwall	44	b Toshack	11	
A. Coxon	c and b Johnson	19	lbw b Toshack	0	
†T. G. Evans	c Miller b Johnston	9	not out	24	
J. C. Laker	c Tallon b Johnson	28	b Lindwall	0	
A. V. Bedser	b Lindwall	9	c Hassett b Johnston	9	
D. V. P. Wright	not out	13	c Lindwall b Toshack	4	
Extras	(lb 3, nb 4)	7	(b 16, lb 4)	20	
Total		215	Total	186	

FALL OF WICKETS

AUSTRALIA

Wkt	1st	2nd
1st	3	122
2nd	87	296
3rd	166	296
4th	173	329
5th	216	416
6th	225	445
7th	246	460
8th	275	—
9th	320	—
10th	350	—

ENGLAND

Wkt	1st	2nd
1st	17	42
2nd	32	52
3rd	46	65
4th	46	106
5th	133	133
6th	134	133
7th	145	141
8th	186	141
9th	197	158
10th	215	186

Umpires: C. N. Woolley,
D. Davies

ENGLAND	1st Innings				2nd Innings			
	O	M	R	W	O	M	R	W
Bedser	43	14	100	4	34	6	112	1
Coxon	35	10	90	2	28	3	82	1
Edrich	8	0	43	1	2	0	11	0
Wright	21·3	8	54	1	19	4	69	1
Laker	7	3	17	0	31·2	6	111	2
Yardley	15	4	35	2	13	4	36	2
Compton					3	0	11	0

AUSTRALIA	1st Innings				2nd Innings			
	O	M	R	W	O	M	R	W
Lindwall	27·4	7	70	5	23	9	61	3
Johnston	22	4	43	2	33	15	62	2
Johnson	35	13	72	3	2	1	3	0
Toshack	18	11	23	0	20·1	6	40	5

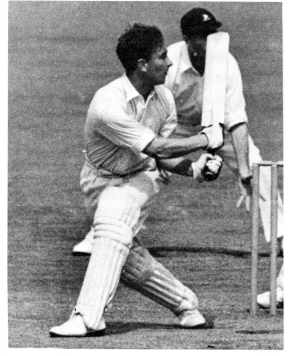

115. D. C. S. Compton

116. R. R. Lindwall

117. **Australia 1948**
Back row: R. R. Lindwall, K. R. Miller, W. A. Brown. *Middle row:* W. F. Ferguson (scorer), R. N. Harvey, D. T. Ring, E. R. H. Toshack, W. A. Johnston, R. A. Saggers, S. G. Barnes, K. O. E. Johnson (manager). *Front:* S. J. E. Loxton, R. A. Hamence, A. L. Hassett, D. G. Bradman (capt.), C. L. McCool, A. R. Morris, I. W. Johnson.

1948 Third Test, Old Trafford

July 8, 9, 10, 12, 13
Toss: England   *Result:* Match Drawn

Two down with three to play, England badly needed to win at Old Trafford, and but for the weather they might have done so. Extravagant claims, however, were later exposed by events at Leeds. Certainly a great game of cricket was spoiled. Lindwall and Johnston soon unsettled the early England batting, and the biggest disaster came when Compton, struggling with Edrich to redeem another bad start, changed his mind when he heard a call of 'no-ball' and tried to hook a Lindwall bouncer but was late with his shot, the ball flying to his head by way of the bat's edge. He was led off the field, and at 32 for 2 with one man injured Crapp came in to play his first innings in Test cricket. (England had made four changes, dropping Hutton, who had not inspired confidence at Lord's, substituting Emmett, and bringing in Crapp, Pollard and Young for Coxon, Laker and Wright. Australia played Loxton for Brown.)

English batsmen had lost the habit of playing fast bowling, and with no one to retaliate it was inevitable that the Australian fast men should pitch the ball where they pleased; but in this match the bouncers were overdone. Edrich, who had done nothing in the series so far, was one player who could not be intimidated, and he and the left-handed Crapp struggled through to lunch, when England were 57 for 2. 50 minutes after lunch, with the score at 87 for 2, the second new ball became due. It soon accounted for Crapp and Dollery, and half an hour later, when Edrich was caught at the wicket after battling for 3 hours 10 minutes for 32, England were 119 for 5. At this point Compton, fortified by two stitches and an unspecified amount of brandy, joined his captain. Yardley was out after tea, but Evans batted boldly for 75 minutes, and at stumps England were 231 for 7, Compton 64 not out.

Compton and Bedser, continuing next morning, put on 121 before Bedser was run out, but the innings soon ended then. Compton batted for 5 hours 27 minutes and was missed three times, all very difficult chances, to a keeper whose hands were raw from taking the bouncers.

Barnes, whose fielding at short leg was a feature of the series, was badly hurt when Pollard swept a Johnson off-spinner straight at him, and Johnson, perhaps as a punishment, was sent in first. He failed, Bradman was late to Pollard and lbw, and Australia, 126 for 3 at the end of the second day, found Bedser and Pollard too much for them next morning and were all out soon after lunch 142 behind. In this dangerous situation Miller was at last persuaded to bowl, and he bowled very fast; but Washbrook was undisturbed by the bumpers, and England at stumps were 174 for 3, 316 in front with two days left. The fourth day was washed out, there was no play until 2.15 on the fifth, and with two more breaks for rain the game jerked to a disappointing end.

ENGLAND

C. Washbrook	b Johnston	11	not out	85	
G. M. Emmett	c Barnes b Lindwall	10	c Tallon b Lindwall	0	
W. J. Edrich	c Tallon b Lindwall	32	run out	53	
D. C. S. Compton	not out	145	c Miller b Toshack	0	
J. F. Crapp	lbw b Lindwall	37	not out	19	
H. E. Dollery	b Johnston	1			
*N. W. D. Yardley	c Johnson b Toshack	22			
†T. G. Evans	c Johnston b Lindwall	34			
A. V. Bedser	run out	37			
R. Pollard	b Toshack	3			
J. A. Young	c Bradman b Johnston	4			
Extras	(b 7, lb 17, nb 3)	27	(b 9, lb 7, w 1)	17	
Total		**363**	**Total** (3 wkts dec)	**174**	

AUSTRALIA

A. R. Morris	c Compton b Bedser	51	not out	54	
I. W. Johnson	c Evans b Bedser	1	c Crapp b Young	6	
*D. G. Bradman	lbw b Pollard	7	not out	30	
A. L. Hassett	c Washbrook b Young	38			
K. R. Miller	lbw b Pollard	31			
S. G. Barnes	retired hurt	1			
S. J. E. Loxton	b Pollard	36			
†D. Tallon	c Evans b Edrich	18			
R. R. Lindwall	c Washbrook b Bedser	23			
W. A. Johnston	c Crapp b Bedser	3			
E. R. H. Toshack	not out	0			
Extras	(b 5, lb 4, nb 3)	12	(nb 2)	2	
Total		**221**	**Total** (1 wkt)	**92**	

FALL OF WICKETS

ENGLAND

Wkt	1st	2nd
1st	22	1
2nd	28	125
3rd	96	129
4th	97	—
5th	119	—
6th	141	—
7th	216	—
8th	337	—
9th	352	—
10th	363	—

AUSTRALIA

Wkt	1st	2nd
1st	3	10
2nd	13	—
3rd	82	—
4th	135	—
5th	139	—
6th	172	—
7th	208	—
8th	219	—
9th	221	—
10th	—	—

Umpires: F. Chester, D. Davies

AUSTRALIA	1st Innings					2nd Innings			
	O	M	R	W		O	M	R	W
Lindwall	40	8	99	4	..	14	4	37	1
Johnston	45·5	13	67	3	..	14	3	34	0
Loxton	7	0	18	0	..	8	1	29	0
Toshack	41	20	75	2	..	12	5	26	1
Johnson	38	16	77	0	..	7	3	16	0
Miller					..	14	7	15	0

ENGLAND	1st Innings					2nd Innings			
	O	M	R	W		O	M	R	W
Bedser	36	12	81	4	..	19	12	27	0
Pollard	32	9	53	3	..	10	8	6	0
Edrich	7	3	27	1	..	2	0	8	0
Yardley	4	0	12	0	..				
Young	14	5	36	1	..	21	12	31	1
Compton					..	9	3	18	0

1948 Fourth Test, Leeds

July 22, 23, 24, 26, 27
Toss: England *Result:* Australia won by seven wickets

Hutton, returning for Emmett, took part in two century opening stands, and indeed England began so well that despite interruptions for rain they made 268 for 2 on the first day, Washbrook being out just before stumps for 143. Bedser, sent in as night-watchman, helped Edrich to add 155 next day, Edrich completing a patient century, but after passing 420 with only two men out England were all out for 496. By the close Australia were 63 for 1.

Light rain enlivened the pitch on the third morning and Hassett and Bradman were both dismissed by Pollard. The 19-year-old Harvey, whose fielding and throwing had been superb, then joined Miller, and they put on 121 in the next 95 minutes, Miller sweeping and driving Laker for 6 and playing a stream of strokes while Harvey followed his example so well that he was first to his 50. Harvey made a century in his first Test (he had replaced the injured Barnes), and Loxton, who hit five sixes, batted only 2¼ hours for his 93. Even so 8 wickets were down for 355, but Lindwall, who escaped a stumping chance, took Australia to 457 for 9 by the close. Laker, although heavily punished, always looked likely to take wickets, but England missed the steadiness of Young. Cranston, an all-rounder, had replaced Dollery.

England, with a lead of 38, began the task of consolidation next morning, and in 105 minutes before lunch Hutton and Washbrook put on 72. Both were out during the afternoon to attacking strokes, but Edrich and Compton were tied down, and when the new ball was taken at 167 the match was in the balance. The run rate then accelerated, and although wickets tumbled after tea, Evans, Bedser and Laker hit out fruitfully towards the close. Five minutes' batting on the last morning allowed Yardley to apply the heavy roller to hasten the breaking up of the wicket, and then Australia went in wanting 404 in 344 minutes to win.

Mixing periodic mistakes that should have cost them their wickets with strokes that continually pierced the field, Morris and Bradman took Australia to 121 for 1 at lunch after the dismissal of Hassett. The catalogue of English errors is too long to record; but Evans had a disastrous day behind the stumps, and although Compton did enough as a bowler to have won the match he wilted later under a determined assault from Morris, and Young was badly missed. England's demoralisation is indicated by the frequency of boundaries: Morris had 20 in his century, while Bradman hit 29 fours *and no threes.* These two put on 301, and Australia won with 12 minutes to spare.

ENGLAND

L. Hutton	b Lindwall	81	c Bradman b Johnson	57	
C. Washbrook	c Lindwall b Johnston	143	c Harvey b Johnston	65	
W. J. Edrich	c Morris b Johnson	111	lbw b Lindwall	54	
A. V. Bedser	c and b Johnson	79	(9)c Hassett b Miller	17	
D. C. S. Compton	c Saggers b Lindwall	23	(4)c Miller b Johnston	66	
J. F. Crapp	b Toshack	5	(5)b Lindwall	18	
*N. W. D. Yardley	b Miller	25	(6)c Harvey b Johnston	7	
K. Cranston	b Loxton	10	(7)c Saggers b Johnston	0	
†T. G. Evans	c Hassett b Loxton	3	(8)not out	47	
J. C. Laker	c Saggers b Loxton	4	not out	15	
R. Pollard	not out	0			
Extras	(b 2, lb 8, w 1, nb 1)	12	(b 4, lb 12, nb 3)	19	
Total		**496**	**Total** (8 wkts dec)	**365**	

AUSTRALIA

A. R. Morris	c Cranston b Bedser	6	c Pollard b Yardley	182	
A. L. Hassett	c Crapp b Pollard	13	c and b Compton	17	
*D. G. Bradman	b Pollard	33	not out	173	
K. R. Miller	c Edrich b Yardley	58	lbw b Cranston	12	
R. N. Harvey	b Laker	112	not out	4	
S. J. E. Loxton	b Yardley	93			
I. W. Johnson	c Cranston b Laker	10			
R. R. Lindwall	c Crapp b Bedser	77			
†R. A. Saggers	st Evans b Laker	5			
W. A. Johnston	c Edrich b Bedser	13			
E. R. H. Toshack	not out	12			
Extras	(b 9, lb 14, nb 3)	26	(b 6, lb 9, nb 1)	16	
Total		**458**	**Total** (3 wkts)	**404**	

FALL OF WICKETS

ENGLAND

Wkt	1st	2nd
1st	168	129
2nd	268	129
3rd	423	232
4th	426	260
5th	447	277
6th	473	278
7th	486	293
8th	490	330
9th	496	—
10th	496	—

AUSTRALIA

Wkt	1st	2nd
1st	13	57
2nd	65	358
3rd	68	396
4th	189	—
5th	294	—
6th	329	—
7th	344	—
8th	355	—
9th	403	—
10th	458	—

Umpires: F. Chester,
H. G. Baldwin

AUSTRALIA	1st Innings					2nd Innings			
	O	M	R	W		O	M	R	W
Lindwall	38	10	79	2	..	26	6	84	2
Miller	17·1	2	43	1	..	21	5	53	1
Johnston	38	13	86	1	..	29	5	95	4
Toshack	35	6	112	1	..				
Loxton	26	4	55	3	..	10	2	29	0
Johnson	33	9	89	2	..	21	2	85	1
Morris	5	0	20	0	..				

ENGLAND	1st Innings					2nd Innings			
	O	M	R	W		O	M	R	W
Bedser	31·2	4	92	3	..	21	2	56	0
Pollard	38	6	104	2	..	22	6	55	0
Cranston	14	1	51	0	..	7·1	0	28	1
Edrich	3	0	19	0	..				
Laker	30	8	113	3	..	32	11	93	0
Yardley	17	6	38	2	..	13	1	44	1
Compton	3	0	15	0	..	15	3	82	1
Hutton					..	4	1	30	0

1948 Fifth Test, Oval

August 14, 16, 17, 18
Toss: England   *Result:* Australia won by an innings and 149 runs

But for the weather England might well have won at Old Trafford; but for missed chances and faulty selection they must surely have won at Leeds. But any doubts about Australia's overwhelming superiority were resolved at the Oval, where England were crushed despite some good bowling by Bedser, Hollies and Young. Although the start was delayed until noon the match was virtually over by lunch-time, when England were 29 for 4.

The weather was still unsettled after heavy rain and when Yardley won the toss he had no alternative but to bat. In a humid atmosphere, but on a sodden pitch, Lindwall, Miller and Johnston, backed up by wonderful catching, dismissed England in 2 hours 27 minutes for 52. Yet throughout the innings Hutton looked safe and assured, and it was a shock when he was last out, to a diving left-handed catch by Tallon from a perfectly good leg glance.

In an hour's batting Morris and Barnes passed the England score without loss, and it was not until Hollies bowled that England got a wicket; at 117 Barnes, groping forward, was caught behind. Bradman went in just before six o'clock to an emotional reception and was bowled second ball by a googly, and at stumps Australia were 153 for 2.

With Sunday intervening the wicket dried out completely, and it was a fine performance by England to get Australia out for the addition of 236 runs, especially as 73 of these came in the stand between Morris and Hassett that had begun on the Saturday. The other Australian batsmen, indeed, ranked as no more than partners for Morris, whose innings was faultless. His cover-driving and hooking frequently beat the field, and he never looked like losing his wicket; in the finish he ran himself out. 337 behind, England lost Dewes at 20, but Hutton and Edrich stayed till stumps at 54 for 1.

On Tuesday morning Edrich was bowled by a glorious express from Lindwall that whipped back from the off; Lindwall was acknowledged by this time as a truly great fast bowler. Compton was strangely uncertain, but at lunch England were not quite dead at 121 for 2. Compton was caught at slip after lunch from a hard cut, and Miller, serving up everything from fast to slow, eventually bowled Hutton, who had batted 4¼ hours for 64. Hampered by rain and bad light after having had all the worst of the conditions from the start, England then limped to an innings defeat. Washbrook missed this match through injury, but the selectors were strongly criticised for the side they chose.

ENGLAND

L. Hutton	c Tallon b Lindwall	30	c Tallon b Miller	64	
J. G. Dewes	b Miller	1	b Lindwall	10	
W. J. Edrich	c Hassett b Johnston	3	b Lindwall	28	
D. C. S. Compton	c Morris b Lindwall	4	c Lindwall b Johnston	39	
J. F. Crapp	c Tallon b Miller	0	b Miller	9	
*N. W. D. Yardley	b Lindwall	7	c Miller b Johnston	9	
A. J. Watkins	lbw b Johnston	0	c Hassett b Ring	2	
†T. G. Evans	b Lindwall	1	b Lindwall	8	
A. V. Bedser	b Lindwall	0	b Johnston	0	
J. A. Young	b Lindwall	0	not out	3	
W. E. Hollies	not out	0	c Morris b Johnston	0	
Extras	(b 6)	6	(b 9, lb 4, nb 3)	16	
Total		**52**	**Total**	**188**	

AUSTRALIA

S. G. Barnes	c Evans b Hollies	61
A. R. Morris	run out	196
*D. G. Bradman	b Hollies	0
A. L. Hassett	lbw b Young	37
K. R. Miller	st Evans b Hollies	5
R. N. Harvey	c Young b Hollies	17
S. J. E. Loxton	c Evans b Edrich	15
R. R. Lindwall	c Edrich b Young	9
†D. Tallon	c Crapp b Hollies	31
D. T. Ring	c Crapp b Bedser	9
W. A. Johnston	not out	0
Extras	(b 4, lb 2, nb 3)	9
Total		**389**

FALL OF WICKETS

ENGLAND

Wkt	1st	2nd
1st	2	20
2nd	10	64
3rd	17	125
4th	23	153
5th	35	164
6th	42	167
7th	45	178
8th	45	181
9th	47	188
10th	52	188

AUSTRALIA

Wkt	1st	2nd
1st	117	—
2nd	117	—
3rd	226	—
4th	243	—
5th	265	—
6th	304	—
7th	332	—
8th	359	—
9th	389	—
10th	389	—

Umpires: H. G. Baldwin, D. Davies

AUSTRALIA	1st Innings					2nd Innings			
	O	M	R	W		O	M	R	W
Lindwall	16·1	5	20	6	..	25	3	50	3
Miller	8	5	5	2	..	15	6	22	2
Johnston	16	4	20	2	..	27·3	12	40	4
Loxton	2	1	1	0	..	10	2	16	0
Ring					..	28	13	44	1

ENGLAND	1st Innings					2nd Innings			
	O	M	R	W		O	M	R	W
Bedser	31·2	9	61	1	..				
Watkins	4	1	19	0	..				
Young	51	16	118	2	..				
Hollies	56	14	131	5	..				
Compton	2	0	6	0	..				
Edrich	9	1	38	1	..				
Yardley	5	1	7	0	..				

December 1, 2, 4, 5
Toss: Australia   *Result:* Australia won by 70 runs

The retirement of Bradman and the absence of Barnes were serious deprivations for Australia, but their bowling strength was intact; indeed it was augmented by that character beloved of cricket fiction, the mystery bowler. Iverson, tall and burly, awkward with the bat and in the field, had taken 46 wickets in his first Sheffield Shield season the previous year at the age of 34; now his unorthodox finger action and splendid control made him the outstanding spinner of the series. England for their part had the best batsman in Hutton and the best bowler in Bedser, and the selectors struck lucky with Brown, who was not their first or even their second choice; but Compton, following an operation on his knee, had a wretched series, and Washbrook found the slower wickets with their lack of bounce inimical to his style. With the young supporting batsmen failing, and with Edrich condemned for some supposed misdemeanour and left behind, the batting was fatally weak. Injuries during the tour compelled Brown to ask for reinforcements and Statham and Tattersall were flown out, but they played no significant part in the campaign.

After a bad start in the preliminary matches England on the first day at Brisbane dismissed Australia for 228. Harvey was in zealous mood after the early loss of Moroney, and at lunch Australia were 69 for 1; but after lunch Morris was lbw to Bedser, Miller was never happy against Wright, and Harvey was brilliantly caught by Evans on the leg side standing up. Hassett was beaten by a ball that pitched on the leg stump and hit the top of the off, Brown picked up two useful wickets, and the innings was finished off with the second new ball. Bad light ended play before England could begin their reply.

Heavy rain on the uncovered pitch washed out the Saturday, but by skilful batting on the third morning after a late start Washbrook and Simpson made 28. All England's work was then discounted as the innings became a procession on an impossible wicket. At 68 for 7 Brown declared, and the Australians fared even worse, Hassett declaring at 32 for 7. England were left with 70 minutes' batting before stumps, and 193 to win.

Simpson was yorked by Lindwall first ball, but Washbrook and Dewes held on for a time. An appeal against the light failed, and 3 wickets were lost in the last 10 minutes, by which time England were 30 for 6. Hutton, held back to stiffen the middle, made a memorable attempt next morning under improved conditions to steer England towards victory, but the damage already done was too great.

AUSTRALIA

J. A. R. Moroney	c Hutton b Bailey	0	lbw b Bailey		0
A. R. Morris	lbw b Bedser	25	c Bailey b Bedser		0
R. N. Harvey	c Evans b Bedser	74	(6)c Simpson b Bedser		12
K. R. Miller	c McIntyre b Wright	15	(7)c Simpson b Bailey		8
*A. L. Hassett	b Bedser	8	lbw b Bailey		3
S. J. E. Loxton	c Evans b Brown	24	(4)c Bailey b Bedser		0
R. R. Lindwall	c Bedser b Bailey	41	(8)not out		0
†D. Tallon	c Simpson b Brown	5			
I. W. Johnson	c Simpson b Bailey	23	(3)lbw b Bailey		8
W. A. Johnston	c Hutton b Bedser	1			
J. Iverson	not out	1			
Extras	(b 5, lb 3, nb 3)	11	(nb 1)		1
Total		**228**	**Total** (7 wkts dec)		**32**

ENGLAND

R. T. Simpson	b Johnston	12	b Lindwall		0
C. Washbrook	c Hassett b Johnston	19	c Loxton b Lindwall		6
†T. G. Evans	c Iverson b Johnston	16	(6)c Loxton b Johnston		5
D. C. S. Compton	c Lindwall b Johnston	3	(9)c Loxton b Johnston		0
J. G. Dewes	c Loxton b Miller	1	(3)b Miller		9
L. Hutton	not out	8	(8)not out		62
A. J. W. McIntyre	b Johnston	1	run out		7
*F. R. Brown	c Tallon b Miller	4	(10)c Loxton b Iverson		17
T. E. Bailey	not out	1	(4)c Johnston b Iverson		7
A. V. Bedser			(5)c Harvey b Iverson		0
D. V. P. Wright			c Lindwall b Iverson		2
Extras	(lb 2, nb 1)	3	(b 6, nb 1)		7
Total	(7 wkts dec)	**68**	**Total**		**122**

FALL OF WICKETS

AUSTRALIA

Wkt	1st	2nd
1st	0	0
2nd	69	0
3rd	116	0
4th	118	12
5th	129	19
6th	156	31
7th	172	32
8th	219	—
9th	226	—
10th	228	—

ENGLAND

Wkt	1st	2nd
1st	28	0
2nd	49	16
3rd	52	22
4th	52	23
5th	56	23
6th	57	30
7th	67	46
8th	—	46
9th	—	77
10th	—	122

Umpires: A. N. Barlow,
H. Elphinston

ENGLAND	1st Innings					2nd Innings			
	O	M	R	W		O	M	R	W
Bailey	12	4	28	3	..	7	2	22	4
Bedser	16·5	4	45	4	..	6·5	2	9	3
Wright	16	0	81	1	..				
Brown	11	0	63	2	..				

AUSTRALIA	1st Innings					2nd Innings			
	O	M	R	W		O	M	R	W
Lindwall	1	0	1	0	..	7	3	21	2
Johnston	11	2	35	5	..	11	2	30	2
Miller	10	1	29	2	..	7	3	21	1
Iverson					..	13	3	43	4

1950–51 Second Test, Melbourne

December 22, 23, 26, 27
Toss: Australia   *Result:* Australia won by 28 runs

In a heavy atmosphere helping swerve, on a pitch that had been covered for some days against heavy rain and was assisting the seam bowlers, England had another wonderful first day. Bedser bowled for 80 minutes before lunch and 50 minutes after, Bailey had a long spell in the afternoon and came back for the last 40 minutes, and Brown and Close, both bowling at medium pace, picked up a wicket apiece. Bedser was particularly deadly against the left-handers, and at one point he beat Harvey five times in an over, but it was after lunch, when Bedser and Bailey changed ends, that the Australian batting faltered. Some overs of uncertain length from Wright either side of tea helped Hassett to his 50, and he and Loxton put on 84 after 4 wickets had fallen for 93; but with 40 minutes left Bedser and Bailey came back with the second new ball and Australia were all out for 194, the last wicket falling on the stroke of 6.0.

With the wicket more friendly on the second day, although the ball was inclined to keep low, England missed a wonderful chance of building up a strong position. So ineptly did they perform against determined out-cricket that 6 wickets were down for 61; then Brown played a rousing innings while Bailey defended, and 65 runs were put on in 70 minutes, after which Evans played Bailey's role at first and then followed his captain's example. England's lead of 3 runs had been turned into a deficit of 22 by the close.

After a two-day break for Sunday and Christmas Day, Archer and Morris resumed for Australia. Wright, so erratic in the first innings, struck a length and had Morris lbw. Archer and Harvey were still together at lunch, but at 99 Archer was caught in the gully. Harvey backed up too strongly and Washbrook threw down the bowler's wicket, Miller played outside a Bailey in-swinger, and Brown came on and got 4 wickets in succession. Australia were all out soon after tea for 181, leaving England 179 to win.

In the last 55 minutes Lindwall, bowling very fast, made even Miller look medium pace; but it was Iverson and Johnson who began the erosion of England's chances by getting Washbrook and Bailey before stumps. Next morning Lindwall found Simpson late on the back stroke, and at a time when daring was needed only Hutton played his shots, Brown and Evans, who ought to have gone in earlier, both falling to the new ball. In a palpitating finish Australia always seemed to have just enough runs in hand.

AUSTRALIA

Batsman	1st Innings	Runs	2nd Innings	Runs
K. A. Archer	c Bedser b Bailey	26	c Bailey b Bedser	46
A. R. Morris	c Hutton b Bedser	2	lbw b Wright	18
R. N. Harvey	c Evans b Bedser	42	run out	31
K. R. Miller	lbw b Brown	18	b Bailey	14
*A. L. Hassett	b Bailey	52	c Bailey b Brown	19
S. J. E. Loxton	c Evans b Close	32	c Evans b Brown	2
R. R. Lindwall	lbw b Bailey	8	c Evans b Brown	7
†D. Tallon	not out	7	lbw b Brown	0
I. W. Johnson	c Parkhouse b Bedser	0	c Close b Bedser	23
W. A. Johnston	c Hutton b Bedser	0	b Bailey	6
J. Iverson	b Bailey	1	not out	0
Extras	(b 4, lb 2)	6	(b 10, lb 5)	15
Total		194		181

ENGLAND

Batsman	1st Innings	Runs	2nd Innings	Runs
R. T. Simpson	c Johnson b Miller	4	b Lindwall	23
C. Washbrook	lbw b Lindwall	21	b Iverson	8
J. G. Dewes	c Miller b Johnston	8	(5)c Harvey b Iverson	5
L. Hutton	c Tallon b Iverson	12	c Lindwall b Johnston	40
W. G. A. Parkhouse	c Hassett b Miller	9	(6)lbw b Johnston	28
D. B. Close	c Loxton b Iverson	0	(7)lbw b Johnston	1
*F. R. Brown	c Johnson b Iverson	62	(8)b Lindwall	8
T. E. Bailey	b Lindwall	12	(3)b Johnson	0
†T. G. Evans	c Johnson b Iverson	49	b Lindwall	2
A. V. Bedser	not out	4	not out	14
D. V. P. Wright	lbw b Johnston	2	lbw b Johnston	2
Extras	(b 8, lb 6)	14	(b 17, lb 2)	19
Total		197		150

FALL OF WICKETS

AUSTRALIA

Wkt	1st	2nd
1st	6	43
2nd	67	99
3rd	89	100
4th	93	126
5th	177	131
6th	177	151
7th	192	151
8th	193	156
9th	193	181
10th	194	181

ENGLAND

Wkt	1st	2nd
1st	11	21
2nd	33	22
3rd	37	52
4th	54	82
5th	54	92
6th	61	95
7th	126	122
8th	153	124
9th	194	134
10th	197	150

Umpires: G. C. Cooper, R. Wright

ENGLAND	1st Innings O	M	R	W	2nd Innings O	M	R	W
Bailey	17·1	5	40	4	15	3	47	2
Bedser	19	3	37	4	16·3	2	43	2
Wright	8	0	63	0	9	0	42	1
Brown	9	0	28	1	12	2	26	4
Close	6	1	20	1	1	0	8	0

AUSTRALIA	1st Innings O	M	R	W	2nd Innings O	M	R	W
Lindwall	13	2	46	2	12	1	29	3
Miller	13	0	39	2	5	2	16	0
Johnston	9	1	28	2	13·7	1	26	4
Iverson	18	3	37	4	20	4	36	2
Johnson	5	1	19	0	13	3	24	1
Loxton	4	1	14	0				

118. J. Iverson

119. L. Hutton

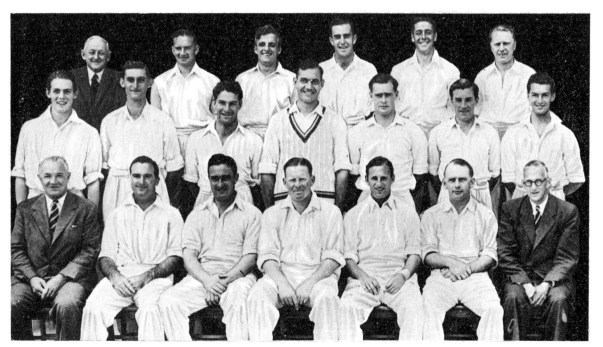

120. England 1950–51
Back row: W. F. Ferguson (scorer), A. J. W. McIntyre, R. Berry, W. G. A. Parkhouse, T. E. Bailey, W. E. Hollies. *Middle row:* D. S. Sheppard, J. J. Warr, J. G. Dewes, A. V. Bedser, D. B. Close, D. V. P. Wright, R. T. Simpson. *Front:* Brig. M. A. Green (joint-manager), T. G. Evans, D. C. S. Compton, F. R. Brown (capt.), L. Hutton, C. Washbrook, J. H. Nash (joint-manager).

January 5, 6, 8, 9
Toss: England   *Result:* Australia won by an innings and 13 runs

Brown's move to stiffen the England middle batting by dropping Hutton in the order, sound in theory, had only succeeded in starving his best batsman of partners, and with Compton back after missing the second Test through a swollen knee Brown restored Hutton and Washbrook as an opening pair. The change was an improvement up to a point; Washbrook left to a great slip catch by Miller at 34, but on an easy pitch on which the bumpers died as soon as they bounced England were 65 for 1 at lunch. Hutton batted superbly, using his feet to drive Iverson, and although Simpson was troubled at first by Johnson he was more himself after lunch. But just when England were moving into a dominant position Miller came back to get Hutton lbw with a ball that whipped in from the off, and three balls later he dismissed Compton with a similar ball. Parkhouse and Brown added 50, and England were 211 for 5 at the close.

Stepping in to the spinners, Brown hit 7 boundaries in the first 50 minutes next morning; but he was eventually bowled hitting at Lindwall, and further disasters came when Bailey had his thumb broken by a ball that lifted and Wright tore a tendon trying to escape being run out. England thus went into the field with three bowlers—Bedser, Brown and Warr—and two substitutes. Morris was at once bowled

behind his legs by Bedser, but Archer and Hassett survived some difficult chances and were still together at stumps, when Australia were 110 for 1.

England's performance on the third day was heroic; apart from six overs from Compton in the final session, Brown permutated any two from three bowlers, and of the 68 8-ball overs England bowled in the day Brown sent down 22 and Bedser and Warr 20 each. More than this, they held Australia so well that 6 wickets were down for 252 at tea. But Johnson, joining a restrained Miller, survived some awkward overs from Brown, and against an exhausted attack these two added 106 before stumps. Miller completed his hundred next morning, and Australia gained a lead of 136.

That morning, with the wicket wearing, Brown had reverted to leg spin; and when England went in again Iverson got Hutton, Washbrook and Simpson in 18 overs for 26 runs. Then after a short rest he came back to finish off the match by getting Brown, Bedser and Warr. Bowling with his middle finger folded down and flicking his off-spinner, Iverson pushed the ball through too quickly to be got at, and only Compton played him well. Despite their magnificent showing in the field England thus lost the Ashes and the rubber.

ENGLAND

Batsman	1st Innings		2nd Innings		
L. Hutton	lbw b Miller	62	c Tallon b Iverson	9	
C. Washbrook	c Miller b Johnson	18	b Iverson	34	
R. T. Simpson	c Loxton b Miller	49	c Tallon b Iverson	0	
D. C. S. Compton	b Miller	0	c Johnson b Johnston	23	
W. G. A. Parkhouse	c Morris b Johnson	25	run out	15	
*F. R. Brown	b Lindwall	79	b Iverson	18	
T. E. Bailey	c Tallon b Johnson	15	(8) not out	0	
†T. G. Evans	not out	23	(7) b Johnson	14	
A. V. Bedser	b Lindwall	3	b Iverson	4	
J. J. Warr	b Miller	4	b Iverson	0	
D. V. P. Wright	run out	0	absent hurt	—	
Extras	(lb 10, nb 2)	12	(b 1, lb 5)	6	
Total		**290**	**Total**	**123**	

AUSTRALIA

K. A. Archer	c Evans b Bedser	48
A. R. Morris	b Bedser	0
*A. L. Hassett	c Bedser b Brown	70
R. N. Harvey	b Bedser	39
K. R. Miller	not out	145
S. J. E. Loxton	b Bedser b Brown	17
†D. Tallon	lbw b Bedser	18
I. W. Johnson	b Brown	77
R. R. Lindwall	lbw b Brown	1
W. A. Johnston	run out	0
J. Iverson	run out	1
Extras	(b 3, lb 7)	10
Total		**426**

FALL OF WICKETS

ENGLAND		
Wkt	1st	2nd
1st	34	32
2nd	128	40
3rd	128	45
4th	137	74
5th	187	91
6th	258	119
7th	267	119
8th	281	123
9th	286	123
10th	290	—

AUSTRALIA		
Wkt	1st	2nd
1st	1	—
2nd	122	—
3rd	122	—
4th	190	—
5th	223	—
6th	252	—
7th	402	—
8th	406	—
9th	418	—
10th	426	—

Umpires: A. N. Barlow,
H. Elphinston

AUSTRALIA	1st Innings				2nd Innings			
	O	M	R	W	O	M	R	W
Lindwall	16	0	60	2	4	1	12	0
Miller	15·7	4	37	4	6	2	15	0
Johnson	31	8	94	3	10	2	32	1
Johnston	21	5	50	0	13	6	31	1
Iverson	10	1	25	0	19·4	8	27	6
Loxton	5	0	12	0				

ENGLAND	1st Innings				2nd Innings			
	O	M	R	W	O	M	R	W
Bedser	43	4	107	4				
Warr	36	4	142	0				
Brown	44	4	153	4				
Compton	6	1	14	0				

1950–51 Fourth Test, Adelaide

February 2, 3, 5, 6, 7, 8
Toss: Australia   *Result:* Australia won by 274 runs

On a slow, easy-paced wicket, and in intense heat, Australia scored 254 for 3 on the first day after losing Archer without a run on the board. A passive but intelligent innings from Hassett, who protected Morris from his bête noire Bedser (four dismissals out of five in the series so far) helped Australia towards recovery, after which Morris and a fortunate Harvey put on 110, Wright as so often being unable to find the edge of the bat. Morris after a cramped start began to play freely, and after Bedser had bowled Harvey with the new ball Miller kept Morris company somewhat unsurely until the close. Morris was then 140 not out. England had Tattersall in for the injured Bailey, while the 20-year-old Burke replaced Loxton for Australia.

England did well to finish off the Australian innings for the addition of 117 next day; Wright got some lift off a length and Tattersall bowled well in his first Test. Morris, who made 206, was last out, sacrificing his wicket going for a big hit. England went in at 3.50, and Washbrook was soon caught at backward square leg. But Simpson batted coolly and Hutton was at his most fluent, his only mistake being when he danced out to a Johnson off-break and missed; Tallon missed it too. Half an hour from the close Simpson played on and Compton came in to play out time.

Not out 56 overnight, Hutton made exactly a hundred runs next day in what was possibly his greatest innings. Watching Iverson on to the bat and deflecting, or jumping in to drive through the covers, he showed complete mastery, and the other batsmen looked outclassed. A last-wicket stand with Wright added 53, after which the Australian team applauded him off the field.

99 in front, Australia lost 3 wickets for 95; but a long stand between Miller and Harvey on the fourth afternoon ruled out an England victory. Australia were 285 for 5 at stumps, and on the fifth day, with Brown off the field following a motor accident and Compton skippering, Burke, scoring mostly by deflections, took his overnight 37 not out to 101 before Hassett declared. The time was then 2.45.

The wicket was still good and the heat intense, and England seemed to have every hope of saving the game. Hutton and Washbrook put on 74, but Hutton was caught off a hard hook, and Washbrook and Compton were both out before stumps. Simpson and Sheppard batted soundly and sensibly through the last morning until Simpson drove wildly at the last ball before lunch; after that resistance soon ceased.

AUSTRALIA

K. A. Archer	c Compton b Bedser	0	c Bedser b Tattersall	32	
A. R. Morris	b Tattersall	206	run out	16	
*A. L. Hassett	c Evans b Wright	43	lbw b Wright	31	
R. N. Harvey	b Bedser	43	b Brown	68	
K. R. Miller	c Brown b Wright	44	b Wright	99	
J. W. Burke	b Tattersall	12	not out	101	
I. W. Johnson	c Evans b Bedser	16	c Evans b Warr	3	
R. R. Lindwall	lbw b Wright	1	run out	31	
†D. Tallon	b Tattersall	1	c Hutton b Compton	5	
W. A. Johnston	c Hutton b Wright	0	not out	9	
J. Iverson	not out	0			
Extras	(b 2, lb 1, w 1, nb 1)	5	(b 7, lb 1)	8	
Total		371	Total (8 wkts dec)	403	

ENGLAND

L. Hutton	not out	156	c sub (S. J. E. Loxton) b Johnston	45	
C. Washbrook	c Iverson b Lindwall	2	lbw b Johnston	31	
R. T. Simpson	b Johnston	29	c Burke b Johnston	61	
D. C. S. Compton	c Tallon b Lindwall	5	c sub (S. J. E. Loxton) b Johnston	0	
D. S. Sheppard	b Iverson	9	lbw b Miller	41	
*F. R. Brown	b Miller	16	absent hurt	—	
†T. G. Evans	c Burke b Johnston	13	(6)c Johnson b Miller	21	
A. V. Bedser	lbw b Iverson	7	(7)c Morris b Miller	0	
R. Tattersall	c Harvey b Iverson	0	(8)c Morris b Johnson	6	
J. J. Warr	b Johnston	0	(9)b Johnson	0	
D. V. P. Wright	lbw b Lindwall	14	(10)not out	0	
Extras	(b 15, lb 5, nb 1)	21	(b 15, lb 3, w 2, nb 3)	23	
Total		272	Total	228	

FALL OF WICKETS

AUSTRALIA

Wkt	1st	2nd
1st	0	26
2nd	95	79
3rd	205	95
4th	281	194
5th	310	281
6th	357	297
7th	363	367
8th	366	378
9th	367	—
10th	371	—

ENGLAND

Wkt	1st	2nd
1st	7	74
2nd	80	90
3rd	96	90
4th	132	181
5th	161	221
6th	195	221
7th	206	228
8th	214	228
9th	219	228
10th	272	—

Umpires: A. N. Barlow, A. F. Cocks

ENGLAND	1st Innings					2nd Innings			
	O	M	R	W		O	M	R	W
Bedser	26	4	74	3	..	25	6	62	0
Warr	16	2	63	0	..	21	0	76	1
Wright	25	1	99	4	..	21	2	109	2
Tattersall	25.5	5	95	3	..	27	2	116	1
Brown	3	0	24	0	..	3	1	14	1
Compton	1	0	11	0	..	4.6	1	18	1

AUSTRALIA	1st Innings					2nd Innings			
	O	M	R	W		O	M	R	W
Lindwall	13.3	0	51	3	..	10	2	35	0
Miller	13	2	36	1	..	13	4	27	3
Johnson	15	2	38	0	..	25.6	6	63	2
Iverson	26	4	68	3	..				
Johnston	25	4	58	3	..	27	4	73	4
Burke					..	3	1	7	0

1950-51 Fifth Test, Melbourne

February 23, 24, 26, 27, 28
Toss: Australia   *Result:* England won by eight wickets

As in the first two Tests, England made a promising start by bowling Australia out cheaply on the first day; but their own reply, after beginning strongly, faded badly. A great innings by Simpson, and magnificent bowling by Bedser, then put them on the way to their first victory since 1938.

On a good pitch Australia thanks to Morris and Hassett had reached 111 for 1 in just under 3 hours when Brown, whose bruised shoulder had not fully recovered, put himself on because of an injury to Bailey and, bowling at medium pace from the Richmond end, sent back Morris, Harvey and Miller, so that Australia were suddenly 123 for 4. Harvey and Miller were out to consecutive balls, an over intervening. Hole stopped the hat trick, and with Bailey off the field and Hassett at his composed best, Australia seemed likely to recover. But Bedser proved irresistible with the new ball, and with wickets falling fast Hassett was compelled to play his shots. A succession of graceful cuts and drives took him to 92, but then Hutton brought off a great one-handed slip catch wide to his right. Australia at stumps were 206 for 8.

There was no play on the Saturday through rain—the second Saturday washed out in the series—but the wicket had recovered on the Monday, and Australia were soon disposed of. Hutton and Washbrook

put on 40 in 32 minutes, Hutton and Simpson played the spinners confidently after Hutton had twice been missed at slip, and at tea England were 160 for 1; but Hole then bowled Hutton with an off-spinner and Lindwall and Miller, in a determined effort to preserve Australia's record, swept aside the middle batting with the new ball. England were only one run ahead with 6 men out at stumps, but on the third morning Simpson made 64 of the 74 added with Tattersall for the last wicket and England led by 103.

Going in again at 2.40 on the fourth day, Australia lost 2 quick wickets. Harvey's answer was to attack, and he and Hassett added 81 before Wright, after a long and accurate spell, got Harvey lbw. Brown came on and deceived Miller just as he had done in the first innings, but Hassett and Hole stayed till stumps, when Australia were 26 in front with 6 wickets to go.

On the fifth morning Wright bowled Hassett with a perfectly pitched leg-break, and although Hole carried Australia's hopes into the afternoon, Bedser got 3 of the last 4 wickets to bring his series total to 30. Hutton then played with absolute certainty until England had made the 95 they needed to win.

AUSTRALIA

Batsman	1st Innings dismissal		2nd Innings dismissal	
J. W. Burke	c Tattersall b Bedser	11	c Hutton b Bedser	1
A. R. Morris	lbw b Brown	50	lbw b Bedser	4
*A. L. Hassett	c Hutton b Brown	92	b Wright	48
R. N. Harvey	c Evans b Brown	1	lbw b Wright	52
K. R. Miller	c and b Brown	7	c and b Brown	0
G. B. Hole	b Bedser	18	b Bailey	63
I. W. Johnson	lbw b Bedser	1	c Brown b Wright	0
R. R. Lindwall	c Compton b Bedser	21	b Bedser	14
†D. Tallon	c Hutton b Bedser	1	not out	2
W. A. Johnston	not out	12	b Bedser	1
J. Iverson	c Washbrook b Brown	0	c Compton b Bedser	0
Extras	(b 2, lb 1)	3	(b 2, lb 8, w 1, nb 1)	12
Total		**217**	Total	**197**

ENGLAND

Batsman	1st Innings dismissal		2nd Innings dismissal	
L. Hutton	b Hole	79	not out	60
C. Washbrook	c Tallon b Miller	27	c Lindwall b Johnston	7
R. T. Simpson	not out	156	run out	15
D. C. S. Compton	c Miller b Lindwall	11	not out	11
D. S. Sheppard	c Tallon b Miller	1		
*F. R. Brown	b Lindwall	6		
†T. G. Evans	b Miller	1		
A. V. Bedser	b Lindwall	11		
T. E. Bailey	c Johnson b Iverson	5		
D. V. P. Wright	lbw b Iverson	3		
R. Tattersall	b Miller	10		
Extras	(b 9, lb 1)	10	(lb 2)	2
Total		**320**	Total (2 wkts)	**95**

FALL OF WICKETS

AUSTRALIA

Wkt	1st	2nd
1st	23	5
2nd	111	6
3rd	115	87
4th	123	89
5th	156	142
6th	166	142
7th	184	192
8th	187	196
9th	216	197
10th	217	197

ENGLAND

Wkt	1st	2nd
1st	40	32
2nd	171	62
3rd	204	—
4th	205	—
5th	212	—
6th	213	—
7th	228	—
8th	236	—
9th	246	—
10th	320	—

Umpires: A. N. Barlow, H. Elphinston

ENGLAND	1st Innings					2nd Innings			
	O	M	R	W		O	M	R	W
Bedser	22	5	46	5	..	20·3	4	59	5
Bailey	9	1	29	0	..	15	3	32	1
Brown	18	4	49	5	..	9	1	32	1
Wright	9	1	50	0	..	15	2	56	3
Tattersall	11	3	40	0	..	5	2	6	0

AUSTRALIA	1st Innings					2nd Innings			
	O	M	R	W		O	M	R	W
Lindwall	21	1	77	3	..	2	0	12	0
Miller	21·7	5	76	4	..	2	0	5	0
Johnston	12	1	55	0	..	11	3	36	1
Iverson	20	4	52	2	..	12	2	32	0
Johnson	11	1	40	0	..	1	0	1	0
Hole	5	0	10	1	..	1	0	3	0
Hassett					..	0·6	0	4	0

Averages: 1950-51

AUSTRALIA

BATTING

	M.	Inns.	N.O.	Runs	H.S.	Av.
K. R. Miller	5	9	1	350	145*	43·75
J. W. Burke	2	4	1	125	101*	41·66
A. L. Hassett	5	9	0	366	92	40·66
R. N. Harvey	5	9	0	362	74	40·22
A. R. Morris	5	9	0	321	206	35·66
K. A. Archer	3	5	0	152	48	30·40
I. W. Johnson	5	9	0	151	77	16·77
R. R. Lindwall	5	9	1	124	41	15·50
S. J. E. Loxton	3	5	0	75	32	15·00
D. Tallon	5	8	2	39	18	6·50
W. A. Johnston	5	8	2	29	12*	4·83
J. Iverson	5	7	3	3	1*	0·75

PLAYED IN ONE TEST: J. A. R. Moroney 0 and 0, G. B. Hole 18 and 63

BOWLING

	Overs	Mds.	Runs	Wkts.	Av.
J. Iverson	138·4	29	320	21	15·23
K. R. Miller	106·6	23	301	17	17·70
W. A. Johnston	153·7	29	422	22	19·18
R. R. Lindwall	99·3	10	344	15	22·93
I. W. Johnson	111·6	23	311	7	44·42

ALSO BOWLED: S. J. E. Loxton 9–1–26–0, J. W. Burke 3–1–7–0, G. B. Hole 6–0–13–1, A. L. Hassett 0·6–0–4–0.

ENGLAND

BATTING

	M.	Inns.	N.O.	Runs	H.S.	Av.
L. Hutton	5	10	4	533	156*	88·83
R. T. Simpson	5	10	1	349	156*	38·77
F. R. Brown	5	8	0	210	79	26·25
W. G. A. Parkhouse	2	4	0	77	28	19·25
T. G. Evans	5	9	1	144	49	18·00
C. Washbrook	5	10	0	173	34	17·30
D. S. Sheppard	2	3	0	51	41	17·00
T. E. Bailey	4	7	2	40	15	8·00
D. C. S. Compton	4	8	1	53	23	7·57
A. V. Bedser	5	8	2	43	14*	7·16
J. G. Dewes	2	4	0	23	9	5·75
R. Tattersall	2	3	0	16	10	5·33
D. V. P. Wright	5	7	1	23	14	3·83
J. J. Warr	2	4	0	4	4	1·00

PLAYED IN ONE TEST: D. B. Close 0 and 1, A. J. W. McIntyre 1 and 7.

BOWLING

	Overs	Mds.	Runs	Wkts.	Av.
T. E. Bailey	75·1	18	198	14	14·14
A. V. Bedser	195	34	482	30	16·06
F. R. Brown	109	12	389	18	21·61
D. V. P. Wright	103	6	500	11	45·45

ALSO BOWLED: R. Tattersall 68·5–12–257–4, J. J. Warr 73–6–281–1, D. B. Close 7–1–28–1, D. C. S. Compton 11·6–2–43–1.

Averages: 1953

ENGLAND

BATTING

	M.	Inns.	N.O.	Runs	H.S.	Av.
L. Hutton	5	9	1	443	145	55·37
W. J. Edrich	3	5	1	156	64	39·00
W. Watson	3	5	0	168	109	33·60
D. C. S. Compton	5	8	1	234	61	33·42
T. E. Bailey	5	7	0	222	71	31·71
J. H. Wardle	3	4	2	57	29*	28·50
P. B. H. May	2	3	0	85	39	28·33
T. W. Graveney	5	7	0	169	78	24·14
T. G. Evans	5	7	2	117	44*	23·40
R. T. Simpson	3	5	1	74	31	18·50
J. C. Laker	3	4	0	64	48	16·00
A. V. Bedser	5	6	3	38	22*	12·66
D. Kenyon	2	4	0	29	16	7·25
G. A. R. Lock	2	3	0	21	9	7·00

PLAYED IN ONE TEST: F. R. Brown 22 and 28, J. B. Statham 17*, R. Tattersall 2, F. S. Trueman 10.

BOWLING

	Overs	Mds.	Runs	Wkts.	Av.
A. V. Bedser	265·1	58	682	39	17·48
G. A. R. Lock	61	20	165	8	20·62
J. C. Laker	58·5	11	212	9	23·55
J. H. Wardle	155·3	58	344	13	26·46
T. E. Bailey	143	33	387	8	48·37

ALSO BOWLED: F. R. Brown 52–11–135–4, D. C. S. Compton 3–0–21–1, J. B. Statham 43–10–88–2, R. Tattersall 28–5–81–3, F. S. Trueman 26·3–4–90–4.

AUSTRALIA

BATTING

	M.	Inns.	N.O.	Runs	H.S.	Av.
A. L. Hassett	5	10	0	365	115	36·50
R. N. Harvey	5	10	0	346	122	34·60
A. R. Morris	5	10	0	337	89	33·70
G. B. Hole	5	10	0	273	66	27·30
K. R. Miller	5	9	0	223	109	24·77
R. G. Archer	3	5	1	95	49	23·75
A. K. Davidson	5	10	2	182	76	22·75
R. R. Lindwall	5	9	0	159	62	17·66
J. H. de Courcy	3	6	1	81	41	16·20
G. R. A. Langley	4	6	0	55	18	9·16
J. C. Hill	2	4	2	12	8*	6·00
R. Benaud	3	5	0	15	7	3·00
W. A. Johnston	3	6	6	22	9*	—

PLAYED IN ONE TEST: D. T. Ring 18 and 7, D. Tallon 0 and 15.

BOWLING

	Overs	Mds.	Runs	Wkts.	Av.
R. R. Lindwall	240·4	62	490	26	18·84
J. C. Hill	66	18	158	7	22·57
A. K. Davidson	125·1	42	212	8	26·50
K. R. Miller	186	72	303	10	30·30
W. A. Johnston	174	67	343	7	49·00

ALSO BOWLED: R. G. Archer 69·3–27–95–4, R. Benaud 68–19–174–2, G. B. Hole 17–8–33–0, R. N. Harvey 3–2–2–0, A. L. Hassett 1–0–4–0, A. R. Morris 3·5–0–15–1, D. T. Ring 43–7–127–2.

1953 First Test, Trent Bridge

June 11, 12, 13, 15, 16
Toss: Australia   *Result*: Match Drawn

Although there was much interference from the weather, the fluctuations of this series made it the most exciting for many years. England had not won a home series for 27 years, Australia had held the Ashes for 19, and England's struggles to avoid defeat at Lord's and Leeds, sandwiched between the excitements of Trent Bridge and Old Trafford, brought the story to a cliff-hanger climax at the Oval. It was not to be expected that Australia would equal their achievements of 1948, but Lindwall was still a great bowler, Morris, Hassett, Harvey and Miller were all great players, and there were promising newcomers in Benaud, Davidson, Archer and Hole. In a series of modest scoring Hole was certainly not a failure, but the all-rounders were disappointing, and the spin attack was so little respected that four fast bowlers were picked for the final Test, leaving the spin to Johnston. For England Hutton and Bedser were again outstanding, Bailey was incomparable as a match-saver, and Laker and Lock proved irresistible at the Oval.

The mutual respect between the two sides was demonstrated on a shortened first day as England bowled to defensive fields and Australia took 92 overs to reach 157 for 3. Morris and Harvey fell to the second

new ball, but Hassett was still there with 67 not out. Handicapped by a wet ball, England made little headway next morning; but when the third new ball was taken after lunch Bedser and Bailey took the last 6 wickets in 40 minutes for 5 runs. Hassett batted 6 hours 34 minutes.

The humid conditions suited Lindwall equally well and England were soon 17 for 3. Hutton and Graveney added 59, but in appalling light England slid to 92 for 6 at stumps. Bailey stayed for 100 minutes and Wardle for an hour, but Australia eventually gained a lead of 105.

Morris and Hole seemed to have survived the opening spell when Bedser hit Hole's off stump; an hour later Australia were 68 for 5, all to Bedser. Morris was eventually bowled behind his legs at 81 for 6, of which he had made 60, but an attempt by the later batsmen to hit their way out of trouble failed and Australia were all out for 123. Bedser's match figures were 14 for 99.

England wanted 229 to win and there were more than 2 days left; by stumps they were 42 for 1. But the fourth day was washed out, and there was no more play until after tea on the final day. In an atmosphere of anti-climax, with no hope of victory on the deadened turf, England batted safely through the last 2 hours.

AUSTRALIA

G. B. Hole	b Bedser	0	b Bedser	5	
A. R. Morris	lbw b Bedser	67	b Tattersall	60	
*A. L. Hassett	b Bedser	115	c Hutton b Bedser	5	
R. N. Harvey	c Compton b Bedser	0	c Graveney b Bedser	2	
K. R. Miller	c Bailey b Wardle	55	c Kenyon b Bedser	5	
R. Benaud	c Evans b Bailey	3	b Bedser	0	
A. K. Davidson	b Bedser	4	c Graveney b Tattersall	6	
†D. Tallon	b Bedser	0	c Simpson b Tattersall	15	
R. R. Lindwall	c Evans b Bailey	0	c Tattersall b Bedser	12	
J. C. Hill	b Bedser	0	c Tattersall b Bedser	4	
W. A. Johnston	not out	0	not out	4	
Extras	(b 2, lb 2, nb 1)	5	(lb 5)	5	
Total		**249**	**Total**	**123**	

ENGLAND

*L. Hutton	c Benaud b Davidson	43	not out	60	
D. Kenyon	c Hill b Lindwall	8	c Hassett b Hill	16	
R. T. Simpson	lbw b Lindwall	0	not out	28	
D. C. S. Compton	c Morris b Lindwall	0			
T. W. Graveney	c Benaud b Hill	22			
P. B. H. May	c Tallon b Hill	9			
T. E. Bailey	lbw b Hill	13			
†T. G. Evans	c Tallon b Davidson	8			
J. H. Wardle	not out	29			
A. V. Bedser	lbw b Lindwall	2			
R. Tattersall	b Lindwall	2			
Extras	(b 5, lb 3)	8	(b 8, lb 4, w 2, nb 2)	16	
Total		**144**	**Total** (1 wkt)	**120**	

FALL OF WICKETS

AUSTRALIA

Wkt	1st	2nd
1st	2	28
2nd	124	44
3rd	128	50
4th	237	64
5th	244	68
6th	244	81
7th	246	92
8th	247	106
9th	248	115
10th	249	123

ENGLAND

Wkt	1st	2nd
1st	17	26
2nd	17	—
3rd	17	—
4th	76	—
5th	82	—
6th	92	—
7th	107	—
8th	121	—
9th	136	—
10th	144	—

Umpires: D. Davies, Harold Elliott

ENGLAND	1st Innings					2nd Innings			
	O	M	R	W		O	M	R	W
Bedser	38·3	16	55	7	..	17·2	7	44	7
Bailey	44	14	75	2	..	5	1	28	0
Wardle	35	16	55	1	..	12	3	24	0
Tattersall	23	5	59	0	..	5	0	22	3

AUSTRALIA	1st Innings					2nd Innings			
	O	M	R	W		O	M	R	W
Lindwall	20·4	2	57	5	..	16	4	37	0
Johnston	18	7	22	0	..	18	9	14	0
Hill	19	8	35	3	..	12	3	26	1
Davidson	15	7	22	2	..	5	1	7	0
Benaud					..	5	0	15	0
Morris					..	2	0	5	0

121. **A. L. Hassett**

122. **A. V. Bedser**

123. **Australia 1953**
Back row: G. R. A. Langley, K. R. Miller, D. T. Ring, W. A. Johnston, J. C. Hill. *Middle row:* G. A. Davies (manager), R. Benaud, G. B. Hole, C. C. McDonald, R. G. Archer, D. Tallon, A. K. Davidson, W. F. Ferguson (scorer). *Front:* I. D. Craig, J. H. de Courcy, A. L. Hassett (capt.), A. R. Morris, R. N. Harvey, R. R. Lindwall.

1953 Second Test, Lord's

Test no. 160

June 25, 26, 27, 29, 30
Toss: Australia   *Result:* Match Drawn

'... some of the best and most exciting cricket that I have ever watched has been when batsmen with pluck and skill have batted hour by hour against the bowlers, fighting for the draw.' So wrote umpire Robert Thoms in *Wisden* in 1890; and Lord's 1953 was a shining example.

Both sides made changes. England recalled Brown, chairman of selectors, and included Watson and Statham for Tattersall, Simpson and May. For Australia Langley kept wicket and Ring replaced Hill. The first day was mostly Australia's. Four chances were missed, the easiest being Hassett's to Hutton at slip when he was 55, and at tea Australia were 180 for 1. But Harvey was out soon after, Hassett on reaching his hundred retired with cramp, and England rode their luck as Wardle got Hole, Benaud and Miller cheaply; at stumps Australia were 263 for 5.

Although Hutton dropped two more catches and had to go off for repairs, Australia lost their last 5 wickets for 83. Fine driving and cutting by the left-handed Davidson accounted for most of these. Kenyon failed, but Hutton and Graveney raised England to 177 for 1. The strokes were locked away for the last hour, but the stand equalled England's best since the war. Graveney was yorked first thing next morning, but a hostile spell with the new ball was skilfully contained by Hutton and Compton, Hutton making 145. A familiar collapse followed his dismissal, 6 wickets falling after lunch for 54.

26 behind, Australia soon lost Hassett, but Miller made 58 of Australia's close of play score of 96 for 1. Next morning it was Morris who scored the faster, and it was not until Compton was put on in desperation that a wicket fell. Then the game changed again as Miller was out for 109 and Brown, turning his leg-breaks down the slope, took 3 wickets in 15 balls. But an onslaught by Lindwall boosted Australia's lead to 342, and he then took the ball and removed Kenyon and Hutton. At stumps England were 20 for 3.

England thus began the final day facing defeat. Compton and Watson resisted stubbornly, but after 95 minutes Johnston got Compton with a faster ball that kept low. There were still nearly 5 hours left when Bailey joined Watson, but at tea they were still together, having survived spinners and new ball alike, and they were not parted until 5.50, when Watson edged a googly to slip; his 109, in his first Test, lasted 5¾ hours. When Bailey left 5 minutes later after batting 4¼ hours, Australia still had a chance; but England's apprehensions soon receded under the weight of a bold assault from Brown.

AUSTRALIA

*A. L. Hassett	c Bailey b Bedser	104	c Evans b Statham	3	
A. R. Morris	st Evans b Bedser	30	c Statham b Compton	89	
R. N. Harvey	lbw b Bedser	59	(4)b Bedser	21	
K. R. Miller	b Wardle	25	(3)b Wardle	109	
G. B. Hole	c Compton b Wardle	13	lbw b Brown	47	
R. Benaud	lbw b Wardle	0	c Graveney b Bedser	5	
A. K. Davidson	c Statham b Bedser	76	c and b Brown	15	
D. T. Ring	lbw b Wardle	18	lbw b Brown	7	
R. R. Lindwall	b Statham	9	b Bedser	50	
†G. R. A. Langley	c Watson b Bedser	1	b Brown	9	
W. A. Johnston	not out	3	not out	0	
Extras	(b 4, lb 4)	8	(b 8, lb 5)	13	
Total		**346**	**Total**	**368**	

ENGLAND

*L. Hutton	c Hole b Johnston	145	c Hole b Lindwall	5	
D. Kenyon	c Davidson b Lindwall	3	c Hassett b Lindwall	2	
T. W. Graveney	b Lindwall	78	c Langley b Johnston	2	
D. C. S. Compton	c Hole b Benaud	57	lbw b Johnston	33	
W. Watson	st Langley b Johnston	4	c Hole b Ring	109	
T. E. Bailey	c and b Miller	2	c Benaud b Ring	71	
F. R. Brown	c Langley b Lindwall	22	c Hole b Benaud	28	
†T. G. Evans	b Lindwall	0	not out	11	
J. H. Wardle	b Davidson	23	not out	0	
A. V. Bedser	b Lindwall	1			
J. B. Statham	not out	17			
Extras	(b 11, lb 1, w 1, nb 7)	20	(b 7, lb 6, w 2, nb 6)	21	
Total		**372**	**Total** (7 wkts)	**282**	

FALL OF WICKETS

AUSTRALIA

Wkt	1st	2nd
1st	65	3
2nd	190	168
3rd	225	227
4th	229	235
5th	240	248
6th	280	296
7th	291	305
8th	330	308
9th	331	362
10th	346	368

ENGLAND

Wkt	1st	2nd
1st	9	6
2nd	177	10
3rd	279	12
4th	291	73
5th	301	236
6th	328	246
7th	328	282
8th	332	—
9th	341	—
10th	372	

Umpires: F. S. Lee
H. G. Baldwin

ENGLAND

	1st Innings O	M	R	W		2nd Innings O	M	R	W
Bedser	42·4	8	105	5	..	31·5	8	77	3
Statham	28	7	48	1	..	15	3	40	1
Brown	25	7	53	0	..	27	4	82	4
Bailey	16	2	55	0	..	10	4	24	0
Wardle	29	8	77	4	..	46	18	111	1
Compton					..	3	0	21	1

AUSTRALIA

	1st Innings O	M	R	W		2nd Innings O	M	R	W
Lindwall	23	4	66	5	..	19	3	26	2
Miller	25	6	57	1	..	17	8	17	0
Johnston	35	11	91	2	..	29	10	70	2
Ring	14	2	43	0	..	29	5	84	2
Benaud	19	4	70	1	..	17	6	51	1
Davidson	10·5	2	25	1	..	14	5	13	0
Hole					..	1	1	0	0

218

1953 Third Test, Old Trafford

July 9, 10, 11, 13, 14
Toss: Australia   *Result:* Match Drawn

All wicket-keepers throughout Test history have had their bad days, but few single mistakes can have been more costly than the dropping of Harvey by Evans standing back to Bailey when the batsman had scored 4. Had it been held the match might have gone very differently. As it was Harvey, although playing and missing several times at first, took part in a stand of 173 with Hole after 3 wickets had fallen for 48, finally making 122 before being well caught on the leg side standing up by the man who had let him off earlier.

England went into the field with only four bowlers, and one of these, Laker, pulled a muscle straight away. Yet they made an exciting if somewhat fortunate start. Play did not begin until 2.50 after heavy rain, and the wicket was too sodden to help batsman or bowler: but after 15 minutes Morris played on, the ball trickling on to the stumps; at 48 Bailey yorked Hassett; and at the same total Miller played on just as Morris had done. Harvey's period of uncertainty followed, and at tea Australia were 81 for 3. There were two breaks for rain before stumps, by which time Australia had made 151 for 3 off 52 overs, Harvey 60, Hole 41.

Only 28 overs were bowled on the second day, most of them before lunch; but there was time for Harvey to reach his hundred, and when rain stopped play Australia were 221 for 3. Play began on the third day at noon, and it was soon apparent that the wicket was less friendly. Australia were 290 for 6 at lunch, and a declaration then might have embarrassed England a good deal; but Hassett took no chances and batted on, and with de Courcy hitting out gaily the total reached 318. England lost Edrich and Graveney cheaply and were 32 for 2, but by that time the wicket had eased and Hutton and Compton added 94. Both were out just before stumps, however, when England still needed 43 to save the follow on.

A blank fourth day seemed to leave the game dead; but the fifth was full of excitement, England's 6th wicket falling with 20 still needed to save the follow on. But Simpson and Bailey added 40, and although Hill showed that the wicket was taking spin a robust innings from Evans helped England to a creditable 276. There was a sensational finish as the Australians collapsed to 35 for 8, only Davidson showing any ability to cope with the turning ball; but by then the Australians were not inclined to take matters too seriously.

AUSTRALIA

*A. L. Hassett	b Bailey	26	c Bailey b Bedser	8	
A. R. Morris	b Bedser	1	c Hutton b Laker	0	
K. R. Miller	b Bedser	17	st Evans b Laker	6	
R. N. Harvey	c Evans b Bedser	122	(7) b Wardle	0	
G. B. Hole	c Evans b Bedser	66	(4) c Evans b Bedser	2	
J. H. de Courcy	lbw b Wardle	41	(5) st Evans b Wardle	8	
A. K. Davidson	st Evans b Laker	15	(6) not out	4	
R. G. Archer	c Compton b Bedser	5	lbw b Wardle	0	
R. R. Lindwall	c Edrich b Wardle	1	b Wardle	4	
J. C. Hill	not out	8	not out	0	
†G. R. A. Langley	c Edrich b Wardle	8			
Extras	(b 6, lb 1, nb 1)	8	(lb 3)	3	
Total		**318**	**Total** (8 wkts)	**35**	

ENGLAND

*L. Hutton	lbw b Lindwall	66
W. J. Edrich	c Hole b Hill	6
T. W. Graveney	c de Courcy b Miller	5
D. C. S. Compton	c Langley b Archer	45
J. H. Wardle	b Lindwall	5
W. Watson	b Davidson	16
R. T. Simpson	c Langley b Davidson	31
T. E. Bailey	c Hole b Hill	27
†T. G. Evans	not out	44
J. C. Laker	lbw b Hill	5
A. V. Bedser	b Morris	10
Extras	(b 8, lb 8)	16
Total		**276**

FALL OF WICKETS

AUSTRALIA

Wkt	1st	2nd
1st	15	8
2nd	48	12
3rd	48	18
4th	221	18
5th	256	31
6th	285	31
7th	290	31
8th	291	35
9th	302	—
10th	318	—

ENGLAND

Wkt	1st	2nd
1st	19	—
2nd	32	—
3rd	126	—
4th	126	—
5th	149	—
6th	149	—
7th	209	—
8th	231	—
9th	243	—
10th	276	—

Umpires: D. Davies,
Harold Elliott

ENGLAND		1st Innings				2nd Innings		
	O	M	R	W	O	M	R	W
Bedser	45	10	115	5	4	1	14	2
Bailey	26	4	83	1				
Wardle	28·3	10	70	3	5	2	7	4
Laker	17	3	42	1	9	5	11	2

AUSTRALIA		1st Innings				2nd Innings		
	O	M	R	W	O	M	R	W
Lindwall	20	8	30	2				
Archer	15	8	12	1				
Hill	35	7	97	3				
Miller	24	11	38	1				
Davidson	20	4	60	2				
Harvey	3	2	2	0				
Hole	2	0	16	0				
Morris	1	0	5	1				

1953 Fourth Test, Leeds

July 23, 24, 25, 27, 28
Toss: Australia   *Result:* Match Drawn

Misfortune had always dogged England at Leeds. In 1899 Briggs had had his seizure, in 1909 Jessop strained his back, in 1921 Hobbs was stricken with appendicitis. In 1926 Carr put Australia in and then dropped Macartney, in 1930 and 1934 Bradman made over 300, and in 1938 Bradman and O'Reilly stole the Ashes. Then in 1948 Australia made 404 to win on the final day. What misfortunes were in store this time?

Hassett put England in, and Lindwall with his second ball bowled Hutton. The pitch had been softened by rain, but after lunch it played well enough. Yet Hutton, Edrich, Compton and Graveney were out for 98 (of which Graveney made 55), Simpson was struck on the elbow and had to retire, Watson limped off after being bowled off his ankle, and Bailey, sent back by Evans, wrenched his knee trying to escape being run out. England's 142 for 7 off 96 overs was the lowest ever in a day's play in England, though 25 minutes were lost through rain.

On a pitch that was still spongy England were finished off next morning for 167. Bedser then got Morris and Hassett, Bailey, bowling off a shortened run, dismissed Miller, and Australia were 84 for 3; but Harvey and Hole, doubling the score, took Australia into the lead.

The later batting collapsed to the new ball, but thanks to a useful last-wicket stand Australia led by 99.

Edrich was the senior partner in an opening stand of 57 on the third morning; but at 62 for 1 rain intervened. On the fourth day, with rain again interrupting play, England struggled on a freshened pitch and at stumps were 177 for 5—only 78 in front. And on the last day Compton, 60 not out overnight, was unable to continue at first through a swollen hand. Yet thanks to a marathon effort by Bailey and fine off driving by Laker, England had virtually saved the game when Bailey was last out after 4 hours 22 minutes to the last ball before tea.

Wanting 177 in 115 minutes, Australia were prepared to show interest; and when 14 runs came off Lock's first over (he opened with Bedser) they played their luck. Harvey and Hole put on 57 in half an hour, and when Davidson joined Hole only 66 were wanted in 45 minutes with 7 wickets left. But Bailey, back to his long run and taking his time, bowled wide of the leg stump, Hole was well caught by Graveney on the boundary from a shot that would otherwise have gone for six, and the target was put out of reach.

ENGLAND

Batsman	1st Innings		2nd Innings	
*L. Hutton	b Lindwall	0	c Langley b Archer	25
W. J. Edrich	lbw b Miller	10	c de Courcy b Lindwall	64
T. W. Graveney	c Benaud b Miller	55	b Lindwall	3
D. C. S. Compton	c Davidson b Lindwall	0	lbw b Lindwall	61
W. Watson	b Lindwall	24	c Davidson b Miller	15
R. T. Simpson	c Langley b Lindwall	15	c de Courcy b Miller	0
T. E. Bailey	run out	7	c Hole b Davidson	38
†T. G. Evans	lbw b Lindwall	25	c Lindwall b Miller	1
J. C. Laker	c Lindwall b Archer	10	c Benaud b Davidson	48
G. A. R. Lock	b Davidson	9	c Morris b Miller	8
A. V. Bedser	not out	0	not out	3
Extras	(b 8, lb 4)	12	(b 1, lb 8)	9
Total		167		275

AUSTRALIA

Batsman	1st Innings		2nd Innings	
*A. L. Hassett	c Lock b Bedser	37	b Lock	4
A. R. Morris	c Lock b Bedser	10	st Evans b Laker	38
R. N. Harvey	lbw b Bailey	71	(4)lbw b Bedser	34
K. R. Miller	c Edrich b Bailey	5		
G. B. Hole	c Lock b Bedser	53	(3)c Graveney b Bailey	33
J. H. de Courcy	lbw b Lock	10	not out	13
R. Benaud	b Bailey	7		
A. K. Davidson	c Evans b Bedser	2	(5)not out	17
R. G. Archer	not out	31		
R. R. Lindwall	b Bedser	9		
†G. R. A. Langley	c Hutton b Bedser	17		
Extras	(b 4, lb 8, w 2)	14	(b 3, lb 4, w 1)	8
Total		266	Total (4 wkts)	147

FALL OF WICKETS

ENGLAND

Wkt	1st	2nd
1st	0	57
2nd	33	62
3rd	36	139
4th	98	167
5th	108	171
6th	110	182
7th	133	239
8th	149	244
9th	167	258
10th	167	275

AUSTRALIA

Wkt	1st	2nd
1st	27	27
2nd	70	54
3rd	84	111
4th	168	117
5th	183	—
6th	203	—
7th	203	—
8th	208	—
9th	218	—
10th	266	—

Umpires: F. Chester, F. S. Lee

AUSTRALIA	1st Innings				2nd Innings			
	O	M	R	W	O	M	R	W
Lindwall	35	10	54	5	54	19	104	3
Miller	28	13	39	2	47	19	63	4
Davidson	20·4	7	23	1	29·4	15	36	2
Archer	18	4	27	1	25	12	31	1
Benaud	8	1	12	0	19	8	26	0
Hole					3	1	6	0

ENGLAND	1st Innings				2nd Innings			
	O	M	R	W	O	M	R	W
Bedser	28·5	2	95	6	17	1	65	1
Bailey	22	4	71	3	6	1	9	1
Lock	23	9	53	1	8	0	48	1
Laker	9	1	33	0	2	0	17	1

1953 Fifth Test, Oval

August 15, 17, 18, 19

Toss: Australia *Result:* England won by eight wickets

In 1953, as in 1926, the position was that Australia had won the first three post-war series and that the Ashes were at stake at the Oval in the 20th match since the war. Six days were allotted, but the extra day did not tempt the England selectors to think defensively: they played four bowlers plus Bailey, dropping Simpson to make room for Trueman, and they replaced Watson, the hero of Lord's, with May. Australia had Johnston fit again for the first time since Lord's, and he replaced Benaud. With the spinners expected to get some help later in the game, England were better equipped to take advantage; yet when Hassett won the toss for the fifth time running the threat from Laker and Lock seemed greatly diminished.

The see-saw of the series continued through the first morning as Australia recovered to 98 for 2 at lunch, with Hassett and Harvey entrenched, after losing Morris and Miller for 41. Morris was out to Bedser for the 18th time in the 20 post-war Tests. But during lunch a shower enlivened the wicket, and with Trueman fast and accurate and Bedser still getting some movement, Hassett, Harvey and—after another short shower—de Courcy were quickly disposed of. Hole batted freely for a time while Archer defended, but by 3.45 both were out and Australia were 160 for 7. At this point Lindwall joined David-son. Both were missed off Laker, but by fine cover-driving Lindwall injected so much life into the dying innings that another 105 runs were made—47 with Davidson, 38 with Langley and 30 with Johnston. In dismissing Archer, Bedser took his 39th wicket of the series, beating Tate's record. England survived two overs from Lindwall and Miller before bad light stopped play, Hutton ducking to a vicious Lindwall bouncer and losing his cap, which fell just beyond the bails.

Edrich got England going next morning, after which Hutton and May put on exactly 100; then Johnston, changing to slow-medium spin, dismissed them both. England were struggling, and when Lindwall got Compton and Graveney after tea the match had swung towards Australia. Evans played a typical innings, but England were chiefly indebted to Bailey for their precarious lead of 31.

Overnight showers had laid the dust, but when the sun dried the wicket on the third day Laker and Lock caused an astonishing collapse, Australia reeling from 50-odd for 1 to 85 for 6. Some thrilling hitting by Archer only delayed the end, and England were left with 132 to win. Johnston, bowling his spinners from one end while Lindwall and Miller closed the other, found the edge of the bat many times, but Edrich steered England to victory.

AUSTRALIA

*A. L. Hassett	c Evans b Bedser	53	lbw b Laker	10		
A. R. Morris	lbw b Bedser	16	lbw b Lock	26		
K. R. Miller	lbw b Bailey	1	(5)c Trueman b Laker	0		
R. N. Harvey	c Hutton b Trueman	36	b Lock	1		
G. B. Hole	c Evans b Trueman	37	(3)lbw b Laker	17		
J. H. de Courcy	c Evans b Trueman	5	run out	4		
R. G. Archer	c and b Bedser	10	c Edrich b Lock	49		
A. K. Davidson	c Edrich b Laker	22	b Lock	21		
R. R. Lindwall	c Evans b Trueman	62	c Compton b Laker	12		
†G. R. A. Langley	c Edrich b Lock	18	c Trueman b Lock	2		
W. A. Johnston	not out	9	not out	6		
Extras	(b 4, nb 2)	6	(b 11, lb 3)	14		
Total		**275**	Total	**162**		

ENGLAND

*L. Hutton	b Johnston	82	run out	17
W. J. Edrich	lbw b Lindwall	21	not out	55
P. B. H. May	c Archer b Johnston	39	c Davidson b Miller	37
D. C. S. Compton	c Langley b Lindwall	16	not out	22
T. W. Graveney	c Miller b Lindwall	4		
T. E. Bailey	b Archer	64		
†T. G. Evans	run out	28		
J. C. Laker	c Langley b Miller	1		
G. A. R. Lock	c Davidson b Lindwall	4		
F. S. Trueman	b Johnston	10		
A. V. Bedser	not out	22		
Extras	(b 9, lb 5, w 1)	15	(lb 1)	1
Total		**306**	Total (2 wkts)	**132**

FALL OF WICKETS

AUSTRALIA

Wkt	1st	2nd
1st	38	23
2nd	41	59
3rd	107	60
4th	107	61
5th	118	61
6th	160	85
7th	160	135
8th	207	140
9th	245	144
10th	275	162

ENGLAND

Wkt	1st	2nd
1st	37	24
2nd	137	88
3rd	154	—
4th	167	—
5th	170	—
6th	210	—
7th	225	—
8th	237	—
9th	262	—
10th	306	—

Umpires: D. Davies, F. S. Lee

ENGLAND	1st Innings					2nd Innings			
	O	M	R	W		O	M	R	W
Bedser	29	3	88	3	..	11	2	24	0
Trueman	24·3	3	86	4	..	2	1	4	0
Bailey	14	3	42	1	..				
Lock	9	2	19	1	..	21	9	45	5
Laker	5	0	34	1	..	16·5	2	75	4

AUSTRALIA	1st Innings					2nd Innings			
	O	M	R	W		O	M	R	W
Lindwall	32	7	70	4	..	21	5	46	0
Miller	34	12	65	1	..	11	3	24	1
Johnston	45	16	94	3	..	29	14	52	0
Davidson	10	1	26	0	..				
Archer	10·3	2	25	1	..	1	1	0	0
Hole	11	6	11	0	..				
Hassett					..	1	0	4	0
Morris					..	0·5	0	5	0

November 26, 27, 29, 30, December 1
Toss: England *Result:* Australia won by an innings and 154 runs

Leaving behind three of the bowlers who had won the Ashes at the Oval 15 months earlier, and discarding a fourth after the first Test, England yet contrived to find a pair of opening bowlers comparable for destructive ability with any of the great pairs of the past. Tyson, chosen in preference to Trueman because of his exceptional pace, and Statham, one of the most persistently accurate of all fast bowlers, operating on wickets that had more grass and a less even bounce than in previous years, proved the decisive factors. Hutton's shrewdness as a captain compensated for his decline as a batsman, but he played at least one decisive innings, and Compton after breaking a finger in the first Test came back strongly; but the main batting confrontation was provided by Cowdrey and May. There was no falling off in the Australian bowling, England always having to fight for runs, and the matches were closely contested; but the injection of confidence the Australian batting received in the first Test quickly wore off, only three batsmen reaching 50 (once each) in the remaining Tests. England thus won the rubber for the first time in Australia for 22 years and only the fifth time this century.

Misled by the behaviour of the wicket in the match with Queensland

a week earlier, when the pitch had been well-grassed and lively at the start, Hutton put Australia in; but from the first few deliveries it was clear that the wicket was lifeless. The selection of the side had been based on the same false premise, England taking the field without a slow bowler—for the only time in Test history except for Melbourne in 1932-33, when they suffered their only defeat of the tour.

England were soon on the defensive, the out-cricket suffered from the absence of Evans (injured), several catches were dropped, Compton broke a finger in the boundary railings chasing a slice to third man, and at stumps Australia were 208 for 2. Morris and Harvey, the not out batsmen, were both put down when the new ball was taken next morning; and as they passed their centuries and opened out their rediscovered form on the series seemed likely to be immense.

Facing a total of 601 for 8 declared, England in 40 minutes collapsed to 25 for 4; it was clear that Lindwall and Miller were still great bowlers. Cowdrey and Bailey, punctuating long turgid periods with an occasional burst of shots, put on 82, and when England followed on there was some notable defiance from Edrich and May; but nothing could erase the humiliation of England's first 40 minutes' batting against that overwhelming score.

AUSTRALIA

L. E. Favell	c Cowdrey b Statham	23
A. R. Morris	c Cowdrey b Bailey	153
K. R. Miller	b Bailey	49
R. N. Harvey	c Bailey b Bedser	162
G. B. Hole	run out	57
R. Benaud	c May b Tyson	34
R. G. Archer	c Bedser b Statham	0
R. R. Lindwall	not out	64
†G. R. A. Langley	b Bailey	16
*I. W. Johnson	not out	24
W. A. Johnston	did not bat	
Extras	(b 11, lb 7, nb 1)	19
Total	(8 wkts dec)	**601**

ENGLAND

		1st inns		2nd inns
*L. Hutton	c Langley b Lindwall	4	lbw b Miller	13
R. T. Simpson	b Miller	2	run out	9
W. J. Edrich	c Langley b Archer	15	b Johnston	88
P. B. H. May	b Lindwall	1	lbw b Lindwall	44
M. C. Cowdrey	c Hole b Johnston	40	b Benaud	10
T. E. Bailey	b Johnston	88	c Langley b Lindwall	23
F. H. Tyson	b Johnson	7	not out	37
A. V. Bedser	b Johnson	5	c Archer b Johnson	5
†K. V. Andrew	b Lindwall	6	b Johnson	5
J. B. Statham	b Johnson	11	(11)c Harvey b Benaud	14
D. C. S. Compton	not out	2	(10)c Langley b Benaud	0
Extras	(b 3, lb 6)	9	(b 7, lb 2)	9
Total		**190**	**Total**	**257**

FALL OF WICKETS

AUSTRALIA
Wkt	1st	2nd
1st	51	
2nd	123	—
3rd	325	—
4th	456	—
5th	463	—
6th	464	—
7th	545	—
8th	572	—
9th	—	—
10th	—	—

ENGLAND
Wkt	1st	2nd
1st	4	22
2nd	10	23
3rd	11	147
4th	25	163
5th	107	181
6th	132	220
7th	141	231
8th	156	242
9th	181	243
10th	190	257

Umpires: M. J. McInnes,
C. Hoy

ENGLAND	1st Innings				2nd Innings			
	O	M	R	W	O	M	R	W
Bedser	37	4	131	1				
Statham	34	2	123	2				
Tyson	29	1	160	1				
Bailey	26	1	140	3				
Edrich	3	0	28	0				

AUSTRALIA	1st Innings				2nd Innings			
	O	M	R	W	O	M	R	W
Lindwall	14	4	27	3	17	3	50	2
Miller	11	5	19	1	12	2	30	1
Archer	4	1	14	1	15	4	28	0
Johnson	19	5	46	3	17	5	38	2
Benaud	12	5	28	0	8·1	1	43	3
Johnston	16·1	5	47	2	21	8	59	2

124. R. N. Harvey

125. F. H. Tyson

126. **England 1954-55**
Back row: H. Dalton (masseur), M. C. Cowdrey, J. H. Wardle, J. B. Statham, T. W. Graveney, R. Appleyard, J. V. Wilson,
J. E. McConnon, F. H. Tyson, P. J. Loader, K. V. Andrew, G. Duckworth (scorer). *Front:* R. T. Simpson, T. G. Evans, P. B. H. May,
L. Hutton (capt.), C. G. Howard (manager), A. V. Bedser, W. J. Edrich, T. E. Bailey.

1954-55 Second Test, Sydney

December 17, 18, 20, 21, 22
Toss: Australia   *Result:* England won by 38 runs

Hutton's determination to have a two-pronged spearhead and the need for a balanced attack dictated the dropping of Bedser and Simpson, while Graveney came in for the injured Compton. For Australia, Hole and Davidson replaced Miller and Johnson (injured). Morris, deputising for Johnson, put England in on a patchy wicket: however unsound historically, with England still suffering from the hangover of Brisbane it looked good psychology. At lunch England were 34 for 2.

England were going steadily afterwards when Hutton glanced Johnston and Davidson dived to take a wonderful catch; England then collapsed before the Australian fast attack and were 111 for 9 when Statham joined Wardle in the best stand of the innings. Only four more overs were possible, in the last of which Morris was caught off one that flew; even so his policy looked justified.

The only criticism of England's out-cricket on the second day was the over rate: but the 51·6 overs bowled proved enough to dismiss Australia. Softened up by Bailey after a promising start and then harried by Tyson and Statham, they were all out for 228, their lead, though useful enough, being restricted to 74. But for Archer's charmed life against Tyson this might have been less.

England seemed in a hopeless position just before lunch on the third day at 55 for 3; but May and Cowdrey put on 116, and at stumps

England had made 204 for 4 off 70 overs. When five more wickets fell next morning for 46 runs, however, and Tyson was knocked out by a Lindwall bouncer, England seemed lost. But Statham was concerned in another valuable last-wicket partnership, Morris again shunning spin, and Australia were left wanting 223.

In a violent opening burst Statham beat both openers repeatedly before getting Morris, and with Tyson bowling at a terrific pace despite his injury Australia lived dangerously. But when these two tired Hutton went on the defensive, and by the close Australia at 72 for 2 were within 151 of victory.

Next morning Tyson, with a bump on the back of his head the size of an egg, swung the game England's way with two paralysing yorkers to dismiss Burke and Hole, and although the wicket was now easy Australia were blasted out. Much more controlled off a shortened run, Tyson bowled just about as fast as humanly possible, and he and Statham showed what they had learnt from Lindwall (bouncers apart) about bowling a full length around the off stump. A great innings by Harvey, and yet another last-wicket stand, threatened England to the end, but after 90 minutes sustained pace in the afternoon and with 39 still wanted Tyson finally got Johnston.

ENGLAND

*L. Hutton	c Davidson b Johnston	30	c Benaud b Johnston	28		
T. E. Bailey	b Lindwall	0	c Langley b Archer	6		
P. B. H. May	c Johnston b Archer	5	b Lindwall	104		
T. W. Graveney	c Favell b Johnston	21	c Langley b Johnston	0		
M. C. Cowdrey	c Langley b Davidson	23	c Archer b Benaud	54		
W. J. Edrich	c Benaud b Archer	10	b Archer	29		
F. H. Tyson	b Lindwall	0	b Lindwall	9		
†T. G. Evans	c Langley b Archer	3	c Lindwall b Archer	4		
J. H. Wardle	c Burke b Johnston	35	lbw b Lindwall	8		
R. Appleyard	c Hole b Davidson	8	not out	19		
J. B. Statham	not out	14	c Langley b Johnston	25		
Extras	(lb 5)	5	(lb 6, nb 4)	10		
Total		**154**	**Total**	**296**		

AUSTRALIA

L. E. Favell	c Graveney b Bailey	26	c Edrich b Tyson	16
*A. R. Morris	c Hutton b Bailey	12	lbw b Statham	10
J. W. Burke	c Graveney b Bailey	44	b Tyson	14
R. N. Harvey	c Cowdrey b Tyson	12	not out	92
G. B. Hole	b Tyson	12	b Tyson	0
R. Benaud	lbw b Statham	20	c Tyson b Appleyard	12
R. G. Archer	c Hutton b Tyson	49	b Tyson	6
A. K. Davidson	b Statham	20	c Evans b Statham	5
R. R. Lindwall	c Evans b Tyson	19	b Tyson	8
†G. R. A. Langley	b Bailey	5	b Statham	0
W. A. Johnston	not out	0	c Evans b Tyson	11
Extras	(b 5, lb 2, nb 2)	9	(lb 7, nb 3)	10
Total		**228**	**Total**	**184**

FALL OF WICKETS

ENGLAND

Wkt	1st	2nd
1st	14	18
2nd	19	55
3rd	58	55
4th	63	171
5th	84	222
6th	85	232
7th	88	239
8th	99	249
9th	111	250
10th	154	296

AUSTRALIA

Wkt	1st	2nd
1st	18	27
2nd	65	34
3rd	100	77
4th	104	77
5th	122	102
6th	141	122
7th	193	127
8th	213	136
9th	224	145
10th	228	184

Umpires: M. J. McInnes, R. Wright

AUSTRALIA	1st Innings					2nd Innings			
	O	M	R	W		O	M	R	W
Lindwall	17	3	47	2	..	31	10	69	3
Archer	12	7	12	3	..	22	9	53	3
Davidson	12	3	34	2	..	13	2	52	0
Johnston	13·3	1	56	3	..	19·3	2	70	3
Benaud					..	19	3	42	1

ENGLAND	1st Innings					2nd Innings			
	O	M	R	W		O	M	R	W
Statham	18	1	83	2	..	19	6	45	3
Bailey	17·4	3	59	4	..	6	0	21	0
Tyson	13	2	45	4	..	18·4	1	85	6
Appleyard	7	1	32	0	..	6	1	12	1
Wardle					..	4	2	11	0

1954-55 Third Test, Melbourne

Test no. 166

December 31, January 1, 3, 4, 5
Toss: England   *Result:* England won by 128 runs

Australia hit back at once after their Sydney defeat with some magnificent bowling by Miller (returning for Davidson), so that England were soon 41 for 4. Despite a suspect knee Miller took full advantage of some dampness in the wicket to get Hutton, Edrich and Compton in 90 minutes sustained malevolence before lunch, his figures then reading 9 overs, 8 maidens, 5 runs (two scoring strokes), 3 wickets. Meanwhile Lindwall, almost as fierce, got May caught, like Compton, off his glove.

Cowdrey began with an edged boundary between third slip and gully, but this was his only false stroke. As at Brisbane he and Bailey revived England's fortunes, getting behind the rising ball and putting on 74, but the wicket eased after the first hour. Surviving the early horrors through perfect technique, the 22-year-old Cowdrey made 50 out of 69 and 100 out of 158. Evans too batted with discretion, helping to add 54, but after Cowdrey was bowled behind his legs by an off-break the tail folded up to Archer.

Next day, on an improved wicket whose most serious fault was that the occasional ball kept low, Australia struggled to 65 for 4 at lunch. Statham and Tyson got the openers, Miller fell to a great diving catch by Evans, Hole was beaten for speed by a full toss. When Appleyard bowled Harvey after lunch Australia were 92 for 5.

With a great chance of a substantial first innings lead, England now allowed Australia to recover. Clumsy ground fielding, fast bowlers who had tired in great heat, a compact innings by Maddocks (deputising for Langley), and possibly Hutton's reluctance to bat again that evening, all contributed, and by stumps Australia had reached 188 for 8. The tempo was again slow and England bowled only 54 overs against Australia's 67·6 the previous day.

When England went in again Hutton and Edrich cleared the arrears, and then May, after an anxious first over, made the ball hum through the deep-set off-side field, so that at stumps England were 159 for 3. On the fourth day Johnston found a ball of curving flight to dismiss May, but Bailey held the middle together for 165 minutes, Evans and Wardle hit profitably, and Australia were set 240 to win. 75 for 2 at stumps, with 165 wanted, they were in much the same position as at Sydney. But early on the fifth morning an acrobatic leg-side catch by Evans dismissed Harvey, after which Tyson's pace and hostility proved irresistible. In 51 balls he took 6 for 16, Australia losing their last 8 wickets for 36.

ENGLAND

*L. Hutton	c Hole b Miller	12	lbw b Archer	42
W. J. Edrich	c Lindwall b Miller	4	b Johnston	13
P. B. H. May	c Benaud b Lindwall	0	b Johnston	91
M. C. Cowdrey	b Johnson	102	b Benaud	7
D. C. S. Compton	c Harvey b Miller	4	c Maddocks b Archer	23
T. E. Bailey	c Maddocks b Johnston	30	not out	24
†T. G. Evans	lbw b Archer	20	c Maddocks b Miller	22
J. H. Wardle	b Archer	0	b Johnson	38
F. H. Tyson	b Archer	6	c Harvey b Johnston	6
J. B. Statham	b Archer	3	c Favell b Johnston	0
R. Appleyard	not out	1	b Johnston	6
Extras	(b 9)	9	(b 2, lb 4, w 1)	7
Total		**191**	**Total**	**279**

FALL OF WICKETS
ENGLAND

Wkt	1st	2nd
1st	14	40
2nd	21	96
3rd	29	128
4th	41	173
5th	115	185
6th	169	211
7th	181	257
8th	181	273
9th	190	273
10th	191	279

AUSTRALIA

L. E. Favell	lbw b Statham	25	b Appleyard	30
A. R. Morris	lbw b Tyson	3	c Cowdrey b Tyson	4
K. R. Miller	c Evans b Statham	7	(5)c Edrich b Tyson	6
R. N. Harvey	b Appleyard	31	c Evans b Tyson	11
G. B. Hole	b Tyson	11	(6)c Evans b Statham	5
R. Benaud	c sub (J. V. Wilson) b Appleyard	15	(3)b Tyson	22
R. G. Archer	b Wardle	23	b Statham	15
†L. V. Maddocks	c Evans b Statham	47	b Tyson	0
R. R. Lindwall	b Statham	13	lbw b Tyson	0
*I. W. Johnson	not out	33	not out	4
W. A. Johnston	b Statham	11	c Evans b Tyson	0
Extras	(b 7, lb 3, nb 2)	12	(b 1, lb 13)	14
Total		**231**	**Total**	**111**

AUSTRALIA

Wkt	1st	2nd
1st	15	23
2nd	38	57
3rd	43	77
4th	65	86
5th	92	87
6th	115	97
7th	134	98
8th	151	98
9th	205	110
10th	231	111

Umpires: M. J. McInnes, C. Hoy

AUSTRALIA	1st Innings				2nd Innings			
	O	M	R	W	O	M	R	W
Lindwall	13	0	59	1	18	3	52	0
Miller	11	8	14	3	18	6	35	1
Archer	13·6	4	33	4	24	7	50	2
Benaud	7	0	30	0	8	2	25	1
Johnston	12	6	26	1	24·5	2	25	5
Johnson	11	3	20	1	8	2	25	1

ENGLAND	1st Innings				2nd Innings			
	O	M	R	W	O	M	R	W
Tyson	21	2	68	2	12·3	1	27	7
Statham	16·3	0	60	5	11	1	38	2
Bailey	9	1	33	0	3	0	14	0
Appleyard	11	3	38	2	4	1	17	1
Wardle	6	0	20	1	1	0	1	0

1954-55 Fourth Test, Adelaide

January 28, 29, 31, February 1, 2
Toss: Australia   *Result:* England won by five wickets

One down in the series, Australia had Davidson in for Lindwall, injured. McDonald came in for Favell, and with Morris he gave Australia a fine start, the lunch score being 51 for 0. But after lunch Tyson got one to lift off a length to dismiss Morris, and McDonald was caught at slip off Appleyard. Burke left at 115, and then Bailey, hitherto held in reserve, had a confident Harvey caught at first slip. Miller and Benaud then took Australia to 161 for 4—off 58 overs—at stumps. The shade temperature was 100 degrees and Hutton made 18 bowling changes in the day.

Australia lost 3 wickets for 60 in the pre-lunch session next day, two of them to Appleyard, and when Davidson was eighth out at 229 England's performance on a perfect pitch could hardly be faulted. But Maddocks and Johnson, by sensible, robust methods and good running, put on 92 in 95 minutes, and Australia totalled 323. England gained some solace from a bright start by Hutton and Edrich, but it was noticeable that both were troubled by Johnson. At stumps England were 57 for 0.

The third day produced a great tussle between the spin of Johnson and Benaud and the skill and concentration of Hutton, Cowdrey and Compton; of the 81 overs bowled in the day the quick men bowled

only 10. (Archer had pulled a muscle.) Coming together at 63 for 2, Hutton and Cowdrey put on 99 in 165 minutes, Hutton being out just before tea to a freak catch by Davidson close in off a hard hook. 169 for 3 at tea, England added 61 in the final session without losing a wicket; but Johnson had held back the new ball, and on the fourth morning it accounted for Cowdrey and Compton for 2 runs. England owed much to Bailey, Evans (37 in 36 minutes) and Wardle for their lead of 18.

On a wicket unhelpful to fast bowling Hutton tried Appleyard when the Australian openers had made 24; and Appleyard immediately caught and bowled Morris and followed by getting Burke and Harvey before stumps, when Australia were 69 for 3. Statham's third ball next morning ended McDonald's workmanlike innings, and on a wicket still more suited to spin than pace Statham and Tyson swept the rest of the Australian batting aside, England being left with only 94 to win.

Miller rekindled Australia's dying hopes by getting Hutton, Edrich and Cowdrey in 3 overs for 12 runs; and at 49 he brought off a glorious catch at extra cover to dismiss May. But Lindwall was absent, Johnson had hurt his arm, and Compton and Bailey took England to the brink of victory.

AUSTRALIA

					FALL OF WICKETS

C. C. McDonald	c May b Appleyard	48	b Statham	29	AUSTRALIA
A. R. Morris	c Evans b Tyson	25	c and b Appleyard	16	
J. W. Burke	c May b Tyson	18	b Appleyard	5	
R. N. Harvey	c Edrich b Bailey	25	b Appleyard	7	
K. R. Miller	c Bailey b Appleyard	44	b Statham	14	
R. Benaud	c May b Appleyard	15	(7)lbw b Tyson	1	
†L. V. Maddocks	run out	69	(6)lbw b Statham	2	
R. G. Archer	c May b Tyson	21	c Evans b Tyson	3	
A. K. Davidson	c Evans b Bailey	5	lbw b Wardle	23	
*I. W. Johnson	c Statham b Bailey	41	(11)not out	3	
W. A. Johnston	not out	0	(10)c Appleyard b Tyson	3	
Extras	(b 3, lb 7, nb 2)	12	(b 4, lb 1)	5	
Total		**323**	**Total**	**111**	

Wkt	1st	2nd
1st	59	24
2nd	86	40
3rd	115	54
4th	129	69
5th	175	76
6th	182	77
7th	212	79
8th	229	83
9th	321	101
10th	323	111

ENGLAND

*L. Hutton	c Davidson b Johnston	80	c Davidson b Miller	5	
W. J. Edrich	b Johnson	21	b Miller	0	
P. B. H. May	c Archer b Benaud	1	c Miller b Johnston	26	
M. C. Cowdrey	c Maddocks b Davidson	79	c Archer b Miller	4	
D. C. S. Compton	lbw b Miller	44	not out	34	
T. E. Bailey	c Davidson b Johnston	38	lbw b Johnston	15	
†T. G. Evans	c Maddocks b Benaud	37	not out	6	
J. H. Wardle	c and b Johnson	23			
F. H. Tyson	c Burke b Benaud	1			
R. Appleyard	not out	10			
J. B. Statham	c Maddocks b Benaud	0			
Extras	(b 1, lb 2, nb 4)	7	(b 3, lb 4)	7	
Total		**341**	**Total** (5 wkts)	**97**	

ENGLAND

Wkt	1st	2nd
1st	60	3
2nd	63	10
3rd	162	18
4th	232	49
5th	232	90
6th	283	—
7th	321	—
8th	323	—
9th	336	—
10th	341	—

Umpires: M. J. McInnes,
R. Wright

ENGLAND	1st Innings				2nd Innings			
	O	M	R	W	O	M	R	W
Tyson	26.1	4	85	3	15	2	47	3
Statham	19	4	70	0	12	1	38	3
Bailey	12	3	39	3				
Appleyard	23	7	58	3	12	7	13	3
Wardle	19	5	59	0	4.2	1	8	1

AUSTRALIA	1st Innings				2nd Innings			
	O	M	R	W	O	M	R	W
Miller	11	3	34	1	10.4	2	40	3
Archer	3	0	12	0	4	0	13	0
Johnson	36	17	46	2				
Davidson	25	8	55	1	2	0	7	0
Johnston	27	11	60	2	8	2	20	2
Benaud	36.6	6	120	4	6	2	10	0
Burke	2	0	7	0				

1954-55 Fifth Test, Sydney

February 25, 26, 28, March 1, 2, 3
Toss: Australia   *Result:* Match Drawn

With the Ashes won, Graveney replaced Edrich. Lindwall and Favell returned for Australia, Burge and Watson were included, and Morris, Burke, Archer and Johnston stood down. Much of the Test Match atmosphere was dissipated by the downpours which caused the first three scheduled days to be abandoned, and when play eventually started there were only 13 hours 10 minutes left. Yet there was some superb cricket.

Although the pitch had been covered the rain had seeped through, and when he won the toss Johnson put England in. As it happened the pitch was a beauty, and despite the loss of Hutton to the fourth ball of the match Graveney at once began to drive in classical style. The first 90 minutes brought 95 runs, 58 to Graveney, and he ran to his hundred in 2½ hours with four 4s in one over from Miller. But a brilliant caught and bowled by Johnson dismissed him soon after, Cowdrey was out first ball, and when May edged Benaud to slip in the last over England were 196 for 4.

In 90 minutes before lunch next day Compton and Bailey added only 51; but Compton's last 62 runs came in 80 minutes, after which interest centred on whether Lindwall could get his 100th wicket. After he had dismissed Evans, Bailey gave him his wicket, and Hutton then declared. Lindwall thus became the only fast bowler to achieve this distinction.

Australia's new opening pair put on 52, but Wardle bowled Watson with a chinaman, Favell was late on the back stroke to Tyson, and at stumps, with only a day to go, Australia were 82 for 2.

In the earlier matches Wardle had filled the role of defensive bowler while the fast bowlers were rested; but on the final day, giving the ball plenty of air, he showed what he could do in a more attacking style. After Harvey had been caught and bowled, Miller run out through a bad call by McDonald, and McDonald himself dismissed after a scratchy but determined innings, Wardle sent back Burge, Benaud and Maddocks, and Australia at 202 for 8 still needed 20 to avoid following on. Taking the new ball proved abortive so Hutton restored Wardle, and at 217 he beat Davidson. Lindwall and Johnson then got within one run of the target before Johnson was run out.

With only 2 hours left there was little chance of a result, but Wardle took 3 more wickets and puzzled all the batsmen, his figures on the last day being 28·4, 3, 115, 7. Australian ineptitude against spin caused even more surprise than their failures against pace; but another staunch innings from McDonald suggested that this resolute player had come to stay.

ENGLAND

*L. Hutton	c Burge b Lindwall	6
T. W. Graveney	c and b Johnson	111
P. B. H. May	c Davidson b Benaud	79
M. C. Cowdrey	c Maddocks b Johnson	0
D. C. S. Compton	c and b Johnson	84
T. E. Bailey	b Lindwall	72
†T. G. Evans	c McDonald b Lindwall	10
J. H. Wardle	not out	5
F. H. Tyson	⎱	
R. Appleyard	⎰ did not bat	
J. B. Statham		
Extras	(b 1, lb 3)	4
Total	(7 wkts dec)	**371**

AUSTRALIA

	1st Innings			2nd Innings	
W. Watson	b Wardle	18	c Graveney b Statham	3
C. C. McDonald	c May b Appleyard	72	c Evans b Graveney	37
L. E. Favell	b Tyson	1	c Graveney b Wardle	9
R. N. Harvey	c and b Tyson	13	c and b Wardle	1
K. R. Miller	run out	19	b Wardle	28
P. J. Burge	c Appleyard b Wardle	17	not out	18
R. Benaud	b Wardle	7	b Hutton	22
†L. V. Maddocks	c Appleyard b Wardle	32		
A. K. Davidson	c Evans b Wardle	18		
*I. W. Johnson	run out	11		
R. R. Lindwall	not out	2		
Extras	(b 10, lb 1)	11		
Total		**221**	**Total** (6 wkts)	**118**

FALL OF WICKETS

	ENGLAND	
Wkt	1st	2nd
1st	6	—
2nd	188	—
3rd	188	—
4th	196	—
5th	330	—
6th	359	—
7th	371	—
8th	—	—
9th	—	—
10th	—	—

	AUSTRALIA	
Wkt	1st	2nd
1st	52	14
2nd	53	27
3rd	85	29
4th	129	67
5th	138	87
6th	147	118
7th	157	—
8th	202	—
9th	217	—
10th	221	—

Umpires: M. J. McInnes, R. Wright

AUSTRALIA	1st Innings				2nd Innings			
	O	M	R	W	O	M	R	W
Lindwall	20·6	5	77	3	..			
Miller	15	1	71	0	..			
Davidson	19	3	72	0	..			
Johnson	20	5	68	3	..			
Benaud	20	4	79	1	..			

ENGLAND	1st Innings				2nd Innings			
	O	M	R	W	O	M	R	W
Tyson	11	1	46	2	..	5	2	20	0
Statham	9	1	31	0	..	5	0	11	1
Appleyard	16	2	54	1	..				
Wardle	24·4	6	79	5	..	12	1	51	3
Graveney					..	6	0	34	1
Hutton					..	0·6	0	2	1

Averages: 1954-55

AUSTRALIA

BATTING	M.	Inns.	N.O.	Runs	H.S.	Av.
I. W. Johnson	4	6	4	116	41	58·00
C. C. McDonald	2	4	0	186	72	46·50
R. N. Harvey	5	9	1	354	162	44·25
A. R. Morris	4	7	0	223	153	31·85
L. V. Maddocks	3	5	0	150	69	30·00
R. R. Lindwall	4	6	2	106	64*	26·50
K. R. Miller	4	7	0	167	49	23·85
J. W. Burke	2	4	0	81	44	20·35
L. E. Favell	4	7	0	130	30	18·57
G. B. Hole	3	5	0	85	57	17·00
R. G. Archer	4	7	0	117	49	16·71
R. Benaud	5	9	0	148	34	16·44
A. K. Davidson	3	5	0	71	23	14·20
G. R. A. Langley	2	3	0	21	16	7·00
W. A. Johnston	4	6	2	25	11	6·25

PLAYED IN ONE TEST: W. Watson 18 and 3, P. J. Burge 17 and 18*.

BOWLING	Overs	Mds.	Runs	Wkts.	Av.
R. G. Archer	97·6	32	215	13	16·53
I. W. Johnson	111	37	243	12	20·25
W. A. Johnston	141·4	37	423	19	22·26
K. R. Miller	88·4	28	243	10	24·30
R. R. Lindwall	130·6	28	381	14	27·21
R. Benaud	116·7	23	377	10	37·70

ALSO BOWLED: A. K. Davidson 71–16–220–3, J. W. Burke 2–0–7–0.

ENGLAND

BATTING	M.	Inns.	N.O.	Runs	H.S.	Av.
T. W. Graveney	2	3	0	132	111	44·00
P. B. H. May	5	9	0	351	104	39·00
D. C. S. Compton	4	7	2	191	84	38·20
T. E. Bailey	5	9	1	296	88	37·00
M. C. Cowdrey	5	9	0	319	102	35·44
L. Hutton	5	9	0	220	80	24·44
W. J. Edrich	4	8	0	180	83	22·50
R. Appleyard	4	5	3	44	19*	22·00
J. H. Wardle	4	6	1	109	38	21·80
T. G. Evans	4	7	1	102	37	17·00
J. B. Statham	5	7	1	67	25	11·16
F. H. Tyson	5	7	1	66	37*	11·00

PLAYED IN ONE TEST: R. T. Simpson 2 and 9, K. V. Andrew 6 and 5, A. V. Bedser 5 and 5.

BOWLING	Overs	Mds.	Runs	Wkts.	Av.
R. Appleyard	79	22	224	11	20·36
F. H. Tyson	151	16	583	28	20·82
J. H. Wardle	70·6	15	229	10	22·90
J. B. Statham	143·3	16	499	18	27·72
T. E. Bailey	73·4	8	306	10	30·60

ALSO BOWLED: A. V. Bedser 37–4–131–1, W. J. Edrich 3–0–28–0, T. W. Graveney 6–0–34–1, L. Hutton 0·6–0–2–1.

Averages: 1956

ENGLAND

BATTING	M.	Inns.	N.O.	Runs	H.S.	Av.
P. B. H. May	5	7	2	453	101	90·60
Rev. D. S. Sheppard	2	3	0	199	113	66·33
P. E. Richardson	5	8	0	364	104	45·50
C. Washbrook	3	3	0	104	98	34·66
M. C. Cowdrey	5	8	0	244	81	30·50
T. E. Bailey	4	5	1	117	33*	29·25
T. G. Evans	5	7	1	115	47	19·16
G. A. R. Lock	4	4	1	46	25*	15·33
T. W. Graveney	2	4	1	41	18	13·66
W. Watson	2	4	0	32	18	8·00
J. C. Laker	5	6	1	37	12	7·40
A. S. M. Oakman	2	2	0	14	10	7·00
F. S. Trueman	2	3	0	9	7	3·00
J. B. Statham	3	4	2	0	0*	0·00

PLAYED IN ONE TEST: R. Appleyard 1*, J. H. Wardle 0 and 0, D. J. Insole 5, D. C. S. Compton 94 and 35*, F. H. Tyson 3, A. E. Moss played in one Test but did not bat.

BOWLING	Overs	Mds.	Runs	Wkts.	Av.
J. C. Laker	283·5	127	442	46	9·60
F. S. Trueman	75	13	184	9	20·44
G. A. R. Lock	237·2	115	337	15	22·46
J. B. Statham	106	35	184	7	26·28
T. E. Bailey	108·5	39	223	6	37·16

ALSO BOWLED: A. E. Moss 4–3–1–0, R. Appleyard 30–10–49–2, J. H. Wardle 27–9–59–1, A. S. M. Oakman 8–3–21–0, T. W. Graveney 6–3–6–0, F. H. Tyson 14–5–34–1.

AUSTRALIA

BATTING	M.	Inns.	N.O.	Runs	H.S.	Av.
J. W. Burke	5	10	1	271	65	30·11
R. Benaud	5	9	1	200	97	25·00
C. C. McDonald	5	10	0	243	89	24·30
K. R. Miller	5	10	0	203	61	22·55
R. N. Harvey	5	10	0	197	69	19·70
R. R. Lindwall	4	6	4	36	22*	18·00
P. J. Burge	3	6	1	84	35*	16·80
I. D. Craig	2	4	0	55	38	13·75
K. D. Mackay	3	6	0	73	38	12·16
G. R. A. Langley	3	4	2	21	14	10·50
R. G. Archer	5	8	0	82	33	10·25
A. K. Davidson	2	1	0	8	8	8·00
I. W. Johnson	5	9	1	61	17	7·62
L. V. Maddocks	2	4	0	6	4	1·50

PLAYED IN ONE TEST: P. Crawford 0* and 0.

BOWLING	Overs	Mds.	Runs	Wkts.	Av.
K. R. Miller	205·1	44	467	21	22·23
R. G. Archer	207·4	67	451	18	25·05
R. R. Lindwall	100·1	29	238	7	34·00
R. Benaud	154	48	330	8	41·25
I. W. Johnson	119	32	303	6	50·50

ALSO BOWLED: P. Crawford 4·5–2–4–0, A. K. Davidson 20–2–56–2, J. W. Burke 8–4–20–0, K. D. Mackay 24–6–44–1.

1956 First Test, Trent Bridge

June 7, 8, 9, 11, 12
Toss: England   *Result:* Match Drawn

In one of the wettest summers on record, after an abnormally dry spring, wickets were unpredictable and spin bowlers flourished. The Australians, disrupted by injuries, were a weak batting side, and in winning the toss four times out of five England had the best of the conditions. Yet it is not possible to explain the success of Laker without conceding his greatness. England were even weaker in batting and were only saved by a treble of selectorial gambles which reintroduced Washbrook, Sheppard and Compton to Test cricket; yet Australian spin bowlers exerted little influence on the Tests. The bowling honours went to Miller and Archer, Benaud and Johnson taking only 14 wickets between them, at prohibitive cost. Australia went into the first Test without a single win against the counties and having suffered their first defeat by a county since 1912; in the course of this defeat Laker took all ten wickets on the first day. Yet on the morning of the third Test they looked to have the rubber almost won. England used Cowdrey as an opener and he and Richardson did well, but the batsman who dominated the series, head and shoulders above all others, was May.

The retirement of Hutton, Compton's knee trouble, and injuries to Tyson, Statham and Trueman, obliged England to rebuild their side. Australia for their part fielded much the same side as towards the end of the previous series, but the loss of Lindwall and Davidson—up to that point their best bowlers—through injuries during the game was an even more crippling blow.

Only about 3½ hours' play was possible on the first day, in which England scored 134 for 2 off 63 overs. There was no play at all on the second day, and when play restarted at 1.30 on the Saturday some fine batting by Richardson and May was followed by ineffectual attempts to force the pace against Miller and Archer. An earlier declaration might have served England better, as Australia at stumps were 19 for 2.

Laker and Lock resumed next morning, but the wicket although damp was not difficult. Harvey's defiant 64 lasted 3 hours 20 minutes. Richardson and Cowdrey then put on 129 before stumps, England thus leading by 198.

On the last day Australia were left 258 to win in 4 hours. They set their sights on survival, but when 3 wickets fell to the spinners for 41 England seemed poised for victory. Burke and Burge then batted skilfully through the last 2 hours, and although the wicket was unresponsive their display suggested that Australian technique against spin had improved with the experience gained so far.

ENGLAND

P. E. Richardson	c Langley b Miller	81	c Langley b Archer	73		
M. C. Cowdrey	c Miller b Davidson	25	c Langley b Miller	81		
T. W. Graveney	c Archer b Johnson	8	(4)not out	10		
*P. B. H. May	c Langley b Miller	73				
W. Watson	lbw b Archer	0	(3)c Langley b Miller	8		
T. E. Bailey	c Miller b Archer	14				
†T. G. Evans	c Langley b Miller	0	(5)not out	8		
J. C. Laker	not out	9				
G. A. R. Lock	lbw b Miller	0				
R. Appleyard	not out	1				
A. E. Moss	did not bat					
Extras	(b 5, lb 1)	6	(b 4, lb 1, w 2, nb 1)	8		
Total	(8 wkts dec)	**217**	**Total** (3 wkts dec)	**188**		

AUSTRALIA

C. C. McDonald	lbw Lock	1	c Lock b Laker	6
J. W. Burke	c Lock b Laker	11	not out	58
R. N. Harvey	lbw b Lock	64	b Lock	3
P. J. Burge	c sub (J. M. Parks) b Lock	7	(5)not out	35
K. R. Miller	lbw b Laker	0	(4)lbw b Laker	4
R. G. Archer	c Lock b Appleyard	33		
R. Benaud	b Appleyard	17		
*I. W. Johnson	c Bailey b Laker	12		
R. R. Lindwall	c Bailey b Laker	0		
†G. R. A. Langley	not out	0		
A. K. Davidson	absent hurt			
Extras	(lb 3)	3	(b 10, lb 3, nb 1)	14
Total		**148**	**Total** (3 wkts)	**120**

FALL OF WICKETS

ENGLAND

Wkt	1st	2nd
1st	53	151
2nd	72	163
3rd	180	178
4th	181	—
5th	201	—
6th	203	—
7th	213	—
8th	214	—
9th	—	—
10th	—	—

AUSTRALIA

Wkt	1st	2nd
1st	10	13
2nd	12	18
3rd	33	41
4th	36	—
5th	90	—
6th	110	—
7th	148	—
8th	148	—
9th	148	—
10th	—	—

Umpires: T. J. Bartley, J. S. Buller

AUSTRALIA	1st Innings					2nd Innings		
	O	M	R	W	O	M	R	W
Lindwall	15	4	43	0				
Miller	33	5	69	4	19	2	58	2
Davidson	10	1	22	1				
Archer	31	10	51	2	9	0	46	1
Johnson	14	7	26	1	12	2	29	0
Burke	1	1	0	0	3	1	6	0
Benaud					18	4	41	0

ENGLAND	1st Innings					2nd Innings		
	O	M	R	W	O	M	R	W
Moss	4	3	1	0				
Bailey	3	1	8	0	9	3	16	0
Laker	29·1	11	58	4	30	19	29	2
Lock	36	16	61	3	22	11	23	1
Appleyard	11	4	17	2	19	6	32	0
Graveney					6	3	6	0

1956 Second Test, Lord's

June 21, 22, 23, 25, 26
Toss: Australia   *Result:* Australia won by 185 runs

The signs for Australia at Lord's were hardly propitious. Lindwall and Davidson were absent, Crawford, a replacement, broke down in his opening spell, and Harvey, their leading batsman, failed in both innings. Yet they played like a team and won on their merits. England brought in Trueman, Statham and Wardle for Moss, Appleyard and Lock, and Australia's other replacement was Mackay.

The pitch was easy and at lunch Australia were 70 for 0, Bailey, off the seam, getting the most life. McDonald, with his short back-lift, and Burke, meticulously behind the line, took their opening stand to 137, but both were missed in the forties by May. Shortly before tea Bailey came back and at once got McDonald and Harvey, and when Burke was stumped after tea the game was even. 55 minutes were then lost through bad light, but there was time for May to miss another slip catch before stumps, when Australia were 180 for 3.

Next morning Statham and Trueman found that extra yard of pace and Burge was soon bowled, which introduced the gum-chewing Mackay. Miller batted 50 minutes for 9 before being bowled by Trueman, and Australia made only 55 during the morning's play. Their last 7 wickets fell in uncharacteristic fashion for 105 in 61·1 overs, Mackay batting 2 hours 40 minutes for 38.

After a calm beginning Richardson and Graveney both fell to Miller. Cowdrey went to a memorable catch in the gully by Benaud, and at stumps England were 74 for 3. Next morning England progressed somewhat uncertainly to 126 for 4 when Johnson for the first time tried spin. Benaud at once dismissed May and Evans, and this proved the turning point, Miller and Archer coming back after lunch to finish off the innings.

114 ahead, Australia added another 36 before McDonald was brilliantly taken in the gully by Cowdrey. Harvey just escaped a pair only to fall to another incredible catch soon afterwards, this time off Trueman, who also dismissed Burke, Burge (a yorker) and Archer to make Australia 79 for 5. Miller, applauded all the way to the wicket, rewarded the crowd with a brief flashback to his 1945 form, but at stumps Australia, 115 for 6, were only 229 in front.

After a hectic start next morning Benaud settled to a great display of judicious hitting; he made 50 in 73 minutes and 90 before lunch, being out soon afterwards to the new ball. Mackay played his part with 31 in 265 minutes, and England were set 372 to win. 72 for 2 at stumps, they faced the last day in much the same position as in 1953; but after fighting hard all morning they succumbed soon after lunch.

AUSTRALIA

C. C. McDonald	c Trueman b Bailey	78	c Cowdrey b Bailey	26	
J. W. Burke	st Evans b Laker	65	c Graveney b Trueman	16	
R. N. Harvey	c Evans b Bailey	0	c Bailey b Trueman	10	
P. J. Burge	b Statham	21	b Trueman	14	
K. R. Miller	b Trueman	28	(7)c Evans b Trueman	30	
K. D. Mackay	c Bailey b Laker	38	(5)c Evans b Statham	31	
R. G. Archer	b Wardle	28	(6)c Evans b Bailey	1	
R. Benaud	b Statham	5	c Evans b Trueman	97	
*I. W. Johnson	c Evans b Trueman	6	lbw b Bailey	17	
†G. R. A. Langley	c Bailey b Laker	14	not out	7	
P. Crawford	not out	0	lbw b Bailey	0	
Extras	(lb 2)	2	(b 2, lb 2, nb 4)	8	
Total		**285**	**Total**	**257**	

ENGLAND

P. E. Richardson	c Langley b Miller	9	c Langley b Archer	21	
M. C. Cowdrey	c Benaud b Mackay	23	lbw b Benaud	27	
T. W. Graveney	b Miller	5	c Langley b Miller	18	
*P. B. H. May	b Benaud	63	(5)c Langley b Miller	53	
W. Watson	c Benaud b Miller	6	(4)b Miller	18	
T. E. Bailey	b Miller	32	c Harvey b Archer	18	
†T. G. Evans	st Langley b Benaud	0	c Langley b Miller	20	
J. C. Laker	b Archer	12	c Langley b Archer	4	
J. H. Wardle	c Langley b Archer	0	b Miller	0	
F. S. Trueman	c Langley b Miller	7	b Archer	2	
J. B. Statham	not out	0	not out	0	
Extras	(lb 14)	14	(lb 5)	5	
Total		**171**	**Total**	**186**	

FALL OF WICKETS

AUSTRALIA

Wkt	1st	2nd
1st	137	36
2nd	137	47
3rd	151	69
4th	185	70
5th	196	79
6th	249	112
7th	255	229
8th	265	243
9th	285	257
10th	285	257

ENGLAND

Wkt	1st	2nd
1st	22	35
2nd	32	59
3rd	60	89
4th	87	91
5th	128	142
6th	128	175
7th	161	180
8th	161	184
9th	170	184
10th	171	186

Umpires: F. S. Lee,
E. Davies

ENGLAND	1st Innings					2nd Innings			
	O	M	R	W		O	M	R	W
Statham	35	9	70	2	..	26	5	59	1
Trueman	28	6	54	2	..	28	2	90	5
Bailey	34	12	72	2	..	24·5	8	64	4
Laker	29·1	10	47	3	..	7	3	17	0
Wardle	20	7	40	1	..	7	2	19	0

AUSTRALIA	1st Innings					2nd Innings			
	O	M	R	W		O	M	R	W
Miller	34·1	9	72	5	..	36	12	80	5
Crawford	4·5	2	4	0	..				
Archer	23	9	47	2	..	31·2	8	71	4
Mackay	11	3	15	1	..				
Benaud	9	2	19	2	..	28	14	27	1
Johnson					..	4	2	3	0

127. K. R. Miller

128. J. C. Laker

129. Australia 1956

Back row: J. Wilson, K. D. Mackay, A. K. Davidson, P. J. Burge, P. Crawford, R. Benaud, R. G. Archer, R. N. Harvey. *Middle row:* G. R. A. Langley, K. R. Miller, I. W. Johnson (capt.), R. R. Lindwall, C. C. McDonald, J. W. Burke. *Front:* I. D. Craig, L. V. Maddocks, J. Rutherford.

1956 Third Test, Leeds

Test no. 171

July 12, 13, 14, 16, 17
Toss: England *Result:* England won by an innings and 42 runs

Australia had been showing improved form against the counties, but the return of Lindwall, barely fit, was more than counter-balanced by Miller's inability to bowl due to a sore knee. Langley, injured, was replaced by Maddocks. Dismayed by their batting failures England replaced Graveney and Watson with Washbrook and Insole, and on a pitch notoriously unfriendly to fast bowling they brought in Oakman for Statham. Lock returned for Wardle. Of these changes the only one that drew criticism was the reappearance of Washbrook at the age of 41.

Four days before the game the wicket was under water; but at the start it looked good. For the first hour, however, the ball moved off the seam, and Archer, getting plenty of lift with his high action, beat Cowdrey, Oakman and Richardson, and after 65 minutes England were 17 for 3. Had Miller been able to bowl they might have been in worse trouble; as it was Johnson had to turn to Mackay and Benaud.

Washbrook from the start batted with complete outward assurance, and May showed the classical poise of the great player. The first mistake came when Washbrook, at 44, banged a short ball from Johnson at Miller in the covers, but Miller saw it too late. May should have been caught and bowled by Mackay when 83, but no wicket fell until 6.25, when May played a tennis shot at a high full toss and

was caught at fine leg. In a partnership that swung the series, he and Washbrook had put on 187. 90 not out overnight, Washbrook missed his hundred, but Bailey and Evans put on 53 before Lindwall, bowling now at somewhere near top pace, finished off the tail. England's 325 had taken 167·4 overs.

Some bare patches on the wicket, and a long spell in which Benaud had sometimes turned the ball sharply, lent drama to the appearance, after Trueman had beaten McDonald, of first Laker and then Lock. Six wickets fell for 69, but Miller and Benaud held on until stumps. The wicket was helping spin but only Laker and Lock could have got such results.

Rain on Saturday and Sunday deadened the pitch, and when play started at 12.45 on the Monday Miller and Benaud took Australia within 34 of saving the follow on. But after Benaud had pulled Laker to deep mid-wicket the tail collapsed. The turf was still wet when Australia batted again and they fought desperately, being 93 for 2 at stumps off 57 overs, Harvey 40, Miller 24. All went well next morning for 50 minutes, but then Laker got one to turn and lift and Miller's 2¼-hour struggle ended. The remaining batsmen lacked the skill for mere survival, but Harvey by superb footwork and conceptration resisted for 4½ hours.

ENGLAND

P. E. Richardson	c Maddocks b Archer	5
M. C. Cowdrey	c Maddocks b Archer	0
A. S. M. Oakman	b Archer	4
*P. B. H. May	c Lindwall b Johnson	101
C. Washbrook	lbw b Benaud	98
G. A. R. Lock	c Miller b Benaud	21
D. J. Insole	c Mackay b Benaud	5
T. E. Bailey	not out	33
†T. G. Evans	b Lindwall	40
J. C. Laker	b Lindwall	5
F. S. Trueman	c and b Lindwall	0
Extras	(b 4, lb 9)	13
Total		**325**

AUSTRALIA

C. C. McDonald	c Evans b Trueman	2	b Trueman	6
J. W. Burke	lbw b Lock	41	b Laker	16
R. N. Harvey	c Trueman b Lock	11	c and b Lock	69
P. J. Burge	lbw b Laker	2	(5)lbw b Laker	5
K. D. Mackay	c Bailey b Laker	2	(8)b Laker	2
K. R. Miller	b Laker	41	(4)c Trueman b Laker	26
R. G. Archer	b Laker	4	(9)c Washbrook b Lock	1
R. Benaud	c Oakman b Laker	30	(6)b Laker	1
†L. V. Maddocks	c Trueman b Lock	0	(10)lbw Lock	0
*I. W. Johnson	c Richardson b Lock	0	(7)c Oakman b Laker	3
R. R. Lindwall	not out	0	not out	0
Extras	(b 4, lb 6)	10	(b 7, lb 4)	11
Total		**143**	**Total**	**140**

FALL OF WICKETS

ENGLAND

Wkt	1st	2nd
1st	2	—
2nd	8	—
3rd	17	—
4th	204	—
5th	226	—
6th	243	—
7th	248	—
8th	301	—
9th	321	—
10th	325	—

AUSTRALIA

Wkt	1st	2nd
1st	2	10
2nd	40	45
3rd	59	108
4th	59	120
5th	63	128
6th	69	136
7th	142	138
8th	143	140
9th	143	140
10th	143	140

Umpires: J. S. Buller,
D. Davies

AUSTRALIA	1st Innings				2nd Innings			
	O	M	R	W	O	M	R	W
Lindwall	33·4	11	67	3	..			
Archer	50	24	68	3	..			
Mackay	13	3	29	0	..			
Benaud	42	9	89	3	..			
Johnson	29	8	59	1	..			

ENGLAND	1st Innings				2nd Innings			
	O	M	R	W	O	M	R	W
Trueman	8	2	19	1	11	3	21	1
Bailey	7	2	15	0	7	2	13	0
Laker	29	10	58	5	41·3	21	55	6
Lock	27·1	11	41	4	40	23	40	3

1956 Fourth Test, Old Trafford

July 26, 27, 28, 30, 31
Toss: England   *Result:* England won by an innings and 170 runs

Hopes for a fast, true wicket were perhaps naive following earlier persistent rains. The final cutting disclosed dry patches, and the Australians did not hide their disappointment. Much of their subsequent failure may indeed have been psychological; yet when the weather gave opportunities for recovery great resolution was shown. The match was only surrendered in the final session of the last day after the most remarkable piece of bowling in the history of cricket.

Sheppard replaced Insole, but Graveney's absence through injury allowed Oakman to retain his place. Australia brought in Craig for Burge. On a lifeless wicket Richardson and Cowdrey put on 174, Sheppard and May 93, and at stumps England were 307 for 3. Sheppard completed a mature hundred next day, Evans hit 47 in 29 minutes, and although the wicket was already taking spin England totalled 459.

Australia began their reply at 2.30, and Laker and Lock took up the attack at 3.10. Half an hour later they changed ends. Nothing happened for 15 minutes; then McDonald was caught at leg slip. 80 minutes later, tea interval included, Australia were all out. The ball certainly turned, but there was no sudden deterioration in the wicket; the batting simply folded.

65 minutes were left for play. At 28 McDonald retired temporarily

with knee trouble, and Harvey came in only to hit a full toss straight to mid-wicket. Curiously this was the only wicket to fall. Rain allowed only 45 minutes' play on the Saturday, Australia losing Burke; and on the Monday the conditions were so unpleasant that only 19·2 overs were bowled, McDonald and Craig adding 27.

Play began 10 minutes late on the last day after further rain in the night, and at lunch McDonald and Craig were still together: each had then been batting more than 4 hours. But just before lunch the sun came out, and 15 minutes after the interval Craig was lbw, after which Mackay, Miller and Archer all left without scoring. Benaud then stayed with McDonald for 75 minutes until tea, Laker and Lock changing ends without effect.

McDonald was out to the second ball after tea after a stay of 5 hours 37 minutes, and with the ball turning more quickly now than at any time, Laker, back at the Stretford end, took the last 3 wickets to complete all 10. Lock in 55 overs failed to take a wicket. Laker took all his wickets in both innings from the same end. The game was so full of paradoxes as to defy rational analysis, but to quote Ian Johnson: "When the controversy and the side issues of the match are forgotten, Laker's wonderful bowling will remain."

ENGLAND

P. E. Richardson	c Maddocks b Benaud	104
M. C. Cowdrey	c Maddocks b Lindwall	80
Rev. D. S. Sheppard	b Archer	113
*P. B. H. May	c Archer b Benaud	43
T. E. Bailey	b Johnson	20
C. Washbrook	lbw b Johnson	6
A. S. M. Oakman	c Archer b Johnson	10
†T. G. Evans	st Maddocks b Johnson	47
J. C. Laker	run out	3
G. A. R. Lock	not out	25
J. B. Statham	c Maddocks b Lindwall	0
Extras	(b 2, lb 5, w 1)	8
Total		**459**

AUSTRALIA

C. C. McDonald	c Lock b Laker	32	c Oakman b Laker	89
J. W. Burke	c Cowdrey b Lock	22	c Lock b Laker	33
R. N. Harvey	b Laker	0	c Cowdrey b Laker	0
I. D. Craig	lbw b Laker	8	lbw b Laker	38
K. R. Miller	c Oakman b Laker	6	(6)b Laker	0
K. D. Mackay	c Oakman b Laker	0	(5)c Oakman b Laker	0
R. G. Archer	st Evans b Laker	6	c Oakman b Laker	0
R. Benaud	c Statham b Laker	0	b Laker	18
R. R. Lindwall	not out	6	c Lock b Laker	8
†L. V. Maddocks	b Laker	4	(11)lbw b Laker	2
*I. W. Johnson	b Laker	0	(10)not out	1
Extras		0	(b 12, lb 4)	16
Total		**84**	Total	**205**

FALL OF WICKETS

ENGLAND

Wkt	1st	2nd
1st	174	—
2nd	195	—
3rd	288	—
4th	321	—
5th	327	—
6th	339	—
7th	401	—
8th	417	—
9th	458	—
10th	459	—

AUSTRALIA

Wkt	1st	2nd
1st	48	28
2nd	48	55
3rd	62	114
4th	62	124
5th	62	130
6th	73	130
7th	73	181
8th	78	198
9th	84	203
10th	84	205

Umpires: F. S. Lee, E. Davies

AUSTRALIA	1st Innings				2nd Innings			
	O	M	R	W	O	M	R	W
Lindwall	21·3	6	63	2				
Miller	21	6	41	0				
Archer	22	6	73	1				
Johnson	47	10	151	4				
Benaud	47	17	123	2				

ENGLAND	1st Innings				2nd Innings			
	O	M	R	W	O	M	R	W
Statham	6	3	6	0	16	10	15	0
Bailey	4	3	4	0	20	8	31	0
Laker	16·4	4	37	9	51·2	23	53	10
Lock	14	3	37	1	55	30	69	0
Oakman					8	3	21	0

1956 Fifth Test, Oval

August 23, 24, 25, 27, 28
Toss: England   *Result:* Match Drawn

Compton's return after an operation to remove his right knee-cap, the farewell appearance of Lindwall and Miller, Tyson, fit at last, operating with Statham in a Test against Australia for the first time in England, Laker's chance to beat Bedser's record—these, with the Ashes decided, seemed the attractions of the final Test. Yet the game had more than sentimental interest: by winning it Australia could still square the rubber. Davidson played for the first time since the first Test, Langley replaced Maddocks, and the other players omitted were Mackay, Bailey and Oakman.

When Lindwall got Cowdrey caught behind off a late out-swinger to the fifth ball of the match, another England batting failure seemed in prospect. But after 20 minutes a shower drove the players off, and when they returned the outfield was wet and the shine disappeared. Richardson and Sheppard put on 52; but Sheppard was out just before lunch, Richardson was caught behind afterwards for the seventh time in the series, and Compton returned to Test cricket at 66 for 3.

It was nearly 15 minutes before Compton got off the mark; but from then on he played all his shots in a remarkable souvenir of his best days. But after making 94 out of 156 added with May he was beautifully caught at leg slip 15 minutes from stumps; and in the closing minutes in failing light England lost 3 more wickets, slumping to 223

for 7 at stumps. The innings was soon finished off next morning, and once again England owed everything to May and the judgment of the selectors.

McDonald was brilliantly caught at leg slip in Tyson's first over, but overnight rain encouraged May to turn to Laker and Lock, and by mid-afternoon, when Miller joined Harvey, Australia were 47 for 5. Setting himself to deal with Laker, Harvey stayed 2½ hours, after which, as the wicket eased, Miller and Benaud added 43 and Miller and Lindwall 48. Australia did well to get within 45 runs of England's score.

More rain overnight gave Australia a last chance of saving the rubber, but although Davidson and Archer turned to spinners on a drying pitch neither they nor Johnson and Burke bowled accurately enough to counter bold play by Richardson and Sheppard. England were 76 for 1 when the rain returned; no more play was possible until after lunch on the last day.

Unwilling to offer Australia a chance of sharing the rubber, May batted on until 4.10, leaving himself 2 hours in which to bowl Australia out. Three wickets fell quickly, but Craig, Miller and Johnson resisted long enough to make a draw certain.

ENGLAND

P. E. Richardson	c Langley b Miller	37	c Langley b Lindwall	34	
M. C. Cowdrey	c Langley b Lindwall	0	c Benaud b Davidson	8	
Rev. D. S. Sheppard	c Archer b Miller	24	c Archer b Miller	62	
*P. B. H. May	not out	83	not out	37	
D. C. S. Compton	c Davidson b Archer	94	not out	35	
G. A. R. Lock	c Langley b Archer	0			
C. Washbrook	lbw b Archer	0			
†T. G. Evans	lbw b Miller	0			
J. C. Laker	c Archer b Miller	4			
F. H. Tyson	c Davidson b Archer	3			
J. B. Statham	b Archer	0			
Extras	(w 2)	2	(b 3, lb 3)	6	
Total		**247**	**Total** (3 wkts dec)	**182**	

AUSTRALIA

C. C. McDonald	c Lock b Tyson	3	lbw b Statham	0	
J. W. Burke	b Laker	8	lbw b Laker	1	
R. N. Harvey	c May b Lock	39	c May b Lock	1	
I. D. Craig	c Statham b Lock	2	c Lock b Laker	7	
*I. W. Johnson	b Laker	12	(6)c Lock b Laker	10	
A. K. Davidson	c May b Laker	8			
K. R. Miller	c Washbrook b Statham	61	(5)not out	7	
R. G. Archer	c Tyson b Laker	9			
R. Benaud	b Statham	32	(7)not out	0	
R. R. Lindwall	not out	22			
†G. R. A. Langley	lbw b Statham	0			
Extras	(b 6)	6	(b 1)	1	
Total		**202**	**Total** (5 wkts)	**27**	

FALL OF WICKETS

ENGLAND

Wkt	1st	2nd
1st	1	17
2nd	53	100
3rd	66	108
4th	222	—
5th	222	—
6th	222	—
7th	223	—
8th	231	—
9th	243	—
10th	247	—

AUSTRALIA

Wkt	1st	2nd
1st	3	0
2nd	17	1
3rd	20	5
4th	35	10
5th	47	27
6th	90	—
7th	111	—
8th	154	—
9th	202	—
10th	202	—

Umpires: D. Davies, T. J. Bartley

AUSTRALIA	1st Innings					2nd Innings			
	O	M	R	W		O	M	R	W
Lindwall	18	5	36	1	..	12	3	29	1
Miller	40	7	91	4	..	22	3	56	1
Davidson	5	1	16	0	..	5	0	18	1
Archer	28·2	7	53	5	..	13	3	42	0
Johnson	9	2	28	0	..	4	1	7	0
Benaud	9	2	21	0	..	1	0	10	0
Burke					..	4	2	14	0

ENGLAND	1st Innings					2nd Innings			
	O	M	R	W		O	M	R	W
Statham	21	8	33	3	..	2	1	1	1
Tyson	14	5	34	1	..				
Laker	32	12	80	4	..	18	14	8	3
Lock	25	10	49	2	..	18·1	11	17	1

1958-59 First Test, Brisbane

December 5, 6, 8, 9, 10
Toss: England   *Result:* Australia won by eight wickets

Beginning with the banishment of Wardle after he had been an original choice and ending with the withdrawal of Laker from the fourth Test and the absence of Statham from the fifth, England faced disaster after disaster. In between there were injuries to Watson, Milton and Subba Row, the latter missing the entire series. An outcry against the negative cricket of the opening Test, and mounting controversy over umpiring, throwing and drag, made England's unavailing struggles seem all the more squalid; controversies apart, Australia played by far the better cricket. Davidson and Benaud had advanced to greatness with the ball, McDonald's application brought him over 500 runs, and the only new batsman of Test class to emerge was the Australian O'Neill. The English bowling was good but the batting was too weak to support it, and there was no Washbrook, Sheppard or Compton to turn to when things went wrong. Basing their main assault on left-arm pace over the wicket running across the bat, Australia found nearly all the England batsmen at fault, and by holding their catches they magnified still further the disparity between the sides.

In Meckiff's third over Milton was bowled by an in-swinging yorker, and without addition Richardson was caught off the outside edge. Graveney, dropped at slip when 1, stayed with May till lunch, but at 62 Davidson again had him playing down the wrong line and this time the catch was taken. May went to a fine catch by Grout, Cowdrey got one that lifted, and at 83 for 6 the innings was mangled irretrievably. An attempt to hit before the greenness in the wicket disappeared might then have paid England better, but they pottered instead and McDonald and Burke had to face only 2 overs that night.

The pitch gave less help on the second day, but after lunch Australia were made to struggle. 156 for 6 at the close, they were held on the third day to a lead of 52. By stumps Australia had bowled another 51 overs and England had crawled to 92 for 2.

Defensive bowling, and England's objective of wearing out a wicket that was never plumb, produced further wearisome cricket, and by the time Bailey left on the fourth day he had batted 7½ hours for 68. Graveney was tragically run out, Cowdrey went to a doubtful catch, and the only relief lay in the observance of the actions of Meckiff and Burke, on view for a time at opposite ends.

With 147 needed Burke outdid even Bailey for stubbornness, but a fine innings by O'Neill in which bat was at last put to ball brought the first touch of sanity into a mockery of a game.

ENGLAND

Batsman	1st dismissal		2nd dismissal	
P. E. Richardson	c Mackay b Davidson	11	c and b Benaud	8
C. A. Milton	b Meckiff	5	c Grout b Davidson	17
T. W. Graveney	c Grout b Davidson	19	(4)run out	36
*P. B. H. May	c Grout b Meckiff	26	(5)lbw b Benaud	4
M. C. Cowdrey	c Kline b Meckiff	13	(6)c Kline b Meckiff	28
T. E. Bailey	st Grout b Benaud	27	(3)b Mackay	68
†T. G. Evans	c Burge b Davidson	4	lbw b Davidson	4
G. A. R. Lock	c Davidson b Benaud	5	b Meckiff	1
J. C. Laker	c Burke b Benaud	13	b Benaud	15
J. B. Statham	c Grout b Mackay	2	c McDonald b Benaud	3
P. J. Loader	not out	6	not out	0
Extras	(lb 1, w 1, nb 1)	3	(b 10, lb 4)	14
Total		**134**		**198**

AUSTRALIA

Batsman	1st dismissal		2nd dismissal	
C. C. McDonald	c Graveney b Bailey	42	c Statham b Laker	15
J. W. Burke	c Evans b Loader	20	not out	28
R. N. Harvey	lbw b Loader	14	c Milton b Lock	23
N. C. O'Neill	c Graveney b Bailey	34	not out	71
P. J. Burge	c Cowdrey b Bailey	2		
K. D. Mackay	c Evans b Laker	16		
*R. Benaud	lbw b Loader	16		
A. K. Davidson	lbw b Laker	25		
†A. T. W. Grout	b Statham	2		
I. Meckiff	b Loader	5		
L. F. Kline	not out	4		
Extras	(b 4, lb 1, nb 1)	6	(b 2, lb 3, nb 5)	10
Total		**186**	**Total** (2 wkts)	**147**

FALL OF WICKETS

ENGLAND

Wkt	1st	2nd
1st	16	28
2nd	16	34
3rd	62	96
4th	75	102
5th	79	153
6th	83	161
7th	92	169
8th	112	190
9th	116	198
10th	134	198

AUSTRALIA

Wkt	1st	2nd
1st	55	20
2nd	65	58
3rd	88	—
4th	94	—
5th	122	—
6th	136	—
7th	162	—
8th	165	—
9th	178	—
10th	186	—

Umpires: M. J. McInnes, C. Hoy

AUSTRALIA	1st Innings					2nd Innings			
	O	M	R	W		O	M	R	W
Davidson	16	4	36	3	..	28	12	30	2
Meckiff	17	5	33	3	..	19	7	30	2
Mackay	8	1	16	1	..	9	6	7	1
Benaud	18·4	9	46	3	..	39·2	10	66	4
Kline					..	14	4	34	0
Burke					..	10	5	17	0

ENGLAND	1st Innings					2nd Innings			
	O	M	R	W		O	M	R	W
Statham	20	2	57	1	..	6	1	13	0
Loader	19	4	56	4	..	9	1	27	0
Bailey	13	2	35	3	..	5	1	21	0
Laker	10·1	3	15	2	..	17	3	39	1
Lock	10	4	17	0	..	14·7	5	37	1

1958-59 Second Test, Melbourne

Test no. 175

December 31, January 1, 2, 3, 5
Toss: England   *Result:* Australia won by eight wickets

From the third over England were struggling against odds. Moving the ball away late, Davidson had Richardson caught behind, beat Watson for pace, and then had Graveney lbw to a swinging full toss—all in six balls. Yet England recovered so well that only one more wicket fell all day, by which time they were 173 for 4, May 89, Cowdrey 28. Bailey, who opened with Richardson, actually outscored May while he was in, and indeed May was uncertain at first and should have been caught and bowled by Benaud in the last over before lunch; but he eventually achieved absolute mastery, and his century, completed on the second morning, kept England in the game. With Cowdrey he helped to put on 118. Classical left-arm pace bowling by Davidson and some very fast projections from Meckiff with the second new ball, backed up by magnificent fielding, held England to 259 all out after they had passed 200 with four wickets down.

When Burke was bowled by Statham offering no stroke it seemed that once again the attack might make good the batting deficiency; but with McDonald sound and Harvey brilliant the close of play score reached 96 for 1 (Harvey 60). On the third day Harvey took most of the morning to play himself in; but after lunch he and O'Neill added 118 in 2 hours 20 minutes, O'Neill's share being only 37. After reaching his hundred Harvey accelerated, and when Australia reached 250 with this pair still together, the new ball a worn relic and Statham and Loader tiring, a huge Australian total looked certain. But the two fast bowlers still had something left: O'Neill was caught behind and Harvey bowled, Simpson and Benaud went without scoring, and with Australia suddenly 262 for 6 the match was transformed.

The tail could not last against the pace and accuracy of Statham next morning and Australia were all out for 308—49 in front. On a pitch still fast and true, the England batsmen had a second chance to take a grip on the game. Yet within an hour they were 27 for 4, at tea they were 57 for 6, and by 5.30 they were all out. May was criticised for placing himself and Cowdrey as low as 5 and 6, and the rout was accentuated by a galaxy of brilliant catches; but the chief destroyer was Meckiff. His jerky action and erratic delivery made him difficult to pick up, and with no respite from Davidson at the other end England were dismissed for 87—their lowest score in Australia since 1903-4. Australia were left with only 39 to win.

ENGLAND

P. E. Richardson	c Grout b Davidson	3	c Harvey b Meckiff	2	
T. E. Bailey	c Benaud b Meckiff	48	c Burke b Meckiff	14	
W. Watson	b Davidson	0	b Davidson	7	
T. W. Graveney	lbw b Davidson	0	c Davidson b Meckiff	3	
*P. B. H. May	b Meckiff	113	c Davidson b Meckiff	17	
M. C. Cowdrey	c Grout b Davidson	44	c Grout b Meckiff	12	
†T. G. Evans	c Davidson b Meckiff	4	run out	11	
G. A. R. Lock	st Grout b Benaud	5	c and b Davidson	6	
J. C. Laker	not out	22	c Harvey b Davidson	3	
J. B. Statham	b Davidson	13	not out	8	
P. J. Loader	b Davidson	1	b Meckiff	0	
Extras	(b 1, lb 2, w 3)	6	(b 1, lb 1, nb 2)	4	
Total		259	Total	87	

AUSTRALIA

C. C. McDonald	c Graveney b Statham	47	lbw b Statham	5	
J. W. Burke	b Statham	3	not out	18	
R. N. Harvey	b Loader	167	(4)not out	7	
N. C. O'Neill	c Evans b Statham	37			
K. D. Mackay	c Evans b Statham	18			
R. B. Simpson	lbw b Loader	0			
*R. Benaud	lbw b Statham	0			
A. K. Davidson	b Statham	24			
†A. T. W. Grout	c May b Loader	8	(3)st Evans b Laker	12	
I. Meckiff	b Statham	0			
L. F. Kline	not out	1			
Extras	(lb 3)	3			
Total		308	Total (2 wkts)	42	

FALL OF WICKETS

ENGLAND

Wkt	1st	2nd
1st	7	3
2nd	7	14
3rd	7	21
4th	92	27
5th	210	44
6th	218	57
7th	218	71
8th	233	75
9th	253	80
10th	259	87

AUSTRALIA

Wkt	1st	2nd
1st	11	6
2nd	137	26
3rd	255	—
4th	257	—
5th	261	—
6th	262	—
7th	295	—
8th	300	—
9th	300	—
10th	308	—

Umpires: M. J. McInnes, R. Wright

AUSTRALIA	1st Innings					2nd Innings			
	O	M	R	W		O	M	R	W
Davidson	25.5	7	64	6	..	15	2	41	3
Meckiff	24	4	69	3	..	15.2	3	38	6
Mackay	9	2	16	0	..				
Benaud	29	7	61	1	..	1	0	4	0
Kline	11	2	43	0	..				

ENGLAND	1st Innings					2nd Innings			
	O	M	R	W		O	M	R	W
Statham	28	6	57	7	..	5	1	11	1
Loader	27.2	4	97	3	..	5	1	13	0
Bailey	16	0	50	0	..				
Laker	12	1	47	0	..	4	1	7	1
Lock	17	2	54	0	..	3.1	1	11	0

236

130. P. B. H. May

131. R. Benaud

132. England 1958-59
Back row: D. Montague (masseur), C. A. Milton, W. Watson, P. E. Richardson, R. Swetman, G. Duckworth (scorer). *Middle row:* G. A. R. Lock, J. B. Statham, P. J. Loader, R. Subba Row, T. W. Graveney, F. H. Tyson, F. S. Trueman. *Front:* F. R. Brown (manager), T. E. Bailey, M. C. Cowdrey, P. B. H. May (capt.), T. G. Evans, J. C. Laker, E. D. R. Eagar (assistant-manager).

1958-59 Third Test, Sydney

January 9, 10, 12, 13, 14, 15
Toss: England   *Result:* Match Drawn

On a slow, lifeless wicket England's openers (Bailey and Milton this time) again failed. Graveney and May stayed until lunch and put on 68 in all, but then May fell to a spectacular catch in the covers. Graveney, driving at Benaud, was caught in the gully, Dexter, preferred to Watson, was lbw offering no stroke, and 91 for 2 had become 98 for 5. May and Dexter fell to Slater (seamers and off-spinners), who was replacing Kline. Other changes were Favell for Simpson, Swetman for Evans (injured), and Trueman for Loader.

Cowdrey seemed well set when he was beaten by Benaud at 155 for 6, but Swetman batted for over 2½ hours, and after Cowdrey left he received good support from Lock. Heavy rain restricted play next day to 1¼ hours, in which England's last 4 wickets, thanks to brilliant catching, fell for 29. There was time for 3 torrid overs of speed before the close, which Australia were lucky to survive.

Next morning in great heat May soon turned to Laker and Lock. Burke went cheaply, a restrained Harvey was eventually bowled anticipating Laker's turn, and when McDonald after three hours of concentration got a nasty one from Lock Australia were 87 for 3. But England failed to pour on the pressure, the catching compared badly

with Australia's, and O'Neill and Favell were allowed to work out the contrasting problems of Laker and Lock in their own way. This they did by putting bat to ball, and by stumps Australia had recovered to 184 for 3.

England began the fourth day well, and at 208 for 6 Australia's advantage had gone. May then took the new ball; but although the bat was beaten no wicket fell, and when the spinners returned Davidson and Mackay were set. Their stand of 115 re-established Australia's ascendancy, and when England slid to 64 for 3 on the fifth morning, still 74 behind, defeat looked imminent. Yet with the Ashes still to play for the spectre of a last-day collapse against spin haunted Benaud, and when May and Cowdrey settled in to a match-saving stand he went on the defensive, showing what he had learnt from England about negative cricket. Meckiff was off with a strained tendon, and Benaud himself had a sore spinning finger, but Cowdrey's hundred took 6 hours 2 minutes—the slowest century on record in these matches —and England were not able to declare until 110 minutes from time. That Benaud's fears were not merely neurotic was shown when Laker took two early wickets, but Harvey and O'Neill played out time.

ENGLAND

Batsman	1st Innings dismissal	Runs	2nd Innings dismissal	Runs
T. E. Bailey	lbw b Meckiff	8	c sub (R. B. Simpson) b Benaud	25
C. A. Milton	c Meckiff b Davidson	8	c Davidson b Benaud	8
T. W. Graveney	c Harvey b Benaud	33	lbw b Davidson	22
*P. B. H. May	c Mackay b Slater	42	b Burke	92
M. C. Cowdrey	c Harvey b Benaud	34	not out	100
E. R. Dexter	lbw b Slater	1	c Grout b Benaud	11
†R. Swetman	c Mackay b Benaud	41	lbw b Burke	5
G. A. R. Lock	lbw b Mackay	21	(9)not out	11
F. S. Trueman	c Burke b Benaud	18	(8)st Grout b Benaud	0
J. C. Laker	c Harvey b Benaud	2		
J. B. Statham	not out	0		
Extras	(b 4, lb 5, w 2)	11	(b 11, lb 1, w 1)	13
Total		219	Total (7 wkts dec)	287

AUSTRALIA

Batsman	1st Innings dismissal	Runs	2nd Innings dismissal	Runs
C. C. McDonald	c Graveney b Lock	40	b Laker	16
J. W. Burke	c Lock b Laker	12	b Laker	7
R. N. Harvey	b Laker	7	not out	18
N. C. O'Neill	c Swetman b Laker	77	not out	7
L. E. Favell	c Cowdrey b Lock	54		
K. D. Mackay	b Trueman	57		
*R. Benaud	b Laker	6		
A. K. Davidson	lbw b Lock	71		
†A. T. W. Grout	c Statham b Laker	14		
K. N. Slater	not out	1		
I. Meckiff	b Lock	2		
Extras	(b 5, lb 10, nb 1)	16	(b 6)	6
Total		357	Total (2 wkts)	54

FALL OF WICKETS

ENGLAND		
Wkt	1st	2nd
1st	19	30
2nd	23	37
3rd	91	64
4th	97	246
5th	98	262
6th	155	269
7th	194	270
8th	200	—
9th	202	—
10th	219	—

AUSTRALIA		
Wkt	1st	2nd
1st	26	22
2nd	52	33
3rd	87	—
4th	197	—
5th	199	—
6th	208	—
7th	323	—
8th	353	—
9th	355	—
10th	357	—

Umpires: M. J. McInnes, C. Hoy

AUSTRALIA	1st Innings					2nd Innings			
	O	M	R	W		O	M	R	W
Davidson	12	3	21	1	..	33	11	65	1
Meckiff	15	2	45	1	..	3	1	7	0
Benaud	33·4	10	83	5	..	33	7	94	4
Slater	14	4	40	2	..	18	5	61	0
Mackay	8	3	19	1	..	11	2	21	0
Burke					..	11	3	26	2

ENGLAND	1st Innings					2nd Innings			
	O	M	R	W		O	M	R	W
Statham	16	2	48	0	..	2	0	6	0
Trueman	18	3	37	1	..	4	1	9	0
Lock	43·2	9	130	4	..	11	4	23	0
Laker	46	9	107	5	..	8	3	10	2
Bailey	5	0	19	0	..				

1958-59 Fourth Test, Adelaide

January 30, 31, February 2, 3, 4, 5
Toss: England   *Result:* Australia won by ten wickets

When Laker reported unfit England were almost bound to rely on pace, and May put Australia in. But the fate of the Ashes was virtually decided as McDonald and Burke put on 171. After the first half hour England's only chance came when Burke was apparently caught at the wicket off his glove, but umpire McInnes, the object of much scepticism during the tour, gave him not out. Australia at stumps were 200 for 1.

Next morning in great heat England failed to take a wicket, but McDonald (torn thigh muscle) did not appear after lunch, and England took their chance, 5 wickets falling in the next 3½ hours for 135. Statham proved once again that he was England's best fast bowler, but forceful cricket from O'Neill and Benaud took Australia to 403 for 6. Umpire McInnes appeared to make another mistake when Mackay was appealed against for a catch at the wicket, but sensing this Mackay walked out. Next morning McDonald gave his wicket away after Burke, his runner, had seemed to be run out.

When England began their reply Richardson (replacing the injured Milton) offered no stroke to the second ball from Lindwall (replacing the injured Meckiff) and was lbw. Davidson yorked Bailey, and England were 11 for 2. May and Cowdrey made 63 in the next 68

minutes, but May was out before stumps, when England were 115 for 3.

On the fourth day Cowdrey and Graveney stood firm until lunch, the main threat seeming to come from the speed of the giant Rorke, whose drag brought him closer to the batsman than any other bowler. The lunch-time 170 for 3 quickly became 188 for 9 as Rorke got Cowdrey and Graveney and Benaud spun out the tail. Evans was a passenger with a broken finger, and only a last-wicket stand of 52 between Watson and Statham averted a rout.

Although without Davidson (sprained ankle), Benaud made England follow on, and Watson, last out, stayed for the last 75 minutes with Richardson, who suddenly for the first time in the series began to play well. England again went through the morning session without loss, but after lunch a fine running catch at deep mid-wicket dismissed Watson. Richardson after 3¾ hours didn't go far enough across when padding up, and Cowdrey was bowled off his pads, but May and Graveney resisted sternly until May got a horrible shooter.

198 for 5 at stumps and still 38 behind, England refused to give up. Graveney, who batted for 5 hours in all, kept the innings going until 3.30 on the last day, but he was never able to take command and Australia were left with only 35 to win.

AUSTRALIA

						FALL OF WICKETS

		1st Innings		2nd Innings	
C. C. McDonald	b Trueman	170			
J. W. Burke	c Cowdrey b Bailey	66	not out	16	
R. N. Harvey	run out	41			
N. C. O'Neill	b Statham	56			
L. E. Favell	b Statham	4	not out	15	
K. D. Mackay	c Evans b Statham	4			
*R. Benaud	b Trueman	46			
A. K. Davidson	c Bailey b Tyson	43			
†A. T. W. Grout	lbw b Trueman	9			
R. R. Lindwall	b Trueman	19			
G. F. Rorke	not out	2			
Extras	(b 2, lb 8, w 4, nb 2)	16	(b 4, lb 1)	5	
Total		476	Total (0 wkts)	36	

FALL OF WICKETS

AUSTRALIA

Wkt	1st	2nd
1st	171	—
2nd	276	—
3rd	286	—
4th	294	—
5th	369	—
6th	388	—
7th	407	—
8th	445	—
9th	473	—
10th	476	—

ENGLAND

	1st Innings		2nd Innings	
P. E. Richardson	lbw b Lindwall	4	lbw b Benaud	43
T. E. Bailey	b Davidson	4	(6)c Grout b Lindwall	6
*P. B. H. May	b Benaud	37	lbw b Rorke	59
M. C. Cowdrey	b Rorke	84	b Lindwall	8
T. W. Graveney	c Benaud b Rorke	41	not out	53
W. Watson	b Rorke	25	(2)c Favell b Benaud	40
F. S. Trueman	c Grout b Benaud	0	c Grout b Davidson	0
G. A. R. Lock	c Grout b Benaud	2	b Rorke	9
F. H. Tyson	c and b Benaud	0	c Grout b Benaud	33
†T. G. Evans	c Burke b Benaud	4	(11)c Benaud b Davidson	0
J. B. Statham	not out	36	(10)c O'Neill b Benaud	2
Extras	(lb 2, nb 1)	3	(b 5, lb 5, w 3, nb 4)	17
Total		240	Total	270

ENGLAND

Wkt	1st	2nd
1st	7	89
2nd	11	110
3rd	74	125
4th	170	177
5th	173	198
6th	180	199
7th	184	222
8th	184	268
9th	188	270
10th	240	270

Umpires: M. J. McInnes, R. Wright

ENGLAND	1st Innings					2nd Innings			
	O	M	R	W		O	M	R	W
Statham	23	0	83	3		4	0	11	0
Trueman	30·1	6	90	4		3	1	3	0
Tyson	28	1	100	1					
Bailey	22	2	91	1					
Lock	25	0	96	0		2	0	8	0
Cowdrey						1·3	0	9	0

AUSTRALIA	1st Innings					2nd Innings			
	O	M	R	W		O	M	R	W
Davidson	12	0	49	1		8·3	3	17	2
Lindwall	15	0	66	1		26	6	70	2
Rorke	18·1	7	23	3		34	7	78	2
Benaud	27	6	91	5		29	10	82	4
O'Neill	2	1	8	0					
Burke						4	2	6	0

1958-59 Fifth Test, Melbourne

February 13, 14, 16, 17, 18
Toss: Australia   *Result:* Australia won by nine wickets

Benaud's reasons for sending England in were tangible enough: the return of Meckiff gave him four fast bowlers, and there were green patches on the wicket. Statham, England's leading bowler, was injured and so was Loader, Milton had gone home for treatment, and Watson sprained a muscle just before the game. Laker and Dexter returned, and Mortimore replaced Lock.

Lindwall's first ball lifted off a length and accounted for Bailey, and at 13 May got another lifter and was caught in the gully. Richardson and Cowdrey were together at lunch, but afterwards Cowdrey was caught at slip off an attacking stroke. Graveney lasted 80 minutes before pushing Benaud to mid on, and Dexter was out first ball. When Richardson, after his best innings of the series, hit a long hop back to Benaud England were 128 for 7. It was left to two of the bowlers, Mortimore and Trueman, to take advantage of a tiring pace attack and bring England within reach of 200 at stumps.

At 12.45 next morning Australia were batting against an erratic Tyson and an unlucky Trueman. At 41, however, Tyson got Burke, and then, changing ends, he began to bowl rhythmically and well. McDonald had several escapes, one of them when he was given not out after a bail was dislodged when he glanced Trueman for four; the

umpire was *not* McInnes, who on being passed over had retired. Tenacious and imperturbable, McDonald batted well later and was 98 not out at stumps, when Australia, despite the loss of Harvey and O'Neill (first ball) to Trueman at 83, seemed firmly in control at 150 for 3.

On the third morning Mackay, who had helped to add 71, was caught off Laker, and McDonald when 103 was dropped behind off the same bowler. Laker had his revenge later, Davidson was meanwhile bowled by Mortimore just when he was beginning to look dangerous, and Australia at lunch, with four wickets to fall, were only 15 runs on. But the afternoon session proved the most prolific of the series as Benaud and Grout added 100, and with Benaud monopolising the strike after Grout was out Australia gained a lead of 146.

Before the close Lindwall yorked Bailey with an in-swinger and beat May with an out-swinger, and England were off on a familiar road. In 45 minutes next morning Cowdrey by magnificent driving made 42 but was then run out; photographs of the incident did not confirm the decision. Graveney, too, played his shots before being beautifully caught low down at slip by Harvey; this and some belligerence from Trueman took the match into the fifth day.

ENGLAND

P. E. Richardson	c and b Benaud	68	lbw b Benaud	23	
T. E. Bailey	c Davidson b Lindwall	0	b Lindwall	0	
*P. B. H. May	c Benaud b Meckiff	11	c Harvey b Lindwall	4	
M. C. Cowdrey	c Lindwall b Davidson	22	run out	46	
T. W. Graveney	c McDonald b Benaud	19	c Harvey b Davidson	54	
E. R. Dexter	c Lindwall b Meckiff	0	c Grout b Davidson	6	
†R. Swetman	c Grout b Davidson	1	lbw b Lindwall	9	
J. B. Mortimore	not out	44	b Rorke	11	
F. S. Trueman	c and b Benaud	21	b Rorke	36	
F. H. Tyson	c Grout b Benaud	9	c Grout b Rorke	6	
J. C. Laker	c Harvey b Davidson	2	not out	5	
Extras	(b 4, w 4)	8	(b 9, lb 3, w 2)	14	
Total		**205**	Total	**214**	

AUSTRALIA

C. C. McDonald	c Cowdrey b Laker	133	not out	51	
J. W. Burke	c Trueman b Tyson	16	lbw b Tyson	13	
R. N. Harvey	c Swetman b Trueman	13	not out	1	
N. C. O'Neill	c Cowdrey b Trueman	0			
K. D. Mackay	c Graveney b Laker	23			
A. K. Davidson	b Mortimore	17			
*R. Benaud	c Swetman b Laker	64			
†A. T. W. Grout	c Trueman b Laker	74			
R. R. Lindwall	c Cowdrey b Trueman	0			
I. Meckiff	c and b Trueman	2			
G. F. Rorke	not out	0			
Extras	(b 5, lb 4)	9	(lb 4)	4	
Total		**351**	Total (1 wkt)	**69**	

FALL OF WICKETS

ENGLAND		
Wkt	1st	2nd
1st	0	0
2nd	13	12
3rd	61	78
4th	109	105
5th	112	131
6th	124	142
7th	128	158
8th	191	172
9th	203	182
10th	205	214

AUSTRALIA		
Wkt	1st	2nd
1st	41	66
2nd	83	—
3rd	83	—
4th	154	—
5th	207	—
6th	209	—
7th	324	—
8th	327	—
9th	329	—
10th	351	—

Umpires: R. Wright,
L. Townsend

AUSTRALIA	1st Innings					2nd Innings			
	O	M	R	W		O	M	R	W
Davidson	12·5	2	38	3	..	21	1	95	2
Lindwall	14	2	36	1	..	11	2	37	3
Meckiff	15	2	57	2	..	4	0	13	0
Rorke	6	1	23	0	..	12·4	2	41	3
Benaud	17	5	43	4	..	6	1	14	1

ENGLAND	1st Innings					2nd Innings			
	O	M	R	W		O	M	R	W
Trueman	25	0	92	4	..	6·7	0	45	0
Tyson	20	1	73	1	..	6	0	20	1
Bailey	14	2	43	0	..				
Laker	30·5	4	93	4	..				
Mortimore	11	1	41	1	..				

Averages: 1958-59

AUSTRALIA

BATTING	M.	Inns.	N.O.	Runs	H.S.	Av.
C. C. McDonald	5	9	1	520	170	65·00
N. C. O'Neill	5	7	2	282	77	56·40
R. N. Harvey	5	9	3	291	167	48·50
L. E. Favell	2	3	1	73	54	36·50
A. K. Davidson	5	5	0	180	71	36·00
J. W. Burke	5	10	3	199	66	28·42
R. Benaud	5	5	0	132	64	26·40
K. D. Mackay	5	5	0	118	57	23·60
A. T. W. Grout	5	6	0	119	74	19·83
R. R. Lindwall	2	2	0	19	19	9·50
I. Meckiff	4	4	0	9	5	2·25

PLAYED IN TWO TESTS: L. Kline 4* and 1*, G. F. Rorke 2* and 0*.
PLAYED IN ONE TEST: P. J. Burge 2, R. B. Simpson 0, K. N. Slater 1*.

BOWLING	Overs	Mds.	Runs	Wkts.	Av.
I. Meckiff	112·2	24	292	17	17·17
R. Benaud	233·2	65	584	31	18·83
A. K. Davidson	183·5	45	456	24	19·00
G. F. Rorke	70·5	17	165	8	20·62
K. D. Mackay	45	14	79	3	26·33
R. R. Lindwall	66	10	209	7	29·85

ALSO BOWLED: L. Kline 25–6–77–0, J. W. Burke 25–10–49–2, K. N. Slater 32–9–101–2, N. C. O'Neill 2–1–8–0.

ENGLAND

BATTING	M.	Inns.	N.O.	Runs	H.S.	Av.
M. C. Cowdrey	5	10	1	391	100*	43·44
P. B. H. May	5	10	0	405	113	40·50
T. W. Graveney	5	10	1	280	54	31·11
P. E. Richardson	4	8	0	162	68	20·25
T. E. Bailey	5	10	0	200	68	20·00
W. Watson	2	4	0	72	40	18·00
J. B. Statham	4	7	3	64	36*	16·00
R. Swetman	2	4	0	56	41	14·00
F. S. Trueman	3	6	0	75	36	12·50
J. C. Laker	4	7	2	62	22*	12·40
F. H. Tyson	2	4	0	48	33	12·00
C. A. Milton	2	4	0	38	17	9·50
G. A. R. Lock	4	8	1	60	21	8·57
T. G. Evans	3	6	0	27	11	4·50
E. R. Dexter	2	4	0	18	11	4·50
P. J. Loader	2	4	2	7	6*	3·50

PLAYED IN ONE TEST: J. B. Mortimore 44* and 11.

BOWLING	Overs	Mds.	Runs	Wkts.	Av.
J. C. Laker	127·6	24	318	15	21·20
J. B. Statham	104	12	286	12	23·83
P. J. Loader	60·2	10	193	7	27·57
F. S. Trueman	87	11	277	9	30·77
F. H. Tyson	54	2	193	3	64·33
T. E. Bailey	75	7	259	4	64·75
G. A. R. Lock	126·2	25	376	5	75·20

ALSO BOWLED: M. C. Cowdrey 1·3–0–9–0, J. B. Mortimore 11–1–41–1.

Averages: 1961

ENGLAND

BATTING	M.	Inns.	N.O.	Runs	H.S.	Av.
R. Subba Row	5	10	0	468	137	46·80
K. F. Barrington	5	9	1	364	83	45·50
D. A. Allen	4	6	3	132	42*	44·00
E. R. Dexter	5	9	0	378	180	42·00
P. B. H. May	4	8	1	272	95	38·85
G. Pullar	5	10	1	287	63	31·88
M. C. Cowdrey	4	8	0	168	93	21·00
J. T. Murray	5	8	0	160	40	20·00
J. B. Statham	4	7	4	59	18	19·96
J. A. Flavell	2	3	2	14	14	14·00
F. S. Trueman	4	6	0	60	25	10·00
R. Illingworth	2	3	0	28	15	9·33
G. A. R. Lock	3	5	0	39	30	7·80

PLAYED IN ONE TEST: M. J. K. Smith 0 and 1*, H. L. Jackson 8, D. B. Close 33 and 8.

BOWLING	Overs	Mds.	Runs	Wkts.	Av.
H. L. Jackson	44	16	83	4	20·75
E. R. Dexter	79·4	16	223	9	24·77
F. S. Trueman	164·4	21	529	20	26·45
D. A. Allen	134	53	354	13	27·23
J. B. Statham	201·4	41	501	17	29·47
R. Illingworth	55·3	17	126	3	42·00
J. A. Flavell	82·4	17	231	5	46·20
G. A. R. Lock	107	33	250	3	83·33

ALSO BOWLED: D. B. Close 8–1–33–0.

AUSTRALIA

BATTING	M.	Inns.	N.O.	Runs	H.S.	Av.
W. M. Lawry	5	8	0	420	130	52·50
P. J. Burge	5	8	1	332	181	47·42
R. N. Harvey	5	8	0	338	114	42·25
B. C. Booth	2	3	0	126	71	42·00
N. C. O'Neill	5	8	0	324	117	40·50
A. K. Davidson	5	8	3	151	77*	30·20
G. D. McKenzie	3	5	2	75	34	25·00
R. B. Simpson	5	8	0	191	76	23·87
K. D. Mackay	5	7	0	158	64	22·57
C. C. McDonald	3	5	0	95	54	19·00
R. Benaud	4	6	1	45	36*	9·00
A. T. W. Grout	5	7	1	47	30	7·83

PLAYED IN TWO TESTS: F. M. Misson 25*. PLAYED IN ONE TEST: R. A. Gaunt 3

BOWLING	Overs	Mds.	Runs	Wkts.	Av.
A. K. Davidson	280·2	86	572	23	24·86
G. D. McKenzie	129	36	323	11	29·36
R. Benaud	214·3	76	488	15	32·53
R. B. Simpson	92·4	37	229	7	32·71
K. D. Mackay	273	87	525	16	32·81
F. M. Misson	76	18	243	7	34·71

ALSO BOWLED: R. A. Gaunt 46–10–86–3, R. N. Harvey 1–1–0–0, N. C. O'Neill 4–1–13–0.

1961 First Test, Edgbaston

June 8, 9, 10, 12, 13
Toss: England *Result:* Match Drawn

Both sides were regrouping after the retirement or exclusion of seasoned players. The batting looked even, dominated in each case, as it turned out, by a left-hander playing in his first series. Davidson and Benaud were great bowlers for Australia, Statham and Trueman for England; but otherwise the bowling was weak. To paper over the holes in their attack Australia found the ideal instrument in Mackay; England found no such stand-by. But where Australia had the greatest apparent advantage was in the robustness of her later batting, and to this was added an adventurous vitality and self-confidence which England could rarely match. Both sides suffered from injuries, the most serious befalling Benaud, who for long periods was far below his best and who missed the Lord's Test; yet curiously enough his absence from this encounter was a blessing in disguise for Australia, making room for a third seam bowler. England misjudged the pitch at Lord's and played two spinners, and this probably cost them the game. Despite his injury Benaud proved an inspiring leader, never more so than in the game at Old Trafford which decided the Ashes. The dusty wickets of 1956 were replaced by green-tops on which winning the toss proved a doubtful advantage: the side batting second always led on first innings.

The first day was showery, with several interruptions: thus Davidson was able to bowl without relief until 4.30. The chief damage, however, was done by the stealthy seamers of Mackay; the wicket suited him perfectly. After a confident beginning Pullar lost his leg stump at 36, Dexter tried to assert himself but was caught close in, and England were soon fighting for survival; at stumps they were 180 for 8. They did not last long next morning, and after a sound start Harvey and O'Neill revelled in the off-spin attack, 149 being added in the afternoon. The close of play score of 359 for 5 off 102 overs meant that for the rest of the match England would be struggling to avoid defeat.

Only 3¼ hours' play was possible on the third day, and only 47 overs were bowled on the Monday, when England's phlegmatic openers put on 93. Dexter made a precarious start against Benaud and was missed off Davidson, but England began the last day 106 for 1—215 behind.

Dexter's concentration, questioned so far, proved equal to all demands and he batted 5 hours 44 minutes for 180. Subba Row made a solid 112, and Australia's hopes finally evaporated during a stand of 161 between Dexter and Barrington. Frustrated of victory by the weather, Benaud was able to bowl only 9 painful overs on the last day; but England's escape was meritorious enough.

ENGLAND

G. Pullar	b Davidson	17	c Grout b Misson		28
R. Subba Row	c Simpson b Mackay	59	b Misson		112
E. R. Dexter	c Davidson b Mackay	10	st Grout b Simpson		180
*M. C. Cowdrey	b Misson	13	b Mackay		14
K. F. Barrington	c Misson b Mackay	21	not out		48
M. J. K. Smith	c Lawry b Mackay	0	not out		1
R. Illingworth	c Grout b Benaud	15			
†J. T. Murray	c Davidson b Benaud	16			
D. A. Allen	run out	11			
F. S. Trueman	c Burge b Benaud	20			
J. B. Statham	not out	7			
Extras	(b 3, lb 3)	6	(lb 18)		18
Total		**195**	**Total** (4 wkts)		**401**

AUSTRALIA

W. M. Lawry	c Murray b Illingworth	57
C. C. McDonald	c Illingworth b Statham	22
R. N. Harvey	lbw b Allen	114
N. C. O'Neill	b Statham	82
P. J. Burge	lbw b Allen	25
R. B. Simpson	c and b Trueman	76
A. K. Davidson	c and b Illingworth	22
K. D. Mackay	c Barrington b Statham	64
*R. Benaud	not out	36
†A. T. W. Grout	c Dexter b Trueman	5
F. M. Misson	did not bat	
Extras	(b 8, lb 4, nb 1)	13
Total	(9 wkts dec)	**516**

FALL OF WICKETS

ENGLAND

Wkt	1st	2nd
1st	36	93
2nd	53	202
3rd	88	239
4th	121	400
5th	121	—
6th	122	—
7th	153	—
8th	156	—
9th	181	—
10th	195	—

AUSTRALIA

Wkt	1st	2nd
1st	47	—
2nd	106	—
3rd	252	—
4th	299	—
5th	322	—
6th	381	—
7th	469	—
8th	501	—
9th	516	—
10th	—	—

Umpires: J. S. Buller,
F. S. Lee

AUSTRALIA	1st Innings				2nd Innings			
	O	M	R	W	O	M	R	W
Davidson	26	6	70	1	31	10	60	0
Misson	15	6	47	1	28	6	82	2
Mackay	29	10	57	4	41	13	87	1
Benaud	14.3	8	15	3	20	4	67	0
Simpson					34	12	87	1

ENGLAND	1st Innings				2nd Innings			
	O	M	R	W	O	M	R	W
Trueman	36.5	1	136	2				
Statham	43	6	147	3				
Illingworth	44	12	110	2				
Allen	24	4	88	2				
Dexter	5	1	22	0				

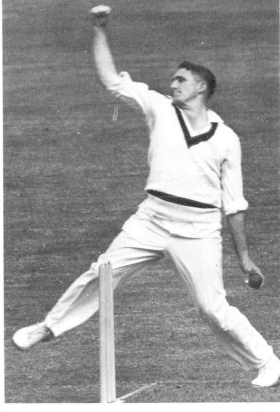

133. F. S. Trueman

134. A. K. Davidson

135. **Australia 1961**
Back row: A. E. James (masseur), R. B. Simpson, L. F. Kline, R. A. Gaunt, F. M. Misson, W. M. Lawry, I. W. Quick, G. D. McKenzie, P. J. Burge, N. C. O'Neill, B. N. Jarman, J. D. Cameron (scorer). *Front:* B. C. Booth, A. T. W. Grout, A. K. Davidson, R. C. Steele (treasurer), R. Benaud (capt.), S. G. Webb (manager), R. N. Harvey, C. C. McDonald, K. D. Mackay.

1961 Second Test, Lord's

June 22, 23, 24, 26
Toss: England   *Result:* Australia won by five wickets

The pitch was full of life from the start and the ball fizzed through at varying heights. Yet thanks to three dropped catches England had reached 87 for 1 just before lunch when Mackay had Subba Row lbw. In the next over Dexter was caught near the square leg umpire, and England went into lunch 87 for 3.

May was back in the England side after missing the first Test through injury, and he and Cowdrey were settling down when Davidson got one to leave May as it lifted. Barrington was caught at second slip, and at 127 Cowdrey was 6th out when he was caught off his glove. The tail fought hard and added another 79, but England were all out for 206. Statham then bowled McDonald and Trueman got Simpson, but Lawry and Harvey held on until stumps, when Australia were 42 for 2. No spin was used all day.

The pitch was not much easier on the second day and the Australian batsmen were hit many times. At 81 Harvey was caught at slip, and with no third seam bowler Cowdrey tried Dexter, who in-slanted one past O'Neill. Burge thus joined Lawry at a crisis, and with Lawry getting behind the line and Burge also showing what a fine player he had become, 95 runs were added before Burge hooked too late at a Statham bouncer. Soon afterwards Lawry completed his hundred;

although beaten several times by Statham he displayed wonderful tenacity and his was a great innings. England hit back to get 8 wickets down for 238 but were then frustrated by a 9th wicket stand between Mackay and the 20-year-old McKenzie which took Australia to 286 for 8. With Misson also showing surprising technique, Australia lasted another 85 minutes next morning and gained a lead of 134.

There followed another England batting failure. After a bright start Subba Row was caught behind driving. Dexter had the misfortune to be bowled off his thigh, Pullar chased a wide one, and an apprehensive Cowdrey gave a catch to cover. When May left to another rising ball and Illingworth failed England were 144 for 6, only 10 runs in front. Barrington and Murray by sensible play added 34 before stumps and another 13 next morning, but the new ball precipitated the end and Australia wanted only 69 to win.

In a vengeful burst of ferocity Statham and Trueman had four wickets down for 19, and off the last ball before lunch Burge was missed off Statham; but after lunch a relaxed Burge steered Australia to victory. A survey of the Lord's pitch after the game revealed depressions, causing the effect of a 'ridge'.

ENGLAND

Batsman	1st Innings		2nd Innings	
G. Pullar	b Davidson	11	c Grout b Misson	42
R. Subba Row	lbw b Mackay	48	c Grout b Davidson	8
E. R. Dexter	c McKenzie b Misson	27	b McKenzie	17
*M. C. Cowdrey	c Grout b McKenzie	16	c Mackay b Misson	7
P. B. H. May	c Grout b Davidson	17	c Grout b McKenzie	22
K. F. Barrington	c Mackay b Davidson	4	lbw b Davidson	66
R. Illingworth	b Misson	13	c Harvey b Simpson	0
†J. T. Murray	lbw b Mackay	18	c Grout b McKenzie	25
G. A. R. Lock	c Grout b Davidson	5	b McKenzie	1
F. S. Trueman	b Davidson	25	c Grout b McKenzie	0
J. B. Statham	not out	11	not out	2
Extras	(lb 9, w 2)	11	(b 1, lb 10, w 1)	12
Total		**206**		**202**

AUSTRALIA

Batsman	1st Innings		2nd Innings	
W. M. Lawry	c Murray b Dexter	130	c Murray b Statham	1
C. C. McDonald	b Statham	4	c Illingworth b Trueman	14
R. B. Simpson	c Illingworth b Trueman	0	(6)c Illingworth b Statham	15
*R. N. Harvey	c Barrington b Trueman	27	(3)c Murray b Trueman	4
N. C. O'Neill	b Dexter	1	(4)b Statham	0
P. J. Burge	c Murray b Statham	46	(5)not out	37
A. K. Davidson	lbw b Trueman	6	not out	0
K. D. Mackay	c Barrington b Illingworth	54		
†A. T. W. Grout	lbw b Dexter	0		
G. D. McKenzie	b Trueman	34		
F. M. Misson	not out	25		
Extras	(b 1, lb 12)	13		
Total		**340**	**Total (5 wkts)**	**71**

FALL OF WICKETS

ENGLAND

Wkt	1st	2nd
1st	26	33
2nd	87	63
3rd	87	67
4th	111	80
5th	115	127
6th	127	144
7th	156	191
8th	164	199
9th	167	199
10th	206	202

AUSTRALIA

Wkt	1st	2nd
1st	5	15
2nd	6	15
3rd	81	19
4th	88	19
5th	183	58
6th	194	—
7th	238	—
8th	238	—
9th	291	—
10th	340	—

Umpires: C. S. Elliott, W. E. Phillipson

AUSTRALIA	1st Innings					2nd Innings			
	O	M	R	W		O	M	R	W
Davidson	24·3	6	42	5	..	24	8	50	2
McKenzie	26	7	81	1	..	29	13	37	5
Misson	16	4	48	2	..	17	2	66	2
Mackay	12	3	24	2	..	8	6	5	0
Simpson					..	19	10	32	1

ENGLAND	1st Innings					2nd Innings			
	O	M	R	W		O	M	R	W
Statham	44	10	89	2	..	10·5	3	31	3
Trueman	34	3	118	4	..	10	0	40	2
Dexter	24	7	56	3	..				
Lock	26	13	48	0	..				
Illingworth	11·3	5	16	1	..				

244

1961 Third Test, Leeds

July 6, 7, 8

Toss: Australia   *Result:* England won by eight wickets

The wicket played as unevenly as the surface was patchy, and Australia by winning the toss seemed to have gained a decisive advantage; at tea on the first day they had laid the foundations of what seemed a winning total. England, without Statham, seemed at a serious disadvantage; but Trueman covered his absence with fire and inspiration. Both sides made a change of captaincy, May (the original choice for the series) taking over from Cowdrey and Benaud returning. Jackson was playing in his first Test against Australia at the age of 40.

The determination of McDonald and Lawry was clear as they took the score to 65 before McDonald was out shortly before lunch. Of the first 87 overs, 56 were bowled by Allen and Lock, which showed what May thought of the pitch; but McDonald and Harvey continually went down the wicket to kill the spin. After McDonald left O'Neill batted equally well, and at tea Australia were 183 for 2. The new ball was due, and as there was no sign of a break-through May took it. The result astonished everyone. Bowling with increasing hostility as wickets fell, Trueman took 5 wickets for 16 in 6 overs, and with Jackson getting Burge and Mackay, Australia lost seven wickets for 21 in 50 minutes. Davidson and McKenzie then added 29, but Australia were all out for 237.

England needed a good start and Pullar and Subba Row put on 59—50 of them on the second morning. Davidson cut down his pace to suit the wicket, but although Benaud was sometimes troublesome his injured shoulder reduced his effectiveness and the other Australians bowled too short. Punishing an erratic Simpson—although missed off him when hitting a full toss to mid-wicket—Cowdrey showed his best form, and he and Pullar added 86 for the second wicket. The new ball accounted for Pullar, and at 223 Cowdrey, seeing Langridge hesitate after an appeal for a leg-side catch, walked out as Mackay had done in the previous series. 238 for 4 at stumps—one run in front—England collapsed next day and their lead would have been negligible but for a bold attack on Benaud by Lock.

Jackson in his first over bowled McDonald with a break-back, and Lawry at 49 was caught behind off Allen's first ball; but Harvey and O'Neill had cleared the arrears and were re-establishing Australia's position when Trueman came back and, bowling off-cutters off a shortened run, got 5 wickets before the tea interval without conceding a run. There was no recovery, and England won comfortably by 8 wickets.

AUSTRALIA

C. C. McDonald	st Murray b Lock	54	b Jackson	1	
W. M. Lawry	lbw b Lock	28	c Murray b Allen	28	
R. N. Harvey	c Lock b Trueman	73	c Dexter b Trueman	53	
N. C. O'Neill	c Cowdrey b Trueman	27	c Cowdrey b Trueman	19	
P. J. Burge	c Cowdrey b Jackson	5	lbw b Allen	0	
K. D. Mackay	lbw b Jackson	6	(9)c Murray b Trueman	0	
R. B. Simpson	lbw b Trueman	2	(6)Trueman	3	
A. K. Davidson	not out	22	(7)c Cowdrey b Trueman	7	
*R. Benaud	b Trueman	0	(8)b Trueman	0	
†A. T. W. Grout	c Murray b Trueman	3	c and b Jackson	7	
G. D. McKenzie	b Allen	8	not out	0	
Extras	(b 7, lb 2)	9	(lb 2)	2	
Total		237	Total	120	

ENGLAND

G. Pullar	b Benaud	53	not out	26
R. Subba Row	lbw b Davidson	35	b Davidson	6
M. C. Cowdrey	c Grout b McKenzie	93	c Grout b Benaud	22
*P. B. H. May	c and b Davidson	26	not out	8
E. R. Dexter	b Davidson	28		
K. F. Barrington	c Simpson b Davidson	6		
†J. T. Murray	b McKenzie	6		
F. S. Trueman	c Burge b Davidson	4		
G. A. R. Lock	b McKenzie	30		
D. A. Allen	not out	5		
H. L. Jackson	run out	8		
Extras	(lb 5)	5		
Total		299	Total (2 wkts)	62

FALL OF WICKETS

AUSTRALIA

Wkt	1st	2nd
1st	65	4
2nd	113	49
3rd	187	99
4th	192	102
5th	196	102
6th	203	105
7th	203	109
8th	204	109
9th	208	120
10th	237	120

ENGLAND

Wkt	1st	2nd
1st	59	14
2nd	145	45
3rd	190	—
4th	223	—
5th	239	—
6th	248	—
7th	252	—
8th	286	—
9th	291	—
10th	299	—

Umpires: J. S. Buller, John Langridge

ENGLAND	1st Innings					2nd Innings			
	O	M	R	W		O	M	R	W
Trueman	22	5	58	5	..	15.5	5	30	6
Jackson	31	11	57	2	..	13	5	26	2
Allen	28	12	45	1	..	14	6	30	2
Lock	29	5	68	2	..	10	1	32	0

AUSTRALIA	1st Innings					2nd Innings			
	O	M	R	W		O	M	R	W
Davidson	47	23	63	5	..	11	6	17	1
McKenzie	27	4	64	3	..	5	0	15	0
Mackay	22	4	34	0	..	1	0	8	0
Benaud	39	15	86	1	..	6	1	22	1
Simpson	14	5	47	0	..				

1961 Fourth Test, Old Trafford

July 27, 28, 29, 31, August 1
Toss: Australia   *Result:* Australia won by 54 runs

The side that wins a match like this one—and with it the Ashes—will never forget the joy and thrill of it; for the side that loses, the poignancy of defeat must remain almost unbearable even in retrospect. England had Close in for Cowdrey (throat infection), Statham was back, and Flavell replaced Lock, leaving only one top-class spinner. Australia had Booth for McDonald (also injured); but most significant was the improved fitness of Benaud.

The wicket was green and the atmosphere suited swing. Simpson was caught behind in Statham's first over, but Lawry was soon driving confidently. Harvey, too, looked dangerous before being brilliantly caught at slip. O'Neill was given a nauseatingly painful time by Flavell before knocking his wicket over avoiding a Trueman bouncer, and soon after lunch Burge was bowled. When rain fell at 2.40 Australia were 124 for 4, Lawry 64 not out. May's policy next morning was to bowl Statham out, holding Trueman in reserve, and, with fine support from Dexter, Statham responded so well that Australia were dismissed for 190.

England soon lost Subba Row and Dexter, but the wicket was easier and May and Pullar added 111. 187 for 3 at stumps, England grafted their way next day to a worthwhile lead. But chasing quick runs after tea they lost their last 3 wickets cheaply, and at stumps Australia had fought their way back to 63 for 0 (114 behind).

Missed at slip by Subba Row when he was 25, Lawry carried on next day to 102. Harvey, looking for runs despite Australia's precarious position, was dropped twice before being caught behind, and O'Neill and Burge were also in forceful mood. Yet when the 6th wicket fell Australia were only 119 ahead. Mackay and Davidson then added 35 in the last hour.

Allen took 3 of the outstanding wickets on the last morning in 15 balls and the match looked won. But Davidson, after defending grimly, suddenly hit Allen for 20 in one over, including two huge off-drives for 6, and 98 runs were added for the last wicket.

Their grip on the game loosened, England faced the formidable task of making 256 to win at 67 an hour. A magnificent 76 in 84 minutes from Dexter brought the game to a gripping climax, but Benaud went round the wicket and aimed at the bowler's footmarks, and after dismissing Dexter he bowled May round his legs second ball. Close used methods that could only have been applauded had they succeeded, Subba Row was yorked last ball before tea, and Barrington and the tail between them could not save the game, Australia winning a remarkable match with 20 minutes to spare.

AUSTRALIA

W. M. Lawry	lbw b Statham	74	c Trueman b Allen	102	
R. B. Simpson	c Murray b Statham	4	c Murray b Flavell	51	
R. N. Harvey	c Subba Row b Statham	19	c Murray b Dexter	35	
N. C. O'Neill	hit wkt b Trueman	11	c Murray b Statham	67	
P. J. Burge	b Flavell	15	c Murray b Dexter	23	
B. C. Booth	c Close b Statham	46	lbw b Dexter	9	
K. D. Mackay	c Murray b Statham	11	c Close b Allen	18	
A. K. Davidson	c Barrington b Dexter	0	not out	77	
*R. Benaud	b Dexter	2	lbw b Allen	1	
†A. T. W. Grout	c Murray b Dexter	2	c Statham b Allen	0	
G. D. McKenzie	not out	1	b Flavell	32	
Extras	(b 4, lb 1)	5	(b 6, lb 9, w 2)	17	
Total		**190**	**Total**	**432**	

ENGLAND

G. Pullar	b Davidson	63	c O'Neill b Davidson	26	
R. Subba Row	c Simpson b Davidson	2	b Benaud	49	
E. R. Dexter	c Davidson b McKenzie	16	c Grout b Benaud	76	
*P. B. H. May	c Simpson b Davidson	95	b Benaud	0	
D. B. Close	lbw b McKenzie	33	c O'Neill b Benaud	8	
K. F. Barrington	c O'Neill b Simpson	78	lbw b Mackay	5	
†J. T. Murray	c Grout b Mackay	24	c Simpson b Benaud	4	
D. A. Allen	c Booth b Simpson	42	c Simpson b Benaud	10	
F. S. Trueman	c Harvey b Simpson	3	c Benaud b Simpson	8	
J. B. Statham	c Mackay b Simpson	4	b Davidson	8	
J. A. Flavell	not out	0	not out	0	
Extras	(b 2, lb 4, w 1)	7	(b 5, w 2)	7	
Total		**367**	**Total**	**201**	

FALL OF WICKETS
AUSTRALIA

Wkt	1st	2nd
1st	8	113
2nd	51	175
3rd	89	210
4th	106	274
5th	150	290
6th	174	296
7th	185	332
8th	185	334
9th	189	334
10th	190	432

ENGLAND

Wkt	1st	2nd
1st	3	40
2nd	43	150
3rd	154	150
4th	212	158
5th	212	163
6th	272	171
7th	358	171
8th	362	189
9th	367	193
10th	367	201

Umpires: John Langridge, W. E. Phillipson

ENGLAND	1st Innings					2nd Innings			
	O	M	R	W		O	M	R	W
Trueman	14	1	55	1	..	32	6	92	0
Statham	21	3	53	5	..	44	9	106	1
Flavell	22	8	61	1	..	29·4	4	65	2
Dexter	6·4	2	16	3	..	20	4	61	3
Allen					..	38	25	58	4
Close					..	8	1	33	0

AUSTRALIA	1st Innings					2nd Innings			
	O	M	R	W		O	M	R	W
Davidson	39	11	70	3	..	14·4	1	50	2
McKenzie	38	11	106	2	..	4	1	20	0
Mackay	40	9	81	1	..	13	7	33	1
Benaud	35	15	80	0	..	32	11	70	6
Simpson	11·4	4	23	4	..	8	4	21	1

1961 Fifth Test, Oval

August 17, 18, 19, 21, 22
Toss: England   *Result:* Match Drawn

England's hopes of squaring the rubber received a severe jolt on the first morning, in which they lost 4 wickets for 67. Trueman, who got the blame for the rough into which Benaud had pitched at Old Trafford, was left out, but Cowdrey and Lock returned. For Australia, Gaunt replaced the injured McKenzie.

The ball was swinging and there was some early life in the wicket, and England after 50 minutes were 20 for 3. But May and Dexter played their strokes and had added 47 when just on lunch-time Dexter slashed fatally at a widish ball. The batting in the afternoon was inevitably cautious as May and Barrington worked for a recovery, and in 3 hours they put on 80 before May skied Benaud into the covers going for a big hit. Barrington batted 3¼ hours for 53, Murray 110 minutes for 27, and at stumps England off 104 overs had made only 210 for 8. Firm-footed hitting and mis-hitting brought another 46 runs next morning, and then Australia were pegged back by Statham and Flavell, 2 wickets falling for 15. But shortly after lunch O'Neill was missed by Barrington at slip off Statham, and that was England's last chance.

Wonderful running which turned singles into twos and twos into threes, and superb footwork which enabled O'Neill to play many of his drives far down the pitch, made the afternoon's batting the finest of the series. O'Neill made 82 in the session, and in 3 hours 40 minutes Australia made as many as England had done in 6 hours the previous day. When O'Neill left at 211 Burge in his contrasting style took over, sweeping and hooking so effectively that by stumps Australia were 290 for 4; but May's handling of the attack drew strong criticism, particularly his failure to take the new ball when O'Neill was out. He delayed it for another 54 runs, by which time the stylish Booth, too, was established.

Although an hour was lost on the third day through rain Australia added another 204 and had time for 15 overs at England, in which 30 were made without loss. The fourth day was also rain-interrupted, but at the end of it England were facing defeat at 155 for 4, still 83 behind with a day to go. Subba Row and Barrington, however, played through till lunch and added 172 in all. Batting with a runner through a strain, Subba Row lasted 7 hours 40 minutes, while Barrington was in 4¾ hours. England were still only 45 runs on with 2½ hours left when these two were out; but with Davidson hurt and McKenzie absent, and the wicket too slow for Benaud, Murray and Allen held on.

ENGLAND

G. Pullar	b Davidson	8	c Grout b Mackay	13	
R. Subba Row	lbw b Gaunt	12	c and b Benaud	137	
M. C. Cowdrey	c Grout b Davidson	0	(5)c Benaud b Mackay	3	
*P. B. H. May	c Lawry b Benaud	71	c O'Neill b Mackay	33	
E. R. Dexter	c Grout b Gaunt	24	(3)c Gaunt b Mackay	0	
K. F. Barrington	c Grout b Gaunt	53	c O'Neill b Benaud	83	
†J. T. Murray	c O'Neill b Mackay	27	c Grout b Benaud	40	
G. A. R. Lock	c Grout b Mackay	3	c Benaud b Mackay	0	
D. A. Allen	not out	22	not out	42	
J. B. Statham	b Davidson	18	not out	9	
J. A. Flavell	c Simpson b Davidson	14			
Extras	(b 1, lb 2, w 1)	4	(b 6, lb 3, w 1)	10	
Total		**256**	**Total (8 wkts)**	**370**	

AUSTRALIA

W. M. Lawry	c Murray b Statham	0
R. B. Simpson	b Allen	40
R. N. Harvey	lbw b Flavell	13
N. C. O'Neill	c sub (M. J. Stewart) b Allen	117
P. J. Burge	b Allen	181
B. C. Booth	c Subba Row b Lock	71
K. D. Mackay	c Murray b Flavell	5
A. K. Davidson	lbw b Statham	17
*R. Benaud	b Allen	6
†A. T. W. Grout	not out	30
R. A. Gaunt	b Statham	3
Extras	(b 10, lb 1)	11
Total		**494**

FALL OF WICKETS

ENGLAND

Wkt	1st	2nd
1st	18	33
2nd	20	33
3rd	20	83
4th	67	90
5th	147	262
6th	193	283
7th	199	283
8th	202	355
9th	238	—
10th	256	—

AUSTRALIA

Wkt	1st	2nd
1st	0	—
2nd	15	—
3rd	88	—
4th	211	—
5th	396	—
6th	401	—
7th	441	—
8th	455	—
9th	472	—
10th	494	—

Umpires: C. S. Elliott,
F. S. Lee

AUSTRALIA	1st Innings					2nd Innings			
	O	M	R	W		O	M	R	W
Davidson	34·1	8	83	4	..	29	7	67	0
Gaunt	24	3	53	3	..	22	7	33	0
Benaud	17	4	35	1	..	51	18	113	3
Mackay	39	14	75	2	..	68	21	121	5
Simpson	4	2	6	0	..	2	0	13	0
O'Neill					..	4	1	13	0
Harvey					..	1	1	0	0

ENGLAND	1st Innings					2nd Innings			
	O	M	R	W		O	M	R	W
Statham	38·5	10	75	3	..				
Flavell	31	5	105	2	..				
Dexter	24	2	68	0	..				
Allen	30	6	133	4	..				
Lock	42	14	102	1	..				

1962-63 First Test, Brisbane

November 30, December 1, 3, 4, 5
Toss: Australia   *Result:* Match Drawn

The best cricket matches are not staged; they happen. But the pressures on the two captains to produce entertainment were never stronger than in this series, following as it did the memorable series between Australia and the West Indies of 1960-61. In the event neither captain had the resources to make good his promises, and mutual respect between two evenly-matched sides plus a succession of slow wickets combined to produce a series that, although not deserving the calumny it received, fell short of expectation. Outstanding for England were Dexter, Barrington, Trueman and Titmus, while for Australia Davidson was still a highly dangerous bowler, McKenzie was approaching greatness, and Benaud—like Dexter for England—was a latent, inhibiting threat dominating the strategy of the series. The England selectors' precept that fielding would be a major consideration in selection was not adhered to, and it was in this department that England were outclassed; the result was that the Australian batting, sustained by dropped catches, never failed.

A fine opening spell by Trueman gave England a good start, and although Simpson made 50 and Booth and Davidson added 54 for the sixth wicket, England seemed in control when the new ball was taken at 208 for 6. But the 6-hour day in operation for the first time in Australia helped the batting side, and with Booth making 113 Australia were 323 for 7 at stumps. It was 90 minutes next day before Mackay and Benaud, the overnight not outs, were separated, and Australia totalled 404.

Pullar and Sheppard survived early escapes to make 62 together, and Dexter hit his first 50 in 68 minutes, but both he and Cowdrey were out before stumps, when England were 169 for 4. The crisis came after the loss of Smith, the night-watchman, to the new ball next morning; but Barrington and Parfitt held on, though their tedious methods (roughly four hours each) angered the crowd.

16 for 0 overnight, Australia reached 362 for 4 at the end of the fourth day, thanks to dropped catches, sluggish fielding, and the enterprise of O'Neill and Harvey. Yet on a slow wicket it was not until the last session that they scored at over a run a minute, Lawry staying 4 hours 20 minutes for his 98. Benaud declared first thing next morning, leaving England 378 to win at 63 an hour, and after a century opening stand there was a point in mid-afternoon when Dexter was going so strongly that an England win looked possible. But the new ball changed the complexion, and in the last 40 minutes it was England who were staving off defeat. Dexter's 99 took only 2 hours 47 minutes.

AUSTRALIA

W. M. Lawry	c Smith b Trueman	5	c Sheppard b Titmus	98	
R. B. Simpson	c Trueman b Dexter	50	c Smith b Dexter	71	
N. C. O'Neill	c Statham b Trueman	19	lbw b Statham	56	
R. N. Harvey	b Statham	39	c Statham b Dexter	57	
P. J. Burge	c Dexter b Trueman	6	not out	47	
B. C. Booth	c Dexter b Titmus	112	not out	19	
A. K. Davidson	c Trueman b Barrington	23			
K. D. Mackay	not out	86			
*R. Benaud	c Smith b Knight	51			
G. D. McKenzie	c and b Knight	4			
†B. N. Jarman	c Barrington b Knight	2			
Extras	(b 5, lb 1, nb 1)	7	(b 4, lb 10)	14	
Total		**404**	**Total** (4 wkts dec)	**362**	

ENGLAND

G. Pullar	c and b Benaud	33	c and b Davidson	56	
Rev. D. S. Sheppard	c McKenzie b Benaud	31	c Benaud b Davidson	53	
*E. R. Dexter	b Benaud	70	b McKenzie	99	
M. C. Cowdrey	c Lawry b Simpson	21	c and b Benaud	9	
K. F. Barrington	c Burge b Benaud	78	c McKenzie b Davidson	23	
†A. C. Smith	c Jarman b McKenzie	21			
P. H. Parfitt	c Davidson b Benaud	80	(6) c Jarman b McKenzie	4	
F. J. Titmus	c Simpson b Benaud	21	(7) not out	3	
B. R. Knight	c Davidson b McKenzie	0	(8) not out	4	
F. S. Trueman	c Jarman b McKenzie	19			
J. B. Statham	not out	8			
Extras	(b 4, lb 2, w 1)	7	(b 15, lb 10, nb 2)	27	
Total		**389**	**Total** (6 wkts)	**278**	

FALL OF WICKETS

AUSTRALIA

Wkt	1st	2nd
1st	5	136
2nd	46	216
3rd	92	241
4th	101	325
5th	140	—
6th	194	—
7th	297	—
8th	388	—
9th	392	—
10th	404	—

ENGLAND

Wkt	1st	2nd
1st	62	114
2nd	65	135
3rd	145	191
4th	169	257
5th	220	257
6th	297	261
7th	361	—
8th	362	—
9th	362	—
10th	389	—

Umpires: C. J. Egar,
E. F. Wykes

ENGLAND	1st Innings					2nd Innings			
	O	M	R	W		O	M	R	W
Statham	16	1	75	1	..	16	1	67	1
Trueman	18	0	76	3	..	15	0	59	0
Knight	17.5	2	65	3	..	14	1	63	0
Titmus	33	8	91	1	..	26	3	81	1
Dexter	10	0	46	1	..	16	0	78	2
Barrington	12	3	44	1	..				

AUSTRALIA	1st Innings					2nd Innings			
	O	M	R	W		O	M	R	W
Davidson	21	4	77	0	..	20	6	43	3
McKenzie	25.3	2	78	3	..	20	4	61	2
Mackay	28	7	55	0	..	7	0	28	0
Benaud	42	12	115	6	..	27	7	71	1
Simpson	18	6	52	1	..	7	0	48	0
O'Neill	1	0	5	0	..	2	2	0	0

136. **K. F. Barrington**

137. **R. B. Simpson**

138. **England 1962–63**

Back row: K. F. Barrington, F. J. Titmus, B. R. Knight, J. T. Murray, P. H. Parfitt. *Middle row:* W. R. Watkins (scorer), A. C. Smith, G. Pullar, T. W. Graveney, J. D. F. Larter, L. J. Coldwell, R. Illingworth, D. A. Allen, S. Cowan (masseur). *Front:* A. V. Bedser (assistant-manager), F. S. Trueman, M. C. Cowdrey, E. R. Dexter (capt.), J. B. Statham, Rev. D. S. Sheppard, His Grace the Duke of Norfolk (manager).

1962–63 Second Test, Melbourne

December 29, 31, January 1, 2, 3
Toss: Australia   *Result:* England won by 7 wickets

On a day of great heat and humidity Australia did well to reach 263 for 7 after being 164 for 6. Again it was the final session that saw them recover, and again the architects were Davidson, Mackay and Benaud. An uncharacteristic innings by Simpson helped Australia to 93 for 1 at lunch; the bat was beaten so many times that the score seemed unreal. O'Neill, Harvey and Lawry all left in quick succession afterwards, and Booth and Burge never really established themselves, but then came the rescue act, though England would have been in a happier position had Sheppard taken a catch from Benaud in the last over. England bowled only 73 overs in the day.

Australia added another 53 next morning, and there was just time before the interval for Davidson to produce an unplayable ball for Sheppard and another to shave Dexter's stumps; and after lunch Pullar was not so lucky. But a wonderful stand of 175 in 198 minutes between Dexter and Cowdrey restored the position. Batsmen and bowlers alike were exhausted when Dexter, playing for the morrow, was caught at slip, again missing his hundred. At stumps England were 210 for 3, Cowdrey 94.

The new ball had been safely negotiated next morning when Cowdrey was caught off a long hop, and Barrington was beaten by a break-back at 255 for 5; but Graveney played with refreshing confidence until he ran himself out. Davidson then mopped up the tail. Lawry and Simpson soon devoured England's slender lead, but Trueman in an inspired spell got Simpson and O'Neill and at tea Australia were 40 for 2. Harvey, going for a fourth run, was beaten by a great 90-yard throw by Pullar, Burge met a shooter from Statham, and although Sheppard again dropped a catch in the last over Australia at stumps were 105 for 4.

Despite a chanceless century from Booth and an obstinate 57 from Lawry in 5 hours—he too got a shooter—England never relaxed their grip on the fourth day. But a setback came when, needing 234 to win on a wicket on which the occasional ball still kept low, they lost Pullar and were 9 for 1 at stumps.

Sheppard had dropped two vital catches and had scored a duck in the first innings, and if any man needed to redeem himself he did: now he added 124 with Dexter. Australia had their chance when Dexter was run out; but Cowdrey was missed at slip at 149 and Sheppard at the wicket at 151, and England won with 1¼ hours to spare. On the final day not a single wicket fell to a bowler.

AUSTRALIA

W. M. Lawry	b Trueman	52	b Dexter	57	
R. B. Simpson	c Smith b Coldwell	38	b Trueman	14	
N. C. O'Neill	c Graveney b Statham	19	c Cowdrey b Trueman	0	
R. N. Harvey	b Coldwell	0	run out	10	
P. J. Burge	lbw b Titmus	23	b Statham	14	
B. C. Booth	c Barrington b Titmus	27	c Trueman b Statham	103	
A. K. Davidson	c Smith b Trueman	40	c Smith b Titmus	17	
K. D. Mackay	lbw b Titmus	49	lbw b Trueman	9	
*R. Benaud	c Barrington b Titmus	36	c Cowdrey b Trueman	4	
G. D. McKenzie	b Trueman	16	b Trueman	0	
†B. N. Jarman	not out	10	not out	11	
Extras	(b 2, lb 4)	6	(b 4, lb 5)	9	
Total		**316**	**Total**	**248**	

ENGLAND

Rev. D. S. Sheppard	lbw b Davidson	0	run out	113	
G. Pullar	b Davidson	11	c Jarman b McKenzie	5	
*E. R. Dexter	c Simpson b Benaud	93	run out	52	
M. C. Cowdrey	c Burge b McKenzie	113	not out	58	
K. F. Barrington	lbw b McKenzie	35	not out	0	
T. W. Graveney	run out	41			
F. J. Titmus	c Jarman b Davidson	15			
†A. C. Smith	not out	6			
F. S. Trueman	c O'Neill b Davidson	6			
J. B. Statham	b Davidson	1			
L. J. Coldwell	c Benaud b Davidson	1			
Extras	(b 4, lb 4, nb 1)	9	(b 5, lb 3, nb 1)	9	
Total		**331**	**Total** (3 wkts)	**237**	

FALL OF WICKETS

AUSTRALIA

Wkt	1st	2nd
1st	62	30
2nd	111	30
3rd	112	46
4th	112	69
5th	155	161
6th	164	193
7th	237	212
8th	289	228
9th	294	228
10th	316	248

ENGLAND

Wkt	1st	2nd
1st	0	5
2nd	19	129
3rd	194	233
4th	254	—
5th	255	—
6th	292	—
7th	315	—
8th	324	—
9th	327	—
10th	331	—

Umpires: C. J. Egar,
W. Smyth

ENGLAND

	1st Innings				2nd Innings			
	O	M	R	W	O	M	R	W
Trueman	23	1	83	3	20	1	62	5
Statham	22	2	83	1	23	1	52	2
Coldwell	17	2	58	2	25	2	60	0
Barrington	6	0	23	0	5	0	22	0
Dexter	6	1	10	0	9	2	18	1
Titmus	15	2	43	4	14	4	25	1
Graveney	3	1	10	0				

AUSTRALIA

	1st Innings				2nd Innings			
	O	M	R	W	O	M	R	W
Davidson	23·1	4	75	6	19	2	53	0
McKenzie	29	3	95	2	20	3	58	1
Mackay	6	2	17	0	9	0	34	0
Benaud	18	3	82	1	14	1	69	0
Simpson	7	1	34	0	2	0	10	0
O'Neill	5	1	19	0				
Booth					0·2	0	4	0

1962-63 Third Test, Sydney

January 11, 12, 14, 15
Toss: England   *Result:* Australia won by eight wickets

A lifeless pitch, a slow outfield, and magnificent ground fielding retarded England's progress on the first day. Sheppard's cheap dismissal and some early uncertainty by Dexter were further inhibiting factors. England were without Graveney with a virus infection, and Parfitt replaced him, while Coldwell was preferred to Allen and Murray displaced Smith. Australia had Shepherd and Guest for Burge and Mackay.

When Dexter was out 15 minutes before lunch he and Pullar had put on 61 in 85 minutes. Dropped when 43 at slip off Guest, Pullar batted nearly 3½ hours for 53, but Cowdrey and Barrington put on 69 in quick time, and when Cowdrey was caught like Pullar off a long hop after batting 2 hours 40 minutes England were reasonably well placed at 201 for 4. Parfitt was then out pushing forward to Simpson, Barrington and Murray were beaten by Davidson with the second new ball, and that was 221 for 7. Although Titmus (missed twice) and Trueman put on 51, England were all out next morning for 279.

For a long time when Australia batted things went badly for England. Even the early dismissal of Lawry had its attendant misfortune, Murray diving to take a brilliant catch only to sprain his shoulder. Parfitt took over behind the stumps. Harvey began by giving a difficult chance to slip; at 32 he drove Titmus straight to Sheppard at extra cover, who dropped it; and Sheppard was again at fault when misjudging a lofted Harvey sweep. Meanwhile Simpson was batting in his most compact style, and the score had reached 174 when Titmus, varying his pace and flight and floating the occasional ball away, took the wickets of Harvey, Simpson, O'Neill and Booth in 58 balls for 5 runs. Australia at stumps were 212 for 5, and the game was wide open again. Simpson, having taken 5 for 57 in England's innings, batted 4 hours for 91.

Thanks largely to the burly Shepherd and a last wicket stand of 39, Australia gained a lead of 40 on the third morning, but the match still looked evenly poised. Within 45 minutes, however, the genius of Davidson and Simpson's greatness at slip had won the match for Australia. Swinging the ball both ways very late at a pace little short of genuinely fast, Davidson—as he often did with the new ball—looked almost unplayable, and this time England did not escape the consequences. Pullar, Dexter and Sheppard were all his victims, Cowdrey was caught at slip off Benaud's first ball, and although England struggled to 86 for 6 that night, and Murray batted 100 minutes for 3, Australia were left with only 65 to win.

ENGLAND

Batsman	Dismissal 1st	Runs	Dismissal 2nd	Runs
G. Pullar	c Benaud b Simpson	53	b Davidson	0
Rev. D. S. Sheppard	c McKenzie b Davidson	3	c Simpson b Davidson	12
*E. R. Dexter	c Lawry b Benaud	32	c Simpson b Davidson	11
M. C. Cowdrey	c Jarman b Simpson	85	c Simpson b Benaud	8
K. F. Barrington	lbw b Davidson	35	b McKenzie	21
P. H. Parfitt	c Lawry b Simpson	0	c O'Neill b McKenzie	28
F. J. Titmus	b Davidson	32	c Booth b O'Neill	6
†J. T. Murray	lbw b Davidson	0	not out	3
F. S. Trueman	b Simpson	32	c Jarman b McKenzie	9
J. B. Statham	c Benaud b Simpson	0	b Davidson	2
L. J. Coldwell	not out	2	c Shepherd b Davidson	0
Extras	(lb 3, w 2)	5	(b 2, lb 2)	4
Total		**279**		**104**

AUSTRALIA

Batsman	Dismissal 1st	Runs	Dismissal 2nd	Runs
W. M. Lawry	c Murray b Coldwell	8	b Trueman	8
R. B. Simpson	b Titmus	91	not out	34
R. N. Harvey	c Barrington b Titmus	64	lbw b Trueman	15
B. C. Booth	c Trueman b Titmus	16	not out	5
N. C. O'Neill	b Titmus	3		
B. K. Shepherd	not out	71		
†B. N. Jarman	run out	0		
A. K. Davidson	c Trueman b Titmus	15		
*R. Benaud	c and b Titmus	15		
G. D. McKenzie	lbw b Titmus	4		
C. Guest	b Statham	11		
Extras	(b 10, lb 11)	21	(b 5)	5
Total		**319**	**Total** (2 wkts)	**67**

FALL OF WICKETS

	ENGLAND	
Wkt	1st	2nd
1st	4	0
2nd	65	20
3rd	132	25
4th	201	37
5th	203	53
6th	221	71
7th	221	90
8th	272	100
9th	272	104
10th	279	104

	AUSTRALIA	
Wkt	1st	2nd
1st	14	28
2nd	174	54
3rd	177	—
4th	187	—
5th	212	—
6th	216	—
7th	242	—
8th	274	—
9th	280	—
10th	319	—

Umpires: W. Smyth, L. Rowan

AUSTRALIA	1st Innings					2nd Innings			
	O	M	R	W		O	M	R	W
Davidson	24·5	7	54	4	..	10·6	2	25	5
McKenzie	15	3	52	0	..	14	3	26	3
Guest	16	0	51	0	..	2	0	8	0
Benaud	16	2	60	1	..	19	10	29	1
Simpson	15	3	57	5	..	4	2	5	0
O'Neill					..	7	5	7	1

ENGLAND	1st Innings					2nd Innings			
	O	M	R	W		O	M	R	W
Trueman	20	2	68	0	..	6	1	20	2
Statham	21·2	2	67	1	..	3	0	15	0
Coldwell	15	1	41	1	..				
Titmus	37	14	79	7	..				
Barrington	8	0	43	0	..				
Dexter					..	3·2	0	27	0

1962–63 Fourth Test, Adelaide

January 25, 26, 28, 29, 30
Toss: Australia   *Result:* Match Drawn

All square in the series, it was perhaps inevitable that the two sides should concentrate on parity for the final Test. Thus Australia recalled Mackay, while England substituted Illingworth for Coldwell. Graveney returned for Parfitt, Smith deputised for Murray, and Grout, recovered from injury, took over from Jarman.

After Simpson had been well caught on the leg side by Smith in the second over, and Lawry bowled between bat and pad by Illingworth, Harvey was missed twice off consecutive balls, the first to Cowdrey at slip, the second a straightforward chance to Sheppard at fine leg 30 yards from the bat. Harvey survived another chance before lunch, and after he and Booth had added 85, O'Neill appeared to give a catch to short leg. Harvey and O'Neill then showed their finest form of the series, playing the off-spinners so well that 120 runs were added in the afternoon. In the end both batsmen fell as much from exhaustion as anything, and at stumps Australia were 322 for 5.

Australia's last 5 wickets fell for 71 next morning, and then Davidson and McKenzie raised Australia's hopes with a ferocious opening burst. Pullar was bowled, Barrington was horribly uncertain against Davidson, and Sheppard too was lucky to survive. But in his fourth over Davidson pulled a hamstring, and this gave the batsmen a breather. Even then England got into difficulties, though the luck ran against

them as Cowdrey appeared to get a bad decision and Graveney got a nasty lifter. It was left to Dexter to strike a defiant note with two straight sixes off Simpson before stumps at 192 for 5.

Only 3 hours play was possible on the third day, in which England reached 328 for 9, thanks to a workmanlike innings by Titmus (missed when 34) and a quick 38 from Trueman. England were soon out on the fourth morning, and after a short break for rain Statham and Trueman made the ball lift much as McKenzie had done; but after Lawry and Harvey had gone cheaply Simpson and Booth added 133.

So well did England contain Australia that their lead at the day's end, with 4 wickets left, was 287—not enough, with Davidson unfit, for a declaration, even though Sheppard and Illingworth were both unwell. Indeed Benaud, helped by a bad miss by Titmus in the first over next morning, and with an eye to Dexter's potential, batted on till lunch.

With 105 minutes left England at 122 for 4 were far from safe, and Illingworth was summoned from his sick-bed; but Barrington and Graveney saw the day out, and a match riddled with missed opportunities ended tamely, though Barrington reached a splendid 100 in under 3 hours.

AUSTRALIA

W. M. Lawry	b Illingworth	10	c Graveney b Trueman	16	
R. B. Simpson	c Smith b Statham	0	c Smith b Dexter	71	
R. N. Harvey	c Statham b Dexter	154	c Barrington b Statham	6	
B. C. Booth	c Cowdrey b Titmus	34	c Smith b Dexter	77	
N. C. O'Neill	c Cowdrey b Dexter	100	c Cowdrey b Trueman	23	
A. K. Davidson	b Statham	46	(10)b Statham	2	
B. K. Shepherd	c Trueman b Statham	10	(6)c Titmus b Dexter	13	
K. D. Mackay	c Smith b Trueman	1	(7)c Graveney b Trueman	3	
*R. Benaud	b Dexter	16	(8)c Barrington b Trueman	48	
G. D. McKenzie	c Sheppard b Titmus	15	(9)c Smith b Statham	13	
†A. T. W. Grout	not out	1	not out	16	
Extras	(lb 5, w 1)	6	(b 1, lb 4)	5	
Total		**393**	**Total**	**293**	

ENGLAND

G. Pullar	b McKenzie	9	c Simpson b McKenzie	3	
Rev. D. S. Sheppard	st Grout b Benaud	30	c Grout b Mackay	1	
K. F. Barrington	b Simpson	63	not out	132	
M. C. Cowdrey	c Grout b McKenzie	13	run out	32	
*E. R. Dexter	c Grout b McKenzie	61	c Simpson b Benaud	10	
T. W. Graveney	c Booth b McKenzie	22	not out	36	
F. J. Titmus	not out	59			
R. Illingworth	c Grout b McKenzie	12			
†A. C. Smith	c Lawry b Mackay	13			
F. S. Trueman	c Benaud b Mackay	38			
J. B. Statham	b Mackay	1			
Extras	(b 5, lb 5)	10	(b 4, w 5)	9	
Total		**331**	**Total** (4 wkts)	**223**	

FALL OF WICKETS

AUSTRALIA

Wkt	1st	2nd
1st	2	27
2nd	16	37
3rd	101	170
4th	295	175
5th	302	199
6th	331	205
7th	336	228
8th	366	254
9th	383	258
10th	393	293

ENGLAND

Wkt	1st	2nd
1st	17	2
2nd	84	4
3rd	117	98
4th	119	122
5th	165	—
6th	226	—
7th	246	—
8th	275	—
9th	327	—
10th	331	—

Umpires: C. J. Egar,
A. Mackley

ENGLAND	1st Innings				2nd Innings			
	O	M	R	W	O	M	R	W
Trueman	19	1	54	1	23·3	3	60	4
Statham	21	5	66	3	21	2	71	3
Illingworth	20	3	85	1	5	1	23	0
Dexter	23	1	94	3	17	0	65	3
Titmus	20·1	2	88	2	24	5	69	0

AUSTRALIA	1st Innings				2nd Innings			
	O	M	R	W	O	M	R	W
Davidson	3·4	0	30	0				
McKenzie	33	3	89	5	14	0	64	1
Mackay	27·6	8	80	3	8	2	13	1
Benaud	18	3	82	1	15	3	38	1
Simpson	8	1	40	1	10	1	50	0
O'Neill					8	0	49	0
Lawry					1	1	0	0
Harvey					1	1	0	0

1962–63 Fifth Test, Sydney

Test no. 188

February 15, 16, 18, 19, 20
Toss: England   *Result:* Match Drawn

For only the third time since five-Test series began in Australia, the rubber was still undecided when the final match began. The omens were propitious as England chose five bowlers and Australia brought in Burge and Hawke for Shepherd and Mackay; but a slow pitch and a lush outfield, plus the natural inhibitions of the players in the deciding game, throttled enterprise, and a belated attempt at resuscitation on the final day only aggravated the crowd's disappointment.

Sending Cowdrey in first looked an attacking move until his role was revealed as the counter to Davidson's opening spell. This perfectly reasonable tactic got the innings away to a defensive start; the tactic failed, and the innings never properly recovered. With Davidson wary of his hamstring and Hawke keeping a defensive length, the cricket was wretchedly colourless as Dexter and Barrington fought back after 2 wickets had fallen for 39, and England made only 195 for 5 in the day. Next day Trueman batted 110 minutes for 30. Barrington had only 4 fours in his 101, and England's 321 took 9½ hours.

The start of Australia's innings looked more promising as the batsmen attempted to play strokes, but the loss of Lawry at 28 had a depressing effect, and Simpson spent 2 hours over 30. At stumps Australia were 74 for 3. 70 minutes were lost through rain and bad light on the third day, in which Australia advanced to 285 for 6. Some wonderful footwork by O'Neill against high-class off spin kept the score moving; but Burge, who dominated the innings after O'Neill left, should have been caught at the wicket off Statham when he was 63. Burge batted 5½ hours for his 103, and by adding 64 on the fourth morning Australia gained a lead of 28. Trueman was absent with a muscle strain.

With Cowdrey suffering from an insect bite, Illingworth opened with Sheppard, and as England tried to establish a commanding position Benaud used Davidson in a defensive role the whole afternoon. England with some luck reached 165 for 3 despite bad light; and the policy on the last morning was for Barrington to stay there while the other batsmen attacked. England finally declared at lunch, leaving Australia 241 to win in 4 hours.

Australia adopted much the same tactics, with Lawry as the stabiliser. But only 32 runs came in the first hour, and although Harvey and O'Neill showed willing, 4 wickets fell for 70, after which Lawry and Burge closed up the game. Lawry batted 4 hours for his 45, and the game ended to catcalls and jeers. For the first time in Australia, a five-match series had ended in stalemate.

ENGLAND

Rev. D. S. Sheppard..	c and b Hawke............	19	c Harvey b Benaud........	68
M. C. Cowdrey......	c Harvey b Davidson......	2	(5)c Benaud b Davidson......	53
K. F. Barrington.....	c Harvey b Benaud........	101	c Grout b McKenzie.......	94
*E. R. Dexter........	c Simpson b O'Neill.......	47	st Grout b Benaud........	6
T. W. Graveney......	c Harvey b McKenzie.....	14	(6)c and b Davidson......	3
R. Illingworth.......	c Grout b Davidson.......	27	(2)c Hawke b Benaud.......	18
F. J. Titmus........	c Grout b Hawke.......	34	not out................	12
F. S. Trueman.......	c Harvey b Benaud.......	30	c Harvey b McKenzie......	8
†A. C. Smith.......	b Simpson................	6	c Simpson b Davidson.....	1
D. A. Allen.........	c Benaud b Davidson......	14		
J. B. Statham.......	not out................	17		
Extras...........	(b 4, lb 6).............	10	(b 1, lb 4)...........	5
Total...........	....	**321**	**Total** (8 wkts dec).......	**268**

AUSTRALIA

W. M. Lawry.......	c Smith b Trueman.......	11	not out................	45
R. B. Simpson.......	c Trueman b Titmus.......	32	b Trueman...........	0
B. C. Booth.........	b Titmus............	11	(5)b Allen............	0
N. C. O'Neill......	c Graveney b Allen.......	73	c Smith b Allen........	17
P. J. Burge.........	lbw b Titmus.........	103	(6)not out............	52
R. N. Harvey.......	c sub (P.H.Parfitt) b Statham	22	(3)b Allen............	28
A. K. Davidson......	c Allen b Dexter..........	15		
*R. Benaud..........	c Graveney b Allen.......	57		
G. D. McKenzie.....	c and b Titmus...........	0		
N. J. N. Hawke.....	c Graveney b Titmus......	14		
†A. T. W. Grout.....	not out............	0		
Extras...........	(b 6, lb 5).............	11	(b 4, lb 6).........	10
Total...........	....	**349**	**Total** (4 wkts).........	**152**

FALL OF WICKETS

ENGLAND

Wkt	1st	2nd
1st	5	40
2nd	39	137
3rd	129	145
4th	177	239
5th	189	247
6th	224	249
7th	276	257
8th	286	268
9th	293	—
10th	321	—

AUSTRALIA

Wkt	1st	2nd
1st	28	0
2nd	50	39
3rd	71	70
4th	180	70
5th	231	—
6th	271	—
7th	299	—
8th	303	—
9th	347	—
10th	349	—

Umpires: C. J. Egar, L. Rowan

AUSTRALIA

	1st Innings					2nd Innings			
	O	M	R	W		O	M	R	W
Davidson........	25·6	4	43	3	..	28	1	80	3
McKenzie........	27	4	57	1	..	8	0	39	2
Hawke.........	20	1	51	2	..	9	0	38	0
Benaud.........	34	9	71	2	..	30	8	71	3
Simpson........	18	4	51	1	..	4	0	22	0
O'Neill.........	10	0	38	1	..				
Harvey.........					..	3	0	13	0

ENGLAND

	1st Innings					2nd Innings			
	O	M	R	W		O	M	R	W
Trueman.........	11	0	33	1	..	3	0	6	1
Statham.........	18	1	76	1	..	4	1	8	0
Dexter.........	7	1	24	1	..	4	1	11	0
Titmus.........	47·2	9	103	5	..	20	7	37	0
Allen............	43	15	87	2	..	19	11	26	3
Illingworth.......	5	1	15	0	..	10	5	8	0
Barrington.......					..	8	3	22	0
Graveney........					..	4	0	24	0

Averages: 1962-63

AUSTRALIA

BATTING	M.	Inns.	N.O.	Runs	H.S.	Av.
P. J. Burge	3	6	2	245	103	61·25
B. C. Booth	5	10	2	404	112	50·50
B. K. Shepherd	2	3	1	94	71*	47·00
R. B. Simpson	5	10	1	401	91	44·55
R. N. Harvey	5	10	0	395	154	39·50
K. D. Mackay	3	5	1	148	86*	37·00
N. C. O'Neill	5	9	0	310	100	34·44
W. M. Lawry	5	10	1	310	98	34·44
R. Benaud	5	7	0	227	57	32·42
A. K. Davidson	5	7	0	158	46	22·57
N. J. N. Hawke	1	1	0	14	14	14·00
B. N. Jarman	3	4	2	23	11*	11·50
C. Guest	1	1	0	11	11	11·00
G. D. McKenzie	5	7	0	52	16	7·42
A. T. W. Grout	2	3	3	17	16*	–

BOWLING	Overs	Mds.	Runs	Wkts.	Av.
A. K. Davidson	175·6	30	480	24	20·00
G. D. McKenzie	205·3	25	619	20	30·95
R. Benaud	233	58	688	17	40·47
N. J. N. Hawke	29	1	89	2	44·50
R. B. Simpson	93	18	369	8	46·12
K. D. Mackay	85·6	19	227	4	56·75
N. C. O'Neill	33	8	118	2	59·00

ALSO BOWLED: C. Guest 18–0–59–0, R. N. Harvey 4–1–13–0, W. M. Lawry 1–1–0–0, B. C. Booth 0·2–0–4–0.

ENGLAND

BATTING	M.	Inns.	N.O.	Runs	H.S.	Av.
K. F. Barrington	5	10	2	582	132*	72·75
E. R. Dexter	5	10	0	481	99	48·10
M. C. Cowdrey	5	10	1	394	113	43·77
F. J. Titmus	5	8	3	182	59*	36·40
Rev. D. S. Sheppard	5	10	0	330	113	33·00
T. W. Graveney	3	5	1	116	41	29·00
P. H. Parfitt	2	4	0	112	80	28·00
G. Pullar	4	8	0	170	56	21·25
F. S. Trueman	5	7	0	142	38	20·28
R. Illingworth	2	3	0	57	27	19·00
D. A. Allen	1	1	0	14	14	14·00
A. C. Smith	4	5	1	47	21	11·75
J. B. Statham	5	6	2	29	17*	7·25
B. R. Knight	1	2	1	4	4*	4·00
J. T. Murray	1	2	1	3	3*	3·00
L. J. Coldwell	2	3	1	3	2*	1·50

BOWLING	Overs	Mds.	Runs	Wkts.	Av.
D. A. Allen	62	26	113	5	22·60
F. S. Trueman	158·3	9	521	20	26·05
F. J. Titmus	236·3	54	616	21	29·33
E. R. Dexter	95·2	6	373	11	33·90
B. R. Knight	31·5	3	128	3	42·66
J. B. Statham	165·2	16	580	13	44·61
L. J. Coldwell	57	5	159	3	53·00
R. Illingworth	40	9	131	1	131·00
K. F. Barrington	39	6	154	1	154·00

ALSO BOWLED: T. W. Graveney 7–1–34–0.

Averages: 1964

ENGLAND

BATTING	M.	Inns.	N.O.	Runs	H.S.	Av.
K. F. Barrington	5	8	1	531	256	75·85
G. Boycott	4	6	0	291	113	48·50
E. R. Dexter	5	8	0	384	174	48·00
M. C. Cowdrey	3	5	1	188	93*	47·00
J. H. Edrich	3	4	0	161	120	40·25
P. J. Sharpe	2	3	1	71	35*	35·50
J. M. Parks	5	7	0	207	68	29·57
R. W. Barber	1	2	0	53	29	26·50
F. J. Titmus	5	8	0	138	56	17·25
P. H. Parfitt	4	5	0	73	32	14·60
F. S. Trueman	4	6	1	42	14	8·40

PLAYED IN TWO TESTS: T. W. Cartwright 4 and 0, L. J. Coldwell 0*, 0* and 6*, J. A. Flavell 7, 5 and 5, N. Gifford 5, 1* and 1.
PLAYED IN ONE TEST: D. A. Allen 21 and 3, J. B. Mortimore 12, F. E. Rumsey 3*, K. Taylor 9 and 15, J. S. E. Price 0* and 1.

BOWLING	Overs	Mds.	Runs	Wkts.	Av.
F. S. Trueman	133·3	25	399	17	23·47
N. Gifford	83	35	140	5	28·00
F. J. Titmus	202	92	301	10	30·10
E. R. Dexter	49	7	118	3	39·33
L. J. Coldwell	64	14	158	4	39·50
T. W. Cartwright	139	55	228	5	45·60
F. E. Rumsey	35·5	4	99	2	49·50
J. S. E. Price	66	6	250	4	62·50
J. A. Flavell	49·2	8	136	2	68·00

ALSO BOWLED: J. B. Mortimore 49–13–122–0, D. A. Allen 16–8–22–1, R. W. Barber 6–1–23–0, K. Taylor 2–0–6–0, K. F. Barrington 1–0–4–0, G. Boycott 1–0–3–0.

AUSTRALIA

BATTING	M.	Inns.	N.O.	Runs	H.S.	Av.
R. B. Simpson	5	8	2	458	311	76·33
P. J. Burge	5	8	1	322	160	46·00
B. C. Booth	5	8	3	210	98	42·00
T. R. Veivers	5	5	1	159	67*	39·75
W. M. Lawry	5	9	1	317	106	39·62
N. J. N. Hawke	5	4	2	66	37	33·00
N. C. O'Neill	4	6	1	156	47	31·20
I. R. Redpath	5	8	1	216	58*	30·85
A. T. W. Grout	5	5	0	84	37	16·80
G. D. McKenzie	5	5	1	14	10	3·50
G. E. Corling	5	4	1	5	3	1·66

PLAYED IN ONE TEST: R. M. Cowper 2.

BOWLING	Overs	Mds.	Runs	Wkts.	Av.
G. D. McKenzie	251	61	654	29	22·55
N. J. N. Hawke	242·1	80	496	18	27·55
G. E. Corling	193·1	50	447	12	37·25
T. R. Veivers	228·1	73	444	11	40·36
R. B. Simpson	60	19	159	1	159·00

ALSO BOWLED: N. C. O'Neill 10–6–37–0.

1964 First Test, Trent Bridge

June 4, 5, 6, 8, 9
Toss: England   *Result:* Match Drawn

Bad luck with the weather in what was otherwise a fine summer, and a victory at Leeds half-way through the series by the side holding the Ashes—with its inevitable reaction of 'what we have we hold'—combined to make this an unusually frustrating and disappointing series. The Australians were not highly rated, they were an undistinguished fielding side and had only a moderate record against the counties; but their batting was strong enough for Cowper, who averaged over 50 in first-class matches, to be left out of all the Tests except one, and the bowling, led by McKenzie and the fast-medium Hawke, always troubled England except at Manchester, where the wicket was the best seen since the war. The Australians themselves must have been satisfied with their team; anyway they never changed it, except on one occasion through injury. Thus Burge, although in unimpressive form, was persevered with on the grounds of class and temperament, and he rewarded his captain with the innings that won the series. England as usual were beset by batting crises; yet Edrich and Cowdrey, who missed one Test each through injury, were each dropped from another, and Graveney although in wonderful form was again excluded. Trueman at 33 was England's best bowler.

With Edrich reporting unfit shortly before the start, Dexter was forced to improvise for an opener. After rain had delayed the start by 25 minutes the ball moved off the seam and occasionally flew, but Titmus stayed with Boycott for 50 minutes. Just before he was out Titmus collided with the bowler and fell when answering a call for a quick single, but although the ball was thrown in quickly Grout turned his back on the stumps. England were 52 for 1 when rain stopped play.

A further 95 minutes were lost on the second day, in which England added 164 for the loss of 7 wickets. Again the ball seamed and flew, but the Australian bowlers lacked control, while Cowdrey showed superb defensive technique. The third day was washed out altogether, and on the fourth morning Dexter declared.

Although the wicket was easier the ball was still seaming, and Australia in getting within 48 of England's score owed much to Simpson. As Boycott had fractured a finger Dexter opened with Titmus, and he hit 56 out of 71 in 78 minutes before stumps.

Ideally England needed quick runs on the last morning; but they were not quite safe from defeat, and Dexter was not able to declare until 7 minutes after lunch. With 2½ hours remaining, 202 still wanted, and O'Neill hurt, Australia were in some danger at 40 for 2; but then the rain returned.

ENGLAND

G. Boycott	c Simpson b Corling	48	lbw b McKenzie	17	
F. J. Titmus	c Redpath b Hawke	16	(1)c O'Neill b McKenzie	68	
*E. R. Dexter	c Grout b Hawke	9	(3)b McKenzie	33	
M. C. Cowdrey	b Hawke	32	(4)lbw b Corling	33	
K. F. Barrington	c Lawry b Veivers	22	c and b Veivers	1	
P. J. Sharpe	not out	35	(5)c Hawke b Veivers	19	
†J. M. Parks	c Booth b Veivers	15	(7)c Grout b McKenzie	4	
F. S. Trueman	c Simpson b Veivers	0	(8)lbw b McKenzie	3	
D. A. Allen	c Grout b McKenzie	21	(10)not out	0	
L. J. Coldwell	not out	0	(9)c Booth b Corling	7	
J. A. Flavell	did not bat				
Extras	(b 5, lb 11, nb 2)	18	(b 2, lb 2, w 1, nb 3)	8	
Total	(8 wkts dec)	**216**	**Total** (9 wkts dec)	**193**	

AUSTRALIA

W. M. Lawry	c Barrington b Coldwell	11	run out	3	
I. R. Redpath	b Trueman	6	c Parks b Flavell	2	
N. C. O'Neill	b Allen	26	retired hurt	24	
P. J. Burge	lbw b Trueman	31	not out	4	
B. C. Booth	run out	0	not out	6	
*R. B. Simpson	c Barrington b Titmus	50			
T. R. Veivers	c Trueman b Flavell	8			
G. D. McKenzie	c Parks b Coldwell	4			
N. J. N. Hawke	not out	10			
†A. T. W. Grout	c Parks b Coldwell	13			
G. E. Corling	b Trueman	3			
Extras	(lb 1, nb 5)	6	(nb 1)	1	
Total		**168**	**Total** (2 wkts)	**40**	

FALL OF WICKETS

ENGLAND

Wkt	1st	2nd
1st	38	90
2nd	70	95
3rd	90	147
4th	135	174
5th	141	179
6th	164	180
7th	165	186
8th	212	187
9th	—	193
10th	—	—

AUSTRALIA

Wkt	1st	2nd
1st	8	3
2nd	37	25
3rd	57	—
4th	61	—
5th	91	—
6th	118	—
7th	137	—
8th	141	—
9th	165	—
10th	168	—

Umpires: J. S. Buller, C. S. Elliott

AUSTRALIA	1st Innings				2nd Innings			
	O	M	R	W	O	M	R	W
McKenzie	28	7	53	1	24	5	53	5
Corling	23	7	38	1	15·5	4	54	2
Hawke	35	15	68	3	19	5	53	0
Veivers	16	2	39	3	8	0	25	2

ENGLAND	1st Innings				2nd Innings			
	O	M	R	W	O	M	R	W
Trueman	20·3	3	58	3	5	0	28	0
Coldwell	22	3	48	3				
Allen	16	8	22	1				
Flavell	16	3	28	1	4·2	0	11	1
Titmus	4	1	6	1				

1964 Second Test, Lord's

June 18, 19, 20, 22, 23
Toss: England   *Result:* Match Drawn

Roughly half the playing time had been lost at Trent Bridge; and when the first two days were washed out at Lord's the Board of Control suggested an extra half-hour on the last three days. But Australia, holding the Ashes, refused. Edrich returned for the injured Boycott, Parfitt replaced Allen, and with the Lord's slope in mind Gifford came in for Flavell. Dexter put Australia in on winning the toss, but the pitch was never difficult. At lunch Australia were 79 for 3.

Two magnificent catches by Parfitt, one diving at backward short leg to dismiss Redpath and another from a slash into the gully, brought Australia to 88 for 6 in the afternoon; but the left-handed Veivers, combining dour defence with robust hitting, frustrated England for 2½ hours. McKenzie helped him put on 44 before Trueman came back to break the stand, 31 more were added with Grout, and Australia at 176 all out had wriggled off the hook. Dexter, opening with Edrich, was then yorked second ball, and England at stumps were 26 for 1.

Australia turned the tables next morning as Cowdrey was dismissed in the fourth over and Barrington was lbw at 42 for 3. Some good running by Edrich and Parfitt restored England's spirits, but when Corling found a good one for Parfitt England were 83 for 4. Sharpe

then batted so well with Edrich that a substantial lead still seemed possible; but at 138 Hawke had Sharpe lbw, and Parks after a bright start was beautifully caught by Simpson running back from slip after an edged skier. At 170 for 6 England thus depended very much on Edrich and Titmus for a worthwhile lead, and at tea, with the new ball just taken, they were 201 for 6, Edrich 103. Altogether they put on 57, and England gained a lead of 70; but Lawry and Redpath made a steady start, after which Redpath and O'Neill stood firm until stumps at 49 for 1.

At this point there was little likelihood that the last day would bring a result; but Dexter's tactics next morning in not using a spinner for well over an hour and bowling Coldwell for the first 105 minutes puzzled many, especially as the wicket seemed likely by then to favour spin rather than speed. Titmus came on for his first over of the innings at 114 for 2, after which Redpath stayed on 36 for 53 minutes before being lbw sweeping, and Burge too lost his wicket to Titmus before lunch. An earlier recourse to spin might have embarrassed Australia a good deal more; but as it happened the match was washed out soon after lunch.

AUSTRALIA

W. M. Lawry	b Trueman	4	c Dexter b Gifford	20
I. R. Redpath	c Parfitt b Coldwell	30	lbw b Titmus	36
N. C. O'Neill	c Titmus b Dexter	26	c Parfitt b Trueman	22
P. J. Burge	lbw b Dexter	1	c Parfitt b Titmus	59
B. C. Booth	lbw b Trueman	14	not out	2
*R. B. Simpson	c Parfitt b Trueman	0	not out	15
T. R. Veivers	b Gifford	54		
G. D. McKenzie	b Trueman	10		
†A. T. W. Grout	c Dexter b Gifford	14		
N. J. N. Hawke	not out	5		
G. E. Corling	b Trueman	0		
Extras	(b 8, lb 5, nb 5)	18	(b 8, lb 4, nb 2)	14
Total		**176**	**Total** (4 wkts)	**168**

ENGLAND

*E. R. Dexter	b McKenzie	2
J. H. Edrich	c Redpath b McKenzie	120
M. C. Cowdrey	c Burge b Hawke	10
K. F. Barrington	lbw b McKenzie	5
P. H. Parfitt	lbw b Corling	20
P. J. Sharpe	lbw b Hawke	35
†J. M. Parks	c Simpson b Hawke	12
F. J. Titmus	b Corling	15
F. S. Trueman	b Corling	8
N. Gifford	c Hawke b Corling	5
L. J. Coldwell	not out	6
Extras	(lb 7, nb 1)	8
Total		**246**

FALL OF WICKETS
AUSTRALIA

Wkt	1st	2nd
1st	8	35
2nd	46	76
3rd	58	143
4th	84	148
5th	84	—
6th	88	—
7th	132	—
8th	163	—
9th	167	—
10th	176	—

ENGLAND

Wkt	1st	2nd
1st	2	—
2nd	33	—
3rd	42	—
4th	83	—
5th	138	—
6th	170	—
7th	227	—
8th	229	—
9th	235	—
10th	246	—

Umpires: J. F. Crapp, J. S. Buller

ENGLAND		1st Innings				2nd Innings			
	O	M	R	W		O	M	R	W
Trueman	25	8	48	5	..	18	6	52	1
Coldwell	23	7	51	1	..	19	4	59	0
Gifford	12	6	14	2	..	17	9	17	1
Dexter	7	1	16	2	..	3	0	5	0
Titmus	17	6	29	0	..	17	7	21	2

AUSTRALIA		1st Innings				2nd Innings			
	O	M	R	W		O	M	R	W
McKenzie	26	8	69	3	..				
Corling	27·3	9	60	4	..				
Hawke	16	4	41	3	..				
Veivers	9	4	17	0	..				
Simpson	21	8	51	0	..				

139. P. J. Burge

140. E. R. Dexter

141. Australia 1964
Back row: A. E. James (masseur), N. J. N. Hawke, G. E. Corling, J. W. Martin, R. M. Cowper, A. N. Connolly, D. Sherwood (scorer). *Middle row:* R. H. D. Sellers, T. R. Veivers, J. Potter, J. A. Ledward (treasurer). G. D. McKenzie, I. R. Redpath, B. N. Jarman. *Front:* P. J. Burge, N. C. O'Neill, R. B. Simpson (capt.), R. C. Steele (manager), B. C. Booth, W. M. Lawry, A. T. W. Grout.

1964 Third Test, Leeds

July 2, 3, 4, 6, 7
Toss: England   *Result:* Australia won by seven wickets

As at Manchester in 1961, so at Leeds in 1964, Australia climbed from the precipice of defeat to the pinnacle of victory. Dexter's decision to take the new ball with Australia 187 for 7 in reply to England's 268 will always be debated; more questionable, perhaps, was his failure to restore Titmus and Gifford for a full hour. The last 3 Australian wickets added 211, and a fatal final session on the third day left England's second innings in ruins, Australia winning by 7 wickets. Boycott returned for Sharpe, Flavell replaced Coldwell, and other changes were Taylor for Cowdrey and Cowper for O'Neill, both unfit. Taylor had played a fine innings of 160 for Yorkshire against the Australians just before the second Test.

A good wicket and fast outfield somewhat flattered England's lunch score of 112 for 2, Dexter 57 not out; but in the afternoon, with conditions more favourable to swing, England lost 3 wickets cheaply. Parfitt and Parks survived some early mistakes and at tea England were 199 for 5; but the new ball accounted for Parfitt and Titmus. Parks was eventually caught at mid-wicket after batting 2¼ hours. The Australian catching reached a high standard, and Hawke in his final spell took 4 for 30. Bad light then ended play 10 minutes early.

Feeling that the initiative was being surrendered too easily, Simpson opened with Lawry, and they made 50 in the first hour before Simpson played on trying to cut. No further wicket fell for nearly 2 hours as Lawry batted at his best and Redpath stayed; but Redpath was not confronted with Titmus for 50 minutes, and once this move was made the innings atrophied. Redpath's discomfiture, indeed, probably accounted for his mistake in running out Lawry at 124; and with Redpath playing on and Booth being stumped Australia were 154 for 4. Trueman came back to bowl Cowper—a tactical success that was overlooked later—and after tea Veivers and McKenzie fell to Titmus. At 178 for 7 the scene was set for Burge and Hawke.

The first 7 overs of the new ball produced 42 runs; Burge reached his 100 off the penultimate ball of the day; and Hawke was caught off the last. They had added 105 in 99 minutes. Next morning a dispirited England conceded another 106 runs before Burge's magnificent innings ended.

Edrich and Barrington showed plenty of fight in a stand of 75 after Boycott had been brilliantly caught and Parfitt had broken a knuckle first ball, but both were out before stumps, and Dexter too. Australia needed only 109 to win, Flavell was absent injured, and Titmus and Gifford could do no more than hint at what might have been had the target been more distant.

ENGLAND

Batsman	1st dismissal	1st	2nd dismissal	2nd
G. Boycott	c Simpson b Corling	38	c Simpson b Corling	4
J. H. Edrich	c Veivers b McKenzie	3	c Grout b McKenzie	32
*E. R. Dexter	c Grout b McKenzie	66	(5)c Redpath b Veivers	17
K. F. Barrington	b McKenzie	29	lbw b Veivers	85
P. H. Parfitt	b Hawke	32	(3)c Redpath b Hawke	6
K. Taylor	c Grout b Hawke	9	(8)b Veivers	15
†J. M. Parks	c Redpath b Hawke	68	(6)c Booth b McKenzie	23
F. J. Titmus	c Burge b McKenzie	3	(9)c Cowper b Corling	14
F. S. Trueman	c Cowper b Hawke	4	(10)not out	12
N. Gifford	not out	1	(7)b McKenzie	1
J. A. Flavell	c Redpath b Hawke	5	c Simpson b Corling	5
Extras	(lb 9, nb 1)	10	(b 6, lb 6, w 1, nb 2)	15
Total		**268**	**Total**	**229**

AUSTRALIA

Batsman	1st dismissal	1st	2nd dismissal	2nd
W. M. Lawry	run out	78	c Gifford b Trueman	1
*R. B. Simpson	b Gifford	24	c Barrington b Titmus	30
I. R. Redpath	b Gifford	20	not out	58
P. J. Burge	c sub (A. Rees) b Trueman	160	b Titmus	8
B. C. Booth	st Parks b Titmus	4	not out	12
R. M. Cowper	b Trueman	2		
T. R. Veivers	c Parks b Titmus	8		
G. D. McKenzie	b Titmus	0		
N. J. N. Hawke	c Parfitt b Trueman	37		
†A. T. W. Grout	lbw b Titmus	37		
G. E. Corling	not out	2		
Extras	(b 1, lb 8, w 2, nb 6)	17	(b 1, lb 1)	2
Total		**389**	**Total** (3 wkts)	**111**

FALL OF WICKETS

ENGLAND

Wkt	1st	2nd
1st	17	13
2nd	74	88
3rd	129	145
4th	138	156
5th	163	169
6th	215	184
7th	232	192
8th	260	199
9th	263	212
10th	268	229

AUSTRALIA

Wkt	1st	2nd
1st	50	3
2nd	124	45
3rd	129	64
4th	154	—
5th	157	—
6th	178	—
7th	178	—
8th	283	—
9th	372	—
10th	389	—

Umpires: W. F. F. Price,
C. S. Elliott

AUSTRALIA

	1st Innings				2nd Innings			
	O	M	R	W	O	M	R	W
McKenzie	26	7	74	4	28	8	53	3
Hawke	31·3	11	75	5	13	1	28	1
Corling	24	7	50	1	17·5	6	52	3
Veivers	17	3	35	0	30	12	70	3
Simpson	5	0	24	0	1	0	11	0

ENGLAND

	1st Innings				2nd Innings			
	O	M	R	W	O	M	R	W
Trueman	24·3	2	98	3	7	0	28	1
Flavell	29	5	97	0				
Gifford	34	15	62	2	20	5	47	0
Dexter	19	5	40	0	3	0	9	0
Titmus	50	24	69	4	27	19	25	2
Taylor	2	0	6	0				

1964 Fourth Test, Old Trafford

July 23, 24, 25, 27, 28
Toss: Australia   *Result:* Match Drawn

The England selectors made four changes in the team for Old Trafford —where England had to win to retain any hope of regaining the Ashes. Most radical was the dropping of Trueman. Parfitt was retained, to the exclusion of Cowdrey, and five bowlers were chosen, three of them for the first time against Australia. For Simpson, one up with two to play, this was the one match he mustn't lose; and by winning the toss on a perfect wicket he took a long stride towards his goal.

An overcast sky carried a threat of swing which did not materialise, and only Cartwright had the openers playing and missing; he at least was moving the ball off the pitch. Simpson gave a difficult chance to Parks on the leg side when 33, but otherwise he was the safer—and the slower—of the two. When Lawry was run out at 5.10 they had put on a record 201, and at stumps Australia were 253 for 2 (off 122 overs) and the Ashes were nearly safe. Simpson was 109, his first century against England in 25 innings; Cartwright's analysis was 43—17—76—1. It was a game in which figures were to matter more than anything.

On the second day Australia added 317 for the loss of another 2 wickets, taking them to 570 for 4. Simpson, 265 not out, had made 156 in the day. Cartwright bowled 34 more overs for 52 runs and one

wicket; Barrington and Parfitt were not called upon at all. The declaration that might otherwise have come that evening was obliterated by the long shadow of the Ashes; Australia at that point could still conceivably have lost the game, and with it their advantage. The situation—and the wicket—left Simpson little alternative but to carry on.

Australia added 84 in an hour next morning before declaring, Simpson hitting out towards the end of his 12 hours 42 minutes at the wicket. His had been the longest innings ever played against England. When England went in 50 minutes before lunch they needed 457 to save the follow on; their close of play score of 162 for 2, with Edrich and Boycott out, was only mildly encouraging.

On the fourth day Englishmen followed the play with morbid fascination as Dexter and Barrington, by methods similar to Australia's, and helped by some slack fielding, added another 210. Partisan yearnings that one of them might beat Simpson's individual score, and that Australia's mammoth total might be eclipsed, went unsatisfied, but a reply of over 600, while doing little for cricket's image, left the honours even. Veivers' 95.1 overs in a single innings beat all records for these games.

AUSTRALIA

W. M. Lawry	run out	106	not out	0
*R. B. Simpson	c Parks b Price	311	not out	4
I. R. Redpath	lbw b Cartwright	19		
N. C. O'Neill	b Price	47		
P. J. Burge	c Price b Cartwright	34		
B. C. Booth	c and b Price	98		
T. R. Veivers	c Edrich b Rumsey	22		
†A. T. W. Grout	c Dexter b Rumsey	0		
G. D. McKenzie	not out	0		
N. J. N. Hawke	} did not bat			
G. E. Corling				
Extras	(b 1, lb 9, nb 9)	19		
Total	(8 wkts dec)	**656**	**Total** (0 wkts)	**4**

ENGLAND

G. Boycott	b McKenzie	58
J. H. Edrich	c Redpath b McKenzie	6
*E. R. Dexter	b Veivers	174
K. F. Barrington	lbw b McKenzie	256
P. H. Parfitt	c Grout b McKenzie	12
†J. M. Parks	c Hawke b Veivers	60
F. J. Titmus	c Simpson b McKenzie	9
J. B. Mortimore	c Burge b McKenzie	12
T. W. Cartwright	b McKenzie	4
J. S. E. Price	b Veivers	1
F. E. Rumsey	not out	3
Extras	(b 5, lb 11)	16
Total		**611**

FALL OF WICKETS

AUSTRALIA		
Wkt	1st	2nd
1st	201	—
2nd	233	—
3rd	318	—
4th	382	—
5th	601	—
6th	646	—
7th	652	—
8th	656	—
9th	—	—
10th	—	—
ENGLAND		
Wkt	1st	2nd
1st	15	—
2nd	126	—
3rd	372	—
4th	417	—
5th	560	—
6th	589	—
7th	594	—
8th	602	—
9th	607	—
10th	611	—

Umpires: J. S. Buller,
W. F. Price

ENGLAND	1st Innings				2nd Innings			
	O	M	R	W	O	M	R	W
Rumsey	35.5	4	99	2				
Price	45	4	183	3				
Cartwright	77	32	118	2				
Titmus	44	14	100	0	1	1	0	0
Dexter	4	0	12	0				
Mortimore	49	13	122	0				
Boycott	1	0	3	0				
Barrington					1	0	4	0

AUSTRALIA	1st Innings				2nd Innings			
	O	M	R	W	O	M	R	W
McKenzie	60	15	153	7				
Corling	46	11	96	0				
Hawke	63	28	95	0				
Simpson	19	4	59	0				
Veivers	95.1	36	155	3				
O'Neill	10	0	37	0				

1964 Fifth Test, Oval

August 13, 14, 15, 17, 18
Toss: England   *Result:* Match Drawn

The England selectors restored Cowdrey and Trueman, adding greatly as it happened to the interest of the game. Barber, who a week earlier had made a hundred before lunch against the Australians for Warwickshire, displaced Edrich, whose fighting century at Lord's was thus temporarily eclipsed. Price and Cartwright were retained. By winning this match England could still square the rubber.

Getting first knock proved a dubious advantage; the ball moved off the seam, the bounce was uneven, and the light was dull. Indeed an appeal against the light was turned down before England went in to lunch at 81 for 2. Dexter and Cowdrey were both caught projecting strokes at shortish balls when they appeared set, Parfitt failed to dig out a McKenzie yorker, playing it on to his stumps, and although Barrington struggled on until he was 8th out at 173, not a single stand was worth as much as 30 after the opening partnership. England were all out for a dismal 182, and Hawke, bowling in-swingers and leg cutters in Bedser vein, took 6 for 47. The day was then shortened by nearly 90 minutes by bad light, Australia making 3 for 0.

Setting out to make the rubber safe and to build a winning lead, Australia batted with a solidity and purpose on the second day that was bound to be tedious to English watchers. By stumps they had made 245 for 5 off 123 overs, a fraction under 2 runs an over, and for much of the day they scored even slower than this, the first hundred runs taking 69 overs. But in this period some good bowling and the uneven bounce kept them struggling. Had Trueman taken a fairly easy chance from Booth at backward square leg they would have been 123 for 4; but England were never on terms after that.

Grout having gone in overnight, Veivers appeared at no. 8, and his power and discrimination again served Australia well. But the game did not really come to life until Trueman suddenly found a good one to beat Redpath and had McKenzie caught by Cowdrey at slip next ball. Lunch intervened, and the hat trick was averted, but another Cowdrey slip catch brought Trueman his 300th wicket in all Tests.

Australia's 379 had taken 9 hours, and England were 197 behind; but Boycott and Barber put on 80, and England were 132 for 2 at stumps. The fourth day was England's as they fought to build up a lead for a last-day declaration against tactics that inevitably became more and more defensive, and by stumps they were 184 ahead; but a final day abandoned through rain was a sad though apposite requiem.

ENGLAND

G. Boycott	b Hawke	30	c Redpath b Simpson	113	
R. W. Barber	b Hawke	24	lbw b McKenzie	29	
*E. R. Dexter	c Booth b Hawke	23	c Simpson b McKenzie	25	
M. C. Cowdrey	c Grout b McKenzie	20	(5)not out	93	
K. F. Barrington	c Simpson b Hawke	47	(6)not out	54	
P. H. Parfitt	b McKenzie	3			
†J. M. Parks	c Simpson b Corling	10			
F. J. Titmus	c Grout b Hawke	8	(4)b McKenzie	56	
F. S. Trueman	c Redpath b Hawke	14			
T. W. Cartwright	c Grout b McKenzie	0			
J. S. E. Price	not out	0			
Extras	(lb 3)	3	(b 6, lb 4, nb 1)	11	
Total		**182**	**Total** (4 wkts)	**381**	

AUSTRALIA

*R. B. Simpson	c Dexter b Cartwright	24
W. M. Lawry	c Trueman b Dexter	94
N. C. O'Neill	c Parfitt b Cartwright	11
P. J. Burge	lbw b Titmus	25
B. C. Booth	c Trueman b Price	74
I. R. Redpath	b Trueman	45
†A. T. W. Grout	b Cartwright	20
T. R. Veivers	not out	67
G. D. McKenzie	c Cowdrey b Trueman	0
N. J. N. Hawke	c Cowdrey b Trueman	14
G. E. Corling	c Parfitt b Trueman	0
Extras	(b 4, lb 1)	5
Total		**379**

FALL OF WICKETS

ENGLAND		
Wkt	*1st*	*2nd*
1st	44	80
2nd	61	120
3rd	82	200
4th	111	255
5th	117	—
6th	141	—
7th	160	—
8th	173	—
9th	174	—
10th	182	—

AUSTRALIA		
Wkt	*1st*	*2nd*
1st	45	—
2nd	57	—
3rd	96	—
4th	202	—
5th	245	—
6th	279	—
7th	343	—
8th	343	—
9th	367	—
10th	379	—

Umpires: C. S. Elliott,
J. F. Crapp

AUSTRALIA	1st Innings					2nd Innings			
	O	M	R	W		O	M	R	W
McKenzie	26	6	87	3	..	38	5	112	3
Corling	14	2	32	1	..	25	4	65	0
Hawke	25·4	8	47	6	..	39	8	89	0
Veivers	6	1	13	0	..	47	15	90	0
Simpson					..	14	7	14	1

ENGLAND	1st Innings					2nd Innings			
	O	M	R	W		O	M	R	W
Trueman	33·3	6	87	4	..				
Price	21	2	67	1	..				
Cartwright	62	23	110	3	..				
Titmus	42	20	51	1	..				
Barber	6	1	23	0	..				
Dexter	13	1	36	1	..				

1965-66 First Test, Brisbane

December 10, 11, 13, 14, 15
Toss: Australia   *Result:* Match Drawn

For the second successive time in Australia the rubber was halved; and for the second successive series there was serious interference from the weather. The loss of a full day's play in both the first and fifth Tests precluded a result in either. Both sides had their strengths and weaknesses, and although England had slightly the better of the series they were hardly worth victory. Their batting was exceptionally strong but their bowling, depleted by injuries, was correspondingly weak, and their only success came on a wearing wicket after batting first. It was Parks' misfortune to miss the chance that probably cost England the Ashes; he should perhaps have been played as a batsman, where he was one of the successes of the tour, making way for Murray behind the stumps. Smith's close catching was a factor in the victory at Sydney, but his prestige waned with his loss of batting form. Three times Lawry stood between England and the decisive advantage that presages victory; Simpson and Walters, too, were great players, and Burge and Cowper each played a match-saving innings. After some early uncertainty the Australian spin attack was mastered; but Hawke bowled consistently well and McKenzie, dropped but then recalled for the vital fourth Test when his replacement was injured, showed that his apparent decline had been no more than temporary.

A crop of injuries seriously weakened the two sides at Brisbane: Simpson and McKenzie were absent, Cowdrey was unwell, and Jones and Larter could not be considered. England suffered further when Russell, his thumb already strapped following a fracture, split his hand while fielding. On a rain-reduced first day Australia made 79 for 1 off 36 overs, and the second day was washed out entirely. England began the third day well when Brown beat Cowper and Burge, and at 125 Booth hit one hard back at Titmus; but with Brown off afterwards with a strained muscle and Barber conceding 42 runs off 5 overs, Lawry and Walters added 187. Surviving a confident appeal for a catch at the wicket on the first day, and missed shortly afterwards off Titmus at slip, Lawry batted 7 hours, while the 19-year-old Walters, with a century in his first Test, showed exceptional coolness and footwork in a stay of 5 hours 20 minutes.

Australia left themselves 11 hours in which to bowl England out twice; and England, needing 294 to save the follow on, batted with such timidity that at 115 for 4 they looked in real danger. But a great attacking innings by Parks restored their faith in themselves, and although they followed on they finished the match strongly.

AUSTRALIA

W. M. Lawry	c Parks b Higgs	166	
I. R. Redpath	b Brown	17	
R. M. Cowper	c Barrington b Brown	22	
P. J. Burge	b Brown	0	
*B. C. Booth	c and b Titmus	16	
K. D. Walters	c Parks b Higgs	155	
T. R. Veivers	not out	56	
N. J. N. Hawke	not out	6	
†A. T. W. Grout	⎫		
P. I. Philpott	⎬ did not bat		
P. J. Allan	⎭		
Extras	(lb 2, nb 3)	5	
Total	(6 wkts dec)	**443**	

ENGLAND

R. W. Barber	c Walters b Hawke	5	c Veivers b Walters	34	
G. Boycott	b Philpott	45	not out	63	
J. H. Edrich	c Lawry b Philpott	32	c Veivers b Philpott	37	
K. F. Barrington	b Hawke	53	c Booth b Cowper	38	
*M. J. K. Smith	b Allan	16	not out	10	
†J. M. Parks	c Redpath b Philpott	52			
F. J. Titmus	st Grout b Philpott	60			
D. A. Allen	c Cowper b Walters	3			
D. J. Brown	b Philpott	3			
K. Higgs	lbw b Allan	4			
W. E. Russell	not out	0			
Extras	(b 4, nb 3)	7	(b 2, lb 2)	4	
Total		**280**	**Total** (3 wkts)	**186**	

FALL OF WICKETS

AUSTRALIA

Wkt	1st	2nd
1st	51	—
2nd	90	—
3rd	90	—
4th	125	—
5th	312	—
6th	431	—
7th	—	—
8th	—	—
9th	—	—
10th	—	—

ENGLAND

Wkt	1st	2nd
1st	5	46
2nd	75	114
3rd	86	168
4th	115	—
5th	191	—
6th	221	—
7th	232	—
8th	253	—
9th	272	—
10th	280	—

Umpires: C. J. Egar, L. Rowan

ENGLAND	1st Innings				2nd Innings			
	O	M	R	W	O	M	R	W
Brown	21	4	71	3	..			
Higgs	30	6	102	2	..			
Titmus	38	9	99	1	..			
Allen	39	12	108	0	..			
Barber	5	0	42	0	..			
Boycott	4	0	16	0	..			

AUSTRALIA	1st Innings				2nd Innings			
	O	M	R	W	O	M	R	W
Allan	21	6	58	2	..	3	0	25	0
Hawke	16	7	44	2	..	10	2	16	0
Walters	10	1	25	1	..	5	1	22	1
Philpott	28·1	3	90	5	..	14	1	62	1
Cowper	7	4	7	0	..	6	0	20	1
Veivers	11	1	49	0	..	12	1	37	0

1965-66 Second Test, Melbourne

December 30, 31, January 1, 3, 4
Toss: Australia   *Result:* Match Drawn

Simpson, Australia's appointed captain, was able to play at Melbourne, and McKenzie returned for Allan, but doubt about Hawke's fitness contributed to his replacement by Connolly. Cowdrey returned for Russell, but Brown and Higgs, England's opening bowlers at Brisbane, were both unfit, and they were replaced by Jones and Knight—the latter having reinforced the touring party three weeks earlier. A weakened English attack thus faced Australia at virtually full strength.

At lunch on the first day Australia were 78 for 0. At 93 Simpson pulled Allen to square leg, and Burge failed, but the left-handers Lawry and Cowper added 94 in 90 minutes. With Lawry's departure Cowper slowed down, and at stumps Australia were 278 for 4 off 79 overs.

With Jones and Knight sharing one end and Titmus at the other, Australia lost their last 6 wickets next day in 2¼ hours for 80. England galloped away to an exciting start, 86 coming off the first 13 overs, but McKenzie, after taking a fine catch at square leg to dismiss Boycott, characteristically found some extra life in the wicket after tea to get Barber caught off his glove. Edrich's misjudgment of the spin-bowlers' length compelled frequent adjustments, but he and Barrington had taken England to 208 for 2 at stumps.

England added 308 on the third day for the loss of 5 more wickets, Edrich reaching a persevering hundred and Cowdrey, his timing faultless, making 104 in 3¼ hours. Parks' lofted off drives were just what was needed after tea, and England finished next morning with a lead of exactly 200; but Simpson and Lawry gave Australia another splendid start, and when rain stopped play 10 minutes after tea Australia were 131 for 1.

On the last morning Cowper was lbw offering no stroke, and half an hour later, with 37 still wanted to make England bat again, Lawry was caught at backward short leg. In the next half-hour Burge and Booth added 13 nervous runs before Allen bowled Booth off his pads, and Australia were only 4 runs ahead when Barber drew Burge out of his ground only for Parks to miss the stumping. Smith took the new ball after lunch, but it was a despairing move. Once again Burge, his place in the side threatened, played a match-decisive innings, and Walters, in compiling his second century in three Test innings, helped him to add 198 in just over 3 hours. Long before they were parted Australia were safe.

AUSTRALIA

*R. B. Simpson	c Edrich b Allen	59	c Barrington b Knight	67	
W. M. Lawry	c Cowdrey b Allen	88	c Smith b Barber	78	
P. J. Burge	b Jones	5	(4)c Edrich b Boycott	120	
R. M. Cowper	c Titmus b Jones	99	(3)lbw b Jones	5	
B. C. Booth	lbw b Jones	23	b Allen	10	
K. D. Walters	c Parks b Knight	22	c and b Barrington	115	
T. R. Veivers	run out	19	st Parks b Boycott	3	
P. I. Philpott	b Knight	10	b Knight	2	
†A. T. W. Grout	c Barber b Knight	11	c Allen b Barrington	16	
G. D. McKenzie	not out	12	run out	2	
A. N. Connolly	c Parks b Knight	0	not out	0	
Extras	(b 2, lb 7, nb 1)	10	(b 1, lb 3, w 1, nb 3)	8	
Total		**358**	**Total**	**426**	

ENGLAND

G. Boycott	c McKenzie b Walters	51
R. W. Barber	c Grout b McKenzie	48
J. H. Edrich	c and b Veivers	109
K. F. Barrington	c Burge b Veivers	63
M. C. Cowdrey	c Connolly b Cowper	104
*M. J. K. Smith	c Grout b McKenzie	41
†J. M. Parks	c Cowper b McKenzie	71
B. R. Knight	c Simpson b McKenzie	1
F. J. Titmus	not out	56
D. A. Allen	c Grout b Connolly	2
I. J. Jones	b McKenzie	1
Extras	(b 4, lb 5, w 2)	11
Total		**558**

not out	5
not out	0

Total (0 wkts) **5**

FALL OF WICKETS

AUSTRALIA

Wkt	1st	2nd
1st	93	120
2nd	109	141
3rd	203	163
4th	262	176
5th	297	374
6th	318	382
7th	330	385
8th	342	417
9th	352	426
10th	358	426

ENGLAND

Wkt	1st	2nd
1st	98	—
2nd	110	—
3rd	228	—
4th	333	—
5th	409	—
6th	443	—
7th	447	—
8th	540	—
9th	551	—
10th	558	—

Umpires: C. J. Egar,
W. Smyth

ENGLAND

	1st Innings					2nd Innings			
	O	M	R	W		O	M	R	W
Jones	24	4	92	3	..	20	1	92	1
Knight	26.5	2	84	4	..	21	4	61	2
Titmus	31	7	93	0	..	22	6	43	0
Allen	20	4	55	2	..	18	3	48	1
Barber	6	1	24	0	..	17	0	87	1
Barrington					..	7.4	0	47	2
Boycott					..	9	0	32	2
Smith					..	2	0	8	0

AUSTRALIA

	1st Innings					2nd Innings			
	O	M	R	W		O	M	R	W
McKenzie	35.2	3	134	5	..	1	0	2	0
Connolly	37	5	125	1	..	1	0	3	0
Philpott	30	2	133	0	..				
Walters	10	2	32	1	..				
Simpson	16	4	61	0	..				
Veivers	12	3	46	2	..				
Cowper	3	0	16	1	..				

142. M. C. Cowdrey

143. W. M. Lawry

144. **England 1965-66**

Back row: J. T. Ikin (assistant to manager), D. J. Brown, J. D. F. Larter, K. Higgs, J. Jennings (masseur). *Middle row:* P. H. Parfitt, G. Boycott, W. E. Russell, R. W. Barber, I. J. Jones, B. R. Knight, J. H. Edrich. *Front:* J. M. Parks, F. J. Titmus, M. C. Cowdrey, M. J. K. Smith (capt.), S. C. Griffith (manager), K. F. Barrington, D. A. Allen, J. T. Murray.

1965-66 Third Test, Sydney

January 7, 8, 10, 11
Toss: England   *Result:* England won by an innings and 93 runs

After eight draws in the previous nine Tests the indications seemed more favourable at Sydney, where the wicket was known to be helpful to spin. England chose two fast bowlers in support of Titmus and Allen, and Australia included two wrist-spinners as a contrast to McKenzie and Hawke. England for the first time were at full strength, but Australia were without Simpson.

An opening partnership of 234 between Barber and Boycott, inferior only to that of Hobbs and Rhodes in 1911-12 (323) and Hobbs and Sutcliffe in 1924-25 (283), took England half-way to victory. At 31 Boycott was missed by Sincock at leg slip off McKenzie; but there was no other discernible chance. 93 for 0 at lunch, England added 141 in the afternoon. Barber's hundred came in 3 hours 10 minutes, and when he was second out at 303 he had virtually won the match for his side.

It was as well, even so, that Edrich stood firm against McKenzie in the final session, as England lost Barrington, Cowdrey and Smith to Hawke and the second new ball. Next morning Edrich, scratching at times with his usual imperturbability, kept going for his second hundred in successive Test innings—completed with a straight drive

for six off Philpott. The final screw was turned as Allen and Jones put on 55 for the last wicket.

The ball was not yet turning and it was the England fast bowlers who made the breach. Lawry, Thomas, Booth and Burge—the latter to a great catch by Parks off the inside edge—were all out before stumps, when Australia were 113 for 4, Cowper 46 not out. Cowper batted 4 hours 10 minutes for his 60; but his surrendering of the initiative before the ball started to turn may not have been the best thing for his side. Australia were 174 for 5 at lunch; but immediately after the interval, when the new ball was taken, Brown took three wickets in one over, and Australia were all out for 221.

Following on 267 behind, Australia survived the opening burst but then fell apart. Thomas swept and was caught at slip off the top edge, Cowper cracked a long hop to mid-wicket, and Lawry failed to respond to a Burge call, running Burge out. Booth batted well for a time, and on the fourth day, with Titmus and Allen in harness, Walters for over two hours showed how to play the turning ball; but helped by Smith's cool leadership and fearless close catching England won early that afternoon.

ENGLAND

G. Boycott	c and b Philpott	84
R. W. Barber	b Hawke	185
J. H. Edrich	c and b Philpott	103
K. F. Barrington	c McKenzie b Hawke	1
M. C. Cowdrey	c Grout b Hawke	0
*M. J. K. Smith	c Grout b Hawke	6
D. J. Brown	c Grout b Hawke	1
†J. M. Parks	c Grout b Hawke	13
F. J. Titmus	c Grout b Walters	14
D. A. Allen	not out	50
I. J. Jones	b Hawke	16
Extras	(b 3, lb 8, w 2, nb 2)	15
Total		**488**

AUSTRALIA

W. M. Lawry	c Parks b Jones	0	c Cowdrey b Brown	33
G. Thomas	c Titmus b Brown	51	c Cowdrey b Titmus	25
R. M. Cowper	st Parks b Allen	60	c Boycott b Titmus	0
P. J. Burge	c Parks b Brown	6	run out	1
*B. C. Booth	c Cowdrey b Jones	8	b Allen	27
D. J. Sincock	c Parks b Brown	29	(7)c Smith b Allen	27
K. D. Walters	st Parks b Allen	23	(6)not out	35
N. J. N. Hawke	c Barber b Brown	0	(9)c Smith b Titmus	2
†A. T. W. Grout	b Brown	0	(10)c Smith b Allen	3
G. D. McKenzie	c Cowdrey b Barber	24	(11)c Barber b Titmus	12
P. I. Philpott	not out	5	(8)lbw b Allen	5
Extras	(b 7, lb 8)	15	(b 3, lb 1)	4
Total		**221**	**Total**	**174**

FALL OF WICKETS

ENGLAND

Wkt	1st	2nd
1st	234	—
2nd	303	—
3rd	309	—
4th	309	—
5th	317	—
6th	328	—
7th	358	—
8th	395	—
9th	433	—
10th	488	—

AUSTRALIA

Wkt	1st	2nd
1st	0	46
2nd	81	50
3rd	105	51
4th	105	86
5th	155	86
6th	174	119
7th	174	131
8th	174	135
9th	203	140
10th	221	174

Umpires: C. J. Egar, L. Rowan

AUSTRALIA	1st Innings				2nd Innings			
	O	M	R	W	O	M	R	W
McKenzie	25	2	113	0				
Hawke	33·7	6	105	7				
Walters	10	1	38	1				
Philpott	28	3	86	2				
Sincock	20	1	98	0				
Cowper	6	1	33	0				

ENGLAND	1st Innings				2nd Innings			
	O	M	R	W	O	M	R	W
Jones	20	6	51	2	7	0	35	0
Brown	17	1	63	5	11	2	32	1
Boycott	3	1	8	0				
Titmus	23	8	40	0	17·3	4	40	4
Barber	2·1	1	2	1	5	0	16	0
Allen	19	5	42	2	20	8	47	4

1965-66 Fourth Test, Adelaide

January 28, 29, 31, February 1
Toss: England   *Result:* Australia won by an innings and 9 runs

After their exertions in successive Tests at Melbourne and Sydney the tourists had three minor matches, two of them in the holiday atmosphere of Tasmania; but although relaxation was needed, this may not have been an ideal preliminary to the vital fourth Test. The Australian preparations, on the other hand, were abrasive and designed to be therapeutic; five of their Sydney team were discarded. Simpson, fit again, replaced Booth, Chappell came in for Cowper, Stackpole (leg-breaks) and Veivers were the chosen spinners, and McKenzie was dropped for Allan. As it happened, a late injury to Allan forced McKenzie's recall; but the corrective effect was there.

England had been lucky to win the toss at Sydney; now, under very different conditions, they won it again. In a humid atmosphere the ball moved in the air and off the pitch, and a chastened McKenzie forced Barber to play on in his first over. Boycott retaliated with three boundaries off Hawke, but in Hawke's second over he left to a wonderful catch by Chappell high up at slip. Edrich struggled for 45 minutes before fatally chasing a widish one, and England were 33 for 3. Barrington and Cowdrey fought their way back to 69 for 3 by lunch.

After lunch, with Barrington at his soundest and Cowdrey at his most composed, came a tragic and wretched misunderstanding:

Cowdrey was misled by a shout from the wicket-keeper into thinking that Barrington had called him for a run. He rushed down the pitch and was easily run out. Smith, Parks and Titmus all gave promise of resistance in turn, but the revitalised Australians never lost their grip on the game, and England at stumps were 240 for 9. When they were all out next morning the reprieved McKenzie had taken 6 for 48.

Just as England's openers rammed home the advantage at Sydney, so now did Simpson and Lawry in a match-winning stand of 244, beating their own record of 201 at Old Trafford in 1964. This was run-a-minute cricket, with the running forcing Smith to bring in his fielders and open the gaps. Simpson should have been run out when 32 and caught off a mishit sweep when 84; but after that his only mistakes were due to exhaustion. He batted for 9 hours.

Capturing Australia's last 7 wickets for 183 on the third day, England went in again 275 behind. Boycott was beaten by a break-back and Barber and Edrich fell to injudicious strokes, but Barrington and Cowdrey held on until stumps at 64 for 3. They had reached 114 on the fourth morning when Cowdrey edged Stackpole; but even before that England's task had looked beyond them.

ENGLAND

G. Boycott	c Chappell b Hawke	22	lbw b McKenzie	12	
R. W. Barber	b McKenzie	0	c Grout b Hawke	19	
J. H. Edrich	c Simpson b McKenzie	5	c Simpson b Hawke	1	
K. F. Barrington	lbw b Walters	60	c Chappell b Hawke	102	
M. C. Cowdrey	run out	38	c Grout b Stackpole	35	
*M. J. K. Smith	b Veivers	29	c McKenzie b Stackpole	5	
†J. M. Parks	c Stackpole b McKenzie	49	run out	16	
F. J. Titmus	lbw b McKenzie	33	c Grout b Hawke	53	
D. A. Allen	c Simpson b McKenzie	2	not out	5	
D. J. Brown	c Thomas b McKenzie	1	c and b Hawke	0	
I. J. Jones	not out	0	c Lawry b Veivers	8	
Extras	(lb 2)	2	(lb 2, nb 8)	10	
Total		**241**	**Total**	**266**	

AUSTRALIA

*R. B. Simpson	c Titmus b Jones	225
W. M. Lawry	b Titmus	119
G. Thomas	b Jones	52
T. R. Veivers	c Parks b Jones	1
P. J. Burge	c Parks b Jones	27
K. D. Walters	c Parks b Brown	0
I. M. Chappell	c Edrich b Jones	17
K. R. Stackpole	c Parks b Jones	43
N. J. N. Hawke	not out	20
†A. T. W. Grout	b Titmus	4
G. D. McKenzie	lbw b Titmus	1
Extras	(b 4, lb 3)	7
Total		**516**

FALL OF WICKETS

ENGLAND

Wkt	1st	2nd
1st	7	23
2nd	25	31
3rd	33	32
4th	105	114
5th	150	123
6th	178	163
7th	210	244
8th	212	253
9th	222	257
10th	241	266

AUSTRALIA

Wkt	1st	2nd
1st	244	—
2nd	331	—
3rd	333	—
4th	379	—
5th	383	—
6th	415	—
7th	480	—
8th	501	—
9th	506	—
10th	516	—

Umpires: C. J. Egar,
L. Rowan

AUSTRALIA

	1st Innings					2nd Innings			
	O	M	R	W		O	M	R	W
McKenzie	21.7	4	48	6	..	18	4	53	1
Hawke	23	2	69	1	..	21	6	54	5
Walters	14	0	50	1	..	9	0	47	0
Stackpole	5	0	30	0	..	14	3	33	2
Chappell	4	1	18	0	..	22	4	53	0
Veivers	13	3	24	1	..	3.7	0	16	1

ENGLAND

	1st Innings					2nd Innings			
	O	M	R	W		O	M	R	W
Jones	29	3	118	6	..				
Brown	28	4	109	1	..				
Boycott	7	3	33	0	..				
Titmus	37	6	116	3	..				
Allen	21	1	103	0	..				
Barber	4	0	30	0	..				

1965-66 Fifth Test, Melbourne

February 11, 12, 14, 15, 16
Toss: England   *Result:* Match Drawn

Had the deciding Test been at Sydney, where the tourists had won the third Test by an innings and beaten New South Wales by 9 wickets, England must have won the series; but it was Melbourne's turn for two Tests, and England accordingly played a third seam bowler and dropped Allen. No doubt Knight's form with the bat influenced them as well. Australia too seemed to be insuring against defeat when they played Cowper for Burge. England's advantage in batting first was jeopardised when Boycott went for a short run at the end of an over although Barber loudly declined; Boycott had already taken 60 of the first 80 balls bowled. Boycott himself was out soon afterwards and England were 41 for 2.

After lunch the atmosphere changed entirely as Barrington made the fastest hundred of the series—102 off 122 balls in 2½ hours. 130 runs were added in the afternoon, and when Barrington was out soon after tea his partnership with Edrich had produced 178 in even time. His wicket fell to the plain-looking fast-medium of Walters, who almost had Cowdrey caught at slip before he had scored. Later he got Edrich and had Smith caught behind trying to glance. 254 for 5 looked like crisis point, especially when McKenzie and Hawke came on with the new ball, but Cowdrey and Parks made 58 in the last hour and England were 312 for 5 off 78 overs.

Cowdrey and Parks added another 80 next morning, and at lunch England were 419 for 7; but after lunch Australia successfully applied the brake. The declaration left them half-an-hour's batting before tea, in which Simpson was bowled by a beauty that started on the middle and just took the off; and directly after tea Thomas was caught at slip driving at Jones. But a slow over rate deadened the tempo, and Australia at stumps were 101 for 2.

Heavy overnight rain meant a soggy ball next morning, trouble with the run-ups, no spin before lunch, and another slow over rate. Lawry and Cowper met everything with the middle of the bat, and England waited for mistakes that never came. The second new ball was already half an hour old when Lawry was caught in the gully having made 592 runs in the series, the highest since Bradman in 1946-47. Australia at stumps were 333 for 3, and nothing short of a quick break-through next morning could resuscitate the game.

As it happened the fourth day was washed out, and the fifth would have been posthumous but for England's unflagging efforts in the field and Cowper's slow progress towards a record-breaking score. He batted for 12 hours 7 minutes.

ENGLAND

Batsman	Dismissal	Score	2nd Innings	Score
G. Boycott	c Stackpole b McKenzie	17	lbw b McKenzie	1
R. W. Barber	run out	17	b McKenzie	20
J. H. Edrich	c McKenzie b Walters	85	b McKenzie	3
K. F. Barrington	c Grout b Walters	115	not out	32
M. C. Cowdrey	c Grout b Walters	79	not out	11
*M. J. K. Smith	c Grout b Walters	0		
†J. M. Parks	run out	89		
F. J. Titmus	not out	42		
B. R. Knight	c Grout b Hawke	13		
D. J. Brown	c and b Chappell	12		
I. J. Jones	not out	4		
Extras	(b 9, lb 2, nb 1)	12	(lb 2)	2
Total	(9 wkts dec)	**485**	**Total** (3 wkts)	**69**

AUSTRALIA

W. M. Lawry	c Edrich b Jones	108
*R. B. Simpson	b Brown	4
G. Thomas	c Titmus b Jones	19
R. M. Cowper	b Knight	307
K. D. Walters	c and b Barber	60
I. M. Chappell	c Parks b Jones	19
K. R. Stackpole	b Knight	9
T. R. Veivers	b Titmus	4
N. J. N. Hawke	not out	0
†A. T. W. Grout	} did not bat	
G. D. McKenzie		
Extras	(b 6, lb 5, nb 2)	13
Total	(8 wkts dec)	**543**

FALL OF WICKETS

ENGLAND		
Wkt	*1st*	*2nd*
1st	36	6
2nd	41	21
3rd	219	34
4th	254	—
5th	254	—
6th	392	—
7th	419	—
8th	449	—
9th	474	—
10th	—	—

AUSTRALIA		
Wkt	*1st*	*2nd*
1st	15	—
2nd	36	—
3rd	248	—
4th	420	—
5th	481	—
6th	532	—
7th	543	—
8th	543	—
9th	—	—
10th	—	—

Umpires: C. J. Egar, L. Rowan

AUSTRALIA	*1st Innings* O	M	R	W		*2nd Innings* O	M	R	W
McKenzie	26	5	100	1		6	2	17	3
Hawke	35	5	109	1		4	1	22	0
Walters	19	3	53	4		2	0	16	0
Simpson	5	1	20	0					
Stackpole	10	2	43	0		3	0	10	0
Veivers	15	3	78	0					
Chappell	17	4	70	1		2	0	2	0

ENGLAND	*1st Innings* O	M	R	W		*2nd Innings* O	M	R	W
Brown	31	3	134	1					
Jones	29	1	145	3					
Knight	36·2	4	105	2					
Titmus	42	12	86	1					
Barber	16	0	60	1					

Averages: 1965-66

AUSTRALIA

BATTING	M.	Inns.	N.O.	Runs	H.S.	Av.
R. B. Simpson	3	4	0	355	225	88·75
W. M. Lawry	5	7	0	592	166	84·57
R. M. Cowper	4	6	0	493	307	82·16
K. D. Walters	5	7	1	410	155	68·33
G. Thomas	3	4	0	147	52	36·75
P. J. Burge	4	6	0	159	120	26·50
K. R. Stackpole	2	2	0	52	43	26·00
T. R. Veivers	4	5	1	83	56*	20·75
I. M. Chappell	2	2	0	36	19	18·00
B. C. Booth	3	5	0	84	27	16·80
N. J. N. Hawke	4	5	3	28	20	14·00
G. D. McKenzie	4	5	1	51	24	12·75
P. I. Philpott	3	4	1	22	10	7·33
A. T. W. Grout	5	5	0	34	16	6·80

PLAYED IN ONE MATCH: A. N. Connolly 0 and 0*, I. R. Redpath 17, D. J. Sincock 29 and 27. P. J. Allan did not bat.

BOWLING	Overs	Mds.	Runs	Wkts.	Av.
N. J. N. Hawke	142·7	29	419	16	26·18
G. D. McKenzie	133·1	20	467	16	29·18
K. D. Walters	79	8	283	9	31·44
R. M. Cowper	22	5	76	2	38·00
P. J. Allan	24	6	83	2	41·50
P. I. Philpott	100·1	9	371	8	46·37
K. R. Stackpole	32	5	116	2	58·00
T. R. Veivers	66·7	11	250	4	62·50
A. N. Connolly	38	5	128	1	128·00
I. M. Chappell	45	9	143	1	143·00

ALSO BOWLED: R. B. Simpson 21–5–81–0, D. J. Sincock 20–1–98–0.

ENGLAND

BATTING	M.	Inns.	N.O.	Runs	H.S.	Av.
K. F. Barrington	5	8	1	464	115	66·28
F. J. Titmus	5	6	2	258	60	64·50
M. C. Cowdrey	4	6	1	267	104	53·40
J. M. Parks	5	6	0	290	89	48·33
J. H. Edrich	5	8	0	375	109	46·87
G. Boycott	5	9	2	300	84	42·85
R. W. Barber	5	9	1	328	185	41·00
D. A. Allen	4	5	2	62	50*	20·66
M. J. K. Smith	5	7	1	107	41	17·83
I. J. Jones	4	5	2	29	16	9·66
B. R. Knight	2	2	0	14	13	7·00
D. J. Brown	4	5	0	17	12	3·40

PLAYED IN ONE MATCH: K. Higgs 4, W. E. Russell 0*.

BOWLING	Overs	Mds.	Runs	Wkts.	Av.
K. F. Barrington	7·4	0	47	2	23·50
B. R. Knight	83·7	10	250	8	31·25
I. J. Jones	129	15	533	15	35·53
D. J. Brown	108	14	409	11	37·18
G. Boycott	23	4	89	2	44·50
D. A. Allen	137	33	403	9	44·77
K. Higgs	30	6	102	2	51·00
F. J. Titmus	210·3	52	517	9	57·44
R. W. Barber	55·1	2	261	3	87·00

ALSO BOWLED: M. J. K. Smith 2–0–8–0.

Averages: 1968

ENGLAND

BATTING	M.	Inns.	N.O.	Runs	H.S.	Av.
B. L. D'Oliveira	2	4	1	263	158	87·66
J. H. Edrich	5	9	0	554	164	61·55
K. F. Barrington	3	4	1	170	75	56·66
T. W. Graveney	5	9	1	337	96	41·12
C. Milburn	2	3	0	109	83	36·33
M. C. Cowdrey	4	6	0	215	104	35·83
G. Boycott	3	5	0	162	49	32·40
E. R. Dexter	2	4	0	97	38	24·25
B. R. Knight	2	3	1	34	27*	17·00
A. P. E. Knott	5	8	1	116	33	16·57
R. Illingworth	3	4	0	51	27	12·75
J. A. Snow	5	6	1	56	19	11·20
D. J. Brown	4	4	0	17	14	4·25
D. L. Underwood	4	4	4	69	45*	—

PLAYED IN ONE TEST: D. L. Amiss 0 and 0, R. W. Barber 20 and 46, K. Higgs 2 and 0, P. I. Pocock 6 and 10, R. M. Prideaux 64 and 2, K. W. R. Fletcher 0 and 23*.

BOWLING	Overs	Mds.	Runs	Wkts.	Av.
D. L. Underwood	209·5	103	302	20	15·10
B. L. D'Oliveira	39	20	49	3	16·33
B. R. Knight	40·4	16	85	4	21·25
R. Illingworth	183·2	82	291	13	22·39
P. I. Pocock	58	15	156	6	26·00
R. W. Barber	21	1	87	3	29·00
J. A. Snow	203	44	508	17	29·88
D. J. Brown	144	34	401	12	33·41

ALSO BOWLED: K. Higgs 58·3–19–121–2, K. F. Barrington 8–1–26–1, E. R. Dexter 8–0–28–0.

AUSTRALIA

BATTING	M.	Inns.	N.O.	Runs	H.S.	Av.
W. M. Lawry	4	7	1	270	135	45·00
I. M. Chappell	5	10	2	348	81	43·50
K. D. Walters	5	9	0	343	86	38·11
I. R. Redpath	5	10	0	310	92	31·00
R. M. Cowper	4	8	1	191	57	27·28
A. P. Sheahan	5	9	1	213	88	26·62
R. J. Inverarity	2	4	0	99	56	24·75
B. N. Jarman	4	7	1	88	41	14·66
E. W. Freeman	2	3	0	37	21	12·33
J. W. Gleeson	5	8	1	52	19	7·42
G. D. McKenzie	5	8	1	32	12	4·57
N. J. N. Hawke	2	3	0	7	5	2·33
A. N. Connolly	5	8	5	5	3	1·66

PLAYED IN ONE TEST: H. B. Taber 16, A. A. Mallett 43* and 0.

BOWLING	Overs	Mds.	Runs	Wkts.	Av.
A. N. Connolly	267·1	75	591	23	25·69
R. M. Cowper	103	36	241	8	30·12
E. W. Freeman	67·5	17	186	6	31·00
A. A. Mallett	61	15	164	5	32·80
J. W. Gleeson	193·5	65	417	12	34·75
G. D. McKenzie	264	77	595	13	45·76

ALSO BOWLED: I. M. Chappell 33–9–84–1, N. J. N. Hawke 58–18–115–1, K. D. Walters 16–7–27–0, R. J. Inverarity 1–0–3–0.

1968 First Test, Old Trafford

June 6, 7, 8, 10, 11
Toss: Australia   *Result:* Australia won by 159 runs

This was the youngest touring party ever to visit England, and if fielding alone could have won the series they would have done so; in fact they halved the rubber—for the third time in four series—and retained the Ashes. The weather, which caused the loss of 49 of their first 60 hours' scheduled cricket and 100 hours altogether, gave them a wry compensation by intervening in four of the five Tests and helping them to escape defeat in three. England recovered well as a team from a dismal start, but except for one purple patch at Lord's their fielding and catching were unworthy of an international side, and it was this deficiency as much as the weather that cost them the Ashes.

Despite the paucity of cricket the Australians had arrived at a settled combination and it was England who were wrestling with selection problems at Old Trafford. Of 14 possibles they eventually left out Brown, Cartwright and Underwood, leaving only three specialist bowlers, plus Barber and D'Oliveira, who had taken 7 wickets between them that season. Barber had come in on Barrington's withdrawal.

England made a great start when Redpath was lbw to Snow and Cowper chopped Snow on to his wicket: 29 for 2. Walters edged Higgs perilously close to D'Oliveira at slip, but soon he was cutting and driving surely and playing the ball off his toes wide of mid on. Australia at lunch were 77 for 2, and in the first over afterwards Lawry struck two telling blows when he hit Pocock for 4 and 6. In 10 overs Pocock conceded 44, and the threat he presented, on a wicket that was never quite plumb, was scotched for the moment. When Barber dismissed Walters and Lawry (the latter off a long hop), Australia were 174 for 4; but Sheahan and Chappell took them to 319 for 4 at stumps.

In 85 minutes on the second day Australia lost their last 6 wickets for 85; and despite interruptions for rain which freshened the pitch it took them 3¼ hours to separate Boycott and Edrich. But after Edrich had been run out by a brilliant Walters return England collapsed. On this wicket Lawry was content for England to avert the follow on, and when Australia batted again they owed much to Walters, whose display against Pocock's off spin (6 for 79) was masterly. 413 to win was an impossible target but Edrich, Graveney and Barber all applied themselves, and on the last day D'Oliveira played an innings whose merit was somewhat obscured by England's hopeless position. England had the worst of the conditions, but nothing but bad batting could account for the disparity in first innings scores.

AUSTRALIA

*W. M. Lawry	c Boycott b Barber	81	c Pocock b D'Oliveira	16	
I. R. Redpath	lbw b Snow	8	lbw b Snow	8	
R. M. Cowper	b Snow	0	c and b Pocock	37	
K. D. Walters	lbw b Barber	81	lbw b Pocock	86	
A. P. Sheahan	c D'Oliveira b Snow	88	c Graveney b Pocock	8	
I. M. Chappell	run out	73	c Knott b Pocock	9	
†B. N. Jarman	c and b Higgs	12	b Pocock	41	
N. J. N. Hawke	c Knott b Snow	5	c Edrich b Pocock	0	
G. D. McKenzie	c Cowdrey b D'Oliveira	0	c Snow b Barber	0	
J. W. Gleeson	c Knott b Higgs	0	run out	2	
A. N. Connolly	not out	0	not out	2	
Extras	(lb 7, nb 2)	9	(b 2, lb 9)	11	
Total		**357**	**Total**	**220**	

ENGLAND

G. Boycott	c Jarman b Cowper	35	c Redpath b McKenzie	11	
J. H. Edrich	run out	49	c Jarman b Cowper	38	
*M. C. Cowdrey	c Lawry b McKenzie	4	c Jarman b McKenzie	11	
T. W. Graveney	c McKenzie b Cowper	2	c Jarman b Gleeson	33	
D. L. Amiss	c Cowper b McKenzie	0	b Cowper	0	
R. W. Barber	c Sheahan b McKenzie	20	c Cowper b Hawke	46	
B. L. D'Oliveira	b Connolly	9	not out	87	
†A. P. E. Knott	c McKenzie b Cowper	5	lbw b Connolly	4	
J. A. Snow	not out	18	c Lawry b Connolly	2	
K. Higgs	lbw b Cowper	2	c Jarman b Gleeson	0	
P. I. Pocock	c Redpath b Gleeson	6	lbw b Gleeson	10	
Extras	(b 9, lb 3, w 3)	15	(b 5, lb 6)	11	
Total		**165**	**Total**	**253**	

FALL OF WICKETS

AUSTRALIA

Wkt	1st	2nd
1st	29	24
2nd	29	24
3rd	173	106
4th	174	122
5th	326	140
6th	341	211
7th	351	211
8th	353	214
9th	357	214
10th	357	220

ENGLAND

Wkt	1st	2nd
1st	86	13
2nd	87	25
3rd	89	91
4th	90	91
5th	97	105
6th	120	185
7th	137	215
8th	137	218
9th	144	219
10th	165	253

Umpires: C. S. Elliott, J. S. Buller

ENGLAND

		1st Innings				2nd Innings		
	O	M	R	W	O	M	R	W
Snow	34	5	97	4	17	2	51	1
Higgs	35·3	11	80	2	23	8	41	0
D'Oliveira	25	11	38	1	5	3	7	1
Pocock	25	5	77	0	33	10	79	6
Barber	11	0	56	2	10	1	31	1

AUSTRALIA

		1st Innings				2nd Innings		
	O	M	R	W	O	M	R	W
McKenzie	28	11	33	3	18	3	52	2
Hawke	15	7	18	0	8	4	15	1
Connolly	28	15	26	1	13	4	35	2
Gleeson	6·3	2	21	1	30	14	44	3
Cowper	26	11	48	4	39	12	82	2
Chappell	1	0	4	0	2	0	14	0

145. A. N. Connolly

146. J. H. Edrich

147. Australia 1968
Back row: A. E. James (masseur), E. W. Freeman, R. J. Inverarity, A. A. Mallett, L. E. Truman (treasurer), D. A. Renneberg, A. P. Sheahan, L. R. Joslin, J. W. Gleeson, D. Sherwood (scorer). *Front:* I. M. Chappell, I. R. Redpath, N. J. N. Hawke, R. M. Cowper, W. M. Lawry (capt.), R. J. Parish (manager), G. D. McKenzie, A. N. Connolly, K. D. Walters, H. B. Taber.

1968 Second Test, Lord's

June 20, 21, 22, 24, 25
Toss: England   *Result:* Match Drawn

Anxious to put the memory of Old Trafford behind them, England made five changes at Lord's, Milburn, Barrington, Knight, Brown and Underwood replacing Amiss, D'Oliveira, Barber, Higgs and Pocock. England had made 15 for the loss of Edrich when rain stopped play; on the resumption there was an hour to go till lunch, and with the ball lifting nastily from just short of a length England seemed certain to lose more wickets. But Boycott and Milburn, by sound technique and a contempt for physical discomfort, saw England through to the interval at 53 for 1. A storm then washed out play for the day.

Next morning Milburn attacked the bowling with such ferocity that it was difficult to evaluate to what extent the pitch had recovered, though it had certainly improved. McKenzie, driven and hooked for 4 in his first over, was taken off after his second. Cowper, Australia's most successful bowler at Old Trafford, was pulled high into the grandstand first ball. In 80 minutes Milburn added 67 to his overnight 16 before he was caught on the square leg boundary off a Gleeson leg-spinner trying for another six. Soon afterwards Boycott was caught at short extra from one which stopped, and at lunch England were 156 for 3.

15 minutes were lost in the afternoon through bad light, but Cowdrey and Barrington put on 97 by determined play before Cowdrey was caught off a McKenzie lifter. Soon afterwards Barrington was hit on the finger and had to retire. Jarman, too, chipped a bone: there was still plenty of life in the pitch. Graveney tried to accelerate in the evening but England had pottered to 314 for 5 by stumps. Only 13½ overs were possible next day, in which England added 37, Cowdrey declaring on the fourth morning.

With conditions to their liking the England quicker bowlers hardly wasted a ball. Cowdrey set an attacking field, and for once England took their chances. A great one-handed catch on the leg side in Brown's first over got rid of Lawry; Redpath was taken low at slip in Brown's next. Cowper, driving, edged to Graveney; Knight had Sheahan taken at the wicket, then threw himself sideways in the gully to catch Walters. Cowdrey took three slip catches, Jarman got a painful blow on his damaged finger, and Australia were all out for 78. Cool defence by Lawry and Redpath took advantage of the bowlers' inevitable reaction when Australia followed on, but even so Australia faced the final day needing 273 to avoid an innings defeat. More heavy rain, however, cut play down to 2 hours 25 minutes, and Cowdrey gave best to the weather 17 minutes from time.

ENGLAND

J. H. Edrich	c Cowper b McKenzie	7
G. Boycott	c Sheahan b McKenzie	49
C. Milburn	c Walters b Gleeson	83
*M. C. Cowdrey	c Cowper b McKenzie	45
K. F. Barrington	c Jarman b Connolly	75
T. W. Graveney	c Jarman b Connolly	14
B. R. Knight	not out	27
†A. P. E. Knott	run out	33
J. A. Snow	not out	0
D. J. Brown	} did not bat	
D. L. Underwood		
Extras	(b 7, lb 5, w 1, nb 5)	18
Total	(7 wkts dec)	**351**

AUSTRALIA

*W. M. Lawry	c Knott b Brown	0	c Brown b Snow	28
I. R. Redpath	c Cowdrey b Brown	4	b Underwood	53
R. M. Cowper	c Graveney b Snow	8	c Underwood b Barrington	32
K. D. Walters	c Knight b Brown	26	b Underwood	0
A. P. Sheahan	c Knott b Knight	6	not out	0
I. M. Chappell	lbw b Knight	7	not out	12
N. J. N. Hawke	c Cowdrey b Knight	2		
G. D. McKenzie	b Brown	5		
J. W. Gleeson	c Cowdrey b Brown	14		
†B. N. Jarman	retired hurt	0		
A. N. Connolly	not out	0		
Extras	(lb 2, nb 4)	6	(nb 2)	2
Total		**78**	**Total** (4 wkts)	**127**

FALL OF WICKETS

ENGLAND

Wkt	1st	2nd
1st	10	—
2nd	142	—
3rd	147	—
4th	244	—
5th	271	—
6th	330	—
7th	351	—
8th	—	—
9th	—	—
10th	—	—

AUSTRALIA

Wkt	1st	2nd
1st	1	66
2nd	12	93
3rd	23	97
4th	46	115
5th	52	—
6th	58	—
7th	63	—
8th	78	—
9th	78	—
10th	—	—

Umpires: J. S. Buller, A. E. Fagg

AUSTRALIA

	1st Innings				2nd Innings			
	O	M	R	W	O	M	R	W
McKenzie	45	18	111	3	..			
Hawke	35	7	82	0	..			
Connolly	26·3	8	55	2	..			
Walters	3	2	2	0	..			
Cowper	8	2	40	0	..			
Gleeson	27	11	43	1	..			

ENGLAND

	1st Innings				2nd Innings			
	O	M	R	W	O	M	R	W
Snow	9	5	14	1	..	12	5	30	1
Brown	14	5	42	5	..	19	9	40	0
Knight	10·4	5	16	3	..	16	9	35	0
Underwood					..	18	15	8	2
Barrington					..	2	0	12	1

1968 Third Test, Edgbaston

July 11, 12, 13, 15, 16
Toss: England   *Result:* Match Drawn

Again England, although reaching a position of unassailable strength, had to give best to the weather. The first day was washed out entirely, and England, without Milburn (injured) and playing five specialist bowlers including Knight, made understandably cautious progress on the second day, only 65 runs being made before lunch. Brilliant fielding, and a fine spell by Gleeson, also contributed to the slow rate. But when Boycott was out (36 in 154 minutes), Cowdrey showed superb form, while Edrich batted soundly for 4 hours 20 minutes. Freeman, who had displaced Hawke, got Edrich and Barrington with the second new ball, but Graveney too was in touch and 67 runs came in the last 70 minutes, England closing at 258 for 3. After reaching 50 Cowdrey went lame, but his stroke-play seemed little affected.

England's scoring rate was again restricted by the fielding on the third day. Cowdrey got his hundred in his 100th Test, but Graveney, to whom a hundred must have meant at least as much, missed his. The later batsmen failed to press home England's advantage and in 3½ hours only 151 were added. In a fiery opening spell Brown disposed of Redpath (bowled) and Lawry (broken finger), but Cowper and Chappell survived a half-chance each and batted so well that at stumps Australia were 109 for 1 off 40 overs.

England's chances of a win looked modest at this point; and although Snow bowled Cowper next morning, Chappell and Walters reduced the threat of a follow on (200 runs in this series) in a stand of 44. But when Chappell was bowled leg stump at 165 after an admirable 71 in 3¼ hours, Graveney, captaining in Cowdrey's absence, somehow conjured up an atmosphere of crisis. Underwood turned one from leg to bowl Sheahan, and although Taber survived the half-hour till lunch, the last 5 wickets fell to spin for 29 runs.

England's need now was quick runs, and although McKenzie, deputising for Lawry, bowled 18 overs in succession without a break except for the tea interval, and although the fielding was as keen as ever, England made 142 for 3 off 42 overs, Graveney promoting himself to no. 3 and helping Edrich put on 74 in 55 minutes.

The pitch was still good, and when the last day began Australia, 9 for 0 overnight, needed 321 to win in 6 hours; they were a long way from defeat, but the declaration underlined England's superiority. After Redpath had been beaten by Snow, Graveney turned again to spin. The Australian tactics were for Cowper to thwart Underwood while Chappell smothered Illingworth; but 45 minutes after Redpath's dismissal the rain came again.

ENGLAND

J. H. Edrich	c Taber b Freeman	88	c Cowper b Freeman	64	
G. Boycott	lbw b Gleeson	36	c Taber b Connolly	31	
*M. C. Cowdrey	b Freeman	104			
K. F. Barrington	lbw b Freeman	0			
T. W. Graveney	b Connolly	96	(3)not out	39	
B. R. Knight	c Chappell b Connolly	6	(4)b Connolly	1	
†A. P. E. Knott	b McKenzie	4	(5)not out	4	
R. Illingworth	lbw b Gleeson	27			
D. J. Brown	b Connolly	0			
J. A. Snow	c Connolly b Freeman	19			
D. L. Underwood	not out	14			
Extras	(b 4, lb 6, w 1, nb 4)	15	(lb 2, nb 1)	3	
Total		**409**	**Total** (3 wkts dec)	**142**	

AUSTRALIA

*W. M. Lawry	retired hurt	6			
I. R. Redpath	b Brown	0	lbw b Snow	22	
R. M. Cowper	b Snow	57	(1)not out	25	
I. M. Chappell	b Knight	71	(3)not out	18	
K. D. Walters	c and b Underwood	46			
A. P. Sheahan	b Underwood	4			
†H. B. Taber	c Barrington b Illingworth	15			
E. W. Freeman	b Illingworth	6			
G. D. McKenzie	not out	0			
J. W. Gleeson	c Illingworth b Underwood	2			
A. N. Connolly	b Illingworth	0			
Extras	(b 1, lb 10, nb 2)	13	(lb 1, nb 2)	3	
Total		**222**	**Total** (1 wkt)	**68**	

FALL OF WICKETS

ENGLAND		
Wkt	1st	2nd
1st	80	57
2nd	188	131
3rd	189	134
4th	282	—
5th	293	—
6th	323	—
7th	374	—
8th	374	—
9th	376	—
10th	409	—

AUSTRALIA		
Wkt	1st	2nd
1st	10	44
2nd	121	—
3rd	165	—
4th	176	—
5th	213	—
6th	213	—
7th	219	—
8th	222	—
9th	222	—
10th	—	—

Umpires: C. S. Elliott, H. Yarnold

AUSTRALIA	1st Innings					2nd Innings			
	O	M	R	W		O	M	R	W
McKenzie	47	14	115	1	..	18	1	57	0
Freeman	30·5	8	78	4	..	9	2	23	1
Connolly	35	8	84	3	..	15	3	59	2
Gleeson	46	19	84	2	..				
Cowper	7	1	25	0	..				
Walters	7	3	8	0	..				

ENGLAND	1st Innings					2nd Innings			
	O	M	R	W		O	M	R	W
Snow	17	3	46	1	..	9	1	32	1
Brown	13	2	44	1	..	6	1	15	0
Knight	14	2	34	1	..				
Underwood	25	9	48	3	..	8	4	14	0
Illingworth	22	10	37	3	..	5·2	2	4	0

1968 Fourth Test, Leeds

July 25, 26, 27, 29, 30
Toss: Australia   *Result:* Match Drawn

Cowdrey, Boycott and Milburn were all absent through injury, and the weakened English side was reconstructed to include another batsman, Knight being dropped. A compensating factor was that Australia were without Lawry.

For a side whose main interest was to avoid defeat and thus retain the Ashes the first day went uncommonly well for Australia. Lawry's replacement was quickly despatched, but Redpath, batting no. 3, went for his shots while Cowper defended; his innings was an extraordinary mixture of brilliance and fallibility. Meanwhile Illingworth bowled 9 overs for 1 run—mostly to Cowper, who was dropped at the wicket off Snow. Three difficult chances to Fletcher at slip also went down. Cowper reached double figures just before lunch, when Australia were 75 for 1.

Redpath continued to ride his luck until he hit across Illingworth at 152 for 3. More chances had meanwhile gone begging, Walters being missed three times, and when a break-through seemed possible at 188 for 4 Chappell and Sheahan added 60. 258 for 5 in the day, modest enough, represented bitter disappointment for England.

Australia's last 5 wickets fell next day for 57, and by tea-time Edrich and Prideaux had made 82 together off 41 overs, their progress restricted by a defensive field. When they began to accelerate Prideaux went to

a fine running catch, Edrich was caught behind, and Dexter was bowled. Barrington joined Graveney at 141 for 3 with only Fletcher of the batsmen to come.

Next day even Graveney could not find his touch, Barrington batted 3 hours for 49, and after passing 200 with 3 wickets down England found themselves 241 for 9, all hope of regaining the Ashes apparently gone. But intelligent cricket by Underwood and Brown brought England within 13 of Australia's total.

A wet ball did not help England on the vital fourth morning, and at lunch Australia, 92 for 2 overnight, were 172 for 3. But after lunch the spinners made Australia fight hard; Chappell batted more than 4 hours and Walters 3 hours 20 minutes. When their stand of 79 was broken Sheahan was dropped at long leg by Snow. An hour was lost through rain and bad light, and 55 minutes of the final day were gone before the last wicket fell, another dropped catch delaying the end. England then needed 326 at 66 an hour.

On a worn wicket on which spin might at any time have menaced them their efforts were unsuccessful, though there was a point in mid-afternoon when Edrich and Graveney seemed to be going well enough. But Jarman relied on McKenzie and Connolly, and although this may have saved England from defeat it denied them victory.

AUSTRALIA

R. M. Cowper	b Snow	27	st Knott b Illingworth	5
R. J. Inverarity	b Snow	8	lbw b Illingworth	34
I. R. Redpath	b Illingworth	92	c Edrich b Snow	48
K. D. Walters	c Barrington b Underwood	42	c Graveney b Snow	56
I. M. Chappell	b Brown	65	c Barrington b Underwood	81
A. P. Sheahan	c Knott b Snow	38	st Knott b Illingworth	31
*†B. N. Jarman	c Dexter b Brown	10	st Knott b Illingworth	4
E. W. Freeman	b Underwood	21	b Illingworth	10
G. D. McKenzie	lbw b Underwood	5	c Snow b Illingworth	10
J. W. Gleeson	not out	2	c Knott b Underwood	7
A. N. Connolly	c Graveney b Underwood	0	not out	0
Extras	(lb 4, nb 1)	5	(b 13, lb 8, nb 5)	26
Total		**315**	**Total**	**312**

ENGLAND

J. H. Edrich	c Jarman b McKenzie	62	c Jarman b Connolly	65
R. M. Prideaux	c Freeman b Gleeson	64	b McKenzie	2
E. R. Dexter	b McKenzie	10	b Connolly	38
*T. W. Graveney	c Cowper b Connolly	37	c and b Cowper	41
K. F. Barrington	b Connolly	49	not out	46
K. W. R. Fletcher	c Jarman b Connolly	0	not out	23
†A. P. E. Knott	lbw b Freeman	4		
R. Illingworth	c Gleeson b Connolly	6		
J. A. Snow	b Connolly	0		
D. J. Brown	b Cowper	14		
D. L. Underwood	not out	45		
Extras	(b 1, lb 7, nb 3)	11	(b 8, lb 7)	15
Total		**302**	**Total (4 wkts)**	**230**

FALL OF WICKETS

AUSTRALIA

Wkt	1st	2nd
1st	10	28
2nd	104	81
3rd	152	119
4th	188	198
5th	248	273
6th	268	281
7th	307	283
8th	309	296
9th	315	311
10th	315	312

ENGLAND

Wkt	1st	2nd
1st	123	4
2nd	136	81
3rd	141	134
4th	209	168
5th	215	—
6th	235	—
7th	237	—
8th	241	—
9th	241	—
10th	302	—

Umpires: J. S. Buller, A. E. Fagg

ENGLAND	1st Innings					2nd Innings			
	O	M	R	W		O	M	R	W
Snow	35	3	98	3	..	24	3	51	2
Brown	35	4	99	2	..	27	5	79	0
Illingworth	29	15	47	1	..	51	22	87	6
Underwood	27.4	13	41	4	..	45.1	22	52	2
Dexter	7	0	25	0	..	1	0	3	0
Barrington					..	6	1	14	0

AUSTRALIA	1st Innings					2nd Innings			
	O	M	R	W		O	M	R	W
McKenzie	39	20	61	2	..	25	2	65	1
Freeman	22	6	60	1	..	6	1	25	0
Gleeson	25	5	68	1	..	11	4	26	0
Connolly	39	13	72	5	..	31	10	68	2
Cowper	18	10	24	1	..	5	0	22	1
Chappell	4	1	6	0	..	5	3	6	0
Inverarity					..	1	0	3	0

1968 Fifth Test, Oval

August 22, 23, 24, 26, 27
Toss: England   *Result:* England won by 226 runs

When Australia were 85 for 5 at lunch on the final day and facing defeat, the storm that flooded the Oval seemed an appropriate curtain to England's luckless campaign in quest of the Ashes. But the unexpected drama of the last 75 minutes, after a squad of volunteers had mopped up the deluge, provided scenes as memorable as any in the long history of the Oval. Cowdrey and Milburn returned for England, Barrington and Fletcher making room for them, and D'Oliveira came in at the last moment for the injured Prideaux. Lawry returned to captain Australia, while an injury to Cowper reprieved Inverarity and encouraged the preference of Mallett over Freeman.

Some brilliant stops by Sheahan at cover may have exasperated Milburn; aiming yet again for the off boundary he was yorked at 28. Dexter found the going tough, and when Mallett beat Cowdrey after lunch in his first over in Test cricket England were 113 for 3. Fortunately Graveney was soon into his stride, Edrich punched the shorter balls unerringly, and some venturesome clumps by D'Oliveira in the last half hour lifted the total to 272 for 4, Edrich 130 not out.

The second day belonged to D'Oliveira. Missed by Jarman when 31, he made no other mistake until reaching his hundred. He went on to make 158, being entirely responsible for such acceleration as England achieved. Australia were left with 70 minutes' batting and soon lost Inverarity; at stumps they were 43 for 1.

The batsman who dominated the third day was Lawry. After he and Redpath had taken Australia to 120 for 1 at lunch, 5 wickets fell in the afternoon for 76; but at stumps, when Australia were 264 for 7, Lawry was 135 not out. 31 were still needed to save the follow on, and although Lawry left early next day, Mallett and Gleeson held on. Mallett batted for over 3 hours in all.

England resumed with a volley of shots from Milburn and Dexter, and although some consolation was later necessary Australia were set 352 to win at 54 an hour. In 35 minutes before stumps they lost Lawry and Redpath; and next morning the final inroads seemed to have been made when Chappell and Walters fell to Underwood. But Inverarity and Sheahan showed plenty of fight; and then came lunch and the storm.

It was D'Oliveira who made the vital break-through when he bowled Jarman with only 35 minutes to go. After that, with the wicket drying, and in spite of more missed chances, Underwood was irresistible. The margin, however, was only 6 minutes: had the Australians not shunned loitering, gardening, and all other acts of gamesmanship, England would never have won.

ENGLAND

J. H. Edrich	b Chappell	164	c Lawry b Mallett	17	
C. Milburn	b Connolly	8	c Lawry b Connolly	18	
E. R. Dexter	b Gleeson	21	b Connolly	28	
*M. C. Cowdrey	lbw b Mallett	16	b Mallett	35	
T. W. Graveney	c Redpath b McKenzie	63	run out	12	
B. L. D'Oliveira	c Inverarity b Mallett	158	c Gleeson b Connolly	9	
†A. P. E. Knott	c Jarman b Mallett	28	run out	34	
R. Illingworth	lbw b Connolly	8	b Gleeson	10	
J. A. Snow	run out	4	c Sheahan b Gleeson	13	
D. L. Underwood	not out	9	not out	1	
D. J. Brown	c Sheahan b Gleeson	2	b Connolly	1	
Extras	(b 1, lb 11, w 1)	13	(lb 3)	3	
Total		**494**		**181**	

AUSTRALIA

*W. M. Lawry	c Knott b Snow	135	c Milburn b Brown	4	
R. J. Inverarity	c Milburn b Snow	1	lbw b Underwood	56	
I. R. Redpath	c Cowdrey b Snow	67	lbw b Underwood	8	
I. M. Chappell	c Knott b Brown	10	lbw b Underwood	2	
K. D. Walters	c Knott b Brown	5	c Knott b Underwood	1	
A. P. Sheahan	b Illingworth	14	c Snow b Illingworth	24	
†B. N. Jarman	st Knott b Illingworth	0	b D'Oliveira	21	
G. D. McKenzie	b Brown	12	(9)c Brown b Underwood	0	
A. A. Mallett	not out	43	(8)c Brown b Underwood	0	
J. W. Gleeson	c Dexter b Underwood	19	b Underwood	5	
A. N. Connolly	b Underwood	3	not out	0	
Extras	(b 4, lb 7, nb 4)	15	(lb 4)	4	
Total		**324**		**125**	

FALL OF WICKETS

ENGLAND

Wkt	1st	2nd
1st	28	23
2nd	84	53
3rd	113	67
4th	238	90
5th	359	114
6th	421	126
7th	458	149
8th	468	179
9th	489	179
10th	494	181

AUSTRALIA

Wkt	1st	2nd
1st	7	4
2nd	136	13
3rd	151	19
4th	161	29
5th	185	65
6th	188	110
7th	237	110
8th	269	110
9th	302	120
10th	324	125

Umpires: C. S. Elliott, A. E. Fagg

AUSTRALIA	1st Innings					2nd Innings			
	O	M	R	W		O	M	R	W
McKenzie	40	8	87	1	..	4	0	14	0
Connolly	57	12	127	2	..	22.4	2	65	4
Walters	6	2	17	0	..				
Gleeson	41.2	8	109	2	..	7	2	22	2
Mallett	36	11	87	3	..	25	4	77	2
Chappell	21	5	54	1	..				

ENGLAND	1st Innings					2nd Innings			
	O	M	R	W		O	M	R	W
Snow	35	12	67	3	..	11	5	22	0
Brown	22	5	63	3	..	8	3	19	1
Illingworth	48	15	87	2	..	28	18	29	1
Underwood	54.3	21	89	2	..	31.3	19	50	7
D'Oliveira	4	2	3	0	..	5	4	1	1

The results – series by series

Season	M	Won by E	Won by A	D	England captain	Australian captain
1876-77	2	1	1	0	James Lillywhite, jnr.	D. W. Gregory
1878-79	1	0	1	0	Lord Harris	D. W. Gregory
1880	1	1	0	0	Lord Harris	W. L. Murdoch
1881-82	4	0	2	2	A. Shaw	W. L. Murdoch
1882	1	0	1	0	A. N. Hornby	W. L. Murdoch
1882-83	4	2	2	0	Hon. Ivo Bligh	W. L. Murdoch
1884	3	1	0	2	†Lord Harris	W. L. Murdoch
1884-85	5	3	2	0	A. Shrewsbury	†T. P. Horan
1886	3	3	0	0	A. G. Steel	H. J. H. Scott
1886-87	2	2	0	0	A. Shrewsbury	P. S. McDonnell
1887-88	1	1	0	0	W. W. Read	P. S. McDonnell
1888	3	2	1	0	†W. G. Grace	P. S. McDonnell
1890	2	2	0	0	W. G. Grace	W. L. Murdoch
1891-92	3	1	2	0	W. G. Grace	J. McC. Blackham
1893	3	1	0	2	†W. G. Grace	J. McC. Blackham
1894-95	5	3	2	0	A. E. Stoddart	†G. Giffen
1896	3	2	1	0	W. G. Grace	G. H. S. Trott
1897-98	5	1	4	0	†A. C. MacLaren	G. H. S. Trott
1899	5	0	1	4	†A. C. MacLaren	J. Darling
1901-02	5	1	4	0	A. C. MacLaren	†J. Darling
1902	5	1	2	2	A. C. MacLaren	J. Darling
1903-04	5	3	2	0	P. F. Warner	M. A. Noble
1905	5	2	0	3	Hon. F. S. Jackson	J. Darling
1907-08	5	1	4	0	†F. L. Fane	M. A. Noble
1909	5	1	2	2	A. C. MacLaren	M. A. Noble
1911-12	5	4	1	0	J. W. H. T. Douglas	C. Hill
1912	3	1	0	2	C. B. Fry	S. E. Gregory
1920-21	5	0	5	0	J. W. H. T. Douglas	W. W. Armstrong
1921	5	0	3	2	†Hon. L. H. Tennyson	W. W. Armstrong
1924-25	5	1	4	0	A. E. R. Gilligan	H. L. Collins
1926	5	1	0	4	†A. W. Carr	†H. L. Collins
1928-29	5	4	1	0	†A. P. F. Chapman	J. Ryder
1930	5	1	2	2	†A. P. F. Chapman	W. M. Woodfull
1932-33	5	4	1	0	D. R. Jardine	W. M. Woodfull
1934	5	1	2	2	†R. E. S. Wyatt	W. M. Woodfull
1936-37	5	2	3	0	G. O. Allen	D. G. Bradman
1938	4	1	1	2	W. R. Hammond	D. G. Bradman
1946-47	5	0	3	2	†W. R. Hammond	D. G. Bradman
1948	5	0	4	1	N. W. D. Yardley	D. G. Bradman
1950-51	5	1	4	0	F. R. Brown	A. L. Hassett
1953	5	1	0	4	L. Hutton	A. L. Hassett
1954-55	5	3	1	1	L. Hutton	†I. W. Johnson
1956	5	2	1	2	P. B. H. May	I. W. Johnson
1958-59	5	0	4	1	P. B. H. May	R. Benaud
1961	5	1	2	2	†P. B. H. May	†R. Benaud
1962-63	5	1	1	3	E. R. Dexter	R. Benaud
1964	5	0	1	4	E. R. Dexter	R. B. Simpson
1965-66	5	1	1	3	M. J. K. Smith	†R. B. Simpson
1968	5	1	1	3	†M. C. Cowdrey	†W. M. Lawry
In England	96	26	25	45		
In Australia	107	40	55	12		
Total	**203**	**66**	**80**	**57**		

†In these series there was more than one captain, the captain given being he who led the side most times.

The results

Of the 203 games, England have won 66, Australia 80 and 57 have been drawn.

The following was the position after certain landmarks:

	Won by E	Won by A	Drawn
After 50 Tests	26	18	6
After 100 Tests	40	41	19
After 150 Tests	55	62	33
After 200 Tests	65	80	55

The biggest difference in victories between the sides is 15 wins ahead by Australia after Old Trafford, 1968. England's longest lead is 11, after Sydney (first Test), 1897-98.

The sides were level with 40 wins each after the 1920-21 series, and were level again on four other occasions up to and including the third Test at Melbourne in 1936-37. Australia went ahead at Adelaide in the following match and England have not had parity since.

On two occasions has a side won 7 or more successive matches:

A won 8 successive matches   Sydney 1920-21 to Headingley 1921
E won 7 successive matches   Melbourne 1884-85 to Sydney 1887-88

The only occasion on which a side has won every match in a five-match series is when Australia did so in 1920-21.

Longest unbeaten sequence:

A in 14 successive matches   Brisbane 1946-47 to Adelaide 1950-51
A in 13 successive matches   Sydney 1920-21 to Adelaide 1924-25
A in 10 successive matches   Sydney 1962-63 to Melbourne 1965-66
A in 9 successive matches   Melbourne 1897-98 to Oval 1899
E in 9 successive matches   Trent Bridge 1926 to Adelaide 1928-29

The grounds

Twelve grounds have been used for these matches – seven in England and five in Australia.

In England	First match	Tests	Won by E	Won by A	Drawn
Oval	1880	24	12	4	8
Lord's	1884	22	5	8	9
Old Trafford	1884	20	4	4	12
Headingley	1899	14	2	5	7
Trent Bridge	1899	11	2	3	6
Edgbaston	1902	4	1	0	3
Sheffield	1902	1	0	1	0
		96	26	25	45

In Australia	First match	Tests	Won by E	Won by A	Drawn
Melbourne C.G.	1876-77	40	15	20	5
Sydney C.G.	1881-82	39	16	20	3
Adelaide Oval	1884-85	19	6	11	2
Brisbane C.G. (Woolloongabba)	1932-33	8	2	4	2
Brisbane (Exhibition Ground)	1928-29	1	1	0	0
		107	40	55	12

	First match	Tests	Won by E	Won by A	Drawn
In England	1880	96	26	25	45
In Australia	1876-77	107	40	55	12
		203	66	80	57

The Oval and Melbourne are the only grounds that have staged a Test on every Test-playing tour to the respective countries.

The Test ground at Sydney (now Sydney Cricket Ground, no. 1) has been variously known as the Civil and Military Ground, the Association Ground, and Moore Park. The trustees of the New South Wales Cricket Association changed the name to Sydney Cricket Ground in 1894.

The most recent ground to be introduced to England-Australia Test cricket is at Brisbane. The decision to play a Test at Brisbane on all MCC tours of Australia was taken at a meeting of the Australian Board of Control for International Cricket held at Melbourne in September 1927, Sydney and Melbourne foregoing a Test on alternate tours.

As from the 1961 series, a rota system has been in operation in England whereby Trent Bridge and Edgbaston are respectively omitted as Test venues on alternate Australian tours. This followed a Board of Control decision at Lord's on March 8, 1955.

At a Board of Control meeting at Lord's on November 24, 1930, a sub-committee was appointed to consider the question whether there were grounds in England, other than those then used for Test matches, suitable to stage such games. No other grounds were given Test status as a result of these deliberations. (The sub-committee was appointed following a suggestion by W. L. Kelly, the manager of the 1930 Australian team in England.)

The toss

In the 203 games, England have won the toss 105 times and Australia 98. The following was the position after certain landmarks:

	Toss won by E	Toss won by A
After 50 Tests	22 times	28 times
After 100 Tests	49 times	51 times
After 150 Tests	76 times	74 times
After 200 Tests	103 times	97 times

At no time has the difference between the sides, as regards the toss, been more than seven – and this position has occurred three times: after the 89th match (Adelaide, 1911-12, when Australia led by 48 to 41); after the 201st match (Edgbaston, 1968, when England led by 104 to 97); and after the Oval match of 1968, which is the present position.

Over the course of the series each country has been more successful at home, as the following table shows:

		Toss won by E	Toss won by A
In England	96 matches	56 times	40 times
In Australia	107 matches	49 times	58 times
	203 matches	**105** times	**98** times

The following captains won the toss in all five Tests of a series:

Hon. F. S. Jackson (E)   in 1905
M. A. Noble (A)   in 1909
A. L. Hassett (A)   in 1953

A. Shaw (E) won the toss in all four games in 1881-82, as did W. R. Hammond (E) in 1938. A. L. Hassett (A) won the toss in nine of his ten matches as captain.

On four occasions has a side won four matches in a series despite also losing the toss four times in that series: Australia in 1901-02, England in 1932-33, Australia in 1948 and Australia in 1958-59.

L. Hutton (E), in 1953, is the only captain who has lost the toss in all five Tests and yet won the series.

Longest sequence in winning the toss:

		Successful captain
8 by A	Edgbaston 1909 to Adelaide 1911-12	M.A.Noble(5), C.Hill(3)
7 by A	Adelaide 1950-51 to Oval 1953	A.L.Hassett
7 by E	Headingley 1956 to Adelaide 1958-59	P.B.H.May

Highest totals

ENGLAND

903 for 7 dec.	Oval	1938
658 for 8 dec.	Trent Bridge	1938
636	Sydney	1928-29
627 for 9 dec.	Old Trafford	1934
611	Old Trafford	1964
589	Melbourne	1911-12
577	Sydney	1903-04
576	Oval	1899
558	Melbourne	1965-66
551	Sydney	1897-98
548	Melbourne	1924-25
524	Sydney	1932-33
521	Brisbane	1928-29
519	Melbourne	1928-29
501	Adelaide	1911-12

England's highest totals on the other regular Test grounds are as follows:

Headingley	496	1948
Lord's	494	1938
Edgbaston	409	1968

The longest innings for England in point of time is 15 hours 17 minutes, occupied by their 903 for 7 dec. at the Oval in 1938.

AUSTRALIA

729 for 6 dec.	Lord's	1930
701	Oval	1934
695	Oval	1930
659 for 8 dec.	Sydney	1946-47
656 for 8 dec.	Old Trafford	1964
645	Brisbane	1946-47
604	Melbourne	1936-37
601 for 8 dec.	Brisbane	1954-5?
600	Melbourne	1924-25
586	Sydney	1894-95
584	Headingley	1934
582	Adelaide	1920-21
581	Sydney	1920-21
573	Adelaide	1897-98
566	Headingley	1930
564	Melbourne	1936-37
551	Oval	1884
543 for 8 dec.	Melbourne	1965-66
536	Melbourne	1946-47
520	Melbourne	1897-98
516 for 9 dec.	Edgbaston	1961
516	Adelaide	1965-66
509	Trent Bridge	1948
506	Adelaide	1907-08

The longest innings for Australia in point of time is 12 hours 58 minutes, occupied by their 656 for 8 dec. at Old Trafford in 1964.

Highest second innings totals

ENGLAND

475	Melbourne	1894-95
441	Trent Bridge	1948
437	Sydney	1894-95
436	Oval	1926
426 for 5 dec.	Trent Bridge	1905
412	Adelaide	1932-33
411	Sydney	1924-25
401 for 4	Edgbaston	1961

AUSTRALIA

582	Adelaide	1920-21
581	Sydney	1920-21
564	Melbourne	1936-37
536	Melbourne	1946-47
506	Adelaide	1907-08
485	Sydney	1903-04
476	Adelaide	1911-12
460 for 7 dec.	Lord's	1948
452	Sydney	1924-25
433	Adelaide	1936-37
432	Old Trafford	1961
427 for 6 dec.	Trent Bridge	1938
426	Melbourne	1965-66
422	Sydney	1907-08
411	Adelaide	1894-95
408	Sydney	1907-08
†404 for 3	Headingley	1948
403 for 8 dec.	Adelaide	1950-51

†To win match. This is the only innings total to reach 400 and thereby bring victory to a side. The only other fourth-innings total to reach 400 is England's 411 at Sydney in 1924-25.

In only one of the 203 matches have *both* sides reached 400 in their second innings – in the first Test at Sydney in 1924-25.

It was not until 1938 that Australia reached 400 in a second innings in England, their previous best having been 349 at the Oval in 1893. Of the 96 matches played in England, a second-innings total of 400 has been reached only eight times.

Highest totals in fourth innings

To win match

404 for 3 by A	Headingley	1948
332 for 7 by E	Melbourne	1928-29
315 for 6 by A	Adelaide	1901-02
298 for 4 by E	Melbourne	1894-95
287 for 5 by A	Melbourne	1928-29
282 for 9 by E	Melbourne	1907-08
276 for 4 by A	Sydney	1897-98
275 for 8 by A	Sydney	1907-08
263 for 9 by E	Oval	1902

In all the above matches, except those at the Oval in 1902 and at Headingley in 1948, the side batting last had unlimited time at their disposal.

To draw

310 for 7 (needing 551 total) by E	Melbourne	1946-47
282 for 7 (needing 343 total) by E	Lord's	1953
278 for 6 (needing 378 total) by E	Brisbane	1962-63

Australia's highest fourth-innings total in a drawn match is 224 for 7 (needing 402 to win) at Headingley in 1905.

To lose

411 (losing by 193 runs) by E	Sydney	1924-25
370 (losing by 119 runs) by E	Adelaide	1920-21
363 (losing by 11 runs) by E	Adelaide	1924-25
336 (losing by 12 runs) by A	Adelaide	1928-29
335 (losing by 93 runs) by A	Trent Bridge	1930
333 (losing by 94 runs) by A	Melbourne	1894-95
323 (losing by 365 runs) by E	Melbourne	1936-37
292 (losing by 70 runs) by A	Sydney	1911-12
291 (losing by 146 runs) by E	Sydney	1911-12
290 (losing by 81 runs) by E	Melbourne	1924-25
281 (losing by 377 runs) by E	Sydney	1920-21
278 (losing by 216 runs) by E	Adelaide	1903-04
253 (losing by 159 runs) by E	Old Trafford	1968

In three successive matches in 1924-25 – at Sydney, Melbourne and Adelaide – England scored 411, 290 and 363 respectively in the fourth innings (on each occasion batting for more than six hours), losing each time.

Lowest totals

ENGLAND

45	Sydney	1886-87	75	Melbourne	1894-95
52	Oval	1948	77	Oval	1882
53	Lord's	1888	77	Sydney	1884-85
61	Melbourne	1901-02	84	Oval	1896
61	Melbourne	1903-04	87	Headingley	1909
62	Lord's	1888	87	Melbourne	1958-59
65	Sydney	1894-95	95	Old Trafford	1884
72	Sydney	1894-95	99	Sydney	1901-02

Also note:

76 for 9 dec.	Melbourne	1936-37
68 for 7 dec.	Brisbane	1950-51

England's lowest second-innings totals are their 62 at Lord's in 1888 and 72 at Sydney in 1894-95.

The shortest innings for England in point of time is 68 minutes, occupied by their 61 at Melbourne in 1901-02.

AUSTRALIA

36	Edgbaston	1902	63	Oval	1882
42	Sydney	1887-88	65	Oval	1912
44	Oval	1896	66	Brisbane	1928-29
53	Lord's	1896	68	Oval	1886
58	Brisbane	1936-37	70	Old Trafford	1888
60	Lord's	1888	74	Edgbaston	1909

78	Lord's	1968	84	Sydney	1886-87
80	Oval	1888	84	Old Trafford	1956
80	Sydney	1936-37	86	Old Trafford	1902
81	Old Trafford	1888	91	Oval	1893
82	Sydney	1887-88	92	Oval	1890
83	Sydney	1882-83	97	Sydney	1886-87

Also note:

| 32 for 7 dec. | Brisbane | 1950-51 |
| 35 for 8 | Old Trafford | 1953 |

Australia's lowest second-innings totals are their 44 at the Oval in 1896 and 58 at Brisbane in 1936-37.

The shortest innings for Australia in point of time is 71 minutes, occupied by their 58 at Brisbane in 1936-37.

Totals of less than 100 in each innings

42 and 82	by A	Sydney	1887-88
53 and 62	by E	Lord's	1888
81 and 70	by A	Old Trafford	1888
65 and 72	by E	Sydney	1894-95

Also note:

101 and 77	by E	Oval	1882
80 and 100	by A	Oval	1888
100 and 95 for 8	by E	Oval	1890
61 and 101	by E	Melbourne	1903-04

Highest match aggregates

The first Test to produce an aggregate of 1,000 runs was the first match of the 1881-82 series at Melbourne. The first to do so in England was at Old Trafford in 1896.

The progressive match aggregate record is as follows:

1,049 runs for 33 wkts	Melbourne	1881-82
1,514 .. .. 40 ..	Sydney	1894-95
1,541 .. .. 35 ..	Sydney	1903-04
1,753 .. .. 40 ..	Adelaide	1920-21

The progressive record in England is:

1,073 runs for 37 wkts	Old Trafford	1896
1,182 .. .. 25 ..	Oval	1899
1,601 .. .. 29 ..	Lord's	1930
1,723 .. .. 31 ..	Headingley	1948

The highest match aggregates are as follows:

1,753 runs for 40 wkts	Adelaide	1920-21	in 6 days' play
1,723 .. .. 31 ..	Headingley	1948	in 5 days' play
1,619 .. .. 40 ..	Melbourne	1924-25	in 7 days' play
1,611 .. .. 40 ..	Sydney	1924-25	in 7 days' play
1,601 .. .. 29 ..	Lord's	1930	in 4 days' play
1,562 .. .. 37 ..	Melbourne	1946-47	in 6 days' play
1,554 .. .. 35 ..	Melbourne	1928-29	in 8 days' play
1,541 .. .. 35 ..	Sydney	1903-04	in 6 days' play
1,514 .. .. 40 ..	Sydney	1894-95	in 6 days' play
1,502 .. .. 29 ..	Adelaide	1946-47	in 6 days' play
1,497 .. .. 37 ..	Melbourne	1928-29	in 7 days' play
1,496 .. .. 24 ..	Trent Bridge	1938	in 4 days' play
1,494 .. .. 37 ..	Oval	1934	in 4 days' play
1,467 .. .. 40 ..	Adelaide	1924-25	in 7 days' play
1,433 .. .. 30 ..	Brisbane	1962-63	in 5 days' play
1,422 .. .. 40 ..	Adelaide	1928-29	in 7 days' play

The highest match aggregate on the other regular Test grounds are:

| 1,307 runs for 20 wkts | Old Trafford | 1934 | in 4 days' play |
| 1,112 .. .. 23 .. | Edgbaston | 1961 | in 5 days' play |

Lowest match aggregates

The lowest aggregates in completed matches are as follows:

291 runs for 40 wkts	Lord's	1888	in 2 days' play
323 .. .. 30 ..	Old Trafford	1888	in 2 days' play
363 .. .. 40 ..	Oval	1882	in 2 days' play
374 .. .. 40 ..	Sydney	1887-88	in 3 days' play
389 .. .. 38 ..	Oval	1890	in 2 days' play
392 .. .. 40 ..	Oval	1896	in 3 days' play

The three matches of the 1888 series produced respectively aggregates of 291, 497 and 323 runs. These matches followed immediately the one at Sydney in 1887-88 which produced 374 runs.

The lowest aggregates in completed matches this century are as follows:

450 runs for 34 wkts	Brisbane	1950-51	in 3 days' play
451 .. .. 30 ..	Edgbaston	1909	in 3 days' play
521 .. .. 30 ..	Trent Bridge	1921	in 2 days' play
542 .. .. 39 ..	Melbourne	1903-04	in 3 days' play

Biggest victories

Innings and 579 runs	England won	Oval	1938
Innings and 332 runs	Australia won	Brisbane	1946-47
Innings and 230 runs	England won	Adelaide	1891-92
Innings and 225 runs	England won	Melbourne	1911-12
Innings and 217 runs	England won	Oval	1886
Innings and 200 runs	Australia won	Melbourne	1936-37

Altogether England have won by an innings on 18 occasions and Australia on 12. England recorded nine innings victories in these matches before Australia recorded her first.

England won by an innings in successive matches in both 1886 and 1888; Australia did so in both 1897-98 and 1946-47.

The two largest victories (above) were recorded in successive matches, though the Second World War intervened.

The only series in which a side has won by an innings and then lost the next match by an innings is that of 1965-66, when England won the third Test at Sydney by an innings and 93 runs and lost the fourth Test at Adelaide by an innings and 9 runs.

At the Oval in 1938 L. Hutton's innings of 364 in itself exceeded the combined totals of Australia (201 and 123).

The biggest victories by runs have been:

675 runs	England won	Brisbane	1928-29
562 runs	Australia won	Oval	1934
409 runs	Australia won	Lord's	1948
382 runs	Australia won	Adelaide	1894-95
377 runs	Australia won	Sydney	1920-21
365 runs	Australia won	Melbourne	1936-37
338 runs	England won	Adelaide	1932-33
322 runs	England won	Brisbane	1936-37
308 runs	Australia won	Melbourne	1907-08
307 runs	Australia won	Sydney	1924-25

In matches limited by time, the biggest victories with time in hand have been:

England won with 15 hours 17 mins to spare	Oval	1953
Australia won with 13 hours 30 mins to spare	Brisbane	1950-51
England won with 12 hours 13 mins to spare	Headingley	1961

Each of the above three matches was won with more than two full playing days to spare. The only other matches to be so concluded were the second and third Tests (at Melbourne and Sydney – both won by Australia) of 1950-51. Thus three successive matches in this series finished in this manner.

Close finishes

1 wkt	England won at the Oval	1902
1 wkt	England won at Melbourne	1907-08
2 wkts	England won at the Oval	1890
2 wkts	Australia won at Sydney	1907-08
3 runs	Australia won at Old Trafford	1902
6 runs	Australia won at Sydney	1884-85

7 runs	Australia won at the Oval	1882
10 runs	England won at Sydney	1884-85
11 runs	Australia won at Adelaide	1924-25
12 runs	England won at Adelaide	1928-29
13 runs	England won at Sydney	1886-87

England won at the Oval in 1968 with six minutes to spare.

Australia won at Trent Bridge in 1934 with 10 minutes to spare.

Australia won at Headingley in 1948 with 12 minutes to spare.

At Melbourne, in the second Test of 1907-08, the match would have resulted in a tie had G. R. Hazlitt hit the stumps from cover point when England's last pair went for a hurried single. As it was, S. F. Barnes' single brought England a one-wicket victory.

Duration of matches

LONGEST

8 days	Melbourne	1928-29	Fifth Test
†7 days	Sydney	1911-12	Fifth Test
7 days	Sydney	1924-25	First Test
7 days	Melbourne	1924-25	Second Test
7 days	Adelaide	1924-25	Third Test
7 days	Melbourne	1928-29	Third Test
7 days	Adelaide	1928-29	Fourth Test

†No play on third and sixth days because of rain.

Up to the Second World War all Tests in Australia were played to a finish, except those of 1876-77, which were limited to four days; that of 1878-79, which was limited to three days; those of 1881-82, when the first Test, arranged for three days, was extended into the fourth day by agreement, the second and third, arranged for four days, had provision for extension, if necessary, and the fourth, arranged for four days, was limited to that duration; and the final Test of 1891-92, which was limited to six days (but was in fact completed in four). From 1946-47 to 1958-59 (inclusive) Tests were limited to six days, and in 1962-63 and 1965-66 they were limited to five, total playing time (30 hours) remaining the same.

In England, all Tests prior to 1912 were limited to three days. The final Test of that year at the Oval was a 'timeless' Test and lasted four days.* With the exception of 'timeless' Tests in England (see below), all Tests up to and including 1926 were limited to three days, those from 1930 to 1938 (inclusive) to four days, and those from 1948 to 1968 (inclusive) to five days.

'Timeless' Tests in England have been as follows:

*1912	Oval	Lasted four days
1926	Oval	Lasted four days
†1930	Oval	Lasted six days
1934	Oval	Lasted four days
1938	Oval	Lasted four days

*The 1912 Oval Test nominally began as a 'timeless' Test, the Board of Control having previously ruled that in the circumstances applying to the match it would 'be played to a finish.' However, during the course of the match itself the Board of Control deemed it to be a six-day match.

†No play on fifth day because of rain.

At Sydney in 1954-55, England rejected an Australian request to add two days to the fifth Test to make up for some of the time lost by rain. (No play was possible on the first three days.)

At Lord's in 1964, at an emergency meeting on the second scheduled day of the match, Australia rejected an English proposal that an extra 30 minutes' cricket be added to each of the remaining three scheduled days. (No play was possible on the first two days.)

At a meeting of the first-class county captains at Lord's on 8. December, 1902, it was proposed that henceforth Test matches in England should consist of a series of three games, with a week set apart for each game. Though carried by the county captains, the proposal was later rejected and the status quo remained, with a provision in 1905 (for the first time) that the fifth Test would be played to a finish if the result of the rubber depended on it.

After the first four Tests of the 1953 series had been drawn, the English and Australian Boards of Control added an extra day to the fifth Test at the Oval, which was thus a six-day match (though finished in four).

At both meetings of the Imperial Cricket Conference in 1926 – at Lord's on 31 May and at the Oval on 28 July – the Australian representatives requested that consideration be given to allocating four days for future Test matches in England. (The second meeting took place on the day following the fourth successive drawn Test in the 1926 series.) As a result of a meeting at Lord's, on 4 January, 1929, of the Advisory County Cricket Committee – the matter of duration of Tests in England having been placed in their hands by the Board of Control – MCC recommended to the Australian Board of Control that four days be allotted to each of the first four Tests of 1930, the fifth to be played to a finish if neither side, after four Tests, has an advantage. The Australian Board of Control approved this proposal.

SHORTEST

The shortest match (in which there was a result) was at Old Trafford in 1888, when England won before lunch (at 1.55) on the second day.

The following matches have produced a result within two days:

Oval	1882	Australia won by 7 runs
Lord's	1888	Australia won by 61 runs
Oval	1888	England won by innings and 137 runs
Old Trafford	1888	England won by innings and 21 runs
Oval	1890	England won by 2 wickets
Trent Bridge	1921	Australia won by 10 wickets

In the fourth Test at Sydney in 1894-95, Australia won by an innings and 147 runs within two playing days, no play having taken place on the scheduled second day through rain.

In 1888 all three Tests of the series ended in two days.

The most recent Tests to be completed in three days are those at Headingley in 1961 (England won by 8 wickets) and at Headingley in 1938 (Australia won by 5 wickets). At Brisbane in 1950-51 Australia won by 70 runs within three playing days, no play having taken place on the scheduled second day through rain.

The shortest matches in which there was actual play (but in which there was no result) are as follows:

50 minutes' play	Trent Bridge	1926
105 minutes' play	Lord's	1902

Most appearances

Thirty-six players – 15 Englishmen and 21 Australians – have appeared in 25 or more England-Australia Tests, as follows:

ENGLAND		AUSTRALIA	
41 Tests	W. Rhodes	52 Tests	S. E. Gregory
41 Tests	J. B. Hobbs	42 Tests	W. W. Armstrong
35 Tests	J. McC. Blackham	41 Tests	C. Hill
35 Tests	M. C. Cowdrey	40 Tests	V. T. Trumper
33 Tests	W. R. Hammond	39 Tests	M. A. Noble
32 Tests	A. A. Lilley	38 Tests	W. A. S. Oldfield
32 Tests	F. E. Woolley	37 Tests	D. G. Bradman
31 Tests	J. Briggs	37 Tests	R. N. Harvey
31 Tests	T. G. Evans	35 Tests	J. McC. Blackham
29 Tests	T. W. Hayward	33 Tests	J. J. Kelly
28 Tests	E. H. Hendren	31 Tests	G. Giffen
28 Tests	D. C. S. Compton	31 Tests	H. Trumble
27 Tests	H. Sutcliffe	31 Tests	J. Darling
27 Tests	L. Hutton	30 Tests	W. Bardsley
26 Tests	J. T. Tyldesley	29 Tests	K. R. Miller
		29 Tests	R. R. Lindwall
Among Englishmen, J. B.		28 Tests	A. C. Bannerman
Hobbs appeared in most		27 Tests	R. Benaud
matches in Australia – 24.		26 Tests	C. G. Macartney
Among Australians, S. E.		25 Tests	W. M. Woodfull
Gregory appeared in most		25 Tests	A. K. Davidson
matches in England – 29.			

Most consecutive appearances

40 consecutive Tests	V. T. Trumper	for A	1899 to 1911–12
39	M. A. Noble	for A	1897–98 to 1909
37	R. N. Harvey	for A	1948 to 1962–63
36	S. E. Gregory	for A	1891–92 to 1903–04
33	J. J. Kelly	for A	1896 to 1905
33	W. R. Hammond	for E	1928–29 to 1946–47
29	F. E. Woolley	for E	1909 to 1926
28	D. G. Bradman	for A	1932–33 to 1948
25	C. Hill	for A	1901–02 to 1907–08
25	W. M. Woodfull	for A	1926 to 1934

Of the 36 players who appeared in 25 or more Tests, C. G. Macartney made the fewest consecutive appearances (10).

S. E. Gregory's 36 consecutive appearances stretched over nine successive series – the record number.

J. McC. Blackham (A) appeared in the greatest number of different series (or seasons) – 16. He is followed by S. E. Gregory (15). The record for England is shared by J. Briggs and W. Rhodes, who each appeared in 11 different series.

Most runs in a day by a side

					Playing time	Overs bowled in day
475 for 2	by A	Oval	1934	1st day	5 hrs 50 mins	100
458 for 3	by A	Headingley	1930	1st day	5 hrs 52 mins	134
†455 for 1	by A	Headingley	1934	2nd day	6 hrs 20 mins	138·2
435 for 4	by E	Oval	1899	1st day	5 hrs 52 mins	††152
422 for 4	by E	Trent Bridge	1938	1st day	5 hrs 45 mins	125

†Australia took their score from 39 for 3 to 494 for 4.

††This figure is an approximation based on the entire innings, no record being available of the number of overs bowled on the first day.

Australia scored 366 for 3 on the first day at Headingley in 1926 *after being put in*. (The runs were scored in 4¾ hours, rain stopping play early).

At Lord's in 1930 the four days' play produced respectively 405, 424, 423 and 349 runs, the aggregates on the last three days being shared by both sides.

The greatest number of runs scored in a day in Australia (where shorter playing hours have obtained) is 355 for 6 by Australia on the first day at Adelaide in 1903–04. In the first Test at Sydney in 1903–04 successive days' play produced 351 runs (third day) and 350 runs (fourth day).

Fewest runs in a day

					Overs bowled in day
106	Brisbane	1958–59	4th day	E 92–2 to 198	68·2
122	Brisbane	1958–59	3rd day	A 156–6 to 186: E 92–2	64·1
122	Melbourne	1958–59	4th day	A 282–6 to 308: E 87: A 9–1	†48·4

†During the entire day's play only 1 over was bowled by a slow bowler.

On each of the above days the scheduled playing time was 5 hours and there were no interruptions through weather. In the first instance, however, when England scored 106 runs, the day's play was 3 minutes under 5 hours, England's innings ending just before the scheduled close. Similarly, in each of the other two cases play was a few minutes short because the respective overnight innings ended shortly before lunch.

The first four days' play at Brisbane in 1958–59 produced respectively 142, 148, 122 and 106 runs – an average of 129·5 runs per day. The overs bowled were 61·4, 57, 64·1 and 68·2 respectively.

Not until the first day of the fourth Test of the 1958–59 series were as many as 200 runs scored in a day, Australia scoring exactly 200 (for 1) at Adelaide. England bowled only 56 overs in this entire first day, and only 54 overs in the entire second day.

The fewest runs in a day in England is 142 (for 7) off 96 overs in 335 minutes (25 minutes lost through rain) by England on the first day at Headingley in 1953. England scored 38 for 3 before lunch in 100 minutes (rain having delayed the start for 20 minutes); 54 between lunch and tea in 105 minutes (tea being early because of a shower); and 50 between tea and the close in 130 minutes.

On the fifth day at Old Trafford in 1956 Australia scored 121 (for 8) – taking their score from 84 for 2 to 205 – in 4 hours 47 minutes, off 96 overs. (Ten minutes were lost at the start of the day through unfitness of pitch, and 63 minutes at the end because the match finished.)

Most runs by a side before lunch

						Time
196 (for 6 wkts)	by E	Old Trafford	1896	109–4 to 305	on 3rd day	130 mins
174 (for 1 wkt)	by E	Oval	1921	129–4 to 303–5	on 2nd day	147 mins
173 (for 1 wkt)	by A	Old Trafford	1902	Start to 173–1	on 1st day	113 mins
169 (for 7 wkts)	by A	Headingley	1905	Start to 169–7	on 2nd day	150 mins
169 (for 0 wkt)	by E	Trent Bridge	1938	Start to 169–0	on 1st day	120 mins

Scoring rates per 100 balls

		ENGLAND			AUSTRALIA					ENGLAND			AUSTRALIA		
Series	Tests	Runs scored	Balls received	Runs per 100 balls	Runs scored	Balls received	Runs per 100 balls	Series	Tests	Runs scored	Balls received	Runs per 100 balls	Runs scored	Balls received	Runs per 100 balls
1876–77	2	687	1541	44·58	730	2019	36·15	1888	3	604	1411	42·80	507	1380	36·73
1878–79	1	273	548	49·81	275	650	42·30	1890	2	505	1456	34·68	502	1761	28·50
1880	1	477	978	48·77	476	1008	47·22	1891–92	3	1385	3137	44·15	1281	4604	27·82
1881–82	4	1832	4617	39·67	1439	3918	36·27	1893	3	1412	3161	44·66	1149	2211	51·96
1882	1	178	507	35·10	185	572	32·34	1894–95	5	2399	5798	41·37	2822	5911	47·74
1882–83	4	1470	3582	41·03	1378	3795	36·31	1896	3	1168	2329	50·15	1100	2447	44·95
1884	3	1085	2405	45·11	1107	2563	43·15	1897–98	5	2622	6254	41·92	2691	5529	48·67
1884–85	5	1916	4323	44·32	1822	5527	32·96	1899	5	2075	4327	47·97	2475	5488	45·09
1886	3	1117	3189	35·02	792	2430	32·59	1901–02	5	2118	5292	40·02	2260	4950	45·65
1886–87	2	534	1686	31·67	450	1533	29·35	1902	5	1646	3563	46·19	1395	2982	46·78
1887–88	1	250	700	35·71	124	429	28·90	1903–04	5	2333	5669	41·15	2424	4744	51·09

Series	Tests	ENGLAND Runs scored	ENGLAND Balls received	ENGLAND Runs per 100 balls	AUSTRALIA Runs scored	AUSTRALIA Balls received	AUSTRALIA Runs per 100 balls
1905	5	2788	6092	45·76	1862	3381	55·07
1907-08	5	2584	5654	45·70	3187	6379	49·96
1909	5	1568	3758	41·72	2101	4393	47·82
1911-12	5	2833	6008	47·15	2679	5290	50·64
1912	3	933	2302	40·52	472	1306	36·14
1920-21	5	2779	5656	49·13	3368	6244	53·93
1921	5	2243	4469	50·19	1979	3502	56·51
1924-25	5	3067	7150	42·89	3630	8698	41·73
1926	5	2076	4932	42·09	1833	4577	40·04
1928-29	5	3757	9775	38·43	3069	8402	36·52
1930	5	2765	6221	44·44	2886	6378	45·24
1932-33	5	2726	7296	37·36	2490	4960	50·20
1934	5	2494	6721	37·10	3218	6276	51·27
1936-37	5	2416	6297	38·51	2785	6206	44·87
1938	4	2643	5291	49·95	2137	4212	50·73
1946-47	5	2866	7598	37·72	3374	6666	50·61
1948	5	2645	6783	38·99	2981	6405	46·54
1950-51	5	1865	5032	37·06	2249	5140	43·75
1953	5	2074	5983	34·66	2289	5016	45·63
1954-55	5	2176	6075	35·81	2128	4515	47·13
1956	5	1975	5057	39·05	1611	5400	29·83
1958-59	5	2113	6358	33·23	2026	5173	39·16
1961	5	2559	6699	38·19	2400	5263	45·60
1962-63	5	2761	7025	39·30	2903	7135	40·68
1964	5	2326	5937	39·17	2091	5380	38·86
1965-66	5	2578	5792	44·50	2681	6287	42·64
1968	5	2527	6389	39·55	2148	5840	36·78
	203	**94223**	**228823**	**41·17**	**93961**	**214875**	**43·72**

Note: The scoring rates shown take no account of no-balls and wides, which would in all cases slightly reduce the rate.

Youngest players

18 years 232 days	T. W. Garrett	for A	Melbourne	1876-77
19 .. 96 ..	C. Hill	for A	Lord's	1896
19 .. 100 ..	G. R. Hazlitt	for A	Sydney	1907-08
19 .. 149 ..	A. A. Jackson	for A	Adelaide	1928-29
19 .. 197 ..	G. E. Palmer	for A	Oval	1880
19 .. 252 ..	J. J. Ferris	for A	Sydney	1886-87
19 .. 257 ..	R. G. Archer	for A	Old Trafford 1953
19 .. 287 ..	A. C. Bannerman	for A	Melbourne	1878-79
19 .. 288 ..	R. N. Harvey	for A	Headingley	1948
19 .. 298 ..	P. S. McDonnell	for A	Oval	1880
19 .. 301 ..	D. B. Close	for E	Melbourne	1950-51
19 .. 332 ..	S. J. McCabe	for A	Trent Bridge 1930
19 .. 354 ..	K. D. Walters	for A	Brisbane	1965-66
19 .. 363 ..	G. D. McKenzie	for A	Lord's	1961

It will be observed that only one Englishman has played against Australia before his 20th birthday, though D. C. S. Compton was 20 years and 18 days when he made his debut at Trent Bridge in 1938. He is still the youngest player to represent England in these matches at home.

Oldest players

W. G. Grace (E) was aged 50 when he played in 1899; J. Southerton (E) was 49 in 1876-77; H. Ironmonger (A) was 49 in 1932-33; W. Rhodes (E) was 48 in 1926; J. B. Hobbs (E) was 47 in 1930; F. E. Woolley (E) was 47 in 1934; H. Strudwick (E) was 46 in 1926; D. D. J. Blackie (A) was 46 in 1928-29.

The oldest player to represent Australia in England is H. Carter, who was aged 43 in 1921.

In his 50th year, in 1921, C. B. Fry was invited to captain England, but he declined. He was, however, among those named to appear in the Lord's Test that year (under J. W. H. T. Douglas's captaincy) but on the eve of the match he withdrew, being dissatisfied with his form.

J. B. Hobbs (aged 47 in 1930) is the oldest player to appear throughout an entire five-match series.

G. Geary (E) at Trent Bridge in 1934 and H. L. Jackson (E) at Headingley in 1961 both opened the bowling at the age of 40.

J. B. Hobbs scored six centuries for England after the age of 40. W. W. Armstrong (A) and C. G. Macartney (A) each scored three, and E. H. Hendren (E) and W. Bardsley (A) each one. D. G. Bradman (A), A. L. Hassett (A) and J. Ryder (A) were each in their 40th year when they scored their final century in these matches. T. W. Graveney (E), at the age of 41, scored 96 at Edgbaston in 1968.

Oldest players on debut

49 years 119 days	J. Southerton	for E	Melbourne	1876-77
46 .. 253 ..	D. D. J. Blackie	for A	Sydney	1928-29
45 .. 237 ..	H. Ironmonger	for A	Brisbane	1928-29

41 years 337 days	E. R. Wilson	for E	Sydney	1920-21
40 .. 92 ..	H. L. Jackson	for E	Headingley	1961
40 .. 57 ..	L. B. Fishlock	for E	Sydney	1946-47

A. Wood (E) reached the age of 40 on the day after the conclusion of his first, and only, Test against Australia (Oval, 1938).

The captains

ENGLAND	Debut as captain	Series as captain	M	W	L	D	Toss won	Toss lost
A. C. MacLaren	1897-98	5	22	4	11	7	11	11
W. G. Grace	1888	6	13	8	3	2	4	9
P. B. H. May	1956	3	13	3	6	4	9	4
J. W. H. T. Douglas	1911-12	3	12	4	8	0	6	6
L. Hutton	1953	2	10	4	1	5	2	8
E. R. Dexter	1962-63	2	10	1	2	7	6	4
A. P. F. Chapman	1926	3	9	6	1	2	5	4
A. E. Stoddart	1893	3	8	3	4	1	2	6
W. R. Hammond	1938	2	8	1	3	4	6	2
A. Shrewsbury	1884-85	2	7	5	2	0	3	4
N. W. D. Yardley	1946-47	2	6	0	5	1	5	1
M. C. Cowdrey	1961	2	6	1	2	3	5	1
P. F. Warner	1903-04	1	5	3	2	0	2	3
Hon. F. S. Jackson	1905	1	5	2	0	3	5	0
A. E. R. Gilligan	1924-25	1	5	1	4	0	1	4
R. E. S. Wyatt	1930	2	5	1	2	2	4	1
D. R. Jardine	1932-33	1	5	4	1	0	1	4
G. O. Allen	1936-37	1	5	2	3	0	2	3
F. R. Brown	1950-51	1	5	1	4	0	1	4
M. J. K. Smith	1965-66	1	5	1	1	3	3	2
Lord Harris	1878-79	3	4	2	1	1	2	2
A. Shaw	1881-82	1	4	0	2	2	4	0
Hon. Ivo Bligh	1882-83	1	4	2	2	0	3	1
A. G. Steel	1886	2	4	3	1	0	2	2
A. W. Carr	1926	1	4	0	0	4	2	2
F. L. Fane	1907-08	1	3	1	2	0	1	2
C. B. Fry	1912	1	3	1	0	2	3	0
Hon. L. H. Tennyson	1921	1	3	0	1	2	2	1
Jas. Lillywhite, jnr	1876-77	1	2	1	1	0	0	2
A. N. Hornby	1882	2	2	0	1	1	1	1
A. O. Jones	1907-08	1	2	0	2	0	1	1
W. W. Read	1887-88	1	1	1	0	0	0	1
J. C. White	1928-29	1	1	0	1	0	1	0
C. F. Walters	1934	1	1	0	0	1	0	1
T. W. Graveney	1968	1	1	0	0	1	0	1
		203	**66**	**80**	**57**	**105**	**98**

Between 1887-88 (when the long run of amateur England captains began) and 1963 (when the amateur-professional distinction in English first-class cricket was abolished) L. Hutton was the only professional to captain England against Australia. However, two professionals in this period assumed the captaincy in the field on the indisposition of the appointed captain – J. B. Hobbs at Old Trafford in 1926 and D. C. S. Compton at Adelaide in 1950-51.

AUSTRALIA	Debut as captain	Series as captain	M	W	L	D	Toss won	Toss lost
D. G. Bradman	1936-37	4	19	11	3	5	6	13
J. Darling	1899	4	18	5	4	9	5	13
W. L. Murdoch	1880	7	16	5	7	4	7	9
M. A. Noble	1903-04	3	15	8	5	2	11	4
W. M. Woodfull	1930	3	15	5	6	4	8	7
R. Benaud	1958-59	3	14	6	2	6	6	8
W. W. Armstrong	1920-21	2	10	8	0	2	4	6
A. L. Hassett	1950-51	2	10	4	2	4	9	1
I. W. Johnson	1954-55	2	9	2	4	3	3	6
J. McC. Blackham	1884-85	4	8	3	3	2	4	4
G. H. S. Trott	1896	2	8	5	3	0	5	3
H. L. Collins	1924-25	2	8	4	2	2	5	3
R. B. Simpson	1964	2	8	2	0	6	2	6
P. S. McDonnell	1886-87	3	6	1	5	0	4	2
C. Hill	1911-12	1	5	1	4	0	3	2
J. Ryder	1928-29	1	5	1	4	0	2	3
G. Giffen	1894-95	1	4	2	2	0	3	1
W. M. Lawry	1968	1	4	1	1	2	1	3
D. W. Gregory	1876-77	2	3	2	1	0	2	1
H. J. H. Scott	1886	1	3	0	3	0	1	2
S. E. Gregory	1912	1	3	0	1	2	0	3
T. P. Horan	1884-85	1	2	0	2	0	1	1
H. Trumble	1901-02	1	2	2	0	0	1	1
W. Bardsley	1926	1	2	0	0	2	1	1
B. C. Booth	1965-66	1	2	0	1	1	1	1
H. H. Massie	1884-85	1	1	1	0	0	1	0
A. R. Morris	1954-55	1	1	0	1	0	1	0
R. N. Harvey	1961	1	1	1	0	0	0	1
B. N. Jarman	1968	1	1	0	0	1	1	0
			203	80	66	57	98	105

Of Australia's 29 captains, all have been chosen while playing for either New South Wales or Victoria except five – Giffen, Darling, Hill, Bradman and Jarman (all South Australia).

The only occasion on which *both* the regular captains did not play in a Test was at Headingley in 1968, when M. C. Cowdrey (who had been appointed for the series) and W. M. Lawry both stood down through injury, the sides being led by T. W. Graveney (who had captained England in the field in the previous Test at Edgbaston during Cowdrey's indisposition) and B. N. Jarman.

W. W. Armstrong captained Australia in eight successive victories (they were his first eight matches as captain) – the record sequence for a captain in these matches.

M. A. Noble, in his first 13 matches as captain, never took part in a draw.

YOUNGEST AND OLDEST CAPTAINS
The youngest player to captain England was the Hon. Ivo Bligh, who was 23 years 292 days at Melbourne in 1882-83. The youngest Australian captain in these matches was W. L. Murdoch, who was 24 years 324 days at the Oval in 1880.

The oldest player to captain England was W. G. Grace, who was 50 years 318 days on the opening day at Trent Bridge in 1899. The oldest player on his first appearance as captain for England is T. W. Graveney, who was 41 years 39 days at Headingley in 1968. (Both W. G. Grace, in 1888, and C. B. Fry, in 1912, first captained England at the age of 40.)

The oldest player to captain Australia was W. Bardsley, who was 42 years 229 days on the opening day at Old Trafford in 1926. Bardsley

is also the oldest player on his first appearance as captain for Australia, being 42 years 215 days at Headingley in 1926. (S. E. Gregory, in 1912, was 42 – but younger than Bardsley – and W. W. Armstrong, in 1920-21, was 41 when first captaining Australia.)

CAPTAINS ON DEBUT
The following players captained their country on their first appearance in England-Australia Tests:
England: Hon. Ivo Bligh, F. R. Brown, A. W. Carr, J. W. H. T. Douglas, F. L. Fane, A. E. R. Gilligan, Lord Harris, Jas. Lillywhite, jnr. (in first Test of all), C. F. Walters, P. F. Warner and R. E. S. Wyatt.
Australia: D. W. Gregory (in first Test of all).
Six players were captain in *every* England-Australia Test in which they appeared: Hon. Ivo Bligh (4 matches), A. W. Carr (4), A. E. R. Gilligan (5), Lord Harris (4), Jas. Lillywhite, jnr. (2) – all for England; and D. W. Gregory (3 matches) for Australia.

CONSECUTIVE TESTS AS CAPTAIN
The following have captained their country in most consecutive England-Australia Tests:

19 consecutive Tests by D. G. Bradman (A)	1936-37 to 1948
15 consecutive Tests by W. M. Woodfull (A)	1930 to 1934
14 consecutive Tests by W. L. Murdoch (A)	1880 to 1884-85
14 consecutive Tests by A. C. MacLaren (E)	1899 to 1902

BEST PERFORMANCES BY CAPTAINS
Batting: Of the 64 captains in England-Australia Tests, D. G. Bradman (A), in his 19 matches as captain, has scored most runs (2,432), most centuries (10) and has the highest average (90·07).

These performances are unapproached by any English captain, only two of whom have reached 1,000 runs – A. C. MacLaren (1,156 runs, average 35·03) and P. B. H. May (1,091 runs, average 54·55). The highest average by an English captain is the Hon. F. S. Jackson's 70·28 (in five matches). The greatest number of centuries by an English captain is two – by A. C. MacLaren (in 1897-98 and 1901-02), Hon. F. S. Jackson (both in 1905) and P. B. H. May (in 1956 and 1958-59).

Among Australians, Bradman's record is likewise unapproached. Only one other captain has reached 1,000 runs – M. A. Noble (1,002 runs, average 38·53). The best averages, after Bradman's, are 81·30 by R. B. Simpson and 56·00 by W. W. Armstrong. Armstrong made three centuries (all in 1920-21) as captain against England, W. L. Murdoch two (in 1880 and 1884), A. L. Hassett two (both in 1953) and R. B. Simpson two (in 1964 and 1965-66).

D. G. Bradman, P. B. H. May and R. B. Simpson share the distinction of scoring centuries while captain in both England and Australia. Bradman actually scored as many as *five* centuries in each country as captain.

The highest aggregate by a captain in a series is 810 runs by D. G. Bradman in 1936-37; his 680 in 1946-47 is second. The highest by an England captain is 492 by the Hon. F. S. Jackson in 1905.

The highest innings played by a captain have been:

311	R. B. Simpson	for A	Old Trafford	1964
270	D. G. Bradman	for A	Melbourne	1936-37
240	W. R. Hammond	for E	Lord's	1938
234	D. G. Bradman	for A	Sydney	1946-47
225	R. B. Simpson	for A	Adelaide	1965-66
212	D. G. Bradman	for A	Adelaide	1936-37
211	W. L. Murdoch	for A	Oval	1884

A. E. Stoddart's 173 at Melbourne in 1894-95 is the highest by an England captain in Australia.

In only four matches have *both* captains scored a century – at Lord's in 1930, 1938 and 1953, and at Old Trafford in 1964.

Bowling: Most wickets by a captain in an innings have been:

7-100	M. A. Noble	for A	Sydney	1903-04
6- 70	R. Benaud	for A	Old Trafford	1961
6-115	R. Benaud	for A	Brisbane	1962-63
6-155	G. Giffen	for A	Melbourne	1894-95
5- 26	G. Giffen	for A	Sydney	1894-95

5- 36	G. O. Allen	for E	Brisbane	1936-37
5- 46	J. W. H. T. Douglas	for E	Melbourne	1911-12
5- 49	F. R. Brown	for E	Melbourne	1950-51
5- 52	Hon. F. S. Jackson	for E	Trent Bridge	1905
5- 62	H. Trumble	for A	Melbourne	1901-02
5- 76	G. Giffen	for A	Adelaide	1894-95
5- 83	R. Benaud	for A	Sydney	1958-59
5- 91	R. Benaud	for A	Adelaide	1958-59

No captain has taken 10 wickets in a match, and only one – R. Benaud – has taken 9: he did it twice, in successive matches in 1958-59 – 9-177 at Sydney and 9-173 at Adelaide.

R. Benaud's 31 wickets (average 18·83) in 1958-59 is the record aggregate for a captain in a series.

The greatest number of wickets taken by an English captain in a match is 8 (for 107) by G. O. Allen at Brisbane in 1936-37, and F. R. Brown's 18 wickets (average 21·61) in 1950-51 is the record aggregate for an English captain in a series.

Captains who sent opponents in

The following captains put their opponents in to bat on winning the toss:

P. S. McDonnell (A)	Sydney	1886-87	Lost by 13 runs
P. S. McDonnell (A)	Sydney	1887-88	Lost by 126 runs
G. Giffen (A)	Melbourne 1894-95		Lost by 94 runs
A. E. Stoddart (E)	Sydney	1894-95	Lost by inns and 147 runs
A. C. MacLaren (E)	Melbourne 1901-02		Lost by 229 runs
A. O. Jones (E)	Sydney	1907-08	Lost by 49 runs
M. A. Noble (A)	Lord's	1909	Won by 9 wickets
J. W. H. T. Douglas (E)	Melbourne 1911-12		Won by inns and 225 runs
A. W. Carr (E)	Headingley 1926		Drawn
A. L. Hassett (E)	Headingley 1953		Drawn
L. Hutton (E)	Brisbane	1954-55	Lost by inns and 154 runs
A. R. Morris (A)	Sydney	1954-55	Lost by 38 runs
I. W. Johnson (A)	Sydney	1954-55	Drawn
P. B. H. May (E)	Adelaide	1958-59	Lost by 10 wickets
R. Benaud (A)	Melbourne 1958-59		Won by 9 wickets
E. R. Dexter (E)	Lord's	1964	Drawn

P. S. McDonnell, G. Giffen and A. R. Morris each put their opponents in to bat in their first match as captain in England-Australia Tests. (In Morris's case it was his only Test as captain.)

In 1954-55 – at Brisbane and Sydney – the captains put their opponents in to bat in successive matches, as did the captains at Adelaide and Melbourne in 1958-59.

Declarations

England have declared on 32 occasions in these matches and Australia on 19.

Declarations in Australia before matches were limited in duration were comparatively rare, there being only 4 instances up to the Second World War: the first did not occur until 1928-29. Altogether there have been 17 declarations in Australia and 34 in England.

In England the laws of cricket on declarations – but not experimental rules – have applied to all Tests against Australia with the exception of those of 1956, when law 15 was in abeyance and the experimental rule allowing a captain to declare on the first day applied. In fact, there has never been a first-day declaration in these matches.

Declaration landmarks

1893: First declaration in a Test in England (by A. E. Stoddart at Lord's).

1899: First declaration by Australia (by J. Darling at Trent Bridge).

1902: First declaration on second day and also first declaration of a first innings (by A. C. MacLaren at Edgbaston).

1905: First declaration to bring victory (by Hon. F. S. Jackson at Trent Bridge).

1928-29: First declaration in a Test in Australia (by A. P. F. Chapman at Brisbane).

1934: First declaration in both innings (by R. E. S. Wyatt at Old Trafford).

1936-37: First declaration by both captains (by D. G. Bradman and G. O. Allen at Melbourne).

1938: First declaration by both captains in England (by W. R. Hammond and D. G. Bradman at Trent Bridge).

In the third Test at Melbourne in 1936-37 both captains declared on the same day (within 143 minutes of each other). At Brisbane in 1950-51 both captains again declared on the same day (within 79 minutes of each other).

The only time a side has won in the face of a third-innings declaration is at Headingley in 1948, when Australia won by 7 wickets after England had declared at 365 for 8.

The lowest total at which an innings has been declared is 32 for 7 by Australia at Brisbane in 1950-51. England's lowest is 68 for 7, in the same match.

Most runs

	Tests	Inns	N.O.	Runs	H.S.	Av.
D. G. Bradman (A)	37	63	7	5,028	334	89·78
J. B. Hobbs (E)	41	71	4	3,636	187	54·26
W. R. Hammond (E)	33	58	3	2,852	251	51·85
H. Sutcliffe (E)	27	46	5	2,741	194	66·85
C. Hill (A)	41	76	1	2,660	188	35·46
L. Hutton (E)	27	49	6	2,428	364	56·46
R. N. Harvey (A)	37	68	5	2,416	167	38·34
V. T. Trumper (A)	40	74	5	2,263	185*	32·79
S. E. Gregory (A)	52	92	7	2,193	201	25·80
M. C. Cowdrey (E)	35	62	4	2,186	113	37·68
W. W. Armstrong (A)	42	71	9	2,172	158	35·03
K. F. Barrington (E)	23	39	6	2,111	256	63·96
A. R. Morris (A)	24	43	2	2,080	206	50·73

Only two players have reached an aggregate of 2,000 runs in one country – D. G. Bradman (2,674 runs in England and 2,354 runs in Australia) and J. B. Hobbs (2,493 runs in Australia).

J. B. Hobbs, H. Sutcliffe, D. G. Bradman, L. Hutton, A. R. Morris, R. N. Harvey and K. F. Barrington all exceeded 1,000 runs in both England and Australia.

Apart from D. G. Bradman's 2,674 runs in England, only five other Australians – S. J. McCabe, C. G. Macartney, A. R. Morris, R. N. Harvey and W. M. Lawry – have scored 1,000 runs in England, the highest among these five being 1,055 by McCabe. Bradman's record is also 1,259 ahead of the nearest Englishman, the Hon. F. S. Jackson (in one more Test than Bradman) having scored 1,415 runs in England.

Most centuries

A total of 297 centuries have been scored in the 203 matches – 143 for England, and 154 for Australia. The longest sequence of matches in which no century was recorded is 9 (first Test of 1886-87 to first Test of 1891-92 inclusive).

The centuries have been scored as follows:

	For E	For A	Total
In England	66	64	130
In Australia	77	90	167
	143	**154**	**297**

For England 60 batsmen have scored a century, and 57 have done so for Australia.

The following have scored most centuries:

19 centuries	D. G. Bradman	for A	in 37 Tests
12 centuries	J. B. Hobbs	for E	in 41 Tests
9 centuries	W. R. Hammond	for E	in 33 Tests
8 centuries	H. Sutcliffe	for E	in 27 Tests
8 centuries	A. R. Morris	for A	in 24 Tests
7 centuries	M. Leyland	for E	in 20 Tests
7 centuries	W. M. Lawry	for A	in 24 Tests
6 centuries	V. T. Trumper	for A	in 40 Tests
6 centuries	W. M. Woodfull	for A	in 25 Tests

6 centuries R. N. Harvey for A in 37 Tests
5 centuries A. C. MacLaren for E in 35 Tests
5 centuries Hon. F. S. Jackson for E in 20 Tests
5 centuries C. G. Macartney for A in 26 Tests
5 centuries W. H. Ponsford for A in 20 Tests
5 centuries D. C. S. Compton for E in 28 Tests
5 centuries L. Hutton for E in 27 Tests

5 centuries K. F. Barrington for E in 23 Tests
5 centuries M. C. Cowdrey for E in 35 Tests

D. G. Bradman (A) scored the greatest number of centuries in England (11), followed by the Hon. F. S. Jackson (E) with 5.

J. B. Hobbs (E) scored the greatest number of centuries in Australia (9), followed by D. G. Bradman (A) with 8.

Centuries

ENGLAND

Score	Player	Venue	Year
132*	R. Abel	Sydney	1891-92
120	L. E. G. Ames	Lord's	1934
185	R. W. Barber	Sydney	1965-66
134	W. Barnes	Adelaide	1884-85
129	C. J. Barnett	Adelaide	1936-37
126	C. J. Barnett	Trent Bridge	1938
132*	K. F. Barrington	Adelaide	1962-63
101	K. F. Barrington	Sydney	1962-63
256	K. F. Barrington	Old Trafford	1964
102	K. F. Barrington	Adelaide	1965-66
115	K. F. Barrington	Melbourne	1965-66
113	G. Boycott	Oval	1964
103*	L. C. Braund	Adelaide	1901-02
102	L. C. Braund	Sydney	1903-04
121	J. Briggs	Melbourne	1884-85
140	J. T. Brown	Melbourne	1894-95
121	A. P. F. Chapman	Lord's	1930
102†	D. C. S. Compton	Trent Bridge	1938
147 } 103*	D. C. S. Compton	Adelaide	1946-47
184	D. C. S. Compton	Trent Bridge	1948
145*	D. C. S. Compton	Old Trafford	1948
102	M. C. Cowdrey	Melbourne	1954-55
100*	M. C. Cowdrey	Sydney	1958-59
113	M. C. Cowdrey	Melbourne	1962-63
104	M. C. Cowdrey	Melbourne	1965-66
104	M. C. Cowdrey	Edgbaston	1968
180	E. R. Dexter	Edgbaston	1961
174	E. R. Dexter	Old Trafford	1964
158	B. L. D'Oliveira	Oval	1968
173†	K. S. Duleepsinhji	Lord's	1930
120†	J. H. Edrich	Lord's	1964
109	J. H. Edrich	Melbourne	1965-66
103	J. H. Edrich	Sydney	1965-66
164	J. H. Edrich	Oval	1968
119	W. J. Edrich	Sydney	1946-47
111	W. J. Edrich	Headingley	1948
287†	R. E. Foster	Sydney	1903-04
144	C. B. Fry	Oval	1905
152†	W. G. Grace	Oval	1880
170	W. G. Grace	Oval	1886
111	T. W. Graveney	Sydney	1954-55
119†	G. Gunn	Sydney	1907-08
122*	G. Gunn	Sydney	1907-08
102*	W. Gunn	Old Trafford	1893
251	W. R. Hammond	Sydney	1928-29
200	W. R. Hammond	Melbourne	1928-29
119* } 177	W. R. Hammond	Adelaide	1928-29
113	W. R. Hammond	Headingley	1930
112	W. R. Hammond	Sydney	1932-33
101	W. R. Hammond	Sydney	1932-33
231*	W. R. Hammond	Sydney	1936-37
240	W. R. Hammond	Lord's	1938
169*	J. Hardstaff, jnr.	Oval	1938
130	T. W. Hayward	Old Trafford	1899
137	T. W. Hayward	Oval	1899
114	J. W. Hearne	Melbourne	1911-12
127*	E. H. Hendren	Lord's	1926
169	E. H. Hendren	Brisbane	1928-29
132	E. H. Hendren	Old Trafford	1934
126*	J. B. Hobbs	Melbourne	1911-12
187	J. B. Hobbs	Adelaide	1911-12
178	J. B. Hobbs	Melbourne	1911-12
107	J. B. Hobbs	Lord's	1912
122	J. B. Hobbs	Melbourne	1920-21
123	J. B. Hobbs	Adelaide	1920-21
115	J. B. Hobbs	Sydney	1924-25
154	J. B. Hobbs	Melbourne	1924-25
119	J. B. Hobbs	Adelaide	1924-25
119	J. B. Hobbs	Lord's	1926
100	J. B. Hobbs	Oval	1926
142	J. B. Hobbs	Melbourne	1928-29
126	K. L. Hutchings	Melbourne	1907-08
100†	L. Hutton	Trent Bridge	1938
364	L. Hutton	Oval	1938
122*	L. Hutton	Sydney	1946-47
156*	L. Hutton	Adelaide	1950-51
145	L. Hutton	Lord's	1953
103	F. S. Jackson	Oval	1893
118	F. S. Jackson	Oval	1899
128	Hon. F. S. Jackson	Old Trafford	1902
144*	Hon. F. S. Jackson	Headingley	1905
113	Hon. F. S. Jackson	Old Trafford	1905
104	G. L. Jessop	Oval	1902
137†	M. Leyland	Melbourne	1928-29
109	M. Leyland	Lord's	1934
153	M. Leyland	Old Trafford	1934
110	M. Leyland	Oval	1934
126	M. Leyland	Brisbane	1936-37
111*	M. Leyland	Melbourne	1936-37
187	M. Leyland	Oval	1938
130	A. C. MacLaren	Melbourne	1894-95
109	A. C. MacLaren	Sydney	1897-98
124	A. C. MacLaren	Adelaide	1897-98
116	A. C. MacLaren	Sydney	1901-02
140	A. C. MacLaren	Trent Bridge	1905
117	H. Makepeace	Melbourne	1920-21
104	P. B. H. May	Sydney	1954-55
101	P. B. H. May	Headingley	1956
113	P. B. H. May	Melbourne	1958-59
182*	C. P. Mead	Oval	1921
102†	Nawab of Pataudi	Sydney	1932-33
216*	E. Paynter	Trent Bridge	1938
154*†	K. S. Ranjitsinhji	Old Trafford	1896
175	K. S. Ranjitsinhji	Sydney	1897-98
117	W. W. Read	Oval	1884
179	W. Rhodes	Melbourne	1911-12
104	P. E. Richardson	Old Trafford	1956
135	A. C. Russell	Adelaide	1920-21
101	A. C. Russell	Old Trafford	1921
102*	A. C. Russell	Oval	1921
105	J. Sharp	Oval	1909
113	Rev. D. S. Sheppard	Old Trafford	1956
113	Rev. D. S. Sheppard	Melbourne	1962-63
105*	A. Shrewsbury	Melbourne	1884-85
164	A. Shrewsbury	Lord's	1886
106	A. Shrewsbury	Lord's	1893
156*	R. T. Simpson	Melbourne	1950-51
135*	A. G. Steel	Sydney	1882-83
148	A. G. Steel	Lord's	1884
134	A. E. Stoddart	Adelaide	1891-92
173	A. E. Stoddart	Melbourne	1894-95
112†	R. Subba Row	Edgbaston	1961
137	R. Subba Row	Oval	1961
115†	H. Sutcliffe	Sydney	1924-25
176 } 127	H. Sutcliffe	Melbourne	1924-25
143	H. Sutcliffe	Melbourne	1924-25
161	H. Sutcliffe	Oval	1926
135	H. Sutcliffe	Melbourne	1928-29
161	H. Sutcliffe	Oval	1930
194	H. Sutcliffe	Sydney	1932-33
138	J. T. Tyldesley	Edgbaston	1902
100	J. T. Tyldesley	Headingley	1905
112*	J. T. Tyldesley	Oval	1905
149	G. Ulyett	Melbourne	1881-82
117	A. Ward	Sydney	1894-95
109†	W. Watson	Lord's	1953
112	C. Washbrook	Melbourne	1946-47
143	C. Washbrook	Headingley	1948
133*	F. E. Woolley	Sydney	1911-12
123	F. E. Woolley	Sydney	1924-25

†scored on debut

AUSTRALIA

Score	Player	Venue	Year
133*	W. W. Armstrong	Melbourne	1907-08
158	W. W. Armstrong	Sydney	1920-21
121	W. W. Armstrong	Adelaide	1920-21
123*	W. W. Armstrong	Melbourne	1920-21
118	C. L. Badcock	Melbourne	1936-37
165*†	C. Bannerman	Melbourne	1876-77
136 } 130	W. Bardsley	Oval	1909
193*	W. Bardsley	Lord's	1926
234	S. G. Barnes	Sydney	1946-47
141	S. G. Barnes	Lord's	1948
128	G. J. Bonnor	Sydney	1884-85
112	B. C. Booth	Brisbane	1962-63
103	B. C. Booth	Melbourne	1962-63
112	D. G. Bradman	Melbourne	1928-29
123	D. G. Bradman	Melbourne	1928-29
131	D. G. Bradman	Trent Bridge	1930
254	D. G. Bradman	Lord's	1930
334	D. G. Bradman	Headingley	1930
232	D. G. Bradman	Oval	1930
103*	D. G. Bradman	Melbourne	1932-33
304	D. G. Bradman	Headingley	1934
244	D. G. Bradman	Oval	1934
270	D. G. Bradman	Melbourne	1936-37

212	D. G. Bradman	Adelaide	1936-37	115	A. L. Hassett	Trent Bridge	1953	182	A. R. Morris	Headingley	1948
169	D. G. Bradman	Melbourne	1936-37	104	A. L. Hassett	Lord's	1953	196	A. R. Morris	Oval	1948
144*	D. G. Bradman	Trent Bridge	1938	112	H.S.T.L.Hendry	Sydney	1928-29	206	A. R. Morris	Adelaide	1950-51
102*	D. G. Bradman	Lord's	1938	188	C. Hill	Melbourne	1897-98	153	A. R. Morris	Brisbane	1954-55
103	D. G. Bradman	Headingley	1938	135	C. Hill	Lord's	1899	153*	W. L. Murdoch	Oval	1880
187	D. G. Bradman	Brisbane	1946-47	119	C. Hill	Sheffield	1902	211	W. L. Murdoch	Oval	1884
234	D. G. Bradman	Sydney	1946-47	160	C. Hill	Adelaide	1907-08	133	M. A. Noble	Sydney	1903-04
138	D. G. Bradman	Trent Bridge	1948	124	T. P. Horan	Melbourne	1881-82	117	N. C. O'Neill	Oval	1961
173*	D. G. Bradman	Headingley	1948	140	F. A. Iredale	Adelaide	1894-95	100	N. C. O'Neill	Adelaide	1962-63
105	W. A. Brown	Lord's	1934	108	F. A. Iredale	Old Trafford	1896	116	C. E. Pellew	Melbourne	1920-21
133	W. A. Brown	Trent Bridge	1938	164†	A. A. Jackson	Adelaide	1928-29	104	C. E. Pellew	Adelaide	1920-21
206*	W. A. Brown	Lord's	1938	147	C. Kelleway	Adelaide	1920-21	110†	W. H. Ponsford	Sydney	1924-25
181	P. J. Burge	Oval	1961	100	A. F. Kippax	Melbourne	1928-29	128	W. H. Ponsford	Melbourne	1924-25
103	P. J. Burge	Sydney	1962-63	130	W. M. Lawry	Lord's	1961	110	W. H. Ponsford	Oval	1930
160	P. J. Burge	Headingley	1964	102	W. M. Lawry	Old Trafford	1961	181	W. H. Ponsford	Headingley	1934
120	P. J. Burge	Melbourne	1965-66	106	W. M. Lawry	Old Trafford	1964	266	W. H. Ponsford	Oval	1934
101*†| J. W. Burke	Adelaide	1950-51	166	W. M. Lawry	Brisbane	1965-66	143*	V. S. Ransford	Lord's	1909
104†	H. L. Collins	Sydney	1920-21	119	W. M. Lawry	Adelaide	1965-66	100	A. J. Richardson	Headingley	1926
162	H. L. Collins	Adelaide	1920-21	108	W. M. Lawry	Melbourne	1965-66	138	V. Y. Richardson	Melbourne	1924-25
114	H. L. Collins	Sydney	1924-25	135	W. M. Lawry	Oval	1968	201*	J. Ryder	Adelaide	1924-25
307	R. M. Cowper	Melbourne	1965-66	100	R. R. Lindwall	Melbourne	1946-47	112	J. Ryder	Melbourne	1928-29
101	J. Darling	Sydney	1897-98	134	J. J. Lyons	Sydney	1891-92	102	H. J. H. Scott	Oval	1884
178	J. Darling	Adelaide	1897-98	170	C. G. Macartney	Sydney	1920-21	311	R. B. Simpson	Old Trafford	1964
160	J. Darling	Sydney	1897-98	115	C. G. Macartney	Headingley	1921	225	R. B. Simpson	Adelaide	1965-66
104†	R. A. Duff	Melbourne	1901-02	133*	C. G. Macartney	Lord's	1926	108	J. M. Taylor	Sydney	1924-25
146	R. A. Duff	Oval	1905	151	C. G. Macartney	Headingley	1926	143	G. H. S. Trott	Lord's	1896
100	J.H.W. Fingleton	Brisbane	1936-37	109	C. G. Macartney	Old Trafford	1926	135*	V. T. Trumper	Lord's	1899
136	J.H.W. Fingleton	Melbourne	1936-37	187*	S. J. McCabe	Sydney	1932-33	104	V. T. Trumper	Old Trafford	1902
161	G. Giffen	Sydney	1894-95	137	S. J. McCabe	Old Trafford	1934	185*	V. T. Trumper	Sydney	1903-04
107†	H. Graham	Lord's	1893	112	S. J. McCabe	Melbourne	1936-37	113	V. T. Trumper	Adelaide	1903-04
105	H. Graham	Sydney	1894-95	232	S. J. McCabe	Trent Bridge	1938	166	V. T. Trumper	Sydney	1907-08
100	J. M. Gregory	Melbourne	1920-21	104*	C. L. McCool	Melbourne	1946-47	113	V. T. Trumper	Sydney	1911-12
201	S. E. Gregory	Sydney	1894-95	170	C. C. McDonald	Adelaide	1958-59	155†	K. D. Walters	Brisbane	1965-66
103	S. E. Gregory	Lord's	1896	133	C. C. McDonald	Melbourne	1958-59	115	K. D. Walters	Melbourne	1965-66
117	S. E. Gregory	Oval	1899	147	P. S. McDonnell	Sydney	1881-82	141	W. M. Woodfull	Headingley	1926
112	S. E. Gregory	Adelaide	1903-04	103	P. S. McDonnell	Oval	1884	117	W. M. Woodfull	Old Trafford	1926
116†	R. J. Hartigan	Adelaide	1907-08	124	P. S. McDonnell	Adelaide	1884-85	111	W. M. Woodfull	Sydney	1928-29
112†	R. N. Harvey	Headingley	1948	112	C. E. McLeod	Melbourne	1897-98	107	W. M. Woodfull	Melbourne	1928-29
122	R. N. Harvey	Old Trafford	1953	141*	K. R. Miller	Adelaide	1946-47	102	W. M. Woodfull	Melbourne	1928-29
162	R. N. Harvey	Brisbane	1954-55	145*	K. R. Miller	Sydney	1950-51	155	W. M. Woodfull	Lord's	1930
167	R. N. Harvey	Melbourne	1958-59	109	K. R. Miller	Lord's	1953				
114	R. N. Harvey	Edgbaston	1961	155	A. R. Morris	Melbourne	1946-47	†scored on debut			
154	R. N. Harvey	Adelaide	1962-63	122 } 124* }	A. R. Morris	Adelaide	1946-47				
128	A. L. Hassett	Brisbane	1946-47								
137	A. L. Hassett	Trent Bridge	1948	105	A. R. Morris	Lord's	1948				

Quickest time to 1,000 runs

1 year 223 days after debut	D. G. Bradman (A)	Headingley	1930
1 year 224 days after debut	W. R. Hammond (E)	Headingley	1930
1 year 238 days after debut	H. Sutcliffe (E)	Oval	1926
1 year 241 days after debut	A. R. Morris (A)	Headingley	1948

The above four players also reached their 1,000th run in the fewest Tests and the fewest innings, as follows:

D. G. Bradman	in 7th Test and 13th innings	Headingley	1930
W. R. Hammond	in 8th Test and 14th innings	Headingley	1930
A. R. Morris	in 9th Test and 16th innings	Headingley	1948
H. Sutcliffe	in 10th Test and 15th innings	Oval	1926

The youngest player to reach 1,000 runs is D. G. Bradman (A), aged 21 years 318 days at Headingley in 1930. The youngest Englishman to reach 1,000 runs is W. R. Hammond, aged 27 years 23 days at Headingley in 1930. (Bradman and Hammond reached their 1,000 runs on successive days.)

The quickest time to 2,000 runs is 5 years 233 days after debut by D. G. Bradman (A) at Headingley in 1934. The quickest by an Englishman is 7 years 350 days by H. Sutcliffe at Sydney in 1932-33.

D. G. Bradman (A) holds the record for reaching 2,000 runs in the fewest Tests (17) and the fewest innings (29). The best by an Englishman is by H. Sutcliffe (19 Tests and 31 innings).

The youngest player to reach 2,000 runs is D. G. Bradman (A), aged 25 years 328 days at Headingley in 1934. The youngest Englishman to reach 2,000 runs is W. R. Hammond, aged 33 years 183 days at Sydney in 1936-37.

Most runs in a series

		Tests	Inns.	N.O.	Runs	H.S.	Av.	100s	50s	0s
D. G. Bradman (A)	1930	5	7	0	974	334	139·14	4	0	0
W. R. Hammond (E)	1928-29	5	9	1	905	251	113·12	4	0	0
D. G. Bradman (A)	1936-37	5	9	0	810	270	90·00	3	1	2
D. G. Bradman (A)	1934	5	8	0	758	304	94·75	2	1	0
H. Sutcliffe (E)	1924-25	5	9	0	734	176	81·55	4	2	1
A. R. Morris (A)	1948	5	9	1	696	196	87·00	3	3	0
D. G. Bradman (A)	1946-47	5	8	1	680	234	97·14	2	3	1
J. B. Hobbs (E)	1911-12	5	9	1	662	187	82·75	3	1	0
W. M. Lawry (A)	1965-66	5	7	0	592	166	84·57	3	2	1
K. F. Barrington (E)	1962-63	5	10	2	582	132*	72·75	2	3	0
V. T. Trumper (A)	1903-04	5	10	1	574	185*	63·77	2	3	1
J. B. Hobbs (E)	1924-25	5	9	0	573	154	63·66	3	2	1
W. H. Ponsford (A)	1934	4	7	1	569	266	94·83	2	1	0
D. C. S. Compton (E)	1948	5	10	1	562	184	62·44	2	2	1
H. L. Collins (A)	1920-21	5	9	0	557	162	61·88	2	3	0
J. H. Edrich (E)	1968	5	9	0	554	164	61·55	1	4	0
J. M. Taylor (A)	1924-25	5	10	0	541	108	54·10	1	4	1
J. Darling (A)	1897-98	5	8	0	537	178	67·12	3	0	0
L. Hutton (E)	1950-51	5	10	4	533	156*	88·83	1	4	0
K. F. Barrington (E)	1964	5	8	1	531	256	75·85	1	2	0
C. Hill (A)	1901-02	5	10	0	521	99	52·10	0	4	1
C. C. McDonald (A)	1958-59	5	9	1	519	170	64·87	2	1	0
W. A. Brown (A)	1938	4	8	1	512	206*	73·14	2	1	0
D. G. Bradman (A)	1948	5	9	2	508	173*	72·57	2	1	2
J. B. Hobbs (E)	1920-21	5	10	0	505	123	50·50	2	1	0
A. R. Morris (A)	1946-47	5	8	1	503	155	71·85	3	1	0

D. G. Bradman (A) reached 500 runs in a series most times – five. J. B. Hobbs (E) did so three times.

D. G. Bradman (A), A. R. Morris (A) and K. F. Barrington (E) are the only batsmen to score 500 runs in a series in both England and Australia.

C. Hill (A), in 1901-02 (above), exceeded 500 runs without scoring a century. The highest aggregate in a series by an Englishman without including a century is 481 by E. R. Dexter in 1962-63: like Hill, his highest score was 99.

Highest average in a series *(Qualification: 3 completed innings)*

		Inns.	N.O.	Runs	H.S.	100s	Av.
D. G. Bradman (A)	1930	7	0	974	334	4	139·14
L. Hutton (E)	1938	4	0	473	364	2	118·25
W. R. Hammond (E)	1928-29	9	1	905	251	4	113·12
D. G. Bradman (A)	1938	6	2	434	144*	3	108·50
E. Paynter (E)	1938	6	2	407	216*	1	101·75
D. G. Bradman (A)	1946-47	8	1	680	234	2	97·14
W. H. Ponsford (A)	1934	7	1	569	266	2	94·83
D. G. Bradman (A)	1934	8	0	758	304	2	94·75
C. G. Macartney (A)	1926	6	1	473	151	3	94·60
P. B. H. May (E)	1956	7	2	453	101	1	90·60
D. G. Bradman (A)	1936-37	9	0	810	270	3	90·00

C. G. Macartney in 1926 (above) broke his own record average of 86·66 in 1920-21, which in turn broke J. B. Hobbs' 82·75 in 1911-12.

Hobbs' average remained the best by an Englishman for 17 years (until 1928-29, above).

D. G. Bradman (A) averaged 90 or over in four successive series – a performance unapproached by any other player.

A series average of 80 or over has been achieved five times by D. G. Bradman (A) and twice by J. B. Hobbs, H. Sutcliffe and L. Hutton for England and C. G. Macartney for Australia.

J. B. Hobbs was aged 43 when he averaged 81·00 in 1926.

D. G. Bradman (A) averaged 50 or over in eight different series; J. B. Hobbs (E) and H. Sutcliffe (E) each did so in six. (Bradman and Sutcliffe *never* failed to average above 50 in any series in which they took part.)

D. G. Bradman (A) and L. Hutton (E) each headed the combined averages in three different series.

Highest individual innings

Twenty-seven double-centuries have been scored – 8 for England and 19 for Australia:

	6s	5s	4s					
364	–	–	35	out of 770 in 797 mins	L. Hutton	for E	Oval	1938
334	–	–	46	out of 506 in 383 mins	D. G. Bradman	for A	Headingley	1930
311	1	–	23	out of 646 in 762 mins	R. B. Simpson	for A	Old Trafford	1964
307	–	–	20	out of 507 in 727 mins	R. M. Cowper	for A	Melbourne	1965-66
304	2	–	43	out of 511 in 430 mins	D. G. Bradman	for A	Headingley	1934
287	–	–	37	out of 504 in 419 mins	R. E. Foster	for E	Sydney	1903-04
270	–	–	22	out of 452 in 458 mins	D. G. Bradman	for A	Melbourne	1936-37
266	–	1	27	out of 574 in 460 mins	W. H. Ponsford	for A	Oval	1934
256	–	–	26	out of 468 in 683 mins	K. F. Barrington	for E	Old Trafford	1964
254	–	–	25	out of 423 in 339 mins	D. G. Bradman	for A	Lord's	1930
251	–	–	30	out of 459 in 461 mins	W. R. Hammond	for E	Sydney	1928-29
244	1	–	32	out of 451 in 316 mins	D. G. Bradman	for A	Oval	1934
240	–	–	32	out of 437 in 367 mins	W. R. Hammond	for E	Lord's	1938
234	–	–	17	out of 564 in 642 mins	S. G. Barnes	for A	Sydney	1946-47
234	–	–	24	out of 405 in 393 mins	D. G. Bradman	for A	Sydney	1946-47

	6s	5s	4s					
232	–	–	16	out of 411 in 438 mins	D. G. Bradman	for A	Oval	1930
232	I	–	34	out of 300 in 235 mins	S. J. McCabe	for A	Trent Bridge	1938
231*	–	–	27	out of 399 in 460 mins	W. R. Hammond	for E	Sydney	1936-37
225	I	–	18	out of 480 in 545 mins	R. B. Simpson	for A	Adelaide	1965-66
216*	I	I	26	out of 414 in 319 mins	E. Paynter	for E	Trent Bridge	1938
212	–	–	14	out of 401 in 437 mins	D. G. Bradman	for A	Adelaide	1936-37
211	–	–	24	out of 479 in 485 mins	W. L. Murdoch	for A	Oval	1884
206*	–	I	22	out of 422 in 369 mins	W. A. Brown	for A	Lord's	1938
206	–	–	23	out of 371 in 462 mins	A. R. Morris	for A	Adelaide	1950-51
201*	I	I	12	out of 371 in 395 mins	J. Ryder	for A	Adelaide	1924-25
201	–	–	28	out of 371 in 243 mins	S. E. Gregory	for A	Sydney	1894-95
200	–	–	17	out of 336 in 398 mins	W. R. Hammond	for E	Melbourne	1928-29

D. G. Bradman (A) scored most double-centuries – 8; he is followed by W. R. Hammond (E) with 4. Bradman, Hammond and R. B. Simpson (A) all reached a score of 200 or more in both England and Australia.

The two double-centuries by R. B. Simpson (311 and 225) were his only three-figure innings. R. E. Foster, E. Paynter and R. M. Cowper each scored 200 or more as his only three-figure score.

R. B. Simpson scored 311 and R. M. Cowper scored 307 as their maiden centuries in these matches. The highest maiden century for England is 287 by R. E. Foster.

W. R. Hammond's 251 and 200 (above) were scored in consecutive innings, as were D. G. Bradman's 304 and 244.

D. G. Bradman (A) is the only batsman to make three scores of 200 or more in a series (254, 334, 232 in 1930).

In the 1938 series the record number of five scores of 200 or more were recorded.

The nearest innings to a double-century without reaching it is 196 by A. R. Morris (A) at the Oval in 1948. The nearest innings to a double-century by a batsman who *never* recorded such a score in these matches is 194 by H. Sutcliffe (E) at Sydney in 1932-33.

Century in each innings

136	and 130	W. Bardsley	for A	Oval	1909
176	and 127	H. Sutcliffe	for E	Melbourne	1924-25
119*	and 177	W. R. Hammond	for E	Adelaide	1928-29
147	and 103*	D. C. S. Compton	for E	Adelaide	1946-47
122	and 124*	A. R. Morris	for A	Adelaide	1946-47

The instances by Compton and Morris (above) occurred in the same match.

H. Sutcliffe (above) was playing in only his second Test against Australia, having scored 59 and 115 in his first.

The following came close to performing the feat:

124	and 83	P. S. McDonnell	for A	Adelaide	1884-85
106	and 81	A. Shrewsbury	for E	Lord's	1893
98	and 97	C. Hill	for A	Adelaide	1901-02
95	and 93	F. E. Woolley	for E	Lord's	1921
201*	and 88	J. Ryder	for A	Adelaide	1924-25
101	and 94	K. F. Barrington	for E	Sydney	1962-63

C. Hill and F. E. Woolley (above) are the only batsmen to score two nineties in the same match.

J. Ryder (above) and D. G. Bradman (244 and 77 for Australia at the Oval in 1934) are the only batsmen to score a double-century and a fifty in the same match.

H. Sutcliffe (E) on six occasions scored 50 or more in each innings of a match. A. R. Morris (A) and K. F. Barrington (E) each did so four times.

Three centuries in successive innings

115, 176 and 127	H. Sutcliffe	for E	1924-25
133*, 151, 109	C. G. Macartney	for A	1926
155, 122 and 124*	A. R. Morris	for A	1946-47

D. G. Bradman (A), in 1936-37, 1938, 1946-47, scored a century in each of eight successive matches in which he batted. (The eight centuries were scored in twelve innings.)

D. G. Bradman (A), in 1928-29, 1930, scored a century in each of four successive matches. No other batsman has achieved this, though W. R. Hammond (E) in 1928-29 scored four centuries in three successive matches.

Both W. R. Hammond (in 1928-29) and D. G. Bradman (in 1934) scored double-centuries in successive innings.

J. H. Edrich (E) is the only batsman to score five successive fifties in one series – 88, 64, 62, 65, 164 in 1968. P. B. H. May (E) also scored five successive fifties, but they were spread over two series – 79, 73, 63, 53, 101 in 1954-55, 1956.

Carrying bat through innings

J. E. Barrett	67* out of 176 in 4 hrs 38 mins	for A	Lord's	1890
R. Abel	132* out of 307 in 5 hrs 25 mins	for E	Sydney	1891-92
W. Bardsley	193* out of 383 in 6 hrs 38 mins	for A	Lord's	1926
W. M. Woodfull	30* out of 66 in 1 hr 21 mins	for A	Brisbane	1928-29
W. M. Woodfull	73* out of 193 in 3 hrs 55 mins	for A	Adelaide	1932-33
W. A. Brown	206* out of 422 in 6 hrs 9 mins	for A	Lord's	1938
L. Hutton	156* out of 272 in 6 hrs 10 mins	for E	Adelaide	1950-51

(Australia batted two men short when Woodfull performed the feat in 1928-29, and one man short when he did it in 1932-33.)

In addition to the above, the following were also at the wicket throughout the entire duration of a completed innings, having opened the innings and been last man out:

V. T. Trumper	74 out of 122 in 1 hr 52 mins	for A	Melbourne	1903-04
W. A. Brown	69 out of 201 in 2 hrs 46 mins	for A	Oval	1938
L. Hutton	30 out of 52 in 2 hrs 27 mins	for E	Oval	1948
A. R. Morris	206 out of 371 in 7 hrs 42 mins	for A	Adelaide	1950-51
R. J. Inverarity	56 out of 125 in 4 hrs 8 mins	for A	Oval	1968

(Australia batted two men short when Brown scored his 69.)

Most runs in a day

309	D. G. Bradman	(334)	for A	Headingley	1930	0-309* on 1st day
271	D. G. Bradman	(304)	for A	Headingley	1934	0-271* on 2nd day
244	D. G. Bradman	(244)	for A	Oval	1934	0-244 on 1st day
214	R. E. Foster	(287)	for E	Sydney	1903-04	73*-287 on 3rd day
213	S. J. McCabe	(232)	for A	Trent Bridge	1938	19*-232 on 3rd day
210	W. R. Hammond	(240)	for E	Lord's	1938	0-210* on 1st day
205	W. H. Ponsford	(266)	for A	Oval	1934	0-205* on 1st day

On the first day at the Oval in 1934, two batsmen – D. G. Bradman and W. H. Ponsford (above) – both exceeded 200 runs on the same day.

D. G. Bradman's scores of 304 and 244 (above) were made in consecutive innings.

The greatest number of runs in a day for Australia in Australia is 192 (56*-248*) by D. G. Bradman (270) on the fourth day at Melbourne in 1936-37.

The greatest number of runs made on the *first* day of a match in Australia is 185 (0-185) by R. W. Barber (185) at Sydney in 1965-66. The record for an Australian on the first day in Australia is 182 (0-182*) by C. Hill (188) at Melbourne in 1897-98.

On 20 occasions D. G. Bradman scored 100 or more runs in a single day for Australia against England – in every one of his 19 centuries, and twice in his 232 at the Oval in 1930. (He missed a 21st occasion by a single run.) The nearest approach to this performance is by J. B. Hobbs (E) and A. R. Morris (A), who each scored 100 or more runs in a day seven times in these Tests.

Most boundaries in an innings

6s	5s	4s						
–	–	46	(184)	334	D. G. Bradman	for A	Headingley	1930
2	–	43	(184)	304	D. G. Bradman	for A	Headingley	1934
–	–	37	(148)	287	R. E. Foster	for E	Sydney	1903-04
1	–	34	(142)	232	S. J. McCabe	for A	Trent Bridge	1938
–	–	35	(140)	364	L. Hutton	for E	Oval	1938
1	–	32	(134)	244	D. G. Bradman	for A	Oval	1934
–	–	33	(132)	182	A. R. Morris	for A	Headingley	1948
–	–	32	(128)	240	W. R. Hammond	for E	Lord's	1938
–	–	31	(124)	180	E. R. Dexter	for E	Edgbaston	1961
–	–	30	(120)	160	J. Darling	for A	Sydney	1897-98
–	–	30	(120)	251	W. R. Hammond	for E	Sydney	1928-29
1	2	26	(120)	178	J. Darling	for A	Adelaide	1897-98
–	–	29	(116)	173*	D. G. Bradman	for A	Headingley	1948
1	1	26	(115)	216*	E. Paynter	for E	Trent Bridge	1938
–	1	27	(113)	266	W. H. Ponsford	for A	Oval	1934
–	–	28	(112)	201	S. E. Gregory	for A	Sydney	1894-95
–	1	27	(108)	231*	W. R. Hammond	for E	Sydney	1936-37
–	–	26	(104)	185*	V. T. Trumper	for A	Sydney	1903-04
–	–	26	(104)	256	K. F. Barrington	for E	Old Trafford	1964
–	–	25	(100)	187*	S. J. McCabe	for A	Sydney	1932-33
–	–	25	(100)	254	D. G. Bradman	for A	Lord's	1930

D. G. Bradman five times scored 100 or more runs in an innings in boundaries.

The greatest number of runs in boundaries in an innings at Melbourne is 90 (1 six, 21 fours) by K. L. Hutchings (E) in his 126 in 1907-08. (C. Hill hit 1 five and 21 fours in his 188 in 1897-98; J. B. Hobbs hit 22 fours in his 178 in 1911-12; D. G. Bradman hit 22 fours in his 270 in 1936-37.)

The greatest number of runs in boundaries in an innings at Brisbane is 84 (2 sixes, 18 fours) by A. R. Morris (A) in his 153 in 1954-55. (W. M. Lawry hit 20 fours in his 166 in 1965-66.)

The greatest number of runs scored in boundaries by a side in a single innings is 345 (1 five, 85 fours) in England's 903 for 7 dec. at the Oval in 1938. (In addition, there were 4 fours in byes and 1 four in leg-byes, making a grand total of 365 runs in boundaries.)

High percentage of runs in boundaries

6s	5s	4s						
–	–	7	(28)	30	G. A. R. Lock	for E	Headingley	1961
–	–	8	(32)	35	T. J. D. Kelly	for A	Melbourne	1876-77
–	–	8	(32)	37	A. Shrewsbury	for E	Oval	1884
1	–	7	(34)	42	A. L. Hassett	for A	Lord's	1938
–	–	9	(36)	43	P. S. McDonnell	for A	Oval	1880
–	–	10	(40)	53	G. Geary	for E	Trent Bridge	1934
1	1	8	(43)	57	J. Darling	for A	Oval	1905
–	–	11	(44)	62	F. E. Woolley	for E	Oval	1912
1	–	10	(46)	66	D. G. Bradman	for A	Adelaide	1932-33
1	–	11	(50)	69	C. J. Barnett	for E	Brisbane	1936-37
–	–	13	(52)	69*	M. A. Noble	for A	Oval	1899
–	–	14	(56)	70	H. Trumble	for A	Sydney	1897-98
–	–	14	(56)	76	J. Worrall	for A	Headingley	1899
–	–	14	(56)	76*	D.C.S.Compton	for E	Lord's	1938
1	–	13	(58)	76	A. K. Davidson	for A	Lord's	1953
1	–	13	(58)	76	E. R. Dexter	for E	Old Trafford	1961
–	–	15	(60)	75	J. Worrall	for A	Oval	1899
–	1	14	(61)	79	J. T. Tyldesley	for E	Sydney	1901-02
–	1	15	(65)	79	R. H. Spooner	for E	Oval	1905
1	–	15	(66)	88	S. J. McCabe	for A	Trent Bridge	1934
5	–	9	(66)	93	S. J. E. Loxton	for A	Headingley	1948
–	1	17	(73)	104	G. L. Jessop	for E	Oval	1902
–	–	19	(76)	101	J. Darling	for A	Sydney	1897-98
–	–	20	(80)	116	A. C. MacLaren	for A	Sydney	1901-02
–	–	20	(80)	117	W.W. Read	for E	Oval	1884
–	–	22	(88)	132	E. H. Hendren	for E	Old Trafford	1934
1	–	21	(90)	126	K. L. Hutchings	for E	Melbourne	1907-08
–	–	24	(96)	143	G. H. S. Trott	for A	Lord's	1896
–	–	30	(120)	160	J. Darling	for A	Sydney	1897-98
–	–	33	(132)	182	A. R. Morris	for A	Headingley	1948

When J. Darling (160, above) reached his century, he had hit 20 fours. Likewise, A. R. Morris had hit 20 fours when he reached his century in his 182 (above). These are the record boundary figures on a player reaching three figures.

R. H. Spooner, in his 79 (above), had hit 1 five and 10 fours when he reached his half-century (52*).

J. J. Lyons, in his 31 for Australia at the Oval in 1893, scored 20 (4, 4, 4, 4, 4) from 5 consecutive balls he received (the first 2 from J. Briggs and the last 3 from W. H. Lockwood, being caught off the next ball).

W. J. Edrich, in his 54 for England at Headingley in 1948, scored 18 (4, 4, 4, 6) in 4 successive balls from I. W. Johnson.

A. R. Morris, in his 182 (above), hit 7 fours in the course of 9 successive balls received from D. C. S. Compton.

G. A. R. Lock, in his 30 (above), hit 7 fours in the course of 11 balls (all from R. Benaud).

Most boundaries in a day

6s	5s	4s							
–	–	42	(168)	D. G. Bradman	(0-309*)	for A	Headingley	1st day	1930
2	–	39	(168)	D. G. Bradman	(0-271*)	for A	Headingley	2nd day	1934
1	–	32	(134)	D. G. Bradman	(0-244)	for A	Oval	1st day	1934
–	–	33	(132)	A. R. Morris	(0-182)	for A	Headingley	5th day	1948
1	–	31	(130)	S. J. McCabe	(19*-232)	for A	Trent Bridge	3rd day	1938
–	–	30	(120)	J. Darling	(0-160)	for A	Sydney	4th day	1897-98
–	–	30	(120)	R. E. Foster	(73*-287)	for E	Sydney	3rd day	1903-04
–	–	30	(120)	E. R. Dexter	(5*-180)	for E	Edgbaston	5th day	1961
1	2	26	(120)	J. Darling	(0-178*)	for A	Adelaide	1st day	1897-98

The greatest number of runs scored in boundaries (from the bat) by a side in one day is 264 (66 fours) by Australia on the fifth day at Headingley in 1948, in their 404 for 3. (In addition, there were 1 four in byes and 1 four in leg-byes, making a grand total of 272 runs in boundaries.)

Most boundaries before lunch

6s	5s	4s							
–	–	17	(68)	K. S. Ranjitsinhji	(41*-154*)	for E	Old Trafford	3rd day	1896
–	–	16	(64)	D. G. Bradman	(0-105*)	for A	Headingley	1st day	1930
–	–	15	(60)	C. G. Macartney	(0-112*)	for A	Headingley	1st day	1926
–	–	14	(56)	J. Darling	(0-68*)	for A	Sydney	4th day	1897-98
–	–	14	(56)	V. T. Trumper	(0-103*)	for A	Old Trafford	1st day	1902
–	–	14	(56)	C. J. Barnett	(0-98*)	for E	Trent Bridge	1st day	1938

D. G. Bradman's 16 fours before lunch (above) is the greatest number scored in a two-hour pre-lunch period.

Hundreds before lunch

								Time
K. S. Ranjitsinhji	(154*)	for E	Old Trafford	1896	41*-154*	on 3rd day		130 mins
V. T. Trumper	(104)	for A	Old Trafford	1902	0-103*	on 1st day		113 mins
C. P. Mead	(182*)	for E	Oval	1921	19*-128*	on 2nd day		147 mins
C. G. Macartney	(151)	for A	Headingley	1926	0-112*	on 1st day		116 mins
D. G. Bradman	(334)	for A	Headingley	1930	0-105*	on 1st day		112 mins

Macartney's performance (above) was achieved after Australia had been put in and had lost a wicket to the first ball of the match.

The greatest number of runs scored for England before lunch on the first day is 98, by C. J. Barnett (126) at Trent Bridge in 1938: Barnett reached his century off the first ball after lunch.

The greatest number of runs scored before lunch in Australia is 84 (0-84*) in 85 mins by J. J. Lyons (134) on the third day at Sydney in 1891-92.

The greatest number of runs scored between lunch and tea is 127 (105*-232) by S. J. McCabe (232) on the third day at Trent Bridge in 1938. This is also the record number of runs scored in a single session of play on any day in England-Australia Tests.

The greatest number of runs scored between tea and close of play is 113 (15*-128) by G. J. Bonnor (128) on the second day at Sydney in 1884-85. This is also the record number of runs scored in a single session of play in these matches in Australia.

The greatest number of runs scored between the start of play and tea is 220 (0-220*) by D. G. Bradman (334) on the first day at Headingley in 1930. (This exceeds the record in Australia by as many as 62 – J. Darling having scored 158 (0-158*) on the fourth day at Sydney in 1897-98. Bradman's figure also exceeds the record in Australia for a *first* day by as many as 73 – R. W. Barber having scored 147 (0-147*) between the start of play and tea on the first day at Sydney in 1965-66.)

The greatest number of runs scored between lunch and close of play is 204 (105*-309*) by D. G. Bradman (334) on the first day at Headingley in 1930.

On five occasions D. G. Bradman scored 100 or more runs in a single session of play, as follows:

54*-155*	between tea and close on 2nd day	in 254	Lord's	1930
0-105*	between start and lunch on 1st day	in 334	Headingley	1930
105*-220*	between lunch and tea on 1st day	in 334	Headingley	1930
169*-271*	between tea and close on 2nd day	in 304	Headingley	1934
43*-150*	between lunch and tea on 1st day	in 244	Oval	1934

D. G. Bradman is the only player in these matches to score a century before lunch and then go on to score a further 100 runs between lunch and tea on the same day (in his 334 at Headingley in 1930).

Youngest and oldest century-scorers

The following centuries were scored by batsmen under the age of 21:

19 years 152 days	A. A. Jackson	164 for A	Adelaide	1928-29
19 years 290 days	R. N. Harvey	112 for A	Headingley	1948
19 years 357 days	K. D. Walters	155 for A	Brisbane	1965-66
20 years 14 days	K. D. Walters	115 for A	Melbourne	1965-66
20 years 19 days	D. C. S. Compton	102 for E	Trent Bridge	1938
20 years 129 days	D. G. Bradman	112 for A	Melbourne	1928-29
20 years 197 days	D. G. Bradman	123 for A	Melbourne	1928-29
20 years 240 days	J. W. Burke	101* for A	Adelaide	1950-51
20 years 317 days	C. Hill	188 for A	Melbourne	1897-98
20 years 324 days	J. W. Hearne	114 for E	Melbourne	1911-12

The youngest player to score a double-century is D. G. Bradman (A), who was 21 years 307 days in his 254 at Lord's in 1930.

The youngest player to score a triple-century is D. G. Bradman (A), who was 21 years 318 days in his 334 at Headingley in 1930.

The youngest player to score a double-century for England is L. Hutton, who was 22 years 60 days in his 364 at the Oval in 1938: he reached his triple-century on the same day.

The highest average in a series by a player under the age of 21 is 69·00 by A. A. Jackson (A) in 1928-29.

The highest aggregate in a series by a player under the age of 21 is 468 by D. G. Bradman (A) in 1928-29.

The oldest player to score a century is J. B. Hobbs (E), who was 46 years 83 days when he made 142 at Melbourne in 1928-29.

The oldest player to score a century for Australia is W. Bardsley, who was 42 years 201 days when he reached his century in his 193* at Lord's in 1926.

The oldest players to score a century for the first time in these matches are:

38 years 173 days	H. Makepeace	117	for E	Melbourne	1920-21
37 years 353 days	A. J. Richardson	100	for A	Headingley	1926
37 years 144 days	E. H. Hendren	127*	for E	Lord's	1926

The oldest Australian to do so in Australia is G. Giffen, who was 35 years 279 days when he scored 161 at Sydney in 1894-95.

Altogether (including the above instances) 21 Englishmen and 14 Australians have scored their maiden century in these matches at the age of 30 or over.

The oldest player to make a century on debut in these matches is W. Watson (E) who was 33 years 115 days when he scored 109 at Lord's in 1953.

The oldest player to score a double-century as his maiden three-figure innings is E. Paynter (E) who was 36 years 218 days when he scored 216* at Trent Bridge in 1938. The oldest Australian to do so is J. Ryder, who was 35 years 162 days when he scored 201* at Adelaide in 1924-25.

Centuries by batsmen low in order

At number 10 in order:

117	W. W. Read	for E	Oval	1884
104	R. A. Duff	for A	Melbourne	1901-02

At number 9 in order:

160	C. Hill	for A	Adelaide	1907-08
100	J. M. Gregory	for A	Melbourne	1920-21
100	R. R. Lindwall	for A	Melbourne	1946-47

The only occasion on which numbers 8 and 9 in the order both scored centuries was at Adelaide in 1907-08, when in Australia's second innings R. J. Hartigan (number 8) scored 116 and C. Hill (number 9) scored 160.

The highest innings by a number 11 batsman have been:

50	F. R. Spofforth	for A	Melbourne	1884-85
46*	A. A. Mailey	for A	Sydney	1924-25
45*	W. W. Armstrong	for A	Melbourne	1901-02
45*	D. L. Underwood	for E	Headingley	1968
43*	W. Attewell	for E	Adelaide	1891-92
40*	W. Rhodes	for E	Sydney	1903-04

At Sydney, in the first Test of 1924-25, A. A. Mailey, at number 11 in each innings, batted 87 minutes for 21 and 79 minutes for 46*, the respective tenth-wicket partnerships in these times yielding 62 (with W. A. S. Oldfield) and 127 (with J. M. Taylor). Later in the series, in the first innings at Adelaide, Mailey (again at number 11) batted 77 minutes for 27, J. Ryder and he adding 73 for the tenth wicket.

Most sixes in an innings

Five by S. J. E. Loxton (93) for A Headingley 1948

On two occasions J. Darling (A) hit five balls in an innings out of the playing area, but at that time 6s were awarded only for hits out of the ground. The innings were his 51 at Old Trafford in 1902 (two 6s and three 4s out of playing area), and his 73 at Old Trafford in 1905 (five 4s out of playing area).

Apart from Loxton (above), no player has hit more than three actual over-the-boundary 6s (as such) in an innings. Those who have hit three such 6s are:

A. P. F. Chapman	(121)	for E	Lord's	1930
R. E. S. Wyatt	(78)	for E	Adelaide	1932-33
W. J. O'Reilly	(37*)	for A	Sydney	1936-37
W. M. Lawry	(106)	for A	Old Trafford	1964

(A. P. F. Chapman, in his 121, above, also had another scoring-stroke for 6 which included four overthrows.)

W. J. O'Reilly (above) hit his three 6s in the course of an innings lasting 44 minutes.

In addition to the above, the following batsmen hit the equivalent of three or more 6s in an innings, when over-the-boundary hits were not awarded 6 runs:

4 fives	G. J. Bonnor	(85)	for A	Melbourne	1882-83
3 fives	G. J. Bonnor	(34)	for A	Melbourne	1882-83
3 fives	G. J. Bonnor	(128)	for A	Sydney	1884-85
1 six, 2 fives	J. Darling	(178)	for A	Adelaide	1897-98
3 fours[1]	J. Worrall	(75)	for A	Oval	1899
3 fours[2]	G. L. Jessop	(102)	for E	Oval	1902

[1]All out of playing area. [2]All into pavilion.

The first two instances by G. J. Bonnor (above) occurred in successive matches.

G. Ulyett (67) hit the first ball he received out of the playing area (for 5) in England's second innings at Sydney in 1881-82.

The greatest number of 6s hit by a side in an innings is seven, in Australia's 458 at Headingley in 1948 (five by S. J. E. Loxton, two by K. R. Miller). This is also the greatest number of 6s hit in a day.

S. J. E. Loxton and J. Darling, in their innings mentioned above, also hold the record (5) for the greatest number of 6s (or the equivalent) by a player in a match.

The greatest number of 6s recorded altogether by both sides in a single match is 12 (seven by Australia, five by England) at Headingley in 1948.

K. R. Miller (A) hit at least one over-the-boundary 6 on seven of the nine grounds on which he played – Lord's, the Oval, Old Trafford, Headingley, Sydney, Adelaide and Brisbane.

In England, up to and including the 1909 series, it was the normal (but not invariable) practice to award 4 runs for a hit out of the playing area, and 6 runs for a hit right out of the ground. Before the start of the 1905 Tests, the Australian captain, J. Darling, publicly declared that he would like 6 runs awarded for an over-the-boundary hit in that summer's series. However, at a meeting of the Board of Control at Lord's, on 26 May 1905, it was decided that 'owing to the different arrangements on the different grounds, it would not be expedient to lay down any hard and fast rule that a hit to the boundary should count four and a hit over the boundary six'. Since the 1912 series all hits over the boundary in England have counted 6, following the approval of a resolution (relating to all first-class cricket in England) passed by the Advisory County Cricket Committee on 21 March 1910.

In Australia, up to and including the 1903-04 series, 5 runs were awarded for a hit out of the playing area (the batsmen thereupon changing ends) and 6 runs for a hit right out of the ground. By the start of the 1907-08 series, all Test grounds in Australia had adopted the practice of awarding 6 runs for all over-the-boundary hits, and this position has obtained ever since.

Big hits

1880, Oval: G. J. Bonnor (2) hit A. Shaw a measured 115 yards from the pavilion wicket to long-on, but was caught by G. F. Grace after the batsmen had crossed three times.

1881-82, Sydney: P. S. McDonnell (147) drove a ball from W. Bates over the pavilion. (This was not the present members' stand, or pavilion, which was erected in 1886.)

1882-83, Melbourne: G. J. Bonnor (85) hit four balls out of the playing area – the first two off A. G. Steel into the pavilion reserve, the third (off W. Bates) into the crowd, and the fourth (off W. W. Read, bowling lobs) again into the pavilion reserve. The hit off Read, had it not struck a tree, 'would have gone over the outer fence for 6'.

1882-83, Melbourne: W. Bates (28) hit a ball from G. E. Palmer which, according to some accounts, went 'clean out of the ground'. However, 5 runs were awarded for the hit, which was therefore out of the playing area only.

Big hits (continued)

1882-83, Melbourne: G. J. Bonnor (34) hit three balls out of the playing area, this making seven such hits by him in two successive Tests.

1884, Oval: H. J. H. Scott (102) hit a ball from A. G. Steel to the roof of the pavilion.

1891-92, Sydney: A. E. Stoddart (27) made a huge hit – for 5 – off C. T. B. Turner into the reserve.

1891-92, Adelaide: A. E. Stoddart (134) made two great drives (for 5 each) off C. T. B. Turner and G. Giffen, both into the members' reserve. Both hits were in the course of three balls received by Stoddart.

1893, Oval: J. J. Lyons (31) drove W. H. Lockwood to the roof of the pavilion, whence the ball bounced over and into the road on the other side. (Off the next ball Lyons just failed to carry the pavilion, the ball landing on the roof of the members' enclosure.)

1894-95, Adelaide: A. E. Trott (38*) hit a ball from W. H. Lockwood which landed in a buggy on the carriage-drive outside the embankment.

1894-95, Sydney: J. Darling (31) hit a ball from J. Briggs over the heads of the crowd into the tennis-courts behind the pavilion, the estimated carry being 120 yards.

1897-98, Adelaide: J. Darling (178) pulled a ball from J. Briggs over the square-leg boundary and out of the ground. (This was alleged to have been the first out-of-the-ground hit ever made in a first-class match at the Adelaide Oval.) The stroke put up Darling's century – the only time a century has been reached in England-Australia matches with a hit out of the ground.

1902, Old Trafford: J. Darling (51) hit two 6s out of the ground, both off W. Rhodes – the first into the road adjoining the railway booking-office, and the second into the road at the other end.

1902, Oval: G. L. Jessop (104) three times drove H. Trumble into the pavilion, including twice in one over.

1905, Trent Bridge: W. W. Armstrong (27) on-drove a ball from B. J. T. Bosanquet over the grandstand at the Radcliffe Road end, the ball landing in Radcliffe Road.

1909, Old Trafford: A. Cotter (17) straight-drove C. Blythe out of the ground for 6, the ball clearing Warwick Road and landing in Paulin's field. The hit was off the third ball Cotter received.

1932-33, Sydney: W. R. Hammond (75*) on-drove W. J. O'Reilly high into the upper deck of the pavilion grandstand, the ball then cannoning into the luncheon-room.

1936-37, Sydney: W. J. O'Reilly (37*) made a huge drive off H. Verity to the 'Hill' end of the ground.

1946-47, Brisbane: K. R. Miller (79) hit D. V. P. Wright over long-on to the roof of the members' stand, whence the ball bounced back on to the field.

1946-47, Adelaide: K. R. Miller (141*) on the fourth morning hit a 6 off the first ball of the day (a no-ball by D. V. P. Wright), the ball landing among the members' friends in the enclosure on the square-leg boundary.

1948, Headingley: K. R. Miller (58) hit a ball from J. C. Laker which pitched at the foot of the trees at the Kirkstall Lane end.

1948, Headingley: S. J. E. Loxton (93) on-drove K. Cranston high into the pavilion. Later in the same innings Loxton hit J. C. Laker for a carry of about 125 yards towards the foot of the trees at the Kirkstall Lane end.

1950-51, Sydney: K. R. Miller (145*) off-drove J. J. Warr over the sightscreen to the foot of the Noble Stand.

1954-55, Adelaide: J. H. Wardle (23) hit R. Benaud for 6 over long-on, the estimated carry of the hit being between 110 and 120 yards.

1964, Lord's: G. D. McKenzie (10) made a square-leg hit out of the ground off L. J. Coldwell, the ball bouncing on the roof of the Mound Stand, whence it dropped into St. John's Wood Road, striking a passer-by (Mr Richard Horton, aged 55, of Camden Town, London) in the face and breaking his spectacles.

Fast innings

31* in 13 mins	W. P. Howell	for A	Sydney	1901-02
30 .. 13 ..	C. Bannerman	for A	Melbourne	1876-77
35 .. 14 ..	W. P. Howell	for A	Sydney	1901-02
30 .. 17 ..	G. A. R. Lock	for E	Headingley	1961
35 .. 21 ..	G. L. Jessop	for E	Melbourne	1901-02
33 .. 23 ..	J. J. Lyons	for A	Lord's	1890
37 .. 24 ..	L. Hutton	for E	Sydney	1946-47
42* .. 25 ..	A. P. F. Chapman	for E	Headingley	1926
37 .. 25 ..	A. Shrewsbury	for E	Oval	1884
47 .. 29 ..	T. G. Evans	for E	Old Trafford	1956
51* .. 37 ..	J. W. Hitch	for E	Oval	1921
55 .. 45 ..	J. J. Lyons	for A	Lord's	1890
62 .. 50 ..	V. T. Trumper	for A	Sheffield	1902
62* .. 55 ..	G. A. Lohmann	for E	Oval	1888
104 .. 77 ..	G. L. Jessop	for E	Oval	1902
232 .. 235 ..	S. J. McCabe	for A	Trent Bridge	1938

The only player to have both his innings in the same match included in the above list is J. J. Lyons (55 and 33 at Lord's in 1890).

Apart from G. L. Jessop's 104 (above), the only other innings of 100 or over that has been scored at a run a minute or better (over its entire length) is G. J. Bonnor's 128 in 115 minutes for Australia at Sydney in 1884-85. S. J. McCabe's 232 (above) came very close.

The following innings began at a fast rate:

W. P. Howell	hit first 23 in 5 mins in 35	at Sydney	1901-02
J. T. Brown	hit first 26 in 12 mins in 140	at Melbourne	1894-95
A. E. Stoddart	hit first 20 in 12 mins in 24	at Lord's	1893
H. H. Massie	hit first 26 in 13 mins in 43	at Melbourne	1882-83
A. P. F. Chapman	hit first 40 in 15 mins in 42*	at Headingley	1926

Fastest fifties

28 mins	J. T. Brown	(140)	for E	Melbourne	1894-95
35 mins	J. W. Hitch	(51*)	for E	Oval	1921
36 mins	J. J. Lyons	(55)	for A	Lord's	1890
36 mins	J. Ryder	(79)	for A	Sydney	1928-29
40 mins	J. Darling	(160)	for A	Sydney	1897-98
40 mins	V. T. Trumper	(62)	for A	Sheffield	1902
43 mins	G. L. Jessop	(104)	for E	Oval	1902
46 mins	D. G. Bradman	(254)	for A	Lord's	1930
46 mins	R. R. Lindwall	(50)	for A	Lord's	1953
47 mins	R. W. V. Robins	(61)	for E	Melbourne	1936-37
48 mins	F. S. Jackson	(103)	for E	Oval	1893
48 mins	G. L. Jessop	(55)	for E	Sheffield	1902
49 mins	R. B. Minnett	(90)	for A	Sydney	1911-12
49 mins	D. G. Bradman	(334)	for A	Headingley	1930

S. J. McCabe, in his 232 for Australia at Trent Bridge in 1938, scored the fourth fifty of his innings (150* to 202*) in 24 minutes – the fastest time for any single fifty.

The fastest time for a player's score to be taken from fifty to a century is 32 minutes – by G. L. Jessop (E) in his 104 at the Oval in 1902, and by J. M. Taylor (A) in his 108 at Sydney in 1924-25.

Fastest centuries

75 mins	G. L. Jessop	(104)	for E	Oval	1902
91 mins	J. Darling	(160)	for A	Sydney	1897-98
94 mins	V. T. Trumper	(185*)	for A	Sydney	1903-04
95 mins	J. T. Brown	(140)	for E	Melbourne	1894-95
99 mins	D. G. Bradman	(334)	for A	Headingley	1930
100 mins	G. J. Bonnor	(128)	for A	Sydney	1884-85

V. T. Trumper (A) and D. G. Bradman (A) are the only batsmen to reach a century within 2 hours twice. Bradman actually did it in successive Tests (at Lord's and Headingley in 1930).

Fastest double-centuries

214 mins D. G. Bradman (334) for A Headingley 1930
223 mins S. J. McCabe (232) for A Trent Bridge 1938
234 mins D. G. Bradman (254) for A Lord's 1930
241 mins S. E. Gregory (201) for A Sydney 1894-95
283 mins D. G. Bradman (244) for A Oval 1934

The fastest double-century by an Englishman is in 306 minutes, by E. Paynter (216*) at Trent Bridge in 1938.

The fastest triple-century is in 336 minutes, by D. G. Bradman (334) for Australia at Headingley in 1930. (The only triple-century for England was reached in 662 minutes by L. Hutton at the Oval in 1938.)

Longest innings

The longest innings in point of time have been:

13 hours 17 mins L. Hutton (E) 364 Oval 1938
12 .. 42 .. R. B. Simpson (A) 311 Old Trafford 1964
12 .. 7 .. R. M. Cowper (A) 307 Melbourne 1965-66
11 .. 23 .. K. F. Barrington (E) 256 Old Trafford 1964
10 .. 42 .. S. G. Barnes (A) 234 Sydney 1946-47
9 .. 5 .. R. B. Simpson (A) 225 Adelaide 1965-66
8 .. 7 .. C. C. McDonald (A) 170 Adelaide 1958-59
8 .. 5 .. W. L. Murdoch (A) 211 Oval 1884
8 .. 1 .. E. R. Dexter (E) 174 Old Trafford 1964

Three of the above instances occurred in the same match (at Old Trafford, 1964).

The longest innings played for England in Australia is 7 hours 41 mins by W. R. Hammond (251 at Sydney, 1928-29).

The longest innings played in these matches without reaching a century is 7 hours 38 mins by T. E. Bailey (68 at Brisbane, 1958-59).

Four-day Innings

Owing to bad weather I. D. Craig's 38 for Australia at Old Trafford in 1956 was spread over four days (8*, 10*, 24*, 38). C. C. McDonald's 89 in the same Australian innings was also spread over four days, but he had retired hurt early in the innings (11 ret. ht., 15*, 25*, 89).

Three-day Innings

A. C. Bannerman 70 for A Sydney 1881-82 15*, 59*, 70
P. S. McDonnell 147 for A Sydney 1881-82 0*, 72*, 147
A. C. Bannerman 94 for A Sydney 1882-83 1*, 68*, 94
A. C. Bannerman 91 for A Sydney 1891-92 0*, 67*, 91
J. T. Tyldesley 97 for E Melbourne 1903-04 46*, 97*, 97
G. Gunn 122*for E Sydney 1907-08 50*, 77*, 122*
W. Rhodes 179 for E Melbourne 1911-12 23*, 157*, 179
C. B. Fry 42 for E Lord's 1912 24*, 41*, 42
C. Kelleway 147 for A Adelaide 1920-21 19*, 115*, 147
H. Sutcliffe 127 for E Melbourne 1924-25 12*, 114*, 127
W. R. Hammond 251 for E Sydney 1928-29 33*, 201*, 251
W. R. Hammond 200 for E Melbourne 1928-29 12*, 169*, 200
W. R. Hammond 113 for E Headingley 1930 61*, 73*, 113
G. Duckworth 33 for E Headingley 1930 0*, 15*, 33
D. G. Bradman 232 for A Oval 1930 27*, 130*, 232
D. G. Bradman 270 for A Melbourne 1936-37 56*, 248*, 270
D. G. Bradman 212 for A Adelaide 1936-37 26*, 174*, 212
L. Hutton 364 for E Oval 1938 160*, 300*, 364
S. G. Barnes 234 for A Sydney 1946-47 21*, 109*, 234
A. R. Morris 155 for A Melbourne 1946-47 14*, 132*, 155
D. C. S. Compton 184 for E Trent Bridge 1948 36*, 154*, 184
R. N. Harvey 122 for A Old Trafford 1953 60*, 105*, 122
G. B. Hole 66 for A Old Trafford 1953 41*, 66*, 66
R. Subba Row 112 for E Edgbaston 1961 5*, 68*, 112
R. Subba Row 137 for E Oval 1961 19*, 69*, 137
F. J. Titmus 59*for E Adelaide 1962-63 2*, 57*, 59*
P. J. Burge 103 for A Sydney 1962-63 0*, 98*, 103
R. B. Simpson 311 for A Old Trafford 1964 109*, 265*, 311
K. F. Barrington 256 for E Old Trafford 1964 20*, 153*, 256
R. M. Cowper 307 for A Melbourne 1965-66 32*, 159*, 307
W. M. Lawry 135 for A Oval 1968 19*, 135*, 135

C. C. McDonald's 170 for Australia at Adelaide in 1958-59 was also spread over three days, but he had retired hurt during the innings (112*, 149 ret. ht., 170).

W. R. Hammond's scores of 251 and 200 (above) were made in successive Test innings.

Due to stoppages for bad light and rain as well as the normal intervals, D. C. S. Compton's 184 (above) stretched over nine separate periods of play.

Longest period on field of play

27 hours 59 mins R. B. Simpson for A Old Trafford 1964
  (Whole match except for 16 mins)
27 hours 52 mins H. Sutcliffe for E Melbourne 1924-25
  (Whole match except for 86 mins)
26 hours 39 mins W. R. Hammond for E Adelaide 1928-29
  (Whole match except for 230 mins)
24 hours 28 mins K. F. Barrington for E Old Trafford 1964
  (Whole match except for 227 mins)
23 hours 12 mins L. Hutton for E Adelaide 1950-51
  (Whole match except for 230 mins)
22 hours 50 mins R. M. Cowper for A Melbourne 1965-66
  (Whole match except for 46 mins)
22 hours 26 mins S. G. Barnes for A Sydney 1946-47
  (Whole match except for 63 mins)
21 hours 9 mins W. M. Lawry for A Oval 1968
  (Whole match except for 354 mins)
21 hours 4 mins E. R. Dexter for E Old Trafford 1964
  (Whole match except for 431 mins)

H. Sutcliffe (E), in scoring 176 and 127 at Melbourne in 1924-25, batted in all for 13 hours 30 minutes – the longest time that any player has batted in an England-Australia match.

The longest time that any Australian has batted in these matches is 12 hours 47 minutes by R. B. Simpson in his innings of 311 and 4* at Old Trafford in 1964.

The following players were on the field for the longest period from the commencement of a match:

First 23 hours 12 mins of play L. Hutton for E Adelaide 1950-51
First 18 hours 50 mins of play W. A. Brown for A Oval 1938
First 18 hours 31 mins of play W. A. Brown for A Lord's 1938
First 18 hours 5 mins of play W. M. Lawry for A Oval 1968
First 17 hours 33 mins of play R. Abel for E Sydney 1891-92

L. Hutton (E), at Adelaide in 1950-51, was on the field continuously from the start of the match until 4.45 p.m. on the fifth day. The best performance for Australia in this regard is by W. A. Brown at Lord's in 1938: Brown was on the field from the start of the match until exactly 5 p.m. on the fourth day (90 minutes from the end of the match).

Slow innings

0* in 46 mins J. Briggs for E Adelaide 1897-98
0* .. 51 .. A. P. Sheahan for A Lord's 1968
4 .. 74 .. A. P. E. Knott for E Headingley 1968
4 .. 80 .. A. C. Bannerman for A Sydney 1886-87
5 .. 85 .. A. C. Bannerman for A Oval 1888
3* .. 100 .. J. T. Murray for E Sydney 1962-63
14 .. 115 .. A. C. Bannerman for A Melbourne 1882-83
9 .. 120 .. W. Newham for E Sydney 1887-88
15* .. 120 .. A. C. Bannerman for A Sydney 1886-87
15 .. 130 .. T. E. Bailey for E Sydney 1950-51
10* .. 133 .. T. G. Evans for E Adelaide 1946-47
19* .. 142 .. W. L. Murdoch for A Melbourne 1882-83
24* .. 163 .. T. E. Bailey for E Melbourne 1954-55
32 .. 184 .. W. J. Edrich for E Old Trafford 1948
27 .. 186 .. M. C. Cowdrey for E Lord's 1956
34 .. 225 .. W. H. Scotton for E Oval 1886
41 .. 240 .. A. C. Bannerman for A Melbourne 1891-92
28* .. 250 .. J. W. Burke for A Brisbane 1958-59

38	in 259 mins	I. D. Craig	for A	Old Trafford	1956
38	.. 262 ..	T. E. Bailey	for E	Headingley	1953
31	.. 264 ..	K. D. Mackay	for A	Lord's	1956
40	.. 289 ..	H. L. Collins	for A	Old Trafford	1921
57	.. 304 ..	W. M. Lawry	for A	Melbourne	1962-63
53*	.. 308 ..	T. W. Graveney	for E	Adelaide	1958-59
89	.. 320 ..	M. A. Noble	for A	Old Trafford	1899
82	.. 345 ..	W. H. Scotton	for E	Adelaide	1884-85
90	.. 345 ..	W. H. Scotton	for E	Oval	1884
98	.. 350 ..	D. R. Jardine	for E	Adelaide	1928-29
100*	.. 365 ..	M. C. Cowdrey	for E	Sydney	1958-59
115	.. 394 ..	A. L. Hassett	for A	Trent Bridge	1953
91	.. 448 ..	A. C. Bannerman	for A	Sydney	1891-92
68	.. 458 ..	T. E. Bailey	for E	Brisbane	1958-59
234	.. 642 ..	S. G. Barnes	for A	Sydney	1946-47

At Sydney in 1886-87 A. C. Bannerman (A) scored 15* in 2 hours in the first innings and 4 in 80 minutes in the second. At Melbourne in 1891-92 he scored 45 in 3¼ hours in the first innings and 41 in 4 hours in the second. In the following match (at Sydney), in his 91, Bannerman scored from only 5 of the 204 balls he received from W. Attewell.

The fewest runs scored by a batsman in a complete day's play (uninterrupted) is 67 (0*-67*) by A. C. Bannerman (A) on the third day at Sydney in 1891-92, in his innings of 91: the playing time was 4 hours 55 minutes. The fewest number scored by an English batsman is 102 (12*-114*) by H. Sutcliffe in 4 hours 53 minutes on the sixth day at Melbourne in 1924-25, in his innings of 127. (Both these records came very close to being broken on the fourth day at Brisbane in 1958-59 when T. E. Bailey scored 41 runs (27*-68) before being out seven minutes before the close of a 5-hour day: in his innings of 68 he scored from only 40 of the 426 balls he received.)

A. C. Bannerman (A) scored only 7 runs (12*-19*) in the entire period between lunch and tea (105 minutes) on the third day at Melbourne in 1891-92, in his 41. He made only one scoring stroke (a hit for 3) in one period of an hour during the afternoon.

C. Kelleway (A), in his 61 in 4½ hours at Lord's in 1912, remained at 0* for 37 minutes and later in his innings batted for periods of 25, 20 and 20 minutes without scoring a run. He was 9* after an hour, 20* after 2 hours, and reached 52* in 4 hours 10 minutes.

H. L. Collins (A), in his 40 at Old Trafford in 1921, scored only 5 runs (17*-22*) in the last hour before lunch on the final day. At one period he did not score for 40 minutes, and he scored only 18 (22*-40*) in the entire afternoon period of play.

K. D. Mackay (A), in his 31 at Lord's in 1956, had scored 9* in 100 minutes at the close of the third day, going on to score 18 in his first 3 hours at the wicket. He reached 30* after 4¼ hours.

M. C. Cowdrey (E), in his 27 at Lord's in 1956, made only four scoring strokes (1, 1, 2, 4) in the last 2 hours of the fourth day's play. Between 5 p.m. and the close at 6.30 he scored a 2 off R. G. Archer (at 5.30) and a 4 off K. R. Miller (at 6.10). He had scored 21* in 155 minutes at close of play.

T. E. Bailey (E), in his 68 at Brisbane in 1958-59, scored 8 runs (27*-35*) before lunch on the fourth day – see next section – and 15 runs (35*-50*) between lunch and tea. During the entire afternoon period of 110 minutes he made eight scoring strokes from the 27 overs bowled while England added. 47. He remained at 47* for 48 minutes.

J. W. Burke (A), in his 28* at Brisbane in 1958-59, scored 9 runs (0-9*) before lunch on the fifth day – see next section – and 12 runs (9*-21*) out of 54 added off 23 overs in 110 minutes between lunch and tea. During the afternoon session he made nine scoring strokes (eight of them singles) and at the tea interval his 21* had taken 200 minutes. After tea he finished his innings with seven successive singles in 50 minutes.

(*The instances relating to Bailey & Burke, above, were on successive days.*)

A. P. Sheahan (A), at Lord's in 1968, scored off only two of the 70 balls he received in the match, in the course of 87 minutes at the wicket. In his first innings (6) he made scoring strokes of 4 and 2 off 26 balls in 36 minutes, and in his second innings (0*) he received 44 balls in 51 minutes.

Fewest runs before lunch

Only players who were at the wicket throughout the entire pre-lunch period are included in the following table:

8 (27*-35*) in 1½ hrs on 4th day: T. E. Bailey (E) at Brisbane, 9 December 1958. (Bailey scored off only 6 balls during the morning (1, 2, 1, 1, 1, 2) while England went from 92 for 2 to 111 for 4, 19 being added off 21 overs.)

8 (8*-16*) in 80 mins (start delayed 10 mins through a second application of the roller on pitch) on 4th day: W. J. Edrich (E) at Brisbane, 3 December 1946. (England went from 21 for 1 to 56 for 3, only 29 runs coming from the bat during the morning. Edrich scored off only 3 balls – 3, 1, 4 – all morning.)

9 (0-9*) in 1½ hrs on 5th day: J. W. Burke (A) at Brisbane, 10 December 1958. (Australia began their second innings at start of play and were 42 for 1 at lunch, off 18 overs. Burke scored off only 8 balls (1, 1, 1, 2, 1, 1, 1, 1) during the morning.)

10 (0*-10*) in 1½ hrs on 6th day: T. G. Evans (E) at Adelaide, 6 February 1947. (England went from 274 for 8 to 340 for 8, adding 66 off 196 balls – 24 overs, including 4 no-balls – Evans scoring off only 5 of the 77 balls he received during the morning, hitting only one boundary.)

11 (59*-70*) in 80 mins on 3rd day: A. C. Bannerman (A) at Sydney, 6 March 1882. (Australia went from 146 for 3 to 215 for 3.)

13 (28*-41*) in 1½ hrs on 6th day: P. E. Richardson (E) at Adelaide, 4 February 1959. (England went from 43 for 0 to 87 for 0.)

13 (28*-41*) in 1½ hrs on 6th day: T. W. Graveney (E) at Adelaide, 5 February 1959. (England went from 198 for 5 to 229 for 7, only 2 fours, both by Graveney, being scored all morning.)

13 (0-13*) in 1½ hrs on 4th day: W. L. Murdoch (A) at Sydney, 21 February 1883. (Australia began their second innings at start of play and were 39 for 0 at lunch. Murdoch scored off only 7 balls – 1, 2, 1, 4, 2, 2, 1 – all morning.)

14 (32*-46*) in 1½ hrs on 3rd day: C. C. McDonald (A) at Melbourne, 2 January 1959. (Australia went from 96 for 1 to 135 for 1, only 1 four – by R. N. Harvey – being hit all morning.)

15 (0-15*) in 2 hrs on 1st day: R. M. Cowper (A) at Headingley, 25 July 1968. (Australia began their innings at start of play and were 75 for 1 at lunch. Cowper scored off only 10 of the 90 balls he received before lunch, scoring his 15* while 35 overs (14 maidens) were bowled. He remained at 5* for 35 mins, while 11 overs were bowled and scored his first boundary after 118 mins.)

16 (41*-57) in 2 hrs on 4th day: W. M. Lawry (A) at Melbourne, 2 January 1963. (Australia went from 105 for 4 to 161 for 5, Lawry being out to the last ball before lunch. He scored 6 runs in the first hour and altogether hit 3 twos and 10 singles during the morning.)

16 (0-16*) in 112 mins on 1st day: W. H. Scotton (E) at the Oval, 12 August 1886. (England began their innings at start of play and were 56 for 0 at lunch.)

17 (9*-26*) in 2 hrs on 4th day: K. D. Mackay (A) at Lord's, 25 June 1956. (Australia went from 115 for 6 to 221 for 6, R. Benaud scoring 87 of the 106 added. Mackay scored off only 12 balls during the morning – 1 four, 2 twos and 9 singles.)

17 (73*-90*) in 1½ hrs on 5th day: D. R. Jardine (E) at Adelaide, 6 February 1929. (England went from 206 for 2 to 261 for 2.)

17 (81*-98*) in 1½ hrs on 2nd day: A. L. Hassett (A) at Brisbane, 30 November 1946. (Australia went from 292 for 2 to 371 for 3, Hassett scoring only one boundary all morning.)

18 (39*-57*) in 1½ hrs on 4th day: J. H. W. Fingleton (A) at Melbourne, 5 January 1937. (Australia went from 194 for 5 to 252 for 5, Fingleton scoring only one boundary all morning.)

The fewest number of runs made in a 2½-hour pre-lunch period is 22 (0-22*) by H. L. Collins (A) on the 3rd day at Old Trafford, July 26, 1921. Australia began their innings at start of play and were 69 for 4 at lunch. Of the 54 overs bowled during the morning, 31 were maidens.

The Brisbane and Adelaide Tests of 1958-59 each provided an instance for the above table on successive days.

Slowest fifties

357 mins	T. E. Bailey	(68)	for E	Brisbane	1958-59
275 mins	W. M. Lawry	(57)	for A	Melbourne	1962-63
258 mins	T. W. Graveney	(53*)	for E	Adelaide	1958-59
250 mins	C. Kelleway	(61)	for A	Lord's	1912
249 mins	D. R. Jardine	(56)	for E	Adelaide	1932-33

The slowest time for a player's score to be taken from fifty to a century is 212 minutes – by A. L. Hassett (A) in his 128 at Brisbane in 1946-47. The slowest by an English player is 201 minutes by W. Watson in his 109 at Lord's in 1953.

The slowest time for any single fifty at any stage of an innings is 357 minutes by T. E. Bailey (above).

Slowest centuries

362 mins	M. C. Cowdrey	(100*)	for E	Sydney	1958-59
350 mins	W. M. Lawry	(135)	for A	Oval	1968
346 mins	A. L. Hassett	(115)	for A	Trent Bridge	1953
344 mins	A. L. Hassett	(128)	for A	Brisbane	1946-47
330 mins	R. B. Simpson	(311)	for A	Old Trafford	1964

On three occasions H. Sutcliffe (E), A. L. Hassett (A) and W. M. Lawry (A) took five hours or more to reach a century. Two of Lawry's instances occurred in the same series (1965-66).

Slowest double-centuries

608 mins	R. B. Simpson	(311)	for A	Old Trafford	1964
570 mins	S. G. Barnes	(234)	for A	Sydney	1946-47
535 mins	R. M. Cowper	(307)	for A	Melbourne	1965-66
518 mins	K. F. Barrington	(256)	for E	Old Trafford	1964
483 mins	R. B. Simpson	(225)	for A	Adelaide	1965-66

The slowest triple-century is in 753 minutes, by R. B. Simpson (311) for Australia at Old Trafford in 1964. The slowest for England (and the only one) is in 662 minutes by L. Hutton at the Oval in 1938.

An hour before breaking duck

95 mins	at 0*	T. G. Evans	(10*)	for E	Adelaide	1946-47
74 mins	at 0*	J. T. Murray	(3*)	for E	Sydney	1962-63
70 mins	at 0*	W. L. Murdoch	(17)	for A	Sydney	1882-83

T. G. Evans (above) had scored 0* in 44 minutes at the close of the fifth day, and, on the following morning, made his first scoring stroke – a 2 off R. R. Lindwall – off the 61st ball he received. Altogether Evans scored off only 5 of the 98 balls he received, his strokes being 2, 1, 2, 1, 4.

J. T. Murray (above) had scored 0* in 44 minutes at the close of the third day, batting with a shoulder injury he had sustained earlier in the match. After 30 minutes on the fourth morning he made his first scoring stroke – a single off G. D. McKenzie. He later scored a 2 off A. K. Davidson, these being the only 2 balls he scored from out of the 100 he received.

W. L. Murdoch (above) was one of Australia's opening batsmen, and thus he holds the record for not scoring for the longest time at the commencement of a side's innings. He began his innings at the start of play on the fourth morning, and did not score his first run until the 113th ball of the innings was bowled.

The following batsmen, having broken their duck, did not score a run for an hour or more at one stage of their innings:

67 mins	at 24*	W. H. Scotton	(34)	for E	Oval	1886
63 mins	at 10*	D. R. Jardine	(24)	for E	Brisbane	1932-33

D. R. Jardine (above) did not score off 82 consecutive balls he received while his score stood at 10*.

The longest period an Australian batsman has batted without adding a run to his score (having broken his duck) is 58 minutes, by H. L. Collins (24) while his score stood at 14* at Lord's in 1926.

Record partnership for each wicket

ENGLAND

				Time
323 for 1st wkt	J. B. Hobbs (178) and W. Rhodes (179)	Melbourne	1911-12	268 mins
382 .. 2nd ..	L. Hutton (364) and M. Leyland (187)	Oval	1938	381 ..
262 .. 3rd ..	W. R. Hammond (177) and D. R. Jardine (98)	Adelaide	1928-29	350 ..
222 .. 4th ..	W. R. Hammond (240) and E. Paynter (99)	Lord's	1938	182 ..
206 .. 5th ..	E. Paynter (216*) and D. C. S. Compton (102)	Trent Bridge	1938	138 ..
215 .. 6th ..	L. Hutton (364) and J. Hardstaff (169*)	Oval	1938	206 ..
143 .. 7th ..	F. E. Woolley (133*) and J. Vine (36)	Sydney	1911-12	147 ..
124 .. 8th ..	E. H. Hendren (169) and H. Larwood (70)	Brisbane	1928-29	118 ..
151 .. 9th ..	W. H. Scotton (90) and W. W. Read (117)	Oval	1884	130 ..
130 .. 10th ..	R. E. Foster (287) and W. Rhodes (40*)	Sydney	1903-04	66 ..

AUSTRALIA

				Time
244 for 1st wkt	R. B. Simpson (225) and W. M. Lawry (119)	Adelaide	1965-66	255 mins
451 .. 2nd ..	W. H. Ponsford (266) and D. G. Bradman (244)	Oval	1934	316 ..
276 .. 3rd ..	D. G. Bradman (187) and A. L. Hassett (128)	Brisbane	1946-47	278 ..
388 .. 4th ..	W. H. Ponsford (181) and D. G. Bradman (304)	Headingley	1934	341 ..
405 .. 5th ..	S. G. Barnes (234) and D. G. Bradman (234)	Sydney	1946-47	393 ..
346 .. 6th ..	J. H. W. Fingleton (136) and D. G. Bradman (270)	Melbourne	1936-37	364 ..
165 .. 7th ..	C. Hill (188) and H. Trumble (46)	Melbourne	1897-98	152 ..
243 .. 8th ..	R. J. Hartigan (116) and C. Hill (160)	Adelaide	1907-08	245 ..
154 .. 9th ..	S. E. Gregory (201) and J. McC. Blackham (74)	Sydney	1894-95	73 ..
127 .. 10th ..	J. M. Taylor (108) and A. A. Mailey (46*)	Sydney	1924-25	79 ..

The record partnerships have been distributed over nine different grounds – five in Australia and four in England. D. G. Bradman (A) shares in five of the record stands.

D. C. S. Compton (E), in 1938, and C. Hill (A), in 1897-98, were both under 21 when they took part in their respective record partnerships.

England's 9th-wicket record (above) has subsisted – so far – for 85 years, the longest period of time any record partnership has subsisted in the history of these matches. Apart from those partnerships shown above (seven in all), the only other record partnership for any wicket that subsisted for 50 or more years was the stand of 180 for the 1st wicket by W. Bardsley and S. E. Gregory at the Oval in 1909 that remained Australia's 1st-wicket record from 11 August 1909 to 23 July 1964.

No record partnership has been established for England since 1938.

The following batsmen have taken part in two record partnerships in the same innings (excluding the first eight Tests, when record partnerships were low and readily broken):

W. L. Murdoch (211), at the Oval in 1884, added 143 for the 2nd wicket with P. S. McDonnell (then the record), and 207 for the 3rd wicket with H. J. H. Scott (then the record);

W. H. Scotton (90), at the Oval in 1884, added 45 for the 4th wicket with A. G. Steel (then joint record), and 151 for the 9th wicket with W. W. Read;

S. E. Gregory (201), at Sydney in 1894-95, added 139 for the 5th wicket with G. Giffen (then the record), and 154 for the 9th wicket with J. McC. Blackham;

R. E. Foster (287), at Sydney in 1903-04, added 192 for the 5th wicket with L. C. Braund (then the record), and 130 for the 10th wicket with W. Rhodes;

W. R. Hammond (240), at Lord's in 1938, added 222 for the 4th wicket with E. Paynter, and 186 for the 6th wicket with L. E. G. Ames (then the record);

L. Hutton (364), at the Oval in 1938, added 382 for the 2nd wicket with M. Leyland, and 215 for the 6th wicket with J. Hardstaff.

Progressive record partnership

The first fifty partnership in these matches was between C. Bannerman and B. B. Cooper, for Australia, in the first Test of all, at Melbourne in 1876-77.

The following table shows the progressive record partnership until the highest stand was recorded, at the Oval in 1934.

77 for 4th wkt	C. Bannerman (165 ret. ht.) and B. B. Cooper (15)	for A	Melbourne	1876-77
88 .. 1st ..	D. W. Gregory (43) and N. Thompson (41)	for A	Melbourne	1876-77
120 .. 2nd ..	W. G. Grace (152) and A. P. Lucas (55)	for E	Oval	1880
137 .. 2nd ..	G. Ulyett (87) and J. Selby (55)	for E	Melbourne	1881-82
199 .. 4th ..	A. C. Bannerman (70) and P. S. McDonnell (147)	for A	Sydney	1881-82
207 .. 3rd ..	W. L. Murdoch (211) and H. J. H. Scott (102)	for A	Oval	1884
210 .. 3rd ..	A. Ward (93) and J. T. Brown (140)	for E	Melbourne	1894-95
221 .. 4th ..	G. H. S. Trott (143) and S. E. Gregory (103)	for A	Lord's	1896
243 .. 8th ..	R. J. Hartigan (116) and C. Hill (160)	for A	Adelaide	1907-08
323 .. 1st ..	J. B. Hobbs (178) and W. Rhodes (179)	for E	Melbourne	1911-12
388 .. 4th ..	W. H. Ponsford (181) and D. G. Bradman (304)	for A	Headingley	1934
451 .. 2nd ..	W. H. Ponsford (266) and D. G. Bradman (244)	for A	Oval	1934

Highest partnerships

Thirty-one partnerships of 200 or over have been recorded – 11 for England and 20 for Australia:

451 for 2nd wkt	W. H. Ponsford (266) and D. G. Bradman (244)	for A	Oval	1934
405 .. 5th ..	S. G. Barnes (234) and D. G. Bradman (234)	for A	Sydney	1946-47
388 .. 4th ..	W. H. Ponsford (181) and D. G. Bradman (304)	for A	Headingley	1934
382 .. 2nd ..	L. Hutton (364) and M. Leyland (187)	for E	Oval	1938
346 .. 6th ..	J. H. W. Fingleton (136) and D. G. Bradman (270)	for A	Melbourne	1936-37
323 .. 1st ..	J. B. Hobbs (178) and W. Rhodes (179)	for E	Melbourne	1911-12
301 .. 2nd ..	A. R. Morris (182) and D. G. Bradman (173*)	for A	Headingley	1948
283 .. 1st ..	J. B. Hobbs (154) and H. Sutcliffe (176)	for E	Melbourne	1924-25
276 .. 3rd ..	D. G. Bradman (187) and A. L. Hassett (128)	for A	Brisbane	1946-47
262 .. 3rd ..	W. R. Hammond (177) and D. R. Jardine (98)	for E	Adelaide	1928-29
249 .. 3rd ..	D. G. Bradman (169) and S. J. McCabe (112)	for A	Melbourne	1936-37
246 .. 3rd ..	E. R. Dexter (174) and K. F. Barrington (256)	for E	Old Trafford	1964
244 .. 1st ..	R. B. Simpson (225) and W. M. Lawry (119)	for A	Adelaide	1965-66
243 .. 8th ..	R. J. Hartigan (116) and C. Hill (160)	for A	Adelaide	1907-08
243 .. 4th ..	D. G. Bradman (232) and A. A. Jackson (73)	for A	Oval	1930
235 .. 2nd ..	W. M. Woodfull (141) and C. G. Macartney (151)	for A	Headingley	1926
234 .. 1st ..	G. Boycott (84) and R. W. Barber (185)	for E	Sydney	1965-66
231 .. 2nd ..	W. M. Woodfull (155) and D. G. Bradman (254)	for A	Lord's	1930
229 .. 3rd ..	D. G. Bradman (334) and A. F. Kippax (77)	for A	Headingley	1930
222 .. 4th ..	W. R. Hammond (240) and E. Paynter (99)	for E	Lord's	1938
221 .. 4th ..	G. H. S. Trott (143) and S. E. Gregory (103)	for A	Lord's	1896
219 .. 1st ..	L. Hutton (100) and C. J. Barnett (126)	for E	Trent Bridge	1938
219 .. 5th ..	R. B. Simpson (311) and B. C. Booth (98)	for A	Old Trafford	1964
215 .. 2nd ..	W. M. Woodfull (111) and H. S. T. L. Hendry (112)	for A	Sydney	1928-29
215 .. 6th ..	L. Hutton (364) and J. Hardstaff (169*)	for E	Oval	1938
212 .. 3rd ..	W. M. Lawry (108) and R. M. Cowper (307)	for A	Melbourne	1965-66
210 .. 3rd ..	A. Ward (93) and J. T. Brown (140)	for E	Melbourne	1894-95
207 .. 3rd ..	W. L. Murdoch (211) and H. J. H. Scott (102)	for A	Oval	1884
206 .. 5th ..	E. Paynter (216*) and D. C. S. Compton (102)	for E	Trent Bridge	1938
202 .. 3rd ..	A. R. Morris (153) and R. N. Harvey (162)	for A	Brisbane	1954-55
201 .. 1st ..	W. M. Lawry (106) and R. B. Simpson (311)	for A	Old Trafford	1964

D. G. Bradman (A) shared in 10 double-century partnerships – the record. No other batsman has taken part in more than three. The record for England is held by L. Hutton (three).

At the Oval in 1938 L. Hutton shared in two double-century partnerships in the same innings (382 and 215 above). At Old Trafford in 1964 R. B. Simpson also shared in two double-century partnerships in the same innings (201 and 219 above). The only other innings of a side to contain two such partnerships was England's innings at Trent Bridge in 1938 (219 and 206 above).

The only partnership to end at 199 was that for the 4th wicket between A. C. Bannerman (70) and P. S. McDonnell (147) for Australia at Sydney in 1881-82.

The greatest number of century partnerships in which one player has participated is 22, by J. B. Hobbs (E). Both H. Sutcliffe (E) and D. G. Bradman (A) shared in 21 century stands.

J. B. Hobbs (E) shared in 16 century partnerships for the 1st wicket – the record number by one player for a particular wicket. H. Sutcliffe (E) shared in 15 century partnerships for the 1st wicket, 11 of them with Hobbs.

In the following instances a batsman took part in three century partnerships in the same innings:

R. E. Foster (287)   for 5th, 9th and 10th wkts   for E   Sydney   1903-04
H. Sutcliffe (194)   for 1st, 2nd and 3rd wkts   for E   Sydney   1932-33
L. Hutton (364)   for 2nd, 3rd and 6th wkts   for E   Oval   1938

In addition to the match at Sydney in 1932-33 (above), the first 3 wickets yielded 100 or more runs in Australia's first innings at Lord's in 1930 and in England's first innings at Headingley in 1948.

The greatest number of century partnerships recorded in a single innings is four – in England's 903 for 7 dec. at the Oval in 1938.

The greatest number of century partnerships in a series is 18 in 1920-21 (11 for Australia, 7 for England).

The greatest number of century partnerships in which one batsman has participated in a series is five, as follows:

H. Sutcliffe (E)   in 1924-25 and 1932-33
D. G. Bradman (A)   in 1930 and 1936-37
J. B. Hobbs (E)   in 1924-25
W. M. Woodfull (A)   in 1930

Fast partnerships

30 for	7th wkt in	8 mins	G. L. Jessop (104) and G. H. Hirst (58)	for E	Oval	1902
36 ..	9th	14 ..	J. J. Kelly (24*) and W. P. Howell (35)	for A	Sydney	1901-02
42*..	9th	16 ..	F. W. Freer (28*) and G. E. Tribe (25*)	for A	Sydney	1946-47
50 ..	1st	21 ..	A. C. MacLaren (25) and G. L. Jessop (35)	for E	Melbourne	1901-02
77 ..	10th	28 ..	S. J. McCabe (232) and L. O'B. Fleetwood-Smith (5*)	for A	Trent Bridge	1938
62 ..	7th	29 ..	Rev. D. S. Sheppard (113) and T. G. Evans (47)	for E	Old Trafford	1956
60 ..	2nd	30 ..	V. T. Trumper (62) and C. Hill (119)	for A	Sheffield	1902
71*..	3rd	37 ..	A. C. Russell (102*) and J. W. Hitch (51*)	for E	Oval	1921
71 ..	4th	40 ..	T. J. E. Andrews (94) and J. M. Taylor (75)	for A	Oval	1921
74 ..	8th	44 ..	D. C. S. Compton (76*) and A. W. Wellard (38)	for E	Lord's	1938
85 ..	8th	46 ..	W. A. Brown (206*) and W. J. O'Reilly (42)	for A	Lord's	1938
102*..	5th	62 ..	E. Tyldesley (78*) and P. G. H. Fender (44*)	for E	Old Trafford	1921
112 ..	8th	65 ..	H. Graham (105) and A. E. Trott (86*)	for A	Sydney	1894-95
111 ..	7th	65 ..	M. Leyland (111*) and R. W. V. Robins (61)	for E	Melbourne	1936-37
110 ..	4th	65 ..	C. B. Fry (60) and A. C. MacLaren (49)	for E	Oval	1899
130 ..	10th	66 ..	R. E. Foster (287) and W. Rhodes (40*)	for E	Sydney	1903-04
109 ..	6th	67 ..	Hon. F. S. Jackson (49) and G. L. Jessop (104)	for E	Oval	1902
107 ..	4th	67 ..	C. Hill (119) and S. E. Gregory (29)	for A	Sheffield	1902
154 ..	9th	73 ..	S. E. Gregory (201) and J. McC. Blackham (74)	for A	Sydney	1894-95
154 ..	8th	88 ..	D. Tallon (92) and R. R. Lindwall (100)	for A	Melbourne	1946-47
158 ..	6th	90 ..	J. T. Tyldesley (112*) and R. H. Spooner (79)	for E	Oval	1905
193 ..	3rd	120 ..	J. Darling (160) and J. Worrall (62)	for A	Sydney	1897-98
206 ..	5th	138 ..	E. Paynter (216*) and D. C. S. Compton (102)	for E	Trent Bridge	1938
210 ..	3rd	145 ..	A. Ward (93) and J. T. Brown (140)	for E	Melbourne	1894-95
231 ..	2nd	154 ..	W. M. Woodfull (155) and D. G. Bradman (254)	for A	Lord's	1930
221 ..	4th	160 ..	G. H. S. Trott (143) and S. E. Gregory (103)	for A	Lord's	1896
249 ..	3rd	163 ..	D. G. Bradman (169) and S. J. McCabe (112)	for A	Melbourne	1936-37
229 ..	3rd	163 ..	D. G. Bradman (334) and A. F. Kippax (77)	for A	Headingley	1930
301 ..	2nd	217 ..	A. R. Morris (182) and D. G. Bradman (173*)	for A	Headingley	1948

H. Graham, in his 105 for Australia at Sydney in 1894-95, shared successive stands of 68 for the 7th wicket in 40 minutes with J. Darling and 112 for the 8th wicket in 65 minutes with A. E. Trott. Graham and Trott put on their first 35 in 15 minutes.

C. G. Macartney and J. M. Taylor, in their stand of 109 for the 4th wicket in 75 minutes at Headingley in 1921, took the total from 200 to 250 in 18 minutes.

E. Tyldesley and P. G. H. Fender, in their stand of 102* for the 5th wicket in 62 minutes at Old Trafford in 1921, put on their first 45 in 20 minutes and had added 81* in 39 minutes at the point of the illegal declaration.

H. Sutcliffe and A. P. F. Chapman, in their stand of 68 for the 3rd wicket in 46 minutes at Sydney in 1924-25, put on their first 50 in 27 minutes.

J. Ryder and J. M. Taylor, in their stand of 63 for the 3rd wicket in 47 minutes at Adelaide in 1924-25, put on their first 50 in 26 minutes.

D. G. Bradman and S. J. McCabe put on 67* for the 5th wicket in the last 37 minutes' play on the second day at Headingley in 1934. Their stand went on to produce 90 in 61 minutes.

M. Leyland and R. W. V. Robins, in their stand of 111 for the 7th wicket in 65 minutes at Melbourne in 1936-37, put on their first 50 in 25 minutes and their first 100 in 59 minutes. The stand having put on 41* at the close of the fifth day, they added 70 in the first 45 minutes on the final morning.

D. G. Bradman and S. J. McCabe, in their stand of 249 for the 3rd wicket in 163 minutes at Melbourne in 1936-37, scored their second 100 together in 63 minutes and their last 100 in 51 minutes.

A. R. Morris and D. G. Bradman scored their first 70 in 42 minutes in their 2nd-wicket stand of 99* (in 91 minutes) at Adelaide in 1946-47.

At the tea interval on the final day at Headingley in 1948, A. R. Morris and D. G. Bradman, for the 2nd wicket, had added 231* in 165 minutes. Altogether they put on 64 in 30 minutes before lunch, 167 in 135 minutes between lunch and tea, and 70 in 52 minutes after tea.

Fast partnerships for first wicket

First-wicket partnerships in England-Australia matches have not been particularly fast, but the following are the most noteworthy:

50 in 21 mins	A. C. MacLaren (25) and G. L. Jessop (35)	for E	Melbourne	1901-02
49 .. 24 ..	L. Hutton (37) and C. Washbrook (41)	for E	Sydney	1946-47
57 .. 33 ..	V. T. Trumper (31) and R. A. Duff (27)	for A	Lord's	1905
56 .. 35 ..	A. C. Bannerman (60) and J. J. Lyons (33)	for A	Old Trafford	1893
54 .. 35 ..	A. C. Bannerman (55) and W. Bruce (22)	for A	Oval	1893
75 .. 45 ..	J. Darling (47) and F. A. Iredale (30)	for A	Oval	1896
66 .. 45 ..	J. J. Lyons (55) and C. T. B. Turner (24)	for A	Lord's	1890
103 .. 76 ..	W. Bardsley (63*) and T. J. E. Andrews (49)	for A	Lord's	1921
135 .. 78 ..	V. T. Trumper (104) and R. A. Duff (54)	for A	Old Trafford	1902
129 .. 88 ..	V. T. Trumper (113) and R. A. Duff (79)	for A	Adelaide	1903-04
158 .. 111 ..	A. C. Russell (102*) and G. Brown (84)	for E	Oval	1921
219 .. 172 ..	L. Hutton (100) and C. J. Barnett (126)	for E	Trent Bridge	1938
323 .. 268 ..	J. B. Hobbs (178) and W. Rhodes (179)	for E	Melbourne	1911-12

V. T. Trumper and R. A. Duff shared two century partnerships for the 1st wicket against England (as above) – scored at an average rate of 95·42 runs per hour.

Most wickets

ENGLAND	Tests	Balls	Mds.	Runs	Wkts	Av.
W. Rhodes	41	5,791	233	2,616	109	24·00
S. F. Barnes	20	5,749	264	2,288	106	21·58
A. V. Bedser	21	7,065	209	2,859	104	27·49
R. Peel	20	5,216	444	1,715	102	16·81
J. Briggs	31	4,941	338	1,993	97	20·54
T. Richardson	14	4,497	191	2,220	88	25·22
M. W. Tate	20	7,686	330	2,542	83	30·62
J. C. Laker	15	4,010	204	1,444	79	18·27
F. S. Trueman	19	4,361	83	1,999	79	25·30
G. A. Lohmann	15	3,301	326	1,002	77	13·01

AUSTRALIA	Tests	Balls	Mds.	Runs	Wkts	Av.
H. Trumble	31	7,895	448	2,945	141	20·88
M. A. Noble	39	6,845	353	2,860	115	24·86
R. R. Lindwall	29	6,728	216	2,559	114	22·44
C. V. Grimmett	22	9,224	426	3,439	106	32·44
G. Giffen	31	6,325	434	2,791	103	27·09
W. J. O'Reilly	19	7,864	439	2,587	102	25·36
C. T. B. Turner	17	5,195	457	1,670	101	16·53
F. R. Spofforth	18	4,185	416	1,731	94	18·41
G. D. McKenzie	22	6,602	219	2,658	89	29·86
K. R. Miller	29	5,717	225	1,949	87	22·40
A. A. Mailey	18	5,199	90	2,935	86	34·12
A. K. Davidson	25	5,996	221	1,996	84	23·76
R. Benaud	27	7,284	289	2,641	83	31·81
G. E. Palmer	17	4,517	452	1,678	78	21·51
W. A. Johnston	17	5,263	224	1,818	75	24·24

AUSTRALIA		Tests	Balls	M	R	W	Av.	5 wkts in inns	10 wkts in match
A. A. Mailey	1920-21	5	1463	27	946	36	26·27	4	2
G. Giffen	1894-95	5	2060	111	820	34	24·11	3	0
M. A. Noble	1901-02	5	1380	68	608	32	19·00	4	1
H. V. Hordern	1911-12	5	1665	43	780	32	24·37	4	2
J. V. Saunders	1907-08	5	1603	52	716	31	23·09	3	0
R. Benaud	1958-59	5	1866	65	584	31	18·83	2	0
C. V. Grimmett	1930	5	2098	78	925	29	31·89	4	1
G. D. McKenzie	1964	5	1536	61	654	29	22·55	2	0
H. Trumble	1901-02	5	1604	93	561	28	20·03	2	0
W. J. O'Reilly	1934	5	2002	128	698	28	24·92	2	1
E. A. McDonald	1921	5	1235	32	668	27	24·74	2	0
W. J. O'Reilly	1932-33	5	2302	144	724	27	26·81	2	1
R. R. Lindwall	1948	5	1337	57	530	27	19·62	2	0
W. A. Johnston	1948	5	1856	92	630	27	23·33	1	0
E. Jones	1899	5	1276	73	657	26	25·26	2	1
H. Trumble	1902	3	1036	55	371	26	14·26	2	2
R. R. Lindwall	1953	5	1444	62	490	26	18·84	3	0
C. V. Grimmett	1934	5	2379	148	668	25	26·72	2	0
W. J. O'Reilly	1936-37	5	1982	89	555	25	22·20	2	0

A. A. Mailey in 1920-21 took the record number of wickets for Australia though he bowled in only four of the five matches in which he played.

W. J. O'Reilly (A) is the only bowler who has taken 25 or more wickets in a series as many as three times. They were, moreover, three successive series.

H. Trumble (A), W. J. O'Reilly (A) and A. V. Bedser (E) are the only bowlers to take 25 or more wickets in a series in both England and Australia.

Of those who have taken 25 or more wickets in a series, the best wicket-frequency rates are as follows:

W. Rhodes (E) took a wicket every 33·29 balls in 1903-04
J. C. Laker (E) took a wicket every 37·02 balls in 1956
H. Trumble (A) took a wicket every 39·84 balls in 1902
H. Larwood (E) took a wicket every 40·06 balls in 1932-33

The best wicket-frequency rate in a series by an Australian in Australia is a wicket every 43·12 balls by M. A. Noble in 1901-02.

The worst wicket-frequency rates among those who have taken 25 or more wickets in a series are:

J. C. White (E) took a wicket every 97·60 balls in 1928-29
C. V. Grimmett (A) took a wicket every 95·16 balls in 1934
W. J. O'Reilly (A) took a wicket every 85·25 balls in 1932-33

Most wickets in a series

ENGLAND		Tests	Balls	M	R	W	Av.	5 wkts in inns	10 wkts in match
J. C. Laker	1956	5	1703	127	442	46	9·60	4	2
A. V. Bedser	1953	5	1591	58	682	39	17·48	5	1
M. W. Tate	1924-25	5	2528	62	881	38	23·18	5	1
S. F. Barnes	1911-12	5	1782	64	778	34	22·88	3	0
H. Larwood	1932-33	5	1322	42	644	33	19·51	2	1
T. Richardson	1894-95	5	1747	63	849	32	26·53	4	0
F. R. Foster	1911-12	5	1660	58	692	32	21·62	3	0
W. Rhodes	1903-04	5	1032	36	488	31	15·74	3	1
J. N. Crawford	1907-08	5	1426	36	742	30	24·73	3	0
A. V. Bedser	1950-51	5	1560	34	482	30	16·06	2	1
F. H. Tyson	1954-55	5	1208	16	583	28	20·82	2	1
R. Peel	1894-95	5	1831	77	721	27	26·70	1	0
W. Voce	1936-37	5	1297	20	560	26	21·53	1	1
A. Fielder	1907-08	4	1299	31	627	25	25·08	1	0
J. C. White	1928-29	5	2440	134	760	25	30·40	3	1

Lowest average in a series (*Qualification: 10 wickets*)

		Tests	Balls	M	R	W	Av.
F. E. Woolley (E)	1912	3	140	7	55	10	5·50
C. V. Grimmett (A)	1924-25	1	251	5	82	11	7·45
R. Peel (E)	1888	3	442	48	181	24	7·54
J. Briggs (E)	1886	3	537	75	132	17	7·76
J. Briggs (E)	1888	3	337	42	94	12	7·83
R. G. Barlow (E)	1886	3	480	70	95	10	9·50
J. C. Laker (E)	1956	5	1703	127	442	46	9·60
W. H. Lockwood (E)	1902	4	487	18	206	17	12·11
C. T. B. Turner (A)	1888	3	656	62	261	21	12·42

(Test series consisting of three or more matches only have been included in the above table).

The lowest average by an English bowler in Australia is 14·14 by T. E. Bailey (14 wickets) in 1950-51.

Wicket-frequency per match

The following tables show the average number of wickets taken per match by all bowlers who have an aggregate of 50 or more wickets in these matches:

ENGLAND

				Av. per match
T. Richardson	88 wkts in 14 matches			6.28
S. F. Barnes	106	..	.. 20	.. 5·30
J. C. Laker	79	..	.. 15	.. 5·26
G. A. Lohmann	77	..	.. 15	.. 5·13
R. Peel	102	..	.. 20	.. 5·10
A. V. Bedser	104	..	.. 21	.. 4·95
H. Larwood	64	..	.. 15	.. 4·26
M. W. Tate	83	..	.. 20	.. 4·15
F. S. Trueman	62	..	.. 15	.. 4·13
W. Bates	50	..	.. 15	.. 3·33
H. Verity	59	..	.. 18	.. 3·27
J. B. Statham	69	..	.. 22	.. 3·13
J. Briggs	97	..	.. 31	.. 3·12
W. Rhodes	109	..	.. 41	.. 2.60
W. Barnes	51	..	.. 21	.. 2·42

AUSTRALIA

				Av. per match
C. T. B. Turner	101 wkts in 17 matches			5·94
W. J. O'Reilly	102	..	.. 19	.. 5·36
J. V. Saunders	64	..	.. 12	.. 5·33
F. R. Spofforth	94	..	.. 18	.. 5·22
C. V. Grimmett	106	..	.. 22	.. 4·81
A. A. Mailey	86	..	.. 18	.. 4·77
G. E. Palmer	78	..	.. 17	.. 4·58
H. Trumble	141	..	.. 31	.. 4·54
W. A. Johnston	75	..	.. 17	.. 4·41
A. Cotter	67	..	.. 16	.. 4·18
G. D. McKenzie	89	..	.. 22	.. 4·04
R. R. Lindwall	114	..	.. 29	.. 3·93
A. K. Davidson	84	..	.. 25	.. 3·36
J. M. Gregory	70	..	.. 21	.. 3·33
E. Jones	60	..	.. 18	.. 3·33
G. Giffen	103	..	.. 31	.. 3·32
R. Benaud	83	..	.. 27	.. 3·07
K. R. Miller	87	..	.. 29	.. 3·00
M. A. Noble	115	..	.. 39	.. 2·94
W. W. Armstrong	74	..	.. 42	.. 1·76

Penetrative career bowling (*Qualification: 25 wickets*)

The following tables show the wicket-frequency rates of the 46 Englishmen and 37 Australians who have taken 25 or more wickets in these matches:

ENGLAND	Balls per wkt	Tests	Balls	Mds.	Runs	Wkts	Av.
B. J. T. Bosanquet	38·80	7	970	10	604	25	24·16
G. A. Lohmann	42·87	15	3301	326	1002	77	13·01
W. Barnes	44·88	21	2289	271	793	51	15·54
W. H. Lockwood	45·81	12	1970	100	884	43	20·55
A. G. Steel	47·03	13	1364	108	605	29	20·86
W. Bates	47·28	15	2364	282	821	50	16·42
J. N. Crawford	47·53	5	1426	36	742	30	24·73
C. Blythe	48·21	9	1977	94	877	41	21·39
W. E. Bowes	48·63	6	1459	41	741	30	24·70
J. C. Laker	50·75	15	4010	204	1444	79	18·27
J. Briggs	50·93	31	4941	338	1993	97	20·54
T. Richardson	51·10	14	4497	191	2220	88	25·22
R. Peel	51·13	20	5216	444	1715	102	16·81
G. Ulyett	51·57	23	2527	286	992	49	20·24
W. Rhodes	53·12	41	5791	233	2616	109	24·00
F. H. Tyson	53·87	8	1724	23	810	32	25·31
S. F. Barnes	54·23	20	5749	264	2288	106	21·58
E. G. Arnold	54·84	8	1371	47	689	25	27·56
F. S. Trueman	55·20	19	4361	83	1999	79	25·30
F. R. Foster	55·70	8	1894	76	742	34	21·82
K. Farnes	56·65	8	2153	58	1065	38	28·02
A. Fielder	57·34	6	1491	42	711	26	27·34
W. Voce	59·75	11	2450	56	1128	41	27·51
J. T. Hearne	61·16	11	2936	209	1070	48	22·29
C. H. Parkin	62·65	9	2005	49	1090	32	34·06
H. Larwood	63·32	15	4053	120	1916	64	29·93
J. W. H. T. Douglas	66·22	7	2318	53	1227	35	35·05
E. Peate	67·61	9	2096	260	682	31	22·00
A. V. Bedser	67·93	21	7065	209	2859	104	27·49
G. H. Hirst	70·87	21	3473	118	1585	49	32·34
R. G. Barlow	72·23	17	2456	315	767	34	22·55
G. O. Allen	72·62	13	3123	58	1603	43	37·27
D. V. P. Wright	77·27	14	3709	61	2039	48	42·47
J. B. Statham	78·33	22	5405	130	2138	69	30·98
T. E. Bailey	78·57	23	3300	105	1373	42	32·69
L. C. Braund	79·67	20	3665	140	1769	46	38·45
H. Verity	83·15	18	4906	256	1657	59	28·08
F. E. Woolley	83·48	32	3590	130	1555	43	36·16
D. A. Allen	89·00	10	2492	120	892	28	31·85
M. W. Tate	92·60	20	7686	330	2542	83	30·62
J. C. White	95·93	7	2974	148	1033	31	33·32
G. Geary	97·33	9	2628	112	963	27	35·66
W. Attewell	105·55	10	2850	326	626	27	23·18
W. R. Hammond	109·94	33	3958	135	1612	36	44·77
G. A. R. Lock	111·03	13	3442	193	1128	31	36·38
F. J. Titmus	119·65	15	4786	198	1434	40	35·85

AUSTRALIA	Balls per wkt	Tests	Balls	Mds	Runs	Wkts	Av.
J. J. Ferris	42·29	8	2030	224	684	48	14·25
F. R. Spofforth	44·52	18	4185	416	1731	94	18·41
J. V. Saunders	51·06	12	3268	108	1620	64	25·31
C. T. B. Turner	51·43	17	5195	457	1670	101	16·53
A. Cotter	51·70	16	3464	63	1916	67	28·59
H. V. Hordern	52·03	5	1665	43	780	32	24·37
H. F. Boyle	54·50	12	1744	175	641	32	20·03
H. Trumble	55·99	31	7895	448	2945	141	20·88
G. E. Palmer	57·91	17	4517	452	1678	78	21·51
R. R. Lindwall	59·01	29	6728	216	2559	114	22·44
M. A. Noble	59·52	39	6845	353	2860	115	24·86
E. Jones	59·66	18	3580	152	1757	60	29·28
E. A. McDonald	60·33	8	1991	42	1060	33	32·12
A. A. Mailey	60·45	18	5199	90	2935	86	34·12
G. Giffen	61·40	31	6325	434	2791	103	27·09
F. Laver	63·97	15	2367	122	964	37	26·05
G. H. S. Trott	65·17	24	1890	48	1019	29	35·13
K. R. Miller	65·71	29	5717	225	1949	87	22·40
J. M. Gregory	69·81	21	4887	109	2364	70	33·77
R. G. Archer	69·85	12	2445	126	761	35	21·74

AUSTRALIA	Balls per wkt	Tests	Balls	Mds	Runs	Wkts	Av.
W. A. Johnston	70·17	17	5263	224	1818	75	24·24
A. K. Davidson	71·38	25	5996	221	1996	84	23·76
L. O'B. Fleetwood-Smith	71·48	7	2359	54	1190	33	36·06
G. D. McKenzie	74·21	22	6602	219	2658	89	29·86
T. W. Garrett	75·22	19	2708	297	970	36	26·94
W. J. O'Reilly	77·09	19	7864	439	2587	102	25·36
C. G. Macartney	79·78	26	2633	120	908	33	27·51
N. J. N. Hawke	85·83	12	3176	128	1119	37	30·24
C. V. Grimmett	87·01	27	9224	426	3439	106	32·44
R. Benaud	87·75	27	7284	289	2641	83	31·81
E. R. H. Toshack	88·17	9	2469	120	801	28	28·60
T. W. Wall	90·25	14	3881	115	1663	43	38·67
C. Kelleway	90·27	18	3340	112	1155	37	31·21
W. W. Armstrong	91·64	42	6782	362	2288	74	30·91
W. P. Howell	100·22	16	3508	229	1243	35	35·51
C. E. McLeod	102·24	17	3374	171	1325	33	40·15
I. W. Johnson	109·33	22	4592	187	1590	42	37·85

Economical career bowling (*Qualification: 1000 balls*)

ENGLAND

Of the 61 Englishmen who have bowled 1000 balls or more, the following have conceded the fewest runs per 100 balls:

	Runs per 100 balls	Tests	Balls	Mds	Runs	Wkts	Av.
W. Attewell	21·96	10	2850	326	626	27	23·18
D. L. Underwood	23·98	4	1259	103	302	20	15·10
A. Shaw	25·93	7	1099	155	285	12	23·75
F. J. Titmus	29·96	15	4786	198	1434	40	35·85
G. A. Lohmann	30·35	15	3301	326	1002	77	13·01
R. Kilner	31·19	7	2164	63	675	24	28·12
R. G. Barlow	31·22	17	2456	315	767	34	22·55
R. Illingworth	31·26	7	1753	109	548	17	32·23
E. Peate	32·53	9	2096	260	682	31	22·00
G. A. R. Lock	32·77	13	3442	193	1128	31	36·38
R. Peel	32·87	20	5216	444	1715	102	16·81

The following have also conceded fewer than 40 runs per 100 balls:
M. W. Tate (33·07), H. Verity (33·77), W. Barnes (34·64), W. Bates (34·72), D. A. Allen (35·79), J. C. Laker (36·00), J. T. Hearne (36·44), G. Geary (36·49), J. C. White (37·76), J. H. Wardle (38·04), F. R. Foster (39·17), G. Ulyett (39·25), J. B. Statham (39·55), B. R. Knight (39·64), S. F. Barnes (39·79).

The least economical English bowler (among those who have bowled 1000 balls or more) is W. J. Edrich, who conceded 60·12 runs per 100 balls.

AUSTRALIA

Of the 62 Australians who have bowled 1000 balls or more, the following have conceded the fewest runs per 100 balls:

	Runs per 100 balls	Tests	Balls	Mds	Runs	Wkts	Av.
E. Evans	26·62	6	1247	166	332	7	47·42
A. J. Richardson	28·75	9	1812	91	521	12	43·41
J. Iverson	28·88	5	1108	29	320	21	15·23
R. K. Oxenham	29·03	3	1202	72	349	7	49·85
H. Ironmonger	29·06	6	2446	155	711	21	33·85
K. D. Mackay	30·86	16	2835	126	875	24	36·45
R. G. Archer	31·12	12	2445	126	761	35	21·74
C. T. B. Turner	32·14	17	5195	457	1670	101	16·53
E. R. H. Toshack	32·44	9	2469	120	801	28	28·60
W. J. O'Reilly	32·89	19	7864	439	2587	102	25·36

The following have also conceded fewer than 40 runs per 100 balls:

A. K. Davidson (33·28), J. J. Ferris (33·69), C. L. McCool (33·72), W. W. Armstrong (33·73), K. R. Miller (33·91), C. G. Macartney (34·48), W. A. Johnston (34·54), C. Kelleway (34·58), I. W. Johnson (34·62), D. D. J. Blackie (35·23), N. J. N. Hawke (35·23), H. S. T. L. Hendry (35·24), R. W. McLeod (35·26), W. P. Howell (35·43), T. W. Garrett (35·81), J. W. Gleeson (35·85), R. Benaud (36·25), T. R. Veivers (36·44), H. F. Boyle (36·75), G. E. Palmer (36·92), C. V. Grimmett (37·28), H. Trumble (37·30), A. N. Connolly (37·70), R. R. Lindwall (38·03), W. J. Whitty (38·24), G. E. Corling (38·56), C. E. McLeod (39·27).

The least economical Australian bowler (among those who have bowled 1000 balls or more) is A. A. Mailey, who conceded 56·45 runs per 100 balls.

Most wickets in an innings

ENGLAND

J. C. Laker*[1]	51·2–23– 53–10	Old Trafford	1956
J. C. Laker*[1]	16·4– 4– 37–9	Old Trafford	1956
G. A. Lohmann	25 –12– 35–8	Sydney	1886-87
H. Verity*[2]	22·3– 8– 43–8	Lord's	1934
G. A. Lohmann	43·2–18– 58–8	Sydney	1891-92
W. Rhodes*[3]	15 – 0– 68–8	Melbourne	1903-04
L. C. Braund	21·3– 6– 81–8	Melbourne	1903-04
T. Richardson	36·1– 7– 94–8	Sydney	1897-98
B. J. T. Bosanquet	32·4– 2–107–8	Trent Bridge	1905
J. C. White	64·5–21–126–8	Adelaide	1928-29
W. Rhodes	11 – 3– 17–7	Edgbaston	1902
F. H. Tyson	12·3– 1– 27–7	Melbourne	1954-55
W. Bates*[4]	26·2–14– 28–7	Melbourne	1882-83
R. Peel	26·2–17– 31–7	Old Trafford	1888
G. Ulyett	39·1–23– 36–7	Lord's	1884
G. A. Lohmann	30·2–17– 36–7	Oval	1886
R. G. Barlow	34·2–20– 40–7	Sydney	1882-83
R. G. Barlow	52 –24– 44–7	Old Trafford	1886
A. V. Bedser*[5]	17·2– 7– 44–7	Trent Bridge	1953
D. L. Underwood	31·3–19– 50–7	Oval	1968
A. V. Bedser*[5]	38·3–16– 55–7	Trent Bridge	1953
W. Rhodes*[3]	15·2– 3– 56–7	Melbourne	1903-04
J. B. Statham	28 – 6– 57–7	Melbourne	1958-59
S. F. Barnes	22·4– 6– 60–7	Sydney	1907-08
H. Verity*[2]	36 –15– 61–7	Lord's	1934
T. Emmett	59 –31– 68–7	Melbourne	1878-79
W. H. Lockwood	50·3–17– 71–7	Oval	1899
W. Bates*[4]	33 –14– 74–7	Melbourne	1882-83
F. J. Titmus	37 –14– 79–7	Sydney	1962-63
S. F. Barnes	64 –17–121–7	Melbourne	1901-02
T. Richardson	68 –23–168–7	Old Trafford	1896

AUSTRALIA

A. A. Mailey	47 – 8–121–9	Melbourne	1920-21
F. Laver	31·3–14– 31–8	Old Trafford	1909
A. E. Trott	27 –10– 43–8	Adelaide	1894-95
H. Trumble	31 –13– 65–8	Oval	1902
M. A. Noble	7·4– 2– 17–7	Melbourne	1901-02
G. R. Hazlitt	21·4– 8– 25–7	Oval	1912
H. Trumble	6·5– 0– 28–7	Melbourne	1903-04
C. T. B. Turner	38 –23– 43–7	Sydney	1887-88
F. R. Spofforth*[1]	28 –15– 44–7	Oval	1882
F. R. Spofforth	41·1–23– 44–7	Sydney	1882-83
F. R. Spofforth*[1]	36·3–18– 46–7	Oval	1882
W. J. O'Reilly	41·4–24– 54–7	Trent Bridge	1934
T. Kendall	33·1–12– 55–7	Melbourne	1876-77
C. G. Macartney	25·3–56– 58–7	Headingley	1909
K. R. Miller	22 – 4– 60–7	Brisbane	1946-47
F. R. Spofforth	35 –16– 62–7	Melbourne	1878-79
R. R. Lindwall	22 – 3– 63–7	Sydney	1946-47
F. Laver	31·3–14– 64–7	Trent Bridge	1905
G. E. Palmer	52·2–25– 65–7	Melbourne	1882-83
G. E. Palmer	58 –36– 68–7	Sydney	1881-82
J. M. Gregory	20 – 1– 69–7	Melbourne	1920-21
E. Jones	36·1–11– 88–7	Lord's	1899

*Same match

298

H. V. Hordern	42·2–11– 90–7	Sydney	1911–12
P. M. Hornibrook	31·2– 9– 92–7	Oval	1930
M. A. Noble	41·1–10–100–7	Sydney	1903–04
N. J. N. Hawke	33·7– 6–105–7	Sydney	1965–66
G. Giffen	52 –14–117–7	Sydney	1884–85

G. Giffen	54 –17–128–7	Oval	1893
A. Cotter	40 – 4–148–7	Oval	1905
G. D. McKenzie	60 –15–153–7	Old Trafford	1964
W. J. O'Reilly	59 – 9–189–7	Old Trafford	1934

Most wickets in a match

19 for 90	J. C. Laker	for E	Old Trafford	1956
15 for 104	H. Verity	for E	Lord's	1934
15 for 124	W. Rhodes	for E	Melbourne	1903–04
14 for 90	F. R. Spofforth	for A	Oval	1882
14 for 99	A. V. Bedser	for E	Trent Bridge	1953
14 for 102	W. Bates	for E	Melbourne	1882–83
13 for 77	M. A. Noble	for A	Melbourne	1901–02
13 for 110	F. R. Spofforth	for A	Melbourne	1878–79
13 for 163	S. F. Barnes	for E	Melbourne	1901–02
13 for 236	A. A. Mailey	for A	Melbourne	1920–21
13 for 244	T. Richardson	for E	Old Trafford	1896
13 for 256	J. C. White	for E	Adelaide	1928–29
12 for 87	C. T. B. Turner	for A	Sydney	1887–88
12 for 89	H. Trumble	for A	Oval	1896
12 for 102	F. Martin	for E	Oval	1890
12 for 104	G. A. Lohmann	for E	Oval	1886
12 for 136	J. Briggs	for E	Adelaide	1891–92
12 for 173	H. Trumble	for A	Oval	1902
12 for 175	H. V. Hordern	for A	Sydney	1911–12

F. R. Spofforth (A) and H. Trumble (A) are the only bowlers to have taken 12 wickets or more in a match on two occasions.

The youngest bowler to take 12 wickets or more in a match is G. A. Lohmann (E), who was 21 years 73 days when he did so at the Oval in 1886. The youngest to do so for Australia is C. T. B. Turner, who was 25 years 90 days at Sydney in 1887–88.

The following have taken 11 wickets in a match:

For England: J. Briggs (1886), R. Peel (1888), T. Richardson (1896), W. H. Lockwood (1902), C. Blythe (1909), M. W. Tate (1924–25), J. C. Laker (1956) and F. S. Trueman (1961).

For Australia: G. E. Palmer (1881–82), F. R. Spofforth (1882–83), M. A. Noble (1902), C. G. Macartney (1909), C. V. Grimmett (1924–25) and W. J. O'Reilly (1934).

The following have taken 10 wickets in a match:

For England: G. A. Lohmann (1886–87 and 1891–92), R. Peel (1887–88), J. Briggs (1893), T. Richardson (1893 and 1897–98), J. T. Hearne (1896), F. E. Woolley (1912), H. Larwood (1932–33), K. Farnes (1934), W. Voce (1936–37), A. V. Bedser (1950–51) and F. H. Tyson (1954–55).

For Australia: G. E. Palmer (1882–83), F. R. Spofforth (1884–85), C. T. B. Turner (1888), G. Giffen (1891–92), E. Jones (1899), H. Trumble (1902), H. V. Hordern (1911–12), A. A. Mailey (1920–21), C. V. Grimmett (1930), W. J. O'Reilly (1932–33 and 1938), L. O'B. Fleetwood-Smith (1936–37) and K. R. Miller (1956).

Most wickets in a day

14 wkts	H. Verity	for E	Lord's	1934	3rd day	6 in 1st	8 in 2nd
12 wkts	J. Briggs	for E	Adelaide	1891–92	3rd day	6 in 1st	6 in 2nd
10 wkts	S. F. Barnes	for E	Melbourne	1901–02	1st day	6 in 1st	4 in 2nd
10 wkts	J. C. Laker	for E	Old Trafford	1956	2nd day	9 in 1st	1 in 2nd

H. Verity's full analysis on the third day at Lord's in 1934 was 44·3–17–80–14.

S. F. Barnes was the only one of the four bowlers (above) who was not aided by a follow-on.

The greatest number of wickets taken by a bowler before lunch is 9 – by R. Peel (E) on the second day at Old Trafford in 1888 (5 in first innings and 4 in second). He was unable to add to his aggregate after lunch, the match already being over.

The greatest number of wickets to fall in a day's play is 27 (for 157 runs) – on the second day at Lord's in 1888: England went from 18 for three to 53, Australia made 60, and England (2nd innings) made 62.

The greatest number of wickets to fall in a day's play in Australia is 25 (for 221 runs) – on the first day of the second Test at Melbourne in 1901–02: Australia scored 112 and 48 for five, and England 61.

On the third day at Brisbane in 1950–51 20 wickets fell (for 102 runs) between lunch and close of play: England went from 28 for 0 to 68 for 7 dec., Australia made 32 for 7 dec., and England (2nd innings) made 30 for six.

Eighteen wickets fell before lunch (for 119 runs) on the second day at Old Trafford in 1888: Australia went from 32 for 2 to 81, and, following on, were out for 70. Nine of the Australian side batted twice in the pre-lunch period on this day.

Ten wickets in a match most times

The feat of taking 10 wickets or more in a match has been performed altogether 59 times – 32 times for England and 27 times for Australia.

4 times	F. R. Spofforth (A)	1878–79, 1882, 1882–83, 1884–85
4 times	T. Richardson (E)	1893, 1896 (twice), 1897–98
3 times	G. A. Lohmann (E)	1886, 1886–87, 1891–92
3 times	J. Briggs (E)	1886, 1891–92, 1893
3 times	H. Trumble (A)	1896, 1902 (twice)
3 times	W. J. O'Reilly (A)	1932–33, 1934, 1938

T. Richardson (E) and H. Trumble (A) are the only bowlers to perform the feat three times in England, and F. R. Spofforth (A) is the only bowler to do so three times in Australia.

The following bowlers performed the feat twice in a series:

T. Richardson	for E	in 1896
H. Trumble	for A	in 1902
H. V. Hordern	for A	in 1911–12
A. A. Mailey	for A	in 1920–21
J. C. Laker	for E	in 1956

All the above five bowlers, with the exception of Hordern, performed the feat in successive matches.

The youngest bowler to take 10 wickets or more in a match is G. E. Palmer (A), who was 20 years 363 days when he took 11 wickets at Sydney in 1881–82. The youngest English bowler to take 10 wickets or more in a match is G. A. Lohmann, who was 21 years 73 days when he took 12 wickets at the Oval in 1886.

R. R. Lindwall (A) is the only bowler who has taken 100 wickets or more in these matches without once reaching a total of 10 wickets in a match. The following have a career aggregate of 50 or more wickets without taking 10 in a match:

England: J. B. Statham (69 wickets), W. Barnes (51).

Australia: R. R. Lindwall (114 wickets), G. D. McKenzie (89), A. K. Davidson (84), R. Benaud (83), W. A. Johnston (75), W. W. Armstrong (74), J. M. Gregory (70), A. Cotter (67), J. V. Saunders (64).

Ten wickets on debut

12 for 102	F. Martin	for E	Oval	1890
10 for 156	T. Richardson	for E	Old Trafford	1893
12 for 175	H. V. Hordern	for A	Sydney	1911-12
11 for 228	M. W. Tate	for E	Sydney	1924-25
11 for 82	C. V. Grimmett	for A	Sydney	1924-25
10 for 179	K. Farnes	for E	Trent Bridge	1934

F. Martin (above) never played against Australia again.

Most runs conceded in an innings

298	(87-11-298-1)	L. O'B. Fleetwood-Smith (A)	Oval 1938
204	(71- 8-204-6)	I. A. R. Peebles (E)	Oval 1930

The greatest number of runs conceded in an innings by an English bowler in Australia is 181 (55·3-13-181-5) by T. Richardson at Sydney in 1894-95.

The greatest number of runs conceded in an innings by an Australian bowler in Australia is 191 (64-14-191-2) by C. V. Grimmett at Sydney in 1928-29.

Most runs conceded in a match

308	(129 and 179)	A. A. Mailey (A)	Sydney	1924-25
302	(160 and 142)	A. A. Mailey (A)	Adelaide	1920-21
298	(167 and 131)	C. V. Grimmett (A)	Brisbane	1928-29
298	(298)	L. O'B. Fleetwood-Smith (A)	Oval	1938
282	(146 and 136)	D. W. Carr (E)	Oval	1909
275	(99 and 176)	A. V. Bedser (E)	Melbourne	1946-47

On 18 occasions – 5 by Englishmen and 13 by Australians – a bowler has conceded 100 or more runs in each innings of a match. A. A. Mailey (A) did so five times.

Bowling unchanged through completed innings

The following pairs of bowlers bowled unchanged throughout a completed innings:

ENGLAND

F. Morley (2 for 34) and R. G. Barlow (7 for 40)	in A's 83	Sydney	1882-83
G. A. Lohmann (7 for 36) and J. Briggs (3 for 28)	in A's 68	Oval	1886
G. A. Lohmann (5 for 17) and R. Peel (5 for 18)	in A's 42	Sydney	1887-88
J. Briggs (6 for 49) and G. A. Lohmann (3 for 46)	in A's 100	Adelaide	1891-92
T. Richardson (6 for 39) and G. A. Lohmann (3 for 13)	in A's 53	Lord's	1896
S. F. Barnes (6 for 42) and C. Blythe (4 for 64)	in A's 112	Melbourne	1901-02
G. H. Hirst (4 for 28) and C. Blythe (6 for 44)	in A's 74	Edgbaston	1909
W. Voce (4 for 16) and G. O. Allen (5 for 36)	in A's 58	Brisbane	1936-37

AUSTRALIA

G. E. Palmer (7 for 68) and E. Evans (3 for 64)	in E's 133	Sydney	1881-82
F. R. Spofforth (5 for 30) and G. E. Palmer (4 for 32)	in E's 77	Sydney	1884-85
C. T. B. Turner (6 for 15) and J. J. Ferris (4 for 27)	in E's 45	Sydney	1886-87
C. T. B. Turner (5 for 36) and J. J. Ferris (5 for 26)	in E's 62	Lord's	1888
G. Giffen (5 for 26) and C. T. B. Turner (4 for 33)	in E's 72	Sydney	1894-95
H. Trumble (3 for 38) and M. A. Noble (7 for 17)	in E's 61	Melbourne	1901-02
J. V. Saunders (5 for 43) and M. A. Noble (5 for 54)	in E's 99	Sydney	1901-02

At Melbourne on 1 January 1902, the opening bowlers for each side performed the feat and moreover did so on the same day.

Of the 15 instances above, the side for which the feat was performed emerged the winner on 13 occasions. The two exceptions were at Sydney in 1886-87 (when Turner and Ferris were on the losing side) and at Melbourne in 1901-02 (when Barnes and Blythe were on the losing side).

Since the Second World War the nearest approach to this performance was at Melbourne in 1958-59, when A. K. Davidson (3 for 41) and I. Meckiff (6 for 38) bowled throughout England's innings of 87 apart from a single over.

At the Oval in 1902, H. Trumble (A) bowled unchanged from the pavilion end right through both England innings of 183 and 263 for 9.

Five wickets in an innings most times

12 times:	S. F. Barnes	for E	in 20 Tests
11 times:	T. Richardson	for E	in 14 Tests
	C. T. B. Turner	for A	in 17 Tests
	C. V. Grimmett	for A	in 22 Tests
9 times:	H. Trumble	for A	in 31 Tests
	M. A. Noble	for A	in 39 Tests
8 times:	W. J. O'Reilly	for A	in 19 Tests
7 times:	F. R. Spofforth	for A	in 18 Tests
	A. V. Bedser	for E	in 21 Tests
	J. Briggs	for E	in 31 Tests
	G. Giffen	for A	in 31 Tests
6 times:	A. Cotter	for A	in 16 Tests
	G. E. Palmer	for A	in 17 Tests
	A. A. Mailey	for A	in 18 Tests
	R. Peel	for E	in 20 Tests
	M. W. Tate	for E	in 20 Tests
	G. D. McKenzie	for A	in 22 Tests
	R. R. Lindwall	for A	in 22 Tests
	W. Rhodes	for E	in 41 Tests
5 times:	W. H. Lockwood	for E	in 12 Tests
	J. V. Saunders	for A	in 12 Tests
	J. C. Laker	for E	in 15 Tests
	G. A. Lohmann	for E	in 15 Tests
	F. S. Trueman	for E	in 19 Tests
	A. K. Davidson	for A	in 25 Tests

The youngest player to take 5 wickets or more in an innings is G. D. McKenzie (A), who was 20 years 2 days at Lord's in 1961. The oldest to do so is D. D. J. Blackie (A), who was 46 years 272 days at Melbourne in 1928-29.

The following have taken 5 wickets or more in *each* innings of a Test:

Three times: J. Briggs (E), T. Richardson (E).

Twice: A. V. Bedser (E), C. V. Grimmett (A), H. V. Hordern (A), J. C. Laker (E), M. A. Noble (A), F. R. Spofforth (A) and C. T. B. Turner (A).

Once: S. F. Barnes (E), W. Bates (E), C. Blythe (E), K. Farnes (E), H. Larwood (E), W. H. Lockwood (E), G. A. Lohmann (E), A. A. Mailey (A), F. Martin (E), K. R. Miller (A), W. J. O'Reilly (A), W. Rhodes (E), M. W. Tate (E), F. S. Trueman (A), H. Verity (E), J. C. White (E) and F. E. Woolley (E).

T. Richardson (E) in 1896 and J. C. Laker (E) in 1956 performed the feat in consecutive Tests in the same series. A. V. Bedser (E) also performed the feat in consecutive Tests, but not in the same series (1950-51 and 1953).

Hat-tricks

F. R. Spofforth   for A   Melbourne   1878-79
    (V. P. F. A. Royle, F. A. Mackinnon, T. Emmett)
W. Bates   for E   Melbourne   1882-83
    (P. S. McDonnell, G. Giffen, G. J. Bonnor)
J. Briggs   for E   Sydney   1891-92
    (W. F. Giffen, S. T. Callaway, J. McC. Blackham)
J. T. Hearne   for E   Headingley   1899
    (C. Hill, S. E. Gregory, M. A. Noble – all "ducks")
H. Trumble   for A   Melbourne   1901-02
    (A. O Jones, J. R. Gunn, S. F. Barnes)
H. Trumble   for A   Melbourne   1903-04
    (B. J. T. Bosanquet, P. F. Warner, A. A. Lilley)
F. R. Spofforth (above) was playing in his second Test.

No bowler has yet succeeded in performing the hat-trick by clean bowling all three batsmen, but R. R. Lindwall (A) clean bowled three men in four balls (see below).

Only Spofforth and Bates (above) performed their hat-tricks in the first innings.

Three wickets in four balls

F. R. Spofforth   for A   Oval   1882
F. R. Spofforth   for A   Sydney   1884-85
W. J. O'Reilly   for A   Old Trafford   1934
W. Voce   for E   Sydney   1936-37
R. R. Lindwall   for A   Adelaide   1946-47
K. D. Mackay   for A   Edgbaston   1961

When W. J. O'Reilly (above) took 3 wickets in 4 balls, they were the first 3 wickets of the match to fall. After the original ball had gone out of shape, the feat was performed in the second over of the replacement ball, H. Sutcliffe having first played a maiden from C. V. Grimmett. O'Reilly then dismissed C. F. Walters, R. E. S. Wyatt and W. R. Hammond in his first 4 deliveries with the replacement ball.

When W. Voce (above) took 3 wickets in 4 balls, they were the first 3 wickets to fall in Australia's first innings – L. P. J. O'Brien, D. G. Bradman and S. J. McCabe – and were all taken with the total at 1. They were taken with the 7th, 8th and 10th balls that Voce bowled.

W. Rhodes took 3 wickets in an over (6 balls) for England at Edgbaston in 1902, dismissing A. J. Hopkins with the first ball, E. Jones with the second, and W. P. Howell with the sixth.

The Hon. F. S. Jackson took 3 wickets in an over (6 balls) for England at Trent Bridge in 1905, dismissing M. A. Noble with the first ball, C. Hill with the fourth, and J. Darling with the sixth.

M. W. S. Sievers took 3 wickets in an over (9 balls, including one no-ball) for Australia at Melbourne in 1936-37, dismissing J. M. Sims with the second ball, R. W. V. Robins with the fourth, and L. E. G. Ames with the ninth.

A. K. Davidson took 3 wickets in an over (8 balls) for Australia at Melbourne in 1958-59, dismissing P. E. Richardson with the first ball, W. Watson with the fifth, and T. W. Graveney with the sixth. They were the first 3 wickets of the match to fall (in the third over of the innings).

R. W. McLeod took 3 wickets in 5 balls (not in the same over) for Australia at Melbourne in 1891-92, they being the first 3 wickets to fall in England's first innings (R. Abel, W. G. Grace and A. E. Stoddart).

All-rounders

Career Records:

The following scored 1,000 runs and took 100 wickets in England-Australia Tests:

	Tests	Runs	Av.	Wkts	Av.	"Double" reached	Match reached
G. Giffen (A)	31	1,238	23·35	103	27·09	Old Trafford, 1896	30th
M. A. Noble (A)	39	1,905	30·72	115	24·86	Oval, 1905	29th
W. Rhodes (E)	41	1,706	31·01	109	24·00	Adelaide, 1920-21	37th

Noble reached the "double" in the fewest Tests. He was also the youngest – at 32 years – to reach the target.

In each of the above three cases the 1,000-run mark was reached before the player took 100 wickets.

It is nearly half a century since the last player reached the target (W. Rhodes on 19 January 1921).

The following scored 1,000 runs and took 50 wickets:

	Tests	Runs	Av.	Wkts	Av.
W. W. Armstrong (A)	42	2,172	35·03	74	30·91
K. R. Miller (A)	29	1,511	33·57	87	22·40

The following scored 500 runs and took 100 wickets:

	Tests	Runs	Av.	Wkts	Av.
H. Trumble (A)	31	838	19·95	141	20·88
R. R. Lindwall (A)	29	795	22·08	114	22·44

W. Barnes (E), W. Bates (E), R. Benaud (A), J. Briggs (E), A. K. Davidson (A), J. M. Gregory (A) and M. W. Tate (E) all scored over 500 runs and took 50 or more wickets. G. H. Hirst (E) and G. Ulyett (E) each missed this double by one wicket.

Series Records:

The following scored 200 runs and took 20 wickets in a series:

	Tests	Runs	Av.	Wkts	Av.
G. Giffen (A)	1894-95	5	475	52·77	34	24·11
L. C. Braund (E)	1901-02	5	256	36·57	21	35·14
F. R. Foster (E)	1911-12	5	226	32·28	32	21·62
J. M. Gregory (A)	1920-21	5	442	73·66	23	24·17
J. M. Gregory (A)	1924-25	5	224	24·88	22	37·09
K. R. Miller (A)	1956	5	203	22·55	21	22·23

In 1894-95 (above) G. Giffen scored more runs and took more wickets than any man in the series on either side. No other player has achieved this even in respect of his own side.

The only player to head both the batting and bowling averages in a series is the Hon. F. S. Jackson (E) in 1905. (His respective averages – 70·28 and 15·46 – were also both superior to Australia's best).

Match Records:

The following scored 100 runs and took 8 wickets in the same match:

G. Giffen (A)	161 & 41	4 for 75 & 4 for 164	Sydney 1894-95
A. E. Trott (A)	38* & 72*	0 for 9 & 8 for 43	Adelaide 1894-95
J. M. Gregory (A)	100	7 for 69 & 1 for 32	Melbourne 1920-21
H. Larwood (E)	70 & 37	6 for 32 & 2 for 30	Brisbane 1928-29
G. O. Allen (E)	35 & 68	3 for 71 & 5 for 36	Brisbane 1936-37

A. E. Trott (above) was making his debut in Test cricket.

Of those players who have taken 10 or more wickets in a match, the following have also scored a half-century in the same Test:

W. Bates (E)	55	7 for 28 & 7 for 74	Melbourne 1882-83
H. Trumble (A)	64* & 7*	8 for 65 & 4 for 108	Oval 1902
F. E. Woolley (E)	62 & 4	5 for 29 & 5 for 20	Oval 1912

On three occasions – the record number – H. Trumble (A) scored a half-century and took 5 or more wickets in an innings in the same Test. G. Giffen (A), M. A. Noble (A) and F. R. Foster (E) each did so twice. Foster did so twice in three matches in 1911-12.

The wicketkeepers

England have been represented by 31 wicketkeepers and Australia by 17. Only the appointed wicketkeepers in each match are listed below.

ENGLAND	Matches	Caught	Stumped	Total
A. A. Lilley	32	65	19	84
T. G. Evans	31	64	11	75
H. Strudwick	17	37	5	42
L. E. G. Ames	17	33	4	37
G. Duckworth	10	23	3	26
J. M. Parks	10	17	4	21
J. T. Murray	6	18	1	19
G. MacGregor	7	14	3	17
A. P. E. Knott	5	11	4	15
R. Pilling	8	10	4	14
A. C. Smith	4	13	0	13
E. J. Smith	7	12	1	13
J. Hunter	5	8	3	11
H. Philipson	5	8	3	11
W. Storer	6	11	0	11

ENGLAND	Matches	Caught	Stumped	Total
E. F. S. Tylecote	6	5	5	10
J. Humphries	3	7	0	7
M. Sherwin	3	5	2	7
R. A. Young	2	6	0	6
G. Brown	3	2	2	4
L. H. Gay	1	3	1	4
R. Swetman	2	3	0	3
A. Wood	1	3	0	3
L. Hone	1	2	0	2
Hon. A. Lyttelton	4	2	0	2
W. F. F. Price	1	2	0	2
H. Wood	1	1	1	2
A. Dolphin	1	1	0	1
P. A. Gibb	1	1	0	1
J. Selby	2	1	0	1
K. V. Andrew	1	0	0	0

AUSTRALIA	Matches	Caught	Stumped	Total
W. A. S. Oldfield	38	59	31	90
A. T. W. Grout	22	69	7	76
†J. McC. Blackham	32	34	24	58
J. J. Kelly	33	39	16	55
H. Carter	21	35	17	52
D. Tallon	15	38	4	42
G. R. A. Langley	9	35	2	37
B. N. Jarman	7	18	0	18
A. H. Jarvis	9	8	9	17
L. V. Maddocks	5	12	1	13
B. A. Barnett	4	3	2	5
H. S. B. Love	1	3	0	3
R. A. Saggers	1	3	0	3
W. Carkeek	3	2	0	2
W. L. Murdoch	1	1	1	2
H. B. Taber	1	2	0	2
F. J. Burton	1	0	1	1

†Blackham also made one catch as a replacement wicketkeeper for W. L. Murdoch in England's second innings at Sydney in 1881-82, his total dismissals while keeping wicket thus being 59.

The youngest wicketkeeper to appear in these matches is G. MacGregor (E), who was aged 20 years 324 days on his debut at Lord's in 1890. The youngest to play for England this century is A. P. E. Knott, who was aged 22 years 58 days at Old Trafford in 1968.

The youngest wicketkeeper to appear for Australia is J. McC. Blackham, who was aged 22 years 309 days on his debut at Melbourne in 1876-77. The youngest to play for Australia this century is W. A. S. Oldfield, who was aged 23 years 99 days at Sydney in 1920-21.

The oldest player to keep wicket is H. Strudwick (E), who appeared in all five Tests in 1926 at the age of 46. (F. E. Woolley, aged 47, kept wicket as a replacement wicketkeeper for L. E. G. Ames in Australia's second innings at the Oval in 1934.)

The oldest player to keep wicket for Australia is H. Carter, who appeared in the first four Tests of 1921 at the age of 43.

A. T. W. Grout (A) made his 50th dismissal (44 ct., 6 st.) in his 12th match – the record. The nearest approach to this is by A. A. Lilley (E), who made his 50th dismissal (45 ct., 5 st.) in his 18th match, though in one he did not have an opportunity of keeping wicket at all because of rain.

T. G. Evans (E) made at least one dismissal in each of the first 23 Tests in which he played.

Most dismissals in an innings

5	(1 ct 4 st)	W. A. S. Oldfield	for A	Melbourne	1924-25
5	(5 ct 0 st)	G. R. A. Langley	for A	Lord's	1956
5	(5 ct 0 st)	A. T. W. Grout	for A	Lord's	1961
5	(5 ct 0 st)	A. T. W. Grout	for A	Sydney	1965-66
5	(3 ct 2 st)	J. M. Parks	for E	Sydney	1965-66

The last two instances above took place in the same match.

Most dismissals in a match

At Lord's in 1956 the wicketkeepers were responsible for 16 of the 40 wickets that fell.

9	(8 ct 1 st)	G. R. A. Langley	for A	Lord's	1956
8	(8 ct 0 st)	J. J. Kelly	for A	Sydney	1901-02
8	(8 ct 0 st)	A. T. W. Grout	for A	Lord's	1961
7	(6 ct 1 st)	T. G. Evans	for E	Lord's	1956
7	(7 ct 0 st)	J. T. Murray	for E	Old Trafford	1961

Most dismissals in a series

21	(20 ct 1 st)	A. T. W. Grout	for A in 5 Tests		1961
20	(16 ct 4 st)	D. Tallon	for A in 5 Tests		1946-47
20	(17 ct 3 st)	A. T. W. Grout	for A in 5 Tests		1958-59
19	(18 ct 1 st)	G. R. A. Langley	for A in 3 Tests		1956
18	(16 ct 2 st)	H. Strudwick	for E in 5 Tests		1924-25
18	(10 ct 8 st)	W. A. S. Oldfield	for A in 5 Tests		1924-25
18	(17 ct 1 st)	J. T. Murray	for E in 5 Tests		1961
17	(8 ct 9 st)	A. A. Lilley	for E in 5 Tests		1903-04
16	(13 ct 3 st)	J. J. Kelly	for A in 5 Tests		1901-02
16	(11 ct 5 st)	T. G. Evans	for E in 5 Tests		1953
16	(15 ct 1 st)	A. T. W. Grout	for A in 5 Tests		1965-66
15	(12 ct 3 st)	W. A. S. Oldfield	for A in 5 Tests		1930
15	(13 ct 2 st)	L. E. G. Ames	for E in 5 Tests		1936-37
15	(12 ct 3 st)	J. M. Parks	for E in 5 Tests		1965-66
15	(11 ct 4 st)	A. P. E. Knott	for E in 5 Tests		1968

D. Tallon (A) in 1946-47 and A. T. W. Grout (A) in 1958-59 each dismissed 20 batsmen in the series of their debut in these matches. J. T. Murray's 18 dismissals in 1961 is the best by an English wicketkeeper in the series of his debut.

Wicketkeepers conceding no byes in high innings

659 for 8 dec.	by A	T. G. Evans (E)	Sydney	1946-47
551	by E	J. J. Kelly (A)	Sydney	1897-98
521	by E	W. A. S. Oldfield (A)	Brisbane	1928-29
489	by A	H. Strudwick (E)	Adelaide	1924-25
443 for 6 dec.	by A	J. M. Parks (E)	Brisbane	1965-66
440	by E	W. A. S. Oldfield (A)	Lord's	1934
421	by A	A. A. Lilley (E)	Lord's	1899
405	by E	W. A. S. Oldfield (A)	Oval	1930
403 for 8 dec.	by E	W. A. S. Oldfield (A)	Oval	1921
401 for 4	by E	A. T. W. Grout (A)	Edgbaston	1961

T. G. Evans in 1946-47 (above) was making his debut in these matches.

W. A. S. Oldfield (A) did not concede a single bye in either of England's innings of 521 and 342 for 8 dec. at Brisbane in 1928-29. In the first five innings played by England in that series Oldfield conceded only three byes while 1,932 runs were scored.

T. G. Evans (E) kept wicket in these matches while Australia scored over 1,000 runs before he conceded his first bye. He conceded no byes in his first two innings (659 for 8 dec. at Sydney and 365 at Melbourne in 1946-47).

G. MacGregor (E) did not concede a single bye in any of the first three innings (all completed) in which he kept wicket – at Lord's and the Oval in 1890.

At Lord's in 1890 neither wicketkeeper (G. MacGregor or J. McC. Blackham) conceded a single bye in any of the four innings, the match aggregate being 618 runs.

T. G. Evans (E) kept wicket for 11 hours 45 minutes in a single innings without conceding a bye (in Australia's 659 for 8 dec., above).

B. A. Barnett (A) conceded only one bye in England's 658 for 8 dec. at Trent Bridge in 1938.

L. E. G. Ames (E) conceded only one bye in Australia's 604 at Melbourne in 1936-37.

The greatest number of byes conceded in an innings is 37 in Australia's 327 at the Oval in 1934. (England's appointed wicketkeeper, L. E. G. Ames, was injured and F. E. Woolley kept wicket in his place.)

The greatest number of byes conceded in an innings by Australia is 24 in England's 353 at Lord's in 1886. (A. H. Jarvis kept wicket).

The greatest number of extras in an innings is 50 – in Australia's 327 at the Oval in 1934, and in England's 903 for 7 dec. at the Oval in 1938.

The greatest number of extras in a match is 94 – at the Oval in 1934. England conceded 83 of them.

Most runs by wicketkeepers

1,116 runs	(av. 23·25)	W. A. S. Oldfield (A)
801 runs	(av. 20·02)	A. A. Lilley (E)
783 runs	(av. 17·79)	T. G. Evans (E)
776 runs	(av. 25·03)	H. Carter (A)
763 runs	(av. 15·89)	J. McC. Blackham (A)
675 runs	(av. 27·00)	L. E. G. Ames (E)
613 runs	(av. 17·51)	J. J. Kelly (A)

(Blackham made a further 37 runs in matches in which he was not wicketkeeper, giving him a total of 800 runs, av. 15·68.)

The highest innings by wicketkeepers are:

120	L. E. G. Ames	for E	Lord's	1934
92	D. Tallon	for A	Melbourne	1946-47
89	J. M. Parks	for E	Melbourne	1965-66
84	A. A. Lilley	for E	Sydney	1901-02
84	G. Brown	for E	Oval	1921
83	L. E. G. Ames	for E	Lord's	1938
82	A. H. Jarvis	for A	Melbourne	1884-85

L. E. G. Ames and J. M. Parks each played five innings of 50 or more.

The fielders

Most catches in an innings

4	L. C. Braund	for E	Sheffield	1902
4	F. E. Woolley	for E	Sydney	1911-12
4	S. J. E. Loxton	for A	Brisbane	1950-51
4	P. B. H. May	for E	Adelaide	1954-55
4	R. N. Harvey	for A	Sydney	1962-63

Most catches in a match

6	A. Shrewsbury	for E	Sydney	1887-88
6	F. E. Woolley	for E	Sydney	1911-12
6	J. M. Gregory	for A	Sydney	1920-21
6	R. N. Harvey	for A	Sydney	1962-63

R. N. Harvey (above) was playing in the final Test of his career.

Most catches in a series

15	J. M. Gregory	for A in 5 Tests	1920-21
12	L. C. Braund	for E in 5 Tests	1901-02
12	W. R. Hammond	for E in 5 Tests	1934

J. M. Gregory (above) held his 15 catches in the series of his debut.

C. Hill (A) held at least one catch in each of the nine series in which he appeared.

In the 1926-63 series R. N. Harvey (A) did not make a catch in any of the first four matches, and then equalled the catching record for both an innings and a match in the fifth.

Most catches in career

For England:

	W. R. Hammond	43 catches in 33 Tests
	W. G. Grace	39 catches in 22 Tests
	L. C. Braund	35 catches in 20 Tests
	F. E. Woolley	34 catches in 32 Tests
	M. C. Cowdrey	34 catches in 35 Tests
	W. Rhodes	34 catches in 41 Tests

(W. G. Grace and F. E. Woolley, above, each made one of their catches while keeping wicket.)

For Australia:

	H. Trumble	45 catches in 31 Tests
	W. W. Armstrong	37 catches in 42 Tests
	R. Benaud	32 catches in 27 Tests
	R. B. Simpson	30 catches in 19 Tests
	J. M. Gregory	30 catches in 21 Tests
	C. Hill	30 catches in 41 Tests

R. B. Simpson (A) held at least one catch in 15 successive Tests in which he played (Headingley 1961 to Adelaide 1965-66).

W. G. Grace (E) held at least one catch in each of the first 12 Tests in which he played (Oval 1880 to Lord's 1890).

The greatest number of matches in which a player has appeared without making a catch is 15, by J. C. Laker (E). The greatest number by an Australian is 7, by L. O'B. Fleetwood-Smith.

The over

The over has consisted of the following number of balls:

IN ENGLAND

4 balls per over from 1880 to 1888	11 matches
5 balls per over from 1890 to 1899	13 matches
6 balls per over from 1902 to 1968	72 matches

IN AUSTRALIA

4 balls per over from 1876-77 to 1887-88	19 matches
6 balls per over from 1891-92 to 1920-21	38 matches
8 balls per over in 1924-25	5 matches
6 balls per over in 1928-29 and 1932-33	10 matches
8 balls per over from 1936-37 to 1965-66	35 matches

The follow on

IN ENGLAND

Series

1880 to 1893	Compulsory	after a deficit of 80 runs
1896 to 1899	Compulsory	after a deficit of 120 runs
1902 to 1961	Optional	after a deficit of 150 runs
1964 to 1968	Optional	after a deficit of 200 runs

IN AUSTRALIA

Series

1876-77 to 1891-92	Compulsory	after a deficit of 80 runs
1894-95 to 1897-98	Compulsory	after a deficit of 120 runs
1901-02	Optional	after a deficit of 150 runs
1903-04 to 1950-51	Optional	after a deficit of 200 runs
1954-55 to 1965-66	Optional	after a deficit of 150 runs

New ball

IN ENGLAND

Prior to the 1909 series there was no provision regarding the taking of a new ball, other than at the commencement of each innings. Since then a new ball has been available as follows:

1909		1948 — After 55 overs
1912		1953 — After 65 overs
1921		1956 — After 200 runs or 75 overs
1926	After 200 runs	1961 — After 200 runs or 85 overs
1930		1964
1934		1968 — After 85 overs
1938		

IN AUSTRALIA

Prior to the 1897-98 series there was no provision regarding the taking of a new ball, other than at the commencement of each innings. Since then a new ball has been available as follows:

1897-98	
1901-02	
1903-04	
1907-08	
1911-12	
1920-21	After 200 runs
1924-25	
1928-29	
1932-33	
1936-37	
1946-47	
1950-51	After 50 overs
1954-55	
1958-59	After 200 runs
1962-63	
1965-66	After 65 overs

Intervals

LUNCHEON INTERVAL

The luncheon interval has always been a regular feature since the commencement of these matches. It has always been at a fixed (i.e. not 'movable') time, though the period between the scheduled start of play and the start of the luncheon interval has varied both in England and Australia.* In accordance with the Playing Conditions pertaining to the various series, the pre-lunch period has frequently varied within the same match. The most common pre-lunch periods in England have been 2 hours or 2½ hours, and in Australia 1½ hours.

*In circumstances where weather has prevented play before lunch, there has frequently been power to take lunch earlier than the fixed time, if the umpires so agree. Occasionally (e.g. at Lord's in 1921), when an obvious finish has been in sight, it has been agreed to play on and finish the match in spite of the luncheon time having arrived.

TEA INTERVAL

In England there was no tea interval in Tests prior to the 1905 series, the match at Trent Bridge that year being the first Test to include such an interval. Since that time it has been a regular feature, incorporated in the Playing Conditions. In the 19 Tests in England between 1880 and 1896 (inclusive) – i.e. all Tests prior to the establishment of the Board of Control – there was neither a tea interval nor an afternoon break for refreshment on the field. However, in 1899 and 1902 it was the usual practice for a brief interval to occur while tea was taken to the players on the field at about 4.30.

In Australia there was no tea interval in the first three Tests played, but since the first Test of the 1881-82 series it has been a regular feature. In both countries, in accordance with the Playing Conditions, the start of the tea interval has been 'movable', and in certain circumstances the interval may not be taken at all. The most common lunch-to-tea periods of play in England have been 2¼ hours or 2 hours 5 minutes, and in Australia 1¾ hours.

Covering of wickets

IN ENGLAND

Prior to the 1926 series there were no regulations regarding the covering of wickets either before or during a match. Since then the position has been as follows:

1926 — The practice in vogue at each ground shall be adhered to so far as covering the wicket prior to the commencement of a Test is concerned.

1930 — The practice in vogue at each ground shall be adhered to so far as covering the whole of the wicket prior to the commencement of a Test is concerned. The wicket shall not be completely covered after play has begun.

1934, 1938, 1948, 1953, 1956 — The wicket shall be completely protected against rain if necessary and as far as practicable 24 hours before the time advertised for the start of a Test or until play begins. After the first ball has been bowled the covers shall not protect more than 3 ft 6 ins in front of the popping crease at each end.

1961 — The whole pitch may be covered only provided no match is actually in progress on the ground at any time before the start of a match and until the first ball is bowled.
The whole pitch shall be covered:
  (a) The night before the match and, if necessary, until the first ball is bowled; and, whenever necessary and possible, at any time prior to that during the preparation of the pitch.
  (b) On each night of the match and, if necessary, throughout Sunday. In addition, in the event of rain during the specified hours of play, the pitch shall be completely covered from the time it is decided that no further play is possible on that day.

1964 — As in 1961, but in the event of rain during the specified hours of play, the umpires shall order the pitch to be completely covered from the time they decide that sufficient rain has fallen on the pitch to ensure no further play being possible on that day.

When this decision is taken the captains shall forthwith abandon play for the day.
Note: During hours of daylight, and provided that it is not raining at the time, the covers should be removed whenever possible: this is particularly desirable when the sheet type cover laid flat on the ground is in use.
The bowling ends will be covered to a distance of 4 ft in front of the popping crease if, during the hours of play, the match is suspended temporarily, owing to weather or light conditions.

1968 — As in 1961, but in the event of rain during the specified hours of play, the umpires shall order the pitch to be completely covered as soon as play has been abandoned for the day. (The note as in 1964 shall apply, as shall the provision regarding the covering of bowling ends, without the words 'or light conditions'.)

IN AUSTRALIA

From 1920-21 to 1950-51 inclusive, the whole of the wicket could be entirely protected prior to the commencement of a match, but after the start only wicket-ends could be covered.

From 1954-55 to 1965-66 inclusive, it was obligatory to protect the whole of the wicket against rain both prior to the commencement of play and for the duration of the match (including the end of each day's play). On Sundays the covering had to be removed and replaced at the times provided for on actual playing days.

Provisions regarding final Test

IN ENGLAND

Prior to 1905 no special provisions were made with regard to the duration of the final Test of a series. Since 1905 the provisions have been as follows:

1905, 1909, 1912, 1921, 1926, 1930 — If prior to the final match neither side has secured an advantage, the final match shall be played to a finish.*

1934 — If after the fourth match neither side has won two matches or if the results are even, the fifth match shall be played to a finish.

1938, 1948 — If after the fourth match the difference in matches won is not greater than one, the fifth match shall be played to a finish.

1953 — No special provision for fifth match (i.e. all five Tests scheduled for 5 days). However, after the fourth Test it was announced that the fifth match would be played (if necessary) over 6 days.

1956, 1961, 1964 — No special provision for fifth match (i.e. all five Tests scheduled for 5 days).

1968 — If after the fourth match the series is level, the fifth match shall be played (if necessary) over 6 days.

*Although the 'play to a finish' clause was present in the playing conditions for 1905, 1909 and 1912, the real intention for the 1905 match (as later declared by the Board of Control) was for a 4-day limit; in 1909 the match was 'to be played to a finish, but the match not to extend beyond the 6th day'; in 1912 the match was deemed to be of a maximum of 6 days' duration after it began.

IN AUSTRALIA

Special provisions regarding the duration of the final Test have only applied since the Second World War, as follows:

1946-47, 1950-51 — If after the fourth match the difference in matches won is not greater than one, the fifth match shall be played to a finish.

1954-55 — If after the fourth match the difference in matches won is not greater than one, the fifth match shall be played (if necessary) over 7 days.

1958-59   If after the fourth match the series is level, the fifth match shall be played (if necessary) over 7 days, the duration extending to 8 days in the event of bad weather causing cessation of play for one or more complete day or days.

1962-63 } No special provision for fifth match (i.e. all five Tests
1965-66 } scheduled for 5 days).

Record match receipts and attendances at major grounds

IN ENGLAND	Record Match Receipts	Record Match Attendance	Record Paying Attendance for Match
Oval	£62,960.5.11 in 1968	115,000* in 1953	98,812 in 1953
Old Trafford	£37,248.0.6 in 1964	140,000* in 1961	120,417 in 1961
Lord's	£72,882.10.0 in 1968	137,915* in 1953	126,909 in 1953
Trent Bridge	£35,424.16.6 in 1956	101,886* in 1948	84,386 in 1948
Headingley	£48,313.19.6 in 1953	158,000* in 1948	123,756 in 1948
Edgbaston	£37,932.5.1 in 1961	83,000* in 1961	72,114 in 1961

*including members

The record receipts for a single day are £19,354.0.0 on the second day at Lord's in 1968.

The record estimated attendance on a single day (including members) is over 40,000 on the second day at Headingley in 1934. (In those days seating accommodation at Headingley was much smaller than today and many spectators stood at the back of the embankments, which made it possible for more people to be admitted.)

IN AUSTRALIA	Record Match Receipts	Record Match Attendance
Melbourne	£68,376.16.0 in 1962-63 (second Test)	350,534* in 1936-37 (third Test)
Sydney	£38,974.17.0 in 1962-63 (third Test)	194,259* in 1946-47 (second Test)
Adelaide	£33,792.4.6 in 1962-63 (fourth Test)	172,346* in 1932-33 (third Test)
Brisbane	£31,421.0.1 in 1958-59 (first Test)	93,143* in 1932-33 (fourth Test)

*including members

The record receipts for a single day are £21,783.2.6 on the second day of the fifth Test at Melbourne in 1965-66.

The record attendance on a single day (including members) is 87,798 on the third day of the third Test at Melbourne in 1936-37.

Note: The figure for match receipts represents the gross gate receipts (including advance sales and pavilion reservations, where applicable) and does not include extraneous receipts such as radio and television fees, score-card sales, car park fees, etc.
The figures for Australia are given in A £.

Record match receipts

The first match in which the receipts reached £4,000 was the fifth Test at Melbourne in 1894-95. Since then the progressive record has been as follows:

£4,003.14.0	Melbourne	1894-95	5th Test
£4,274.10.0	Sydney	1903-04	1st Test
£4,345.11.9	Melbourne	1911-12	2nd Test
£10,386.14.0	Sydney	1920-21	1st Test
£16,205.4.1	Sydney	1924-25	1st Test
£22,628.4.6	Melbourne	1924-25	2nd Test
£23,518.9.0	Lord's	1930	2nd Test
£30,124.0.0	Melbourne	1936-37	3rd Test
£49,751.0.3	Melbourne	1946-47	3rd Test

£57,717.5.0	Lord's	1953	2nd Test
£72,882.10.0	Lord's	1968	2nd Test

The highest receipts for one match are as follows:

IN ENGLAND

£72,882.10.0	Lord's	1968	2nd Test
£62,960.5.11	Oval	1968	5th Test
£57,717.5.0	Lord's	1953	2nd Test
£57,457.7.6	Lord's	1956	2nd Test
£54,516.15.0	Lord's	1964	2nd Test

IN AUSTRALIA

£68,376.16.0	Melbourne	1962-63	2nd Test
£52,225.12.6	Melbourne	1965-66	2nd Test
£49,751.0.3	Melbourne	1946-47	3rd Test
£48,008.1.7	Melbourne	1954-55	3rd Test
£46,791.13.6	Melbourne	1958-59	2nd Test
£40,499.19.6	Melbourne	1965-66	5th Test

Record receipts for series

IN ENGLAND

£242,188.18.5	1968	£196,561.4.6	1964
£201,008.0.9	1956	£190,338.1.6	1961
£200,428.5.9	1953	£159,966.19.4	1948*

*The 1948 figure represents the total receipts of the series before payment of entertainments tax. This duty was payable on the receipts of each of the six England-Australia series in England between 1921 and 1948, inclusive.

The record receipts for a series in England prior to the Second World War were:

£88,313.12.5   1934
£81,287.8.3   1938
£77,270.17.3   1930

(The above figures are before payment of entertainments tax.)

IN AUSTRALIA

£167,016	1965-66	£108,931	1954-55
£144,008	1962-63	£87,963	1936-37
£130,036	1946-47	£75,324	1928-29
£125,252	1958-59	£70,352	1932-33

Record match attendances

IN ENGLAND

Total Attendance			Playing Days	Paying Attendance
158,000	Headingley	1948	5	123,756
151,000	Headingley	1953	5	112,697
140,000	Old Trafford	1961	5	120,417
137,915	Lord's	1953	5	126,909
134,717	Lord's	1956	5	124,439
133,740	Old Trafford	1948	4*	107,712
132,000	Lord's	1948	5	120,177

*No play took place on the fourth scheduled day of the match, though the public were admitted.

The first Test in England at which the total attendance reached 100,000 was at the Oval in 1926, when nearly 103,000 (including members, guests, etc.) were present during the four days. The then record number of 76,472 paid. Just under 115,000 were present during the four days at Lord's in 1930 – a new English record, which was exceeded in 1948 at Lord's (above).

New record aggregate attendance figures were established in three successive Tests in 1948 – at Lord's, Old Trafford and Headingley.

On the fourth day at Headingley in 1948, the gates having been closed ten minutes before the start of play, it was estimated that 20,000 people tried unsuccessfully to get into the ground. The day's play was watched by nearly 40,000.

On the first day at Lord's in 1926, it was estimated that 10,000 people were unable to gain admittance.

On the second day at Lord's in 1938 and on the third day at Lord's in 1956 and the gates were closed as early as 10.45 a.m.

Total Attendance				Playing Days
350,534	Melbourne	1936-37	3rd Test	6
345,361	Melbourne	1946-47	3rd Test	6
300,270	Melbourne	1954-55	3rd Test	5
262,487	Melbourne	1928-29	3rd Test	7
247,831	Melbourne	1962-63	2nd Test	5
239,175	Melbourne	1924-25	2nd Test	7
230,948	Melbourne	1958-59	2nd Test	5
218,064	Melbourne	1928-29	5th Test	8
200,635	Melbourne	1932-33	2nd Test	4
194,259	Sydney	1946-47	2nd Test	6
180,190	Sydney	1950-51	3rd Test	4
172,858	Sydney	1958-59	3rd Test	6
172,346	Adelaide	1932-33	3rd Test	6
170,014	Melbourne	1965-66	2nd Test	5

Record attendances for series

The first series in which the total attendance reached half a million was in 1924-25. That season's record was broken in 1928-29 and broken in turn in 1936-37, the attendance for that series establishing the present record.

933,513[1] in 1936-37
863,608 in 1928-29
846,810 in 1946-47
765,747[2] in 1958-59
761,107 in 1932-33
735,963 in 1962-63
707,510 in 1954-55
687,134[3] in 1924-25

[1] Excluding about 10,000 who watched the last day's play of the fifth Test free of charge.

[2] Excluding about 20,000 who watched the last day's play of the second Test free of charge.

[3] Excluding about 10,000 who watched the last day's play of the third Test free of charge.

The record attendances for a series in England are:
549,650 in 1953
520,114 in 1948

The first Test in Australia at which the total attendance reached 100,000 was the fifth Test at Melbourne in 1894-95, when 103,636 were present during the five days, 63,649 having paid (at that time a world record). On the second day of the match 29,123 people, including members, were present (a world record at that time for a day's crowd at a Test), 21,717 having paid.

The first Test at which the total attendance reached 150,000 was the first Test at Sydney in 1924-25, when 163,453 were present during the seven days, 131,696 having paid.

The first Test at which the total attendance reached 200,000 was the second Test at Melbourne in 1924-25, when 239,175 were present during the seven days, 180,605 having paid.

On the second day of the third Test at Melbourne in 1946-47, when 70,863 were present, the gates were closed although the stands were far from full, certain passages having become congested.

The Press

The first newspaper writer to travel overseas on a Test tour, either to or from England, was Martin Cobbett, of *The Sportsman*, who accompanied the English side in Australia in 1882-83.

E. W. Swanton (between 1930 and 1968) has reported 71 England v Australia Tests (41 in England, 30 in Australia), including all 60 matches since the Second World War.

E. M. Wellings (between 1934 and 1968) has reported 69 England v Australia Tests (39 in England, 30 in Australia), including all 60 matches since the Second World War. He has reported all the last 64 matches (from Trent Bridge 1938 to date) – the record number of consecutive England-Australia Tests reported by one man. All these 64 Tests have been for the same newspaper, the London *Evening News* – another record.

J. H. W. Fingleton (between 1932-33 and 1968) has reported 62 England v Australia Tests (30 in England, 32 in Australia), including all 60 matches since the Second World War. In addition, he played in 8 Tests in Australia – 3 in 1932-33 and 5 in 1936-37 – that he might otherwise have reported. He is the only Australian writer who has reported as many as six Test tours of England.

J. M. Kilburn and E. M. Wellings are the only writers who have reported every England-Australia Test in England since the start of the 1934 series. In Kilburn's case the reporting has been for one newspaper only, the *Yorkshire Post*.

(*The above figures do not include the abandoned Old Trafford Test of 1938*).

Career records

ENGLAND		BATTING						BOWLING						
		Matches	Inns.	N.O.	Runs	H.S.	Av.	Balls	Mdns.	Runs	Wkts.	Av.	Ct	St
Abel, R.	Surrey (1888)	11	19	1	555	132*	30·83	–	–	–	–	–	9	–
Absolom, C. A.	Kent (1878)	1	2	0	58	52	29·00	–	–	–	–	–	–	–
Allen, D. A.	Gloucestershire (1961)	10	14	5	232	50*	25·77	2,492	120	892	28	31·85	2	–
Allen, G. O. B.	Middlesex (1930)	13	21	1	479	68	23·95	3,123	58	1,603	43	37·27	15	–
Ames, L. E. G.	Kent (1932)	17	27	2	675	120	27·00	–	–	–	–	–	33	4
Amiss, D. L.	Warwickshire (1968)	1	2	0	0	0	0·00	–	–	–	–	–	–	–
Andrew, K. V.	Northamptonshire (1954)	1	2	0	11	6	5·50	–	–	–	–	–	–	–
Appleyard, R.	Yorkshire (1954)	5	6	3	45	19*	15·00	812	32	273	13	21·00	4	–
Armitage, T.	Yorkshire (1876)	2	3	0	33	21	11·00	12	0	15	0	–	–	–
Arnold, E. G.	Worcestershire (1903)	8	12	3	144	40	16·00	1,371	47	689	25	27·56	6	–
Attewell, W.	Nottinghamshire (1884)	10	15	6	150	43*	16·66	2,850	326	626	27	23·18	9	–
Bailey, T. E.	Essex (1950)	23	38	4	875	88	25·73	3,300	105	1,373	42	32·69	16	–
Barber, R. W.	Warwickshire (1964)	7	13	1	447	185	37·25	573	4	371	6	61·83	4	–
Barlow, R. G.	Lancashire (1881)	17	30	4	591	62	22·73	2,456	315	767	34	22·55	14	–
Barnes, S. F.	Lancashire (1901)	20	30	5	210	38*	8·40	5,749	264	2,288	106	21·58	7	–
Barnes, W.	Nottinghamshire (1880)	21	33	2	725	134	23·38	2,289	271	793	51	15·54	19	–
Barnett, C. J.	Gloucestershire (1936)	9	16	0	624	129	39·00	148	6	61	0	–	5	–
Barrington, K. F.	Surrey (1961)	23	39	6	2,111	256	63·96	426	7	231	4	57·75	19	–
Bates, W.	Yorkshire (1881)	15	26	2	656	64	27·33	2,364	282	821	50	16·42	9	–
Bean, G.	Sussex (1891)	3	5	0	92	50	18·40	–	–	–	–	–	4	–

		BATTING						BOWLING						
		Matches	Inns.	N.O.	Runs	H.S.	Av.	Balls	Mdns.	Runs	Wkts.	Av.	Ct	St
Bedser, A. V.	Surrey (1946)	21	35	9	373	79	14·34	7,065	209	2,859	104	27·49	11	–
Bligh, Hon. I.	Kent (1882)	4	7	1	62	19	10·33	–	–	–	–	–	7	–
Blythe, C.	Kent (1901)	9	14	4	75	20	7·50	1,977	94	877	41	21·39	2	–
Bosanquet, B. J. T.	Middlesex (1903)	7	14	3	147	27	13·36	970	10	604	25	24·16	9	–
Bowes, W. E.	Yorkshire (1932)	6	7	3	19	10*	4·75	1,459	41	741	30	24·70	–	–
Boycott, G.	Yorkshire (1964)	12	20	2	753	113	41·83	190	4	92	2	46·00	2	–
Bradley, W. M.	Kent (1899)	2	2	1	23	23*	23·00	625	49	233	6	38·83	–	–
Braund, L. C.	Somerset (1901)	20	36	3	830	103*	25·15	3,665	140	1,769	46	38·45	35	–
Brearley, W.	Lancashire (1905)	4	4	2	21	11*	10·50	669	23	355	17	20·88	1	–
Briggs, J.	Lancashire (1884)	31	48	5	809	121	18·81	4,941	338	1,993	97	20·54	11	–
Brockwell, W.	Surrey (1893)	7	12	0	202	49	16·83	582	31	309	5	61·80	6	–
Brown, D. J.	Warwickshire (1965)	8	9	0	34	14	3·77	1,728	68	810	23	35·21	3	–
Brown, F. R.	Northamptonshire (1950)	6	10	0	260	79	26·00	1,184	23	524	22	23·81	5	–
Brown, G.	Hampshire (1921)	3	5	0	250	84	50·00	–	–	–	–	–	2	2
Brown, J. T.	Yorkshire (1894)	8	16	3	470	140	36·15	35	0	22	0	–	7	–
Carr, A. W.	Nottinghamshire (1926)	4	1	0	13	13	13·00	–	–	–	–	–	1	–
Carr, D. W.	Kent (1909)	1	1	0	0	0	0·00	414	3	282	7	40·28	–	–
Cartwright, T. W.	Warwickshire (1964)	2	2	0	4	4	2·00	834	55	228	5	45·60	–	–
Chapman, A. P. F.	Kent (1924)	16	25	3	784	121	35·63	40	1	20	0	–	18	–
Charlwood, H. R. J.	Sussex (1876)	2	4	0	63	36	15·75	–	–	–	–	–	2	–
Christopherson, S.	Kent (1884)	1	1	0	17	17	17·00	136	13	69	1	69·00	–	–
Clark, E. W.	Northamptonshire (1934)	2	3	3	6	2*	–	608	15	324	8	40·50	–	–
Close, D. B.	Yorkshire (1950)	2	4	0	42	33	10·50	104	2	61	1	61·00	3	–
Coldwell, L. J.	Worcestershire (1962)	4	6	4	9	6*	4·50	840	19	317	7	45·28	1	–
Compton, D. C. S.	Middlesex (1938)	28	51	8	1,842	184	42·83	464	8	298	3	99·33	15	–
Cowdrey, M. C.	Kent (1954)	35	62	4	2,186	113	37·68	11	0	9	0	–	34	–
Coxon, A.	Yorkshire (1948)	1	2	0	19	19	9·50	378	13	172	3	57·33	–	–
Cranston, J.	Gloucestershire (1890)	1	2	0	31	16	15·50	–	–	–	–	–	1	–
Cranston, K.	Lancashire (1948)	1	2	0	10	10	5·00	127	1	79	1	79·00	1	–
Crapp, J. F.	Gloucestershire (1948)	3	6	1	88	37	17·60	–	–	–	–	–	6	–
Crawford, J. N.	Surrey (1907)	5	10	1	162	62	18·00	1,426	36	742	30	24·73	6	–
Dean, H.	Lancashire (1912)	2	2	1	0	0	0·00	324	19	97	6	16·16	1	–
Denton, D.	Yorkshire (1905)	1	2	0	12	12	6·00	–	–	–	–	–	–	–
Dewes, J. G.	Middlesex (1948)	3	6	0	34	10	5·66	–	–	–	–	–	–	–
Dexter, E. R.	Sussex (1958)	19	35	0	1,358	180	38·80	1,582	29	742	23	32·26	10	–
Dipper, A. E.	Gloucestershire (1921)	1	2	0	51	40	25·50	–	–	–	–	–	–	–
D'Oliveira, B. L.	Worcestershire (1968)	2	4	1	263	158	87·66	234	20	49	3	16·33	1	–
Dollery, H. E.	Warwickshire (1948)	2	3	0	38	37	12·66	–	–	–	–	–	–	–
Dolphin, A.	Yorkshire (1920)	1	2	0	1	1	0·50	–	–	–	–	–	1	–
Douglas, J. W. H. T.	Essex (1911)	17	28	2	696	75	26·76	2,318	53	1,227	35	35·05	7	–
Druce, N. F.	Surrey (1897)	5	9	0	252	64	28·00	–	–	–	–	–	5	–
Ducat, A. N.	Surrey (1921)	1	2	0	5	3	2·50	–	–	–	–	–	1	–
Duckworth, G.	Lancashire (1928)	10	17	6	163	39*	14·81	–	–	–	–	–	23	3
Duleepsinhji, K. S.	Sussex (1930)	4	7	0	416	173	59·42	–	–	–	–	–	2	–
Durston, F. J.	Middlesex (1921)	1	2	1	8	6*	8·00	202	2	136	5	27·20	–	–
Edrich, J. H.	Surrey (1964)	13	21	0	1,090	164	51·90	–	–	–	–	–	7	–
Edrich, W. J.	Middlesex (1938)	21	39	1	1,184	119	31·15	1,477	24	888	16	55·50	14	–
Emmett, G. M.	Gloucestershire (1948)	1	2	0	10	10	5·00	–	–	–	–	–	–	–
Emmett, T.	Yorkshire (1876)	7	13	1	160	48	13·33	728	92	284	9	31·55	9	–
Evans, A. J.	Kent (1921)	1	2	0	18	14	9·00	–	–	–	–	–	–	–
Evans, T. G.	Kent (1946)	31	53	9	783	50	17·79	–	–	–	–	–	64	11
Fagg, A. E.	Kent (1936)	2	3	0	42	27	14·00	–	–	–	–	–	2	–
Fane, F. L.	Essex (1907)	4	8	0	192	50	24·00	–	–	–	–	–	1	–
Farnes, K.	Essex (1934)	8	10	4	23	7*	3·83	2,153	58	1,065	38	28·02	1	–
Fender, P. G. H.	Surrey (1920)	5	9	1	198	59	24·75	806	16	522	14	37·28	3	–
Fielder, A.	Kent (1903)	6	12	5	78	20	11·14	1,491	42	711	26	27·34	4	–
Fishlock, L. B.	Surrey (1946)	1	2	0	14	14	7·00	–	–	–	–	–	1	–
Flavell, J. A.	Worcestershire (1961)	4	6	2	31	14	7·75	792	25	367	7	52·42	–	–
Fletcher, K. W. R.	Essex (1968)	1	2	1	23	23*	23·00	–	–	–	–	–	–	–
Flowers, W.	Nottinghamshire (1884)	8	14	0	254	56	18·14	858	92	296	14	21·14	3	–
Ford, F. G. J.	Middlesex (1894)	5	9	0	168	48	18·66	210	6	129	1	129·00	5	–
Foster, F. R.	Warwickshire (1911)	8	11	1	281	71	28·10	1,894	76	742	34	21·82	4	–
Foster, R. E.	Worcestershire (1903)	5	9	1	486	287	60·75	–	–	–	–	–	13	–
Freeman, A. P.	Kent (1924)	2	4	2	80	50*	40·00	968	16	459	8	57·37	1	–
Fry, C. B.	Sussex (1899)	18	29	3	825	144	31·73	10	1	3	0	–	11	–
Gay, L. H.	Somerset (1894)	1	2	0	37	33	18·50	–	–	–	–	–	3	1

		BATTING						BOWLING						
		Matches	Inns.	N.O.	Runs	H.S.	Av.	Balls	Mdns.	Runs	Wkts.	Av.	Ct	St
Geary, G.	Leicestershire (1926)	9	15	2	202	66	15·53	2,628	112	963	27	35·66	9	—
Gibb, P. A.	Yorkshire (1946)	1	2	0	24	13	12·00	—	—	—	—	—	1	—
Gifford, N.	Worcestershire (1964)	2	3	1	7	5	3·50	498	35	140	5	28·00	1	—
Gilligan, A. E. R.	Sussex (1924)	5	9	2	64	31	9·14	1,087	14	519	10	51·90	1	—
Goddard, T. W. J.	Gloucestershire (1930)	1	0	0	0	—	—	193	14	49	2	24·50	—	—
Grace, E. M.	Gloucestershire (1880)	1	2	0	36	36	18·00	—	—	—	—	—	1	—
Grace, G. F.	Gloucestershire (1880)	1	2	0	0	0	0·00	—	—	—	—	—	2	—
Grace, W. G.	Gloucestershire (1880)	22	36	2	1,098	170	32·29	663	65	236	9	26·22	39	—
Graveney, T. W.	Gloucestershire (1953)	22	38	4	1,075	111	31·61	140	4	74	1	74·00	17	—
Greenwood, A.	Yorkshire (1876)	2	4	0	77	49	19·25	—	—	—	—	—	2	—
Gunn, G.	Nottinghamshire (1907)	11	21	1	844	122*	42·20	—	—	—	—	—	13	—
Gunn, J. R.	Nottinghamshire (1901)	6	10	2	85	24	10·62	903	54	387	18	21·50	3	—
Gunn, W.	Nottinghamshire (1886)	11	20	2	392	102*	21·77	—	—	—	—	—	5	—
Haig, N. E.	Middlesex (1921)	1	2	0	3	3	1·50	138	4	88	2	44·00	—	—
Haigh, S.	Yorkshire (1905)	4	5	1	40	14	10·00	372	21	139	4	34·75	1	—
Hallows, C.	Lancashire (1921)	1	1	1	16	16*	—	—	—	—	—	—	—	—
Hammond, W. R.	Gloucestershire (1928)	33	58	3	2,852	251	51·85	3,958	135	1,612	36	44·77	43	—
Hardinge, H. T. W.	Kent (1921)	1	2	0	30	25	15·00	—	—	—	—	—	—	—
Hardstaff, J., jnr.	Nottinghamshire (1936)	9	16	1	559	169*	37·26	—	—	—	—	—	2	—
Hardstaff, J., snr.	Nottinghamshire (1907)	5	10	0	311	72	31·10	—	—	—	—	—	1	—
Harris, 4th Lord	Kent (1878)	4	6	1	145	52	29·00	32	1	29	0	—	2	—
Hayes, E. G.	Surrey (1909)	1	2	0	13	9	6·50	36	0	24	0	—	—	—
Hayward, T. W.	Surrey (1896)	29	51	2	1,747	137	35·65	824	38	486	12	40·50	14	—
Hearne, J. T.	Middlesex (1896)	11	17	4	86	18	6·61	2,936	209	1,070	48	22·29	3	—
Hearne, J. W.	Middlesex (1911)	16	24	2	554	114	25·18	2,068	30	1,027	16	64·18	7	—
Hendren, E. H.	Middlesex (1920)	28	48	4	1,740	169	39·54	47	0	31	1	31·00	15	—
Higgs, K.	Lancashire (1965)	2	3	0	6	4	2·00	591	25	223	4	55·75	1	—
Hill, A.	Yorkshire (1876)	2	4	2	101	49	50·50	340	37	130	6	21·66	—	—
Hirst, G. H.	Yorkshire (1897)	21	33	3	744	85	24·80	3,473	118	1,585	49	32·34	11	—
Hitch, J. W.	Surrey (1911)	6	9	2	103	51*	14·71	462	5	325	7	46·42	2	—
Hobbs, J. B.	Surrey (1907)	41	71	4	3,636	187	54·26	124	5	53	0	—	11	—
Hollies, W. E.	Warwickshire (1948)	1	2	1	0	0*	0·00	336	14	131	5	26·20	—	—
Holmes, P.	Yorkshire (1921)	1	2	0	38	30	19·00	—	—	—	—	—	—	—
Hone, L.	Ireland (1878)	1	2	0	13	7	6·50	—	—	—	—	—	2	—
Hopwood, J. L.	Lancashire (1934)	2	3	1	12	8	6·00	462	32	155	0	—	—	—
Hornby, A. N.	Lancashire (1878)	3	6	0	21	9	3·50	28	7	0	1	—	—	—
Howell, H.	Warwickshire (1920)	4	8	6	15	5	7·50	798	18	490	7	70·00	—	—
Humphries, J.	Derbyshire (1907)	3	6	1	44	16	8·80	—	—	—	—	—	7	—
Hunter, J.	Yorkshire (1884)	5	7	2	93	39*	18·60	—	—	—	—	—	8	3
Hutchings, K. L.	Kent (1907)	7	12	0	341	126	28·41	90	1	81	1	81·00	9	—
Hutton, L.	Yorkshire (1938)	27	49	6	2,428	364	56·46	54	1	60	1	60·00	18	—
Ikin, J. T.	Lancashire (1946)	5	10	0	184	60	18·40	56	0	48	0	—	4	—
Illingworth, R.	Yorkshire (1961)	7	10	0	136	27	13·60	1,753	109	548	17	32·23	6	—
Insole, D. J.	Essex (1956)	1	1	0	5	5	5·00	—	—	—	—	—	—	—
Jackson, H. L.	Derbyshire (1961)	1	1	0	8	8	8·00	264	16	83	4	20·75	1	—
Jackson, Hon. F. S.	Yorkshire (1893)	20	33	4	1,415	144*	48·79	1,587	77	799	24	33·29	10	—
Jardine, D. R.	Surrey (1928)	10	18	1	540	98	31·76	6	0	10	0	—	13	—
Jessop, G. L.	Gloucestershire (1899)	13	18	0	433	104	24·05	660	28	346	10	34·60	7	—
Jones, A. O.	Nottinghamshire (1899)	12	21	0	291	34	13·85	228	14	133	3	44·33	15	—
Jones, I. J.	Glamorgan (1965)	4	5	2	29	16	9·66	1,032	15	533	15	35·53	—	—
Jupp, H.	Surrey (1876)	2	4	0	68	63	17·00	—	—	—	—	—	2	—
Jupp, V. W. C.	Sussex (1921)	2	4	0	65	28	16·25	235	4	142	5	28·40	—	—
Keeton, W. W.	Nottinghamshire (1934)	1	2	0	37	25	18·50	—	—	—	—	—	—	—
Kenyon, D.	Worcestershire (1953)	2	4	0	29	16	7·25	—	—	—	—	—	1	—
Kilner, R.	Yorkshire (1924)	7	7	1	174	74	29·00	2,164	63	675	24	28·12	5	—
King, J. H.	Leicestershire (1909)	1	2	0	64	60	32·00	162	5	99	1	99·00	—	—
Kinneir, S. P.	Warwickshire (1911)	1	2	0	52	30	26·00	—	—	—	—	—	—	—
Knight, A. E.	Leicestershire (1903)	3	6	1	81	70*	16·20	—	—	—	—	—	1	—
Knight, B. R.	Essex (1962)	5	7	2	52	27*	10·40	1,168	29	463	15	30·86	2	—
Knight, D. J.	Surrey (1921)	2	4	0	54	38	13·50	—	—	—	—	—	1	—
Knott, A. P. E.	Kent (1968)	5	8	1	116	33	16·57	—	—	—	—	—	11	4
Laker, J. C.	Surrey (1948)	15	23	4	277	63	14·57	4,010	204	1,444	79	18·27	—	—
Larwood, H.	Nottinghamshire (1926)	15	22	4	386	98	21·44	4,053	120	1,916	64	29·93	12	—
Leslie, C. F. H.	Middlesex (1882)	4	7	0	106	54	15·14	96	10	44	4	11·00	1	—
Leyland, M.	Yorkshire (1928)	20	34	4	1,705	187	56·83	395	10	223	1	223·00	7	—
Lilley, A. A.	Warwickshire (1896)	32	47	7	801	84	20·02	25	1	23	1	23·00	65	19

		BATTING						BOWLING						
		Matches	Inns.	N.O.	Runs	H.S.	Av.	Balls	Mdns.	Runs	Wkts.	Av.	Ct	St
Lillywhite, Jas., jnr.	Sussex (1876)	2	3	1	16	10	8·00	340	37	126	8	15·75	1	—
Loader, P. J.	Surrey (1958)	2	4	2	7	6*	3·50	482	10	193	7	27·57	—	—
Lock, G. A. R.	Surrey (1953)	13	20	2	166	30	9·22	3,442	193	1,128	31	36·38	15	—
Lockwood, W. H.	Surrey (1893)	12	16	3	231	52*	17·76	1,970	100	884	43	20·55	4	—
Lohmann, G. A.	Surrey (1886)	15	22	2	203	62*	10·15	3,301	326	1,002	77	13·01	22	—
Lucas, A. P.	Surrey (1878)	5	9	1	157	55	19·62	120	13	54	0	—	1	—
Lyttelton, Hon. A.	Middlesex (1880)	4	7	1	94	31	15·66	48	5	19	4	4·75	2	—
Macaulay, G. G.	Yorkshire (1926)	1	1	0	76	76	76·00	192	8	123	1	123·00	1	—
McGahey, C. P.	Essex (1901)	2	4	0	38	18	9·50	—	—	—	—	—	1	—
MacGregor, G.	Middlesex (1890)	8	11	3	96	31	12·00	—	—	—	—	—	14	3
McIntyre, A. J. W.	Surrey (1950)	1	2	0	8	7	4·00	—	—	—	—	—	1	—
Mackinnon, F. A.	Kent (1878)	1	2	0	5	5	2·50	—	—	—	—	—	—	—
MacLaren, A. C.	Lancashire (1894)	35	61	4	1,931	140	33·87	—	—	—	—	—	29	—
Makepeace, H.	Lancashire (1920)	4	8	0	279	117	34·87	—	—	—	—	—	—	—
Martin, F.	Kent (1890)	1	1	0	1	1	1·00	287	21	102	12	8·50	—	—
Mason, J. R.	Kent (1897)	5	10	0	129	32	12·90	324	13	149	2	74·50	3	—
May, P. B. H.	Surrey (1953)	21	37	3	1,566	113	46·05	—	—	—	—	—	11	—
Mead, C. P.	Hampshire (1911)	7	10	2	415	182*	51·87	—	—	—	—	—	3	—
Mead, W.	Essex (1899)	1	2	0	7	7	3·50	265	24	91	1	91·00	1	—
Midwinter, W. E.	Gloucestershire (1881)	4	7	0	95	36	13·57	776	79	272	10	27·20	5	—
Milburn, C.	Northamptonshire (1968)	2	3	0	109	83	36·33	—	—	—	—	—	2	—
Milton, C. A.	Gloucestershire (1958)	2	4	0	38	17	9·50	—	—	—	—	—	1	—
Mitchell, T. B.	Derbyshire (1932)	3	4	1	14	9	4·66	468	12	285	4	71·25	1	—
Mold, A.	Lancashire (1893)	3	3	1	0	0*	—	491	32	234	7	33·42	1	—
Morley, F.	Nottinghamshire (1880)	4	6	2	6	2*	1·50	972	124	296	16	18·50	4	—
Mortimore, J. B.	Gloucestershire (1958)	2	3	1	67	44*	33·50	382	14	163	1	163·00	1	—
Moss, A. E.	Middlesex (1956)	1	—	—	—	—	—	24	3	1	0	—	—	—
Murray, J. T.	Middlesex (1961)	6	10	1	163	40	18·11	—	—	—	—	—	18	1
Newham, W.	Sussex (1887)	1	2	0	26	17	13·00	—	—	—	—	—	—	—
Nichols, M. S.	Essex (1930)	1	1	1	7	7*	—	126	5	33	2	16·50	—	—
Oakman, A. S. M.	Sussex (1956)	2	2	0	14	10	7·00	48	3	21	0	—	7	—
O'Brien, T. C.	Middlesex (1884)	2	4	0	24	20	6·00	—	—	—	—	—	1	—
Palairet, L. C. H.	Somerset (1902)	2	4	0	49	20	12·25	—	—	—	—	—	2	—
Parfitt, P. H.	Middlesex (1962)	6	9	0	185	80	20·55	—	—	—	—	—	7	—
Parker, C. W. L.	Gloucestershire (1921)	1	1	1	3	3*	—	168	16	32	2	16·00	—	—
Parkhouse, W. G. A.	Glamorgan (1950)	2	4	0	77	28	19·25	—	—	—	—	—	1	—
Parkin, C. H.	Lancashire (1920)	9	15	2	152	36	11·69	2,005	49	1,090	32	34·06	3	—
Parks, J. M.	Sussex (1964)	10	13	2	497	89	38·23	—	—	—	—	—	17	4
Pataudi, Nawab of	Worcestershire (1932)	3	5	0	144	102	28·80	—	—	—	—	—	—	—
Paynter, E.	Lancashire (1932)	7	11	4	591	216*	84·42	—	—	—	—	—	3	—
Peate, E.	Yorkshire (1881)	9	14	8	70	13	11·66	2,096	260	682	31	22·00	2	—
Peebles, I. A. R.	Middlesex (1930)	2	3	2	9	6	9·00	756	17	354	9	39·33	—	—
Peel, R.	Yorkshire (1884)	20	33	4	427	83	14·72	5,216	444	1,715	102	16·81	17	—
Penn, F.	Kent (1880)	1	2	1	50	27*	50·00	12	1	2	0	—	—	—
Philipson, H.	Middlesex (1891)	5	8	1	·63	30	9·00	—	—	—	—	—	8	3
Pilling, R.	Lancashire (1881)	8	13	1	91	23	7·58	—	—	—	—	—	10	4
Pocock, P. I.	Surrey (1968)	1	2	0	16	10	8·00	348	15	156	6	26·00	2	—
Pollard, R.	Lancashire (1948)	2	2	1	3	3	3·00	612	29	218	5	43·60	1	—
Price, J. S. E.	Middlesex (1964)	2	2	1	1	1	1·00	396	6	250	4	62·50	—	—
Price, W. F. F.	Middlesex (1938)	1	2	0	6	6	3·00	—	—	—	—	—	2	—
Prideaux, R. M.	Northamptonshire (1968)	1	2	0	66	64	33·00	—	—	—	—	—	—	—
Pullar, G.	Lancashire (1961)	9	18	1	457	63	26·88	—	—	—	—	—	—	—
Quaife, W. G.	Warwickshire (1899)	7	13	1	228	68	19·00	15	1	6	0	—	4	—
Ranjitsinhji, K. S.	Sussex (1896)	15	26	4	989	175	44·95	97	6	39	1	39·00	13	—
Read, J. M.	Surrey (1882)	15	26	2	447	57	18·62	—	—	—	—	—	8	—
Read, W. W.	Surrey (1882)	17	26	2	680	117	27·20	60	2	63	0	—	16	—
Relf, A. E.	Sussex (1903)	3	5	2	64	31	21·33	448	24	173	7	24·71	4	—
Rhodes, W.	Yorkshire (1899)	41	69	14	1,706	179	31·01	5,791	233	2,616	109	24·00	34	—
Richardson, P. E.	Worcestershire (1956)	9	16	0	526	104	32·87	—	—	—	—	—	1	—
Richardson, T.	Surrey (1893)	14	24	8	177	25*	11·06	4,497	191	2,220	88	25·22	5	—
Richmond, T. L.	Nottinghamshire (1921)	1	2	0	6	4	3·00	114	3	86	2	43·00	—	—
Robins, R. W. V.	Middlesex (1930)	6	10	2	183	61	22·87	960	10	558	14	39·85	2	—
Root, C. F.	Worcestershire (1926)	3	—	—	—	—	—	642	47	194	8	24·25	1	—
Royle, V. P. F. A.	Lancashire (1878)	1	2	0	21	18	10·50	16	1	6	0	—	2	—
Rumsey, F. E.	Somerset (1964)	1	1	1	3	3*	—	215	4	99	2	49·50	—	—
Russell, A. C.	Essex (1920)	6	11	2	474	135*	52·66	—	—	—	—	—	3	—

		BATTING						BOWLING						
		Matches	Inns.	N.O.	Runs	H.S.	Av.	Balls	Mdns.	Runs	Wkts.	Av.	Ct	St
Russell, W. E.	Middlesex (1965)	1	1	1	0	0*	—	—	—	—	—	—	—	—
Sandham, A.	Surrey (1921)	3	5	0	49	21	9·80	—	—	—	—	—	—	—
Schultz, S. S.	Lancashire (1878)	1	2	1	20	20	20·00	34	3	26	1	26·00	—	—
Scotton, W. H.	Nottinghamshire (1881)	15	25	2	510	90	22·17	20	1	20	0	—	4	—
Selby, J.	Nottinghamshire (1876)	6	12	1	256	70	23·27	—	—	—	—	—	1	—
Sharp, J.	Lancashire (1909)	3	6	2	188	105	47·00	183	3	111	3	37·00	1	—
Sharpe, J. W.	Surrey (1890)	3	6	4	44	26	22·00	975	61	305	11	27·72	2	—
Sharpe, P. J.	Yorkshire (1964)	2	3	1	71	35*	35·50	—	—	—	—	—	—	—
Shaw, A.	Nottinghamshire (1876)	7	12	1	111	40	10·09	1,099	155	285	12	23·75	4	—
Sheppard, Rev. D. S.	Sussex (1950)	9	16	0	580	113	36·25	—	—	—	—	—	2	—
Sherwin, M.	Nottinghamshire (1886)	3	6	4	30	21*	15·00	—	—	—	—	—	5	2
Shrewsbury, A.	Nottinghamshire (1881)	23	40	4	1,277	164	35·47	12	2	2	0	—	29	—
Shuter, J.	Surrey (1888)	1	1	0	28	28	28·00	—	—	—	—	—	—	—
Simpson, R. T.	Nottinghamshire (1950)	9	17	2	434	156*	28·93	—	—	—	—	—	5	—
Sims, J. M.	Middlesex (1936)	2	2	0	3	3	1·50	408	2	244	3	81·33	5	—
Sinfield, R. A.	Gloucestershire (1938)	1	1	0	6	6	6·00	378	16	123	2	61·50	—	—
Smith, A. C.	Warwickshire (1962)	4	5	1	47	21	11·75	—	—	—	—	—	13	—
Smith, E. J.	Warwickshire (1911)	7	9	1	69	22	8·62	—	—	—	—	—	12	1
Smith, M. J. K.	Warwickshire (1961)	6	9	2	108	41	15·42	16	0	8	0	—	4	—
Smith, T. P. B.	Essex (1946)	2	4	0	32	24	8·00	376	1	218	2	109·00	1	—
Snow, J. A.	Sussex (1968)	5	6	1	56	19	11·20	1,218	44	508	17	29·88	3	—
Southerton, J.	Surrey (1876)	2	3	1	7	6	3·50	263	24	107	7	15·28	2	—
Spooner, R. H.	Lancashire (1905)	7	11	0	233	79	21·18	—	—	—	—	—	—	—
Statham, J. B.	Lancashire (1953)	22	32	13	236	36*	12·42	5,405	130	2,138	69	30·98	11	—
Steel, A. G.	Lancashire (1880)	13	20	3	600	148	35·29	1,364	108	605	29	20·86	5	—
Stevens, G. T. S.	Middlesex (1926)	2	3	0	63	24	21·00	384	7	184	5	36·80	3	—
Stoddart, A. E.	Middlesex (1887)	16	30	2	996	173	35·57	162	7	94	2	47·00	6	—
Storer, W.	Derbyshire (1897)	6	11	0	215	51	19·54	168	5	108	2	54·00	11	—
Strudwick, H.	Surrey (1911)	17	26	8	149	24	8·27	—	—	—	—	—	37	5
Studd, C. T.	Middlesex (1882)	5	9	1	160	48	20·00	384	60	98	3	32·66	5	—
Studd, G. B.	Middlesex (1882)	4	7	0	31	9	4·42	—	—	—	—	—	8	—
Subba Row, R.	Northamptonshire (1961)	5	10	0	468	137	46·80	—	—	—	—	—	2	—
Sugg, F. H.	Lancashire (1888)	2	2	0	55	31	27·50	—	—	—	—	—	—	—
Sutcliffe, H.	Yorkshire (1924)	27	46	5	2,741	194	66·85	—	—	—	—	—	14	—
Swetman, R.	Surrey (1958)	2	4	0	56	41	14·00	—	—	—	—	—	3	—
Tate, F. W.	Sussex (1902)	1	2	1	9	5*	9·00	96	4	51	2	25·50	—	—
Tate, M. W.	Sussex (1924)	20	30	1	578	54	19·93	7,686	330	2,542	83	30·62	6	—
Tattersall, R.	Lancashire (1950)	3	4	0	18	10	4·50	717	17	338	7	48·28	3	—
Taylor, K.	Yorkshire (1964)	1	2	0	24	15	12·00	12	0	6	0	—	—	—
Tennyson, Hon. L. H.	Hampshire (1921)	4	5	1	229	74*	57·25	—	—	—	—	—	2	—
Thompson, G. J.	Northamptonshire (1909)	1	1	0	6	6	6·00	24	0	19	0	—	2	—
Titmus, F. J.	Middlesex (1962)	15	22	5	578	60	34·00	4,786	198	1,434	40	35·85	9	—
Townsend, C. L.	Gloucestershire (1899)	2	3	0	51	38	17·00	140	5	75	3	25·00	—	—
Trueman, F. S.	Yorkshire (1953)	19	29	1	338	38	12·07	4,361	83	1,999	79	25·30	21	—
Tyldesley, E.	Lancashire (1921)	5	7	1	257	81	42·83	—	—	—	—	—	2	—
Tyldesley, J. T.	Lancashire (1899)	26	46	1	1,389	138	30·86	—	—	—	—	—	12	—
Tyldesley, R.	Lancashire (1924)	3	5	0	17	6	3·40	830	26	370	7	52·85	—	—
Tylecote, E. F. S.	Kent (1882)	6	9	1	152	66	19·00	—	—	—	—	—	5	5
Tyson, F. H.	Northamptonshire (1954)	8	12	1	117	37*	10·63	1,724	23	810	32	25·31	3	—
Ulyett, G.	Yorkshire (1876)	23	36	0	901	149	25·02	2,527	286	992	49	20·24	16	—
Underwood, D. L.	Kent (1968)	4	4	4	69	45*	—	1,259	103	302	20	15·10	2	—
Verity, H.	Yorkshire (1932)	18	27	8	344	60*	18·10	4,906	256	1,657	59	28·08	14	—
Vernon, G. F.	Middlesex (1882)	1	2	1	14	11*	14·00	—	—	—	—	—	—	—
Vine, J.	Sussex (1911)	2	3	2	46	36	46·00	—	—	—	—	—	—	—
Voce, W.	Nottinghamshire (1932)	11	17	6	67	18	6·09	2,450	56	1,128	41	27·51	8	—
Waddington, A.	Yorkshire (1920)	2	4	0	16	7	4·00	276	7	119	1	119·00	1	—
Wainwright, E.	Yorkshire (1893)	5	9	0	132	49	14·66	127	6	73	0	—	2	—
Walters, C. F.	Worcestershire (1934)	5	9	1	401	82	50·12	—	—	—	—	—	5	—
Ward, A.	Lancashire (1893)	7	13	0	487	117	37·46	—	—	—	—	—	1	—
Wardle, J. H.	Yorkshire (1953)	8	12	3	166	38	18·44	1,661	82	632	24	26·33	1	—
Warner, P. F.	Middlesex (1903)	7	13	1	287	79	23·91	—	—	—	—	—	2	—
Warr, J. J.	Middlesex (1950)	2	4	0	4	4	1·00	584	6	281	1	281·00	—	—
Warren, A. R.	Derbyshire (1905)	1	1	0	7	7	7·00	236	9	113	6	18·83	—	—
Washbrook, C.	Lancashire (1946)	17	31	1	996	143	33·20	—	—	—	—	—	7	—
Watkins, A. J.	Glamorgan (1948)	1	2	0	2	2	1·00	24	1	19	0	—	—	—
Watson, W.	Yorkshire (1953)	7	13	0	272	109	20·92	—	—	—	—	—	1	—

		Matches	Inns.	N.O.	Runs	H.S.	Av.	Balls	Mdns.	Runs	Wkts.	Av.	Ct	St
		BATTING						BOWLING						
Webbe, A. J.	Middlesex (1878)	1	2	0	4	4	2·00	—	—	—	—	—	2	—
Wellard, A. W.	Somerset (1938)	1	2	0	42	38	21·00	192	3	126	3	42·00	—	—
White, J. C.	Somerset (1921)	7	12	6	110	29	18·33	2,974	148	1,033	31	33·32	1	—
Whysall, W. W.	Nottinghamshire (1924)	4	7	0	209	76	29·85	16	0	9	0	—	7	—
Wilson, E. R.	Yorkshire (1920)	1	2	0	10	5	5·00	126	5	36	3	12·00	—	—
Wood, A.	Yorkshire (1938)	1	1	0	53	53	53·00	—	—	—	—	—	3	—
Wood, H.	Surrey (1888)	1	1	0	8	8	8·00	—	—	—	—	—	1	1
Wood, R.	Lancashire (1886)	1	2	0	6	6	3·00	—	—	—	—	—	—	—
Woolley, F. E.	Kent (1909)	32	51	1	1,664	133*	33·28	3,590	130	1,555	43	36·16	34	—
Worthington, T. S.	Derbyshire (1936)	3	6	0	74	44	12·33	80	0	78	0	—	3	—
Wright, D. V. P.	Kent (1938)	14	22	7	83	22	5·53	3,709	61	2,039	48	42·47	4	—
Wyatt, R. E. S.	Warwickshire (1930)	12	21	2	633	78	33·31	120	1	98	1	98·00	6	—
Wynyard, E. G.	Hampshire (1896)	1	2	0	13	10	6·50	—	—	—	—	—	—	—
Yardley, N. W. D.	Yorkshire (1946)	10	19	2	402	61	23·64	1,416	37	576	19	30·31	4	—
Young, H.	Essex (1899)	2	2	0	43	43	21·50	556	38	262	12	21·83	1	—
Young, J. A.	Middlesex (1948)	3	5	2	17	9	5·66	936	64	292	5	58·40	2	—
Young, R. A.	Sussex (1907)	2	4	0	27	13	6·75	—	—	—	—	—	6	—

Note: 1. The county given is that mainly associated with the player's Test career v Australia. 2. The year given in brackets indicates either (a) that of the player's first selection for a Test v Australia at home; or (b) that of his selection for an M.C.C. tour resulting in a first appearance v Australia.

AUSTRALIA		Matches	Inns.	N.O.	Runs	H.S.	Av.	Balls	Mdns.	Runs	Wkts.	Av.	Ct	St
		BATTING						BOWLING						
a'Beckett, E. L.	Victoria (1928)	3	5	0	133	41	26·60	936	41	282	3	94·00	4	—
Alexander, G.	Victoria (1880)	2	4	0	52	33	13·00	168	13	93	2	46·50	2	—
Alexander, H. H.	Victoria (1933)	1	2	1	17	17*	17·00	276	3	154	1	154·00	—	—
Allan, F. E.	Victoria (1879)	1	1	0	5	5	5·00	180	15	80	4	20·00	—	—
Allan, P. J.	Queensland (1965)	1	—	—	—	—	—	192	6	83	2	41·50	—	—
Allen, R. C.	New South Wales (1887)	1	2	0	44	30	22·00	—	—	—	—	—	2	—
Andrews, T. J. E.	New South Wales (1921)	13	19	0	541	94	28·47	156	5	116	1	116·00	9	—
Archer, K. A.	Queensland (1950)	3	5	0	152	48	30·40	—	—	—	—	—	—	—
Archer, R. G.	Queensland (1953)	12	20	1	294	49	15·47	2,445	126	761	35	21·74	11	—
Armstrong, W. W.	Victoria (1902)	42	71	9	2,172	158	35·03	6,782	362	2,288	74	30·91	37	—
Badcock, C. L.	South Australia (1936)	7	12	1	160	118	14·54	—	—	—	—	—	3	—
Bannerman, A. C.	New South Wales (1879)	28	50	2	1,108	94	23·08	292	17	163	4	40·75	21	—
Bannerman, C.	New South Wales (1877)	3	6	2	239	165*	59·75	—	—	—	—	—	—	—
Bardsley, W.	New South Wales (1909)	30	49	4	1,487	193*	33·04	—	—	—	—	—	6	—
Barnes, S. G.	New South Wales (1938)	9	14	2	846	234	70·50	314	5	118	1	118·00	5	—
Barnett, B. A.	Victoria (1938)	4	8	1	195	57	27·85	—	—	—	—	—	3	2
Barrett, J. E.	Victoria (1890)	2	4	1	80	67*	26·66	—	—	—	—	—	1	—
Benaud, R.	New South Wales (1953)	27	41	2	767	97	19·66	7,284	289	2,641	83	31·81	32	—
Blackham, J. McC.	Victoria (1877)	35	62	11	800	74	15·68	—	—	—	—	—	36	24
Blackie, D. D. J.	Victoria (1928)	3	6	3	24	11*	8·00	1,260	51	444	14	31·71	2	—
Bonnor, G. J.	Victoria (1880)	17	30	0	512	128	17·06	164	16	84	2	42·00	16	—
Booth, B. C.	New South Wales (1961)	15	26	5	824	112	39·23	2	0	4	0	—	8	—
Boyle, H. F.	Victoria (1879)	12	16	4	153	36*	12·75	1,744	175	641	32	20·03	10	—
Bradman, D. G.	New South Wales (1928)	37	63	7	5,028	334	89·78	92	2	51	1	51·00	20	—
Bromley, E. H.	Victoria (1933)	2	4	0	38	26	9·50	60	4	19	0	—	2	—
Brown, W. A.	New South Wales (1934)	13	24	1	980	206*	42·60	—	—	—	—	—	9	—
Bruce, W.	Victoria (1885)	14	26	2	702	80	29·25	954	71	440	12	36·66	12	—
Burge, P. J. P.	Queensland (1955)	22	37	6	1,179	181	38·03	—	—	—	—	—	10	—
Burke, J. W.	New South Wales (1951)	14	28	5	676	101*	29·39	288	15	83	2	41·50	8	—
Burn, K. E.	Tasmania (1890)	2	4	0	41	19	10·25	—	—	—	—	—	—	—
Burton, F. J.	New South Wales (1887)	2	4	2	4	2*	2·00	—	—	—	—	—	1	1
Callaway, S. T.	New South Wales (1892)	3	6	1	87	41	17·40	471	33	142	6	23·66	—	—
Carkeek, W.	Victoria (1912)	3	2	1	5	5	5·00	—	—	—	—	—	2	—
Carter, H.	New South Wales (1907)	21	35	4	776	72	25·03	—	—	—	—	—	35	17
Chappell, I. M.	South Australia (1966)	7	12	2	384	81	38·40	558	18	227	2	113·50	4	—
Charlton, P. C.	New South Wales (1890)	2	4	0	29	11	7·25	45	1	24	3	8·00	—	—
Chipperfield, A. G.	New South Wales (1934)	9	15	3	356	99	29·66	870	27	409	5	81·80	13	—
Collins, H. L.	New South Wales (1920)	16	26	0	1,012	162	38·92	522	16	236	3	78·66	11	—
Coningham, A. C. Y.	Queensland (1894)	1	2	0	13	10	6·50	186	9	76	2	38·00	—	—
Connolly, A. N.	Victoria (1965)	6	10	6	5	3	1·25	1,907	80	719	24	29·95	2	—
Cooper, B. B.	Victoria (1877)	1	2	0	18	15	9·00	—	—	—	—	—	2	—
Cooper, W. H.	Victoria (1881)	2	3	1	13	7	6·50	466	31	226	9	25·11	1	—
Corling, G. E.	New South Wales (1964)	5	4	1	5	3	1·66	1,159	50	447	12	37·25	—	—

		Matches	Inns.	N.O.	Runs	H.S.	Av.	Balls	Mdns.	Runs	Wkts.	Av.	Ct	St
Cottam, W. J.	New South Wales (1887)	1	2	0	4	3	2·00	—	—	—	—	—	1	—
Cotter, A. B.	New South Wales (1904)	16	29	1	377	45	13·46	3,464	63	1,916	67	28·59	5	—
Coulthard, G.	Victoria (1882)	1	1	1	6	6*	—	—	—	—	—	—	—	—
Cowper, R. M.	Victoria (1964)	9	15	1	686	307	49·00	794	41	317	10	31·70	11	—
Craig, I. D.	New South Wales (1956)	2	4	0	55	38	13·75	—	—	—	—	—	—	—
Crawford, P.	New South Wales (1956)	1	2	1	0	0*	0·00	29	2	4	0	—	—	—
Darling, J.	South Australia (1894)	31	55	2	1,632	178	30·79	—	—	—	—	—	23	—
Darling, L. S.	Victoria (1933)	7	12	0	245	85	20·41	162	7	65	0	—	6	—
Davidson, A. K.	New South Wales (1953)	25	36	5	750	77*	24·19	5,996	221	1,996	84	23·76	23	—
de Courcy, J. H.	New South Wales (1953)	3	6	1	81	41	16·20	—	—	—	—	—	3	—
Donnan, H.	New South Wales (1892)	5	10	1	75	15	8·33	54	2	22	0	—	1	—
Dooland, B.	South Australia (1947)	2	3	0	49	29	16·33	784	9	351	8	43·87	2	—
Duff, R. A.	New South Wales (1902)	19	34	1	1,079	146	32·69	180	8	85	4	21·25	13	—
Eady, C. J.	Tasmania (1896)	2	4	1	20	10*	6·66	223	14	112	7	16·00	2	—
Ebeling, H. I.	Victoria (1934)	1	2	0	43	41	21·50	186	9	89	3	29·66	—	—
Edwards, J. D.	Victoria (1888)	3	6	1	48	26	9·60	—	—	—	—	—	1	—
Emery, S. H.	New South Wales (1912)	2	—	—	—	—	—	114	2	68	2	34·00	—	—
Evans, E.	New South Wales (1881)	6	10	2	82	33	10·25	1,247	166	332	7	47·42	5	—
Fairfax, A. G.	New South Wales (1929)	5	6	2	215	65	53·75	1,010	38	439	14	31·35	10	—
Favell, L. E.	South Australia (1954)	6	10	1	203	54	22·55	—	—	—	—	—	3	—
Ferris, J. J.	New South Wales (1887)	8	16	4	98	20*	8·16	2,030	224	684	48	14·25	4	—
Fingleton, J. H. W.	New South Wales (1932)	12	21	0	671	136	31·95	—	—	—	—	—	7	—
Fleetwood-Smith,L.O'B.	Victoria (1937)	7	9	4	48	16*	9·60	2,359	54	1,190	33	36·06	1	—
Freeman, E. W.	South Australia (1968)	2	3	0	37	21	12·33	407	17	186	6	31·00	1	—
Freer, F. W.	Victoria (1946)	1	1	1	28	28*	—	160	3	74	3	24·66	—	—
Garrett, T. W.	New South Wales (1877)	19	33	6	339	51*	12·55	2,708	297	970	36	26·94	7	—
Gaunt, R. A.	Victoria (1961)	1	1	0	3	3	3·00	276	10	86	3	28·66	1	—
Gehrs, D. R. A.	South Australia (1904)	2	4	0	19	11	4·75	—	—	—	—	—	4	—
Giffen, G.	South Australia (1881)	31	53	0	1,238	161	23·35	6,325	434	2,791	103	27·09	24	—
Giffen, W. F.	South Australia (1887)	3	6	0	11	3	1·83	—	—	—	—	—	1	—
Gleeson, J. W.	New South Wales (1968)	5	8	1	52	19	7·42	1,163	65	417	12	34·75	2	—
Graham, H.	Victoria (1893)	6	10	0	301	107	30·10	—	—	—	—	—	3	—
Gregory, D. W.	New South Wales (1877)	3	5	2	60	43	20·00	20	1	9	0	—	—	—
Gregory, E. J.	New South Wales (1877)	1	2	0	11	11	5·50	—	—	—	—	—	1	—
Gregory, J. M.	New South Wales (1920)	21	30	3	941	100	34·85	4,887	109	2,364	70	33·77	30	—
Gregory, R. G.	Victoria (1937)	2	3	0	153	80	51·00	24	0	14	0	—	1	—
Gregory, S. E.	New South Wales (1890)	52	92	7	2,193	201	25·80	30	0	33	0	—	24	—
Grimmett, C. V.	South Australia (1925)	22	34	6	366	50	13·07	9,224	426	3,439	106	32·44	7	—
Groube, T. U.	Victoria (1880)	1	2	0	11	11	5·50	—	—	—	—	—	—	—
Grout, A. T. W.	Queensland (1958)	22	26	4	301	74	13·68	—	—	—	—	—	69	7
Guest, C.	Victoria (1963)	1	1	0	11	11	11·00	144	0	59	0	—	—	—
Hamence, R. A.	South Australia (1947)	1	2	1	31	30*	31·00	—	—	—	—	—	—	—
Harry, J.	Victoria (1895)	1	2	0	8	6	4·00	—	—	—	—	—	1	—
Hartigan, R. J.	Queensland (1908)	2	4	0	170	116	42·50	12	0	7	0	—	1	—
Hartkopf, A. E. V.	Victoria (1925)	1	2	0	80	80	40·00	240	2	134	1	134·00	—	—
Harvey, M.	Victoria (1947)	1	2	0	43	31	21·50	—	—	—	—	—	—	—
Harvey, R. N.	Victoria (1948)	37	68	5	2,416	167	38·34	56	4	15	0	—	25	—
Hassett, A. L.	Victoria (1938)	24	42	1	1,572	137	38·34	90	2	60	0	—	15	—
Hawke, N. J. N.	South Australia (1963)	12	13	5	115	37	14·33	3,176	128	1,119	37	30·24	6	—
Hazlitt, G. R.	Victoria (1907)	6	9	3	87	34*	14·50	1,107	50	443	16	27·68	4	—
Hendry, H. S. T. L.	Victoria (1921)	9	15	2	284	112	21·84	1,430	65	504	14	36·00	6	—
Hill, C.	South Australia (1896)	41	76	1	2,660	188	35·46	—	—	—	—	—	30	—
Hill, J. C.	Victoria (1953)	2	4	2	12	8*	6·00	396	18	158	7	22·57	1	—
Hodges, J.	Victoria (1877)	2	4	1	10	8	3·33	136	9	84	6	14·00	—	—
Hole, G. B.	South Australia (1951)	9	17	0	439	66	25·82	150	8	46	1	46·00	10	—
Hopkins, A. J.	New South Wales (1902)	17	28	2	434	43	16·69	1,183	47	581	21	27·66	10	—
Horan, T. P.	Victoria (1877)	15	27	2	471	124	18·84	373	45	143	11	13·00	6	—
Hordern, H. V.	New South Wales (1911)	5	10	2	173	49*	21·62	1,165	43	780	32	24·37	5	—
Hornibrook, P. M.	Queensland (1929)	6	7	1	60	26	10·00	1,579	63	664	17	39·05	7	—
Howell, W. P.	New South Wales (1898)	16	24	6	147	35	8·16	3,508	229	1,243	35	35·51	10	—
Inverarity, R. J.	Western Australia (1968)	2	4	0	99	56	24·75	6	0	3	0	—	1	—
Iredale, F. A.	New South Wales (1894)	14	23	1	807	140	36·68	12	0	3	0	—	16	—
Ironmonger, H.	Victoria (1928)	6	12	3	18	8	2·00	2,446	155	711	21	33·85	2	—
Iverson, J.	Victoria (1950)	5	7	3	3	1*	0·75	1,108	29	320	21	15·23	2	—
Jackson, A. A.	New South Wales (1929)	4	6	0	350	164	58·33	—	—	—	—	—	1	—
Jarman, B. N.	South Australia (1962)	7	11	3	111	41	13·87	—	—	—	—	—	18	—

| | | BATTING | | | | | | BOWLING | | | | | | |
		Matches	Inns.	N.O.	Runs	H.S.	Av.	Balls	Mdns.	Runs	Wkts.	Av.	Ct	St
Jarvis, A. H.	South Australia (1885)	11	21	3	303	82	16·83	—	—	—	—	—	9	—
Jennings, C. B.	South Australia (1912)	3	4	1	44	21	14·66	—	—	—	—	—	4	—
Johnson, I. W.	Victoria (1946)	22	35	6	485	77	16·72	4,592	187	1,590	42	37·85	12	—
Johnston, W. A.	Victoria (1948)	17	25	12	138	29	10·61	5,263	224	1,818	75	24·24	4	—
Jones, E.	South Australia (1894)	18	25	1	126	20	5·25	3,580	152	1,757	60	29·28	19	—
Jones, S. P.	New South Wales (1882)	12	24	4	432	87	21·60	262	26	112	6	18·66	12	—
Kelleway, C.	New South Wales (1911)	18	30	2	874	147	31·21	3,340	112	1,155	37	31·21	12	—
Kelly, J. J.	New South Wales (1896)	33	52	17	613	46*	17·51	—	—	—	—	—	39	16
Kelly, T. J. D.	Victoria (1877)	2	3	0	64	35	21·33	—	—	—	—	—	1	—
Kendall, T.	Victoria (1877)	2	4	1	39	17*	13·00	563	56	215	14	15·35	2	—
Kippax, A. F.	New South Wales (1925)	13	23	1	753	100	34·22	72	5	19	0	—	6	—
Kline, L. F.	Victoria (1958)	2	2	2	5	4*	—	200	6	77	0	—	2	—
Langley, G. R. A.	South Australia (1953)	9	13	2	97	18	8·81	—	—	—	—	—	35	2
Laver, F.	Victoria (1899)	15	23	6	196	45	11·52	2,367	122	964	37	26·05	8	—
Lawry, W. M.	Victoria (1961)	24	41	3	1,909	166	50·23	8	1	0	0	—	13	—
Lee, P. K.	South Australia (1933)	1	2	0	57	42	28·50	316	14	163	4	40·75	—	—
Lindwall, R. R.	New South Wales (1946)	29	43	7	795	100	22·08	6,728	216	2,559	114	22·44	17	—
Love, H. S. B.	New South Wales (1933)	1	2	0	8	5	4·00	—	—	—	—	—	3	—
Loxton, S. J. E.	Victoria (1948)	6	8	0	219	93	27·37	450	11	174	3	58·00	7	—
Lyons, J. J.	South Australia (1887)	14	27	0	731	134	27·07	316	17	149	6	24·83	3	—
Macartney, C. G.	New South Wales (1907)	26	42	4	1,640	170	43·15	2,633	120	908	33	27·51	11	—
Mackay, K. D.	Queensland (1956)	16	23	1	497	86*	22·59	2,835	126	875	24	36·45	7	—
Maddocks, L. V.	Victoria (1954)	5	9	0	156	69	17·33	—	—	—	—	—	11	1
Mailey, A. A.	New South Wales (1920)	18	25	8	201	46*	11·82	5,199	90	2,935	86	34·12	12	—
Mallett, A. A.	South Australia (1968)	1	2	1	43	43*	43·00	366	15	164	5	32·80	—	—
Marr, A. P.	New South Wales (1885)	1	2	0	5	5	2·50	48	6	14	0	—	—	—
Massie, H. H.	New South Wales (1881)	9	16	0	249	55	15·56	—	—	—	—	—	5	—
Matthews, T. J.	Victoria (1912)	5	7	0	74	53	10·57	680	28	277	3	92·33	4	—
Mayne, E. R.	Victoria (1912)	1						—	—	—	—	—	—	—
McAlister, P. A.	Victoria (1904)	8	16	1	252	41	16·80	—	—	—	—	—	10	—
McCabe, S. J.	New South Wales (1930)	24	43	3	1,931	232	48·27	2,585	84	1,076	21	51·23	21	—
McCool, C. L.	Queensland (1946)	5	7	2	272	104*	54·40	1,456	27	491	18	27·27	3	—
McCormick, E. L.	Victoria (1936)	7	9	2	35	17*	5·00	1,356	26	661	21	31·47	7	—
McDonald, C. C.	Victoria (1955)	15	28	1	1,043	170	38·62	—	—	—	—	—	4	—
McDonald, E. A.	Victoria (1921)	8	9	4	101	36	20·20	1,991	42	1,060	33	32·12	2	—
McDonnell, P. S.	Victoria (1880)	19	34	1	950	147	28·78	52	1	53	0	—	6	—
McIlwraith, J.	Victoria (1886)	1	2	0	9	7	4·50	—	—	—	—	—	1	—
McKenzie, G. D.	Western Australia (1961)	22	30	5	224	34	8·96	6,602	219	2,658	89	29·86	10	—
McKibbin, T. R.	New South Wales (1895)	5	8	2	88	28*	14·66	1,032	41	496	17	29·17	4	—
McLaren, J. W.	Queensland (1912)	1	2	2	0	0*	—	144	3	70	1	70·00	—	—
McLeod, C. E.	Victoria (1894)	17	29	5	573	112	23·87	3,374	171	1,325	33	40·15	9	—
McLeod, R. W.	Victoria (1892)	6	11	0	146	31	13·27	1,089	67	384	12	32·00	3	—
McShane, P. G.	Victoria (1885)	3	6	1	26	12*	5·20	108	9	48	1	48·00	2	—
Meckiff, I.	Victoria (1958)	4	4	0	9	5	2·25	898	24	292	17	17·17	1	—
Midwinter, W. E.	Victoria (1877)	8	14	1	174	37	13·38	949	102	333	14	23·78	5	—
Miller, K. R.	Victoria (1946)	29	49	4	1,511	145*	33·57	5,717	225	1,949	87	22·40	19	—
Minnett, R. B.	New South Wales (1911)	6	12	0	309	90	25·75	415	15	213	9	23·66	—	—
Misson, F. M.	New South Wales (1961)	2	1	1	25	25*	—	456	18	243	7	34·71	1	—
Moroney, J. A. R.	New South Wales (1950)	1	2	0	0	0	0·00	—	—	—	—	—	—	—
Morris, A. R.	New South Wales (1946)	24	43	2	2,080	206	50·73	71	1	39	1	39·00	8	—
Morris, S.	Victoria (1885)	1	2	1	14	10*	14·00	136	14	73	2	36·50	—	—
Moses, H.	New South Wales (1887)	6	10	0	198	33	19·80	—	—	—	—	—	1	—
Moule, W. H.	Victoria (1880)	1	2	0	40	34	20·00	51	4	23	3	7·66	1	—
Murdoch, W. L.	New South Wales (1877)	18	33	5	896	211	32·00	—	—	—	—	—	13	1
Musgrove, H.	Victoria (1885)	1	2	0	13	9	6·50	—	—	—	—	—	—	—
Nagel, L. E.	Victoria (1932)	1	2	1	21	21*	21·00	262	9	110	2	55·00	—	—
Nash, L. J.	Victoria (1937)	1	1	0	17	17	17·00	197	2	104	5	20·80	2	—
Noble, M. A.	New South Wales (1898)	39	68	6	1,905	133	30·72	6,845	353	2,860	115	24·86	26	—
Nothling, O. E.	Queensland (1928)	1	2	0	52	44	26·00	276	15	72	0	—	—	—
O'Brien, L. P. J.	Victoria (1932)	3	6	0	104	61	17·33	—	—	—	—	—	2	—
O'Connor, J. A.	South Australia (1908)	4	8	1	86	20	12·28	692	24	340	13	26·15	3	—
Oldfield, W. A. S.	New South Wales (1920)	38	62	14	1,116	65*	23·25	—	—	—	—	—	59	31
O'Neill, N. C.	New South Wales (1958)	19	30	3	1,072	117	39·70	364	10	176	2	88·00	10	—
O'Reilly, W. J.	New South Wales (1932)	19	32	6	277	42	10·65	7,864	439	2,587	102	25·36	4	—
Oxenham, R. K.	Queensland (1928)	3	5	0	88	39	17·60	1,202	72	349	7	49·85	—	—
Palmer, G. E.	Victoria (1880)	17	25	4	296	48	14·09	4,517	452	1,678	78	21·51	13	—

| | | BATTING | | | | | | BOWLING | | | | | | |
		Matches	Inns.	N.O.	Runs	H.S.	Av.	Balls	Mdns.	Runs	Wkts.	Av.	Ct	St
Park, R. L.	Victoria (1920)	1	1	0	0	0	0·00	6	0	9	0	—	—	—
Pellew, C. E.	South Australia (1920)	9	13	1	478	116	39·83	78	3	34	0	—	4	—
Philpott, P. I.	New South Wales (1965)	3	4	1	22	10	7·33	801	9	371	8	46·37	2	—
Ponsford, W. H.	Victoria (1924)	20	35	2	1,558	266	47·21	—	—	—	—	—	17	—
Pope, R. J.	New South Wales (1885)	1	2	0	3	3	1·50	—	—	—	—	—	—	—
Ransford, V. S.	Victoria (1907)	15	29	6	893	143*	38·82	19	1	19	0	—	9	—
Redpath, I. R.	Victoria (1964)	11	19	1	543	92	30·16	—	—	—	—	—	13	—
Reedman, J. C.	South Australia (1894)	1	2	0	21	17	10·50	57	2	24	1	24·00	1	—
Richardson, A. J.	South Australia (1924)	9	13	0	403	100	31·00	1,812	91	521	12	43·41	1	—
Richardson, V. Y.	South Australia (1924)	14	25	0	622	138	24·88	—	—	—	—	—	15	—
Rigg, K. E.	Victoria (1937)	3	5	0	118	47	23·60	—	—	—	—	—	2	—
Ring, D. T.	Victoria (1948)	2	3	0	34	18	11·33	426	20	171	3	57·00	—	—
Robertson, W. R.	Victoria (1885)	1	2	0	2	2	1·00	44	3	24	0	—	—	—
Robinson, R. H.	New South Wales (1936)	1	2	0	5	3	2·50	—	—	—	—	—	1	—
Rorke, G. F.	New South Wales (1959)	2	2	2	2	2*	—	565	17	165	8	20·62	—	—
Ryder, J.	Victoria (1920)	17	28	4	1,060	201*	44·16	1,531	54	630	13	48·46	15	—
Saggers, R. A.	New South Wales (1948)	1	1	0	5	5	5·00	—	—	—	—	—	3	—
Saunders, J. V.	Victoria (1902)	12	20	5	34	11*	2·26	3,268	108	1,620	64	25·31	5	—
Scott, H. J. H.	Victoria (1884)	8	14	1	359	102	27·61	28	1	26	0	—	8	—
Sheahan, A. P.	Victoria (1968)	5	9	1	213	88	26·62	—	—	—	—	—	4	—
Shepherd, B. K.	Western Australia (1963)	2	3	1	94	71*	47·00	—	—	—	—	—	1	—
Sievers, M. W. S.	Victoria (1936)	3	6	1	67	25*	13·40	602	25	161	9	17·88	4	—
Simpson, R. B.	New South Wales (1958)	19	31	3	1,405	311	50·17	1,828	79	838	16	52·37	30	—
Sincock, D. J.	South Australia (1966)	1	2	0	56	29	28·00	160	1	98	0	—	—	—
Slater, K. N.	Western Australia (1959)	1	1	1	1	1*	—	256	9	101	2	50·50	—	—
Slight, J.	Victoria (1880)	1	2	0	11	11	5·50	—	—	—	—	—	—	—
Smith, D.	Victoria (1912)	2	3	1	30	24*	15·00	—	—	—	—	—	—	—
Spofforth, F. R.	Victoria (1877)	18	29	6	217	50	9·43	4,185	416	1,731	94	18·41	11	—
Stackpole, K. R.	Victoria (1966)	2	2	0	52	43	26·00	256	5	116	2	58·00	2	—
Taber, H. B.	New South Wales (1968)	1	1	0	16	16	16·00	—	—	—	—	—	2	—
Tallon, D.	Queensland (1946)	15	20	2	340	92	18·88	—	—	—	—	—	38	4
Taylor, J. M.	New South Wales (1920)	18	25	0	957	108	38·28	48	1	26	1	26·00	9	—
Thomas, G.	New South Wales (1966)	3	4	0	147	52	36·75	—	—	—	—	—	1	—
Thompson, N.	New South Wales (1877)	2	4	0	67	41	16·75	112	16	31	1	31·00	3	—
Toshack, E. R. H.	New South Wales (1946)	9	9	5	65	20*	16·25	2,469	120	801	28	28·60	3	—
Travers, J. F.	South Australia (1902)	1	2	0	10	9	5·00	48	2	14	1	14·00	1	—
Tribe, G. E.	Victoria (1946)	3	3	1	35	25*	17·50	760	9	330	2	165·00	—	—
Trott, A. E.	Victoria (1895)	3	5	3	205	85*	102·50	474	17	192	9	21·33	4	—
Trott, G. H. S.	Victoria (1888)	24	42	0	921	143	21·92	1,890	48	1,019	29	35·13	21	—
Trumble, H.	Victoria (1890)	31	55	13	838	70	19·95	7,895	448	2,945	141	20·88	45	—
Trumble, J. W.	Victoria (1885)	7	13	1	243	59	20·25	600	59	222	10	22·20	3	—
Trumper, V. T.	New South Wales (1899)	40	74	5	2,263	185*	32·79	348	18	142	2	71·00	25	—
Turner, C. T. B.	New South Wales (1887)	17	32	4	323	29	11·53	5,195	457	1,670	101	16·53	8	—
Veivers, T. R.	Queensland (1964)	9	10	2	242	67*	30·25	1,904	84	694	15	46·26	5	—
Waite, M. G.	South Australia (1938)	2	3	0	11	8·	3·66	552	23	190	1	190·00	1	—
Wall, T. W.	South Australia (1929)	14	19	4	83	20	5·53	3,881	115	1,663	43	38·67	7	—
Walters, F. H.	Victoria (1885)	1	2	0	12	7	6·00	—	—	—	—	—	2	—
Walters, K. D.	New South Wales (1965)	10	16	1	753	155	50·20	728	15	310	9	34·44	2	—
Ward, F. A.	South Australia (1936)	4	8	2	36	18	6·00	1,268	30	574	11	52·18	1	—
Watson, W.	New South Wales (1955)	1	2	0	21	18	10·50	—	—	—	—	—	—	—
Whitty, W. J.	South Australia (1909)	6	8	4	35	14	8·75	1,302	71	498	15	33·20	2	—
Woodfull, W. M.	Victoria (1926)	25	41	3	1,675	155	44·07	—	—	—	—	—	5	—
Woods, S. M. J.	New South Wales (1888)	3	6	0	32	18	5·33	217	18	121	5	24·20	1	—
Worrall, J.	Victoria (1885)	11	22	3	478	76	25·15	255	29	127	1	127·00	13	—

Note: 1. The State given is that of first appearance in certain cases of dual affiliation. 2. The year given is that of the player's first appearance v England.